The Byzantine Revival

WARREN TREADGOLD

The Byzantine Revival
780-842

STANFORD UNIVERSITY PRESS

Stanford, California

Published with the assistance of
the National Endowment for the Humanities

Stanford University Press, Stanford, California
© 1988 by the Board of Trustees
of the Leland Stanford Junior University
Printed in the United States of America
Original printing 1988
Last figure below indicates year of this printing:
00 99 98 97 96 95 94 93 92 91
CIP data appear at the end of the book

Title-page illustration: The emperor Theophilus
(r. 829–42) and his court. Matritensis graecus 26-2,
fol. 42^v, a twelfth-century manuscript of the
chronicle of John Scylitzes. (Photo: Biblioteca
Nacional, Madrid)

Stanford University Press publications are
distributed exclusively by Stanford University
Press within the United States, Canada, Mexico,
and Central America; they are distributed
exclusively by Cambridge University Press
throughout the rest of the world.

TO IRINA ANDREESCU TREADGOLD
OF THE COSTA-FORII OF THESSALY
AND THE PASPATES OF CHIOS

Preface

Byzantine historians have a tradition of liking decline. Beginning with the foundation of Constantinople in 324, they have overwhelmingly preferred either the first third of Byzantine history, during which the empire lost most of its land, or the last third, during which the empire disappeared altogether. Though recently they have begun to think that those periods were not as decadent as all that, they still shy away from the middle third of Byzantine history, during which the empire recovered so completely from its earlier reverses that it was able to last through a series of new disasters all the way to its fall in 1453. Edward Gibbon got over this embarrassing lack of decline by racing through it in a single chapter. J. B. Bury published a book on the central part of this period in 1912 in which he managed to overlook the empire's revival almost entirely, and his has remained the standard work since then. Only recently have scholars begun to realize that the revival did happen, but they have focused on its cultural aspect alone.

This book is the first general history of the beginning of this political, economic, and cultural revival, which I place between 780 and 842. Its intended audience ranges from the reader who is simply curious about Byzantium to the scholar who has a professional interest in it. The history of these years and the story of the revival are so closely intertwined that any complete study of one must be an almost complete study of the other; since the almost-but-not-quite complete survey is misleading to the outsider and annoying to the specialist, I have tried to be as comprehensive as I can. The common knowledge that can be assumed in this field is at best so small that I have chosen to explain practically everything, so as to write for all interested readers.

The book's plan is two parts analysis to four parts narrative. The first and last chapters, which analyze the empire as it was in 780 and as it had become by 842, provide a measure of how much difference the revival made. The four middle chapters, which correspond to the main changes in government, trace the course of the empire's development in the meantime. Each chapter covers political, social, economic, and cultural history, all of which are integral parts of the story. For example, Irene's religious changes established a new political order and stimulated culture; Nicephorus I's reforms were at once military, institutional, and economic; and Leo V's and Theophilus's religious edicts were influenced by military considerations and had political effects. Scholars who have studied events of only one kind have failed to notice not only these connections but also the gradual advance of the revival as a whole. Since history originally happened in chronological order and in all fields simultaneously, it ought sometimes to be looked at that way.

Although the problem of how a society can emerge from decline plainly arises in modern times as well, in this book, as in my previous work, I have based my conclusions on Byzantine evidence and avoided relying on modern parallels. This approach to Byzantine history has recently won me the criticism of the prominent medievalist Giles Constable, who has declared that study of the sources "should not prevent scholars from asking new questions and seeking new answers" that show Byzantium's relevance to the modern world.* Without endorsing the view that the main use of history is to protect us from false historical analogies, I still believe that to be useful historical knowledge must first be accurate. Those who know Byzantine Greek and study Byzantine texts (as Professor Constable does not) have learned that such research cannot be replaced by any amount of comparison with modern societies.

In transliterating Byzantine names and terms, I use Anglicized forms when plausible ones can be found ("George," "postal logothete") and otherwise Latinized forms ("Constantius," "protovestiarius"). For describing Byzantium, this method seems preferable to transliterating Greek according to its ancient pronunciation (*Geōrgios, logothetēs tou dromou, Kōnstantios, prōtobestiarios*). Forms of this sort, which I have supplied in the Glossary of technical terms at the end, have the advantage of being readily convertible into the Greek alphabet; but they misrepresent the Byzantine pronunciation, which was approximately as in Modern Greek (*Yeoryios, logothetis tou dhromou, Konstandios, protovestiarios*). On the other hand, forms that reflect Byzantine pronunciation are often hard for

---

*See his preface to Alexander Kazhdan's *People and Power in Byzantium* (Washington, D.C., 1982), vii–viii; cf. my "Chronological Accuracy of the *Chronicle* of Symeon the Logothete," *Dumbarton Oaks Papers* 33 (1979): 159.

English-speaking readers to recognize and are inappropriate for referring to the medieval Latin West, to the earlier empire in which Latin was the official language, and to ancient Greece. The forms that I have adopted have earlier English usage on their side and fit most harmoniously into an English text.

I have tried to make the text of this book as straightforward as possible and to argue out historical problems in the notes, or even in books and articles that I have published already and merely cited here. If something in the text is doubtful, as it often is, this will be signaled by an "apparently," a "probably," or another such warning; those readers who are willing to accept my judgment can then get on with the story, while others can turn to the notes or to the books and articles. In an effort to make the references as easy to consult as the unfortunate necessity of endnotes allows, I have grouped related references together and numbered all the notes in a single series, not repeating numbers from chapter to chapter. Since the primary sources are what matter for deciding doubtful questions, I have tried to make my references to them exhaustive. My references to modern secondary literature, however, are selective. If there is a problem that calls for and has received attention from modern scholars, I note the source of any complex arguments that I adopt, but otherwise I usually cite only the most recent work that I find valuable and let its citations introduce the rest of the literature.

The limited references in my notes consequently understate my debts to many earlier works that have guided me through the sources and influenced my ideas in ways too subtle to be easily acknowledged. In most cases I can simply say that I have treated those works as I hope my own will be treated, as aids to knowledge rather than bibliographical items to be catalogued. Special mention must be made, however, of two books that between them cover the whole period treated here, and that I have used much more than my notes show: Paul Speck's *Kaiser Konstantin VI* for the years before 802 and J. B. Bury's *History of the Eastern Roman Empire* for the years afterward. Though their points of view differ from mine, I greatly respect their scholarship.

I have also had profitable conversations about this book with many people, but three stand out. Robert Browning made valuable and encouraging comments on the text and helped me to correct various errors and imprecisions. Cyril Mango has kindly shared with me his profound knowledge and his wide-ranging insights into a number of points. The more work I do, the more I realize the magnitude of my debt to my teacher Ihor Ševčenko, both for the rigorous training he gave me and for the manner in which he shaped my ideas about Byzantium and indeed about history. An oracular remark from him encouraged me to make this a much more ambitious book than it would otherwise have been. I doubt I shall ever outgrow what he taught me, but I hope I am growing into it.

For financial assistance I am happy to thank the Alexander von Humboldt Foundation, the Mellon Foundation, and the Earhart Foundation, which provided fellowships that allowed me to work on this book at the University of Munich, the Free University of Berlin, Stanford University, the University of Bologna, and Oxford University, and to travel throughout the Balkan and Anatolian peninsulas. The Earhart Foundation also provided a grant to pay for the maps and other illustrations. The maps and diagrams were elegantly and professionally redrawn from my archetypes by Mrs. Jean Dowling of the University of Birmingham. My editor, Paul Psoinos, has improved my text by many intelligent and learned suggestions and never once left it worse than I wrote it. Finally, this book is dedicated to my very favorite Byzantine: my wife.

Oxford, January 1986   W. T.

Contents

Tables, Maps, and Illustrations

The Byzantine Revival

CHAPTER ONE

The Empire in 780

During the reign of the emperor Justinian I (527–65)
the Eastern Roman Empire underwent a great change. When Justinian inherited the throne, the empire seemed strong and stable. In marked contrast to the Western Roman Empire, the last of which had already disappeared, the eastern empire had almost exactly the same frontiers in 527 as
it had had at the final division between East and West in 395. The territory
within these frontiers was about as firmly under its government's control
as the slow communications of the time allowed. If the army was a little
less effective than it had been, it was at least as good as the German and
Persian armies it faced, and its elite troops were much superior to theirs.
Though the empire's population, agriculture, and trade had apparently
been declining very gradually for many years, the people could feed
themselves and the government's revenues exceeded its expenses. Since
the eastern empire included few native speakers of Latin, knowledge of
Latin was naturally becoming rarer, but education and literature in Greek,
like art and architecture, remained of relatively high quality and quantity.
So Justinian seemed to have fewer problems than the great majority of the
Roman emperors who had preceded him. Many rulers in his position
would have sat back to enjoy an age of peace and quiet.

Justinian, however, wanted to take advantage of his favorable circumstances by seizing whatever opportunities presented themselves at home
or abroad. When he had the chance, he purchased a supposedly permanent
peace with Persia. When much of the capital of Constantinople burned
down, he rebuilt its public buildings, especially the Great Church of St.
Sophia, on a lavish scale. When he found plausible pretexts, he invaded
North Africa, Italy, and southern Spain, and ultimately conquered them
from their German overlords. These and other initiatives taken by Justi-

nian in diplomacy, building, and war made a very ambitious program, but one that seemed within the empire's means and likely to strengthen the Roman state in the long run.

Such would probably have been the result if a totally unforeseeable disaster had not occurred. Bubonic plague broke out midway through Justinian's reign, appearing in Egypt in 541 and reaching Constantinople in 542; it was to kill large numbers of people in sporadic outbreaks throughout the empire for over two hundred years. The proof that Justinian's plans were not mad is that even with the plague raging he achieved most of what he set out to do, and left a greatly expanded and not obviously collapsing empire at his death. It is conceivable that the empire would have been weaker if Justinian had not tried to do what he did. At any rate, it is not clear that he would have made things much better by abandoning his projects after the plague began. Although Justinian may not be to blame, however, by the end of his reign the empire's stability had been shaken. In retrospect, the east Roman state and civilization had begun a severe decline that was to last for some two centuries.

For the remainder of the sixth century Justinian's successors tried to stop the rot from spreading. They could do nothing about the plague itself and little about its effects on the empire's economy and society, but they kept the administrative machinery going and by and large defended the frontiers. Despite their efforts, the Visigoths took back part of southern Spain, and another German tribe, the Lombards, occupied about half of Italy. The Avars, a Mongol people ruling a subject population of Slavs, raided the empire's land in the Balkans, and the Persians looted Roman Armenia and Syria; but the Romans pushed most of the invaders out after each incursion and even annexed a bit of Persian Armenia. Nonetheless, the empire's resources were barely sufficient to meet its commitments, and its taxpayers and army were under serious strain.

In 602 rebels in the overworked Roman army in the Balkans staged the first violent takeover of the east Roman government since the empire's division more than two centuries before. During the resulting confusion the Avars and Persians closed in. Much of Syria, Armenia, and the Balkans had been lost by 610, when after a civil war the incompetent rulers in Constantinople were overthrown by a leader of considerable ability, the new emperor Heraclius. But the situation became even worse as the Persians conquered the rest of Syria and Egypt. By 626, Constantinople was besieged by Avars on its European side and by Persians on its Asian side, while Heraclius was campaigning against Persia with armies from what was left of Roman Asia Minor and Armenia. If he had lost, the Roman Empire would probably have met its end very soon thereafter.

In a brilliant campaign, Heraclius defeated the Persians on their home ground and forced them to return all their conquests to Roman rule by 629. The war ended as a greater disaster for the Avars and Persians than for the Romans. The Slavs rebelled successfully against the Avars, and the Persian Empire, wracked by a series of rebellions, was conquered entirely by the newly Muslim Arabs. Yet the Roman Empire had been too much weakened by the expenditures and ravages of the recent war, and by the continuing plague, to profit from its enemies' reverses. The Slavs who threw off Avar rule also established themselves in most of the Roman territory in the Balkans; the Arabs who destroyed the Persian Empire also conquered Roman Syria, Egypt, and North Africa. Not even Heraclius could help matters much; the Arab conquests were well begun before his death in 641. The empire's existence was in danger for a second time.

After a feeble beginning, Roman resistance to the Arabs stiffened. Most of the empire's armies from Syria, Egypt, Armenia, and Thrace withdrew into Asia Minor and defended it desperately. Two massive Arab assaults on Constantinople, in 678 and 718, failed, so that at least the capital remained secure. When the Bulgars appeared as a new enemy in Europe, they too were held off. Despite repeated invasions and countless raids by the Arabs, Asia Minor was never wrested from Roman hands, and it, with the part of Thrace around Constantinople and some enclaves along the southern coast of Europe, became a refuge for whatever had been saved from the wreckage of the Roman state. The empire's farmland had been devastated and its cities depopulated; its economy was dislocated and its culture impoverished; its people were demoralized by their many misfortunes and by theological disputes, largely over why God had allowed the misfortunes to happen; and its enemies were still strong. But by the middle of the eighth century nearly everyone realized that the empire was going to survive for the foreseeable future, though it had changed so much that modern scholars usually give it a different name, the "Byzantine" Empire.

The late eighth century proved to be a time of change for the empire comparable in importance to the reign of Justinian—but this time the change was for the better. As before, the empire's fortunes did not turn abruptly at any single date. Certainly the date of the disappearance of the plague is of some significance. The last outbreak in Constantinople ended in 747, and the last within the empire was in southern Italy in 767. Though the empire's decline had been arrested in most respects before the plague ended, to speak of a revival would be premature. The end of the plague in itself merely gave the state an opportunity to repair past damage.

If we are to look for a change of government that helped start the revival—and in the recovery of a state its government normally plays a

1. Leo IV (r. 775–80). Mutinensis graecus 122, fol. 144ʳ, a fifteenth-century manu-script of the chronicle of John Zonaras. This manuscript includes pictures of the Byzantine emperors that despite their poor quality seem to have some portraitive value. (Photo: Biblioteca Estense, Modena)

part—the most significant change came in 780. Interestingly, some Byzantines of these and later times thought of 780 as the beginning of a revival, and though they spoke mostly of a revival of right religious belief, in their minds that affected everything else as well. Even if we dismiss the favor of God as a possible source of social good, we cannot so easily discount the social benefits of men's believing that God favors them. So this year is a reasonable place to start the story of how the Byzantine revival came about.

THE SITUATION

On September 8, 780, the young emperor Leo IV died suddenly at Constantinople under suspicious circumstances. Since his only son, Constantine VI, was just nine years old, power passed to a regent, Leo's widow Irene. Unlike Leo, who seems to have felt that after so many trials the empire needed a rest, Irene had ambitious plans. She was most interested in changing official church doctrine to restore the icons—images of Christ and the saints—to the important place in the empire's religious life from which the prevailing heresy of Iconoclasm had excluded them. But to do so Irene had to favor new men and to encourage new attitudes. In particular, she seized on the idea that under her and her son the empire's political and moral strength would revive.

The new regent was a dignified and determined woman in her late twenties, who had already shown the talent for palace intrigue that was a prerequisite for a successful reign. She had grown up at Athens, then a small fortified town of no special importance, an imperial enclave in Slav-held territory. She was an orphan. Her family, while a distinguished one for Athens, could not have counted for much in the society of the capital. Yet in 769 the emperor Constantine V had chosen Irene to marry to his son Leo. Aside from a wish to avoid allying himself to a family powerful enough to challenge his own, Constantine's motives for selecting Irene remain obscure. They are especially obscure because he was an uncompromising and persecuting iconoclast, while he must at least have suspected that she was a venerator of icons. Before her wedding, he required her to swear over the eucharistic bread and wine never to venerate icons again.[1]

After extracting this oath, Constantine promoted his chosen daughter-in-law without hesitation. He had her brought by sea to the suburban palace of Hieria, across the Bosporus from Constantinople. From there, on All Saints' Day, 769, she sailed to the capital in the midst of a flotilla of imperial warships decked out with silk streamers. She was greeted by an enthusiastic crowd of Constantinopolitans, with whom she seems to have been popular from the start. Two days later, in a church in the Great Palace, the patriarch of Constantinople solemnized Irene's betrothal to the junior emperor Leo. The final ceremonies took place on Sunday, December 17, when, somewhat exceptionally, Constantine V and Leo crowned Irene Augusta just before her marriage rather than afterward. She would therefore have been acclaimed by the people in her own right before the patriarch celebrated her marriage in the Church of St. Stephen, in the Great Palace. Thirteen months after the wedding, on January 14, 771, Irene bore her husband a son, who was named Constantine after his grandfather.[2]

When Leo IV became emperor upon his father's death in 775, he showed signs of being willing to tolerate the use of icons and of favoring monks, who were mostly iconophiles. Leo's relations with Irene were apparently unstrained. After the deposed khan of the Bulgars Telerig took refuge at Constantinople in 776 and received baptism, Leo married his new ally to Irene's sister. For her own part, Irene either found or had appointed some members of the palace staff who were both supporters of hers and iconophiles. When the incumbent patriarch of Constantinople died in February 780, Leo replaced him with an iconophile sympathizer,

Paul of Cyprus, who was as promising a candidate as Irene could have hoped for. Though Leo himself remained an iconoclast, Irene had reason to be satisfied with the direction things were taking until, within two weeks of Paul's consecration as patriarch, a crisis supervened.[3]

Despite some attempt at concealment in our sources that is probably traceable to the time of the events themselves, Irene's part is not open to much doubt. Leo discovered two icons in his wife's private quarters. After investigation, he learned that they had been brought in by iconophiles on the palace staff. The men in question included Jacobus, the official who supervised the Great Palace and its custodians and kept all its keys, Strategius and Theophanes, the chamberlains who guarded the emperor's bedroom and ranked highest among the palace eunuchs, and two other confidential palace servants. Leo saw this case as a very different matter from his earlier gestures toward the iconophiles, because it concerned his control over his own household and with it his personal security. The loyalty of palace servants was always a subject of worry for a Byzantine ruler, since they were ideally placed to assassinate him and determine his successor.

The emperor had all those implicated in supplying the icons flogged, tonsured, paraded in chains down the main street of Constantinople, and briefly imprisoned. Theophanes died during his punishment and became a martyr for the iconophiles; Leo forced the others to become monks. With Irene he was furious and utterly disillusioned. He rebuked her for breaking her oath to his father (in which he seems to have had a rather naive confidence), he quite reasonably ignored her protests that she knew nothing about the icons in her own bedchamber, and he refused to have marital relations with her for the rest of his life. As it turned out, that was not long.

The surviving chronicles, all written by iconophiles, say that six months later Leo developed a mad passion for a votive crown studded with pearls that the emperor Heraclius had donated to the treasury of St. Sophia a century and a half before. Leo seized the crown, but when he tried it on boils broke out on his head, and he died of a severe fever. He was 30 years old. The chroniclers naturally represent his death as God's judgment upon the emperor's greed, blasphemy, and general iniquity; but if he had been poisoned they would not have been interested in recording that. Leo's abrupt and unexpected end rescued Irene from a nearly intolerable disgrace, and relieved from serious danger any of her collaborators who remained in the palace. Later events showed that Irene had few scruples when she was promoting either her devotion to icons or her personal ambitions. She and her remaining supporters probably connived at her husband's murder.[4]

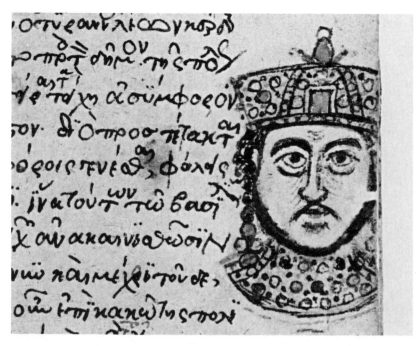

2. Constantine V (r. 741–75). Mutinensis graecus 122, fol. 139ʳ. (Photo: Biblioteca Estense, Modena)

Though after 780 Leo IV was not much regretted or even remembered, the same was not true of Leo's recently deceased father, Constantine V. Admittedly, the results of Constantine's reign of 35 years were not particularly impressive. In his many campaigns against the Bulgars and Arabs he suffered only one or two major defeats, but he did no lasting damage to either enemy and gained no territory for his empire. During his reign central Italy, including Rome, slipped from the empire's possession, leaving Byzantium and the West increasingly estranged from each other. Constantine did amass a large amount of gold, which he spent liberally on his army; but he accomplished this only by limiting other spending strictly and confiscating the property of iconophile monasteries. His enforcement of Iconoclasm made enemies of most men of rank and education, and little art and very little literature were produced during his reign. Nevertheless, Constantine's overpowering personality and sense of purpose made a lasting impression on both his admirers and his detractors. No emperor had aroused such strong feelings since Heraclius a century before. Constantine V Copronymus ("Name of Manure") cast a shadow over his successors until well into the next century.

Constantine owed his picturesquely pejorative epithet to his determined defense of Iconoclasm, the prohibition of the use of religious images that had been introduced by his father, Leo III. Leo III had considered the veneration of icons an abuse, a breach of church discipline that God had punished with the empire's military defeats and other misfortunes. Still, he handled the matter in an edict, not as if it were a true heresy, which would have required the consideration of a church council. Leo did not hunt down people who wanted to venerate icons in private; his quarrel was with those who demanded public use of icons as a necessary part of the faith. The disagreement was nonetheless of consequence, because depictions of Christ and the saints in churches and other public places had long been an important means of making the faith real and comprehensible to many believers. But it was Constantine V, by trying to make Iconoclasm a matter of doctrine and to enforce it upon private religious practice, who exaggerated it into an issue that embittered Byzantine life for nearly a hundred years.

Hindsight is not really necessary to judge Constantine's form of Iconoclasm a failure and a liability to the empire. By Constantine's own showing, venerating icons was not in itself a heresy. He did argue that if an icon represented Christ only as a man it implied the Nestorian heresy that Christ's human nature was separable, whereas if the icon represented Christ as both God and man it implied the Monophysite heresy that Christ had only one nature. But since logically iconophiles could not believe both heresies and did not have to believe either, this argument proved nothing. Even worse, such palpably false charges of heresy against his opponents seemed to imply heresy on his own part. He found it necessary to persecute a large number of outraged subjects, including most of the best-educated and the most devout, especially among the monks. At the very beginning of Constantine's reign, an iconophile-backed rebellion under his brother-in-law Artabasdus had held the capital for two years, demonstrating the Constantinopolitans' discontent with the iconoclast regime. A large iconophile party survived Constantine's persecutions with strengthened determination. At the same time, after Constantine the iconoclasts were also a force to be reckoned with, particularly in the army.[5]

A considerable part of the army that was serving in 780 had been recruited at Constantine's order, and most of it must have served under him on one or another of his many campaigns. By and large, Constantine had shown himself an able commander and tactician, attentive to the needs of his troops and well regarded by them. Though he had not expanded Byzantine territory, expansion does not seem to have been his aim, probably because he found it beyond the empire's strength. Although he was almost indifferent to his losses in central Italy, there was little he could have done about them in any case. The limited success of Constantine's campaigns is a sign less of his limited vision or capacity than of the empire's long-standing military inferiority to its enemies. Constantine's accomplishment was the consolidation of the rough balance of power with the Arabs and Bulgars that Leo III had made possible when he frustrated the Arab siege of Constantinople in 718.

Constantine had had three wives and at least seven children, six of them sons. Leo IV was the only son of Constantine's first wife Irene, the daughter of the khan of the Khazars; she died soon after Leo's birth in January 750. By 752, Constantine had married and been widowed a second time. Though the Church frowned upon any third marriage, Constantine was just 34 and had always asserted his authority over church officials; he quickly married his third wife, Eudocia, and began a new family. The rest of his children were Eudocia's. Leo IV remained his designated heir, but Constantine's eldest sons by Eudocia, Christopher and Nicephorus, were only slightly younger than Leo, and Constantine was apparently much attached to his third wife and her five sons. Except for his daughter Anthusa, however, all his children by Eudocia seem to have had rather undistinguished personalities.[6]

By showing unusual favor to his sons by Eudocia, Constantine created a problem for Leo IV and Leo's own wife and son. In 769, the year in which he was to marry Leo to Irene, Constantine crowned Eudocia Augusta, crowned her two older sons Caesars, and gave her third son the next-highest rank of nobilissimus. The emperor presented the two new Caesars to the people to be acclaimed, then celebrated the event by scattering about a small part of his accumulated gold as he and Leo IV rode from the palace to St. Sophia. This ceremony could easily have given the impression that the younger sons would have some claim to rule along with Leo. When Eudocia's fourth son was born later that year, Constantine made him a nobilissimus as well. Finally, before he died in 775, Constantine committed to the care of Theophanes (the later iconophile martyr) the immense sum of 50,000 pounds of gold as the patrimony of Eudocia's sons. This represented about two years' revenue for the whole empire and was quite possibly more than Constantine left in the regular treasury for Leo, who quickly discovered the secret and confiscated the cash.[7]

As emperor, Leo was understandably wary of his half-brothers. For the first annual payday after his accession, in Holy Week of 776, he summoned not only the officials and troops of the capital but large contingents of the provincial army, which was usually paid in the provinces. After he paid them their salaries and a donative to celebrate his accession,

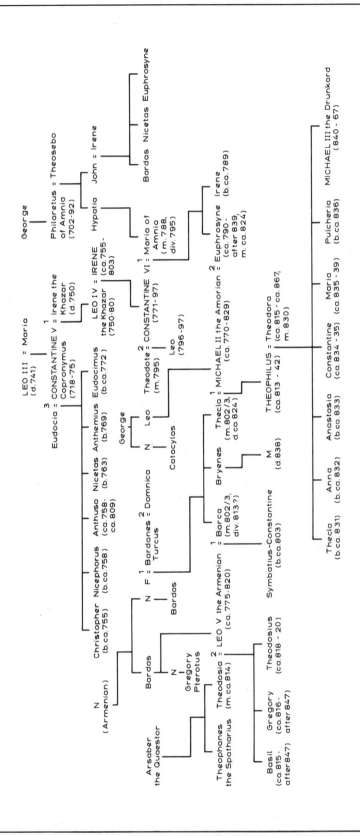

THE ISAURIAN AND AMORIAN DYNASTIES

he encouraged them to stage a supposedly spontaneous demonstration. Joined by many citizens, they demanded that he crown his five-year-old son Constantine VI junior emperor. Leo feigned reluctance on the grounds that if he died early his son might be killed, presumably by his four grandly titled uncles. When the crowd persisted in the demands for which he had paid them, Leo extracted a written oath upon the wood of the True Cross (which he happened to have on hand), by which the senate, the city guilds, and leading military officers and citizens all swore that they would accept no emperors but Leo, Constantine VI, and their descendants. Having thus excluded his half-brothers from the succession, Leo crowned his son on Easter (April 14, 776) in an unusually splendid ceremony. He then felt able to promote his youngest half-brother, Eudocimus, who was a small child and still untitled, to nobilissimus.[8]

No more than a month later, however, the emperor received a report that his half-brother Nicephorus was plotting against him with the support of a number of the imperial bodyguards and grooms. As with the coronation of his son, Leo made a show of consulting the army and people about the punishment of the plotters. Though Nicephorus himself was punished only by the loss of his title of Caesar—perhaps because of his youth, since he was only about eighteen—the others were flogged, tonsured, and exiled to the city of Cherson in the Crimea. Even if this particular plot was not serious, the threat posed to Leo by his half-brothers was real; after Leo's death Irene had still more reason to worry that opponents of her regime might make use of her brothers-in-law.[9]

So Irene's position in September 780 was precarious. She was merely a regent; her son and his uncles had the only hereditary claims to reign as emperors. Irene's iconophilism, which cannot have been a well-kept secret after the scandal earlier that year, was anathema to many of her husband's supporters. The purge of her own supporters on the palace staff had not yet been undone. In her favor, Irene had actual possession of the machinery of government, considerable personal popularity, and the oath that so many of her subjects had recently sworn to Constantine VI on his coronation. The empire she now ruled also had certain favorable prospects for the future, perhaps more favorable under the rule of iconophiles than under that of iconoclasts.

THE TERRITORY

Though in 780 everyone called the state ruled by Irene the Roman Empire, and it was in fact the direct descendant of the empire of Augustus, the modern habit of calling it the "Byzantine Empire" or "Byzantium" has some justification. Constantinople, whose ancient name of Byzan-

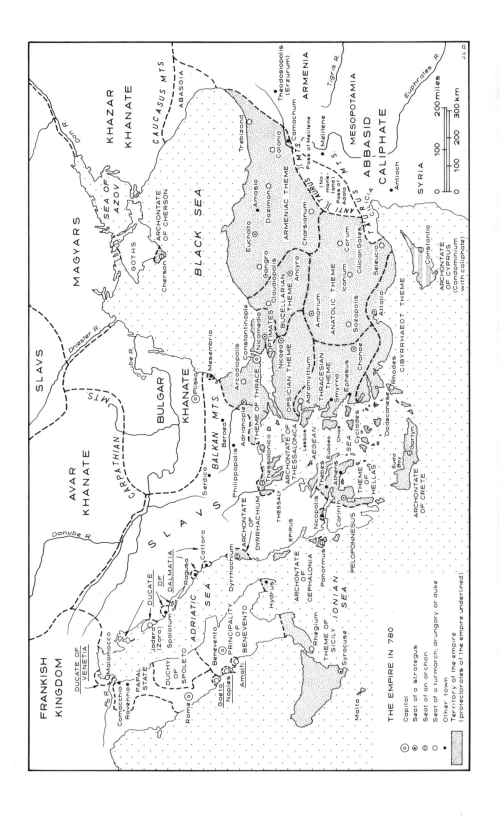

THE EMPIRE IN 780

Capital

Seat of a strategus

Seat of an archon

Seat of a turmarch, drungary, or duke

Other town

Territory of the empire
(protectorates of the empire underlined)

FRANKISH
KINGDOM

PAPAL
STATE

Ravenna
Comacchio

Malamocco
DUCATE OF VENETIA
Jadera (Zara)
Spalatum
Ragusa
Cattaro
DUCATE OF DALMATIA

Po R.
DUCHY OF SPOLETO

Rome

Gaeta
Naples
Amalfi

PRINCIPALITY OF BENEVENTO
Benevento

THEME OF SICILY
Syracuse
Rhegium

Malta

Danube R.

AVAR KHANATE

CARPATHIAN MTS.

SLAVS

Dniester R.

MAGYARS

Don R.

SEA OF AZOV

GOTHS
ARCHONTATE OF CHERSON
Cherson

KHAZAR KHANATE

CAUCASUS MTS.

ABASGIA

ARMENIA

Theodosiopolis (Erzurum)

Tigris R.

Euphrates R.

MESOPOTAMIA

ABBASID CALIPHATE

SYRIA

Antioch

Melitene
Camacum
Pass of Melitene

ARCHONTATE OF CYPRUS (Condominium with caliphate)
Constantia

BLACK SEA

BULGAR KHANATE
Pliska

Danube R.

BALKAN MTS.

Mesembria
Beroea
Serdica
Philippopolis
Adrianople
Arcadiopolis
THEME OF THRACE
Constantinople
OPTIMATES
Nicomedia
Nicaea
OPSICIAN THEME
Adramyttium
Lesbos
Smyrna
Ephesus
Chios

THESSALY
ARCHONTATE OF DYRRHACHIUM
Dyrrhachium
EPIRUS
ARCHONTATE OF THESSALONICA
Thessalonica

Trebizond

Colonia
Amasia
Dazimon
ARMENIAC THEME

Gangra
Claudiopolis
Euchaita
BUCELLARIAN THEME
Ancyra
Charsianum

Amorium
ANATOLIC THEME
Iconium
Corum
Sozopolis
Chonae
THRACESIAN THEME
Cilician Gates
Seleucia
Attalia
CIBYRRHAEOT THEME
Rhodes
Dodecanese

TAURUS MTS.
(No-man's land)
Pass of Adata
CILICIA

ARCHONTATE OF CEPHALONIA
Panormus

Nicopolis
Thebes
Athens
THEME OF HELLAS
Corinth

AEGEAN SEA
Euboea
Cyclades

Suda Bay
ARCHONTATE OF CRETE
Gortyn

ADRIATIC SEA

SLAVS

IONIAN SEA
PELOPONNESUS
Hydrus

200 miles
300 km
100
200
100

J.L.D.

tium was still used by antiquarians, had become the one essential part of the state. By far the empire's largest city, it was the seat of the emperor, the patriarch, and the central bureaucracy and army. Taking possession of Constantinople turned a rebel into an emperor. The capital was the empire's most defensible place, protected by water on two sides and by strong walls on all three. Since its foundation, it was almost the only city or region in the empire that had never fallen to a foreign enemy. Its position at the junction of the major land and sea routes between Europe and Asia and between the Mediterranean and the Black Sea confirmed it as the center of Byzantine trade and manufacturing. Its wealth, population, and power also made it the empire's cultural focus. It dominated the empire more completely than Rome ever had.

The territories that remained to the empire in 780 were precisely those that could be defended most easily from Constantinople. The only large and contiguous Byzantine possessions were the capital's natural hinterlands: the plain of Thrace and the peninsula of Asia Minor. Byzantine Thrace extended to the foothills of the Balkan Mountains, from which the Bulgars and Slavs could raid imperial territory but could not maintain secure bases nearer to the capital. Byzantine Asia Minor extended to the peaks of the Taurus and Antitaurus mountains and the western edge of the Armenian highlands. There Arab armies could break through during most of the year to raid, but they were unable to hold bases on the Byzantine side through more than a few winters, when snow usually closed the passes.

Constantinople had a magnificent port, from which the Byzantines operated a navy slightly stronger than the Arabs' and far stronger than anyone else's. Therefore a series of coastal enclaves and islands stretching from the Crimea to Sicily remained Byzantine. Byzantium also exercised a sort of protectorate over several Italian and Dalmatian ports and claimed an authority over the papacy that the pope had never explicitly disowned. Of the empire's former possessions, Syria, Egypt, and North Africa had been too far from Constantinople and lacked natural defenses against the Arabs; most of the Balkan peninsula had been too poor to support its own defense against the Slavs and Bulgars; and most of Italy, again, had proved too far away. But for the time being, the territory that remained could be kept.

This territory was of two main physical types, which covered areas roughly equal in size but very unequal in economic value and population. The greater part of Byzantine Asia Minor was the Anatolian plateau, a vast but thinly settled frontier region in many ways resembling the American West. It was, and is, in varying degrees mountainous, dry, cold in the winter, and hot in the summer. Though some of it was good for growing grain, most of it was used only to pasture livestock, and a patch in the center was practically a desert. Arab raids, which were overwhelmingly directed against this plateau, made it a particularly unattractive place to live. In contrast, the rest of the empire's territory consisted almost without exception of coastal plains with a mild Mediterranean climate and a considerably denser population. There the land was suitable for raising not only grain but vegetables and the usual Mediterranean vines and olive trees. While this region too suffered raids, it was on the whole safer than the Anatolian plateau. Of course it included Constantinople, and was the region in which most Byzantines lived.[10]

Most Byzantines, though they were of very mixed ethnic background, spoke Greek, and usually they spoke nothing else. Greeks had been living in most of the islands and coastal territories for well over a thousand years. The peoples of the interior of Thrace and Asia Minor had been mostly Hellenized before the disasters of the seventh century, and during the subsequent invasions Greek-speaking refugees from areas lost to the empire had practically completed the process. Greeks had long been present in Sicily and the toe of Italy; by the eighth century, reinforced by refugees from Greece, they were probably in the majority there. The empire's largest linguistic minorities were the Latin speakers in Sicily, southern Italy, and Dalmatia, some Slavs in the Balkans and northwest Asia Minor, and a good many Armenians along the eastern frontier and elsewhere. The most prominent of these were the Armenians, who migrated from the East to seek their fortunes in the army, agriculture, or trade, learning Greek in the process. The empire also had a Greek-speaking Jewish minority of some size, concentrated in Constantinople and other towns and primarily engaged in manufacturing and commerce.

Under the enormous pressure of enemy invasions the empire's territory had come to be organized on a military footing. Its civil provinces had the same boundaries as the districts in which the various divisions of the army were stationed. In Asia Minor, Thrace, eastern Greece, and southern Italy, where the empire still held sizable stretches of land, there were armies called themes, each of which defended a province, also called a theme, with its own administration. The armies contained from 2,000 to 18,000 men. Each theme had a capital, which was the headquarters of its commander, known as a strategus, or general.

The larger themes had subdivisions called turmae, a name that also applied both to the troops and to the land they defended. The commanders of turmae, who often commanded more soldiers than the strategi of the smallest themes, were styled turmarchs. The turmae and the smaller themes were further divided into drungi, which consisted of units of 1,000 men and the corresponding territory under the command of a drungary. The empire's isolated enclaves and islands were organized into archontates, with small garrisons commanded by archons. Only Constantinople itself and the empire's protectorates in Italy and Dalmatia stood outside this system.

In military terms, the most important theme was the Anatolic, whose strategus had the highest rank and the largest army. His jurisdiction covered about half of the Anatolian plateau, through which the Arabs' main invasion routes passed. Although the eastern part of the Anatolic theme was mostly poor land open to devastation by any Arabs who got through the passes, the western part was reasonably fertile and well populated, and had one real city, the strategus's headquarters of Amorium. Next in military importance was the Armeniac theme, with the second-ranking strategus and the second-largest army, covering an area that was probably a bit larger than that of the Anatolic theme and much larger than that of any other jurisdiction. Aside from a narrow strip along the Black Sea that included the port of Trebizond, nearly all the Armeniac theme was sparsely populated plateau, as often raided by the Arabs as the eastern Anatolic theme was. These districts had large numbers of troops because they were good places to stop the Arabs before they reached the main centers of the empire's wealth, which lay elsewhere.[11]

The richest and most populous theme was certainly the Thracesian, though its army ranked a distant third in size. The Thracesian theme included the fertile Aegean coast and the river valleys of western Asia Minor, with many market towns and ports, of which Ephesus and Smyrna were the biggest. Though the Thracesian theme covered less than a seventh of the empire's area, about a quarter of the empire's towns lay within it, easily more than in any other theme. Notwithstanding the relatively small size of the Thracesian army, the theme's wealth made its strategus an important man. In 780 the strategus of the Thracesians was Michael Lachanodracon, an old and trusted comrade of Constantine V who had first assumed his command in 767 and was now the Byzantines' leading general.[12]

The northwestern corner of Asia Minor was occupied by the Opsician and Bucellarian themes. These had been one theme until Artabasdus, count of the Opsician, had used his concentration of troops to seize the capital between 741 and 743. Afterward, Constantine V had prudently divided off the Bucellarian theme from the Opsician, leaving each theme with a fairly modest army, though the head of the Opsician still held the title of count as a memento of his office's former importance. Both themes were generally well-settled and peaceful territories, though determined Arab raiders could occasionally penetrate especially to the Bucellarian theme, which was mostly on the plateau. Each had its headquarters

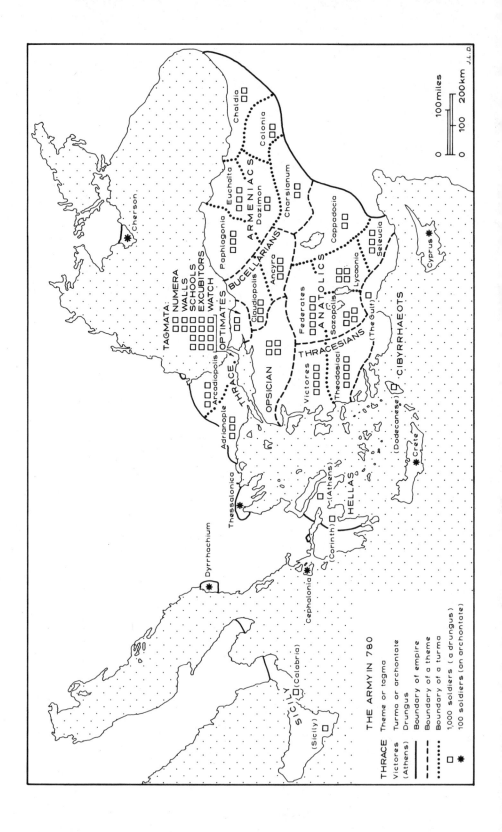

THE ARMY IN 780

THRACE   Theme or tagma
Victores   Turma or archontate
(Athens)   Drungus
     — — — Boundary of empire
     — — — Boundary of a theme
     · · · · · Boundary of a turma
     ▫ 1,000 soldiers (a drungus)
     ✳ 100 soldiers (an archontate)

Map labels:
Cherson
Chaldia
Colonia
Charsianum
Euchaïta
Paphlagonia
Dazimon
ARMENIACS
Cappadocia
Seleucia
BUCELLARIANS
Ancyra
ANATOLICS
Lycaonia
TAGMATA:
   ▫ NUMERA
   ▫ WALLS
   ▫ SCHOOLS
   ▫ EXCUBITORS
   ▫ WATCH
OPTIMATES
Claudiopolis
Federates
Sozopolis
(The Gulf)
Arcadiopolis
THRACE
OPSICIAN
THRACESIANS
CIBYRRHAEOTS
Adrianople
Victores
Theodosiaci
Cyprus
(Dodecanese)
Crete
Thessalonica
HELLAS
(Athens)
(Corinth)
Dyrrhachium
Cephalonia
(Calabria)
SICILY
(Sicily)

at a town of some size, the Opsician at Nicaea and the Bucellarian at Ancyra (modern Ankara).

Across the straits, Thrace formed a single theme with a medium-sized army. Though Thrace had naturally good farmland, in 780 it was just beginning to recover from thorough ravaging by the Slavs and Bulgars, to which Constantine V's wars had put an end for the present. Its capital was probably its largest market town, Adrianople. Though the theme of Thrace nominally included Constantinople, in practice the city was quite independent, since it had its own troops under independent commanders, a civil administration under a city prefect that had existed long before the system of themes, and, of course, the sovereign, who was normally in residence there.

The southern coast of Asia Minor and most of the islands of the Aegean Sea formed the Cibyrrhaeot theme, which instead of a regular army accommodated the empire's main navy. This was a force of some 60 ships with their oarsmen and marines, about half of whom were stationed in the islands and half on the Anatolian coast. The Cibyrrhaeot theme had a number of ports, notably the theme's capital at Attalia, and the islands and the plain around Attalia were fairly fertile and prosperous.

The only other Byzantine territories to rank as themes were the themes of Hellas in eastern Greece and of Sicily in southern Italy, whose armies were small and whose strategi were relatively minor officials. Though these themes were mere fragments of the empire's old possessions in Greece and Italy, they had several fortified towns—including Syracuse in Sicily and the empress Irene's home town of Athens—from which the empire was able to control some of their hinterlands, including all of Sicily.

The archontates were defended by very small garrisons. Crete was the richest archontate. Cyprus was only half Byzantine, demilitarized and sending half its revenues to the emperor and half to the caliph. The other archontates were mere outposts based on one or two isolated strong points: the city of Thessalonica in northern Greece, the town of Cherson in the Crimea, the island of Cephalonia off western Greece, and the town of Dyrrhachium in modern Albania.[13]

The economically and militarily significant part of the empire was thus in Asia Minor and Thrace, roughly the area of modern Turkey. The great bulk of the empire's population, territory, and farmland was there. While the other, fragmentary Byzantine possessions played a role in trade, even in that they were doubtless inferior to the core in Anatolia and Thrace; besides, trade was far less important in the empire's economic life than agriculture. The main military and diplomatic value of Sicily, Hellas, and the archontates was to provide defense against Arab sea power and to keep communications open with the Latin West and the Khazar khanate. They might also have been valuable as bases for reconquering lost Byzantine lands in Italy and the Balkans, but no such reconquest had been attempted for a long time. The empire's military priorities followed from the distribution of its armies: of 80,000 regular troops, 5,000 were stationed in Sicily, Hellas, and the islands, and 75,000 in Thrace and Asia Minor. The army's primary task was defense on land in the East.

Indisputably the empire's strongest enemy was the Arab caliphate, which was so much stronger that the Byzantines might well regard their survival against its opposition as a miracle. In their two sieges of Constantinople the Arabs had come close to conquering the empire outright. In 780 their superiority was still staggering. The caliphate was vastly larger in size: excluding all deserts, it covered about 7 million square kilometers, while the empire covered about 700,000. Further, the Arabs' farmland was generally more fertile, and they had more cities and a better-developed monetary economy. The annual revenue of the caliph al-Mahdī would have amounted to some 35 million Byzantine nomismata, while Irene probably commanded revenues of less than 2 million, though counting revenues in kind would have narrowed the difference somewhat. Of course, the Arabs' state was far more populous. Some recent estimates would put the population of the caliphate at this date at about 30 million and that of the empire at about 7 million. All these advantages naturally affected Arab military power. The largest army the Byzantines could put into the field for a campaign was about 20,000, but the Arabs could field over 100,000 soldiers at a time.[14]

Fortunately for the Byzantines, the caliphs no longer showed much interest in trying to conquer the whole empire. In 750 the Abbasid dynasty had overthrown the Umayyads and moved the caliphal capital from Damascus to Baghdad, and ever since the caliphs' concerns had shifted eastward. Nevertheless, in most years the Arabs conducted both a spring and a summer raid of Byzantine territory. Though the Byzantines sometimes defeated the raiders they had little hope of ending the raids for good, or even of thwarting a determined Arab attempt to take practically any place in Asia Minor. The land remained Byzantine after the raiders had left only by virtue of the system of themes, which made specific troops permanently responsible for holding each district.[15]

To the north, the Bulgars posed a less serious threat than the Arabs, but they were still menacing enough. A race of pagan Turkish warriors, the original Bulgars had made vassals of the native Slavs and Romanians of the lower Danube basin. They did not have an organized state of the same sort as the Byzantines and Arabs, and their numbers, even including their much more numerous vassals, were probably less than a million. But most of the time the Bulgar khan was able to field an army that was a match for the emperor's. In 780, however, after several sharp defeats at the hands of Constantine V, the Bulgars were less threatening than usual, because their army was not yet back to full strength and they were squabbling among themselves. Though Constantine had certainly not crushed Bulgaria, he had provided his heirs with a breathing space before the Bulgars could recover.[16]

West of the Bulgars were tribes of independent, pagan Slavs, whose lands the Byzantines called "Slavinias." The Slavs, who had no unified organization of any kind and were not particularly numerous or warlike, had migrated into Greece some two hundred years before, when the empire had faced more serious invasions elsewhere and the local population had been too small to defend itself. They had pushed the Byzantines out of the entire Greek peninsula except for the walled city of Thessalonica, a few coastal bases, and the theme of Hellas. In the rest of what we call Greece just enough Greek speakers and Christians remained to keep most towns from being utterly abandoned and their names forgotten. Any permanent reacquisition of the Slavinias in Greece would be a problem less of military conquest than of establishing a loyal population of sufficient size to hold the land. In the past no emperor had had a proper opportunity to attempt the resettlement of Greece with Byzantine subjects, especially because much of the land the empire still held had itself been depopulated. But in 780, with the Bulgars quiescent, things were beginning to change.

In Italy, the empire had many claims but few real holdings. In 751 the Lombard kingdom had annexed Ravenna, the capital of Byzantine Italy and the only base north of Calabria that the emperors had actually held with an army. Without a Byzantine garrison in Ravenna, the weak authority that the emperors had kept over several Italian city-states and over the papacy became entirely ineffective. Only the theme of Sicily, with its subject ducate of Calabria in the toe and heel of Italy, could be defended by Byzantine sea power and the modest army of the theme. (The theme of Sardinia, which had briefly served as a place of refuge for the imperial forces that the Arabs had expelled from North Africa, was abandoned before 780, though the empire may have maintained some tenuous links with the independent Sardinians.) The enclaves of Venetia, Naples, Amalfi, and Gaeta, and the Dalmatian ports headed by Jadera (Zara), had no wish to repudiate Byzantine authority, since acknowledging it brought no significant burdens and made trading with the empire somewhat easier. At best, however, they behaved as if they were Byzantine allies rather than possessions.[17]

The position of the papacy was more complex. Since 754, when Pope Paul I had called in the Carolingian Franks to defend Rome against the

Lombards, the papacy had been under Carolingian protection, and the popes were strongly opposed to the Iconoclasm of Constantine V and Leo IV. This disagreement over Iconoclasm, which had caused a church schism between Rome and Constantinople, led the emperors to transfer ecclesiastical jurisdiction over Sicily, Calabria, and what was left of Christian Greece from the papacy to the patriarchate of Constantinople. But the popes had never repudiated Byzantine political authority, and they still hoped that the emperors would abandon Iconoclasm. If they did, the Byzantines might hope to regain some measure of power in central Italy, where in 780 Pope Hadrian I was finding it difficult to secure the formerly Byzantine territories Charlemagne had supposedly ceded to him in 774. Yet the nearest Byzantine possessions were separated from Rome by the independent Lombard principality of Benevento, a minor power attempting to pursue a middle course between the much stronger Carolingians and Byzantines.

Around the Black Sea, the Byzantines had few military problems, since they were the only naval power in the area. Though their base at the Crimean port of Cherson was theoretically vulnerable, it was a useful commercial outlet for the neighboring Khazar khanate, a large, loosely organized power comparable to that of the Bulgars. The only regular state that the Khazars adjoined was the caliphate, with which they shared a border along the Caucasus. As natural enemies of the Arabs, the Khazars were natural allies of the Byzantines. Leo III had formalized the alliance in 733 when he married Constantine V to the Khazar princess Irene, who became the mother of Leo IV. In 780, however, relations with the Khazars were not close, and the prospects for a Byzantine or Khazar offensive in the Caucasus were not promising—at least not in comparison with the empire's opportunities in the Balkans.[18]

THE ADMINISTRATION

During the continuing military crises of the seventh and early eighth centuries, the empire's civil government had become more centralized at Constantinople, while the provinces were coming under military administration. The stages by which the government and army changed are difficult to distinguish and date, but the process was complete well before 780. The main changes must have been brought about by imperial decree, often as a matter of conscious policy. Still, the seventh century in particular had been chaotic, and many times the press of events must have left the emperors with little choice, and little time in which to choose. The resulting machinery of government was workable, and considerably simpler and cheaper than the system it replaced. It was not, however, very efficiently or scrupulously run, and the issue of Iconoclasm had divided and demoralized its civil servants.

The emperor—or now the regent Irene—had ultimate authority over the whole civil and military establishment, and power that in practice was nearly absolute. Legal authority might seem to have been shared by the various members of the imperial family: that is, not only the emperor but also the empress if she had been crowned Augusta, the emperor's son or other heir if he had been crowned junior emperor, and younger sons and other relatives by blood or marriage who held high titles. In practice, however, the senior emperor did what he wished, and no real power belonged to other members of his family, no matter how grandly titled, unless they acquired it by intrigue or force of will.

The patriarch of Constantinople commanded some moral authority independent of the imperial power if he was extremely careful about using it. Nonetheless, if the emperor wanted to replace the patriarch, the emperor could do so, unpleasant though the process might be. The higher civil officials and dignitaries formed a group called the Senate, but in normal times it had a purely ceremonial role, as when it swore loyalty to Constantine VI under Leo IV. It included men whom the emperor consulted, but he seems seldom to have consulted the Senate as a body.

The only important check on the emperor's authority was the fear or reality of revolution, either by palace coup or by armed warfare. In rebellions the opinion of the citizens sometimes counted for something, and the wishes of the soldiers for somewhat more; but generally a handful of civil and military officials made or broke a revolution. If officials failed in a revolt, however, their fate was exile or relegation to a monastery at best and mutilation or execution at worst. Most revolutions did fail: since Leo III had come to power in a successful revolt in 717, eight rebellions or conspiracies had been put down. As a rule, then, if officials disliked a regime they found it prudent to resist passively and unobtrusively, as many iconophile officials resisted the Iconoclasm of Leo III, Constantine V, and Leo IV. Dissent, like corruption, tended to pass undetected if any care was taken to conceal it.[19]

This centralized but not necessarily unified government had its seat in the Great Palace, a large walled district within the capital. The palace housed not only the imperial family and their personal servants but the central bureaucracy and a good-sized garrison. The complex included dozens of buildings connected by corridors and separated by courtyards, containing audience halls, waiting rooms, meeting rooms, offices, banquet halls, bedchambers, churches, kitchens, baths, a small library, a large stable, treasuries, wardrobes, and barracks. Also inside the enclosure were gardens, pleasure pavilions, a private racetrack, and a port with a lighthouse. To the west a passage led to the Hippodrome, where the imperial family showed itself to the people of Constantinople in the imperial box when it watched chariot races. To the north another passage led to the Great Church of the Holy Wisdom, or St. Sophia, where the imperial family appeared in its own gallery to attend Mass. St. Sophia was officially a palace church. The original cathedral had been the nearby Church of the Holy Peace, or St. Irene, but the patriarch and his staff had long been based in St. Sophia and the adjoining patriarchal buildings, and formed part of the palace community.

The community of the Great Palace was formal but not impersonal. The emperor himself paid over a thousand of his higher officials their annual salaries during three days in Lent, and had his chief chamberlain pay the rest during Holy Week. On the twelve days of Christmas the emperor invited the higher officials to dinner in the Banquet Hall of the Nineteen Couches, along with some priests, monks, charioteers from the Hippodrome, and twelve poor men chosen at random each day as an act of charity. Other banquets were held during the rest of the year. There were ceremonies and chariot races on special occasions, often accompanied by presents of money for the officials and sometimes for the clergy, soldiers, and people. The intention was that the emperor's subjects should consider themselves well taken care of, and the higher officials could do so with reason.[20]

The staff of the Great Palace, which now had been purged by Leo IV, enjoyed the most frequent access to the imperial family and usually its greatest confidence, because palace officials were less likely to revolt than civil or military ones. One reason was that the palatine officials were nearly all eunuchs. This custom, originally designed to protect the virtue of the women of the imperial family, had the more important advantage that eunuchs were counted ineligible to hold imperial office themselves and could have no children to conspire for. Another reason for the palace officials' reliability was that they were more dependent on the sovereigns than other officials, since they lacked independent sources of power. Irene, as a woman, had seen much more of the eunuchs than of other officials before she became regent, and she was to make greater use of them than most Byzantine rulers did. Eunuchs could hold nearly any civil or military office, and on the palace staff they were often influential advisers. Some held offices connected with supervising and maintaining the palace and had various subordinates. These included the provestiarius, who had custody of the emperor's regalia and private treasury, the papias, who was custodian of the Great Palace, and the steward of the emperor's table. But the influence of the most important palace officials had little to do with their offices.[21]

Besides the eunuchs, the court included many other officials, some with practical duties and others with mostly honorary ones. Particularly at the emperor's service were the four hundred men of his private bodyguard, who had special robes, insignia, and quarters in the palace. The emperor's private stable, headed by the protostrator, also had a sizable staff of grooms and custodians. Other court officials had higher rank and pay and lighter duties, such as the syncellus, who was the chief adviser of the patriarch of Constantinople and represented the emperor's interest in the Church, and the chartulary of the inkpot, who had custody of the pen and purple ink that the emperor used to sign documents. A characteristically Byzantine official, the master of ceremonies, kept track of the elaborate rituals that the imperial family and its court were supposed to follow. The highest office for a man outside the imperial family was that of magister, a well-paid adviser sometimes entrusted with important missions. There were also purely honorary offices that the emperors bestowed as favors or sold to the wealthy as prestige items.

The actual work of the central administration of the empire was in the hands of a bureaucracy of about 500 men, based in offices in the palace complex. Each of its thirteen bureaus was headed by an official directly responsible to the Crown. Nine of these officials were also supervised by a tenth, the sacellarius, who in 780 was the eunuch John. Though his post was well paid and prestigious, his clerks did the supervising, leaving him free to take on other assignments at the emperor's direction, such as military expeditions, embassies, or even additional offices. In contrast, the nine secretarial officials whom he supervised had heavy responsibilities.

The secretaries with the largest staffs and the main administrative duties were the three senior logothetes. The postal logothete, in 780 a certain Gregory, was most concerned with foreign and domestic policy and most, though not very much, like a minister of state. Supervising and maintaining the post—the imperial communications system of roads and mounted couriers—had traditionally been central to conducting the empire's diplomacy and handling its internal security, all of which fell within this logothete's province. Then the general logothete was a finance minister, in charge of raising cash revenue. He supervised a corps of tax collectors who were essentially private businessmen, collecting the empire's specified land and hearth taxes and trade and market duties in return for a fixed share of the receipts. The general logothete's duties of consulting records and collecting money may seem routine, but his role could be vital, especially because the empire's creaking system of tax collection required constant attention and provided ample opportunities for corruption. Not much later a general logothete, Nicephorus, was to rise from that office directly to the throne. Finally, the military logothete was in

THE CENTRAL BUREAUCRACY

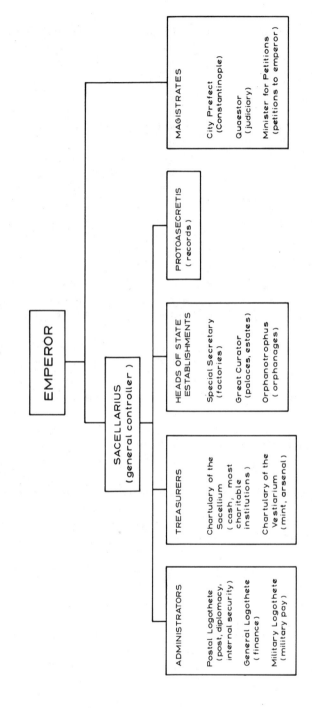

EMPEROR

SACELLARIUS (general controller)

ADMINISTRATORS

Postal Logothete (post, diplomacy, internal security)

General Logothete (finance)

Military Logothete (military pay)

TREASURERS

Chartulary of the Sacellium (cash, most charitable institutions)

Chartulary of the Vestiarium (mint, arsenal)

HEADS OF STATE ESTABLISHMENTS

Special Secretary (factories)

Great Curator (palaces, estates)

Orphanotrophus (orphanages)

PROTOASECRETIS (records)

MAGISTRATES

City Prefect (Constantinople)

Quaestor (judiciary)

Minister for Petitions (petitions to emperor)

charge of distributing pay to the army and navy. John, the sacellarius in 780, later acquired the office of military logothete as well.

The heads of the other secretarial departments seldom took an active part in politics. Perhaps the most important was the protoasecretis, who headed the chancery that drafted and kept the records of all departments; he was generally a man of impressive learning and as such could receive other assignments. More than one protoasecretis won promotion to patriarch of Constantinople despite his lay status, since he was trusted by the Crown and was educated enough to handle theological matters. In 780 the protoasecretis was probably already the future patriarch Tarasius, the most learned man of his time. The other departments were those of two treasurers and three administrators of state establishments. Of the treasurers, the chartulary of the sacellium handled cash and supervised most of the imperial charitable institutions, while the chartulary of the vestiarium handled objects other than cash, supervising the imperial mint and arsenal. The administrators were the special secretary, who ran the imperial factories, the great curator, who administered the emperor's estates and lesser palaces, and the orphanotrophus ("orphan feeder"), who ran the imperial orphanages in the capital.

Three officials known as magistrates were independent of the secretarial departments. Among them were the quaestor, who headed the judiciary, drafted laws, and was sometimes a person of consequence, and the minister for petitions, who transmitted petitions to the emperor. The highest-ranking of the magistrates and indeed of all civil officials was the city prefect, civil governor of the capital. As such, the prefect controlled the capital's trade and manufacturing through his subordinates, who included the heads of the twenty-odd commercial guilds. Despite his high rank, the prefect's job was not a powerful one, since the emperor and other officials exercised so much power in Constantinople that little was left over for him.

Though this bureaucracy may have been what we call "byzantine" in its complexity, it was surprisingly small; including church officials, it might have numbered a thousand men. That it was able to function at all was mostly due to its making the private sector and the army do much of the work of administration. The staffs of the central bureaus consisted mostly of record keepers who kept track of what should be done for the government; agents and messengers who ordered the army, tax collectors, and private citizens to do what should be done; and inspectors who tried to discover whether the orders had been carried out properly. In theory, such a system provided all necessary government at low cost to the state.

About 780, however, the equity and efficiency of the system were not of a high order, particularly when it came to taxation. Constantine V had been on rather bad terms with his civil service and took less interest in it than in his army. As a result, nothing resembling a census seems to have been taken since 733, under Leo III, and the tax records were in disarray. Tax evasion was common among the rich, and the poor complained that the tax collectors made them pay more than they owed. Embezzlement by tax collectors appears to have been widespread, and much of what was legally due from land and hearth taxes and trade duties went uncollected. The problem was probably not only corruption but also the poor education of many civil servants, who lacked the skills needed to prepare and use the regulations and records on which the system depended. The government still worked after a fashion, but possibilities for improving it were vast.[22]

THE ARMY

The Byzantine army comprised the themes, normally stationed in the provinces, and the tagmata, normally stationed in or near Constantinople. In principle, the themes were primarily a defensive force for their own territories, while the tagmata were primarily a mobile force that could reinforce the themes or conduct offensive operations on foreign soil. In practice, both themes and tagmata combined the functions of a garrison and a mobile army, though the tagmata were more mobile than the themes. The distinction between theme and tagma was blurred in the case of the Optimates, a support corps of muleteers associated with the tagmata but stationed in a small district of its own across the straits from Constantinople. The tagmata could also defend Constantinople itself if it was attacked. In 780 the tagmata and Optimates totaled 18,000 soldiers and the themes 62,000.

Though all the officers of the themes and tagmata received an adequate salary and the chief commanders enjoyed a princely one, the common soldiers drew only modest and infrequent cash pay, which was intended to supplement their livelihood rather than to provide it. The thematic soldiers chiefly supported and armed themselves from the income of land grants that they held in return for their military service. For the thematic cavalry these grants were so large that the cavalrymen did not need to work for a living and could provide their own horses and rations while they were on campaign. The infantry had smaller grants, but were probably better off than ordinary peasants. The government made the purchase of armor and weapons easy by producing them at state factories and arranging for them to be sold at warehouses located in the provinces.[23]

Among the tagmatic soldiers, at least the Optimates seem also to have held land grants in their district. But the state supported the tagmata mainly by providing their soldiers with generous monthly living allowances, paid in the form of grain requisitioned from the population. These allowances exceeded the needs of one man, and the surplus could be sold. By these means the soldiers of the tagmata were able to support their families, and the cavalrymen among them were prosperous enough to have squires. Tagmatic soldiers received their arms from the state, which also supplied the cavalry and Optimates with horses and mules and fodder for them. With quarters usually provided by the state as well, the troops of the tagmata were well off, though they were less independent than their fellows in the themes.

Besides the Optimates, who carried the army's baggage on their mules, the empire had three other military departments with support functions. The logothete of the herds and his staff requisitioned the mules and horses for the tagmata from ranches in Asia Minor, then handed the animals over to the department of the count of the stable, which brought them to the area of the capital and distributed them. Though at this time the empire's central naval command had no marines of its own, it had ships and oarsmen, probably already under the drungary of the Fleet, who is first attested a little later. This central fleet transported regular tagmatic or thematic troops on naval expeditions for which the thematic navy did not suffice. Naturally the army also included surveyors, quartermasters, and scouts; there was one medic for every 20 to 25 soldiers in both the tagmata and the themes.

Although the names of the divisions of the tagmata dated from centuries before—most were derived from Latin names given when Latin was still the language of the government—the tagmata as they existed in 780 were largely the creation of Constantine V. Constantine had enlarged them enormously, regularized their command structures, and partly differentiated their functions. His system provided for two tagmata, the Schools and the Excubitors, to form a mobile strike force supported by the Optimates. The domestic of the Schools, the highest-ranking commander of a tagma, could lead expeditions if the emperor did not. When the Schools and Excubitors were not on campaign, they were stationed in the parts of Thrace and Bithynia adjacent to Constantinople, while the Optimates stayed in their own Bithynian territory. The three other tagmata—the Watch, a cavalry corps, and the Numera and the so-called Walls, both infantry—were usually stationed within the city walls. All three formed a garrison and police force for the palace and the city; their commanders were seldom active in politics. The Watch sometimes accompanied the emperor on campaigns, but the Numera and Walls remained in Constantinople, keeping order, tending the city prisons, and guarding against surprise attack.[24]

All the tagmata were organized in much the same way. The chief com-

THE TAGMA OF THE SCHOOLS

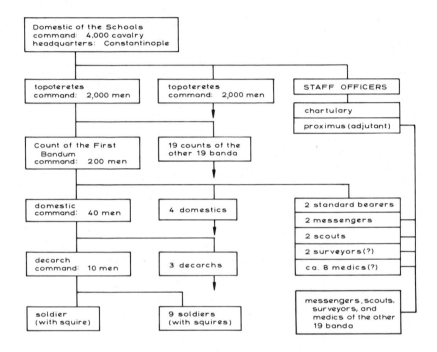

mander of each had the title of domestic, except for the drungary of the Watch and the count of the Walls. Every commander had a clerical staff of two to keep the roll of his tagma and to supervise his corps of messengers. He also had one or two lieutenants, each of whom commanded ten banda of 200 soldiers each. The banda were known by their numbers at this time; about 780 the future hermit Joannicius enrolled in Bandum Eighteen of the Excubitors, and a lead seal survives from a dispatch issued by the commander of Bandum Eight of the Schools. In battle and in parades, each bandum of the four cavalry tagmata was distinguished by its standards—images of Fortune, monograms of Christ, dragons, scepters, and so on—carried by two standard-bearers. Two messengers were attached to each bandum to carry dispatches back and forth. Banda also had variously titled officers commanding brigades of 40 men, subdivided into squadrons of 10 men headed by decarchs. All the officers ranking above decarch were invited to dine with the emperor during the Christmas season, those of each tagma on a different day.[25]

Under Constantine V the tagmata had proved to be loyal and effective troops. In contrast to the more prosperous cavalrymen of the themes, most cavalrymen of the tagmata came from peasant families and had no means of support but that provided by the state; Joannicius had come from a family of farmers and tended pigs before he enlisted. Most, even Joannicius before he saw the error of his ways, were iconoclasts and loyal to Constantine's memory. In 780 the domestic of the Schools, Anthony the Patrician, had held his command since Constantine's reign and possibly since Constantine had created it. The domestic of the Excubitors, another Constantine, had probably also been appointed by Constantine V and was certainly a supporter of his namesake's sons and of Iconoclasm. Accustomed to and indebted to a warlike iconoclast emperor, the tagmata were naturally suspicious of a ruler who was a woman and an iconophile. Irene soon had trouble with them.[26]

The organization of a theme was similar to that of a tagma but more elaborate, because the theme had a role in administration and its widely dispersed troops were harder to keep track of. All the themes were organized according to the same pattern, allowing for the differences in the numbers of their soldiers and some minor differences in titles. A description of the organization of the Thracesian theme will show how the themes functioned.[27]

The strategus of the Thracesians, in 780 Michael Lachanodracon, had his headquarters at the smallish walled town of Chonae in the southeastern part of the theme, the region Arab raiders were most likely to attack. The theme had two turmae of 4,000 men each, the Theodosiaci and the Victores, whose Latin names went back to their origins as Roman legions of the fourth century A.D. The turmarch of the Theodosiaci was based at Chonae with the strategus; the turmarch of the Victores normally resided in the northwestern part of the theme at the port of Adramyttium, and was responsible for the territory of his turma in that sector.

At Chonae the strategus had six staff officers. Of these, the count of the tent was the strategus's principal aide, the chartulary kept the theme's muster-rolls, and the domestic probably supervised the support corps of scouts, surveyors, and quartermasters, who were attached to local units. The strategus's protocancellarius, with a half-dozen subordinate clerks, drafted administrative documents, while the protomandator supervised the theme's 80 messengers, who were spread all over the theme. The strategus also had an elite guard of 100 men known as spatharii, headed by the centarch of the spatharii.[28]

The regular command structure of the theme began with the turmarchs. Under them came the drungaries, each of whom commanded a thousand men. Like strategi and turmarchs, the drungaries had headquarters of their own (at Chonae, Adramyttium, and elsewhere) and were responsible for particular territories. At the regular musterings of the

THE THRACESIAN THEME IN 780

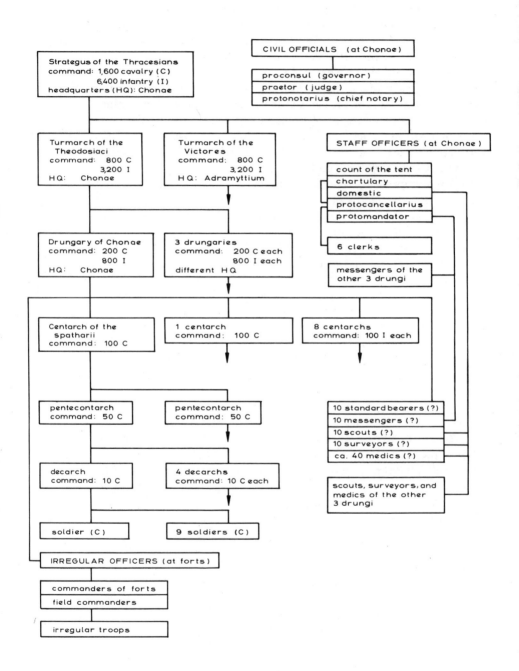

troops at their central camps, the drungaries would determine how many of their drungus's thousand soldiers were ready to serve with their proper equipment, and would punish those who were not. One of the benefactions of St. Philaretus the Almsgiver at about this date was to give a horse to a cavalryman whose own horse had died and left the unfortunate man exposed to the wrath of his drungary.

Apparently each drungus had 200 cavalry and 800 infantry, all spread over the whole territory of the drungus. On campaigns, some of these thousand men served as standard-bearers, messengers, scouts, and surveyors, apparently 10 of each, with about 40 medics. The drungus had three tiers of officers below its drungary: one centarch for every 100 soldiers, one pentecontarch for every 50, and one decarch for every 10. When called up by a drungary, even civilians could serve as irregular troops under their own officers, especially to garrison the theme's forts. Because the Thracesian theme was relatively secure territory, screened from Arab invasion routes by mountains to the east, it had only fifteen fortified places, including the city of Ephesus; themes that were more exposed to attack had more forts. In peacetime, when most of the theme's organization existed only on the chartulary's muster-rolls, the soldiers lived the lives of small landholders on their land grants, except when they were called up for drills. Only the senior officers and a few soldiers at each headquarters stayed on active duty.[29]

When orders came from Constantinople for a campaign, or when the strategus learned that an invasion was likely, he sent out his messengers to the drungaries to order a mobilization. Consulting the names and addresses on the muster-rolls, the drungary sent his own messengers to summon the troops to appear with their arms. Seldom if ever were all the troops sent on campaign, because some were needed for local defense. For a general campaign, contingents from various themes met at specified camps along the main military roads; these contingents then joined the main army, which included some or all of the tagmata of the Schools, Excubitors, and Optimates, as it was led from the capital. Smaller campaigns could be staged with soldiers from the themes alone.

If an enemy attack came unexpectedly, the theme's officers organized the best defense they could, first concentrating their soldiers at a walled town or fort. All but the least threatened drungi had one fortification, and the most exposed had as many as five, usually built on mountains or hills overlooking the cultivated plains. The civilian population escaped to another district, the hills, or the fort with whatever animals, valuables, and other property they could remove. Civilians who served as irregular troops joined in the defense of the fort. If an opportunity presented itself, the defenders could try to pursue or ambush the enemy and to deprive him of his booty. Otherwise, since the Arabs were seldom willing to take the time for a siege and the Slavs and Bulgars knew little of siege warfare, the army and civilian population were safe in the fort, and could reestablish themselves after the raiders had departed. By these means the Byzantines managed to keep possession of their land despite the superior power of the Arabs and the harassment of the Bulgars and Slavs.

The naval theme of the Cibyrrhaeots was in a special category. Its soldiers were marines, who had military land grants comparable to those of cavalrymen. The territory of the Cibyrrhaeot theme, consisting entirely of coastlands and islands, was sheltered from land attacks by other themes, by mountains, and by the sea. The Cibyrrhaeots could defend themselves against naval attacks by the Arabs, to which their theme was particularly exposed. But their fleet's most important function was to serve on expeditions overseas, since the empire lacked a strong central navy. The themes of Sicily and Hellas also had a few ships of their own, but in the eighth century these were primarily used for defensive purposes.

Within his theme, the strategus had full military powers, which he exercised through his staff and his subordinate turmarchs and drungaries. Most judicial and financial powers were in other hands. In 780 the themes still had civil governors, with subordinates who kept their records and served as civil judges; the tax system was run by officials who were independent of both strategus and governor. Though these civil officials acted as representatives of the central government, most of whose departments operated throughout the empire, much was left to the discretion of the strategus. For example, between 771 and 772 Michael Lachanodracon, already strategus of the Thracesians, confiscated and sold all the monasteries in his theme, together with their icons, vestments, plate, books, and lands, and sent the proceeds to the central government. He also reportedly forced every monk and nun under his jurisdiction to marry on penalty of being blinded and exiled. For this Michael won Constantine V's commendation as "a man after my own heart," but the initiative had been Michael's. The main tie of dependence between the strategi and the central government was financial, since with few exceptions all revenues were forwarded to the capital; military payrolls and other appropriations were sent to the themes by the military and postal logothetes. Still, strategi could revolt. Leo III had been strategus of the great Anatolic theme when he seized power in 717.[30]

If the process by which the system of themes developed remains obscure in some respects, its outlines are now fairly clear. As armies, the oldest themes were survivals of the military divisions of the sixth-century empire, with their Latin names Hellenized. The Anatolic theme had been the Army of Oriens, or the East, the Armeniac theme the Army of Armenia, the Opsician theme the armies "in the emperor's presence" around Constantinople, and the Thracesian theme the Army of Thrace. During the military reverses of the early seventh century all these armies except those around Constantinople had been transferred or driven from their original stations into the empire's remaining territory in Asia Minor. Later in the seventh century the theme of Sicily had been separated from the Army of Italy under the exarch of Ravenna; the rest of this army disintegrated in 751. Also in the late seventh century the theme of Hellas appeared, possibly including elements of the mostly destroyed Army of Illyricum. Dating from around 700 were the theme of Thrace, probably formed from part of the Opsician, and the Cibyrrhaeot theme, probably formed from an old naval command instituted by Justinian I. The Bucellarian theme was separated from the Opsician in the mid-eighth century. These were all the themes that existed in 780.

The real questions are when the themes became administrative divisions as well as armies, and when the soldiers came to hold military lands instead of receiving a living wage. The sources say nothing about these changes; but the sources for the seventh century are very poor. Despite many recent and clever arguments that the changes occurred gradually and were completed late, it is likely that they were fairly rapid and early, and date from around 650. Though the themes had civil governors as late as the mid-ninth century, the chaos of the mid-seventh century would soon have led to *de facto* military government in the provinces for most purposes. Similarly, as soon as the empire had suffered its greatest territorial losses in the mid-seventh century it no longer had the revenue to maintain the former level of pay of those soldiers who had not been lost with their old stations but had been withdrawn into Asia Minor. The only possible means of providing for the troops was through land, supplied either by confiscation or from the imperial estates, which were extensive in the sixth century but very small when they are heard of again in the ninth. The military lands may not have been explicitly protected by law until the early tenth century, but the laws of that time make it clear that military lands had existed long before then.[31]

Constantine V had left the themes in good fighting condition, but not necessarily strong enough to risk provoking the Arabs to mount a full-scale attack. In 778, when Leo IV learned that the Arab general Thumama was preparing a more ambitious summer raid than usual, he sent a preventive expedition of troops drawn from all five Asian themes and headed by his father's friend Michael Lachanodracon, strategus of the Thracesians. Crossing the Arab frontier for a campaign of just six days, Michael forced the city of Germanicea to pay tribute, plundered the land, took many of the local Monophysite Christians prisoner, and defeated Thumama, who lost some 2,000 troops and had to abandon his plans for a raid. Leo celebrated a triumph in Constantinople.

The caliph al-Mahdī was enraged, and the next year sent a retaliatory expedition of over 30,000 soldiers against the Anatolic and Opsician themes, and another, probably smaller, against the Armeniac theme. Leo ordered the strategi of Asia Minor not to fight pitched battles, but to evacuate the population to the forts and to call up 3,000 troops from each theme, a total of 15,000; these men were to shadow the enemy, burning the pastures to deny them fodder. The first Arab expedition reached Dorylaeum in the Opsician theme but merely took plunder. The second sacked three forts in the Armeniacs, including the seat of a turmarch at Colonia. Not satisfied with this, the caliph ordered a new Arab base to be fortified at Adata, near the Byzantine frontier, and dispatched two more raiding expeditions. The first, under his son Hārūn al-Rashīd, took and sacked the fort of Semaluus in the Armeniacs after a long siege, but the second, under the unfortunate Thumama, invaded the Thracesians only to be defeated by Lachanodracon with the loss of Thumama's brother. Still unsatisfied, the caliph was planning further expeditions at the time of Leo IV's death.[32]

To fulfill the minimal objective of preventing enemies from permanently conquering Byzantine territory, the themes performed well enough. Year after year the Arabs and Bulgars raided, sacked forts, and killed troops; but the Byzantines reoccupied the land, rebuilt the forts, and replaced the men. Though soldiers died, the land remained, and each gap in the rolls was filled by the dead soldier's son, one of his other relatives, or anyone else who would take over his military land grant and draw his pay. In principle all deaths in battle were to be reported up the chain of command at once and replacements found without delay, and in fact the delays seem to have been fairly short. Only when troops and land were lost together, as when the isolated exarchate of Ravenna fell to the Lombards in 751, did a division of the army disappear, and that happened only in very rare and dire cases. Moreover, the themes were remarkably cheap for the government to support, since the soldiers, who lived off the produce of their farms, were paid less than a living wage.

On the other hand, for purposes of actually keeping raiders out of Byzantine territory, the themes were not at all satisfactory. They did not even make serious efforts to provide such a defense, and as they were constituted in 780 they could scarcely have done so. The main Arab invasion routes passed through either the Cilician Gates or the Pass of Adata into the Anatolic theme or through the Pass of Melitene into the Armeniacs. In 780 the Cilician Gates and the Pass of Adata were defended by the Anatolics' turma of Cappadocia, and the Pass of Melitene by the Armeniacs' turma of Charsianum; each of these turmae apparently had just 2,000 soldiers. Therefore, of the 54,000 troops in Asia Minor only 4,000 were near the crucial frontier passes where Arab raiders might possibly have been stopped. With Byzantine troops deployed in this way, even small bands of Arab raiders could sweep through the passes with little or no opposition.

For purposes of intercepting raiders, furthermore, the themes' command structure was not flexible enough. The problem was not so much that the themes were too large, because in an emergency the individual turmarchs and drungaries seem to have been able to take a good deal of initiative. Even a drungus, however, covered a wide area. The turma of Cappadocia had as many as nineteen widely separated forts, but only two drungi. The thousand soldiers in each drungus were spread all over its territory, with infantry and cavalry living mixed together, though they belonged to different units. No officer lower than a drungary could mobilize troops, because the drungary was the lowest officer with a permanent base. Some time was needed for him to give orders and muster his men, and the Arabs and Bulgars tried not to give advance warning. Thus an effective defense on even a small scale could usually be mounted only after the raiders had penetrated some distance into imperial territory.

There was also the problem that the themes at this time showed a distressing willingness to revolt against the central government. Constantine V, after putting down the revolt of the count of the Opsician Artabasdus, had built up enough personal loyalty among the troops to decrease this danger, but once he and his son were dead it could be expected to reappear. After all, troops who were self-sufficient on their own military estates, and received pay from the central government amounting to about half the wages of a farm hand, had little incentive to back the reigning emperor in a time of revolt. If a soldier simply deserted, of course, he would lose his military land, which he held on condition of doing military service. But if he joined a rebellion backed by his local commanders, he kept his land and only risked losing his cash pay, which was sent out periodically from Constantinople. This was no great deterrent to rebellion, and individual soldiers were seldom punished for participating in large-scale revolts.[33]

In the late eighth century, however, the Byzantine government was probably unable to improve the effectiveness of the themes very much. The themes' total strength was smaller than that of some invading Arab armies; they needed to keep troops in reserve and could not easily spare enough men for a serious static defense at the Arab frontier passes. At the Bulgar frontier, which lacked high mountains and could be crossed almost anywhere, a static defense was out of the question. Dividing the thousand-man drungi into subordinate districts with their own commanders and headquarters would presumably have been possible but would have risked mutiny, because it would have meant turning the themes into a considerably more tightly organized, disciplined, and settled force. Significantly raising the soldiers' pay was possible in the short term because Constantine V had left a large gold reserve, but it would have been very dangerous in the long run unless revenues were greatly increased to cover the added expenditure. Because the army performed its basic functions adequately and its defects were familiar and not easily correctable, the empire lived with it as it was.

THE ECONOMY

After the loss of so much territory and the repeated devastation of the rest, we might expect the empire to have been utterly impoverished, but such does not seem to have been the case. The empire's economy was overwhelmingly agricultural, and agriculture is hard to destroy. The enemy raids do not seem to have damaged Byzantine farmland permanently, though much of it probably lay fallow for a while after its cultivators fled. After the intermittent plagues had come to an end in most of the empire in 747, nothing prevented natural population growth from providing new tillers for underused and abandoned land. At about the same time the empire began to benefit from a general warming of the earth's climate.[34]

By 780 the process of demographic and agricultural recovery must already have been under way. The empire had never had much private trade or manufacturing to lose; some had survived, and whatever had disappeared would have been an insignificant part of the whole economy. More important was the government's share, which included the army, the bureaucracy, and the state industries, and which supported the empire's currency. Through determined efforts, the government had succeeded in keeping up a sizable state revenue and preventing the empire from slipping completely out of a monetary economy into a natural one.

Practically every adult Byzantine used coined money occasionally, if only to pay his taxes. The emperors minted two standard coins: the gold nomisma and the copper follis. These were exchanged at the rate of 288 folles to the nomisma. The nomisma was the foundation of the system and, remarkable to relate, in 780 it was still struck at the standard of 72 to the pound of gold established by Constantine I (306–37). About the size of an American nickel, the nomisma amounted to some eighteen days' wages for a laborer; the law considered a man rich if he had property

7. The main denominations of Byzantine coins in the eighth century, all shown actual size, with the obverse on the left and the reverse on the right. *First row*, The gold nomisma, worth 1/72 of a pound of gold: *obverse*, Constantine V and the future Leo IV; *reverse*, the dead Leo III. *Second row*, The gold semissis, worth 1/2 nomisma: *obverse*, Artabasdus (usurper, 741–43); *reverse*, a cross, with the legend "Jesus Christ conquers." *Third row*, The gold tremissis, worth 1/3 nomisma: *obverse*, Leo III (r. 717–41); *reverse*, the future Constantine V. *Fourth row*, The silver miliaresion, worth 1/12 nomisma: *obverse*, the legend "Constantine [VI] and Irene, Emperors in God"; *reverse*, a cross, with the legend "Jesus Christ conquers." *Fifth row*, The copper follis, worth 1/24 miliaresion: *obverse*, Leo IV and the future Constantine VI; *reverse*, the dead Leo III and Constantine V, with the obsolete mark of value, M (40 [nummi]). *Sixth row*, The copper half-follis. The type is the same as that of the follis, except that it is half the size. The mark of value, M, is therefore meaningless. (Photos: Dumbarton Oaks Byzantine Collection, Washington)

worth 144 nomismata, or two pounds of gold. Even the follis, about the size of a silver dollar, was a valuable coin for a poor man. A laborer in a town earned only fifteen or sixteen folles a day; a farm hand could earn just twelve. One follis could buy a loaf of bread of about a pound at the normal price. The smallest coin was the half-follis. Between follis and nomisma in value were the miliaresion, a silver coin worth 24 folles or one-twelfth of a nomisma, and fractional gold coins worth one-half or one-third of a nomisma; these intermediate coins were somewhat rare. Large sums of gold were usually handled in sealed bags containing nomismata reckoned by their weight in pounds.[35]

This system was better suited to large transactions in gold than to everyday transactions of small sums. Most of all, it met the needs of the state, which collected, kept, and spent gold in large amounts. In 780 the empire's revenues and expenditures appear to have been roughly in balance at about 25,000 pounds of gold a year, or 1.8 million nomismata. The state also held a gold reserve of perhaps twice that much, the sum that had been set aside by Constantine V for his younger sons and that Leo IV had probably kept more or less intact during his short reign. About two-thirds of the state expenditures went for defense, and about half of that for the army payroll, reduced though it was by the system of military lands. Of the other expenditures, some two-thirds went to pay the civil service, mostly as the share of the taxes assigned to the many tax collectors. Around nine-tenths of all revenue came from the hearth and land taxes paid by farmers, with trade and market duties making up about half of the remaining tenth.[36]

This annual collection and disbursement of gold by the state did much to maintain a monetary economy all over the empire. Every farmer had to pay his land and hearth taxes in cash, which averaged about one nomisma a family. As a result, some food, generally livestock or something else moveable with relatively little expense, had to be sold and made available for consumption elsewhere, particularly in nearby towns, instead of being entirely consumed or stored by the producer or bartered with his neighbors. The land tax, which was determined by the quantity and quality of land rather than by how much it produced, provided a powerful incentive not to leave land unused or underexploited. If a landholder defaulted on his taxes, his land was given to his neighbors, who then had to cultivate it and pay the tax. If land was raided or otherwise damaged, however, the state granted a temporary tax exemption.

Since soldiers were settled all over the empire, even in outlying areas, paying them in cash put money into wide circulation. Ordinary soldiers seem to have received one nomisma for each year of service up to full pay of six nomismata a year; the pay scale for officers ascended gradually to the opulent 2,880 nomismata paid to the strategi of the Anatolic, Armeniac, and Thracesian themes. Tax collectors, who took about a tenth of their receipts as their share, traveled widely over the empire and spent money as they went. In Constantinople, the government was by far the largest employer, and paid well, supporting a level of urban life that could hardly have been maintained in any other way. The nine capitals of the themes and the six capitals of the archontates also had officials, garrisons, and law courts in residence, and served as centers for the collection of taxes and the disbursement of payrolls. Fifty-three other towns served as headquarters of turmae and drungi, and many more were strongholds with garrisons; in all these places groups of people were paid by the state. The Church also had courts, income, and expenditures of its own, as well as hundreds of bishops and thousands of priests in towns throughout the empire who probably received some pay in coin. With so much organized support for its towns and economy, Byzantium could not become as backward and rural as most of western Europe was at the time.[37]

Nevertheless, in comparison with the empire of the sixth century the empire in 780 had an economy that was more primitive, in that it was less urban and less monetary. The total cash revenue of the government was about a quarter of what it had been in the sixth century; the revenue per acre had fallen by about a quarter, and the revenue per subject by about two-fifths. By Irene's time the slack had been taken up by taxation in kind, and especially by the military lands, which seem to have replaced imperial estates that had yielded rents in money. The reason that the empire's cash revenues declined is pretty plainly that its subjects were unable to pay more. In 767, under Constantine V, our sources record a monetary panic, during which farmers had to sell their crops at a fifth of the usual price in order to get the money to pay their taxes. Though this situation was aggravated by the Constantine's hoarding of gold, it suggests that the government could exact only so much cash from its subjects, and that farmers managed to save little money from year to year. For most Byzantines, money was above all something needed to pay taxes. The decline in the use of money for small transactions is evident from the decline of the copper coinage; not only had it become much rarer since the sixth century, but the three smallest denominations had been discontinued altogether.[38]

The decline of cities, and with them of trade and manufacturing, made a major difference in the character of economic life. To be sure, the number of settlements called cities had not decreased much within the territory still held by the empire. Most of the names of sixth-century cities are still found in the late eighth century, when about three hundred Byzantine cities had bishops. But the urban population had certainly dropped, both in absolute numbers and as a proportion of the total for the empire.

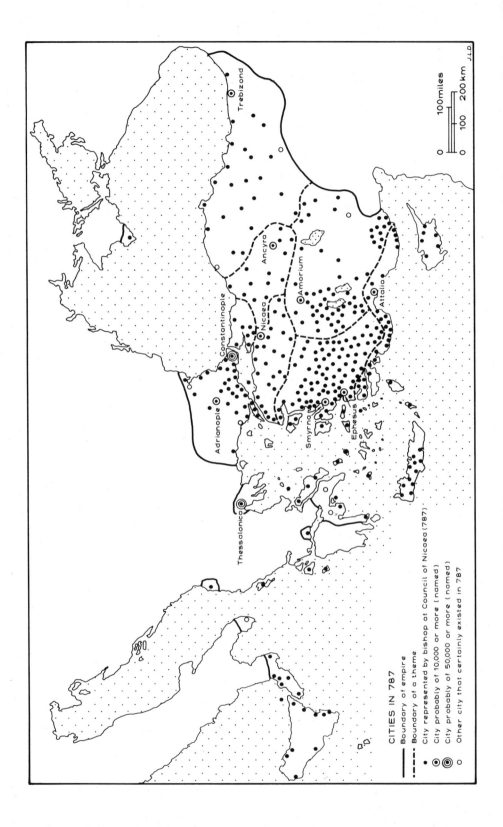

CITIES IN 787

Boundary of empire
Boundary of a theme
City represented by bishop at Council of Nicaea (787)
City probably of 10,000 or more (named)
City probably of 50,000 or more (named)
Other city that certainly existed in 787

Trebizond

Ancyra

Amorium

Constantinople

Nicaea

Attalia

Adrianople

Smyrna

Ephesus

Thessalonica

J.L.D.

100 miles
200 km

0   100
0   100

Within its new boundaries the empire's rural population had probably not fallen a great deal, because refugees, immigrants, and forced settlers had offset the losses from war and disease. But the cities were harder hit than the country by the plague, which spread more rapidly where people lived closer together, and by invasions, which forced many citizens out of Constantinople during sieges and resulted in many other cities' being sacked. The population of Constantinople, probably close to 375,000 at its height before the first plague in 541, might be guessed at about 100,000 in 780.[39]

Demographers have a very rough rule of thumb, based on figures accumulated in modern times, that the second-largest city in a self-contained region is apt to have about half as many people as the largest city, the third-largest about a third as many as the largest, and so on. While this rule is not magic, it provides some sort of test of probability for population figures and estimates. It would suggest that Thessalonica, usually considered the empire's second city, had some 50,000 people. Amorium, which contained some 70,000 people in 838, including about 30,000 troops and some refugees, probably ranked third with a normal population of about 30,000. Ephesus might well have ranked fourth with around 25,000. Adrianople, which held 40,000 people when it was swollen with refugees in 813, would normally have had 20,000 or so, and perhaps ranked fifth. The populations of Ancyra, Smyrna, Nicaea, Attalia, and Trebizond were also probably over 10,000. Smaller places, better called towns than cities, could still have a number of people. When Arab raiders sacked Laodicea Combusta in the Anatolic theme in 770, they took "6,000 captives besides the men of full age," so that its total population was probably some 7,500.[40]

Though all these figures are quite approximate, the average population of the empire's cities in the eighth century appears to be somewhat less than half what it had been in the early sixth century. In fact, the new walls built for Ephesus in the late seventh or early eighth century enclosed a little less than half the area of the old circuit. While scholars have debated passionately about how much Byzantine cities declined during the Dark Ages, their debate seems to be over whether the cities were more than half empty or nearly half full.[41]

The shrinkage of the cities was partly a cause and partly a result of the shrinkage of trade. Even if the original decrease in urban population was the result of plague and invasions, the fact remains that the decreases were not made up once the disasters had passed. As the roads deteriorated, both land and sea travel became less safe, and as the empire's monetary economy was shaken, the countryside sent less food to sustain the cities. Conversely, the shrunken cities needed less food, and had fewer manufactured goods to trade for it. Thus the whole economy shrank. The support that the business of the government, army, and Church provided for the cities was no substitute for a vigorous private sector.

Yet private trade and manufacturing still went on, however reduced their scale. Naturally they were heavily concentrated in Constantinople, which retained its harbors, markets, and commercial quarters devoted to various trades. Guilds, supervised by the city prefect but essentially private, pursued manufacturing, retailing, and service industries of various kinds. Apart from goods for the court, the army, and the navy that were produced by the state factories, the capital's main manufactured products were gold and silver utensils, jewelry, leather goods, silk and linen clothing, perfumes, candles, and soap, all produced by guilds. Copper, lead, and iron utensils were apparently made outside the guild system. Retail guilds dealt with foodstuffs, silk, and manufactured goods imported from the caliphate. Other guilds included notaries, bankers, innkeepers, and agents and contractors.[42]

No doubt the guilds primarily served the city's own citizens, who formed one of the greatest markets in the world; but much of what the guilds sold was imported, and much of what they produced was exported, sometimes outside the empire. The city had a substantial number of shipowners who seem not to have belonged to a regular guild, though they benefited from the restrictions that the government placed on those with whom they did business, including moneylenders. Many of the government's regulations would seem pointlessly restrictive to a modern businessman. On the other hand, the guild system lent stability and legitimacy to trade, which the Byzantines always regarded, sometimes with reason, as a risky and slightly disreputable way of making a living.

Besides Constantinople, a number of other Byzantine ports had a certain share in commerce. Aside from the virtually independent Italian city-states, the empire's chief ports were Thessalonica, Ephesus, Smyrna, Attalia, and Trebizond. Thessalonica, Ephesus, and others held annual trading fairs on the feast days of their patron saints. Attalia and Trebizond were the main centers for trade with the caliphate. Except during the winter, sailings were frequent between the major ports; indeed, communication could not have been maintained among the empire's islands and coastal enclaves in any other way, and transporting bulky goods like grain on land was uneconomical over any long distance. Even on land, however, the government still maintained the main military and post roads in Anatolia, which linked Constantinople with Nicaea, Amorium, Ancyra, Attalia, Trebizond, and the Arab frontier. These roads, though intended to serve military and diplomatic needs, allowed livestock to be driven from the Anatolian plateau to the capital as well. Most long-distance trade was in luxury goods, precious metals, and slaves, but within the empire and near its borders simpler items and foodstuffs went back and forth. The empire had kept control of some of the best land and sea routes in the Mediterranean, and it used them, if only to a moderate extent.[43]

Of course, the empire would have had fairly prosperous agriculture and some trade without any help from its government, and not everything that the government did helped—or helped as much as it would have if it had been done more sensibly, honestly, and efficiently. But on the whole the Byzantine government was an important positive force in the Byzantine economy, as a comparison with the economy of western Europe, which had no such government, should demonstrate. The carefully guarded strength of the Byzantine currency was an important advantage. In this coinage and much else, the imperial government had maintained the skin and bones of an urban and monetary trading economy through the Dark Ages. Now that the empire's population was growing again, its economic decline had been arrested and some economic expansion was practically inevitable. But how much it would increase the power of the Byzantine state largely depended on the ability of the government to turn new private wealth to public advantage.

SOCIETY

Without modern medicine, sanitation, lighting, heating, refrigeration of food, and technology in general, life is hard by our standards; even wealth and a staff of servants do not make up the whole difference. If one is poor under such circumstances, he is likely also to be undernourished, ill-clad, illiterate, superstitious, and prey to all sorts of misery. Such conditions, common today in many parts of the world, were of course universal in premodern times. By most material measures, eighth-century Byzantium was a much worse place to live than the modern United States or western Europe. But it was little if any worse than classical Greece or Renaissance Italy, and rather better than the rest of Europe in the eighth century—provided that the comparison is made between people of comparable social status and comparable places of residence, urban or rural. By emphasizing the wretchedness of conditions that the Byzantines took for granted, some modern scholars have arrived at a picture of Byzantine life that is much too grim.[44]

The empire's only true metropolis was Constantinople, where the effects of the empire's recent difficulties and of their even more recent alleviation must have been particularly evident. In 780 the city's last great plague was only 33 years in the past; a considerable part of the citizenry had been brought in as settlers from Greece and the Aegean islands by Constantine V only 24 years before; and the Aqueduct of Valens, the

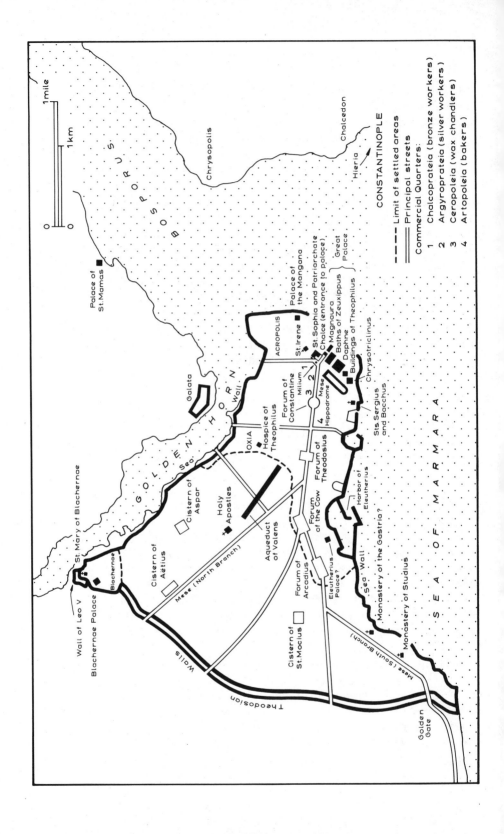

CONSTANTINOPLE

- - - Limit of settled areas
═══ Principal streets
Commercial Quarters:

1 Chalcoprateia (bronze workers)
2 Argyroprateia (silver workers)
3 Ceropoleia (wax chandlers)
4 Artopoleia (bakers)

BOSPORUS

Chrysopolis

Chalcedon

Hieria

GOLDEN HORN

Galata

Palace of St.Mamas

Sea Walls

St.Mary of Blachernae
Wall of Leo V
Blachernae Palace
Blachernae

Cistern of Aëtius
Cistern of Aspar
Holy Apostles

OXIA
Hospice of Theophilus

Forum of Constantine
Milion

ACROPOLIS
Palace of the Mangana
St.Irene
St.Sophia and Patriarchate
Chalce (entrance to palace)
Magnaura
Baths of Zeuxippus
Daphne
Buildings of Theophilus
Great Palace
Chrysotriclinus

Aqueduct of Valens

Forum of the Cow

Forum of Theodosius

Mese
Hippodrome

Sts Sergius and Bacchus

Forum of Arcadius

Eleutherius Palace?

Harbor of Eleutherius

Mese (North Branch)

Cistern of St.Mocius

Mese (South Branch)

Monastery of the Gastria?

Monastery of Studius

Monastery of the Gastria?

Theodosian Walls

Golden Gate

SEA OF MARMARA

1mile
1km

0
0

city's principal source of fresh water, had been restored by Constantine just 13 years earlier. Since the population was probably less than half what it had been at its height—and even then much of the city had not been densely settled—the area within the city walls was naturally full of open spaces and ruins.

Of this area, which is shaped somewhat like a boar's head, the main settled area was in the snout, around a fourth of the whole. This built-up area extended a bit along the coast to the boar's mouth at the Harbor of Eleutherius, and along the southern branch of the main street, the Mese, which ran about a quarter-mile inland from the coast. Even in this section houses were not built high, and neighborhoods tended to be separated from each other by vacant land. Though the shops of some guilds were concentrated in certain districts, other shops, large and small houses, and even palaces seem to have been spread all over the settled area. The rest of the city was very nearly rural, consisting of cultivated fields dotted with a few monasteries, villas, reservoirs, and hamlets.

Although Constantinople had lost some of its cosmopolitan character since the sixth century, its population was still more than sufficient to maintain urban life. The city cannot have had fewer people than Periclean Athens, which with just 15 percent of Constantinople's walled area was probably more bustling but also more cramped and less healthy. As long as Constantinople's population was declining, and houses were being abandoned, the city would have had an appearance of decay, but in 780 this was no longer the case. The population was expanding; new building and rebuilding of houses and shops would have been under way, and the ruins would have been fairly old ones. Though many of the public buildings, especially the very numerous churches, were in disrepair, and some had been abandoned, the walls and some churches had been restored in 740, and the Hippodrome, the government buildings, and the main markets were still functioning. Constantinople was an old city that had once been much bigger, but even now it was not small, and it was gradually growing again.[45]

The city had kept many though not all of the amenities of a large city of late ancient times. The most basic it had: abundant water, a variety of food and other goods for sale, and adequate schools. Less public entertainment was available than before, mostly because of the greater influence of Christian asceticism. But the two racing clubs of the Blues and the Greens still ran chariot races in the Hippodrome on occasion, provided choirs for imperial ceremonies, and probably staged the mime shows, which were interesting enough for some people to find them indecent. Ceremonies involving the imperial family, sometimes held in the Hippodrome, had if anything become more common since the sixth century, and they found an eager audience among the people, as at Irene's reception into the city for her betrothal.

Like the emperor, members of the civil and military aristocracy held great dinner parties in the dining rooms of their palaces, where the guests (sometimes including poor men invited out of charity) reclined at the tables in the ancient fashion. Men of lower classes met at the city's inns over wine and, less often, food. Though women, especially unmarried girls, generally stayed out of public life, that was the rule all over the Mediterranean from ancient until quite recent times. On balance, life in Constantinople was lived somewhat more at home and less in public places in the eighth century than in the sixth, but the differences can easily be exaggerated.[46]

The smaller a city had been before the troubles of the seventh century, the more likely it was to have changed drastically. The two largest cities, Constantinople and Thessalonica, were the only important places that had not fallen to the enemy and so retained the full circuits of their old walls. After other cities fell, their walls were usually rebuilt with a much smaller and more defensible circuit. Those cities that still had populations over ten thousand, like Amorium and Ephesus, had walls that surrounded an urban area with houses, shops, churches, and markets. Ephesus had all these and a port besides within a walled enclosure of about a square kilometer. The empire probably had about ten such cities. There were another 350 or so places called cities because they had bishops, most of which probably had populations of well over a thousand. They would have comprised a number of irregular blocks with houses, shops, inns, more than one church, and a proper marketplace, to which farmers from neighboring villages brought their produce. Outside the more secure regions these towns were generally walled. The ill-fated Laodicea Combusta, which the Arabs were quite proud of sacking, had been a town of this sort.[47]

The great majority of Byzantines, however, lived in thousands of villages, which were grouped around the cities and towns and had populations well under a thousand and sometimes under a hundred. This had always been the pattern in Asia Minor and Greece; even ancient Athens had only been the focal point for dozens of neighboring villages where most Athenian citizens lived. Though the administrative link between the cities and their dependent villages had largely disappeared during the seventh century, the villagers still went to the city to sell their crops, to buy special goods, to take refuge in time of invasion, and to have various matters decided by the bishop or a government official who lived or visited there. The Paphlagonian village of Amnia, for example, as a dependency of the town of Gangra, was subject to the ecclesiastical authority of the bishop and the military authority of the drungary resident at the town.

Most villages would have had a church or two, a smithy, a mill, an inn, and a number of houses with gardens, surrounded by fields and pasture, with woodlands farther out.

Holdings were private, but the landholders were collectively responsible for the taxes assessed on the village. If one of them had died without heirs or abandoned his land, his neighbors generally took over his farm and paid his tax. If an influential landholder escaped paying his assessment, however, the other villagers had to pay a surcharge to make up for his default. Most villagers seem to have worked land that they or their families owned, but some worked others' lands as field hands, in return for food, lodging, and payment in kind. There were also tenants, who usually paid a tenth of their crop as rent plus the equivalent of the land and hearth tax that the owner was supposed to pay for them. There were absentee landlords who lived in the towns, but even a large proprietor might reside in a mansion that dominated a village. Isolated farms seem to have been very rare, as has always been the case in Mediterranean lands, where people are neighborly.[48]

Most Byzantines lived in or near walled enclosures, because the countryside was less safe than before. The regular Arab and Bulgar raids were the beginning but not the end of the problem. The empire's Balkan enclaves also suffered from raids by the independent Slavs, and freebooting Arab pirates raided many coastal regions. After nearly two centuries, these raids had become an accepted part of life in most parts of the empire and had taken their toll on public order. Many of the pirates and thieves were now Byzantine. In these times a landowner might find that farmers from neighboring villages had taken advantage of an Arab raid to seize his outlying tracts, and a man traveling along a high road with only his dog for company was liable to be robbed and murdered by a local highwayman. Maritime law of the period assumed that ships putting in along the coast would often meet with native pirates, brigands, and wreckers. These sorts of crime could have been substantially reduced only by a government with firmer control over its territory.[49]

As people were killed or carried off into slavery, died from the plague, fled natural or man-made disasters, or were forcibly resettled by the government far from their old homes, distinctions of region and class became confused. Now that the empire's population was overwhelmingly Greek-speaking, and Greek dialects were mingled with each other, language and race distinguished people less than before. Both townsmen and villagers found themselves with new neighbors; fortunes were lost and made; land changed hands. Many families died out, and others forgot their genealogies. Scarcely a single Byzantine family could be reliably traced back to the year 600. When family names reappeared, as they were beginning to do in the late eighth century, none were names attested before the gap, and many were not of Greek origin. The Isaurian dynasty itself had no family name, though Irene's relatives did. With dynasties and administrative systems changing, and official shifts from Monotheletism to Orthodoxy and from Orthodoxy to Iconoclasm bringing religious purges, eighth-century Byzantium had become, in part, a new society.[50]

At the top of the social scale, the old Roman senatorial families had vanished, and the empire no longer had a true nobility of birth. As in the modern United States, the upper class was primarily defined by its wealth, and though ideally that wealth should not have been very recently acquired, if it went back a generation or two that was good enough. High offices in the government, the Church, or the army secured a man's place in the aristocracy, and with their high salaries they also brought money if the possessor did not have it already.

Education usually went with being born into a rich family, and lack of education was looked down upon. But being well educated did not by itself put a poor man into the upper class. A reputation for piety and moral behavior was an advantage, and the rich were somewhat more likely to have it than to deserve it—unless they were merchants, whose profession was suspect and whose wealth was relatively modest and insecure. The safest way to be rich was to have a good deal of land, usually in many parcels spread over various districts. Land near the capital in Bithynia was best, because it was less likely to be raided than land in Thrace, and anyone with social pretensions preferred to reside at Constantinople and to have connections at court. As more settled conditions returned and money and land were duly passed on to heirs, this new aristocracy of wealth and office showed signs of developing into a hereditary one. The process, however, had not progressed far by the late eighth century.

Those who did not need to work for a living were a relatively small group, holding a fairly small share of the empire's land and money, though virtually all its high official posts. The empire's mercantile class had always been small, and the disruptions of the seventh century had reduced it further. By comparison, the peasantry seems to have emerged from the troubles better off than before. The considerable number of agricultural slaves of late Roman times appears to have dwindled into insignificance by the eighth century, when most of the few slaves still to be found were domestic servants. The greater independence of the peasants was a natural result of the shrinkage and mobility of the population, which made labor scarcer and more valuable and land less so. Under such circumstances agricultural slaves tended to gain their freedom and most farmers came to hold lands of adequate size and fertility. Land that was less fertile or farther from a fort was often left vacant.

Among the more prosperous farmers were the soldiers, whose military land grants were mostly worked by their relatives or tenants. A cavalryman was supposed to be supported by land worth at least four pounds of gold, twice the amount needed to make a man rich in the eyes of the law and the equivalent of some 77 acres (31 hectares) of good arable. This was twelve times as much as many later Byzantine families found sufficient, and would probably have taken about four plowmen and eight oxen to cultivate. Of course, most eighth-century farming households owned a good deal less land than the families of cavalrymen, if only because they could not work so much; yet lack of land does not seem to have been a common problem. Farm animals, especially oxen for plowing, were harder to come by. The reckoning of a rich farmer's wealth began with his oxen, horses, and other animals rather than his lands, and a poor farmer was more likely to have too few oxen or horses than too small a farm. Thus the hearth tax depended on the household's number of oxen, and one of the main duties of a collector of the land tax was to assign abandoned land to neighboring farmers in order to assure that taxes were paid on it.[51]

Under favorable circumstances, the Byzantine land and hearth taxes were not particularly burdensome. A fairly typical family with one ox and a farm of ten acres planted in wheat could have expected its net crop to be worth some sixteen and a half nomismata, while its taxes would have been a nomisma and a half. In the country, the remaining grain would have been the equivalent of a comfortable income, and would have been supplemented by whatever the family's garden and animals produced.

The taxes, however, were the same every year, though a farm's income varied greatly with the size of the crop and the price it brought. Tax collectors might also demand bribes, overassess the tax by mistake, or assign taxable land to a farmer who had no means of working it. The tax collectors were particularly likely to make demands on ordinary peasants because many richer landholders evaded their taxes through influence, bribery, and fraud, and what one taxpayer did not pay was supposed to be made up by his neighbors. Smallholders could generally manage to supply the taxes in kind on their produce, to do corvée labor for the state, and to borrow from or barter with their neighbors to meet their other needs. During bad times, however—except for raids and natural disasters, for which exceptions were made—monetary taxes could be catastrophic. They were probably the main cause of peasants' going into debt and abandoning their land, which was a major problem for the prosperity of the empire's agriculture.[52]

In a society in which so much had changed or was changing, often for the worse, the Christian faith, as something stable and comforting, had become an even more important part of the lives of most Byzantines than it had been before. Many modern scholars have seen Iconoclasm as an attempt by Leo III and Constantine V to defend their own authority against the growing influence of the iconophile clergy and monks; though this interpretation may not explain everything about Iconoclasm, it must contain a great deal of truth. Of course, the emperors did not set themselves against the Christian religion as such, but rather claimed to be its true defenders against the abuse of icons. No Byzantine ruler could have admitted to his people, or probably to himself, that he was antireligious.[53]

The same Leo III who tried to prohibit the veneration of icons produced the *Ecloga* ("Selection"), a summary of Roman law written in Greek and revised to conform more closely to Christian morality than the old Latin *Code* of Justinian I had done. In particular, the *Ecloga* gave the sacramental view of marriage added support by making fornication illegal, requiring the bride's consent to a marriage as well as the groom's, and severely restricting grounds for divorce. In the name of greater humanity, the *Ecloga* prohibited abortion and considerably reduced the number of crimes punishable by death; but it added one, the practice of homosexuality, and greatly increased the number of crimes punishable by mutilation. All these changes in penalties appear to have been inspired by the Bible, in which God the Father had destroyed Sodom as a place of the most abominable sin and Christ had said that offending parts of the body should be cast off. Despite Leo's heresy, the substance of the *Ecloga* was accepted as a basic legal code by iconophiles and iconoclasts alike for many years to come.[54]

The effect of Christian morality on actual behavior is naturally hard to measure. The *Ecloga* hints at what was condoned even if disapproved. A seducer was fined or whipped, but only if he had seduced a virgin and did not marry her afterwards. Adultery by a wife was grounds for divorce, but adultery by a husband was not, though it was punishable by twelve lashes. In practice, Byzantine sexual morality, in typical Mediterranean fashion, seems to have been concerned mostly with preserving the chastity, or at least the reputation, of wives and unmarried daughters. Yet men were expected to behave discreetly, and divorce and remarriage, except for grave reason, carried a stigma even for a man. Male homosexuality was considered so monstrous a crime that people spoke of it seldom, and then only obliquely. The enemies of Constantine V could think of nothing worse to impute to him than a taste for handsome young men.[55]

To us, a reluctance to put men to death combined with a willingness to maim them may seem an ambiguous sort of humanity. But the Byzantines did feel mutilation was more humane; they also demanded strict proof of guilt and imposed mutilation less often and less brutally than the law allowed. Even most rebels against the emperor, for whom the law prescribed death, were blinded or castrated at worst, and more usually were simply removed from public life by being forced to accept monastic tonsure. Since some of those who were mutilated or tonsured rebelled again, the emperors' reluctance to execute them shows a genuine repugnance for the death penalty. Despite the thievery and murder that went on beyond the government's control, the emperors tried to preserve what they considered a high ideal of Christian justice.

Whatever their failings may have been, most Byzantines were sincerely devout. Nearly everyone accepted the idea that the plagues and invasions had been God's punishment for the Byzantines' sins. Atheism was practically inconceivable; not even the enemies of Constantine V seriously accused him of that. Byzantines also shared the conviction that they would have to answer for their sins after their death, though they hoped to obtain mercy because of their good works in this life, and especially because of their scrupulous devotion to Christ and His saints. The struggle over icons involved for both sides matters more important than their present lives. By defending the sort of worship that they believed God wished to receive, both iconophiles and iconoclasts expected to gain forgiveness of their incidental crimes, and with it everlasting life in a far better world. In the present world, administrators of the Church and the state hoped to build an empire more acceptable to God, which would bring justice and prosperity to its subjects and defeat to its enemies. This hope was not the same thing as patriotism, but it could sometimes have similar effects.

CULTURE

In 780 the Byzantines could look back upon more than two hundred years of seemingly steady decline in their schools, literature, and art. The empire's last period of cultural brilliance had been the reign of Justinian I, which was itself a continuation of the long and vigorous revival of Greek culture in the Roman Empire that had begun in the second century A.D. After Justinian there was a gradual decline in the amount of literature produced, and a far more abrupt decline in the number of literary manuscripts copied, that presumably reflected a shrinking of the reading public. After the reign of Heraclius we no longer hear of a public institution of higher learning at Constantinople, or indeed of schools anywhere in the empire that were sponsored by the state or had more than one teacher.

Secular literature written in the Attic dialect, considered since the second century to be the only fully correct form of Greek, faded out altogether after Heraclius. Other literature was almost exclusively religious, and even it gradually declined in quantity and sophistication. Finally, after

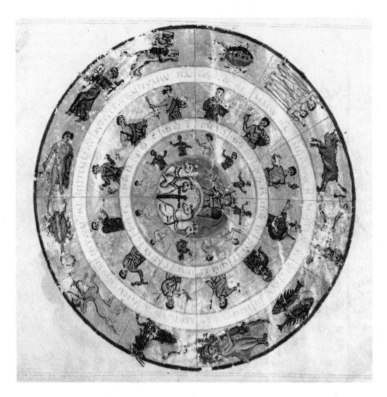

8. Illustrated solar table. Vaticanus graecus 1291, fol. 9ʳ, a manuscript, probably dating between 775 and 780, of the handy tables of Ptolemy. (Photo: Biblioteca Apostolica Vaticana, Vatican City)

the deaths of the theologian St. Germanus in 733 and the homilist Andrew of Crete in 740, literature virtually came to a halt in the empire for 40 years, except for some iconoclast polemics written by the emperor Constantine V himself. St. John of Damascus and certain other Greeks in Arab-held Syria wrote iconophile theology, but they stayed out of imperial territory.

Among the causes of this falling-off of education and literature were Justinian's forbidding pagans to teach, the loss of the cultured cities of Egypt and Syria, and the Byzantines' preoccupation with their many misfortunes, which turned them toward warfare and prayer rather than books. But the principal reason for the decline of the schools and of literature was a decline in the numbers and influence of the group that attended the schools and read and wrote the literature. This group consisted mainly of the civil and ecclesiastical officials of the capital, whose profession required a command of the ordinary literary Greek used in government and church documents, though not necessarily of the more recherché Attic dialect. Under Heraclius, the Atticist historian Theophylact Simocatta had been a high civil official, and later the well-educated St. Germanus, the son of a high civil official, had risen through the ecclesiastical hierarchy to become patriarch of Constantinople.

Until the early seventh century, the civil and religious officialdom had had great political power, often passed on from father to son. During the seventh century, however, these officials gradually lost influence to military officers, who took up a major role in administration under the system of themes and were increasingly relied upon as the empire's military position deteriorated. Then, between 695 and 717, seven violent changes of government brought attendant purges and sometimes executions of the supporters of each emperor who was overthrown. Only the most flexible officials—like St. Germanus, who was willing to condone the Monothelete heresy of one emperor—were able to stay in high positions through all seven purges. Then came Iconoclasm, with further purges of the high officials, who several times conspired against the iconoclast emperors. The elderly Germanus was deposed as patriarch for opposing Iconoclasm. Later chroniclers blame one or another of these purges of well-educated men in high office for the decline of culture in the empire. To crown their misfortunes, the bureaucrats and their teachers, being concentrated in the capital, would have suffered disproportionately from the plague.[56]

Nonetheless, in 780 both Church and state had their full complement of officials, who as we have seen might have numbered about a thousand within Constantinople. Even if they were largely from new families, they needed to be educated men. And they were not the only people in the city with at least a secondary education. Including some monks, nuns, military officers, and wives of civil servants, plus private lawyers, notaries, and of course teachers, the educated probably totaled over 2,000, not an insignificant number in a city of only about 20,000 households.

These people had all learned how to read and write standard literary or *koinē* Greek, which was the language not only of government documents but also of the New Testament and many postclassical authors. Learning to write *koinē* Greek was not easy, because by the eighth century spoken Greek had changed considerably from what it had been in New Testament times, into something closer to Modern Greek. Since the literary language retained the spelling, vocabulary, and grammar of the first century A.D., grammar was the most important subject in a Byzantine secondary school. Some attention was also paid to rhetoric, definable as the art of using and appreciating literary style.

Having learned to read from the Bible at elementary school, secondary school students were supposed to read some of the classics, most of which were written in Attic Greek. The Byzantines' list of classics included the ancient authors best known today, like Homer, Euripides, Aristophanes, and Demosthenes. It also included some later Greek and Christian authors who wrote in a revived Attic dialect, such as Aelius Aristides and St. Gregory of Nazianzus. A select few students in Constantinople then got a smattering of more advanced learning, though they had to get it outside the ordinary secondary schools, generally from learned men who were not professional teachers. For example, about 780 a certain Ignatius, who was later to become a distinguished writer, learned not merely classical poetry but the principles of classical metrics from Tarasius the Protoasecretis. Such specialized literary knowledge, however, appears to have been extremely unusual at this time, and specialized knowledge of mathematics and the natural sciences was rarer still.[57]

Of course, even when the Dark Age was at its darkest, a number of Byzantines outside the educated elite of the capital had received an elementary education and become literate. Even quite low positions in the government, the Church, and commerce required literacy and the ability to do simple arithmetic. Anyone with substantial landholdings or a position of responsibility in the army would have found illiteracy a handicap, since the laws, the system of taxation, and military communications were all written down. Every village had at least a parish priest who could teach children their letters from the Bible, and the larger towns seem to have had secondary schools. Still, outside Constantinople illiteracy was surely the norm, and secondary education a great rarity. Most literature had always been written in urban settings, and if it was to be written again in any quantity it would have to be at Constantinople.[58]

Signs of literary activity were feeble. Yet the city had libraries maintained by the emperor, the patriarch, and various churches, monasteries, and private citizens, which still held the ancient Greek literature that has been directly transmitted to us, plus about as much again that is lost today. The same skills that officials were using to prepare documents could have been used to copy old literary manuscripts and to compose new literary works in the *koinē*. Indeed, those who could read Attic Greek could have imitated it too, given time and effort and a desire to do so.

The principal obstacle in 780 appears to have been that the best-educated Byzantines, who would ordinarily have produced literature, were demoralized. Some of them were even in exile for iconophilism, rebellion, or both. Some of them would have written in defense of the icons, like the educated Greeks of Syria, if they had been able to circulate such works safely. Since this was impossible, they wrote little or nothing.

Constantine V had had to write his own attacks on the icons, and after his death iconoclast literary production seems to have dwindled. The future of Byzantine education and literature looked bleak.[59]

Just as official disapproval of defending icons inhibited literature under Iconoclasm, so official disapproval of creating icons inhibited art. Though the great decrease in the empire's wealth between the later sixth century and the early eighth had inevitably curtailed luxury building and costly art forms, the small, portable religious pictures that we call icons were inexpensive to make. They became extremely popular among a people that sought material and spiritual relief from its troubles through private prayer. Not only churches but also most Byzantine homes had icons, before which worshippers prayed while gazing into the eyes of portraits of Christ, the Virgin, and favorite patron saints. These portraits were supposed to be authentic, carefully transmitted according to a long tradition; when saints appeared to the faithful in dreams they could be recognized from their appearance in icons. For many, the images were an indispensable part of their devotions. Irene herself found them so, to judge from the risk she had run to keep icons in her bedchamber in the palace. To the iconoclasts, of course, the use of icons in Christian worship distracted the worshipper from the substance of the faith; but to sophisticated iconophiles who followed the arguments of John of Damascus, the form of the icon raised the worshipper's thoughts to the heavenly person it represented. Understandably, iconophiles regarded the destruction of an image of Christ as an act of blasphemy against Christ.[60]

When Leo III ordered icons removed and Constantine V ordered them destroyed, neither emperor meant to ban all art, or even quite all religious art. The official ban covered depictions of religious figures, all of which the Byzantines called icons, but not all of these were destroyed, perhaps because their sheer number frustrated the iconoclasts. In many cases Leo and Constantine replaced figural mosaics and frescoes on the walls of churches with mosaics and frescoes of the Cross, which they found fully acceptable. Mosaic crosses dating from Constantine's reign survive today in St. Sophia and St. Irene. Though a depiction of the Cross was religious art of a sort, it was not a sort that gave much scope for creativity, since the Cross could be shown only as a shape, not as an element in a scene of the Crucifixion. Constantine's artists were able to show more virtuosity when they replaced the figural mosaics of the church of St. Mary of the Blachernae in Constantinople with mosaics of trees, birds, and animals, but such art was essentially secular. Constantine also redecorated the Milium, a large vaulted monument in the capital where the empire's roads originated, by substituting scenes of chariot racing in the Hippodrome for pictures of the six ecumenical councils.[61]

9. The constellations, with the northern celestial hemisphere at top, and the southern celestial hemisphere at bottom. Vaticanus graecus 1291, fol. 2ᵛ, 4ᵛ. (Photo: Biblioteca Apostolica Vaticana, Vatican City)

None of this secular art of Constantine's reign seems to have survived, but it was probably not much different from portrayals of similar subjects of a slightly earlier date, which are mostly classical in inspiration, or the slightly later illuminations of a surviving manuscript of the astronomer Ptolemy. Byzantine artists continued to imitate classical models throughout the iconoclast period, and Iconoclasm does not seem to have caused any devastating decline in Byzantine artistic technique. On the other hand, forbidding the creation of religious images ruled out an enormous portion of what artists had done before Iconoclasm, and by asserting that art was inherently incapable of producing true images of Christ and the saints the iconoclasts tended to devalue the artist's whole profession. Making due allowances for the loss of most of the art of the time, we still can hardly maintain that the years before 780 were a time of great achievement in Byzantine art.

Nearly all the building of this period was repair work. After a violent earthquake struck Constantinople and its surrounding area in 740, damaging the city walls and many churches and other buildings as far away as Nicaea, Leo III saw to the repair of the walls at once, and raised the land and hearth tax rates permanently in order to pay for it. Constantine V, who had plenty of money by the middle of his reign, made some repairs to the churches of St. Sophia and St. Irene and, as has been seen, restored the disused Aqueduct of Valens in the capital. For this last project he imported 6,900 workers from Thrace, Asia Minor, and Greece, but he evidently sent them back afterwards. The iconoclasts are known to have dedicated some churches, but these may simply have been churches that were rebuilt after the earthquake. No substantial original works of architecture can be dated to this time.[62]

Even though the empire's resources in the eighth century were inferior to what they had been in the sixth, the vast reserves of gold held by Constantine V and Leo IV could easily have supported much more literature, art, and architecture than was actually produced, especially because literature and most forms of art were relatively inexpensive. But the iconoclast emperors seem to have had little interest in patronage. Neither did wealthy aristocrats often act as patrons under Iconoclasm, except perhaps to commission icons in secret. Constantine V did have a somewhat theatrical streak, which showed in the art he commissioned and the iconoclast theology he wrote. But his main projects were military and dogmatic, and his artistic and literary efforts were merely incidental to his Iconoclasm.

Any major effort to patronize art and literature would have required either cooperating with or trying to replace the empire's cultural elite in Constantinople; but the iconoclast emperors' relations with that elite were uneasy and their interest in culture was marginal. The lack of flourishing literature, art, and architecture at Byzantium was not, of course, directly disadvantageous for the empire's administration or defense. But the main reason for the stagnation of culture—the disaffection and demoralization of the empire's class of administrators—took its toll in disloyalty, corruption, and inefficiency in the Byzantine government.

THE PROSPECTS

The state of the empire in 780 was not all bad. The most recent Byzantine expeditions against the Arabs and Bulgars had ended in victory, and neither the Arabs, the Bulgars, nor anyone else presented a real threat to the empire's survival. The Isaurian dynasty had reached its sixty-third year of rule and made its third transfer of sovereignty from father to son. The army was fairly strong. The treasury had an ample reserve of gold. The population was growing modestly, and since there was plenty of good land to accommodate new farmers agriculture was expanding to match. The fundamental organization of the empire was sound, and if the government did not function very efficiently, it was working about as well as it had at any time since the sixth century. Though the empire had suffered great external losses and internal disruption, the worst of these were in the past. Iconoclasm was only the latest in a series of theological disputes that the empire had always resolved in the end. In most respects, the Byzantines had adjusted to their new situation. Their empire was smaller and poorer than before, but it was tenacious and stable.

The best guess that an impartial and well-informed observer could have made at the time was that the empire would go on pretty much as it was for the foreseeable future. Its traditions, after all, were highly conservative, and the vague idea of most Byzantines that theirs was a universal empire did not take the form of plans to reconquer long-lost territory. During the two centuries from the inauguration of Constantinople in 330 to the accession of Justinian I in 527, the eastern, mainly Greek-speaking part of the empire had changed remarkably little, fighting its foreign and domestic battles without overwhelming victories or defeats. Christianity had advanced gradually but inexorably after its adoption by Constantine I. Art and literature had undergone only a very slow evolution. The population and the economy had registered no more than a slow and slight decline. As we have seen, major changes had begun only when Justinian quite idiosyncratically tried to reconquer the lost Latin West and very unluckily presided over the onset of the plague. Since by 780 the empire had ridden out the plague and the worst assaults of its enemies, it seemed to have returned to its former equilibrium. Though Byzantium was benefiting from some demographic growth, that growth was shared by its neighbors and did not seem likely to alter the balance of power.

In fact, no sudden and sweeping transformation of the empire did follow the year 780, and no crushing disaster overtook either the Byzantines or their adversaries. Nevertheless, Byzantium did not become again the society of little change or scarcely perceptible decline that it had been during its first two hundred years. In the course of the 62 years covered by this book, Byzantium changed from a stagnant society into an expanding one. The change took place within the lifetimes of many people and the memories of some, like the long-lived Joannicius, who was born in 762 and died in 846. And this expansion was only the beginning. The empire was to sustain its political, economic, and cultural revival for almost 300 years, during which it doubled in size. Although this revival was partly the result of fortunate circumstances, it also depended upon the plans of a number of able rulers and administrators, the first of whom was the Augusta Irene.

CHAPTER TWO

The New Regime of Irene, 780-802

For over 22 years Irene wielded great power in the empire, but she was never able to take that power for granted. In September 780, many knowledgeable men who heard of the sudden death of Leo IV and the regency of his widow must have doubted that she would last long. The story that Leo had died of fever after stealing a votive crown from St. Sophia was soon in circulation and, whether it was true or false, publicizing it did nothing to endear Irene to those who had been close to her estranged husband. Since Irene's only right to rule was in the name of her son while he was under age, her regency could be expected to end in a few years when Constantine grew up. To rule even that long, she would have to hold off everyone else who aspired to rule for Constantine or to replace him with one of Leo IV's half-brothers.

Irene kept up certain appearances as a member of the Isaurian dynasty. She duly buried Leo IV in a white marble tomb beside his grandfather, father, and mother in the Church of the Holy Apostles, the traditional burial place of Byzantine emperors. At first she issued coins with portraits of Constantine VI and herself on the obverse and commemorative images of Leo III, Constantine V, and Leo IV on the reverse. But on these coins she and not her son held an orb, the symbol of rule, and she referred to herself as co-ruler with Constantine rather than as regent for him.[63]

The news of Leo IV's death set plotters to work at once. Just 40 days later, on October 16, Irene uncovered a conspiracy against her. As in 776, the plot was to crown Nicephorus, the third son of Constantine V, who was evidently more energetic than his older brother and embittered by the loss of his rank of Caesar. By now Nicephorus was in his early twenties, and had gathered support among men more powerful than the grooms and bodyguards who had backed him before. The most important were

Constantine, domestic of the Excubitors, whose troops could have given the plotters the necessary armed force in the capital, and Gregory, the postal logothete, whose corps of messengers could have summoned troops from the provinces to join the conspiracy. The others named among the ringleaders were Bardas, strategus of the Armeniacs under Constantine V, and Theophylact Rhangabe, drungary of the Dodecanese in the Aegean Sea.

All those implicated seem to have been gathered in Constantinople. Bardas had been out of office for at least two years, and Theophylact was evidently away from his command. Apparently the plot did not touch any active commander of a theme or the chief military commander in Constantinople, the domestic of the Schools Anthony, who had been appointed long ago by Constantine V. Though it was a serious conspiracy, Irene detected it quickly and arrested its members all together. With them she arrested not only their candidate for emperor, Nicephorus, but the other four surviving sons of Constantine V.[64]

No doubt Nicephorus wanted the throne, and he was a natural rallying point for those who did not like Irene or thought she would not last. He was not, however, a candidate very likely to appeal to partisans of the late Leo IV, since he had recently tried to overthrow Leo as well. Moreover, everyone in power had sworn to Leo to defend the succession of his son, Constantine VI. Irene would probably have been more vulnerable to a conspiracy to replace her as regent with Nicephorus's older brother Christopher without deposing Constantine VI. Nicephorus's plot was too hastily conceived and not well enough concealed, like his first attempt, and it played into Irene's hands. It gave her the opportunity to put out of the way not only some of her high-ranking enemies who were plainly guilty, but also Nicephorus's four brothers, who may very well have been as innocent of this conspiracy as they seem to have been of the last. Her discovery of this plot also discouraged those who might have wanted to plot against her in the future.[65]

Irene used her victory prudently. She had the conspirators flogged, tonsured, and exiled to various places. Her five brothers-in-law were ordained as priests, the gentlest possible means of making them ineligible for imperial office, which also meant that those who were not already married could not marry in the future. Christopher's wife, Theodora, now returned to the convent from which she had come; the other brothers seem not yet to have been married, and none seems to have had children. Irene had thus arranged that their side of the family would produce no legitimate heirs. It was presumably at this time that Irene invited Anthusa, probably the twin sister of Nicephorus, to join her as a co-regent. While the offer showed respect for the Isaurian dynasty, it was also reasonably

10. A nomisma of Constantine VI and Irene of the type issued from 780 to 790, shown three times actual size: *obverse*, Constantine and Irene; *reverse*, the dead Leo III, Constantine V, and Leo IV. Such coins obviously give little idea of the emperors' true appearance. (Photos: Dumbarton Oaks Byzantine Collection, Washington)

safe, because Anthusa, who had remained unmarried against her father's wish and devoted herself to charitable works instead, was an iconophile like Irene and had no political ambitions. In fact, she declined the job, but she continued to live in the palace, and Irene's point was made.[66]

The most important office left vacant by the arrest of the conspirators was that of postal logothete, to which Irene promptly appointed Stauracius, her closest ally through most of her reign. Nothing is known about Stauracius's earlier career. He was probably of fairly high rank in 780, because he soon held the very high title of patrician, which men seldom received unless they already held another title. Since he was a eunuch, he is likely to have been a palace servant and to have become acquainted with Irene while she was still in the women's quarters, though he does not seem to have been accused of complicity in the affair of Irene's icons the previous March. If he was not an iconophile by conviction, he chose to act as if he were. With Irene's great confidence in him, as well as the most direct control over the daily business of the government, Stauracius was soon the most powerful man in the empire. Whether or not he had had military experience, he could lead an army, as Irene never presumed to do because of her sex.[67]

Less than four months after her husband's death, Irene used the Christmas Mass in St. Sophia to show off her new independence and security.

Instead of staying in the imperial gallery as was customary, she and her son entered the nave in a grand procession, carrying the votive crown that Leo IV had allegedly seized and tried on at the cost of his life. This Irene restored to the church's treasury, demonstrating how much she disapproved of her late husband's conduct. She then had communion distributed to the people by her five newly ordained brothers-in-law, making it clear that they were now ineligible to rule.[68]

At about this time, word came that a man had found an ancient coffin while digging in Thrace near the outer defenses of the capital. Inside this relic was a corpse, supplied with an engraved tablet that read, "Christ will be born of the Virgin Mary, and I believe in Him. Under the emperors Constantine and Irene, O Sun, you will see me again." The tablet was placed in the treasury of St. Sophia along with the votive crown, proof that some great Greek prophet of the pre-Christian era had been destined to bear witness in the reign of these two highly favored sovereigns. One way or another, Irene had established herself much more firmly after Nicephorus's abortive conspiracy. She did not have to deal with a comparable conspiracy in the capital for some time.[69]

Besides intimidating those who had approved of the old regime of Constantine V and Leo IV, Irene greatly encouraged those who had been disaffected. Most of all she encouraged iconophiles and monks. In the words of a contemporary iconophile monk, during Irene's first year on the throne "the pious began to express themselves freely, the word of God began to spread, those who sought salvation began to renounce the world without hindrance, the glory of God began to be exalted, the monasteries began to be restored, and every good thing began to show itself." And in fact, a number of wealthy and prominent men and women are known to have entered monasteries at the beginning of Irene's reign. Some noble families took the monastic habit together; some landowners near Constantinople converted their country estates into convents. The list of those who became monks includes Theodore of Studius, the most influential abbot of the following period, and Theophanes Confessor, who edited the chronicle from which the preceding quotation comes. The revival that began in 780 was in the first instance a revival of monasticism.[70]

Irene seems to have encouraged people to enter monasteries more by what she was than by anything she did. Theodore of Studius merely says that in Irene's reign, "among other good things, the door to the monastic life was opened to everyone who desired it, though it had long been closed under impious rule." After Constantine V, who had persecuted monks, and Leo IV, who had prevented prominent men from entering monasteries except when he relegated them there as a punishment, Irene's attitude came as a major change. As far as we know, she founded only one monastery herself, and that may have been later in her reign; all the other new monasteries we know of were private foundations. But when the empress let the upper class in Constantinople know that she approved, a respect for monasticism that had been latent among them promptly had its effect. Monasteries held a particular appeal for strict iconophiles, because monks were the group that had remained most staunchly iconophile during the persecutions, while even now those outside monasteries, particularly the secular clergy, had to remain associated with a church hierarchy that was officially iconoclast.[71]

Such a large-scale revival of monasticism was not necessarily a good thing for the Byzantine government. Theophanes and Theodore were educated men from families of civil servants who under normal circumstances would have joined the administration; Theophanes—like Theodore's uncle Plato, who had become a monk before 780—had actually held administrative posts under the iconoclast regime. When such men entered monasteries, they and the descendants whom they might otherwise have had were lost to the state bureaucracy, which already had too few men of education and talent. Earlier Constantine V seems to have opposed monasticism in part because he felt it was depriving him of good civil servants and army officers.[72]

But under present circumstances, especially in the eyes of an iconophile like Irene, the entry of many upper-class Byzantines into monasteries had some advantages. The new monks did not distance themselves far from Byzantine society, but stayed near the capital. Many lived across the straits in Bithynia, where for some time prosperous Constantinopolitans had held land and the Bithynian Mount Olympus had been a monastic center. Some took up residence in monasteries just outside the walls of Constantinople. Most monks, old and new, remained interested in public life, and above all in the issue of Iconoclasm. Now that a ruler had appeared who was sympathetic to the iconophile cause, every convinced iconophile hoped for an official repudiation of Iconoclasm, an end to the schism with other Orthodox Christians, and a restoration of icons to their place in religious life. Irene could depend on iconophiles to use whatever moral authority or personal influence they had in Constantinople in favor of the icons.

The monastic profession left educated men at least as much opportunity for learned pursuits as a government career would have done. As a monk, Theodore of Studius made a thorough study of the lives and works of the Church Fathers, particularly Basil of Caesarea. Theodore's uncle Plato devoted himself to copying manuscripts, especially anthologies of patristic works. At about this time, Theophanes Confessor and Macarius, the abbot of Pelecete, reportedly copied and studied sacred literature every day.[73]

These monks seem to have been interested largely in finding quotations from the Fathers in support of the icons, but in this endeavor they became the first important Byzantine copyists we know of for a good many years. They seldom studied or copied secular literature; the biographer of John of Psicha, another new monk of the time, assures us that though John studied divine letters day and night he never dabbled in Homer, rhetoric, philosophy, astronomy, arithmetic, or any such nonsense as that. But the copying of more manuscripts was the essential condition for any major expansion of Byzantine education. At about this time the future patriarch Nicephorus, then a secretary in the civil service, composed a short history of the period from 602 to 769. Eventually, the research of the new iconophile monks turned out to be the first stage of a general revival of Byzantine learning.[74]

In order to restore the icons, Irene needed not only iconophile monks but iconophile clergy. She had the advantage that the patriarch Paul IV, though he had been appointed by Leo IV, was no friend of Iconoclasm. At his consecration Leo had with great difficulty forced Paul to sign an oath not to venerate icons himself, and this oath Paul did not openly break. But he did what he could to encourage iconophiles and discourage Iconoclasm, and he did not attempt to conceal his views. He and Irene were in a position to fill bishoprics that fell vacant with iconophiles, particularly from among the monks. One staunch iconophile whom they probably appointed was Euthymius, bishop of Sardis, a young man who had been a monk before his consecration. Certainly within a few years a large number of bishops were iconophiles. Some, like Paul, were surely appointees of the previous regime who had known how to keep their mouths shut, but others must have been named as part of a slow, deliberate effort by the new regime. If Irene could stay on the throne long enough, she had every chance of obtaining an iconophile hierarchy.[75]

UNWANTED WARS

Though Irene was soon fairly well established in Constantinople, she could not be sure of the loyalty of her military commanders during the first few years of her reign. Wholesale replacement of her generals might well have set off a revolt in the army; in any event, there were no obvious replacements for them. The only group whom Irene seems to have trusted were the eunuchs of the palace, most of whom were not likely to make good generals. Irene therefore adopted a practice that allowed her to supervise possibly disloyal commanders without dispensing with their services or greatly offending opinion in the army. Leaving most officers in their posts, for important expeditions she would give a palace eunuch whom she trusted a temporary special command over them. Though this was not an ideal solution, it was probably the best that Irene could have found in her circumstances.

In February 781 Irene appointed Elpidius the Patrician as the new strategus of the remote Theme of Sicily, a post he had once held under the old regime. In mid-April, just two months after he had sailed for Sicily, she received a report that he secretly favored the cause of her recently ordained brothers-in-law. The specific accusation was probably that he had been involved in the plot of the ex-Caesar Nicephorus the previous October. Irene immediately dispatched an envoy, Theophilus the Spatharius, to arrest Elpidius and bring him back to the capital. Since Elpidius had left his wife and sons behind in Constantinople, Irene apparently expected him to surrender peacefully.

When the envoy arrived to put him under arrest, however, Elpidius declined to try his luck before Irene, and the Sicilian army, familiar with him from his previous tenure as strategus, stood by him. In an implied invitation to negotiate, Elpidius seems to have allowed Irene's envoy to return unharmed, and does not seem to have declared himself in rebellion. But Irene chose to show firmness rather than compromise with an alleged conspirator. She had Elpidius's family whipped, tonsured, and jailed. For the time being, however, she could spare no troops from the eastern front to send to Sicily. The caliph al-Mahdī, still hungry for revenge after Leo IV's attack on Germanicea, was preparing some major summer raids on Asia Minor from the Arabs' new base at Adata.[76]

In June, anticipating these raids, Irene called up the troops of the themes of Asia Minor and put them under the special command of a palace eunuch, John the Sacellarius. John's office of sacellarius, to which he may have been named by Irene, was a supervisory one, and his role in Asia Minor was also supervisory, since the strategi continued to have direct command over their themes. His mission was to watch the passes over the Taurus and to head off any Arab invasion. The Arabs, commanded by a certain 'Abd al-Kābir, took the most obvious route, and emerged into the Anatolic theme from the Pass of Adata. There they found a large Byzantine force, commanded by Michael Lachanodracon, strategus of the Thracesians, and including Tatzates, strategus of the Bucellarians.

A disorderly battle took place near Caesarea, and after suffering many casualties the Arabs beat a hasty retreat. It was an unusually good defense by the Byzantines and a quite incompetent performance by the Arabs, who since they had enough troops only for a raid in force should have taken care to avoid meeting a large and well-prepared Byzantine army. The caliph was angier than ever, and was persuaded only with difficulty to jail ʿAbd al-Kābir instead of beheading him. The Arabs had no time to mount another campaign that season, but al-Mahdī decided upon a truly formidable expedition for the next summer.[77]

In the meantime, Irene was free to use some of the troops from the Asian themes against Elpidius in Sicily. Probably in the early autumn of 781, she dispatched a substantial expedition under Theodore the Patrician, one of a few palace eunuchs who showed real military ability. Under Theodore's command was a large fleet, most of it probably from the Cibyrrhaeot theme, and a body of soldiers selected from the eastern themes together with their officers. Elpidius had just 2,000 troops spread over Sicily and the toe of Italy, for whom the 2,000 marines of the Cibyrrhaeots would by themselves have been a match. After several battles, Elpidius and his subordinate Nicephorus (probably duke of Calabria) absconded with as much public money as they could find to North Africa, where they obtained favorable terms from the local Arab authorities. Elpidius declared himself emperor, and the Arabs arranged for him to be crowned and robed as one. Though the Arabs did not take Elpidius very seriously, he maintained his claim, eventually making his way to the East, where he was briefly to be heard from again. Sicily and its army returned to the control of Irene's government.[78]

Theodore's expedition to Sicily had not yet returned when the caliph launched his full-scale invasion of Asia Minor in February of 782. The nominal commander was al-Mahdī's young son, Hārūn, but he had experienced officers to assist him. His army was of unprecedented size; the figure that an Arab source gives for it is 95,793 men. The Byzantines had at most 50,000 men in the Anatolian themes, some of whom may have been in Sicily, and 14,000 more in the tagmata, apart from the garrison troops that policed Constantinople. Hārūn's expedition cost the Arabs the equivalent of some 1.6 million Byzantine nomismata, nearly an entire year's revenue for the Byzantine state. Passing through the Cilician Gates and quickly taking the first fort at the frontier, Hārūn advanced across the Anatolic theme by the main military road in the direction of Constantinople. He seems to have avoided sieges, except that on the border of the Opsician theme he left a detachment under his lieutenant al-Rabī to besiege Nacolea and to guard the rear of the main force. Another detachment, under a certain al-Barmakī (a member of the powerful family of the Barmacids), was sent into the Thracesian theme.

11. The Cilician Gates, the Arabs' main route for invasions of the empire, shown from the south. (Photo: Irina Andreescu Treadgold)

From subsequent events it seems likely that this year Irene put her troops under the general command of her most trusted official, the postal logothete Stauracius. Though the various themes were involved in different operations in or near their own territories and under their own commanders, their defenses were coordinated, and at the crucial point Stauracius appears to have been in charge. The Byzantines never attempted to stop as large a force as Hārūn's at the frontier. Now they waited for Hārūn to send out detachments and so to expose his forces to being defeated in detail.

One Byzantine army, perhaps the great army of the Anatolics, fell upon al-Rabī at Nacolea, defeated him, and sent his force fleeing back to the frontier with heavy losses. Michael Lachanodracon led the Thracesians to defend their theme against al-Barmakī at a place called Dareno, perhaps the former Dariucome in the center of the theme's territory. The ensuing battle seems to have been inconclusive, with both sides suffering heavy losses, but the Arabs withdrew afterward. Perhaps near Nicaea, Nicetas, the count of the Opsician, used his cavalry to attack a part of Hārūn's main force under the command of Hārūn's general Yazīd. Nicetas challenged Yazīd to personal combat on horseback, but, after unhorsing him, fell from his own horse and was injured. Nicetas and the Opsician army then fled to Nicomedia, taking refuge with Anthony, domestic of the Schools, who was there in command of the tagmata but did not offer battle to the Arabs. Bypassing Nicomedia, Hārūn advanced to Chrysopolis, just across the Bosporus from Constantinople. Without ships to carry his army across the strait, Hārūn seems to have intended nothing more than to plunder the Asian suburbs of the capital at his leisure.

In the meantime, the rout of al-Rabī had left Hārūn with no troops nearby to secure his rear. The tagmata under Anthony were still undefeated, as were the Bucellarians under their strategus, the Armenian Tatzates; both were close to the road by which Hārūn would have to return. Irene herself ordered the tagmata to cut off Hārūn's retreat. As a result, when the caliph's son made his way back on the main road south of Nicaea through the valley of the Sangarius River, he found that he and his force were surrounded by Byzantines. He faced the tagmata and the Bucellarians, commanded by Anthony and Tatzates under the supervision of Stauracius. Hārūn asked for a truce.

Fortunately for Hārūn, Tatzates hated Stauracius and was ready to turn traitor. By birth an Armenian nobleman, Tatzates had left his home in Arab-occupied Armenia in 760 and joined the army of Constantine V. Constantine had appointed him strategus of the Bucellarians, a command that he had held ever since. But his relations with the new regime of Irene and Stauracius were strained, and his future in Byzantium looked precarious. He secretly asked Hārūn to guarantee a safe passage back to Armenia for himself, his wife, and some of his men; in return he promised to help the Arabs out of their trap. Hārūn naturally agreed. He opened negotiations for a truce with a Byzantine delegation composed of Stauracius, Anthony, and Peter the Magister, a palace official of long standing. When the delegation arrived in the Arab camp, Hārūn managed with Tatzates' help to seize them as hostages. Irene now had to negotiate with Hārūn if she wanted her delegates back. Earlier Hārūn had taken some five thousand other Byzantine prisoners as well.[79]

Irene would probably not have been very sorry to lose Anthony and Peter, both enthusiastic iconoclasts who had loyally served Constantine V. Tatzates, of course, had deserted. But Irene relied heavily on Stauracius. Furthermore, with their commanders in the hands of the enemy, the tagmata and Bucellarians could no longer be relied upon to keep the Arabs surrounded and might well have been defeated. Irene therefore agreed to a truce of three years, on unfavorable terms. Hārūn was to release all his prisoners and leave Byzantine territory. Irene was to supply Hārūn with guides and with markets on his return, and to pay to his father, the caliph, an enormous tribute: 90,000 nomismata each April and 70,000 nomismata each June. The timing of these payments would allow the Arabs to mount a summer raid if they were not made. This settled, Hārūn returned to the caliphate in August of 782, taking with his army an immense plunder of horses, mules, and armor. Irene and Hārūn also exchanged a number of gifts.[80]

Thus Irene muddled through the wars of the first two years of her reign. Two of her generals, Elpidius and Tatzates, had gone over to the Arabs, Byzantines had fought Byzantines in Sicily, and in Asia Minor the Arabs had inflicted many casualties, ravaged the land, and exacted a costly and humiliating truce. Still, no important part of the Byzantine army had risen in a concerted rebellion, and the losses were not intolerably large, especially considering the size of Hārūn's expedition. Though the truce was an expensive one—costing the state nearly a tenth of its revenue over the next three years—it had some advantages for Irene. It assured a period of peace with the Arabs, during which she was able to conduct a gradual purge of the military commanders appointed in the reigns of Constantine V and Leo IV. Michael Lachanodracon may have been demoted because of his half-defeat, and the deserting strategi were of course replaced. After 782 none of the old officers is heard of again in his old post, and most are never heard of at all. No more commanders revolted against Irene, and within a few years all the commanders were thoroughly loyal to her. Although Irene and Stauracius had scarcely wrapped themselves in glory, they had presided over some victories, and they could plausibly blame their losses on disloyal commanders from the previous administration. The new regime would now show what it could do.

OPENINGS TO THE WEST

By Byzantine standards, Irene's foreign policy showed an unusual amount of realism. Her predecessors appear to have felt that Byzantine honor required them to show their standards in Arab territory from time to time. Irene seems to have accepted that the Arabs were stronger and that she had little to gain by provoking them; she stayed almost entirely on the defensive on the eastern front. Irene's predecessors had concerned themselves almost exclusively with the empire's traditional enemies, the Arabs and Bulgars, and had seldom bothered to attack the much weaker Slavs. Perhaps especially because she came from Athens, Irene appears to have realized that the Slavs held a great deal of good land in the Balkans and that their weakness made them attractive opponents rather than despicable ones. The Isaurian emperors had curiously considered the Byzantine exarchate of Ravenna in central Italy not important enough to defend, but too important to concede to the Franks. Irene, with an eye to the Papacy's support for a prospective restoration of the icons, seems to have understood that the Franks had replaced the Byzantines as the main power in central Italy for the foreseeable future and was ready to make friendly overtures to Charlemagne and the popes whom he protected.

Very early in her reign Irene decided to arrange a marriage between her young son and Charlemagne's daughter Rotrud, who was at least three years younger. Because of the two children's ages the marriage could not take place for several years, but Irene saw no reason why goodwill between the Byzantine and Frankish courts should not begin at once. When Charlemagne arrived at Rome to celebrate Easter of 781, he met with ambassadors from Irene, who proposed the marriage. Not surprisingly, Charlemagne accepted. After all, there was no more glorious match in Christendom than the emperor of the Romans, and Charlemagne was well aware of the prestige of Rome.[81]

When Irene received Charlemagne's acceptance, she sent an embassy of particularly high rank to complete the arrangements in the fall of 781. At the head of the embassy was Constans, the new sacellarius. After the success of his special military mission that summer, Irene seems to have transferred the previous sacellarius, John, from his partly honorary office to the more demanding position of military logothete. That his successor was so promptly sent to the Frankish court demonstrates again how light the supervisory duties of the sacellarius were. With Constans were two palace servants, Mamalus the Primicerius and Elissaeus the Notary. Elissaeus, as a eunuch and a man of some learning, was chosen to remain at Aachen to teach little Rotrud to speak and read Greek and to acquaint her with the customs of the Byzantine court. After giving and receiving solemn pledges for the engagement, the ambassadors departed, leaving Elissaeus to his work. Contacts between the two courts continued, and Constantine VI heard enough about Rotrud to fancy himself in love with her.[82]

In the summer of 783, Irene could simply have left her armies to regroup after their losses of the previous year, or she could have attacked the still-disorganized Bulgars. Instead, she sent troops against the Slavs in Greece in the first such Byzantine campaign in many years. She put Stauracius in command of the army, which was large and presumably drawn from several of the themes and tagmata. He was probably chosen not only because he was reliable, but because after his humiliating capture the previous year he needed a victory to refurbish his prestige.

Stauracius conducted a leisurely campaign in little danger from the scattered and outnumbered Slavs. From Constantinople he marched through the theme of Thrace and then to Thessalonica across Slav-held territory, forcing the Slavs there to pay tribute to Irene and acknowledge her sovereignty. During his stay at Thessalonica, he probably began work on a

12. The Church of St. Sophia, Thessalonica, probably begun in 783 by the logothete Stauracius, from a photograph taken in 1890 before the church was altered somewhat. The minaret is a later addition. (Photo: Courtauld Institute, London; and the British School at Athens)

large church of St. Sophia that showed the empire's new interest in the Balkans. From Thessalonica, Stauracius crossed the coastal territory that was subject to the local Byzantine archon and entered Slavic land again in central Greece, where he exacted more tribute and another acknowledgment of subjection to the empire. The logothete next visited the Byzantine theme of Hellas, from which he launched a raid on the Slavs of the Peloponnesus. The raid collected a great amount of booty, much of which these Slavs had presumably taken from the Greeks in their original invasion and subsequent raids. Apparently without attempting to make the Peloponnesian Slavs tributary to the empire, Stauracius marched back the way he had come, with the cooperation of the tribes whom he had subjugated earlier. When he returned to Constantinople in January 784 after a campaign of at least five months, he celebrated a triumph in the Hippodrome.[83]

What had Stauracius accomplished, besides gathering booty and winning some glory for himself? Obviously he overawed the Slavs, and made them less likely to raid Byzantine territory; probably he impressed the

Bulgars without running the risk of actually attacking them. Though some of the Slavs may have continued to pay tribute, it is not clear that Stauracius had demanded more than an immediate payment as he passed through their lands. Quite possibly his soldiers rebuilt or strengthened fortifications in the archontate of Thessalonica and the theme of Hellas, and they may even have retaken a few forts; but the boundaries of both provinces remained essentially the same. In Thrace, however, Stauracius's campaign seems to have altered the situation significantly to the advantage of the Byzantines.

Four months later, in May 784, Irene herself, with Constantine VI and a sizable army, made a tour of Thrace, apparently visiting places that had been cleared of Slavs by Stauracius. It was the closest the empress ever came to leading an army, though she met no enemies and encouraged a festive atmosphere by taking along a traveling orchestra that played organs and other instruments. At the ruined town of Thracian Beroea (modern Stara Zagora), in the region where Slavic, Byzantine, and Bulgar territory met, she ordered the town to be rebuilt and fortified under the name of Irenopolis, which could mean both "City of Irene" and "City of Peace." She then advanced as far as Philippopolis, which is not known to have been in Byzantine hands for almost 200 years, and evidently ordered it to be rebuilt as well. Before she returned to the capital she decreed the restoration of Anchialus, a Black Sea port on the Bulgar frontier that had apparently suffered during the wars of Constantine V with the Bulgars. By these three refoundations Irene both strengthened the Bulgar frontier and extended Byzantine rule perhaps 30 miles west into a sparsely populated area that had been under Slavic control. Most of the inhabitants of the new towns were probably Greeks attracted from elsewhere in the empire by land grants, but some may have been local Slavs.[84]

This modest annexation seems to have been the beginning of a much more ambitious project. Two years later Irene and Constantine were again in Thrace with the tagmata, and a large force from the themes of Asia Minor was operating there as well. By the following year, the Byzantine frontier had reached the Strymon River, about a hundred miles west of Philippopolis and only a few miles from the next Byzantine enclave, around Thessalonica. It was a slow, relatively peaceful expansion, probably involving gradual military occupation and resettlement and no real battles. The sources say very little about it. But evidently Irene was the first Byzantine ruler to make a serious effort to reclaim European territory from the Slavs. Stauracius's campaign seems therefore to have been designed to test and to soften Slavic resistance to eventual conquest, and Irene's triumphal tour of Thrace to inaugurate an open-ended program of

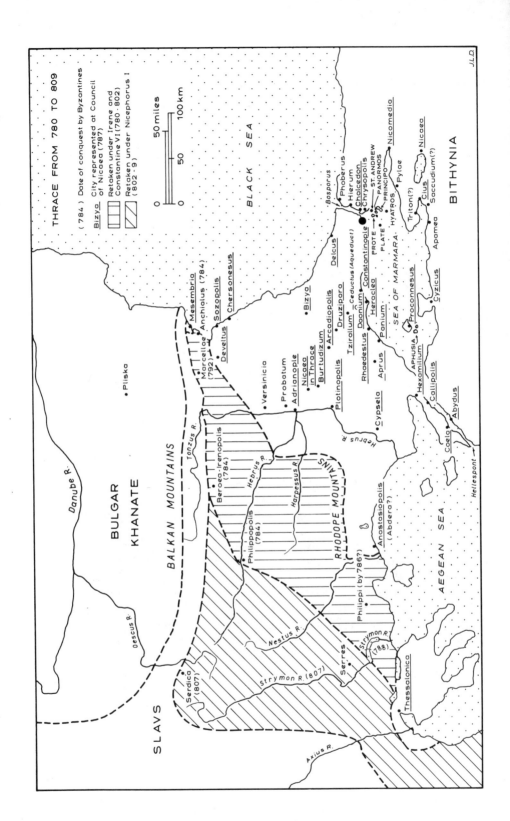

THRACE FROM 780 TO 809

(784) Date of conquest by Byzantines

Bizya City represented at Council of Nicaea (787)

Retaken under Irene and Constantine VI (780-802)

Retaken under Nicephorus I (802-9)

BULGAR KHANATE

SLAVS

BALKAN MOUNTAINS

Danube R.

Oescus R.

Tonzus R.

Pliska

Mesembria

Marcellae Anchialus (784)
(792)

Develtus

Sozopolis

Chersonesus

Versinicia

Probatum

Adrianople

Nicaea
in Thrace

Burtudizum

Plotinopolis

Bizya

Arcadiopolis

Druzipara

Tzirallum

Rhaedestus

Aprus

Cypsela

Ponium

Delcus

Daonium

Ceductus (Aqueduct)

Heraclea

Constantinople

Bosporus

Phoberus

Hierum

Chalcedon
Chrysopolis

ST. ANDREW
PANORMOS

PROTE
PLATE

PRINCIPO

HYATROS

APHUSIA

Hexamilium

Callipolis

Proconnesus

Cyzicus

Apamea

Triton(?)

Cius

Saccudium(?)

Nicaea

Nicomedia

BITHYNIA

SEA OF MARMARA

Pylae

BLACK SEA

Hebrus R.

Harpessus R.

Beroea-Irenopolis
(784)

Philippopolis
(784)

RHODOPE MOUNTAINS

Anastasiopolis

Abdera(?)

Philippi (by 786?)

Nestus R.

Serres

Strymon R.
(788)

Strymon R. (807)

Serdica
(807)

Strymon R. (807)

Thessalonica

AEGEAN SEA

Axius R.

Coela

Abydus

Hellespont

0   50 miles

0   50   100 km

JLD

resettlement of Slavic lands. Though this resettlement was less showy than the great wars of Constantine V, it would offer more substantial and longer-lasting benefits to the empire if it could be sustained.[85]

THE FIRST MOVE AGAINST ICONOCLASM

The first proposal to renounce Iconoclasm officially was made in 784, but not by Irene. For four years the patriarch Paul IV had worked to restore the icons without formally renouncing his oath to Leo IV not to venerate them. He was one of many Byzantines in public life who disliked Iconoclasm but had not gone so far as to refuse to serve under the iconoclast emperors. Since nearly every office-holding iconophile from Irene on down was in a similar position, few could reproach him; and many admired his generosity in almsgiving. But in August 784 Paul became ill, and realized that he was dying. Terrified to face divine judgment without repenting of his temporizing, on August 31 he abruptly abandoned the patriarch's quarters and secretly entered the Monastery of St. Florus in Constantinople, where he abdicated his throne and professed himself a monk.

Entering a monastery was not an unusual step for a dying layman, but it was extraordinary for a patriarch. When Irene discovered where Paul had gone, she and Constantine paid him a visit. She found the distraught patriarch ruing the day when he had accepted his post. He emphasized that the iconoclast emperors had forced the Church of Constantinople into schism with the other Orthodox churches of the West, Egypt, and Syria, and had brought down their anathema upon it. For this the patriarch could not escape responsibility, and he feared that his damnation might be the consequence.

Though Irene had not chosen the time and may even have felt that it was imprudently early, she seized the opportunity to strike at Iconoclasm with the patriarch's help. After speaking with Paul, she sent a picked group of the officials of the senate to the monastery to hear what he had to say. The patriarch called for an ecumenical council to condemn Iconoclasm. The officials, somewhat taken aback, reminded him of his oath to Leo IV. Paul remorsefully acknowledged it, and told them that he prayed God would not punish him for condoning Iconoclasm so long "out of fear of your madness." He expressed the wish that his successor as patriarch should be Tarasius the Protoasecretis, head of the imperial chancery. Soon afterward he died. Paul's deathbed repentence became widely known, and began open discussion among the leading citizens of Constantinople over a possible council.[86]

Sincere though the patriarch evidently was in his repentance, after his meeting with Irene he was presumably cooperating with her. Her record as an iconophile was at least as good as his, since while Paul was keeping his iconoclast oath in public she had broken her own and been discovered and chastised for it. Of course, she was in a position to try to end the continuation of Iconoclasm that had caused him so much remorse. So it is reasonable to think that the dying patriarch agreed with the empress to propose to the delegation of senators that an ecumenical council be held against Iconoclasm and to signal to them that they could discuss that step freely. Otherwise Paul had no reason to press a council upon Irene if she wanted to abolish Iconoclasm by an edict, as Leo III had introduced it; and nothing he could have said would have persuaded the officials to discuss a council openly unless they believed the empress approved. Nor does naming Tarasius as his successor look like an idea that Paul would have had first. Any good iconophile would have suited his purpose, but a cleric would have been best; a loyal civil servant like Tarasius would have appealed chiefly to Irene. By letting Paul speak for her, however, Irene gained the benefit of the dying patriarch's moral authority and avoided exposing herself to the resentment of possible opponents any more than necessary. When Paul spoke of the senators' "madness" he doubtless meant not only outright Iconoclasm, which seems to have been rare among officials, but also reluctance to open the whole bitter question again, which was probably much more common.

After Paul's death Irene decided to organize a demonstration similar to the one that Leo IV had arranged so that the army and people could demand he crown his son co-emperor. After consulting with Tarasius, she invited a large group of senators, clergy, and other citizens to the Magnaura, a subordinate palace within the Great Palace enclosure, to discuss the selection of a new patriarch of Constantinople. The empress began by assuring the assembly that she had not desired Paul's abdication, and would not have consented to it if he had lived. But now that he was dead, she asked them to propose a successor.

Not surprisingly, they declared their unanimous desire for Tarasius and opposition to anyone else. Irene replied that though Tarasius was her choice as well, he had declined, and she invited him to take the floor and explain his reasons. Tarasius spoke at some length, apparently from a prepared text, which has been preserved. He described himself as unworthy, incapable, and a layman, and as such afraid to take on this great office. He was more afraid, however, for a second reason: the Church of Constantinople was in schism with the Orthodox churches of the East and West, and subject to their anathema. This anathema was a terrible thing. He could agree to accept election as patriarch only if the emperors Constantine and Irene and those assembled would agree to hold an ecumenical council to heal the schism.

Most of the crowd shouted their agreement as they were expected to do, yet a minority had the hardihood to shout dissent. Everyone had obviously known in advance that Irene wanted Tarasius and accepted the rulers' right to name whomever they wanted, but some, perhaps the ordinary citizens, were surprised by the proposal of a council. They realized that it would mean a fight over Iconoclasm (though Tarasius had said nothing about Iconoclasm yet), and some either approved of Iconoclasm or wanted to avoid a fight. Tarasius did not let the objection pass without a reply. Assuming a more authoritative manner, he declared that Iconoclasm had been the work of the emperor Leo III, and that the council called by Constantine V had been a mere formality to agree to what Leo had already done. By such arbitrary action, the emperors and council had "dared to put aside, in accordance with their own wishes, an ancient practice handed down in the Church." "But," Tarasius concluded, "the truth of God is not bound, to quote the Apostle." Thus the meeting ended with less agreement than Irene and Tarasius could have hoped for.[87]

Presumably because they realized that they faced considerable opposition, the empress and patriarch-elect moved slowly in their preparations for a council. After being ordained deacon and priest, Tarasius was not consecrated patriarch until Christmas Day 784, after a vacancy in the patriarchate of almost three months. The next step was to announce Tarasius's election and the proposal for a council to the heads of the four other Orthodox patriarchates: Pope Hadrian I and the Orthodox patriarchs of Alexandria, Antioch, and Jerusalem. Tarasius seems to have written first to the three Eastern patriarchs in the hope of reaching them while the peace of 782 with the Arabs was still in effect. Speed was necessary, because Irene was planning to break the peace by withholding the tribute payment due in April 785. Tarasius wrote the same message to each Eastern patriarch, declaring his Orthodoxy on all points including the icons, apologizing for his previous status as a layman, and asking for a letter of reply to be read at the council and two representatives to attend it.

Hostilities with the Arabs broke out too soon for the patriarchs to receive and reply to the letters officially. One letter reached a community of monks in the Egyptian desert, who decided to reply as best they could. They explained that because of the political situation the patriarchs of Alexandria and Antioch could not communicate with the empire safely, while the patriarch of Jerusalem was in exile. As a makeshift, the monks sent a copy of a letter written by a former patriarch of Jerusalem to the patriarchs of Antioch and Alexandria that included a condemnation of

Iconoclasm. They also chose two monks who had served as advisers to the patriarchs of Antioch and Alexandria to take the place of official representatives.[88]

Irene and Tarasius wrote to Pope Hadrian I only on August 29, 785. Tarasius sent approximately the same letter he had sent to the Eastern patriarchs. Irene, writing in Constantine's name as well as her own, proposed that Hadrian attend the council in person if possible, but send legates if he could not. Hadrian wrote back quickly, on October 27, promising to sent legates. Though he was not pleased by the election of a layman to the patriarchate and reiterated papal complaints about Constantine V's removal of Greece and southern Italy from Rome's jurisdiction, the pope was eager for an end to Iconoclasm and made no objection that would delay the council. Irene still proceeded slowly; she did not summon the bishops of the empire to attend the council until well into the next year.[89]

Irene and Tarasius used the year and a half that they allowed themselves between his consecration and the council to strengthen the iconophile cause. Probably quietly, but not secretly, Irene had icons put up in the principal churches and the imperial palace. Tarasius energetically continued both Paul IV's appointments of iconophile clergy and his much-admired generosity to the poor. The new patriarch distributed food and winter clothing to those who needed them, and even began a monthly dole in coin for some. Very soon after his consecration he founded a monastery near Constantinople where iconophiles were trained for the priesthood. He made one of its monks, Michael of Synnada, a metropolitan bishop within two years, and probably named other iconophile bishops as well, since bishops were the ones who would vote at an ecumenical council. The patriarch deputed about a dozen members of the patriarchal staff, including several notaries and the librarian, to search the texts of the Fathers for passages that refuted the iconoclasts and supported the veneration of icons. Tarasius seems to have asked the other bishops and monks invited to the council to make a similar search, thereby continuing the expansion of copying, reading, and studying that had already begun.[90]

Meanwhile, as we have seen, the costly and humiliating peace with the Arabs had ended. Irene had accepted its terms in order to rescue Stauracius and her other captured officials and to allow herself time to appoint generals who were loyal to her. She seems now to have felt that with her generals in place she did not need the peace; she may also have wanted to throw off the humiliation of paying tribute before she confronted the iconoclasts at her council. Neither Irene nor the caliph al-Mahdī seems to have had any wish for full-scale hostilities, and evidently Irene was in no better position to fight the Arabs than she had been before 782. Any prospect of a concerted attack on the caliphate with the Khazars, a strategy that in principle was promising, had faded as the Khazar khan had nearly forgotten that he was supposed to be a Byzantine ally. About 785 a raiding party sent by the khan had seized the fort of Dorus, which belonged to Crimean Goths allied with Byzantium. Though Bishop John of Gotthia had mustered the natives and retaken the fort, the Khazars had then captured him. Irene had no particular strategy in the east, and her failure to pay al-Mahdī the tribute merely brought back the former state of chronic border warfare with the Arabs.[91]

Alī ibn Sulaymān, the energetic governor of the border districts, promptly sent out a cavalry force to make a raid in the summer of 785. The Arabs, probably penetrating through the Pass of Melitene, rode north into the middle of the Armeniac theme. Without meeting serious opposition, they took plunder and captured the monastery of Zobe near Sebastopolis, where they put the abbot Michael and his 36 monks to death for refusing to turn Muslim. While on the whole this was not a particularly destructive raid, the fate of the monks, who were commemorated as martyrs in Constantinople, may have exaggerated its impact for the Byzantines.[92]

That August the caliph al-Mahdī died, and his son al-Hadī began a brief and erratic reign. He dismissed Alī as governor just as Alī was finishing work on Adata, which he had been enlarging and fortifying for five years. During the next winter an unusual amount of snow and rain undermined and partly washed away Adata's sloppily built brick fortifications. Alī's successor was unequal to the emergency. The strategus of the Armeniac theme, an appointee of Irene's who was probably the future emperor Nicephorus, learned of the Arabs' difficulties and advanced on the damaged city. The Arab governor fled with his troops and the rest of the population, leaving the city to the Byzantines, who took considerable booty and completed Adata's destruction. Though the Arabs retaliated with a raid of their own and by building a new stronghold at Tarsus, neither made up for their setback. With her forces' victory at Adata and her gradual conquests in Thrace, Irene now had some solid military achievements to offset her embarrassing defeat in 782.[93]

So matters stood in midsummer of 786, when the ecumenical council was scheduled to meet in Constantinople. Bishops and monks from all over the empire arrived in the capital. Two priests, both named Peter, came from Rome to represent the pope. The two legates sent by the Egyptian monks as makeshift representatives of the patriarchs of Alexandria and Antioch had probably arrived already. Strangely, Irene and

13. The martyrdom of Michael of Zobe and his monks by the Arabs in 785. Vaticanus graecus 1613, p. 77, a manuscript of about the year 1000 of the *Menologium of Basil II*, including illustrations by several painters of the main saints and events commemorated in the Byzantine church calendar. The painter of this scene is Nestor. (Photo: Biblioteca Apostolica Vaticana, Vatican City)

Constantine were away in Thrace with most of the tagmata and many of the troops of the themes when the delegates to the council appeared. No matter how important Irene considered her reconquests and resettlement in Thrace, her presence with the army there at that moment can scarcely have been vital to their success. If she thought that by not being in Constantinople to greet the delegates she would avoid antagonizing those who opposed the council, things did not turn out as she expected.

Though many monks, whose presence was not necessary at councils, had been invited to strengthen the iconophiles' hand, the majority of the bishops must have been appointed by Constantine V and Leo IV, and at least a sizable minority of them either believed in Iconoclasm or wanted to leave the issue alone. They took advantage of Irene's absence to conspire with like-minded laymen in the city, and were in the process of organizing a meeting of their own to plan strategy when Tarasius discovered what they were up to. Informing them that Constantinople had a bishop and they had no right to meet without his knowledge, he invoked his canonical authority to put a stop to any open plotting.

Leaving the troops from the themes to continue their work in Thrace, Irene and Constantine soon returned with the tagmata. The assembly intended to be the Seventh Ecumenical Council was to begin on the morning of August 1 in the monumental Church of the Holy Apostles. On the afternoon of July 31, however, a large body of troops from the tagmata who had just returned with the emperors gathered in the baptistery of the church and began shouting angrily that they would not allow the council to take place. Though the commanders of the tagmata were loyal to Irene, they were unable to restrain many of their junior officers and soldiers, who greatly revered the memory of Constantine V. This group did not want the decrees of Constantine's council overturned, and probably had been incited by the bishops who opposed the new council and by their lay allies. Tarasius consulted Irene and decided to go ahead with the council, evidently in the hope that the situation could be brought under control.

The council met in the church the following morning. Tarasius presided; the emperor and his mother were present as observers. About four hundred bishops and monks seem to have attended. The proceedings had not gone far when a mob of armed troops from the tagmata started to gather in front of the church. They entered the forecourt and pounded on the doors, shouting that they would not allow the council to continue, that Constantine V's decisions could not be changed, and that icons were idols. There was a clear danger that they would try to overthrow Irene. No troops came to her aid.

The empress bowed to necessity and ordered one of her chamberlains to give the order to the council to disperse, adding as he did so, "God's will be done." She angrily made her way back to the palace with her son. While the iconophile bishops and monks scattered, those who had disapproved of the council went out and announced their victory to the mob. The soldiers gradually calmed down, and the riot ended about noon when they became hungry and left to eat. No blood had been shed, and when Irene admitted failure and sent the bishops back to their sees, the immediate danger was over.[94]

Although up to this point Irene had been fairly cautious in her efforts to restore the icons, she seems to have realized that now she had been made to look weak, and if she did not act decisively she could expect to be deposed by someone who looked stronger. She therefore left little time for the bad impression to sink in. She sent Stauracius out to the force drawn from the themes that was still operating in Thrace, and he secured their support for Irene against the rebellious elements in the tagmata. In the city, the empress announced an expedition against the Arabs, and ordered the tagmata to proceed to Malagina, the first camp on the military road to the eastern frontier. She also had the imperial baggage and tent sent there, as if she and Constantine would accompany the expedition themselves. The tagmata followed the orders of their commanders and marched. But Irene did not go to Malagina. She remained in Constantinople, while Stauracius led the troops of the themes from Thrace into the city to secure her position. She then sent orders to Malagina that some 1,500 troops that had taken part in the previous month's riot were to consider themselves cashiered, and were to lay down their arms and return to their places of origin. At the same time, she deposed, exiled, and replaced several iconoclast bishops.

Irene had planned this operation brilliantly. Only about a tenth of the troops at Malagina were being dismissed, no doubt those in units picked out by their commanders as the most seditious. The rest, probably relieved that they were not going to suffer for their failure to oppose the rioters, or even for rioting themselves, abandoned their comrades to their fate. The dismissed soldiers had left their families behind in Constantinople, where they were now in Irene's power. Under the circumstances, the men had little choice but to surrender their arms and disperse to the places in the provinces from which they had been recruited. Their families were then sent out of the capital by boat and allowed to join them. Some of the dismissed soliders who came from the Anatolic theme found places in the theme's army after they returned there, but they caused no further trouble. Over the next few months, Irene recruited new and loyal troops and junior officers to take their places in the tagmata, thus strengthening her hold on the tagmata and on Constantinople. In May of 787, she sent out invitations to a new ecumenical council. Overcoming the failure of her first attempt to restore the icons, Irene emerged from it more powerful than ever.[95]

THE COUNCIL OF NICAEA

This part of Irene's reign showed her at her best. One of her more inspired decisions was to hold the ecumenical council not at Constantinople but at Nicaea in the Opsician theme. By now, holding a council in the capital would probably have been safe, but to call again on the support of the tagmata, which consisted for the most part of the same men as before, might seem to express trust in them that they had not deserved. The choice of Nicaea, the site of the First Ecumenical Council, invited some comparisons that suited Irene's purpose and that few Byzantines could fail to appreciate. She was implicitly comparing her son, Constantine VI, to St. Constantine I, who had held the first council, and herself to Constantine's mother, St. Helen. The iconoclasts were cast in the role of the Arians, the heretics whom the First Council of Nicaea had condemned. Nicaea, located conveniently close to Constantinople, was a reasonably large town, whose Church of St. Sophia was suitable for the gathering. It was the headquarters of the Opsician troops, whose commander, Petronas, was a loyal appointee of Irene's and headed a garrison that proved to be reliable. Nicaea would doubtless have been the best site for the council in the first place.

Irene also decided that she and Constantine VI would not attend the council's opening. Now that she had made it clear that she was determined to have it meet, she could show that she would allow the bishops and abbots to make their own decisions, renouncing the sort of heavy-handed intervention for which Tarasius had denounced Leo III and Constantine V at the Magnaura. The planning and management of the council were Tarasius's responsibility. He arranged for it to meet in seven main sessions from September 24 to October 13, 787, with at least a day between sessions and no meetings on Sundays. The patriarch arrived in Nicaea with the dozen or so members of the patriarchal staff who had made preparations for the council, bringing books, documents, and, doubtless, drafts of the decisions to be voted.

Since the abortive council at Constantinople Irene had wisely kept with her the two legates of the pope and the two monks who were considered representatives of the Eastern patriarchates; they now proceeded to Nicaea. The others who were invited arrived gradually; 252 bishops attended the first session, and 113 more came later. There were also 131 abbots and various other monks and assistants, so that the medium-sized Church of St. Sophia in Nicaea was well filled. Irene's representatives were Petronas, who as count of the Opsician theme was the local military governor, and John the Military Logothete, one of Irene's most trusted palace eunuchs.[96]

Though according to the custom for ecumenical councils the book of the Gospels was placed on the episcopal throne to show that Christ was the true president, the bishops of Sicily immediately called upon Tarasius to preside, and he took firm control of the proceedings. He made a brief opening address, in which he pointedly referred to those bishops who had helped frustrate the previous attempt at holding a council in Constantinople. An imperial secretary then read a letter from Constantine and Irene to the council assuring those assembled that they had full freedom of speech. But nobody needed to be told not to defend Iconoclasm, particularly because immediately afterward nine bishops who had already been excluded as iconoclasts were brought in to ask for admission. They submitted written statements declaring their repentance and condemning

14. The Church of St. Sophia, Nicaea, showing the synthronon in which the presiding bishops sat, with the Gospel book in the central throne, during the Council of Nicaea of 787. (Photo: Irina Andreescu Treadgold)

Iconoclasm and Constantine V's iconoclast Council of Hieria, which some of them had attended. Three were admitted with little trouble; but Tarasius and the monks were a good deal harder on the remaining six— including the bishop of Nicaea himself—all of whom had allegedly held meetings to plot against last year's council at the Church of the Holy Apostles. Their admission was postponed, and the council was adjourned.[97]

Tarasius's exclusion of ten iconoclast bishops (including one, Gregory of Neocaesarea, who had not yet arrived) was a tactic comparable to Irene's dismissal of only a tenth of the tagmata. Obviously, even after a few replacements in the previous year, far more than ten bishops must have been appointees of the iconoclast regime that had ended only seven years before. Many of these bishops must have professed Iconoclasm, and all of them must have condoned it. The ten were presumably chosen either because they were surviving members of the Council of Hieria, not a large group after 33 years, or because they had conspicuously opposed the previous year's council, or for both reasons. Once these men were isolated, other bishops found it easy to prove their Orthodoxy by blaming the designated culprits, who themselves faced deposition and excommunication if they did not recant. Of course, a truly dedicated iconoclast would have stood fast, as many iconophiles had done when Iconoclasm was introduced. Though some bishops whom Irene had already dismissed may have been more dedicated, nothing demonstrates the weakness of Iconoclasm's hold on the Byzantine hierarchy better than the absence of unrepentant iconoclast bishops in 787. The decision of Tarasius and Irene to treat all but open iconoclasts as iconophiles revealed this weakness beautifully.

At the second session of the council the last bishop excluded for Iconoclasm, Gregory of Neocaesarea, requested admission. After Tarasius had questioned him sharply his case was put off along with the other six. The main business of the day was the reading of translations of the replies of Pope Hadrian to the emperors and to Tarasius. Hadrian wrote at length, strongly defending the icons and condemning Iconoclasm and the Council of Hieria. To these sentiments Tarasius gave his wholehearted assent, and the members of the council eagerly expressed their agreement in short declarations and by signing the council's official acts. The third session, in which Gregory of Neocaesarea and the other repentant iconoclasts were finally admitted after some discussion, was given over to reading Tarasius's letter to the Eastern patriarchs and the reply of the Eastern monks. These letters naturally expressed views as resolutely iconophile as the pope's, to which all the members, the repentant Gregory of Neocaesarea foremost among them, hastened to subscribe.[98]

In the fourth session, which began the second week of the council, Tarasius and his assistants presented the results of their research on patristic texts. Their findings were meant to demonstrate that venerating icons was a long-standing tradition of the Church. The patriarchal librarian and notaries read directly from dozens of books, and other members of the council brought forward other books of the Fathers that mentioned icons. Tarasius's assistants showed why they were careful to read from complete volumes when they came to a letter of St. Nilus of Ancyra, which the Council of Hieria had cited to support the iconoclast view that the Cross should be the only image. A complete reading showed that the passage had been quoted out of context, and that Nilus had admitted other sorts of images as well. The former iconoclasts who had attended the Council of Hieria indignantly declared that they had adopted Iconoclasm only because they were deceived by such shameless manipulation. When Euthymius of Sardis, who as a recently appointed bishop could afford to criticize, asked why they had not asked for the original books, Gregory of Neocaesarea and the others could only plead stupidity. The incident served to increase the members' enthusiasm for producing more and more books of the Fathers with passages on icons. After a very long day, Euthymius of Sardis read out a summary of the session's findings, doubtless prepared in advance, which all present signed.[99]

There were still more readings in the fifth session, these designed to expose Iconoclasm as a heresy. One text cited by the Council of Hieria was shown to come from an apocryphal New Testament text that was itself heretical. Gregory of Neocaesarea expressed outrage; when Irene's representative Petronas questioned him, he said no one had been told the origin of the text when it was read at Hieria. Tarasius's assistants then brought forward several books from the patriarchal library from which the iconoclasts had cut out passages about icons, as comparison with other copies showed. The council members were duly indignant. After many readings, one of Tarasius's readers mentioned that he still had fifteen more books on icons in reserve, but the members agreed that they had heard enough. At the end of the session one of the representatives of the Eastern patriarchs submitted a report on how the caliph Yazīd II had forced the Christians in the caliphate to destroy their images on the advice of a Jew, thereby providing the inspiration for the Iconoclasm that broke out soon afterward in Byzantium. Thus Iconoclasm was set down to Jewish and Muslim influence.[100]

The sixth session was entirely prepared by Tarasius and his staff. They arranged for Gregory of Neocaesarea, as a further humiliation, to read out one by one the decrees of the Council of Hieria, after each of which patriarchal assistants presented a refutation of the iconoclast arguments. At the seventh and last session in Nicaea, the prepared decrees of the ecumenical council itself were read out and signed by all the bishops. The session concluded with a series of anathemas against the iconoclasts and acclamations of the Orthodox. Tarasius and the council sent an official letter to the emperors announcing the restoration of church unity; the council sent a similar letter to the clergy of Constantinople.[101]

Now that they had condemned Iconoclasm unequivocally, the council delegates traveled the short distance to Constantinople and received a warm welcome from Irene. She and Constantine then presided over a final session of the council on October 23 in the Magnaura palace, at which they also signed the acts. Apparently this was when the council approved a series of canons on various disciplinary matters, most of them directed against the real or supposed abuses of the iconoclast regime. By enacting various prohibitions, the council indirectly or directly accused the iconoclasts of letting emperors choose bishops (as all emperors did), consecrating churches without relics, converting Jews forcibly, and in partic-

15. The Council of Nicaea of 787. Vaticanus graecus 1613, p. 108. Painter: Pantoleon. If this scene is even partly accurate, it must represent the final session held in Constantinople, since it shows Constantine VI, who was present only then, and a cross in the central throne, which at Nicaea was occupied by the Gospels. In that case the prostrate cleric in the center is being condemned for paying for his ordination, because those accused of Iconoclasm had been readmitted earlier. Even so, the absence of Irene seems to indicate that the painter was poorly informed. (Photo: Biblioteca Apostolica Vaticana, Vatican City)

ular exacting fees from bishops and priests whom they ordained. Clerics who had paid such fees were condemned. Monasteries sold to laymen under Iconoclasm were to be restored. The writings of iconoclasts were to be removed from circulation and deposited in the patriarchal library. Other canons placed restrictions on monks' associations with women, an issue that naturally arose when whole families converted their own properties into monasteries. Monasteries for men associated with monasteries for women were specifically forbidden. The council concluded with more anathemas against the iconoclast clergy—but not against the iconoclast emperors, since the same dynasty was still in power—and acclamations of Constantine and Irene as "the New Constantine and the New Helen." Soon afterward the emperors and Tarasius wrote to Pope Hadrian, enclosing the complete acts of the council.[102]

The members of the Second Council of Nicaea engaged in less theological discussion than those of earlier councils. Tarasius's careful management helped assure that there was no disagreement, and after all, the positive case against Iconoclasm was a fairly simple one. It was true that the use of religious images had a long history in the Church, and that the Church Fathers, aside from objecting to some overzealous use of icons in popular practice, had accepted them as a legitimate part (though not a very important part) of Christian instruction and worship. Once one had accepted the argument of St. John of Damascus and others that the honor paid to an image was meant not for the depiction but for the person depicted, most of the iconoclasts' arguments lost their force. The only strain in earlier Christian theology that really supported Iconoclasm was a strongly antimaterialistic one, bordering on Gnosticism, which had been condemned as heretical long ago. Not even the iconoclasts could defend such ideas openly—though, as the Seventh Ecumenical Council had found, they sometimes quoted heretical texts surreptitiously.

Since by the traditional theological rules the iconoclasts had little case, they had the greatest scope for original theological arguments, such as Constantine V's splendidly sophistical proof that iconophiles were either Nestorians or Monophysites. But in Byzantine theology originality was not a great virtue. So shallow were Iconoclasm's theological roots that it could hardly have become a serious issue without the efforts of the iconoclast emperors. After they died, the only politically important body of iconoclasts were those, mainly in the army, who had little knowledge of theology but a strong loyalty to the memory of their earlier rulers.

Apart from this group, who were to be heard from again, most Byzantines accepted the decrees of the Second Council of Nicaea—many with enthusiasm, others with indifference. The successful completion of the council meant that Irene and her new regime of civil servants and monks were for the time being fully in power, as they could not be said to have been while Iconoclasm was still official doctrine. Though the troops of the tagmata who had rioted in 786 could say that they were defending the official doctrines of the most recent council of the Byzantine Church, now anyone who favored Iconoclasm was simply a rebel. Furthermore, until the Council of Nicaea the entire patriarchate of Constantinople, which was essentially coterminous with the empire, had been officially in schism with the other Orthodox patriarchates; but now this was no longer the case. The healing of the schism strengthened Irene's moral position, both at home and in relations with the papacy.

By and large Irene had Tarasius deal mildly with the clergy ordained in earlier reigns. There were evidently no further depositions for Iconoclasm. Irene used with moderation the council's decree against the bishops and priests who had paid fees when they were consecrated under the iconoclast emperors. On her orders, Tarasius suspended these clerics from their priestly functions for one year, reinstating them in January 789. A

number of monks led by Abbot Sabas of Studius objected that this punishment was too light, and Tarasius himself tried to make it harsher, but
Irene would not permit any change. Irene was thus able to put many former iconoclast clerics on a year's probation for an offense that no one
could conscientiously condone, while at the same time downplaying the
issue of Iconoclasm, which she considered fully settled, and avoiding too
great a humiliation of the defeated party. Considering that Iconoclasm
had been official church doctrine during the entire memory of nearly
every living Byzantine, and had caused great bitterness, considerable persecution, and some deaths, Irene's resolution of the controversy was a surprisingly deft and successful one.[103]

IRENE'S QUARREL WITH CONSTANTINE VI

Although the law had too little power over the Byzantine Crown to set
a specific age at which an emperor should rule without a regent, Constantine VI could certainly have ruled alone by 787, when he was sixteen.
Just over a century before, Justinian II had become emperor without a regent at fifteen; Constantine V had become emperor at twenty-one, and
his third son, Nicephorus, was younger when he first aimed at the throne.
While Irene was obviously in no hurry to step aside, she at least acknowledged that her son was of age to marry. Early in 787, before convoking
the council at Nicaea, she sent an embassy to Charlemagne in Italy to ask
that his daughter Rotrud, now also of marriageable age, be sent to Constantinople to marry Constantine.[104]

Charlemagne, however, refused and put off the marriage indefinitely.
His reasons seem to have been primarily personal. He was so fond of his
daughters that he was never able to bring himself to let any of them marry
and move away from his palace, though later he tolerated their love affairs
with the men of his court. If for his daughters even to leave for a separate
house was too much for him, it is easy to understand his reluctance to let
Rotrud leave for Constantinople, where he could scarcely expect ever to
see her again. He had only agreed to the marriage when her departure was
in the distant and indeterminate future.

Although he meant no diplomatic offense, his refusal to send Rotrud inevitably looked to the Byzantines like a slight. Appearances were particularly bad because when the Byzantine embassy arrived Charlemagne was
just completing a settlement that gave him much greater power over the
Lombard principality of Benevento, which adjoined Byzantine Calabria.
By threatening an invasion, he had forced Prince Arechis of Benevento
to acknowledge Frankish suzerainty, to turn over his entire treasury, and
to surrender hostages, among them his younger son, Grimoald.[105]

Irene was too shrewd a politician to show her displeasure with Charlemagne when she could do nothing against him and might endanger papal participation in the Second Council of Nicaea that autumn. She chose
for the present not to consider the engagement officially broken, as Charlemagne seems not to have formally broken it. When the defeated Arechis
sent her a secret embassy proposing an alliance, however, she was ready
to listen. Arechis offered to recognize Byzantine sovereignty over Benevento if Irene would grant him the title of patrician and send an army to
defend him against Charlemagne. Along with this army Arechis proposed that Irene should send his brother-in-law Adelchis, the pretender to
the throne of Lombard Italy, who had taken refuge at Constantinople after Charlemagne had conquered his kingdom in 774.

Attracted by the possibility of reestablishing some effective Byzantine
power in central Italy, Irene accepted Arechis's proposal in principle. She
sent the strategus of Sicily, Theodore, and two other ambassadors to Arechis in late 787 to grant him the title of patrician and to ask for hostages.
Unfortunately for the proposed alliance, Arechis and his elder son had
both died by the time the embassy arrived, and the heir to the throne was
Charlemagne's hostage Grimoald. Charlemagne allowed Grimoald to
succeed his father the following year only under close supervision by
Frankish agents, making any alliance with Byzantium impossible for the
time being. Pope Hadrian learned of Arechis's earlier negotiations with
Irene and warned Charlemagne.[106]

Irene now decided to do with Constantine's marriage what she had
done with her ecumenical council, and replace a plan that had failed with
another that looked better. She apparently announced that she was the one
who had broken off Constantine's engagement to Rotrud. Instead of a
Frank, Constantine was to have a Byzantine wife, the best and most beautiful in the empire. To find her, Irene sent out a panel of judges to visit the
various parts of the realm and select appropriate candidates from prominent families. They returned in the autumn of 788 with thirteen girls,
whom they presented to Irene, Constantine, and the logothete Stauracius,
so that they could make the final choice of Constantine's bride.[107]

In holding this bride show Irene had not, as one might suppose, let her
fancy overcome her political judgment. Some very shrewd Byzantine rulers followed the custom she had begun four times in the next century, for
every first marriage of a reigning emperor or heir to the throne. Byzantine chronicles, saints' lives, and folklore have scarcely anything but good
to say about the bride shows. Two Byzantine empresses who had been
winners of shows were canonized as saints. The Bible provided a precedent in the bride show in which Ahasuerus chose Esther, surely a worthy
model for an imperial bride. Nor did the custom require that the choice

be made blindly; Irene's judges had made thorough inquiries, and Irene had no intention of allowing Constantine to choose for himself.[108]

The girl whom Irene and Stauracius chose was a certain Maria of Amnia. Maria was the granddaughter of Philaretus the Almsgiver, a magnate of Armenian blood from the Armeniac theme who had lost much of his property in an Arab raid and impoverished himself further by unstinting gifts to the poor. Philaretus was a venerable old man, later honored as a saint, but with neither the resources nor the inclination to play any part in politics. Having received money, honors, and houses in Constantinople, he and his family owed their position to Irene, and could offer no useful support to Constantine against her even if they had wanted to do so. Constantine is said to have deeply regretted his broken engagement to the daughter of the mighty Charlemagne, and he certainly did not like Maria. This is the first time that he is known really to have resented his powerlessness. The ceremony took place in November 788.[109]

Once Constantine's marriage had definitely broken the marriage contract with Charlemagne, Irene was ready to send an army to Benevento to challenge Frankish dominance there. She apparently timed the expedition to come just after Constantine's wedding, and she persisted with it despite two military setbacks closer to home. Since the death of the caliph al-Hadī shortly after the Byzantines' sack of Adata in 786, the new caliph, Hārūn al-Rashīd, had paid little attention to fighting the empire, and the Arabs' annual raids had been minor. But in September 788 they staged a more serious raid on the Anatolic theme. A force from the Anatolics and the Opsician gathered to oppose them at Podandus, just past the Cilician Gates. The Arabs won the ensuing battle, killing some officers and a number of the troops who had found places in the Anatolic army after being dismissed from the tagmata in 786. Though the number lost does not seem to have been immense, the death of Diogenes, an Anatolic turmarch celebrated for his valor, looms large in our report of the battle. If Diogenes was in fact the prototype of the Byzantine epic hero Digenes Acrites, as has been plausibly suggested, his loss must have been keenly felt.[110]

In November, just before the expedition to Benevento landed in Italy, the Bulgars attacked a Byzantine army for the first time since the reign of Constantine V. Philetus, strategus of Thrace, had advanced to the new frontier of his enlarged province on the Strymon River, apparently pursuing Irene's plans for gradual annexation of the Slavic lands to the west. Since he expected no significant opposition from the Slavs, who seem never to have offered any, Philetus encamped without posting sentries. But he had not reckoned with the Bulgars to the north. A Bulgar force took him by surprise and killed him and many of his army. Though the enemy did not follow up their victory, they had already endangered Irene's acquisitions in Thrace. Worse still for Irene, this defeat was likely to give the impression to both Byzantines and Bulgars that she was losing the advantage over the Bulgars that Constantine V had achieved.[111]

Later in November, Irene's expeditionary force arrived in Byzantine Calabria and marched toward the border with Benevento. Though her would-be ally Arechis was dead, Irene had sent along his brother-in-law Adelchis as Arechis had suggested. The head of the Byzantine force was Irene's trusted agent and palace eunuch John the Military Logothete, who since he had been her representative at Nicaea had also resumed his old office of sacellarius. With him was Theodore, the strategus of Sicily who had been an ambassador to Benevento the previous year.

Though John had supervised the successful Byzantine defense against the Arabs in 781, he was not really a soldier. His mission was not to fight the Lombards but to win over as many of them as he could to the Byzantine side by applying pressure and offering support and protection. Irene probably hoped that once she had landed an army in Italy Benevento's new ruler, Grimoald, would be glad to throw off Frankish domination. Unluckily for John, the Byzantines had to fight. Perhaps because the Frankish agents in Benevento were too strong to resist, Grimoald remained faithful to Charlemagne and gathered an army that included a small contingent of Franks. This army met the Byzantine force near the frontier and routed it, killing many, including John, capturing others, and taking a considerable amount of booty. The defeat, following the losses to the Arabs and Bulgars, was highly humiliating for Irene.[112]

Nothing vital had been lost, however, and Irene set about repairing the damage to her army, if not to her prestige. In the same year, about 50,000 Armenians had fled to the empire to escape persecution in the caliphate. Irene and Constantine gave them an official welcome in Constantinople, assigning honors to the nobles and land grants to the commoners. Probably the honors were commands in the themes and the grants were of military land, so that Irene used the Armenians to replace many of the officers and troops lost in her recent defeats. The next year Irene repaired her relations with Grimoald of Benevento, who had now largely freed himself from Frankish domination. In 789 or 790 he made an informal alliance with Byzantium by marrying Euanthia, the sister of Constantine VI's new wife, Maria.[113]

In Thrace, Irene apparently concluded that the empire's expanded territory had too long a frontier for a single commander to defend and divided the theme into two parts. The eastern part, which continued to be called Thrace, included the frontier with the Bulgars and the main routes to the frontier from Constantinople. The remaining territory, the new theme of Macedonia, included the frontier with the Slavs in the west and its approaches from the capital. Irene simply divided the 6,000 men of the old theme of Thrace equally between the two without raising the official strength of the troops in the area; but by appointing two commanders and staffs instead of one she increased the flexibility of the empire's defense on the two frontiers. Further, by naming the new theme "Macedonia" she implied that it was a base for further conquests, because Macedonia proper was actually the Slav-held land to the west of the frontier.[114]

In 790 Constantine turned nineteen. Though he was always present at ceremonial occasions, and all official documents bore his name, he still did not govern, and he had not been able to choose his own wife. Even more humiliating for him, his subjects knew that he was not the real ruler; those who had important business with the government went first to Stauracius the Logothete, not to the emperor. Constantine evidently formed the idea that it was Stauracius, not Irene, who was standing in his way, and that if he could only remove the postal logothete from the government he could rule undisturbed, though with the benefit of his mother's advice.

Constantine's view was not a clear-eyed one. Irene had shown cleverness and determination even before she had appointed Stauracius, and, useful though she found him as an adviser and manager, she was nobody's puppet. But Constantine looked up to his strong-willed mother and did not want to believe that she was unwilling to share power with him. The young emperor had a few allies at court, notably Peter the Magister, who was a former retainer of Constantine V, and two patricians, Theodore Camulianus and Damianus. These three and Constantine agreed on a plot to seize Stauracius and exile him to Sicily, though not to depose Irene.

While the plotters were at work, a major earthquake struck Constantinople on February 9, 790. Most of the inhabitants of the capital fled their houses, camping in tents in the city's open spaces until it was clear that the aftershocks were over. Irene and Constantine took refuge in the Palace of St. Mamas, north of the capital on the European shore of the Bosporus. Amid this confusion, Stauracius discovered Constantine's plot, and told Irene. The empress reacted with the firmness she always showed when her authority was challenged. She ordered the arrest of Constantine's three collaborators, and also of Constantine's former tutor John Picridius, who may have been innocent but was too close to Constantine for Irene to trust. She ordered all four to be flogged and tonsured, exiled John to Sicily and Damianus to a fort near Dyrrhachium, and imprisoned Peter and Theodore in their own houses. She rebuked Constantine harshly and at length, even slapped him, and then kept him confined to his quarters.[115]

Through the spring matters remained in this uneasy state. In early summer, Irene had a stroke of luck. The Arab governor of Egypt had just put down a mutiny among his soldiers, and sent many of the mutineers back to Syria by sea. A Byzantine fleet that was operating off the Syrian coast surprised the Arab ships and captured them together with the troops. It was a welcome little victory after the recent Byzantine defeats at Podandus, on the Strymon, and in Calabria, and it seems to have emboldened Irene. She now took a sterner view of her son's failed conspiracy. Evidently on the ground that Constantine had behaved treasonably, she sent officials to administer an oath to the entire army that as long as she lived they would not allow Constantine to take power. They were further to acclaim the emperors not as "Constantine and Irene," but as "Irene and Constantine." The army began to take the oath without opposition.[116]

This was Irene's boldest move to date. That she succeeded in it even for the moment shows how firmly in control she was. Constantine was emperor, not she. He obviously wanted to rule; neither his age nor any other impediment now disqualified him. Treason was rebellion against the emperor, and only by the most strained interpretation of Irene's regency or co-emperorship could Constantine have been guilty of that. Practically everyone in the empire knew these facts. But the leading government officials and army officers owed their appointments to Irene and had found her faithful to her allies and unforgiving of her opponents. About Constantine they could not be sure, especially because his plan to rule with his mother showed an indecisiveness that offered little security to anyone who supported him against her. Junior officers and officials, however, not to speak of the rank and file of the army, had no such reasons for preferring the empress.

In late summer, while the oath was being administered, the Arabs landed a major expeditionary force on Cyprus, which they controlled jointly with the Byzantines. No doubt they were retaliating for their recent defeat. Irene learned quickly of this expedition, probably from the Byzantine administration on the island, and prepared a defense. Two fleets, that of the Cibyrrhaeots and apparently that of Hellas, and two more army contingents, probably from the Anatolic and Thracesian themes, gathered near Myra in the Cibyrrhaeot theme, each theme's contingent being led by its own strategus.

When the Arabs sailed from Cyprus into the Gulf of Attalia, the Byzantines sighted them and met them in battle somewhere on the west coast of the gulf. While the Arabs remained at sea, the Byzantine land forces could offer no effective help. Since the fleet of Hellas was small, the fighting fell mainly to the Cibyrrhaeots under their strategus Theophilus, who were probably outnumbered. The Arabs put most of the Byzantine ships to flight, surrounded Theophilus's ship, and took him and his crew prisoner. Then they withdrew with their captives. Theophilus had such a reputation for bravery and rectitude that he was later canonized after the caliph Hārūn executed him, though he was not clearly a martyr for the faith.

16. The Arabs' execution of Theophilus, the strategus of the Cibyrrhaeot theme captured in 790. Vaticanus graecus 1613, p. 359. Painter: Pantoleon. (Photo: Biblioteca Apostolica Vaticana, Vatican City)

Some Byzantines blamed the other three strategi for the defeat, saying that they had deserted Theophilus in battle out of envy for his fame.[117]

This loss came at an extremely bad time for Irene. On the whole, she had maintained the empire's military power, but she had been less successful in maintaining its military glory. In 782 the Arabs had captured her senior generals and advisers and forced her to pay tribute. Later the Lombards had killed John the Sacellarius, the Bulgars had killed the strategus of Thrace, and the Arabs had killed the saintly monks of Zobe and the valorous Diogenes the Turmarch. Now they had captured the respected strategus of the Cibyrrhaeots. Compared with these humiliations, Irene's annexations at the expense of the unwarlike Slavs and her lucky capture of the weakened fortress of Adata, militarily significant though they were, seemed paltry triumphs. As a woman, she was unable to win glory for herself by taking the field in person. Most ordinary soldiers remembered fondly how Constantine V had led his armies to victory, and realized that his grandson was now old enough to take his place.

In September of 790, the officials whom Irene had sent to exact the oath excluding Constantine from power reached the Armeniac theme. Because of its remoteness it seems to have been the last to be asked to swear. The soldiers assembled in a recalcitrant mood. They obviously sympathized with Constantine, but, perhaps under the persuasion of their strategus Nicephorus, who was loyal to Irene, they agreed to swear not to be ruled by Constantine during Irene's lifetime, as long as they could continue to acclaim the emperors as "Constantine and Irene," denying Irene the precedence. While this was not a positive act of rebellion, it subtly disputed Irene's position. Choosing to make a show of firmness rather than a tactical concession, Irene rejected the compromise. She sent Alexius Musele, commander of the tagma of the Watch, to repeat the demand that the Armeniacs acclaim her first. Alexius was an Armenian, like many of the Armeniacs, and Irene doubtless chose him for this mission in the hope that he would be well received by them. So he was, but not in the way in which she had hoped.

In a revolutionary atmosphere the assembled soldiers seized Alexius, declared him their new strategus, and deposed and imprisoned their old strategus, Nicephorus. They then proclaimed Constantine VI their only emperor. The news of what the Armeniacs had done spread quickly. Hearing of it, the soldiers of the other four themes of Asia Minor followed the Armeniacs' example and deposed their strategi, two of whom had recently been discredited at the battle in which the Arabs had captured Theophilus, and all of whom were Irene's appointees. Despite their recent oath, these themes too proclaimed Constantine sole emperor. By October the rebellious soldiers had massed at Atroa in the Opsician theme. Irene still held Constantine in captivity, but if she did not release him the rebels obviously meant to march on Constantinople.

Irene now faced a general military uprising of a sort that Byzantium had seldom seen. Though her generals had proved loyal—with the possible exception of Alexius Musele, who had joined the rebellion under compulsion—they had been unable to control their own troops. Well over half the army was in open revolt. Irene could scarcely count on the allegiance of the tagmata, since most of them had failed her in 786 and the commander of the Watch, Musele, was now part of the rebellion. Irene had no taste for a civil war that she would probably lose. She therefore freed Constantine. He made his way to Atroa, where the troops confirmed him as sole emperor and renounced their allegiance to Irene. He then sent word back to the capital, where he was proclaimed sole emperor in the Forum of Constantine on November 10, 790.[118]

CONSTANTINE IN POWER

Constantine's first independent act was to send a delegation from Atroa to the Armeniacs, who had begun the revolt in his favor. His envoys were his former tutor John Picridius, who had somehow returned from his ex-

17. Constantine VI (r. 780–97). Mutinensis graecus 122, fol. 145ʳ. Note that Constantine eventually did grow a short beard, though all coins show him beard-less. (Photo: Biblioteca Estense, Modena)

ile in Sicily, and Michael Lachanodracon, who now emerged from the ob-scurity to which Irene had relegated him. These two had the Armeniacs swear not to acknowledge Irene as empress, an oath that they must have been happy to take, and gave Constantine's sanction to their illegal elec-tion of Alexius Musele as their strategus. Constantine's selection for this mission of Lachanodracon, his grandfather's famous and faithful general, implied that he was trying to live up to the soldiers' expectation that he would bring back the good old days of Isaurian military might. None-theless, Constantine never showed any inclination toward his ancestors' Iconoclasm. The Council of Nicaea had been his as well as Irene's, and he was not about to repudiate it.

In December 790 Constantine returned to the capital to take charge of the government. He conducted a purge of the palace eunuchs through whom Irene had especially ruled, and had Stauracius whipped, tonsured, and exiled to the Armeniac theme. He exiled many other eunuchs as well, including Aëtius the Protospatharius, who was a particularly close confidant of Irene's, although he had not yet taken a conspicuous part in politics. Most other officials, aside from the strategi already deposed, Constantine seems to have left in office. He ordered his mother confined to her Palace of Eleutherius, but surprisingly, he did not formally depose her as his co-emperor, as he had every right to do and as his supporters must have expected he would. He continued to strike coins with her name and portrait, and he did not require her to surrender the portion of the state gold reserve that she had concealed in her palace. By confining her he seems simply to have been taking his revenge for her confining him to his quarters after his earlier conspiracy. He did not exclude her from a role as his adviser in the future, now that she could no longer be under the influence of her eunuchs.[119]

The young emperor, just twenty years old, was eager to show that he could fight. In April 791, five months after his proclamation, he staged a campaign against the Bulgars, doubtless meant to recall his grandfather's many Bulgarian campaigns. Constantine commanded the army in person. Shortly before he reached the Bulgarian frontier, near the Byzantine fort of Probatum, the Bulgars came to meet him under their khan, Kardam. It was late in the day, and the two armies fought only a brief and indecisive battle before nightfall interrupted them. Then, strangely, both withdrew during the night, reportedly each from fear of the other. Perhaps Constantine was unwilling to risk defeat and was satisfied with showing the Byzantine standard, while the Bulgars, who had been forced to defend themselves, were not really prepared to fight and settled for a draw.[120]

In September of the same year Constantine declared an expedition against the Arabs. He collected an army at Amorium, capital of the Anatolic theme, and from there he marched south. His stated objective was Tarsus, the Arabs' main stronghold in Cilicia. But, perhaps because of the early onset of very cold weather, which halted an Arab raid at about the same time, Constantine called off the expedition before he reached the frontier, and returned to Constantinople in October. Thus Constantine, without suffering a defeat, had shown his willingness to march against, if not to grapple with, the empire's two principal enemies. Yet his two half-campaigns began to give the impression that the young emperor did not quite know what he was doing.[121]

Apparently bewildered by his responsibilities, Constantine came under pressure from his mother and his principal officials to restore her to a role in the government. On its face, such a request was outrageous. No adult emperor had ever ruled with his mother before, and Irene's previous be-

18. A nomisma of Constantine VI and Irene of the type issued after 792, shown three times actual size. Note that Constantine VI now has an orb of his own, though he still appears as a beardless youth and the control mark after his inscription indicates that his side of the coin is actually the reverse, which was the less important. On the obverse, Irene too has an orb. (Photos: Dumbarton Oaks Byzantine Collection, Washington)

havior hardly justified special treatment. Since Constantine had failed to depose Irene officially, however, her supporters, playing on Constantine's indecision, could argue that she had only been suspended from power. And obviously she still did have supporters in the government. Though Constantine kept around him and honored those who had backed him from the first, he put scarcely any of them into the empire's principal posts, leaving officials appointed by Irene to administer the empire. Stauracius is the only civil official he is positively known to have replaced. The only one of his close allies upon whom Constantine certainly bestowed an office is Theodore Camulianus, whom he made strategus of the Armeniacs toward the end of 791 to replace Alexius Musele, who was also putatively an ally of Constantine's. When he made this appointment, Constantine summoned Alexius to Constantinople under a guarantee of his safety, and though he then made Alexius a patrician the guarantee would not have been necessary unless Musele's loyalty was in some doubt. Of course, Alexius had been Irene's man until he was forcibly and illegally elected by the troops; but if Constantine distrusted Alexius, he might have distrusted Irene and her active supporters with as much reason.

Yet he took their advice. The day after his twenty-first birthday, on January 15, 792, he reconfirmed Irene as his co-ruler and gave orders for her to be acclaimed with him by the original formula, "Many years to Constantine and Irene!" The honor he accorded his mother was not merely a sentimental gesture; he went so far in accommodating her that he recalled Stauracius from exile. However surprised they may have been, most of the troops and people accepted these measures and made the new acclamation, not presuming to defend Constantine's interests better than he did himself.

The troops of the Armeniacs, however, refused to acclaim Irene and demanded that Alexius Musele be sent back to them. Constantine, without insisting on the acclamation so as to avoid an open confrontation with the Armeniacs, vented his frustration on Alexius. Accusing Alexius of having provoked the Armeniacs' demand as the first step toward making himself emperor, Constantine had the former strategus whipped, tonsured, and imprisoned in the Praetorium. Constantine had heard accusations to support his charge, but the Armeniacs' exasperation at being ordered to acclaim Irene is quite understandable even if Alexius had no part in it. [122]

Ignoring his problems with the Armeniacs, that July Constantine returned to the Bulgarian front. The khan Kardam had been raiding the border areas of the theme of Thrace, apparently in the first raids there since Irene had rebuilt and fortified Beroea-Irenopolis and Anchialus eight years before. Because these two strongholds were nearly a hundred miles apart, Constantine decided to rebuild another between them at Marcellae. He may well have planned this campaign as a peaceful ceremonial tour to inaugurate his new foundation, modeled on the visit that he and Irene had paid to her refoundations in 784. Appropriately for such a tour, he brought along, besides the tagmata and the armies of the themes of Thrace and Macedonia, a number of courtiers and extensive court trappings reminiscent of Irene's traveling orchestra. Unluckily for Constantine, on July 20 Kardam appeared outside Marcellae's new walls with the entire Bulgar army. Constantine was not prepared to fight such a large force; yet his reputation would suffer if he retreated.

Among those in the imperial camp at Marcellae was the court astrologer Pancratius, who assured the emperor that if he fought he would win. Many reasonable Byzantines took such prophecies into account; but, realizing that some prophecies proved false, they also considered more mundane factors. Apparently relying quite blindly on Pancratius's prediction, Constantine sallied out at once against the enemy and lost disastrously. He himself managed to escape to Constantinople, but the Bulgars severely mauled his army, killed many stranded courtiers and imperial bodyguards, and captured the imperial tent and baggage, including money, horses, and assorted ceremonial equipment. Among the dead were Constantine V's old friend Michael Lachanodracon, the strategi Nicetas and Theognostus, who apparently commanded the themes of Thrace and Macedonia, and the inaccurate astrologer. By August some officers and soldiers of the tagmata who had fled to the capital, disillusioned with Constantine VI, met and hastily decided to proclaim Constantine V's son Nicephorus, priest though he was. When the young emperor heard of the plot, he found himself in a desperate position.

If he took uncharacteristically decisive action, that is probably because he followed the advice of Irene and Stauracius, who had no desire to see Nicephorus succeed and had had considerable experience in dealing with conspiracies. At Constantine's order, imperial agents rounded up all five of Constantine V's sons and brought them to the emperor at the Palace of St. Mamas. There he had his agents blind Nicephorus, cut out the tongues of the other four, and blind Alexius Musele. Though none of these men is likely to have been a mover in the plot, the purpose of the mutilation was plainly not to do justice but to dispose of all the obvious candidates to proclaim as emperor in Constantine's place. Once this was done, the plot collapsed.

Of course, Irene and Stauracius bore personal grudges against Alexius, who had been involved in their temporary overthrow, but they may also have been right when they warned Constantine that the plotters in the tagmata would proclaim Alexius if he were not blinded. Even though he seems to have done little or nothing to seek power, the charismatic Armenian had won amazing popularity among the Armeniacs, and the tagmata knew him from the time of his command of the Watch, just two years before. While these drastic and arbitrary punishments of respected personalities must have made Constantine more unpopular, if he had not ordered them he would probably have been not merely unpopular but deposed and mutilated himself.[123]

As it was, the danger was by no means over. In September the Armeniacs, hearing that their hero Alexius had been blinded, put their strategus, Theodore Camulianus, under guard. They chose no new strategus, but rallied around two of their turmarchs. At this news Constantine assembled a force from the other themes under Constantine Artaser, like Alexius an Armenian, and Chrysocheres, strategus of the neighboring Bucellarian theme. The government probably hoped that the Armeniacs would back down under pressure and persuasion, but the success of their previous insubordination had made them bold. In November, they attacked the emperor's force. In a battle in which both sides suffered heavy losses, the Armeniacs were victorious, capturing the loyalists' two commanders and blinding them in revenge. Constantine had to leave the Armeniacs in revolt through the winter, which in their territory was not suitable for campaigns. Fortunately for him, however, their rebellion did not spread. The next spring he was able to march against them with a huge force comprising all available troops from the other themes. On May 25, Pentecost of 793, he met the Armeniacs in battle, and with some help from dissident Armenians within their own ranks he defeated and captured them all.

By now Constantine had learned the lesson that conspirators needed to be dealt with firmly. This rule particularly applied to the Armeniacs, who had been a law unto themselves for more than two and a half years. The emperor executed the Armeniacs' two turmarchs and the bishop of Sinope, apparently their ringleaders. He also found an appropriate way to punish the ordinary soldiers. Dismissing the entire drungus of 1,000 men centered at the theme's headquarters at Euchaïta, who were presumably those most active in the revolts, he confiscated their property and brought them in chains to Constantinople. On June 24 they were paraded through the city with the words "Armeniac conspirator" branded on their foreheads. Finally, Constantine dispersed and exiled them to Sicily and the other islands. Presumably he recruited other soldiers from the civilian population to take their places on the rolls and their military land grants in the Armeniac theme.[124]

The Armeniacs' rebellion had its effect on the empire's ability to defend itself. During the revolt Constantine had apparently agreed to pay the Bulgars an annual tribute to procure peace in Thrace, which he continued to pay after the revolt was over. Soon after the Armeniacs were put down, the Arabs, based at their rebuilt stronghold of Adata, began to take advantage of the confused and demoralized state of the Byzantine troops on the frontier. Arab raiders first arrived at the fort of Camachum on the border of the Armeniac theme, the only Byzantine base east of the Euphrates that had survived earlier attacks. Camachum was garrisoned by some of the Armenians who had betrayed the Armeniac rebellion to Constantine, but they were disappointed that the emperor had not rewarded them and consequently handed over the fort to the Arabs. The raiders went on to take many captives. The loss of Camachum was a serious one, because it was one of a very few Byzantine forts in a location that the Arabs could hold. It remained in Arab hands for almost twenty years.[125]

After this success, the Arabs of Adata took the unusual step of staging a second major raid in the same summer, this one against the Anatolic theme. Crossing the passes, they besieged the important fort of Thebasa on the road to Amorium. The troops of the garrison resisted bravely, even after their water supply had given out and many had died of thirst, but finally they surrendered on terms and were allowed to go. The Arabs took civilian captives and considerable booty in gold and other valuables. They then destroyed the fort, which remained in ruins for twelve years.[126]

Late the next year Sulaymān, emir of Adata and son of the caliph Hārūn, launched an expedition that was still more ambitious, not to say foolhardy. Elpidius, the strategus of Sicily who had fled Irene's army in 782 and proclaimed himself emperor, after years of obscurity had appeared at Adata, probably sent by Hārūn. Sulaymān made use of Elpidius's pretensions by marching out with him, apparently with the avowed aim of putting him on the Byzantine throne. Though the Arabs can scarcely have expected to succeed in this, if a report that the Arab army numbered 40,000 is accurate this was no ordinary raid. Probably the Arabs at least hoped that offering another emperor as an alternative to the unpopular Constantine would encourage some more garrisons to surrender forts to them. Yet the campaign came to nothing. The Arabs had barely passed through the Cilician Gates and reached the fort of Sasima on the road to Ancyra when they ran into an early winter, with heavy snow. Many died, and others suffered frostbitten feet. If Elpidius did them any good, it was only to obtain some help from local Byzantines. The army retreated ignominiously in January of 795.[127]

By this time power at Constantinople seems to have reached an uneasy equilibrium. Though he was now senior emperor, Constantine felt unable to break with his mother and needed her advice, whereas Irene needed her son's consent to rule at all. Apparently the two rulers kept separate circles of supporters and tended to live apart and to busy themselves with different matters. Constantine's favorite residence was the suburban Palace of St. Mamas; his main interests were military, though after he had finally won a victory by putting down the Armeniac revolt he gave his army two years' rest from offensive campaigning. Irene preferred to live at the Palace of Eleutherius, which she had built for herself in the city, and she and her retainers took most interest in domestic affairs. The Great Palace remained the center of government for most purposes, and for most purposes Constantine and Irene cooperated with each other.

CONSTANTINE'S FALL

The first cause of Constantine's quarrel with his mother and Stauracius had been their choice of his wife, Maria, whom he seems to have resented mostly because she had been imposed on him. Maria had been chosen for her extraordinary beauty, and her personality seems to have been innocuous. During six years of marriage, she had borne Constantine two children, though disappointingly for the future of the dynasty both were daughters. Her widely respected grandfather, Philaretus the Almsgiver, had died three years before. The emperor did not like her, and he was unwilling to put up with her now that he ruled. He took as a mistress a woman from his mother's retinue, Theodote, who was a relative of the well-born monks Theodore and Plato of Saccudium. He wanted to make

19. The burial of St. Philaretus the Almsgiver in 792. Vaticanus graecus 1613, p. 218. Painter: Michael the Younger. (Photo: Biblioteca Apostolica Vaticana, Vatican City)

her his wife, and she would have been a suitable consort. But first he had to rid himself of Maria.[128]

Maria's reputation seems to have been sterling enough to discourage her husband from asking the Church to grant him a divorce on the only legal grounds, adultery. Instead, he accused her of trying to poison him. This charge amounted to treason, of which the emperor was the only judge and for which he could exact the death penalty, making himself a widower. Most, however, would have considered capital punishment for the defenseless empress excessive even if they had believed she was guilty, as no one did. In fact, Constantine seems merely to have threatened to execute Maria to pressure the patriarch Tarasius to grant him a divorce. The emperor was only partly successful. After some difficulty he persuaded Maria to enter a convent in January 795, with the consent of Tarasius and Irene. Constantine's problem was that though he was now rid of Maria he was not free to remarry under canon law while she still lived. For the present he let the matter rest.[129]

That April Constantine made his first military expedition since he had put down the Armeniac revolt two years before. He marched against the Arabs, who were evidently raiding the southern part of the Anatolic theme. On May 8, he met part of their force at a place called Anusan, defeated it—probably by sheer weight of numbers—and pursued it as far as a river, which was probably the Lamis, the frontier between the empire and the caliphate. It was not much of a victory, but it was Constantine's first against a foreign enemy, and he savored it as such. Since he had won the battle on the feast of St. John the Apostle, he decided to magnify the triumph by thanking the saint ostentatiously. On his way back to the capital he stopped at Ephesus, where a great church stood over St. John's tomb and an annual trading fair was held at the time of his feast. The emperor prayed at the church and donated to its clergy the tax just collected on that year's fair, a sum of a hundred pounds of gold, or 7,200 nomismata. He then returned to Constantinople.[130]

Apparently feeling more secure after his much-needed triumph, Constantine announced his betrothal to Theodote in August. Before marrying her he crowned her Augusta, a title that his first wife, Maria, had never enjoyed and that Theodote now shared with Irene. Because the marriage was plainly contrary to church law, a regular imperial wedding performed by the patriarch in the Church of St. Stephen in the Great Palace was out of the question. But the emperor found a clergyman of some note to perform the ceremony—Joseph, the steward of St. Sophia and abbot of the Monastery of Cathara. The wedding took place in Constantine's suburban Palace of St. Mamas in September, 40 days after the betrothal. The patriarch Tarasius did not approve, but neither did he discipline his subordinate Joseph or deny Constantine communion after the wedding. The marriage, which was adulterous according to church law, seems to have met with general disapproval, but few people were ready to oppose the emperor openly.[131]

The exceptions were Theodote's relative Theodore and his uncle Plato of Saccudium. The two acted nearly as one, and had jointly headed the Monastery of Saccudium since Plato had resigned as abbot and Theodore had succeeded him, two years before. They now boldly declared the patriarch Tarasius excommunicated, primarily because he had not himself excommunicated the adulterous emperor, but also because he had not prevented Maria's tonsure and Constantine's remarriage. Though Theodore and Plato were unusually strict moralists, it is hard to avoid the conclusion that they led the protest largely to prove that they did not condone the behavior of their relative Theodote. Though Constantine was eager to make up the quarrel, the two monks were not. As they won support from other monks, Constantine found that his remarriage was an issue that would not go away. Irene—who had chosen Maria, always showed respect for monks, and was ambitious to increase her power at her son's expense—discreetly encouraged the protesters. Some even said that she had advised Constantine to divorce Maria in the expectation of such a protest. The young emperor had no obvious means of escaping his difficulties. No doubt he had gone too far in marrying Theodote, but he could scarcely go back now.[132]

Constantine's best hope was to win more glory abroad, and since he had defeated the Arabs the previous year, he now picked a fight with the Bulgar khan, Kardam. In the spring of 796 he did not send the annual tribute that he had agreed to pay soon after Kardam had defeated him at Marcellae in 792. Kardam sent messengers to demand the tribute, threatening to devastate Thrace up to the Golden Gate of Constantinople if he was not paid. With an eye on the impression he made at home, Constantine sent Kardam a package of horse manure with the message, "I have sent you the kind of tribute you deserve. But you are an old man, and I do not want you to exert yourself to come here. Rather I shall go to Marcellae. Come there, and we shall see what God decides."

Constantine collected a sizable army, which included large contingents from Asia Minor, and advanced to Versinicia, not far from the Bulgar frontier. Kardam came with his troops to a nearby forest and encamped there, apparently because he believed that in wooded terrain the emperor could not put his superior numbers to good use. Constantine did not enter the forest, but remained just outside it offering battle for seventeen days. Finally the khan and his army slipped away and escaped to Bulgaria, leaving Constantine with a sort of victory. At least he had paid no tribute and had protected Thrace from devastation. During his expedition the Arabs took advantage of the absence of many of the troops from the east to raid as far as Amorium, but they took no forts and soon returned home with their prisoners and booty.[133]

In Constantinople, Constantine tried to behave as if all were well. Perhaps on July 11, he, Irene, and Tarasius presided over a public celebration to mark the translation to the capital of the supposed relics of the fourth-century martyr St. Euphemia, long believed to have been destroyed under Constantine V but now alleged to have been miraculously rediscovered. As a gesture of favor, the emperor distributed small parts of the saint's body to certain notable citizens, among them his two daughters by Maria, neither of whom can have been more than six years old. In September he went with Irene to Prusa in the Opsician theme for an extended vacation at the baths fed by the local hot springs, taking most of the court and tagmata along but leaving behind Theodote, who was pregnant. At Prusa Constantine tried to arrange a conciliatory meeting with Plato and Theodore, whose monastery was nearby at Saccudium, but they refused to come to him.[134]

During Constantine's stay at Prusa, word came from Constantinople that Theodote had given birth to a son on October 7, apparently prematurely. As the first son and heir to the throne, he was named Leo, continuing the alternation of names in the Isaurian dynasty from father to son. Eager to see his son, the emperor returned to the capital at once by the carriages of the imperial post. Irene and the main part of the court remained behind for a time, evidently at Irene's wish. She used the opportunity to plot her son's downfall.

Irene's influence, which seems always to have been strong in the civil service, was weaker in the army. If she was to overthrow Constantine, she needed the help at least of the tagmata. Their officers were at Prusa, including the most important, the domestic of the Schools, Bardanes Turcus. She began negotiations with them. They listened. Irene made some opportune gifts from the private gold reserve that she retained; she also made some promises. The generals knew that she had kept faith with her supporters in the past, while Constantine had done little for his own supporters and scarcely anything against Irene's. His continuing to rule with his mother seemed an admission of weakness, and he had problems with the Church over his remarriage that he could not resolve. His mediocre military record was not much of a counterweight. Though Irene was too wise to demand that the commanders of the tagmata commit themselves to immediate action, they agreed to stand by her if a propitious time for a rebellion presented itself.

After Irene and the others returned from Prusa, Constantine decided to take stronger measures against Plato and Theodore, since he had gained nothing from his previous forbearance. In February 797 he ordered Bardanes Turcus and John the Count of the Opsician theme to arrest Plato, Theodore, and ten of their monks at Saccudium. The other monks of Saccudium, numbering about a hundred, were scattered. The two generals conducted Plato to Constantinople, where he was imprisoned in the palace. Theodore and the others were beaten and sent into exile at Thessalonica, and the bishops and abbots of monasteries there and along the way were forbidden to converse with them. Still, many defied the order and greeted Theodore and his companions as heroes. Irene quietly did what she could to protect them, a task made easier because one of the generals who arrested them, Bardanes, was her secret ally. Constantine, who habitually trusted his mother more than she deserved, seems to have suspected nothing.[135]

Meanwhile the caliph Hārūn had regained his enthusiasm for fighting the Byzantines, and had built a new Arab stronghold at Anazarbus in Cilicia. Early in 797 Hārūn personally led a raid into the Anatolic theme. This raid apparently provoked Constantine to go out against the Arabs in March, taking with him a highly mobile force of 20,000 men, mostly cavalry picked from the themes and tagmata. Naturally he was accompanied by the officers of the tagmata, who were now secretly allied with Irene. Perhaps because his mother so advised him, he brought along some other allies of hers, including Stauracius. These set to work to subvert the expedition. They bribed some of the soldiers of the Watch, who seem to have been serving as scouts, to report that the Arabs had fled. Constantine accordingly abandoned the campaign and marched back to Constantinople, while Hārūn, finding no opposition, took and destroyed a fort in Cappadocia.[136]

Not long after the emperor returned, he suffered another setback, which he felt more keenly. His infant son, Leo, died on May 1, so that once again he was without an heir. Constantine buried Leo with great mourning. To many, the child's death must have appeared to be a divine judgment on Constantine's adulterous marriage. In August the Arabs, encouraged by their recent success, launched a second summer raid, which penetrated into the Bucellarian theme, the farthest they had gone since 782. Constantine, who was probably depressed, took no immediate action against them.[137]

At this point Irene and the commanders of the tagmata decided that the opportune time had come to overthrow Constantine. To wait longer risked his learning of their intentions, winning a battle that would bolster his reputation, or appointing men who would not join the conspiracy to posts in the tagmata or civil service. As it was, the emperor's fortunes were at a low ebb. His mother's partisans could hardly have had firmer control over the leadership of the tagmata and bureaucracy, and they felt able to do without the active support of the themes. They may also have wanted to take advantage of Constantine's habit of spending the summer at the Palace of St. Mamas, where troops and people in the city who might sympathize with him could not offer him any immediate aid.

The deposition of Constantine was set for Thursday, August 17, when he was to attend chariot races in the Hippodrome and then return by boat to St. Mamas. The conspirators planned to intercept his boat with a ship of their own and to capture him. Though their plans after that are not entirely clear, if they could seize Constantine without alerting anyone who might help him they would be able either to force him to abdicate and enter a monastery or to mutilate or kill him. Irene may have preferred not to be too specific about the fate her son would meet.

After the races Constantine set out by boat, as expected, from the Great Palace to St. Mamas. But as the conspirators bore down upon him in their ship, the emperor—perhaps because he had been warned—realized that something was wrong. He ordered his boat to turn back, and succeeded in reaching the imperial galley, which was evidently at anchor in the port of the Great Palace. Taking with him a few retainers, he boarded the galley at once and sailed across the Sea of Marmara to Pylae in Bithynia. From there he hoped to make his way to the Anatolic theme, where he expected support. Rumors of what had happened seem to have spread quickly in the city. Constantine's wife, Theodote, fled to Triton, another town in Bithynia, and many troops of the tagmata, never easily controlled by their officers during domestic disturbances, took Constantine's part and were eager to join him wherever he was. Constantine remained at Pylae for a day awaiting developments.

Irene held a hurried conference with the officers of the tagmata in the Palace of Eleutherius. She considered sending a delegation of bishops to her son to negotiate her full retirement from politics in return for a guarantee of her safety. But such a plan might not succeed, and would not protect her many allies. These allies included even the retainers who had sailed to Pylae with Constantine, who for the time being were taking no action out of fear that troops who backed the emperor would arrive and kill them if they showed their hand. Those at Irene's conference in the Palace of Eleutherius came to the conclusion that the co-conspirators at Pylae were their only hope.

Accordingly, Irene wrote secretly to her men at Pylae, declaring that if they did not find a way to hand over Constantine to her she would tell him of their part in the conspiracy. Roused by this letter, early on Saturday morning they seized the still-unsuspecting emperor, bundled him back on board the imperial galley, and sailed back with him to the Great Palace in Constantinople. In the middle of the afternoon they imprisoned him in the Purple Room of the palace, the bedchamber of the empress, in which he had been born 26 years before. And there, by the order of Irene and the other conspirators, the retainers put out his eyes, in the process injuring him fatally.[138]

It was hardly a conspiracy of which Irene could be proud. The troops and people had been alerted; Constantine had almost escaped, and his blinding had been forced upon the plotters and had led, almost certainly by accident, to his death. Although the conspirators managed to conceal the death from the people, the news of the blinding alone caused a general shock. After that fateful Saturday many noticed an unusual darkness for seventeen days, and connected the loss of the sun's rays with the loss of Constantine's sight. Others remembered that, almost precisely five years before, Constantine had ordered the blinding of his former ally Alexius Musele, and saw divine retribution in the emperor's fate. Still others thought the punishment was for his adulterous remarriage. But dismay seems to have been a much more common reaction. Even Irene, who during these three days of confusion appears to have lost much of her control

20. A nomisma of the empress Irene (r. 780–802) with her portrait on both sides, shown three times actual size. Mutinensis graecus 122 includes no portrait of Irene, probably because its source was uncomfortable with the idea of a female emperor. (Photos: Dumbarton Oaks Byzantine Collection, Washington)

both over events and over her fellow plotters, showed in her later reign and life a certain weariness that may betray lasting feelings of grief and guilt.[139]

IRENE'S REIGN ALONE

Irene circulated a report that conspirators among her son's retainers had blinded him and left him incapable of ruling, so that she, his co-emperor, had automatically become sole emperor. This story, though not totally fraudulent, was highly dubious. Even if the conspirators had forced Irene's hand to some extent when she had consented to the blinding, she certainly had incited them to rebellion, and did nothing to punish them afterwards. Furthermore, no woman had ever ruled the empire in her own right. An empress left on her own had always felt called upon to make a speedy marriage with a man who then became the emperor. The dynastic principle, which had some moral though no legal force, was not on Irene's side either. She was an Isaurian only by marriage, and four sons of Constantine V still lived with no worse disability than the loss of their tongues. Such mutilation, intended to exclude them from the succession, had not prevented Justinian II from ruling earlier in the same century. But there was no way other than revolt to challenge a new sovereign's right to rule, and for the present Irene had possession of the government. She struck coins with her picture on both sides to make it clear that she ruled alone, and in her acts she used the title "emperor" rather than "empress" to emphasize that there was no emperor but she.[140]

Whatever support Constantine VI had had—and it cannot have been much—quickly evaporated. Theodote retired to a monastery. Irene at once released Plato of Saccudium and recalled his nephew Theodore and his monks from exile. All of them returned to Saccudium. The patriarch Tarasius hastened to depose and defrock Abbot Joseph of Cathara, who had performed Constantine's adulterous marriage to Theodote. Since no one had an interest in taking poor Joseph's part, everyone agreed on condemning him. Tarasius wrote a letter of apology to Plato, and church unity was restored. Irene may not have commanded total loyalty, and many surely thought that Constantine's fate had been cruel, but as far as we know nobody ever rebelled against Irene on Constantine's behalf, or raised the issue of whether he was really blind or really alive.[141]

Irene apparently replaced some of the commanders of the themes appointed by Constantine, but she does not seem to have had to make major changes in other top positions in the government when she took power. Among the officials of the civil service and the tagmata she already commanded almost complete loyalty, as the plot against Constantine had shown. As during her earlier period of rule, her closest advisers were eunuchs, of whom the chief were Stauracius and Aëtius. Both held the rank of patrician, but neither held an office. Now that he was no longer postal logothete Stauracius does not seem to have been clearly more powerful than Aëtius, as he had been before 790.[142]

Stauracius and Aëtius soon began a power struggle behind the throne. The prize was not only influence over Irene's administration, but also influence over the succession. Irene was nearing 50 and evidently had no intention of marrying again; she could name whomever she wanted as her heir. While eunuchs were traditionally considered ineligible to rule, both Stauracius and Aëtius had relatives who were not eunuchs and for whom they aspired to the succession. However, it was not in Irene's interest to make either of her advisers too powerful or to choose an heir whom those who wanted a male emperor could use to displace her. Though some modern historians have thought that Irene was the plaything of Stauracius and Aëtius, it seems more accurate to say that she played them off against each other.[143]

Irene's first problem as sole emperor was to deal with the large-scale Arab raid that her partisans had indirectly encouraged by sabotaging Constantine's spring campaign. The leader of the Arab expedition was ʿAbd al-Malik, a prominent member of the Abbasid house who had long shown a taste for raiding the empire. It was he who had rebuilt Adata in

785 on Hārūn's orders, and he had also led minor raids in 790, 791, and 793, while his son had led a raid in 792. His troops had now spread over a considerable part of the Anatolic and Bucellarian themes and reached as far as Ancyra. Eager for a truce, Irene sent two Byzantine clerics on an embassy to 'Abd al-Malik to try to negotiate one. When this embassy failed, she sent out an army under Aëtius, which had some success against the raiders, perhaps because it caught them off their guard. But Irene had to face the fact that the Arabs' appetite for serious raiding was now aroused, and when it was the empire could do little to oppose them.[144]

In October came a second test for Irene: a predictable conspiracy on behalf of the sons of Constantine V. The conspirators, who do not appear to have included any important officials, arranged for the five princes to escape from the Palace of Therapia several miles up the Bosporus, where they were confined, and to seek refuge in St. Sophia. The conspirators' idea seems to have been that Irene could not remove the suppliants without violating the church's right to give sanctuary, while the princes' presence in the heart of the city would spark a revolt in their favor. A large crowd did gather in the church, but no open rebellion began. Aëtius then arrived and came to an agreement with the princes, guaranteeing their safety if they came out peacefully. Irene honored this pledge, but she exiled the five to Athens, out of reach of any future plotters in the capital. In her home town her uncle Constantine Serantapechus, strategus of Hellas, kept a watchful eye on the last male members of the Isaurian house.[145]

Having established her position at home, Irene was eager for peace abroad both with the Arabs and with the Franks. The Franks were much the easier to win over. Officially the Byzantines had not made peace with them since Irene's ill-fated expedition of 788 against Grimoald of Benevento and his Frankish auxiliaries. When about 790 Grimoald had made an alliance with the Byzantines and married Constantine's sister-in-law Euanthia, the alliance was potentially directed against the Franks. In 794 relations had worsened when a Frankish synod at Frankfurt, relying on a misleading translation of the acts of the Council of Nicaea and acting against the wishes of Pope Hadrian, condemned the council for approving idolatry. No open conflict had broken out, however, and as both powers had lost interest in fighting over southern Italy little reason for tension remained. Already before the fall of Constantine the Byzantines had sent an embassy to Charlemagne, and at the beginning of 798 Irene sent a new embassy, announcing her accession and proposing a formal peace to go with her new government. She merely requested a recognition of the existing political situation and the release of Sisinnius, a brother of the patriarch Tarasius, who had apparently been taken prisoner by the Franks during the campaign of 788. Charlemagne agreed to make peace and returned Sisinnius.[146]

The Arabs, however, who had already rebuffed one Byzantine attempt to make peace, sensed their opponents' weakness and launched a great new raid in September 798. As in the previous year, its leader was 'Abd al-Malik. He divided his force into two parts. The smaller contingent, led by his son 'Abd al-Rahman, reached Ephesus in the Thracesian theme, taking a large number of prisoners and much plunder in an area where no raid had penetrated for many years. The main force, led by 'Abd al-Malik himself, raided the Opsician theme. Some of its raiders seized the imperial stables at Malagina and captured Stauracius's horses and Irene's carriage. Others raided the area of the Monastery of Saccudium, from which Theodore and Plato fled, with many other refugees, to Constantinople. When the army of the Opsician theme under its count, Paul the Patrician, tried to oppose 'Abd al-Malik, it was defeated with heavy losses, and the Arabs added the army's baggage to their booty. All told, it was the most destructive Arab raid since Hārūn's expedition of 782.[147]

Irene therefore tried to conclude peace, as she had in 782. She promptly sent an embassy to the caliph Hārūn under Bishop Euthymius of Sardis, one of her earliest episcopal appointments and a leading participant at the Council of Nicaea. No doubt Euthymius performed his mission ably, but if he offered the same princely tribute as that granted in 782, as Arab dignity appeared to demand, Hārūn's acceptance comes as no surprise. The sum of 160,000 nomismata a year, payable before the summer campaigning season, could be justified in 782 by Irene's need to ransom Stauracius and her other captured officials and to avoid a rout of the leaderless Byzantine army. In 798 it was harder to justify. But evidently Irene had the money to spare and feared, with some reason, that the alternative was a long series of full-scale Arab raids that would be more costly and humiliating than the tribute and would cause great suffering to the people of Asia Minor. She had never been eager for conflict with any power except the unwarlike Slavs, and she seems always to have wanted to be known as a peacemaker.[148]

In March 799 came another ineffectual conspiracy in favor of the pathetic sons of Constantine V. The instigators were apparently dissident soldiers of the theme of Hellas, who plotted with a neighboring Slavic chieftain named Akamir to release the princes and to proclaim one of them emperor. As usual, Irene quickly learned of the plot, probably from her uncle Constantine Serantapechus, the strategus of Hellas, and acted decisively. She sent his son and her cousin, Theophylact, with orders to blind the four princes who had not yet been blinded and to break up the conspiracy. Theophylact followed his orders, and the sons of Constantine V, after being the subjects of five plots, were clearly disqualified from ruling.[149]

Irene had seemingly overcome all challenges and won the freedom to rule as she liked. She even staged a sort of triumphal procession on Easter Monday, April 1, 799. After Mass at the Church of the Holy Apostles, she rode down the main street in a golden carriage drawn by four white horses, scattering gold coins to the people liberally as she went. Each horse was led by a man of patrician rank. The first was Bardanes Turcus, who as domestic of the Schools had helped bring Irene to power and was now strategus of the Thracesians. The others were Nicetas Triphyllius, who was the new domestic of the Schools, Nicetas's brother Sisinnius, who was strategus of Thrace, and an otherwise unknown Constantine Boïlas. It was a grand but rather silly procession, which might have raised doubts about how well the empress was going to manage her officials now that she needed them less urgently.[150]

IRENE'S FALL

During the remainder of her reign Irene showed little of the pragmatism verging on ruthlessness of her earlier dealings at home and abroad. She became increasingly indulgent toward those accused of plotting against her. While she had always shown favor to the Church and especially to the monasteries, she now seems to have carried it to the point of not collecting the taxes due on their secular holdings. She also became increasingly ready to make gifts and financial concessions to the people of Constantinople, beginning with her lavish donative in 799. Her foreign policy was peaceful to the point of impassivity. She tolerated minor Arab raids every year in violation of her expensive peace treaty and let the caliph Hārūn build a new frontier fortress (called Hārūniyyah) undisturbed. She humored the growing imperial pretensions of Charlemagne, and made no further moves to annex Slavic territory. None of these policies was absolutely irresponsible, and most could be defended as philanthropy or as avoiding unnecessary conflict. But for Irene they represented a change of course, the result perhaps of her tiring of rule and declining in health, of a wish to repair her damaged reputation among her subjects, of an eagerness to make up for her past sins before her death, or more probably of all these causes.[151]

Irene's most prescient measure at the time was to establish Plato and Theodore as abbots of the Monastery of Studius in Constantinople. Though their old monastery at Saccudium had not been entirely destroyed in the Arab raid of 798, they were willing to accept Irene's invi-

21. Entrance of the
Monastery of Studius,
Constantinople.
(Photo: Dumbarton Oaks
Byzantine Collection,
Washington)

tation to take over Studius, a stately complex with an illustrious past,
which had lost most of its monks during Constantine V's persecutions.
Now Theodore—whose name was always associated with Studius thereafter—used his position to restore an important monastic presence to the
capital, and under him Studius grew from about 10 to about 700 monks.
Theodore established the sort of monasticism at Studius that had grown
up during the previous eighteen years in Bithynia: communal, austere,
strongly iconophile, and interested in restoring Christian learning to the
flourishing state it had supposedly been in before Iconoclasm. The Monastery of Studius, which kept up its ties with Saccudium, included a
school for novices, a workroom for the copying of manuscripts, and a
growing library. Theodore himself composed many books, including
new monastic regulations designed to promote both asceticism and learning. For all this Irene could take a good deal of credit. She also founded a
new convent of her own on the nearby island of Principo.[152]

In May 799 Irene became gravely ill. Her courtiers, anticipating her
death, began a struggle for the succession. Groups formed around both
Stauracius and Aëtius, but Aëtius seems to have been the more successful
in winning over high officials. He secured the support of Nicetas Tri-

22. Interior of the Monastery of Studius, Constantinople. (Photo: Irina Andre-escu Treadgold)

phyllius, domestic of the Schools, and apparently of Nicetas's brother Si-sinnius, strategus of Thrace. Stauracius's support seems to have been lim-ited to lower-ranking military officers. When Irene started to recover, Aëtius accused Stauracius of plotting to seize the throne, though the charge was probably as true of Aëtius as of Stauracius. Irene held a state council at the Palace of Hieria in the Asian suburbs of Constantinople to consider the accusation. She rebuked Stauracius, but he defended himself and in his turn accused Aëtius and Nicetas. Finally Irene punished no one, and in fact it is difficult to tell whom she should have punished, since she could not safely punish them all. Unfortunately for her, Irene's illness had begun a pattern of intrigue that her recovery did not alter.

Once Stauracius had been outmaneuvered by Aëtius at court, he began plotting with junior officers of the themes and tagmata. He distributed a substantial amount of gold from his private fortune, and presumably made use of connections that he had formed in the army during the course of many years. His main backing was among the Schools, the Excubitors, and the troops of Cappadocia in the Anatolic theme. Apparently he was ready to dispense with his relatives and hoped to become emperor him-self. Though no eunuch had ever ruled in his own right, neither had a woman done so before Irene, and Stauracius may have believed that a eu-nuch was no worse fitted to be emperor than a woman was.

By February 800 Irene had become disturbed enough to hold another state council, this time at the Great Palace, at which Stauracius's enemies, led by Aëtius and Nicetas, convinced her of his guilt. Still she did not punish her old ally harshly, but merely issued an order that no public officials were to converse with him. Aëtius, whom Irene had now named strategus of the Anatolics, was clearly left as her principal adviser. But despite Irene's order, Aëtius's success, and a serious lung disease from which he began to suffer at this time, Stauracius continued to plot. A group of flattering monks and doctors visited him as he lay bedridden at his palace in the capital, always assuring him that he would soon recover and win the throne. By the beginning of June, the officers who supported Stauracius in Cappadocia raised a rebellion against their strategus, Aëtius. But by the time news of the rising reached Constantinople Stauracius had died of his disease, which may have been lung cancer, on June 3. When the news of his death reached the Anatolics two days later, the rebellion collapsed. Though Aëtius and Nicetas were victorious, their alliance does not seem to have survived their victory, which in turn brought little aid to Irene. Irene's courtiers had become so doubtful that her rule could last that plotting had become endemic among them.[153]

While Irene clung to her throne at Byzantium, Pope Leo III crowned Charlemagne emperor of the Romans in Rome on Christmas Day, 800. In Byzantine eyes, as the pope and Charlemagne must have known, the coronation was nothing less than an act of rebellion against the imperial government. The pope argued that the imperial throne was legally vacant, since Constantine VI had been deposed and Irene, as a woman, could not be an emperor—an argument that was decidedly undercut by Charlemagne's earlier recognition of Irene in 798. Yet circumstances forced Leo into some such sophistry, because no one in East or West had any idea as realistic as recognizing the existence of separate western and eastern empires. Instead, they saw the question as one of conflicting claims to a theoretically universal and indivisible Roman Empire. The Byzantine claim had all the historical and constitutional tradition on its side, as every minimally knowledgeable Westerner knew; but Charlemagne held Rome and had more power in the West, and Leo's argument made it possible for him officially to ignore Irene. No doubt Charlemagne and Leo realized that Irene was in no position to take successful military action against them. For the time being, Irene tried to ignore Charlemagne as Charlemagne ignored her. But since the members of the Byzantine administration were aware of Charlemagne's coronation, Irene's declining prestige must have suffered further.[154]

There may therefore have been a bit of desperation in Irene's grant of sweeping tax exemptions to the people of Constantinople and the tagmata in March 801. She abruptly abolished the trading duties paid at the city's markets, which amounted to a tenth of the retail price of all goods. She also reduced the tenth levied on goods on ships bound for the capital that passed the toll stations of Abydus, on the way from the Aegean Sea, and Hierum, on the way from the Black Sea. These measures therefore lowered all prices at Constantinople by at least a tenth, and often by much more, because corrupt tax farmers had exacted as much as a third. Irene also seems to have abolished inheritance taxes for the widows of soldiers, including those of the tagmata, and perhaps for city dwellers in general. Of course the citizens praised Irene loudly.[155]

The impact of these measures on the state revenue can easily be exaggerated—the loss probably amounted to less than half the tribute paid to the Arabs—but it was still a significant sum, and it came on top of other losses of revenue and increases in expenditure. Aside from its denying the tax farmers opportunities for extortion, the measure was hard to justify on grounds of fairness, because the burden of taxation already fell disproportionately on the empire's farmers, and these duties and the inheritance taxes were practically the only levies city dwellers paid. The reductions do seem to have stimulated trade at Constantinople somewhat, but since this trade was now virtually untaxed it could not benefit the treasury much. The tax exemptions were obviously calculated to increase Irene's popularity, so that anyone who thought of deposing her would fear a popular rising in the capital in her favor. And in fact they may have helped keep Irene on her throne for another year and a half. Irene also tried to ward off conspiracies by continuing to give large gifts of money to her leading officials.[156]

After Irene had with difficulty ignored Charlemagne's new imperial title for a year, word came that he was planning to bring it to her attention by making a naval expedition against Sicily. Early in 802 Irene decided to try negotiation, and sent an embassy to Charlemagne under a certain Leo the Spatharius. The Frankish ruler received the Byzantine ambassador with respect, took no further military measures, and by summer sent back legates of his own to Constantinople, bringing an extraordinary proposal for peace. Charlemagne offered to marry Irene and thereby to unite the East and the West. This plan was designed to uphold the principle of the Roman Empire's universality and indivisibility without either side's having to give up any of its claims.

Any real union between the Germanic feudal congeries of Charlemagne and the ancient Byzantine state was of course impossible, and if Charlemagne did not know it many of his advisers surely did. On the other hand, as an unreal solution to an unreal problem the proposal had a certain appeal, at least before the two sides had to spell out what it actually meant. For example, if Charlemagne would have been satisfied with contracting a purely formal marriage during a brief visit to Constantinople—as given Western ideas of a husband's authority he almost certainly would not have been—Irene might have continued to rule with her hand strengthened by Frankish protection. Irene also had to reckon with retaliation from Charlemagne if she gave him a flat refusal, and that she was eager to avoid. The Frankish ambassadors remained in Constantinople for some time while the government considered the matter.

Although the plan was not totally unacceptable to Irene, it was most unwelcome to those courtiers who were hoping to take power after her. Aëtius's plan was now for his brother Leo to succeed the empress, and in case he could not persuade her to name Leo her successor he had assembled a collection of military commands that would be useful in a rebellion. He was now not only strategus of the Anatolics but also count of the Opsician theme, and he had obtained his brother's appointment as strategus of both Thrace and Macedonia; these four themes surrounded Constantinople and had more than a third of the empire's troops. Aëtius repeatedly spoke against the Frankish proposal to Irene, who seems to have been inclined to accept it, at least provisionally. If she did so, Aëtius seemed ready to move against her. A large faction at court, though not in favor of the marriage, feared and resented Aëtius's ambitions as well. It did not wait for Irene to reach a decision.[157]

At about ten o'clock at night on October 31, 802, a group of high officials and dignitaries, accompanied by some officers of the tagmata, arrived at the so-called Bronze House, or Chalce, which formed the outer entrance of the Great Palace. Their leader was Nicephorus, a patrician and the general logothete, almost certainly the same man who had been strategus of the Armeniacs before he was deposed in 790 for backing Irene. In Nicephorus's entourage were seven other patricians, of whom the foremost were Nicetas Triphyllius, still the domestic of the Schools, and his brother Sisinnius, recently displaced as strategus of Thrace by Aëtius's brother Leo. The other patricians were also men of consequence. One was Leo of Sinope, the sacellarius; another was Theoctistus, the quaestor; the rest were Peter, domestic of the Schools earlier in Irene's reign, Gregory, count of the Opsician theme under Leo IV, and Leo Serantapechus, a relative of Irene's.[158]

The members of this formidable delegation announced to the palace guards that they had come on the orders of Irene, who was then at the Palace of Eleutherius. They alleged that she had ordered them to proclaim their leader, Nicephorus, emperor in order to forestall Aëtius's plan to proclaim his brother Leo. Whether or not the guards believed this story, which was after all a fairly plausible one, they willingly joined in proclaiming Nicephorus and admitted him and his company to the Great Palace. Once he was established there, Nicephorus dispatched troops to arrest Irene, who knew nothing of the orders she had supposedly given. About midnight Nicephorus sent out messengers to announce his accession to those he wanted to know of it at once. At dawn he had Irene brought to the Great Palace, and he and his supporters and troops then passed from the palace to St. Sophia, where the patriarch Tarasius crowned him emperor. Some of the people of the city gathered and protested in favor of Irene, but Nicephorus was safely in power.

He then spoke with Irene in the palace. The new emperor declared that he had accepted the throne only reluctantly at the insistence of his supporters, and assured her that she had nothing to fear from him. For her part, Irene accepted her deposition with a dignified resignation, and made a sort of speech for the record. "I take it," she is said to have told Nicephorus, "that God, my helper and champion, glorified me when I was an orphan and raised me to the imperial throne when I was unworthy, and now I blame my fall on myself and my sins." Irene nonetheless reproached Nicephorus for breaking his oath of loyalty to her and recalled that she had trusted him enough to disregard true reports of his plot. But she recognized him as emperor, and asked only to be allowed to continue living in her favorite Palace of Eleutherius. Nicephorus asked in return that she reveal where she had hidden the greater part of the imperial treasury, which she had not trusted him enough to tell him even though he had been her chief finance minister. She gave the requested information, swearing on a relic of the True Cross that she had concealed nothing.

The new emperor could not, however, reasonably run the risk of letting his predecessor reside in the capital under no disabilities. Instead he took the fairly mild measure of exiling her to the Convent of the Mother of God, which she had founded on the nearby island of Principo; there she became the abbess. Thus Irene's reign ended with a bloodless and relatively harmonious transfer of power.[159]

CONTRIBUTIONS OF IRENE'S REIGN

During a long reign in which her right to rule was always in question, her enemies were many, and her allies supported her more out of expediency than devotion, Irene showed remarkable toughness. Orphaned young, self-assured, and sustained by unwavering religious convictions, she seems to have had no loves and few friendships. She had little affection for either her trusting husband or her admiring son, both of whom she plotted against. Her closest allies, among them Stauracius, Aëtius, and Nicephorus, plotted against her in turn. Although her restoration of the icons, her showmanship, and her largesse made her popular among the

monks and commoners of Constantinople and among ordinary iconophiles everywhere, such people did not count for much in politics.
Shrewd and energetic though she was, Irene had to expend much of her
shrewdness and energy simply to stay on her throne. Nevertheless, while
furthering her own ambitions and the cause of the icons, she brought
about a lasting shift in power in the Byzantine government and started a
transformation of the political and cultural life of the empire.

By contrast, Constantine VI did little but get in his mother's way. Of
course, he had few opportunities to pursue sustained policies, since Irene
kept him from power until he was 19, interfered a good deal during his
short reign, and disposed of him when he was 26. Though he demonstrated little ability in ruling and great weakness in dealing with his
mother, he was not utterly incompetent, and given time and freedom
from Irene's influence he might have made an adequate ruler. His main
problem was that he was fashioned of much less stern stuff than Irene,
who in her twenties was already making her way in politics with fewer
advantages than her son was to have. Constantine, Irene, and those
around them realized sooner or later that she was much better suited to
rule than he was, despite the inferiority of her legal claim. And so she
ruled, first in his name, then behind his throne, and finally in his place.
Yet her struggle with him took its toll, and after 787 Irene's finest achievements were behind her. If she had stepped down then, she would have
won herself a reputation of great brilliance, and largely deserved it.

Although Irene showed as much intelligence and determination as
strong emperors like Leo III and Constantine V, she could never rule as
independently as they had. Her real problem was not her son; in the end
his removal actually weakened her position. Her greatest weakness was
that she was a woman, while the Byzantine crown was designed to fit a
man. As a woman, she could not securely rule alone while keeping a
spouse, a son, or another heir in the background, as male emperors commonly did. Byzantine sensibilities would not allow her to lead an army
into battle, though in effect she led the armies that peacefully extended
Byzantine control over Thrace in 784 and 786. She could not lead the
Church as convincingly as a male emperor because she could not be considered a sort of priest, though she took part in certain church ceremonies
and was present at her ill-fated council of 786 and at the last session of the
Seventh Ecumenical Council. In sum, given her subjects' attitudes, she
could not act with the same unquestioned authority as a strong male emperor, who could delegate power with much less danger of losing it.
Aware of this, she made a virtue of necessity and willingly shared power
with her civil service, in the process restoring it to the respected place it
had enjoyed more than a century before.

Irene's primary allies were among the palatine officials, a group that worked with the civil service proper in the Great Palace and shared many of its duties and sometimes its personnel. Irene appointed several palace officials to civil service posts, not only making Stauracius postal logothete but giving the offices of sacellarius and military logothete to the palace eunuch John and later to other eunuchs, Leo and Constans. Though traditionally the officials of the palace and civil service had been fairly distinct from the military officers, especially from the commanders of the themes, Irene also gave several civil officials military commands. First she put the three eunuchs John, Theodore, and Stauracius in charge of military operations in 781, 782, 783, and 788. Later she gave Aëtius command of two themes. While she seems to have appointed the future emperor Nicephorus strategus of the Armeniacs before she made him general logothete, he had probably had experience in the civil service even earlier. Of course, her promotion of her protoasecretis Tarasius to patriarch of Constantinople shows her confidence that he, civil servant though he was, could maneuver the Church through the difficult business of restoring the icons. Though our source material is too thin to provide many more details of what the civil officials did under Irene, their service in these military, diplomatic, ecclesiastical, and administrative assignments seems to prove that she had confidence in them.

Aside from Stauracius and Aëtius, who eventually obtained so much power that they could aspire to overthrow their patroness, Irene's civil servants generally followed their best interests by repaying her trust with fidelity. After 780 they held aloof from conspiracies in favor of Constantine VI and the sons of Constantine V, and apparently even from those begun by Stauracius and Aëtius. When several civil servants finally joined in the successful conspiracy of Nicephorus the General Logothete, they may have felt that Irene's reign was over in any case and they were simply forestalling a conspiracy by Aëtius. Their backing Irene during the conspiracies in 790 and from 796 to 797, and their urging Constantine VI to restore her to power in 792, shows that they were loyal to her even when such loyalty might have been dangerous. Irene clearly had far better relations with her civil officials than the iconoclast emperors had ever had. These good relations extended to monks and bishops from civil service families, many of whom entered monasteries or the church hierarchy during her reign and were probably the empress's most enthusiastic supporters.

Isolated though she may have been as a private person, therefore, Irene was far from isolated as a ruler. She delegated responsibility widely among her officials and enjoyed the support of many monks and others who held no government office. Irene left Tarasius much discretion in deciding how to hold a council to restore the icons, and she gave Stauracius wide powers to clear Thrace of Slavs. The sack of Adata appears to have been entirely due to the initiative of Nicephorus, and Irene relied heavily on advice from Stauracius, Aëtius, and other officials. To a greater extent han in most reigns at Byzantium, then, the accomplishments of Irene's reign were the work of a group. What did this group do for the empire?

In military terms, its record was not glorious. As usual, the numbers of battles won and lost are not by themselves particularly significant, since the empire's defensive system allowed it to replace casualties rapidly and to reassert its control routinely over areas that had been raided. Still, by generally having the best of their battles with the Byzantines during Irene's reign and by collecting a high tribute from her during about a third of it, the Arabs reestablished on both sides of the frontier a reputation for superior strength. Hārūn showed eagerness to press the border war while Irene showed eagerness to avoid it. While the Arabs had several competent military leaders, the Byzantines seemed to have no worthy successor to Michael Lachanodracon, whom Irene retired for political reasons. By showing the Byzantine standard against the Arabs in his three inconclusive expeditions Constantine VI was at least recognizing a problem of prestige that Irene usually ignored.

Aside from the psychological effect of their raids, the Arabs gained some real military advantages by strengthening their fortified positions on the frontier and weakening Byzantine ones. The Arabs built or rebuilt a row of three border strongholds at Anazarbus, Hārūniyyah, and Adata, captured and held the Byzantine border fort of Camachum, and destroyed several other Byzantine border forts, notably Thebasa, which remained in ruins. The Byzantines' only effective opposition to this activity was the temporary capture and sack of Adata, and that was a matter of local rather than central government initiative. Nor does Irene's government seem ever to have tried to enlist the cooperation of the Khazar khan, though in 799 the Khazars invaded the caliphate for reasons of their own. Irene's defense against the Arabs was weaker than that of her three Isaurian predecessors, and though she faced Arab attacks of unusual aggressiveness Irene's government nevertheless deserves some blame for a decline in Byzantine prestige and security in the East.[160]

In the West, Charlemagne's expansion of Frankish power in Italy and his claim to rule the Roman Empire presented new problems for the Byzantines in an area where their influence had been declining for centuries. Unlike her Isaurian predecessors, Irene made some attempts to come to grips with the situation in Italy rather than merely lashing out at the empire's opponents. Marrying Constantine VI to a daughter of Charlemagne was in itself a good idea, and it failed for reasons the imperial government could not have foreseen. After its failure, however, the Byzantines seem to have seriously underestimated Frankish influence over Benevento when they launched their ill-fated expedition of 788. Again, Irene's attempts to negotiate with Charlemagne during her reign alone were sound enough policy, and her government could hardly have anticipated Charlemagne's coronation or his problematical proposal of marriage. The fact that Irene was a woman plainly compromised the empire's standing in the eyes of Charlemagne, the pope, and their advisers, but this was a problem that Irene could do nothing about without relinquishing her position. In any event, Irene lost no territory in Italy and resolved the schism with the pope, and she had little chance to deal with the issue of Charlemagne's imperial title before she was overthrown.

Irene's greatest success in external policy was in the Balkans, where she both gained territory and improved the empire's defenses. The four new Byzantine strongholds of Anchialus, Marcellae, Beroea-Irenopolis, and Philippopolis proved reasonably effective in protecting the Bulgar frontier, and by the end of Irene's reign the Bulgars were behaving themselves without being paid tribute. Irene's annexations at the expense of the Slavs brought into the empire a stretch of fertile land not far from the capital that would modestly increase the empire's population, food supply, and revenue. Incorporated into the new theme of Macedonia with its own military command, the conquered land probably secured overland communications with Thessalonica for the first time since the Slavic invasions. It could also serve as a base for further easy and valuable conquests of territory occupied by the Slavs. Though Constantine VI continued Irene's refoundations by fortifying Marcellae, as far as we know Irene did not continue expansion at the expense of the Slavs during her reign by herself. Perhaps she feared that further expansion, as in 788, would provoke another Bulgar attack that she was not prepared to meet, and certainly she had other preoccupations at the end of her reign. Still, by beginning to reconquer land from the Slavs, as no earlier emperor had done, Irene and Stauracius launched an original and highly promising initiative.

In domestic policy, Irene and Tarasius, after overcoming their setback in 786, managed the restoration of the icons brilliantly. By 802 Iconoclasm had ceased to be a burning issue for most, and the group that overthrew Irene were as good iconophiles as she was. Under Irene the civil service, monks, and ecclesiastical hierarchy had become a highly influential iconophile body. Iconoclast elements in the army were for the present cowed, despite the undeniable fact that the empire had had greater military success under iconoclast rule, which might well give Byzantines the impression that Iconoclasm enjoyed more divine favor. The restoration of the icons, which had been accomplished with far less acrimony than their earlier destruction had caused, brought the empire greater religious peace than it had known for many years. Compared with Iconoclasm, the Moechian Controversy over Constantine VI's remarriage was inconsequential, and with Constantine's fall even it appeared to be over. The Byzantines could now devote their energies to more productive pursuits.

As has been seen, the process of restoring the icons brought with it a revival of scholarship and literature. The movement began with the effort of iconophiles, particularly monks, to show that the use of icons had a firm basis in the works of the Fathers while Iconoclasm had none, a demonstration that required writing theology and copying books as well as research and reading. The composition of histories and saints' lives soon followed, as the iconophiles sought to set the record straight about the iconoclast period. Though such writing still seems to have been on a limited scale, it was nonetheless considerable in comparison with the almost total absence of literature under Iconoclasm. In Irene's reign learning in general began gradually to benefit from the perception that Iconoclasm had been the result of ignorance. Eventually, education and literacy improved and spread. Though this process had not advanced very far by 802, the steady advance of education boded well for the future efficiency of the Byzantine administration and army, which made heavy use of written records, orders, and documents.

Despite the scarcity of the source material it seems safe to say that Irene's reign was a time of economic growth for the empire. With each generation after the end of the plague, the population must have increased. Since the empire was far from being overpopulated, this population growth would have brought more land under cultivation and increased agricultural production and trade, which the Arab raids were not widespread enough seriously to disrupt.

The best indication of Byzantine economic growth that we have is the financial position of the state, which improved in the absence of major economies or reforms. Irene and Constantine's government spent money freely on tribute to the Arabs and Bulgars, public ceremonies, military campaigns, refounding cities, giving public donatives, making presents to officials, and building such structures as the Palace of Eleutherius, the Convent of the Mother of God on Principo, and the Church of St. Sophia at Thessalonica. Constantine lost a substantial sum of money when his camp was captured in 792 by the Bulgars, and in 795 he made a handsome donation to the Church. No major category of spending seems to have been reduced. On the other hand, toward the end of her reign Irene reduced revenue by cutting trade duties, inheritance taxes, and taxes on tenants of church lands. Evidence from both her reign and that of her successor Nicephorus indicates that hers was a time of considerable corruption and inefficiency on the part of tax collectors and other officials and widespread tax evasion by the rich.

We might therefore expect Irene to have run short of gold, especially because Leo IV may have spent part of Constantine V's gold reserve before 780. Nevertheless, 22 years later, Irene still had a sizable reserve to reveal to Nicephorus, over and above the cash on hand that Nicephorus must have known about from his duties as general logothete. Never is there any indication that Irene or Constantine VI was in financial distress, and since Irene was for the most part a prudent ruler, her willingness to spend money probably indicates that she had ample money to spend. Her financial measures contrast markedly with the tax increases, confiscations, tighter fiscal management, and severely restricted expenditures of Leo III and Constantine V, yet it seems clear that her revenue was larger than theirs. This increase in revenue, unmeasurable but plainly significant, appears to reflect a general economic expansion.

It is striking that the man who finally displaced Irene was her finance minister, rather than a leading military commander like Nicetas Triphyllius or a close personal adviser like Aëtius or Stauracius. Apparently under Irene the general logothete was a more than usually important person. He was probably also able to embezzle considerable sums that were useful for organizing a conspiracy. Although as emperor Nicephorus worked tirelessly against official corruption, he showed an expert knowledge of how such corruption worked. His influence seems to have increased along with the empire's wealth.

When Nicephorus overthrew Irene, he did not overthrow her regime. He was backed by her leading officials and even by one of her relatives, and Tarasius and others readily accepted him as Irene's successor. He took over a throne that Irene would probably have lost soon in any case, since her difficulties in ruling as an empress without a colleague or heir had increasingly caught up with her. Having established the empire's officials and monks in power when she restored the icons, afterward she suffered from too many disabilities to lead her new regime very effectively or to reform its failings. Nicephorus was to lead it better.

CHAPTER THREE

The Reforms of Nicephorus I, 802-813

Nicephorus was the first ruler of mature years and wide experience to ascend the throne within living memory. His four predecessors had all been under 30 at their accession and had exercised little responsibility beforehand. Nicephorus was over 50 and had held high office for years. He was able to take command at once, and throughout his reign was fully in charge. He was a strong man, as his admirers and detractors both agreed, and he looked as strong as he was. Large and moderately tall, he had broad shoulders and a protruding stomach, a wide forehead, thick lips, luxuriant hair, and a flowing white beard. All were also agreed on his keen intellect and political sense. Though his reign was not long, it was full of ambitious projects and solid achievements. Nicephorus was a middle-aged man in a hurry.[161]

He had been born about 750 in Cappadocia in the Anatolic theme, the part of the empire most exposed to Arab raids. He was said to be of Arab stock himself, descended from the princely family of the Ghassanids, who in pre-Islamic times had ruled a Christian Arab tribe in the Syrian desert that was allied with the Byzantines. After the Muslim conquest Nicephorus's noble ancestor had reportedly fled to the empire and taken up residence in Cappadocia. Whether or not this report is entirely true, Nicephorus was probably of good family even though he was a provincial.

Nicephorus seems to have held a responsible position in the imperial service by 780. The story goes that Elpidius, the would-be emperor who had last been in Constantinople in that year, remembered Nicephorus as an intelligent man, given to fasting and prayer, with an unusual ability to command. When from his exile among the Arabs Elpidius heard of Nicephorus's accession, he reportedly advised 'Abd al-Malik, the governor of the frontier regions, to throw away his silk robe and put on his armor.

23. Nicephorus I (r. 802–11). Mutinensis graecus 122, fol. 150ʳ. Note the emperor's white beard. (Photo: Biblioteca Estense, Modena)

This story suggests that Nicephorus was indeed the strategus of the Armeniacs who sacked the newly built Arab stronghold of Adata in 786, because that is the only exploit we can attribute to him that made a major impression on the Arabs. After this victory he would have been deposed by his troops in 790 for supporting Irene against Constantine VI, and briefly held under guard.[162]

About 791, Nicephorus married his daughter Procopia to a young noble named Michael Rhangabe. The owner of large inherited estates, Michael was evidently the son of the naval drungary Theophylact Rhangabe, whom Irene had exiled for rebellion in 780. The family had apparently been rehabilitated by the time of Irene's eclipse in 790. Then an alliance of the families of Nicephorus and Rhangabe, who had records of both supporting and opposing Irene, offered some security to both sides in a time when politics were unusually fluid. By 792 Procopia and Michael had given Nicephorus the first of his five grandchildren. At about the same time he had another child of his own, his only surviving son, to whom he gave his own father's name of Stauracius. Nicephorus was subsequently widowed. Before Constantine's fall in 797 Nicephorus became general logothete, presumably through the influence of Irene, and from this powerful office he staged his successful coup. During his earlier career he had probably held other offices of which no record survives. Certainly before 802 he had gained a clear conception of what was wrong with the management of both the army and the empire's finances, along with a determination to put things right.[163]

Nicephorus began his reign with broad support in the bureaucracy and outwardly on good terms with the clergy and army. His coronation, however, had provoked a demonstration in favor of Irene by some of the citizens of Constantinople, who had always liked her and had her to thank for their tax exemptions of the year before. Nicephorus also needed to deal with Aëtius, who was dangerously strong and could only see the change in regime as a blow to his power, though he and the new emperor had had no quarrel previously. Within a month of his coronation, Nicephorus appears to have suspected a plot by Irene and Aëtius, and took precautions against them. He removed Irene from her convent on nearby Principo, where she had to take hurried leave of a flock that she had led for only a few weeks, and sent her to a convent on the island of Lesbos, at a much safer distance. The emperor continued to treat Aëtius with respect, but he retired the ambitious eunuch from his combined command of the Anatolic and Opsician themes.[164]

Nicephorus then brought all five great themes of Asia Minor under an even larger combined command, which he assigned to Bardanes Turcus, previously the strategus of the Thracesian theme alone. He was given the title of monostrategus, used for a single strategus commanding several themes at once. Bardanes—who, to judge from his name and epithet, was of mixed Armenian and Khazar blood—was already well liked by many soldiers and clergy in Asia Minor. His appointment to this enlarged command seems to be a sign that Nicephorus had some anxieties about the loyalty of the Eastern troops and thought that Bardanes was sufficiently loyal and competent to keep them in order.

In Constantinople the emperor at first had his domestic of the Schools, Nicetas Triphyllius, to control the garrison. But Nicephorus's support in the army seems to have been somewhat shaky. At least some people thought that his relations with Nicetas were strained; when Nicetas died suddenly in April 803, there was a rumor that Nicephorus had poisoned him. The rumor is probably false, because Nicephorus was not an unduly suspicious or cautious ruler, and he remained on good terms with the dead man's brother Sisinnius. The emperor chose as the new domestic of the Schools Peter the Patrician, who had held the post under Irene before he had helped put Nicephorus on the throne. Peter proved unshakably loyal.[165]

Nicephorus also had to do something about the Frankish embassy that had come to negotiate Irene's marriage to Charlemagne. Though the situation was delicate, the Franks had to recognize that the proposed marriage was out of the question. The difficulty of sending ambassadors in winter gave Nicephorus time to consider how he should deal with Charlemagne's claim to the title of emperor. In the spring he sent the Frankish embassy back with an embassy of his own, led by a bishop named Michael, who was probably Michael of Synnada. Michael and his colleagues informed Charlemagne of the change in government, assured him of the new government's respect for him and desire for peace, and evidently maintained a diplomatic ambiguity about the question of Charlemagne's title.

The Frankish ruler was content to forget his project for a marriage with Irene and to consider himself at peace with Nicephorus, pending further negotiations. As a gesture of goodwill, he freely recognized the Byzantines' right to Venetia and Dalmatia, which he had conceded to Irene before his coronation as emperor, but of course he continued to insist that he was an emperor. Michael's embassy then returned by way of Rome to Constantinople with a letter from Charlemagne to Nicephorus. The only difficulty was that in replying Nicephorus either had to recognize Charlemagne as emperor, which he would not do, or face war with the Franks. Nicephorus wisely put off his reply, and enjoyed several years of peace while Charlemagne remained in suspense.[166]

As general logothete Nicephorus must have seen a good deal of financial mismanagement without being able to take strong measures against it. His first act after seizing power was to secure possession of the large imperial gold reserve held by Irene. Apparently dissatisfied with its size, he quickly took two measures to increase it. First, he decided not to pay the tribute to the Arabs that fell due in the spring of 803. Though he knew as well as anyone that the Arabs would open hostilities on the frontier when they realized that the money was not forthcoming, he evidently judged that stopping this exorbitant and humiliating payment was worth the probable consequences. Second, he canceled the remissions of urban trade duties and inheritance taxes that Irene had introduced in 801. This was a bold move that endangered the new emperor's popularity, but he seems to have found the exemptions too costly and arbitrary to continue. A man of his experience with state finance and with his provincial origins had good reason to know that the citizens of the capital were comparatively undertaxed.[167]

Nicephorus was also well aware of the problem of corruption. At the very outset of his rule, he created a new law court in the Magnaura palace, where he personally heard complaints by the poor against the rich. The court must have dealt with such matters as taxes that wealthy men avoided through influence and bribery, and so left to be paid by their poorer and weaker neighbors under the communal system of taxation. Nicephorus soon gained a reputation for love of the poor among his partisans, while his enemies decried his oppression of the wealthy. When his enemies denounced him for greed, they seem to have meant only that he collected government revenues diligently, because his own habits were notoriously abstemious, apart from a taste for hunting. He is said to have taken the ascetical George of Amastris as a spiritual director, and friendly sources report that in private, besides fasting and praying, Nicephorus wore shabby clothing and slept upon the ground. With a close relative named Symeon, perhaps a cousin, who was a monk, he enjoyed substantial respect in monastic circles. Despite his reputation for frugality, Nicephorus followed Irene's example of restoring churches around Constantinople.[168]

In the summer of 803 Nicephorus faced the first serious challenge of his reign. Predictably, the Arabs were preparing a raid in retaliation for his withholding their tribute. On May 4, Nicephorus had been thrown by his horse and broken his foot, so that he could not easily go on campaign until he recovered. The responsibility for opposing the Arab raid thus fell upon Bardanes Turcus, the military commander of virtually all of Asia Minor. In July, the Arabs advanced toward the frontier under al-Qāsim, a son of the caliph Hārūn, accompanied by the governor 'Abd al-Malik. When, in response, Bardanes seems to have summoned most of his troops to a staging area in the Anatolic theme, he found them in a rebellious mood. They resented Nicephorus's cancellation of Irene's tax exemptions, which included the exemption of soldiers from inheritance taxes. Since Bardanes had won a reputation for dividing spoils taken from the Arabs generously and fairly, they hoped for better treatment from him. On July 19 the assembled soldiers proclaimed Bardanes emperor. He tried to refuse, and when they finally forced him to accept he claimed to be acting only to defend the interests of Irene.[169]

From the start it was rather a hangdog rebellion. Bardanes never had much stomach for it, and he may really have tried to stay loyal to the emperor as Nicephorus had expected he would. According to a later story, before his proclamation Bardanes had heard a prophecy that his revolt would fail. The Armeniacs, who were under Bardanes' command but had apparently not arrived in the Anatolic theme by the time of the proclamation, remained faithful to Nicephorus. Nevertheless, the rebellion nominally involved nearly half the empire's army, and the soldiers and their candidate for the throne met no serious resistance as they marched on Constantinople.

They encamped just across the strait at the Asian suburb of Chrysopolis and waited eight days in the hope of provoking a rising against Nicephorus in the capital, but no rising came. As Nicephorus continued to collect supporters, news arrived that the empress Irene had died on Lesbos of disease on August 9, removing Bardanes' professed reason for the rebellion. Bardanes and his troops fell back on Malagina, the great supply depot in the Opsician theme, and some rebel leaders began to desert. Among those who joined Nicephorus were two bright young aides whom Bardanes had promoted, and apparently had married to two of his daughters. These were Leo the Armenian and Michael the Amorian—the future emperors Leo V and Michael II.

Not long afterward, Bardanes began to plot to desert his own rebellion. His mediator with Nicephorus was Joseph of Cathara, the priest who had been defrocked for performing the second marriage of Constantine VI. Apparently the unfortunate Joseph had retired to his old monastery of Cathara, not far from Malagina, where he was now available to act as a messenger between Bardanes and Nicephorus. With Joseph's help, Bardanes sent his request for terms to the emperor, who replied with a letter, countersigned by the patriarch Tarasius and several leading officials, pledging that Bardanes and his followers would not be harmed and promising to arrange his escape. After Joseph of Cathara had persuaded Bardanes to accept these minimal assurances, Bardanes slipped out of Malagina on September 8.

He quickly made his way to the Monastery of Heraclium in the nearby port of Cius on the Sea of Marmara. From there he was taken to a ship sent by the emperor and set sail for the nearby island of Prote, where he had previously founded a monastery. While still on board he took the tonsure and habit of a monk, thereby renouncing any eligibility for the throne; and when he arrived on Prote he entered his own monastery and embarked on a strictly ascetic life as the monk Sabas. The revolt thus collapsed, 50 days after it had begun. Nicephorus was enduringly grateful to Joseph for his part in negotiating Bardanes' submission.[170]

Though the emperor kept his pledge and did no bodily harm to the rebels, he enriched the treasury at their expense. He confiscated some of the property of Bardanes and of the officers who had backed the revolt to the end; but he left substantial wealth to Bardanes' wife, Domnica, of which she gave part to the poor and used part to endow her house as a nunnery for herself and her unmarried daughter and stepdaughters. Nicephorus also docked the four themes that had rebelled a year's pay. He further punished some civilians for collaboration, including three bishops who had sees within the area of the rebellion and apparently some monks, who were exiled to the desolate island of Pantellaria beyond Sicily. Some said that the emperor's real grudge against the bishops was that one of them, Euthymius of Sardis, had tonsured a beautiful girl of whom the emperor was enamored; but even if this is so, Euthymius may also have supported Bardanes as the champion of his patroness, Irene. The bishops' exile was in any case very brief. As a conciliatory gesture, Nicephorus allowed Irene's body to be brought back from Lesbos to her convent on Principo, where the nuns buried her in the convent church with every appropriate honor.

The emperor was generous to those who had deserted Bardanes' revolt before its end. He appointed Leo the Armenian and Michael the Amorian to the high posts of turmarch of the Federates and count of the tent in the Anatolic theme, besides awarding them houses in Constantinople, which like their commands had probably been taken from rebels. Nicephorus could hardly afford unnecessary recriminations with his Asian troops, because he had another war to deal with. The Arab raiding party under al-Qāsim, which had besieged two forts in Cappadocia during August and forced the liberation of the Arab prisoners in the area, had proved to be only the first of two. The second was a much larger force under the caliph Hārūn himself. Nicephorus pulled his army together and marched out against the invaders.[171]

For two months the opposing armies stayed well apart from each other in central Asia Minor. The campaign never came to a battle. During this time Hārūn and Nicephorus negotiated by means of letters, of which the Arab and Byzantine sources give accounts that differ in emphasis without being incompatible. According to the Arabs, Nicephorus had earlier written a peremptory letter to Hārūn demanding the return of the tribute paid by Irene, whereupon Hārūn wrote back calling Nicephorus a dog and announcing his invasion; this the Byzantines say nothing about. According to the Byzantines, after Hārūn invaded Nicephorus sent him a conciliatory letter, arguing that his invasion was unjustified, that Mohammed had counseled Muslims to treat Christians as friends, and that though the Arabs already had all the wealth they needed they would be given more if they wished; when Hārūn received this letter and the gifts accompanying it, he agreed to make a truce, gave presents of his own to Nicephorus, and returned marveling at the emperor's wisdom. The Arab sources confirm that Nicephorus proposed a truce in return for tribute, and that Hārūn consented. The tribute that Nicephorus negotiated, which seems to have been fairly moderate, averted a danger that circumstances had left him ill prepared to meet. Since the truce evidently applied only to the rest of 803, the emperor had not committed himself to pay further tribute after he had been able to prepare himself for a fight.[172]

When Nicephorus returned to Constantinople he moved promptly to

24. A nomisma of Nicephorus I and his son Stauracius, shown three times actual size. Since Stauracius appears beardless on all his father's coins, he was probably still in his teens at the end of Nicephorus's reign in 811. (Photos: Dumbarton Oaks Byzantine Collection, Washington)

settle the question of the succession, and celebrated Christmas of 803 by crowning his adolescent son Stauracius in St. Sophia. He then added Stauracius's portrait to his own on imperial coins. Since Stauracius was only about thirteen years old, he naturally had no share in governing as yet. Nicephorus's enemies jeered that Stauracius was sickly, but any ailments he may have had when he was crowned did not prevent him from taking an active part in his father's military expeditions a few years later. He appears to have been consistently obedient to his strong-willed father, a quality that opponents of the government tried to depict as a vice.[173]

All those who had a better claim to rule than Nicephorus and Stauracius were now dead or mutilated. Though Irene's supposed champion, Bardanes Turcus, still lived, she had died and he was settled peacefully in his monastery after a conspicuously unsuccessful rebellion. Nevertheless, in 804 a band of Nicephorus's partisans from Lycaonia in the Anatolic theme broke into Bardanes' island monastery and blinded him. Nicephorus swore to his court that he had had nothing to do with the blinding, made an unsuccessful effort to apprehend and punish the Lycaonians, and remained secluded in the palace for a week as a sign of his grief.

Inevitably rumors circulated that the Lycaonians had acted on the emperor's orders, and that his grieving was a sham to deceive Bardanes' many prominent friends and others who remembered Nicephorus's oath not to harm Bardanes. Others accepted Nicephorus's protestations and believed that he never executed or mutilated a Christian at any time during his reign. Bardanes posed so little threat unblinded, and his blinding was so sure to raise ugly suspicions about the emperor, that Nicephorus may well have been innocent, and the Lycaonians may have acted on their own in what they thought was his interest. Since before the revolt he had strongly favored Bardanes, who had been proclaimed unwillingly and ended his rebellion readily, Nicephorus may even have been sincerely sorry to hear of the attack.[174]

Not long afterward, in August 804, Hārūn sent out a new raid in force through the Cilician Gates into the Anatolic theme. Nicephorus marched out against the Arabs. Before he met them, however, he turned back because of a report that reached him from Constantinople, presumably of a conspiracy. While he was returning to the capital, the Arabs made a surprise attack upon his force at Crasus, near the junction of the Anatolic, Opsician, and Bucellarian themes. Nicephorus himself was almost captured; the Arabs thought that they had wounded him, and that he was rescued only by the heroic efforts of some of his officers. He lost a number of men, and the Arabs claimed to have captured 4,000 of his pack animals. But the raiders did not follow up their advantage, and the defeat, while inglorious for Nicephorus, does not appear to have done much real harm to the Byzantines. The raiders withdrew, whatever disaffection Nicephorus had heard of came to nothing, and soon the emperor found himself more securely established than ever.[175]

NICEPHORUS'S FIRST EXPANSION

Luckily for Nicephorus, the caliph Hārūn was not able to give his full attention to fighting the Byzantines, much as he might have liked to do so. Always forced to struggle to keep control of his central government, in 803 he had conducted an extensive purge, massacring the members of the Barmacid family and imprisoning his able governor of the frontier, ʿAbd al-Malik. Hārūn also had great difficulty administering his outlying provinces. He was receiving a stream of complaints about the governor in his principal recruiting area of Khurāsān in northeastern Iran. In 805 he decided to go to Khurāsān himself.

The caliph therefore arranged a truce with Nicephorus, including an exchange of prisoners at the Lamis River, the Arab-Byzantine border in Cilicia. In return for all the 3,700 or so Arab captives in Byzantine prisons, Nicephorus received a great many, if not all, of the Byzantines taken prisoner in the defeats of the two previous years. Hārūn departed for Khurāsān in April, leaving his young son al-Qāsim in northern Syria to keep an eye on the frontier. Now that Nicephorus could look forward to a year without serious Arab raids, he seized the opportunity eagerly. He moved first not against the Arabs but against the Slavs.[176]

The Byzantine government had left the Slavs of the Greek peninsula relatively undisturbed since the military revolt of 790 had interrupted Irene's and Stauracius's slow annexations at their expense. These annexations had obviously annoyed the neighboring Bulgars, who had shown their displeasure by killing the strategus of Thrace in 788 and had gone on to battle Constantine VI. Further attempts at annexation in the north of Greece were likely to provoke the Bulgars again. But Slavs also held large parts of Greece farther south, in Thessaly, Epirus, and the Peloponnesus, outside the Bulgars' main sphere of interest. Stauracius had raided the Slav-held parts of Thessaly and the Peloponnesus in 783 without meeting serious resistance from either Bulgars or Slavs, taking substantial tribute and plunder. He had not, however, tried to annex the Peloponnesus, though it was weakly held, agriculturally valuable, and, as a virtual island, easily defensible once taken. Nicephorus made the attempt in 805, as soon as he had a respite from civil unrest and Arab raids.

The emperor entrusted the expedition to his strategus of Hellas, who was named Sclerus and came from the frontier area of the Armeniac theme. As strategus of Hellas, Sclerus already had charge of central Greece and the eastern coast of the Peloponnesus. In fact, the headquarters of the theme of Hellas had evidently been for many years in the Peloponnesus at Corinth, which remained the chief Byzantine stronghold against the Peloponnesian Slavs. Sclerus's expedition was not a particularly ostentatious operation; the 2,000-man army of the theme of Hellas probably did most of the work. Nonetheless, the campaign was a great success. Whatever resistance the Slavs put up was crushed. Before the end of the year, Sclerus was able to send word to Nicephorus that all the Slavs had submitted and the entire Peloponnesus was under Byzantine control—for the first time in 218 years, as contemporaries computed it.[177]

Nicephorus was naturally delighted at the news, but he realized that the reconquest was the easier part of the task. The Slavs were ready enough to give in when they faced a serious fight; they had submitted to Sclerus as they had submitted to Stauracius 22 years before. The problem was to keep them from rebelling afterward when they saw no obvious Byzantine military presence. The armies of the Byzantine themes were ill suited to serve as garrison forces, because during most of the year most soldiers lived as civilians on their own holdings. Therefore, though the army of Hellas might, with difficulty, have been able to put down a general Slavic uprising, it was not an effective deterrent to one.

Nicephorus's solution was to settle the Peloponnesus with Byzantines, who would eventually absorb the Slavs. Since most Slavs appear to have been pastoral nomads, the Peloponnesus would have been lightly populated; since much of the peninsula was fertile, if it were brought under cultivation it could accommodate a substantially larger population. Nicephorus therefore embarked on a program of rebuilding the cities of the Peloponnesus and settling them with subjects from other parts of the empire, at the same time attempting to convert the Slavs of the region to Christianity and so to make loyal subjects of them.

At first, Nicephorus brought in voluntary homesteaders, who were no doubt attracted by an open offer of free land and of financial help in bringing it under cultivation. Such an offer by itself had a limited appeal, however, because, even if the danger of Slavic revolt was not widely recognized, land was not particularly scarce in the empire and the Byzantines were a conservative people who were usually reluctant to leave their ancestral homes. Luckily for the program of resettlement, a persistent tradition had it that a number of the Greeks of the eastern Peloponnesus, Calabria, and Sicily were descendants of the original Greek inhabitants of the western Peloponnesus, who had fled the Slavs and Avars in the late sixth and early seventh centuries. In particular, a number of the people of the Calabrian port of Rhegium believed that they were descended from the former inhabitants of the port of Patras on the northern coast of the Peloponnesus, and the people of Monemvasia, a stronghold in the coastal strip of the Peloponnesus that the Byzantines had never lost, believed themselves the descendants of the displaced citizens of Sparta. Allowing for some oversimplification in the retelling over two centuries, such traditions probably had a basis in fact. At any rate, they had a sufficiently powerful influence to make many willing to leave their present homes to reclaim the supposed homeland of their ancestors.

Learning of the community at Rhegium who traced their descent from the citizens of Patras, Nicephorus gave specific orders that they should be transported to the site of their ancestral city. They were led by a priest of theirs named Athanasius, whom Nicephorus named archbishop of Patras toward the end of 805. With the government's help the city was fortified and churches were built or rebuilt in it. Some other Greek settlements were established this early, but Patras was evidently much the largest, the chief Byzantine base in a land still predominantly Slavic. For the present, the reconquered part of the Peloponnesus was apparently attached to the theme of Hellas.[178]

The reconquest of the Peloponnesus was an eminently sensible move, with few costs and great advantages. If ultimately successful, it was sure to increase government revenue as the new population expanded agriculture and trade and paid taxes on them. The annexation shortened the frontier, since it neatly eliminated the border of the theme of Hellas in the Peloponnesus. By providing new anchorages it improved communications with the Byzantine possessions to the west. And yet, for two centuries no Byzantine ruler had attempted to take this highly practicable measure. Since Justinian I, Byzantine emperors had been preoccupied with the East. Whenever they had a breathing space, they had used it to build up their defenses or to deal preemptive strikes against dangerous enemies like the Bulgars or Arabs; such victories increased Byzantine security and glory, traditionally considered the worthiest objectives for an emperor to seek. Since the Slavs were not dangerous, their defeat made little contribution to the empire's defense or prestige. Only one Byzantine source, evidently Peloponnesian in origin, even mentions the campaign that retook the Peloponnesus in 805. The society of the capital hardly noticed the event. But that Nicephorus saw its importance is clear from the promptness with which he began the conquest and the zeal with which he was to follow it up not long afterward.

Nevertheless, Nicephorus was not indifferent to the East, and was far from disdaining opportunities for building up defenses, making preemptive strikes, and winning military laurels. After the exchange of prisoners with the Arabs, Nicephorus made good use of the campaigning season of 805 in the East while Hārūn was away in Khurāsān. He began with a vigorous campaign of rebuilding and strengthening fortresses. Probably in the early spring, Byzantine troops were put to work on the walls of the city of Ancyra in the Bucellarian theme and of the forts of Andrasus and Thebasa in the Anatolic theme. The two forts were near the frontier with Arab Cilicia, the Arabs' usual starting point for raids of Byzantine territory, and Thebasa had lain in ruins since its capture by the Arabs in 793. The Byzantines had made no serious incursions into Arab territory since their capture of Adata in 786, which may well have been an initiative of Nicephorus himself when he was strategus of the Armeniacs. Now, after an interruption of twenty years, Nicephorus was ready to show the Arabs that raiders could cross the frontier from both sides.[179]

Probably late in the summer of 805, Nicephorus sent a good-sized raiding party from the Anatolic theme into Cilicia. The expedition ravaged the countryside and challenged the main strong points, taking prisoners as it went. The Byzantines pillaged the district around the fortress of Anazarbus. They then raided the area around Cilicia's principal fortified town, Mopsuestia, though the garrison of Mopsuestia was able to recover the prisoners taken in its district. The greatest Byzantine success was at Tarsus, which the Arabs had rebuilt and garrisoned only in 786. The Byzantines took the new city and captured its entire garrison before they withdrew. Probably at the same time as this raid, another Byzantine expedition left the Armeniac theme and reached the Arab stronghold of Melitene, which it besieged but did not take. Finally, no doubt at the instigation of Nicephorus, the Christian population of Cyprus rebelled against the Arabs, who governed them jointly with the Byzantines under a long-standing arrangement. As far as we know, Hārūn's son Qāsim took no measures to oppose these attacks.[180]

Although these campaigns of 805 must have been a source of satisfaction to the Byzantines after all the years that they had been passive in the face of Arab raids, Nicephorus's motives in launching them are not fully clear. The expedition to Melitene apparently made an attempt to take the city and perhaps to hold it along with the area between the Taurus and the Antitaurus, in which it was the only major Arab stronghold. While the raiders abandoned Tarsus after they captured it, the next year Hārūn received a report that the Byzantines were thinking of sending a force to fortify and garrison the city. Permanently reoccupying Tarsus would have meant advancing the frontier at least from the Lamis to the Cyanus River, thus annexing the rocky western third of Cilicia with the approaches to the Cilician Gates. The rebellion on Cyprus makes sense only as an attempt to reassert full Byzantine control over the island, which at first seems to have succeeded.[181]

Nicephorus may therefore have been trying to annex a considerable piece of the border region, of which most was a no-man's-land and the rest contained only a few Arab outposts. The territory involved was only a little less defensible than the territories the Byzantines held already; they had long maintained their stake in Cyprus, and they had usually been able to keep possession of the areas of Tarsus and Melitene in the years before the great Arab invasion of 717. Garrisoning Tarsus and Melitene would have partly blocked the main Arab invasion routes across the Taurus into the Byzantine heartland, to the Byzantines' great benefit.[182]

On the other hand, Nicephorus's efforts in 805 were sure to provoke Hārūn, and Hārūn obviously had the resources both to frustrate and to punish them. Nicephorus can scarcely have expected to succeed in advancing the frontier significantly unless Hārūn's problems in Khurāsān and elsewhere within the caliphate monopolized the caliph's attention for years. Though this may have seemed possible, Nicephorus could hardly have believed it was certain. So most probably by his maneuvers Nicephorus was first of all showing the standard, in order to encourage the Byzantines and to dishearten the Arabs, and secondly testing Arab strength, preparing himself to seize any territory that the Arabs proved unable to defend. Rather than a definite attempt at expansion, the campaigns of 805 look like an experiment that the Emperor judged to be worth the risk. If the Arabs attacked in return, that was after all nothing new, and might happen even if the Byzantines kept quiet.

By making any attempts at all to expand his frontiers, Nicephorus was doing something that even aggressive Byzantine rulers had seldom done

25. Patriarch Tarasius and his monastery. Vaticanus graecus 1613, p. 423. Painter: Michael of Blachernae. (Photo: Biblioteca Apostolica Vaticana, Vatican City)

before him. For over two centuries the rule had been that emperors tried to retake only lands that had been lost recently and thus, the Byzantines hoped, temporarily. Irene, by her fairly peaceful, gradual, and modest expansion in Thrace, had broken this old precedent in a small way. Nicephorus's actions in the Peloponnesus and on the eastern frontier began to make Irene's annexations look like a trend. He turned out to have still more ambitious plans in the future.

THE EXPANSION INTERRUPTED

On February 18, 806, the elderly patriarch Tarasius died after a lingering and painful illness. He had adapted himself competently to the changing requirements of Irene, Constantine VI, and Nicephorus, had skillfully brought back and maintained the veneration of icons, and had generally shown a combination of intelligence and pragmatism that gained him Nicephorus's approval. Though Tarasius had been elected patriarch as a lay official he had won the respect of the secular and monastic clergy. Amid general mourning, the emperor reportedly threw himself upon the corpse in his grief, calling Tarasius his adviser and praising his services to the Church and the state. The late patriarch was buried in the monastery that he had founded, which was subsequently known as the Monastery of St. Tarasius. His patriarchate had been a great success. To find a successor as satisfactory to both the emperor and the various clergy and civil servants was probably impossible, if only because no successor could claim the same credit for restoring the icons.[183]

The most distinguished ecclesiastics of the time appear to have been abbots and monks, among whom the outstanding leader was Theodore, abbot of Studius. Theodore was by now not only the head of a large and thriving monastery in Constantinople with four other major monasteries dependent upon it, but a reformer of commanding authority who had introduced a rigorous regime of communal asceticism, hard work, and Christian learning into Byzantine monastic life. On the other hand, Theodore's zeal to maintain strict standards cannot have been universally popular among the clergy, and his unwillingness to compromise for political reasons, evident in the schism that he and his uncle Plato had provoked over the second marriage of Constantine VI, was not what Nicephorus wanted in a patriarch. Yet no other candidate was clearly preeminent.

Having no candidate who was both obvious and suitable, Nicephorus declared that he would hold a free election to the patriarchate. He spent the early weeks of Lent consulting as electors a number of priests, monks, and civil officials, among them Theodore and Plato. To vote for oneself would have been in poor taste. In his highly respectful letter of reply, Theodore professed himself unable to name a candidate who was truly suitable, but he urged Nicephorus to choose the wisest and worthiest man he could find among the bishops, abbots, stylites, and hermits, and certainly no one who was not ordained or tonsured. Since Symeon of Mytilene is the only holy man known to have been living on a pillar at the time, Theodore may have been thinking of him when he said that stylites should descend from their pillars if the common good demanded it. Nonetheless, Theodore avoided excluding himself when it would have been easy to do so. Theodore's uncle Plato did vote for a candidate, and Theodore's later reticence about revealing who it was makes no apparent sense unless it was Theodore. Though some clergy voted with Plato, the rest distributed their votes among a wide variety of candidates, so that the emperor was in effect free to select whomever he wished. The confusion of the electors shows pretty plainly that Nicephorus had not yet expressed a specific preference. He may well have anticipated the deadlock.[184]

Then, despite Theodore's counsel to choose a cleric, the emperor chose a layman, a relatively obscure former civil servant also named Nicephorus. This Nicephorus's official career had begun promisingly under Iconoclasm, although his father had been persecuted as an iconophile under

Constantine V, and before 780 he was already an imperial secretary serving under the protoasecretis Tarasius. Still as a secretary, Nicephorus had been sent by Irene to the Council of Nicaea in 787, where he read aloud the translation of Pope Hadrian's letter. At some time after the council, having risen no higher in the civil hierarchy, the young secretary had gone into prolonged seclusion in a hermitage. Since he did not become a monk, he seems not to have undergone a true conversion, but rather to have made a false step during the maneuvering between Constantine and Irene. The emperor Nicephorus had brought him back into public life only after 803, giving him the not very exalted post of head of the empire's main poorhouse, just outside Constantinople.

The future patriarch's only really extraordinary achievement before 806 was his writing a short history of the seventh and eighth centuries in classicizing Greek. As far as we know, this was the first work in something like Attic Greek, and the first history of comparable scope, that had been written at Byzantium for some 150 years. Otherwise it is not particularly remarkable, as its narrative is bald and dry, its sentiments are conventionally iconophile, and it carefully avoids contemporary controversy by stopping short in 769, just when Irene appeared on the scene. Nevertheless, the book was quite possibly its author's best recommendation for the position of patriarch. It showed Nicephorus to be a man of obvious learning, correct religious views, political discretion, and versatile, if not necessarily brilliant, talent. Apparently these were the qualities that the emperor Nicephorus had liked in Tarasius and sought in Tarasius's successor.[185]

When the choice had been made but before it was officially announced, Plato of Saccudium tried to make the emperor reconsider. In a nocturnal visit to Symeon the Monk, the emperor's relative, Plato seems to have warned that he and Theodore might feel compelled to organize a schism if a layman were selected. The emperor took this warning seriously enough to sequester both Plato and Theodore under arrest until the new patriarch could be safely installed. Leaving little time for the candidate to make the appropriate protestations of his unworthiness, the emperor had him brought by messengers from his poorhouse, which was located across the Golden Horn to the north of the capital, and ordered him to turn monk and cleric as quickly as possible. He was therefore tonsured on Palm Sunday with the sponsorship of the junior emperor, Stauracius. On Holy Thursday the new monk was ordained a deacon, and on Good Friday the new deacon was ordained a priest. On Easter Sunday, April 12, after the liturgy at St. Sophia, he was consecrated patriarch to the unanimous acclaim of the clergy and people present, since Theodore and Plato were not there to dissent or to organize opposition. Then, after an imprisonment of 24 days, the two Studites were released, found that the new patriarch was in office and unlikely to be dislodged, and decided to accept their defeat.[186]

As it happened, the emperor Nicephorus brought forward another measure certain to displease the Studites shortly after the patriarch Nicephorus took office. Joseph of Cathara, the priest whom Tarasius had agreed to defrock in 797 for performing the adulterous marriage of Constantine VI, had done the emperor Nicephorus a valuable service by arranging the surrender of the rebel Bardanes Turcus in 803. Nicephorus had no reason to object to Joseph's previous obedience to Constantine VI, and he was not inclined to let himself be governed by the views of the insubordinate Plato and Theodore. While the patriarch Tarasius lived, to ask him to restore Joseph of Cathara, whom he had already condoned under pressure from Constantine and then condemned under pressure from Irene, would have been too great a humiliation. But the new patriarch, Nicephorus, had never had to take a position on Joseph's case before, and he owed the emperor everything. The emperor accordingly asked him to reopen Joseph's case, recommending restoration to the priesthood in consideration of the unfortunate man's services to the state. To settle the matter the patriarch held a local synod at Constantinople. He invited fourteen other bishops and, by a stroke of someone's genius, Theodore of Studius himself, who because he was not a bishop could not vote. When the bishops voted to readmit Joseph to the priesthood, Theodore kept silent, finding no one else in a mood to support dissent. Joseph took up his old position of steward of St. Sophia under the patriarch Nicephorus.[187]

Theodore and Plato salved their consciences by resolving to avoid communion with the patriarch Nicephorus and others who celebrated the eucharist with Joseph. They relied on their isolation in their monastery and on determined prevarication to avoid the few ceremonial celebrations that they were supposed to attend. By showing himself as determined as the Studites, the emperor had thus overruled them twice without provoking a significant protest, at least for the time being. The emperor of course knew that the Studites were displeased, even if he may not have been sure that they were deliberately avoiding communion with him, and without broaching that issue he sought to conciliate them. Later in 806 he invited Theodore to take part in the election of the abbot of the Monastery of Dalmatus, and probably in the same year he chose Theodore's brother Joseph to be archbishop of Thessalonica, the empire's second city. Theodore attended the election and voted for the winning candidate, Hilarion, while Joseph talked himself into accepting the archbishopric.[188]

At about the time of the patriarch Nicephorus's election, news would have reached Constantinople that the administrators of the Byzantine possessions in the northern Adriatic had submitted to Charlemagne. In Venetia, which had suffered from factional struggles for some time, the two brothers Obelerius and Beatus had established themselves as dukes in 804 and turned to the Franks to secure their power. First they sent a naval expedition to force the leaders of Byzantine Dalmatia to cooperate with them. Then, at the beginning of 806, they arrived at the Frankish court at Thionville with Paul, the duke of Jadera in Dalmatia, and made their submission to Charlemagne. Since Charlemagne felt no obligation to Nicephorus, who still had not answered his letter of 803, he accepted their gifts and their homage, and on February 6 assigned Venetia and Dalmatia to his eldest son, Pepin, as part of his new subkingdom of Italy. Though the Byzantines had had only a very loose jurisdiction over these two fragmentary provinces, and the Franks had acquired no more control, Nicephorus was unwilling to overlook what was technically a rebellion against him. He promptly prepared a naval expedition under Nicetas the Patrician, probably the same man who had served as a strategus of Sicily under Irene. By autumn Nicetas's fleet was reclaiming the Dalmatian ports.[189]

This primarily diplomatic problem was nothing in comparison with the threat from the Arabs. Hārūn had returned from Khurāsān with dismaying swiftness in November 805 to put a stop to Nicephorus's attempts at expansion in the east. In a burst of fury at the emperor's temerity, he decided to direct a summer raid in person, and brought together the largest Abbasid army ever recorded, 135,000 men. This elephantine agglomeration was more than half again as large as the entire strength of the Byzantine themes and tagmata. It must have taken months to assemble, and the Byzantines must have known of its preparations well in advance. It lumbered out of Hārūn's habitual residence of Raqqa on the Euphrates on June 11, 806, under the leadership of the vengeful caliph, who wore a pointed cap with the words "Raider and Pilgrim" written across it. Hārūn also ordered the rebuilding of Tarsus and sent a naval expedition to Cyprus under his admiral Ḥumayd.

If Hārūn had used this mighty force to ravage the Byzantine heartland, he could probably have inflicted damage from which the Byzantines would have taken several years to recover. One of his lieutenants reportedly advised an assault on a major city, but Hārūn took other advice. He intended only to show off his army and to devastate the border area badly enough to put an end to Nicephorus's hopes of refortifying and extending the Byzantine frontier. He therefore concentrated his attacks on Cappadocia, Nicephorus's native land.

After the caliph had passed through the Cilician Gates, he paused at the

crossroads town of Tyana, which seems to have been deserted and un-
defended. There he divided his troops, as he plainly needed to do to allow
them to find supplies. He sent one contingent of some 70,000 under subordinate commanders north into central Cappadocia. This contingent itself divided into detachments that captured Andrasus, just rebuilt by Nicephorus, and two other forts; it then besieged the fortified town of
Cyzistra, and raided as far as the recently refortified city of Ancyra, without attempting to take it. Leaving a much smaller contingent at Tyana to
build a base of operations, including a mosque, Hārūn turned west with
the less than half of his army that remained. The caliph besieged the fortified town of Heraclea, of whose importance he appears to have had an
exaggerated idea, and had a lieutenant take the nearby fort of Thebasa,
also recently rebuilt by Nicephorus. The siege of Heraclea itself lasted a
month, but toward the end of the summer Hārūn captured it. His men
seized such plunder as the town offered, mostly its grain stores, destroyed
the rest, and took all the inhabitants and defenders captive. Meanwhile,
on Cyprus, Ḥumayd wreaked general havoc, and carried 16,000 prisoners
and great booty back to Raqqa.

Though Nicephorus kept his nerve, he could scarcely ignore the tens
of thousands of Arabs who were swarming over the eastern Anatolic
theme and, to judge from their building at Tyana, threatening to winter
there. He led an expedition into Asia Minor himself and apparently defeated some isolated raiders, setting up victory trophies to soothe the injury that Byzantine military pride had sustained. But he wisely stayed out
of the way of the main Arab forces that were so much more numerous
than his own. Instead he sent an embassy of three ecclesiastics, led by Michael of Synnada—probably the same man who had already served ably
as an ambassador to Charlemagne—to negotiate a peace with the caliph.

After prolonged bargaining, they agreed on terms. Nicephorus was to
pay immediately, and afterwards annually, a tribute of 30,006 nomismata,
of which 3 nomismata were a head tax for himself and 3 for his son Stauracius. As the last stipulation shows, this tribute was mostly a symbolic
humiliation; Irene had paid more than four and a half times as much under
the terms of the treaty of 782. Nicephorus also pledged not to rebuild
Heraclea or any of the various forts that the Arabs had destroyed. The
condominium on Cyprus between the Arabs and Byzantines was presumably restored. In return, Hārūn agreed to raise the siege of Cyzistra,
to spare two other places that the Arabs were evidently threatening, and
to evacuate Byzantine territory, including Tyana.

When he dispatched the first tribute payment, Nicephorus asked as a
favor that Hārūn send to him a girl captured at Heraclea who was a candidate for the hand of the junior emperor, Stauracius, along with a tent

and some perfume, presumably for her. Under such circumstances, asking favors seemed a sign of friendship. Hārūn became positively jovial and sent not only the girl, a magnificently equipped tent, and the perfume, but a supply of dates, figs, and raisins, throwing in an antidote for snakebite. Encouraging the caliph's benevolent mood, the emperor sent back a horse laden with 50,000 miliaresia (about 4,200 nomismata), along with 100 brocaded robes, 100 silk robes, twelve falcons, four hunting dogs, and three more horses. But as soon as Hārūn had left Byzantine territory Nicephorus began rebuilding the forts in violation of the treaty, and he never paid the tribute again. For all its size and bluster, Hārūn's raid had done the Byzantines remarkably little harm, and its haul of plunder and tribute was relatively meager.[190]

Nevertheless, the raid accomplished what must have been the caliph's primary purpose: it proved to Nicephorus that the Arabs still had overwhelming military superiority over the Byzantines, and discouraged him from any further efforts at expansion in the east. Obviously Hārūn had seen Nicephorus's operations in 805 as serious threats, and to that extent reports in Syriac and Byzantine sources that Nicephorus impressed the Arabs with his military ability are true. Indeed, they are corroborated by the great pride the Arabic historians take in celebrating Hārūn's limited successes against the emperor. Still, after 806 Nicephorus understood that, whatever internal dissensions plagued the caliphate, they were not crippling enough to allow him to annex Arab territory with impunity. During the rest of his reign he directed his ambitions for conquest toward the Balkans, and took only the usual defensive measures on the frontier in Asia Minor.

NICEPHORUS'S SECOND EXPANSION

In 807 Nicephorus began to follow up his easy success in the Peloponnesus with an attempted annexation and settlement of lands farther north in the Balkan peninsula. Though the Bulgars would be annoyed, they were not comparable in power to the Arabs, and Nicephorus was quite willing to fight them. Besides, for the present the Bulgars were busy with wars to the north, where the dismemberment of the Avar khanate by Charlemagne had provided them with easy marks for conquest. While in the long run Nicephorus may have thought of driving the Bulgars out of the Balkans entirely and restoring the Danube frontier as it had been in the sixth century, for now he seems merely to have wanted the Bulgars cowed so that he could get on with the work of retaking the land to their south that was held by Slavs. He accordingly prepared to lead an expedition against them in the spring of 807, without any provocation that has been recorded. It was to be the beginning of a great project that he would continue for the rest of his reign.

In the meantime, Nicephorus's admiral Nicetas the Patrician had restored and even strengthened the Byzantine position in Dalmatia and Venetia. When the Venetian dukes Obelerius and Beatus had realized that a Byzantine fleet was actually on its way in the fall of 806, they had abandoned their allegiance to the Franks and rediscovered their loyalty to Byzantium. In order to gain what favor they could, they quickly sent a flotilla to help Nicetas recover the Dalmatian coastland that they had themselves detached from the empire the year before. When Nicetas arrived in Venetia toward December, they found him respectful but not unduly trustful. He stayed through the winter to blockade the opposite coast, which the Franks still held, and he inconvenienced Charlemagne's son King Pepin enough to make him agree to a truce lasting until August 807. Before leaving, Nicetas granted Duke Obelerius the court rank of spatharius; but he then took Obelerius's brother, Duke Beatus, and some other Venetians back to Constantinople with him as hostages. Nicephorus soon sent Beatus back with the next-highest rank, consul, and for the present the dukes stayed loyal.[191]

The emperor embarked upon his first expedition against the Bulgars with a force of some size in the spring of 807, but he never reached Bulgaria. When he came to Adrianople, the headquarters of the theme of Macedonia, Nicephorus learned of a conspiracy against him among his bodyguard and the tagmata, who naturally were taking part in the campaign. The conspirators, apparently junior offices, came from Nicephorus's home territory of Cappadocia. Nicephorus had no trouble in foiling their plans, and punished them by whipping, confiscation, and exile. Possibly the conspirators were bitter about the devastation of their homelands in Cappadocia the previous year, and certainly the Arab successes and Nicephorus's humiliating peace had made the emperor look more vulnerable. Though after discovering the conspiracy Nicephorus returned to Constantinople, he apparently left some troops in the area under the strategus of Macedonia. These and the army of the theme of Macedonia, without attacking the Bulgars directly, soon advanced into Slavic territory to the west.[192]

When Hārūn discovered that Nicephorus had broken the treaty by rebuilding the border forts and withholding the tribute, he sent out a spring raid. It was, however, of moderate size, numbering just 10,000 men under Yazīd, a subordinate commander who had taken two forts in the previous year's campaign. This time the Byzantine forces were prepared, and when Yazīd advanced from the recently ruined town of Tarsus to the Cilician Gates he found the Anatolics holding the pass against him. In the ensuing battle the Byzantines defeated the Arabs with heavy losses. Yazīd himself was among the dead.

The news provoked Hārūn to prepare a summer raid to avenge Yazīd. Though the caliph originally intended to lead the raid himself, he changed his mind when he reached the fortified city of Adata, perhaps because of unrest among the local Christians. Once again he divided his forces. He sent one contingent under Yazīd's son to refortify and repopulate Tarsus and so to make sure that the Byzantines would not occupy and fortify it themselves. He stationed another contingent at Adata and a third at Germanicea, apparently to defend them against possible Byzantine attacks. The rest of the army, 30,000 men, set out to make the actual raid under Hārūn's lieutenant Harthama. By this time, however, Nicephorus had arrived in the east with an army to intercept the raiders. Harthama advanced across the mountainous no-man's-land between the Taurus and the Antitaurus, where Nicephorus came to meet him and fought an indecisive battle at an uncertain location. The emperor retreated. Though Harthama claimed victory, he too retreated at once, without gaining any booty. In fact, his men ran so short of provisions that the caliph had to send a relief party to save some of them from starvation.

After returning to Raqqa in July with no further success, Hārūn sent out another expedition by sea under his admiral Ḥumayd. This expedition seems first to have landed in the Peloponnesus and fomented a revolt among the recently subdued Slavs, who ravaged the Greek settlers' lands and besieged their newly refounded city of Patras. In September Ḥumayd attacked the island of Rhodes and took some plunder, but failed to capture the fortified town. Finally, Ḥumayd raided Myra on the south coast of Asia Minor, where he supposedly tried to destroy the wonder-working tomb of its patron, St. Nicholas. While he was there, however, a violent storm arose, which the Byzantines attributed to St. Nicholas's influence. A number of the Arab ships were sunk, and Ḥumayd was forced to withdraw with the rest. Apparently at the same time, the Slavic rebellion in the Peloponnesus was put down by the settlers and the local strategus, who gave credit for their victory to the Apostle Andrew, patron of Patras. With the help of their saints, the Byzantines had ridden out the year's Arab raids without a serious defeat, in sharp contrast to the preceding year. Better than this, Nicephorus had succeeded in rebuilding his forts and repudiating his pledge to pay tribute.[193]

Despite the attention that Nicephorus obviously had to pay to his eastern frontier in 807, he continued his projects for expansion in the West. As with previous advances in the Balkans under both Irene and Nicephorus, this one stirred little interest among the authors of our sources, and its details are accordingly obscure. By early 809, however, it is certain that Byzantine armies were well established in northwestern Thrace. By then they had established a large fortified base at Serdica (Sofia), some 80 miles from Philippopolis, which seems to have been as far as Irene's reconquest had extended. Serdica continued still deeper inland the series of strongholds along the border with the Bulgars that Irene and Constantine VI had built. Now there were five of them—Serdica, Philippopolis, Beroea-Irenopolis, Marcellae, and Anchialus—effectively confining the Bulgars to the north of the Balkan Mountains.

South of Serdica, by 809 the Byzantines evidently held the whole length of the Strymon River, on which they had earlier kept no more than a tenuous presence. At the same time, throughout northern and central Greece the Byzantines appear to have ventured out of their scattered coastal holdings to occupy almost the whole Greek peninsula. Together with Nicephorus's reconquests in the Peloponnesus, these acquisitions nearly doubled Byzantine holdings in the Balkan peninsula. For the time being, the new territories seem to have been added to the existing themes of Macedonia and Hellas, but those themes' armies had been heavily reinforced with troops from other themes or recruits from among the new settlers. By early 809, there were about 12,000 troops in the theme of Macedonia, whose army had totaled just 3,000 before 807.[194]

Once a good-sized army had been assembled, the lands of the weak and disunited Slavs of the Balkans cannot have been difficult to take. As in the Peloponnesian territory that Nicephorus had annexed, the principal problem was to find enough Byzantines to settle the area. Already in the summer of 807, when part of western Thrace had evidently been cleared, Nicephorus was trying one expedient. He gave an extraordinary commission to a certain Bardanius Anemas to round up whatever transients and aliens he could find in the empire. Presumably Bardanius and his men looked for people who were not registered on the tax rolls in their locality. Those taken into custody were transported as colonists to the newly annexed lands in the theme of Macedonia. Serdica in particular gained a civilian population.

Nicephorus was said to be interested in the additional sums that these settlers would pay in taxes, and no doubt he was, since transients and aliens paid no land tax. As soon as they were assigned land, they were added to the tax rolls, though probably with an initial grant of money and a temporary tax exemption to give them a chance to make their farms productive. No doubt the new settlers were a motley crew, including the destitute, vagabonds, and not a few criminals, many of whom came unwillingly to an unfamiliar and dangerous country. But Australia began with no better. Some of the colonists must have been willing enough to make a fresh start on farms of ample size and fertility, largely protected from the Slavs and Bulgars by nearby troops.[195]

This rounding up and settling down of people who were not on the tax rolls is likely to have preceded the new census that Nicephorus began at about this time. September 1, 807, was the beginning of a first year of the indiction, which started a new fifteen-year tax assessment cycle. The last known census, perhaps a partial one, had been ordered 75 years before by Leo III in 732–33, also a first year of the indiction. Since Nicephorus's census was apparently complete by September 809, quite possibly he too began his census with the start of the first indictional year, and spent about two years on the complicated process of revising the tax rolls of the whole empire. While tax collectors and government inspectors had always made revisions in the rolls from year to year to reflect changes in ownership, this was no substitute for a complete revision of the old census. From his tenure as general logothete Nicephorus was familiar with the state that the rolls were in, and he used the opportunity of the new survey to mount a determined attack on tax evasion.[196]

The survey was evidently a thorough one, involving not only counting households and assessing their land, livestock, and slaves, but inquiring into their previous tax payments. While the census went on, inspectors attached to the office of the general logothete seem to have accompanied the tax collectors and assessed additional and back taxes to be collected with the regular payments. To finance the census, which would have required the temporary appointment of extra inspectors, each household paid a fairly modest supplementary roll tax of one-twelfth of a nomisma. Otherwise, the basic tax rates remained what they had been, but were levied much more strictly.

As property was reassessed Nicephorus ordered all permanent tax exemptions to be canceled, thereby clearing away many years' worth of ill-assorted privileges and expanding the tax base significantly. Given that most extraordinary exemptions on the books were probably outdated and arbitrary, this measure must have removed more injustice than it created. Nicephorus also made an effort to collect the inheritance taxes, which after their temporary abolition by Irene had not always been collected with care. Evidently finding it unreasonable that those who had been lucky enough to inherit during Irene's temporary remission should pay nothing, Nicephorus ordered back taxes to be paid on all untaxed inheritances over the past twenty years. Because the inspectors were often unable to document inheritances over such a length of time, Nicephorus enacted a rule that allowed most inheritances to be taxed anyway. If the records showed that a taxpayer had suddenly acquired substantial property, even if he could not be proved to have inherited it, under the new rule he had to surrender a share of the property to the crown, as if he had dug up a pot of gold. Real buried hoards—not uncommon, since rural areas had no banks—were similarly taxable. This rule was subject to the same twenty-year limitation as inheritances.

Nicephorus also took the opportunity of the census to broaden the tax on household slaves, which had long been collected only at the customs station of Abydus on the Hellespont. In consequence, commercia had been levied on the slaves exported from the Mediterranean to Constantinople and the Black Sea coast but not on those exported within the Mediterranean region, an obvious inequity. To correct it, Nicephorus decreed a tax of two nomismata on every household slave recently purchased in this region, which was collected from the purchaser when his property was inspected and an unregistered slave was found. These reforms of the tax on household slaves and the tax on sudden increases in wealth were obviously aimed at the wealthy, though poor men were also affected by the demands for past inheritance taxes.

Another major change made at the time of the census affected church foundations with imperial charters. These establishments, which included the imperial orphanage, hospices, homes for the aged, churches, and monasteries, were usually well endowed with lands farmed by secular tenants. These tenants were legally subject to the hearth tax, which their landlords were bound to pay, but for years the government had not been collecting the tax, probably as a result of the favor Irene had shown to the clergy of the capital. Nicephorus ordered the back taxes to be collected from the first year of his reign, though not from Irene's. Since these institutions do not seem to have had enough cash on hand to pay the arrears, Nicephorus evidently confiscated part of their land in lieu of taxes. Some grumbled that to hold the institutions responsible for back taxes even on the land that they were losing was a sort of double jeopardy, and that the emperor was forcing gold and silver liturgical vessels to be sold. Naturally these measures were unpopular among the leaders of the Church in and around Constantinople, and bishops and other priests and monks began to feel themselves ill used.[197]

In his defense, the emperor could argue that, as in the case of inheritance taxes, he was simply reforming an arbitrary and unfair practice begun by Irene. Such reforms, of course, combined with the cancellation of other exemptions and the discovery of unregistered lands, households, and farm animals, would have brought large sums of money into the treasury while the census continued, and in every year thereafter. Though all this contributed to Nicephorus's reputation for greed among his enemies, it did not damage his reputation among his friends for piety, or even for loving the monks and the poor. After all, Nicephorus's measures primarily affected a few particularly wealthy church foundations and some other wealthy tax evaders. Many other monasteries and private citizens certainly benefited from the census. For one thing, some of them had probably been overassessed, either by accident or because they had lost land that was still entered under their names on the rolls. Much more important, however, was the cancellation of exemptions. When it returned land to the tax rolls, the supplements levied on neighboring taxpayers to make up for the exempted lands would have been reduced and in most cases eliminated. Thus, while Nicephorus increased his revenue, he would actually have decreased the obligations of many taxpayers.

Nicephorus's reoccupation of most of central and northern Greece and his new census and tax assessment were apparently related measures. Even his enemies in Byzantine ruling circles, whose hostility kept them from recognizing much of what he was trying to do, saw that he hoped to gain more revenue from both the new lands and the new assessment. What they did not necessarily see was that an accurate census could be used not only to find out tax evaders, but also to prepare for a transfer of population from Asia Minor to the recently reoccupied Balkans. From the corrected rolls one could learn which regions in Anatolia were so densely settled that if some farmers were moved the rest could still farm the available land; the rolls' corrected names and addresses of taxpayers permitted arrangements to be made for the taxpayers' orderly resettlement elsewhere. Later events were to show that while the census was going on the government must have been drawing up contingency plans for such a resettlement. Ambitious as Nicephorus's present projects were, his future plans went farther.

SIGNS OF OPPOSITION

In December of 807, with his various projects advancing steadily, Nicephorus was ready to provide his son Stauracius with a wife. The junior emperor seems to have been in his middle teens, the usual age for an imperial marriage. Following the example of the empress Irene when she chose a bride for Constantine VI, Nicephorus had decided to select Stauracius's wife in a general competition. To judge from his request in the fall of 806 that Hārūn send him a girl from Heraclea to be a candidate for his son's hand, the emperor was already seeking contestants in that year, though he may have judged it an inauspicious time to hold a bride show because of his recent humiliation by the Arabs. More successful now, he brought together beautiful girls from all over the empire and made his choice. Whether he consulted Stauracius or not is unclear. The winning contestant was Theophano, a relative of the empress Irene and like Irene from Athens. Stauracius married her on December 20.

Nicephorus was obviously trying to associate himself with Irene not only by following the marriage custom that she had introduced but also by choosing a member of her family. This is another proof of Irene's prestige, which had been invoked in the revolt of Bardanes Turcus and was kept alive by those in Constantinople who venerated her as a saint. To be sure, the selection of Theophano raised some doubts that the emperor had made his choice entirely on the basis of virtue and beauty. Nicephorus's detractors declared that Theophano had often slept with a man to whom she had been previously betrothed and that two other contestants were more beautiful—so beautiful that Nicephorus himself celebrated after the wedding by bedding them both. While such gossip would have been easy to invent about a girl who had been engaged and an emperor who was a widower, Nicephorus would have been unlikely to expose his son to ridicule or to risk having a grandson of doubtful legitimacy, though extraordinary temptations might have led him to lapse from his usually ascetic habits. Theophano proved to be a woman of some energy, and no family alliance could enhance the reputation of Nicephorus's dynasty more than a connection with Irene, the patroness of so many of the empire's monks, bishops, and civil servants.[198]

If by marrying Stauracius to Theophano Nicephorus was trying to conciliate those groups, he perceived their discontent accurately. In February of 808, with his usual alertness, the emperor uncovered a new conspiracy against his rule. Its leader and candidate for the throne was the quaestor, Arsaber the Patrician, the empire's chief legal official. The conspirators included some civil servants like Arsaber, bishops, monks, and leading members of the patriarch Nicephorus's staff at St. Sophia— among them the patriarchal secretary and treasurer and the syncellus, the emperor's representative at the patriarchate. It was an odd lot of conspirators: none of them apparently had much power in the administration or any influence over the army, so that the emperor easily apprehended them. Arsaber was known for his piety and learning, and his supporters were from groups that made up the iconophile intelligentsia. The syncellus at the time was probably George, who was then at work on a monumental world chronicle.

The plotters seem also to have been discontented with the patriarch Nicephorus, who was not implicated in the conspiracy though his closest subordinates were conspirators. Probably they were unhappy at the recent restoration of Joseph of Cathara as a priest in their own church of St. Sophia, which implied condoning Joseph's performance of Constantine VI's adulterous marriage. Though it is not certain that the emperor's new census had yet proceeded to the point of his demanding back taxes from the main church foundations around Constantinople and confiscating some of their lands, it seems likely; and in that case this curious conspiracy of so many high-ranking clerics would be much easier to explain. In any event, the clergy of the capital doubtless resented their loss of influence since the days of Irene. Though Theodore of Studius, who was always disdainful of politics, took no part in the plot, his sort of insistence on clerical prerogatives was probably behind it. Merciful to his enemies as usual, the emperor merely subjected Arsaber to whipping, tonsure as a monk, and exile to a monastery in Bithynia. The others were also whipped and exiled, and had their property confiscated.[199]

Though Nicephorus did not directly blame the Studites for the plot, by now he had no doubt that they were refusing communion with him and his patriarch, and he was out of patience with their disaffection. He first took up the case not with the fiercely independent Theodore but with Theodore's brother Joseph, who had shown some flexibility by accepting imperial appointment as archbishop of Thessalonica. The emperor took the matter seriously enough to send his most responsible official, the postal logothete, who demanded that Joseph state his reason for not taking communion with Nicephorus, Stauracius, and the patriarch Nicephorus. Joseph answered, "I have nothing against either our pious emperors or the patriarch, but [only] against the steward [Joseph of Cathara] who married the adulterer and for that reason was deposed in accordance with the holy canons." The logothete, obviously prepared for this reply, told the archbishop that the emperors had no further need of his services.

At Studius, Theodore learned of this interview within two weeks. In some alarm he wrote to his followers at Saccudium to warn that their protest was now known, and he sent convoluted appeals for help to his friends at court. To Theoctistus, who as quaestor had helped put Nicephorus on the throne and as magister was now one of the emperor's two highest-ranking advisers, Theodore proposed a compromise: if Joseph of Cathara would only stop acting as a priest, even if he was not defrocked or removed as steward of St. Sophia, the Studites would abandon their protest. This proposal got nowhere. Theodore and his uncle Plato appealed repeatedly to the monk Symeon, Nicephorus's relative, but Symeon, caught in the middle, could give no clear reply. When Theodore wrote an appeal to the patriarch Nicephorus, the patriarch did not feel able to answer. Theodore and Joseph of Thessalonica both wrote to the emperor asking for an audience, but Nicephorus and Stauracius departed on a military expedition and left them in suspense.[200]

Though this expedition of 808 is known only from a bare mention in one of Theodore's letters, it seems safe to say that it was part of Nicephorus's great expansionary effort in the Balkans. It was probably a relatively peaceful tour of inspection, partly meant to introduce young Stauracius to field operations. The annexations were proceeding successfully, so far without significant resistance from the Bulgars. When the emperor returned from his expedition in the Balkans, he sent another fleet to Dalmatia and Venetia, where the truce with the Franks was expiring. The fleet's commander, Paul the Patrician, visited the Dalmatian ports in the fall of 808 and wintered in Venetia, keeping an eye on a Frankish fleet based on the nearby island of Comacchio, near the mouth of the Po.

Against the Arabs no campaigning was necessary. The caliph Hārūn was in failing health, yet by 808 an open rebellion in Khurāsān urgently required his presence. As in 805, the caliph arranged a truce and exchange of prisoners with Nicephorus before departing for the east. At the exchange of prisoners, which was again held at the Lamis River frontier in Cilicia, the Byzantines delivered to the Arabs just over 2,500 male and female captives, most of them probably taken in the Byzantine raids of 805; the Arabs presumably handed over a similar number of the Byzantines captured in the Arab raids of 806. There may also have been another exchange near the Cilician Gates. Hārūn then left for Khurāsān. This time Nicephorus, chastened by his experience in 806, kept the truce during Hārūn's absence. The emperor had concerns closer to home.[201]

Realizing that Theodore and his Studites were feeling uncomfortable with their grotesquely circumscribed opposition to official church policy, the emperor put increasing pressure on them in the hope of gaining their full submission. He posted soldiers outside the Monastery of Studius, so that the Studites were under virtual house arrest. Then the bishops of Nicaea and Chrysopolis were sent to Theodore to ask him to accept Joseph of Cathara. They argued that the patriarch Tarasius, now acknowledged by all as a saint, had asked Joseph to perform the marriage under a dispensation. "It is the dispensation of a saint," they said; "accept it."

The emperor sent soldiers to bring Theodore, Plato, Joseph of Thessalonica, and another Studite to hear a similar exhortation by Symeon, the monk related to the imperial family whom Theodore had appealed to earlier. The emperor then transferred Theodore and his companions to the Monastery of Sts. Sergius and Bacchus near the palace, where he sent Symeon to talk to them again. By now, however, the Studites had held out too long to be able to submit with dignity. Perhaps Nicephorus saw as much, and mainly intended to isolate them from potential supporters when he gave them so many opportunities to relent.[202]

In January 809 the emperor had the patriarch hold a synod of bishops and abbots to decide how to deal with the Studites. The synod accepted the argument that Joseph of Cathara had performed the marriage under a

26. Theodore of Studius being taken into exile by ship (center) and praying while in exile (left). Vaticanus graecus 1613, p. 175. Painter: Nestor. The Monastery of Studius appears at the right, portrayed in a simplified but recognizable form. Whether the exile shown here is that of 809 or of 815 is not clear. (Photo: Biblioteca Apostolica Vaticana, Vatican City)

dispensation from St. Tarasius—which was not utterly false, insofar as Tarasius had not reprimanded Joseph at the time. Therefore, they decided, Joseph's action had to be accepted, since he had been dispensed by a saint. Enraged by the decision, Theodore burst out, "John the Baptist is dying! The Gospel is being abolished! That is no dispensation!" The members of the synod, who were fully aware that Theodore had been refusing communion with them as well as the emperor, became increasingly exasperated with him and his pretentiously cherished principles. In the end, aside from Joseph of Thessalonica himself, only one bishop is known to have defended Theodore's position. The rest voted to anathematize "those who do not accept the dispensations of the saints," condemning Theodore and his companions and in particular deposing Joseph as archbishop of Thessalonica.

The emperor exiled Theodore, Joseph, and Plato to different islands near Constantinople, and when the other Studites refused to accept the council's decision he expelled them from their monastery and exiled some of them. It was hardly an ideal result for Nicephorus, but the emperor could not regard a monk who presumed to excommunicate him and his patriarch as anything but disloyal, and allowing disloyalty to go unpunished endangered his throne. Although Nicephorus might have compromised earlier, as things stood now most people probably realized that he had done what he had to do.[203]

THE RESETTLEMENT OF GREECE

On March 24, 809, the caliph Hārūn died while on his campaign against the rebels in Khurāsān. His sons al-Amīn and al-Ma'mūn soon began a protracted civil war over the succession, further jeopardizing the unity of the caliphate. Arab power was crippled for a generation, and never recovered completely. As things turned out, the ineffective operations of 807 were to be the last attacks on the empire organized by the Arabs' central government for almost twenty years, though border commanders and various freebooters might conduct campaigns of varying size. Nicephorus was freer than he had ever been to pursue his projects in the Balkans.[204]

At the time of Hārūn's death, the strategus of Macedonia was guarding his theme's new frontier on the river Strymon with a good-sized army. Since Holy Week was approaching, he had received from Constantinople the payroll for all the troops he commanded, including many troops detached from other themes. It was a sum of 1,100 pounds of gold, pay for about 12,000 men. He began by paying the soldiers and officers stationed with him. Since the Slavs to the west were weak, no one anticipated a serious attack. Nevertheless, without warning, a company of Bulgars fell on the army from the west. They massacred most of the soldiers, the strategus, and all the ranking officers of the other themes, and seized the whole payroll and the army's baggage. The Bulgars then withdrew into the lands of the Slavs with their plunder.

At almost the same time, someone in the newly fortified town of Serdica was persuaded to admit a Bulgar force commanded by the khan Krum, who had long been fighting the declining Avars but now attacked the Byzantines for the first time. Krum slaughtered nearly all the soldiers there, reportedly numbering 6,000, along with the civilian population, though some officers managed to escape. After destroying the town he returned to Bulgaria. The Bulgars, achieving complete surprise, had undone in a few days a considerable part of Nicephorus's work in Macedonia during the last two years.[205]

Nicephorus acted at once. As the mobile army of the tagmata and the army of the theme of Thrace were at hand, totaling some 17,000 men, he could depart without delay. On April 3, the Tuesday of Holy Week, the emperor set out for Bulgaria, and quickly arrived at Pliska, the Bulgar capital. Pliska stood among low hills and had only wooden fortifications; as the main Bulgar army seems still to have been in the west, Nicephorus met no resistance. He occupied the town by April 8, when he celebrated Easter in Krum's palace, sending holiday greetings back to Constantinople. Though Pliska was not much of a place, its easy capture was a psychological blow that went a good way toward avenging the massacres on the Strymon and at Serdica.

The emperor took a stern view of the loss of Serdica without a fight. When the officers who had escaped from it sent to ask for a guarantee that they would not be punished, he refused, despite the likelihood that they would desert to Krum and furnish him with information about Byzantine troops and tactics. Since Nicephorus probably suspected that Krum already had such information, possibly from these very men, he received the news of their desertion with equanimity.

The emperor now marched to the ruins of Serdica, which he wanted to rebuild and garrison once again. He realized, however, that orders to reconstruct and man the town would be very unwelcome to his troops, who were already discontented. Though the tagmata normally received their annual pay during Holy Week, in his hurry to depart for Pliska Nicephorus had apparently not taken time to pay them or encumbered himself by taking the money along. Not only were the tagmata impatient to be paid, but as elite troops they were unaccustomed to heavy construction work and to garrison duty away from Constantinople. They were, however, the only troops at hand, because the Bulgars had massacred most of the soldiers of the themes who had performed these tasks before. Nicephorus tried to appeal to the tagmata's *esprit de corps* by having their officers persuade them to volunteer to rebuild Serdica; he hoped at least to avoid the danger of a mutiny if the troops refused. The soldiers, however, discovered what he was up to and mutinied against both the emperor and their officers.

The mutiny began at midday when the soldiers began tearing apart the officers' tents. They then moved on to the tent of Nicephorus himself, where they shouted curses at him for his parsimony and deviousness. But they could not say he was a coward: he had a table brought, stood on it, and confronted the mutineers. With the help of Peter, domestic of the Schools, and another Nicephorus, probably domestic of the Excubitors, the emperor calmed the troops with promises, evidently assuring them that they would return quickly to Constantinople and receive their pay. Some were still not mollified and retreated to a nearby hill, where they remained through the night intermittently crying out "Lord, have mercy!" to emphasize the justice of their complaints. During the night Nicephorus promised donatives to his junior officers, some of whom may well have stirred up the troops by revealing his plans in the first place. The next morning he went to the troops on the hill, strode boldly into the mob, and talked with them, promising them their pay and declaring that he loved them as sons. The army then turned back to Constantinople. Nicephorus may have provoked the mutiny by misplaced perseverance, but he had used the same sort of determination to put it down.

Before he returned to the capital in advance of the troops, the emperor assigned a trusted adviser, Theodosius Salibaras, the job of identifying the principal mutineers by unobtrusively questioning individual soldiers on the return march. These worst offenders Nicephorus summoned to the Palace of St. Mamas north of Constantinople, ostensibly to receive their pay. Instead he had most of them whipped, shorn, and exiled, and the rest of them transported to Chrysopolis in Bithynia, perhaps to be degraded to service as muleteers among the Optimates. Those exiled were probably junior officers, exile hardly being an appropriate punishment for an ordinary soldier. Nicephorus seems to have blamed the mutiny, and the debacles on the Strymon and at Serdica, at least partly on indiscipline and disloyalty in his officer corps.[206]

At this time Nicephorus also suffered a setback in Italy. In the spring, the Byzantine admiral Paul the Patrician had attacked the Frankish fleet on Comacchio, but it had defeated him and forced him to retreat to Venetia. Then he opened negotiations with King Pepin; but the dukes of Venetia, Obelerius and Beatus, refused to cooperate, perhaps fearing that the Franks and Byzantines would remember the dukes' treachery against both sides and join in deposing them. After the negotiations failed, there were even charges that the dukes were planning to attack Paul. Paul withdrew from Venetia in desperation, leaving the province endangered from without and insubordinate within.[207]

The emperor therefore found his projects in the West in jeopardy. The tagmata, besides being disaffected, were by their character poorly suited to the long-term service in the Balkans that was needed. The themes of the West were weak and had suffered heavy casualties. The contingents transferred earlier from the themes of the East to the Balkans had proved ineffective and now had been almost annihilated, making it harder to transfer new troops from the same themes. The recently occupied lands inhabited by Slavs—and Venetia and Dalmatia—seemed ready to fall to an internal rebellion or a Bulgar or Frankish invasion at any time. With their small populations under incomplete Byzantine control, none of these regions could be expected to produce enough revenue to pay for their own defense for the foreseeable future. Radical measures were necessary, either to withdraw from all or part of the territory or to make it more secure.

Accordingly, in the summer of 809, Nicephorus issued a momentous edict whose effects shaped the rest of Byzantine history and have changed the demography of the Balkans up to the present day. No doubt he had been preparing this measure for months, but its precise timing was probably forced upon him by the deteriorating security of his Balkan possessions. He ordered specified families from the other themes to leave their homes and migrate to the new territories in the Balkans. Although these families could take their movable property with them, their land was confiscated by the treasury and sold; in return, they received land grants in the new territories. Both rich and poor had to join the colonists. When a household was selected, every member, from the first through the third generation, had to leave home.

Among those to be resettled, Nicephorus chose a number of the men with the least property to be enrolled as soldiers to defend the Balkans and receive military lands there. The new soldiers' military equipment was to be provided by their former neighbors, who were assessed eighteen and a half nomismata to equip each soldier; in return, the neighbors were to receive the land that the soldiers had formerly owned, dividing it and its tax liability among them, as was customary under the system of collective responsibility for taxes. Some experienced soldiers seem also to have been among the migrants, because this is the most likely time for the transfer of some of the Mardaïtes—descendants of refugees from the caliphate who served as marines—from the Cibyrrhaeot theme to the Peloponnesus. Their former military lands were presumably assigned to new recruits. The migration was to begin at the start of the year of the indiction, on September 1, 809, and to be completed by Easter, March 31, 810.[208]

This was apparently the time at which all the recently acquired Balkan territories were reorganized for administrative purposes. In the south, Nicephorus created a new theme of Peloponnesus, to which he assigned not only the Peloponnesian territory taken from the Slavs in 805 but also the land up to the Isthmus of Corinth that had formed about half of the original theme of Hellas. The Peloponnesian theme included the old capital of Hellas at Corinth, which became the capital of Peloponnesus. The theme of Peloponnesus seems therefore to have received the senior drungus of Hellas that was based at Corinth, with 1,000 men. To this another thousand-man drungus formed of Nicephorus's new recruits was added, probably based at Patras and including new settlements at Sparta and the ports of Methone and Corone. Along with Hellas's capital the theme of Peloponnesus inherited the rank of its strategus, who henceforth outranked the strategus of Hellas.

The remaining theme of Hellas, which kept that name only because it was more appropriate to its geography, retained the junior drungus of the old Hellas in Attica and Euboea. Its headquarters was probably Athens. Hellas then received another drungus of new recruits settled on territory extending from Boeotia into central Greece and southern Thessaly. Their headquarters was probably at Thebes, which seems to have become the theme's capital. Each of these two themes, Peloponnesus and Hellas, was therefore composed half of experienced soldiers long settled on their military land grants, and half of mostly raw recruits just assigned military lands in territory recently opened to settlement.[209]

To the west of Hellas, Nicephorus made Cephalonia a theme instead of an archontate, intending for it to serve not only as a defense against the Slavs and Bulgars but as a base for defending Dalmatia and Venetia. The latter function seems clear from the identity of the first strategus, who was the same Paul the Patrician who had just returned from Venetia with little success. Paul was ordered to prepare for a new expedition to Venetia in 810, when he first appears in the sources with his new title. The Cephalonian theme consisted of two drungi of 2,000 men, primarily marines, who were evidently the few garrison troops of the former archontate of Cephalonia plus some of the new recruits sent to lands taken from the Slavs. Therefore the theme's territory probably included one drungus of the Ionian islands, with its capital on Cephalonia, and another drungus of the adjacent coast and hinterland of Epirus, which like the islands provided suitable land for marines. The headquarters of the second drungus was presumably medieval Nicopolis (the ancient Naupactus), later the capital of an independent theme. Apparently the land of the theme extended to the Pindus Mountains and as far north as Joannina and Adrianopolis (the later Dryinopolis). At the same time, Nicephorus probably tried to bring Dalmatia under closer Byzantine control by turning it into an archontate. When he sent the new strategus of Cephalonia, Paul, to Dalmatia in the spring of 810, the expedition could have brought a few of Nicephorus's new recruits to serve as the archontate's garrison.[210]

Also in late 809 and early 810, Nicephorus almost certainly created the theme of Thessalonica, replacing the archontate there. This new theme lay east of Cephalonia and north of Hellas, and covered northern Thessaly and the southern part of what had been ancient Macedonia, including the Chalcidice. The theme of Thessalonica too had an army of 2,000 men, presumably drawn from the garrison of the old archontate and the recruits of Nicephorus. This theme seems to have extended to meet the theme of Cephalonia at the Pindus near Joannina, and to have included the towns of Beroea in the Aliacmon valley and Larissa in the Pineus valley, the latter perhaps being the headquarters of the theme's junior drungus. At the same time, Nicephorus probably used still more of his recruits to fill those places in the armies of the theme of Macedonia and the other themes that had been left vacant after the recent massacres by the Bulgars and not yet filled through the regular process of replacement. The emperor certainly sent new settlers to the Strymon valley in the Macedonian theme where the Bulgars had attacked, though he seems to have left the region of Serdica unoccupied for the time being.[211]

Finally, at the same time and presumably from the same group of recruits, Nicephorus created a new tagma, the Hicanati. Like the three senior tagmata, it consisted of 4,000 cavalry, each of whom had a squire. Its name seems to be an attempt to Latinize the Greek word for "capable" (hikanos), thus creating a title supposed to sound both glorious and arcane. To this new tagma Nicephorus assigned some of his officers' sons aged fourteen and over, appointing as its nominal commander, the domestic of the Hicanati, his ten-year-old grandson Nicetas Rhangabe. Though the emperor intended for these adolescents to go along on campaigns to gain experience and to lend prestige to the tagma, it was nonetheless a real fighting force. As its actual commander, Nicephorus appointed the experienced and faithful Peter the Patrician, who had served under both him and Irene as domestic of the Schools and had aided in putting down the mutiny among the tagmata the previous spring. Nicephorus's clear purpose in creating the Hicanati was to strengthen the numbers and loyalty of the tagmata by adding a new company on which he could rely.[212]

The emperor undeniably ran a risk of revolt when he issued all these orders in late 809 and early 810. Doubtless they caused great misery to a large part of the population, some of whom were soldiers and some of whom were influential. Many of those ordered to colonize the "lands of the Slavs" were acutely distressed at losing the buildings and lands that their families had owned for generations, and at leaving behind their ancestors' graves. They are said to have blasphemed, prayed for enemy invasions, called their dead ancestors fortunate, and in some cases hanged themselves. While the new land grants were probably large and fertile, since so much land was available for distribution, they were also uncleared and without houses, fences, or farm buildings, besides being vulnerable to attack by Slavs or Bulgars. Worst of all for conservative country dwellers, the land was unfamiliar, as were many of their fellow colonists.

In the one case for which we know some details, Sparta, which had first been settled by people from Monemvasia supposedly descended from ancient Spartans, now also received a mixed population of Armenians, people from the Thracesian theme in western Asia Minor, "Kafirs" (possibly renegade Muslims who had converted to Christianity), and others assembled from still other towns and regions. Nicephorus is said to have given land to Paulician heretics from the Anatolic theme, and the people of the town of Sisium in Cilicia are known to have fled the caliphate and been settled in the empire at just this time. It would have been natural, but not popular, for Nicephorus to include these and other groups of misfits in his great effort at colonization.[213]

Our principal source, who whether he is George Syncellus or Theophanes Confessor is extremely hostile to Nicephorus, bitterly and lengthily decries all the grief that the colonization caused. The only motive he will assign to the emperor in forcing the colonists to leave their homes is a desire to see them die at once so that he could inherit their movable property. Nonetheless, apart from suicides, the outraged chronicler mentions no deaths; he speaks only of spiritual suffering. He says nothing of any mass starvation, of mortality from exposure or fatigue, or even of a general impoverishment of the settlers. Nor was there a revolt. Another source, which is also early, praises the emperor's work of repopulation and rebuilding in the Peloponnesus and his conversion of the local Slavs to Christianity; and for years to come the oral tradition about Nicephorus in the Peloponnesus was favorable.[214]

On the whole, Nicephorus's government appears to have handled this complicated operation with remarkable foresight and efficiency. The recently completed census permitted officials to designate and identify the colonists and to provide for their safe passage and resettlement. Once they arrived at their assigned destinations, they evidently received substantial government assistance in building houses and clearing land. The absence of a general famine probably indicates that the government sent them food from the rest of the Empire until they could produce their own. The rebuilding of the long-ruined towns and churches of the Peloponnesus, beginning with Patras and continuing with Sparta and others, is specifically attributed to Nicephorus; no doubt he contributed money and materials both there and in places for which no information survives.

Some provisions, admittedly, required no direct contributions from the treasury, like the special tax on neighbors to outfit the new recruits. Similarly, Nicephorus donated the lands and other possessions of the Slavs who had rebelled in 807 to the church of Patras, making the Slavs tenants and obliging them to pay rent to the church and to provide for the support of the strategus of Peloponnesus and his household and staff. At any rate, the government's contribution, both in revenues expended and renounced and in planning and organization, was sufficient to make the colonization a success.[215]

It could scarcely have succeeded, however, if the empire's population had not been growing. By 809, the themes of Asia Minor had enough people in them to repopulate and garrison Greece without significantly reducing the area under cultivation in the remainder of the empire. Admittedly, the government often had to force people to buy the confiscated lands. It is reported that in coastal districts, primarily those of Asia Minor, even owners of boats who had always lived by fishing or trading rather than agriculture were forced to buy farmland at a fixed price. The fact remains that, if compelled, the population was able to buy and cultivate the land, apparently nearly all of it.[216]

Of course, the number of those who migrated cannot be precisely estimated. The newly recruited soldiers in the four themes in Greece and in the Hicanati filled about 10,000 new places: if we include some replacements of the thousands of soldiers lost in early 809 the number of recruits would probably rise to around 20,000. With their families, these recruits would have made about 70,000 settlers by themselves. But they were only the poorest colonists, whose land was given to their neighbors to offset the charge for their equipment rather than being sold as was otherwise the rule; they therefore seem to have been in a distinct minority. Perhaps, then, the total number of colonists approached a quarter million. It was certainly adequate to change Greece in a few years from a mainly Slavic country into a mainly Greek one, as the colonists forced the Slavs to accept Christianity, and not long afterward the Greek language. After the colonization the empire's population should have expanded further to spread over the land opened up by the annexations in the Balkans and the departure of the colonists from the rest of the empire.

In the meantime, Nicephorus had added vast new lands in the Balkans to his tax rolls without significantly reducing the lands already registered in other places. For the time being the treasury had to bear the cost of rebuilding and resettlement, no doubt accompanied by temporary tax exemptions while the colonists brought their land into production. In the short run, however, the treasury received the purchase price of the confiscated lands, and in the near future its receipts from the land tax would have increased dramatically. On the other hand, the army had been expanded from 80,000 to 90,000 men, and the military payroll was permanently increased in proportion, from about 600,000 nomismata to about 680,000. Further, Nicephorus seems to have had plans for more operations against the Bulgars, which could only be begun with a large cash reserve to finance them.[217]

Recognizing that the rural population had done its share for the time being, Nicephorus now tried to increase the revenue from the cities, which mainly meant from Constantinople. When he applied there his rule treating suddenly acquired wealth as if it were discovered treasure, however, the results were less equitable and more capricious than they were in agricultural areas. For one thing, the inspection had to be more intrusive. Whereas wealth in land and livestock was easy to inspect, cash and valuables were easily hidden; the inspectors relied on denunciations, sometimes by household slaves, and then searched houses. For another thing, though Byzantine farming tended to increase the farmer's wealth only gradually, so that a doubling of his property in a few years was likely to be the result of an inheritance or the discovery or theft of a pot of gold, the same was hardly true of commerce and trade, in which a single profitable transaction or arrival of valuable cargo could make a man's fortune. Though today no good capitalist considers this sort of success unfair, in Byzantine times it was usually resented as profiteering at best and robbery at worst.

The only taxes that merchants had been paying, however, were the trade duties, which could easily be passed on to the consumer. They paid no income tax, since none existed—a situation that few modern governments allow. Therefore Nicephorus had some justification, not only from the Byzantine point of view but from the modern one, for trying to gain a greater share of mercantile profits for the treasury. Of course, without a uniform system of inspection and assessment, he could scarcely fail to commit injustices. The probably embellished story is told that Nicephorus summoned a chandler who had become wealthy through his own labors, and asked him to place his hand on the emperor's head and declare on oath how much property he had. Daunted by the prospect of touching the emperor, the man tried to decline, but finally swore that he had a hundred pounds of gold, or 7,200 nomismata. Allegedly Nicephorus ordered the money to be brought at once, and asked the unfortunate chandler, "What do you need all this worry for? Have lunch with me, take home a hundred nomismata, and go away content."[218]

If anything, however, Nicephorus was more aware of the uses of trade than most Byzantine emperors. When earlier emperors had accumulated a gold surplus, as most worked hard to do, they had nearly always left it to gather dust in the treasury until it was needed. Quite extraordinarily, Nicephorus invested part of his reserve in trade, though Byzantine ideas of a controlled economy and of the superior majesty of the emperor would not allow him to do so as an ordinary investor. Instead he summoned the leading shipowners of Constantinople and compelled each of them to accept a loan from the state of 12 pounds of gold, or 864 nomismata, at $16\frac{2}{3}$ percent annual interest.

Since this was a fair rate for a maritime loan, the reason it had to be compulsory was apparently that many shipowners did not want to risk so large a sum over and above their usual business. In order to use the money and pay the interest, they had to expand their trade. The end result was probably to stimulate enterprise to the benefit of most traders and consumers alike, while the state received not only the interest but additional trade duties. Though the impact of the loans on the whole economy is likely to have been minor, if only because trade was such a small part of total economic activity, this innovative measure may indicate that Nicephorus was trying to foster a general economic expansion.[219]

Luckily for Nicephorus, the Bulgars seem to have been so shocked by the destruction of Pliska that they did not attack his fledgling themes in the Balkans. It was in the Adriatic that one of Nicephorus's new arrangements was put to the test for the first time. At the beginning of 810 the dukes of Venetia, Obelerius and Beatus, changed sides again and invited King Pepin of Italy to occupy their province with his fleet from Comacchio. Pepin was willing. When he arrived with his fleet and army the dukes surrendered to him, and he occupied most of the settlements of the Venetian Lagoon, including the capital at Malamocco. He then sent his fleet to raid the coast of Dalmatia. Yet a large number of Venetians who opposed the occupation fled by boat to Rialto, an island settlement in the middle of the lagoon that was the part of the province least accessible by land. At first Pepin hoped to starve the refugees out, but they proved to have ample provisions.

Since the lagoon was shallow, Pepin tried to build a makeshift causeway to Rialto from the island of Malamocco across which his army could march. But the Venetians, by bringing up their boats and shooting arrows at the soldiers working on the causeway, were able to drive them off and wreck the little they had built. By now it was late spring, and Paul, the new strategus of Cephalonia, had arrived in Dalmatia with a fleet. Without waiting for Paul to reach Venetia, Pepin withdrew his forces and returned to the mainland, where he soon died, on June 24, 810. Though Paul had brought along legates empowered to negotiate with Pepin, after Pepin's death no Frank in Italy had the authority to make an agreement. The legates went home to report this not-unwelcome news to Nicephorus.

Shortly thereafter Nicephorus sent another legate, Arsaphius the Spatharius, who with the approval of the Venetians deposed Obelerius and Beatus as dukes. Arsaphius exiled Beatus to Jadera; Obelerius had apparently taken refuge with Charlemagne. The Venetians chose Agnellus Particiacus as their new duke and decided to transfer their capital from Malamocco to Rialto, which since that time has been known as the city of Venice. Arsaphius continued on to the court of Charlemagne to open negotiations, since Charlemagne was once more the effective ruler of Italy.[220]

Arsaphius arrived at Aachen in October of 810. Nicephorus appears to have asked him to repeat the performance of Michael of Synnada's embassy of 803 by making a provisional peace without either recognizing Charlemagne's title of emperor or offending Charlemagne by failing to recognize it. This Arsaphius managed to accomplish. Though Charlemagne expressed surprise that his letter of 803 to Nicephorus had received no reply, again he was cordial. He conceded the Byzantines' right to Venetia and agreed to hand over the renegade Duke Obelerius, who by now had betrayed both sides. Arsaphius was thus dismissed with all respect. To avoid having another letter left unanswered, however, this time Charlemagne sent his own embassy to Nicephorus, headed by Haido, the bishop of Basel, to negotiate a formal peace. Haido departed for Constantinople at the beginning of 811, taking Obelerius with him.[221]

In September 810, with affairs in the West taking a promising turn and the Bulgars and the Arabs remarkably quiescent, Nicephorus began the new year of the indiction with more financial measures that affected the cities. Pressing forward with his intention to tax the wealth of merchants, the emperor ordered strict supervision of the sale of all sorts of animals and produce, evidently to enforce the collection of the trade duties. He seems to have uncovered various cases of evasion of the duty, because he subjected some wealthy men to penalties and even confiscation. He also forbade private citizens to make maritime loans at interest, then offered additional loans from the treasury. His evident purpose was to invest more of the empire's gold surplus in a more flexible way, while adjusting the loan to the shipowner's ability to put it to use. Now that maritime loans were an imperial monopoly, shipowners had no choice but to resort to the treasury for money, and no forced loans were necessary.[222]

Just after these measures were enacted, on October 1, 810, an attempt was made to assassinate the emperor. The would-be assassin was a man of no prominence, who entered the palace disguised as a monk and seized the sword of an imperial guard. Two messengers who were standing by and tried to stop the man were seriously wounded before he was taken. When he was tortured to discover whether he had accomplices, even on the rack he swore that he had acted alone in a fit of insanity. Conceivably he told the truth, but deranged assassins were as rare at Byzantium as organized conspiracies were common, and Nicephorus had obviously displeased many people during the preceding few years.[223]

As Nicephorus's reign proceeded, and he found that he could order ever more radical measures and actually make them work, he showed himself more and more willing to court unpopularity. Between 807 and 810 he had in one way or another disturbed the interests or sensibilities of many of the higher clergy, the soldiers of the tagmata, and the merchants of Constantinople, besides many provincials who were adversely affected by his tax reforms and colonization of the Balkans. In manner Nicephorus remained easygoing and genial, and he seems to have kept most of his popularity among the civil service, the chief officers of the army, many monks and lower clergy, and ordinary citizens. But after he had brought about such sweeping changes with evident success it is easy to believe reports that he was proud of his accomplishments. According to one account, at this time he used to criticize those who had reigned before him for being indecisive, and said that no one was stronger than the ruler, if the ruler was ready to rule intelligently. Certainly Nicephorus had done things of which his predecessors had never dreamed.[224]

THE BULGARIAN CATASTROPHE

Nicephorus intended, and apparently had planned for years, to deal the Bulgars a crushing defeat, and quite possibly to annex their territory up to the empire's ancient frontier on the Danube. By 811 the necessary money for a major campaign had been collected by means of the financial measures taken since 807. The rear of such an expedition was protected by the new themes in the Balkans. The tagmata had been strengthened by the new unit of the Hicanati, which a year's training had now readied for service. The campaign of 809, abortive though it had been, had intimidated Krum and his men enough to keep them from attacking Byzantine territory during the period of colonization, and presumably to keep them on the defensive when a new force invaded. No trouble from the Franks or the Arabs seemed in prospect.[225]

As it happened, however, the Arabs did cause trouble. Though they had made only minor raids in 809 and 810, the new caliph, al-Amīn—who was still negotiating with his brother al-Ma'mūn in an effort to avoid open warfare—had shown some interest in the frontier region. He had ordered the fortification and garrisoning of the city of Adana in Cilicia, turning it into another important Arab base. Even after the civil war began in earnest in October 810, the Arabs stationed on the frontier were strong enough to launch raids of some size. In early 811 they sent a raiding party into the Armeniac theme, though the Arabs had generally been reluctant to raid in winter because of the cold. By this unexpected maneuver they surprised the strategus of the Armeniacs, Leo the Armenian.

Since Leo had deserted the rebellion of Bardanes Turcus in 803, he had served with distinction against the Arabs as chief turmarch of the Anatolics and consequently had been rewarded with the command of the Armeniacs. But, as the Armeniac theme had been free of invaders for several years, he seems to have grown lax. Because it was the beginning of Lent, Leo was at Euchaïta, evidently the theme's headquarters, preparing to send out the annual payroll to his soldiers. On February 22, without warning, the Arab raiders swept down upon the town and took it without resistance. While Leo himself escaped, most of the garrison was killed, and the Arabs sacked Euchaïta and carried off the entire payroll of 93,600 nomismata. Nicephorus cashiered Leo and had him flogged, shorn, and exiled for his negligence. The sack of Euchaïta seems to have been so devastating that the emperor transferred the theme's headquarters to Amasia.[226]

Reasonably enough, however, the emperor did not allow this reverse in the East to interrupt his preparations for the Bulgarian expedition. These preparations included some domestic measures that he did not want to postpone. For one thing, he brought Theodore of Studius, his uncle Plato, and the other exiled Studites back to Constantinople. While ostensibly Nicephorus was showing clemency because Plato was seriously ill, he demonstrated a desire for reconciliation by including the others and proposing to restore all of them to the Monastery of Studius after his campaign. Now that they had been punished by two years of exile, Nicephorus seems not to have demanded any concessions from the Studites.[227]

The recall of the Studites appears to have been part of a general effort by Nicephorus to reconcile religious dissidents before he left for Bulgaria. At this time he was especially criticized for tolerating in Asia Minor the different heresies of the Paulicians, who believed in rival good and evil gods, and of the Athingans, who followed certain Jewish practices. In 811 he also allowed an iconoclast hermit named Nicholas to preach in the sparsely populated district just inside the walls of the capital. Naturally the clergy of Constantinople and others who were strict in their Orthodoxy denounced Nicephorus's tolerance. Some grumbled that the emperor must himself be some sort of Paulician, Athingan, or iconoclast, despite his thoroughly Orthodox religious practices and choice of associates.[228]

Also before leaving on his campaign, Nicephorus introduced still more financial measures. Allegedly he ordered his general logothete, Nicetas the Patrician, to increase the taxes of the churches and monasteries and to collect back taxes from the households of his military commanders beginning with the first year of his reign. According to our hostile source, these orders caused general lamentation. When one of the emperor's closest advisers, the patrician Theodosius Salibaras, told him that everyone was crying out against the government, Nicephorus replied, "If God has hardened my heart like Pharaoh's, what good will there be for those under my rule?"

Our informant claims to have heard these words repeated by Theodosius himself, who at the time of writing was safely dead. Unless Nicephorus was being ironic, however, the quotation is quite incredible, and the financial measures and the protest look as if they have been distorted in the telling. While Nicephorus may well have ordered even stricter collection of taxes from certain churches and monasteries, and of back taxes long overdue from certain military officers, he is not likely to have offended any important part of the army just before his greatest campaign. In fact, doubtless because he remembered the mutiny of 809, Nicephorus was particularly careful to treat his army well on this expedition, and the soldiers' morale seems to have been high.[229]

The force Nicephorus assembled was probably the largest the empire had put into the field in living memory. He not only took all the mobile troops of the tagmata, including the Hicanati, but called up the available troops from the themes of Asia Minor and the theme of Thrace. Of these corps' total strength of 71,000 men, the majority evidently went on the expedition. Besides the regular troops, Nicephorus took along a few ordinary subjects of modest means, who brought their own provisions and armed themselves with clubs and slingshots. These seem to have been not conscripts but volunteers, quite possibly drawn from the poor who had benefited by Nicephorus's reforms and were grateful to him. The emperor did not, however, call up the soldiers of the recently established or reorganized themes of the Balkans, or of the recently decimated theme of Macedonia. Since these troops must still have been establishing themselves on newly assigned military lands (as the Hicanati did not need to do), Nicephorus was content to leave them behind to secure his rear.

Besides the officers of the themes and tagmata that were taking part in the campaign, Nicephorus brought along a glittering array of high-ranking courtiers. Among them were his son the junior emperor Stauracius, his son-in-law the curopalates Michael Rhangabe, the magister Theoctistus, and the prefect of Constantinople, whose name is unknown. His adviser Theodosius Salibaras, his old supporter Sisinnius Triphyllius, and even Irene's old adviser Aëtius were there; besides these patricians there were many men with the lesser titles of protospatharius and spatharius. The collection of dignitaries was so complete that the emperor might reasonably be suspected of wanting to assure that none of them plotted against him in his absence, as well as of wanting them present to witness his triumph.[230]

The expedition left Constantinople in May, but it did not invade Bulgaria immediately. Instead Nicephorus encamped at Marcellae, on the frontier, for long enough to let the Bulgars become thoroughly alarmed at the size of the army they faced. The khan Krum, appropriately impressed, sued for peace, but Nicephorus refused whatever terms he offered. To confuse and panic the Bulgars further, Nicephorus apparently made some

27. Stauracius (r. 811). Mutinensis graecus 122, fol. 152ᵛ. The original of this portrait was evidently executed at Stauracius's accession in 811, when he had grown a rudimentary beard. No surviving coins are known to date from his brief reign. (Photo: Biblioteca Estense, Modena)

feints in various directions across the mountainous frontier. Then, on July 11, he struck quickly into Bulgar territory with his entire force and headed for Krum's capital of Pliska, which had been repaired after its sack in 809. By his long delay and feints, he had managed to achieve complete surprise, though Krum's knowledge of the location, strength, and general intentions of the Byzantine army had been confirmed by a household servant of the emperor's who had deserted to the Bulgars.[231]

Arriving at Pliska without warning, Nicephorus put the population to flight and stormed Krum's wooden palace, killing the entire garrison of some 12,000 Bulgars. Krum sent a relief force of perhaps 15,000, which apparently arrived the next day, too late to help the garrison, and the Byzantines virtually annihilated this force as well. Byzantine casualties were few. On July 14, just three days after invading Bulgaria, Nicephorus was able to write back to Constantinople announcing his victories, which he attributed to the advice of his son Stauracius.

When he had taken Pliska earlier, Nicephorus seems not to have found Krum's treasury. This time he made a thorough search and discovered it. Not repeating his mistake of 809 when he had delayed paying the soldiers, he set about distributing the booty at once, and he assigned all the troops shares of the khan's stocks of metal, clothing, and other valuables by referring to the muster rolls of the army. Naturally, he retained for the state treasury the most valuable articles, presumably gold and silver, which he kept in sealed chests. He allowed the exultant soldiers to drink their fill from the khan's wine cellars at a victory banquet, but he ordered the ears and other members of unauthorized looters to be cut off, and did not relax discipline unduly. In a triumphal mood, the emperor strolled about the open passages and terraced buildings within the palace enclosure and thought aloud about building a city named for himself on the site.[232]

Although he believed that he had destroyed most of the Bulgar army, Nicephorus did not imagine that the conquest of Bulgaria was complete as yet. After letting his troops enjoy themselves in Pliska for several days, he ordered the town and palace burned—not a difficult task since they were entirely made of wood—and turned to devastating the countryside. The soldiers destroyed the Bulgars' crops and slaughtered and hamstrung their livestock. Utterly demoralized, Krum sent Nicephorus the message, "Behold, you have conquered. Take whatever you like, and depart in peace." Since, however, it was the Bulgars whom Nicephorus wanted to depart from what he considered Byzantine territory, he took no notice. His plan was to march west across Bulgaria, systematically pillaging the land as he went, until he arrived at Serdica.[233]

In the meantime, Krum had been frantically reinforcing his remaining Bulgars by arming their women and hiring Avars and Slavs as mercenaries. Since this army seems still to have been too weak to face the Byzantines in open battle, the khan resorted to a stratagem, carefully following Nicephorus's movements and relying on the Bulgars' greater familiarity with the country. As the Byzantines made their leisurely way through the foothills of the Balkan range not far from Pliska, they entered one of the valleys of the several small rivers that have their sources in the mountains, perhaps the Tiča. On Thursday, July 24, however, the Byzantine commanders discovered that the Bulgars had hurriedly thrown up and manned log palisades at either end of the valley. With the mountains barring the other two sides, the Byzantines were trapped.

Some of Nicephorus's officers seem to have favored assaulting one of the palisades at once, but the emperor did not agree. In this he may have been right, because the Byzantines' superior numbers would have been of little use in a direct attack on a well-defended position in a narrow pass, whereas they would be more useful if the Bulgars offered open battle or the Byzantines somehow managed to take them by surprise. The officers who disagreed persuaded Stauracius to go to his father's tent to argue for an assault, but Nicephorus held fast to his opinion and grew angry when his son pressed the case for action. The emperor is said to have declared, perhaps predicting the result of attacking the barriers, "Even if we became winged, no one could hope to escape destruction."

The officers seem to have succeeded in preventing panic among the soldiers for the time being by keeping the truth from them. Most of the troops continued recklessly devastating the valley, though a few men who knew, probably officers, deserted and escaped. For two days the Byzantine army remained encamped while the emperor grimly awaited developments. On the night of Friday, July 25, the Bulgars began to shout and clash their weapons around the Byzantine camps, and fear spread as the men began to realize their danger. Before dawn on Saturday morning, the Bulgars attacked.[234]

The first attack, obviously well-planned, fell upon the emperor's camp, which consisted of the tents of the imperial party, the imperial bodyguard, and the tagmata. Though some were just waking up, the scouts seem to have given enough notice for the tagmata to arm hastily before the Bulgars were actually upon them. The themes, whose separate camps were pitched at a distance, did not immediately discover what had happened. During a brief and disorganized resistance, many fell, including the emperor himself and probably his bodyguard. The rest of the tagmata and the imperial party abandoned their camp, took to their horses, and fled. When the themes saw the emperor's camp overrun, they joined the flight as well.

But flight was not so easy. The Bulgars pursued the Byzantines as far as the river, which ran through a marsh. As the Byzantine cavalry tried to ride across, those in front sank into the marshy banks and riverbed, while those immediately behind them tumbled in on top. After many had been trampled and drowned, the marsh and river actually filled with bodies, and the rest of the fugitives and the pursuing Bulgars were able to pass over them. Then, when the surviving Byzantines thought that their escape was finally open, they came to the Bulgars' palisade.

Though the Bulgars had evidently had too few troops to keep it manned, the barrier was sound and high. Some Byzantines, after a vain attempt to make a breach in the logs, dismounted and clambered over the palisade, only to fall into a deep ditch on the other side and break their bones. Other fugitives then set fire to parts of the palisade, and when sections of it began to collapse across the ditch, the Byzantines rode onto them as if over a bridge. But, weakened by the fire, the ropes that tied the logs together gave way and plunged the riders into the ditch beneath. Many were crushed or burned. Only after parts of the ditch had finally filled with wood and corpses could the desperate survivors safely escape to the south.[235]

The casualties were certainly immense. The imperial retinue and the tagmata, who were attacked first and in the rout arrived first at the river and the palisade, appear to have suffered more than the themes. Besides the emperor, the dead included his friends Theodosius Salibaras and Sisinnius Triphyllius, the once-powerful eunuch Aëtius, the prefect of Constantinople, and many other bodyguards and dignitaries. Two of the four commanders of the tagmata were killed, the domestic of the Excubitors and the drungary of the Watch; so were many of the junior officers and ordinary soldiers of the tagmata. The young notables attached to the Hicanati were particularly hard hit, and the acting commander of the Hicanati, Peter the Patrician, was captured by the Bulgars with a large number of other officers and men. The junior emperor, Stauracius, suffered a terrible wound just to the right of his lower spine, though he was brought out alive. By contrast, among the six commanders of themes the strategus of the Anatolics Romanus and the strategus of Thrace died, but the other four seem to have escaped. Nonetheless, many officers and soldiers of the themes were among the fallen.

No one accused the emperor Nicephorus of fleeing, though his enemies said that after he went down in the first encounter with the Bulgars some Byzantines struck him as well. Krum cut the emperor's head from his body and for days hung it on a piece of wood to exhibit to his own people and the Byzantine captives. Then he had the skull stripped of flesh and lined with silver to make a cup, which he used to drink the health of the Slavic chieftains allied with him.[236]

THE REIGN OF STAURACIUS

Nicephorus's defeat and death at the hands of the Bulgars came as a devastating shock to the Byzantines. The magnitude of the defeat, great as it was, was not the main reason for its impact. As a matter of fact, in his victories before his downfall Nicephorus had so battered the Bulgars that they were unable to undertake serious warfare for almost a year, while the Byzantines made up their losses in about the same time. It is not at all clear that the Byzantines lost more men during the campaign than the Bulgars, some 27,000 of whom seem to have died in the two battles at Pliska. Proportionately the Bulgars had almost certainly suffered heavier casualties.

Still, Nicephorus was the first emperor to die in battle with a foreign power since 378, when the Arian heretic Valens died fighting the Visigoths at the battle of Adrianople. Besides, the catastrophic reversal of the Byzantines' fortunes, from an easy triumph to a disgraceful rout under horrific circumstances, thoroughly unnerved the army. After the commander of the Hicanati, Peter the Patrician, and fifty other officers managed to escape from their Bulgar captors, Peter was so disillusioned with the world that he deserted, abandoned his wife and son, and secretly joined Joannicius as a hermit on Mount Olympus in the Opsician theme, letting others believe he was dead. Hagiography records the case of a thematic soldier named Nicholas who escaped in the rout and, similarly affected, also deserted and entered a monastery. A defeat so sudden and complete seemed to most Byzantines an obvious case of divine punishment. Most of the opprobrium that was speedily heaped upon Nicephorus's memory must have been a result of this impression.[237]

Within three days the main body of survivors had gathered at Adrianople. Besides the wounded Stauracius, the survivors of highest rank were Nicephorus's son-in-law Michael Rhangabe and the magister Theoctistus. The senior military officer was Stephen, domestic of the Schools, the only commander of a tagma to survive without being captured. On these and a few other officials the succession depended. By law, Stauracius ought to have been proclaimed, but his injury was so serious that he was in no condition to rule and his recovery was in considerable doubt. Some officials who were friendly to Michael Rhangabe pressed him to let himself be proclaimed emperor, and Theoctistus supported them. But Michael refused out of respect for his oath of loyalty to Nicephorus and Stauracius, and Stephen, the man who could command most authority among the troops, spoke in favor of proclaiming Stauracius on the ground that he might well recover.

Realizing that disunity at such a time would be dangerous, Theoctistus agreed to join Stephen in proclaiming Stauracius, and it was done. Weak as he was, Stauracius roused himself to address the troops. In his speech he was critical of his father, not surprisingly after the disaster that had just occurred and after Nicephorus had rejected Stauracius's advice to break out of the valley at all costs. The soldiers enthusiastically applauded the address and acclaimed him, apparently on July 28.[238]

As he was carried back to Constantinople by litter, the new emperor found that he was paralyzed from the thighs down, and was losing quantities of blood in his urine. Though he did what he could to assert his authority, when his condition became known those about him became increasingly convinced that he would die and behaved accordingly. The patriarch Nicephorus strongly pressed him to appease God by restoring the excessive sums collected by his father, naturally including those taken from the Church. Stauracius, however, firmly told the patriarch that he could return no more than 300 pounds of gold (21,600 nomismata), and even that amount he did not give back immediately.

Since the emperor had no children, the succession was an urgent issue. His sister Procopia wanted her husband Michael Rhangabe to succeed, but Stauracius's wife Theophano had ambitions to rule alone after her husband's death, like her relative Irene. Stauracius tried to put off his decision, probably because he feared that as soon as he made it his chosen successor would push him aside. But his health continued to decline, and the people of Constantinople became so restless in their uncertainty that he feared rioting. A rumor circulated that the wounded emperor was being poisoned by his sister Procopia. Perhaps Stauracius believed it himself; perhaps it was even true. By the end of September, he decided that he should be succeeded by his wife, Theophano, as she wished.[239]

Though the empire's chief officials had their differences, they were united in wanting to prevent the succession of Theophano and another period of insecure rule by a childless woman. Michael Rhangabe was the obvious candidate to put up against her. Therefore the patriarch Nicephorus, the domestic of the Schools Stephen, the magister Theoctistus, and Michael came to an agreement that Michael should be proclaimed. Stauracius quickly forced the issue. Probably because he suspected that Michael was plotting against him, on the evening of October 1 he summoned Stephen the Domestic, whom he still believed to be faithful, and asked him how Michael might be brought from his house and blinded. Stephen advised that it could not be done that night because the Palace of the Mangana, where Michael was living, was too well guarded and defensibly located. Stauracius accepted Stephen's advice and asked him not to reveal their conversation to anyone. Though Stephen told him not to worry, the domestic immediately set about organizing a coup. That very night he ordered the surviving troops of the tagmata to gather in the covered racetrack of the palace and summoned Michael and the ranking civil servants.

At dawn on October 2 the tagmata and the officials duly acclaimed Michael Rhangabe emperor. On his sickbed Stauracius heard and understood the shouts of acclamation, and realized that resistance was pointless. Intending at least to avoid mutilation, he summoned his relative Symeon the Monk at once and accepted tonsure and the monastic habit from him. In the meantime, the patriarch Nicephorus had recognized Michael's acclamation after demanding and receiving his written pledge to uphold Orthodoxy, not to shed Christian blood, and not to introduce any legislation concerning the clergy. Stauracius, who suspected quite rightly that Nicephorus had been part of the plot, sent a strong protest to the patriarch. Nicephorus promptly came to the palace, accompanied by the new emperor and his wife, and counseled Stauracius not to feel distress, because they had acted in despair of his life, not out of treachery. The deposed emperor was not impressed. "You will not find him a better friend," he bitterly told the patriarch. Stauracius was to live on another three miserable months as a monk before he died on January 11, 812, of a gruesome putrefaction in his wound.[240]

THE REIGN OF MICHAEL I

At ten o'clock on the same morning that Stauracius was deposed, the patriarch Nicephorus crowned Michael Rhangabe in St. Sophia to popular rejoicing. The new emperor, who was in his late thirties, looked young, healthy, and handsome, with a round face, a dark complexion, curly black hair, and a beautifully groomed black beard. His family was distinguished, though its name may well be Slavic; and, with Stauracius obviously in no condition to rule, Michael had the best dynastic claim to the throne. He had had some experience in government but not enough to tie him to Nicephorus's unpopular or unsuccessful measures. Mild-mannered, pious, generous, and honest, he had no real enemies. The Church, the bureaucracy, the army, and the people supported him. He lacked only the judgment and decisiveness needed to make even a minimally competent emperor.[241]

Michael's first, and almost only, idea as emperor was to reverse all the unpopular policies of his father-in-law, Nicephorus. He began with Nicephorus's policy of saving money, which had left the treasury comfortably full. After his coronation, he gave the patriarch a princely gift of 3,600 nomismata, and half that sum to the other clergy of St. Sophia. He then compensated all those whom he thought his predecessor had unjustly taxed, and paid a donative to the civil servants of the capital and to the army. On Sunday, October 12, he crowned his wife Procopia Augusta as a sign of the respect and favor he always showed her, and gave even more gifts to the bureaucracy. Apparently on the same occasion, he appropriated 36,000 nomismata for the widows of the soldiers killed in Nicephorus's campaign against the Bulgars. Showing no ill feeling toward the woman who had wanted to exclude him from the succession, he gave large gifts to Stauracius's wife, Theophano. Since she had now become a nun, Michael bestowed on her a splendid palace to convert into a nunnery, where she buried Stauracius when he died. In the words of a contemporary, Michael "enriched all the patricians and officials, the bishops, priests, and monks, the soldiers and the poor, both those in the capital and in the themes, so that in a few days the excessive hoard of Nicephorus, because of which he had met a bad end, was dissipated." Yet ample funds still remained.[242]

At the same time, Michael recalled all those whom Nicephorus had exiled, for whatever reason. Among them was Leo the Armenian, recently

28. Michael I (r. 811–13). Mutinensis graecus 122, fol. 153ʳ. (Photo: Biblioteca Estense, Modena)

dismissed as strategus of the Armeniacs by Nicephorus. Michael now promoted Leo to strategus of the Anatolics, the highest-ranking military command, replacing Romanus, a casualty of the Bulgarian campaign. Not surprisingly, Michael also restored Theodore of Studius, Plato, and the other Studites to their monastery, and reinstated Theodore's brother Joseph as archbishop of Thessalonica. As he wanted to have the entire Church at peace, Michael instructed the patriarch Nicephorus to do something about Joseph of Cathara and about the synod of 809, which had officially condemned the Studites. The patriarch decided to extricate himself from his muddle by deferring to the authority of the pope; but first, Michael had to finish making peace with Charlemagne.[243]

Since the only way to make a final peace with Charlemagne was to recognize him as an emperor, Michael, who, by temperament liked to give people whatever they wanted, was willing to concede the title. By tactfully avoiding the Byzantine title "Emperor of the Romans," Charlemagne had made the concession reasonably easy; after all, the Byzantines had used to recognize the Sassanid shah of Persia as emperor of the Persians without feeling themselves compromised. Michael doubtless learned from the ambassadors whom Charlemagne had recently sent that recognizing him as emperor of the Franks was enough.

So Michael agreed, and sent back the ambassadors to Aachen with an embassy of his own, which was afterward to visit Pope Leo at Rome on behalf of the patriarch. The patriarch wrote a respectful letter to Pope Leo, submitting a statement of his Orthodox beliefs and explaining that he had been unable to write earlier because the emperor Nicephorus, angered by Leo's coronation of Charlemagne, had not allowed it. The Byzantine embassy was led by Bishop Michael of Synnada, already a veteran of embassies to both Franks and Arabs, and Arsaphius, Nicephorus's earlier ambassador to Charlemagne, who was now promoted to protospatharius for his services. They were supposed to reach a complete reconciliation with Charlemagne and the pope. If possible, they were to secure the betrothal of a Frankish princess to Michael's son Theophylact, who was then eighteen, and to obtain the advice of the pope on the controversy over the Studites and Joseph of Cathara. The ambassadors left in November, or thereabouts.[244]

At Christmas of 811, when Michael crowned his son Theophylact in St. Sophia, the emperor was as usual in a generous mood. He endowed the church with golden vessels inlaid with gems and magnificent antique hangings with iconic embroideries; these made a great impression. There were more gifts of money for the patriarch and clergy, this time totaling 9,000 nomismata, and apparently also for the people, who enjoyed the celebration very much. Though some thought that the empress Procopia took too prominent a part in the ceremony and in running the empire generally, everyone applauded the emperor's munificence. Nobody seems to have reflected that only Nicephorus's parsimony had made it possible.[245]

As the emperor appeared willing to do anything the clergy desired, the patriarch, who had been galled by the emperor Nicephorus's toleration of the heretical Athingans and Paulicians of Asia Minor, now sent a detailed report on them to Michael. The patriarch outlined the heretics' beliefs and urged that both groups be punished by death. Since Nicephorus considered the Athingans to be Jews and the Paulicians to be Manichaeans, he saw no contradiction between this advice and the pledge he had obtained from Michael not to shed Christian blood. In January of 812, Michael cheerfully took the advice and issued orders to the ecclesiastical and civil officials of Asia Minor to have Paulicians and Athingans executed. The executions began.

29. A nomisma of Michael I and his son Theophylact, shown three times actual size. (Photos: Dumbarton Oaks Byzantine Collection, Washington)

Though the emperor probably expected all the clergy to applaud his action, he quickly received a protest from none other than Theodore of Studius. A man of principle in every respect, Theodore was shocked at the idea of church courts' sentencing anyone to death, and insisted that heretics must be allowed to live to give them the chance to repent. When Michael found that Theodore disapproved, he hastened to adopt the famous abbot's opinion, and even the patriarch Nicephorus had to agree to it. The emperor therefore issued a new edict merely prohibiting Athingans and Paulicians from practicing their faiths publicly.[246]

So far Michael had almost been able to pretend that the rout in Bulgaria had not happened. Nicephorus's new themes in the Balkans were unaffected by it, because their troops had not taken part in the campaign and the fighting had been far from their borders. In the other themes and the tagmata, according to the usual system of recruitment, sons and other relatives of the dead soldiers came forward to take most of the vacant places, and Michael found others to enroll in the rest. The army therefore suffered no official decline in numbers from Nicephorus's expanded total of 90,000 men, though of course it took some time to enroll all the replacements and to train them properly. The greatest danger was in the themes of Macedonia and Thrace, which adjoined the territory of the newly confident Bulgars. Both themes' armies were still recovering from severe losses to the Bulgars—in Macedonia since 809, when some of its land had also been devastated, and in Thrace since 811. The themes' civilians, many of whom were recent settlers, seem to have been very nervous at the prospect of attacks by the victorious khan Krum. In the spring of 812 Krum besieged Develtus, one of the frontier towns in Thrace. If Develtus fell, the entire frontier region would be in jeopardy.[247]

Roused to action, Michael prepared an expedition against the Bulgars consisting of the tagmata and contingents from the themes of Asia Minor. On June 7 he set out for the frontier. But popular though Michael may have been with most people, he lacked the confidence of his troops. He had taken the Augusta Procopia along for the first stage of the march, reinforcing the rumors that he was subservient to his wife, and his advisers, who included the Studite monks, appear to have known little about warfare. When the news came on the way that the people of Develtus and their bishop had surrendered to Krum and accepted resettlement in Bulgaria, the troops became exasperated with their apparently incompetent leader, refusing to continue their march and shouting insults at Michael. The emperor had to buy off the rioters by giving another donative and canceling the expedition.

Naturally, the news that the troops had mutinied and would not fight encouraged the Bulgars and terrified the Byzantines who lived along the frontier. Without waiting for the Bulgars to arrive, the inhabitants of large stretches of the themes of Thrace and Macedonia, especially the recent colonists, abandoned their homes and fled south. Those whom Irene had settled nearest the frontier at Anchialus, Beroea-Irenopolis, and Philippopolis apparently began the flight. They in turn panicked the people of older settlements farther inland, like Nicaea in Thrace and Probatum, who also deserted their towns. These flights exposed Nicephorus's more recent settlers on the Strymon, evidently including the citizens of Serres, who gladly seized upon this excuse to depart for their former homes in other parts of the empire. As they fled to the southeast, the people of Philippi, which had probably also been resettled by Irene, joined them.

Except for the isolated port of Mesembria on the Black Sea, the whole frontier with Bulgaria thus gave way. Along with all the gains made in Thrace under Irene and Nicephorus, some territory that had been in Byzantine hands before them was deserted as well. The Bulgars began to move into the empty territory without opposition. Now the main inhabited areas of the themes of Macedonia and Thrace, including the region's chief city of Adrianople, were open to Bulgar attack. For the time being, however, the Bulgars stayed out of the area to the south where the population had remained, doubtless joined by most of the refugees from the north.[248]

In Constantinople the news of the army's mutiny and the flight of the inhabitants on the frontier, which was not very far away, made a strong impression. Michael's expensively purchased popularity quickly sank. Some blamed not just Michael's incapacity but his religious views, which did not seem to be winning divine favor. Though a few criticized Michael's recent edict against the Athingans and Paulicians, most found the conclusion that those heretics were correct an uncomfortable one. Others, especially in the tagmata, chose to believe that Michael's iconophilism was at fault. They remembered that the iconoclast Constantine V had repeatedly defeated the Bulgars, and they had now seen the iconophiles Nicephorus and Michael helpless before the same enemy; to iconoclasts, at least, the inference was obvious. One of the hermits who followed the iconoclast preacher Nicholas publicly scraped the paint off an icon of the Virgin. A hastily formed group of conspirators, apparently soldiers, planned to go by night to the island of Panormos near the capital to release the blinded sons of Constantine V, who were imprisoned there. They were to be brought to the mutinous army so that it could proclaim one of them emperor.

Michael's government, however, which understood conspiracy somewhat better than war, learned of the plot and apprehended the plotters. The emperor gave a speech in defense of the icons to the army and transferred the sons of Constantine V to the island of Aphusia, toward the western end of the Sea of Marmara and out of reach of Constantinople. He had the most disaffected soldiers whipped; he seems then to have discharged them from the tagmata and left them to live by begging in the capital. Most of the tagmatic soldiers do not appear to have been ready for a return to Iconoclasm, or at any rate were not ready to be whipped and discharged for defending a failed conspiracy on behalf of some blind nonentities. Michael ordered the tongue of the hermit who had defaced the icon of the Virgin to be cut out, and confined his leader, Nicholas, to a monastery. A report circulated that Nicholas had now repented of his iconoclastic beliefs. In another move against religious dissenters, Michael ordered Leo the Armenian, strategus of the Anatolics, to confiscate the property of the Athingans, whose base was in Leo's theme, and to transport them to other places. After one more address by the emperor to the tagmata, this time at the palace, the immediate danger of rebellion was over.[249]

Thus Michael was still on his throne when his embassy returned from Aachen and Rome in the summer of 812. Michael of Synnada and the other ambassadors had won a warm welcome at Aachen by greeting Charlemagne as emperor in both Latin and Greek. The peace was ratified, including the recognition of Byzantine rights in Venetia and Dalmatia; but the Frankish emperor, who may have drawn a lesson from the failure of earlier projects for marriage between Franks and Byzantines, was not quick to promise a Frankish princess for young Theophylact. Pope Leo had also received the ambassadors graciously, and was glad to send a letter passing judgment on the question of Joseph of Cathara and the Studites. As everyone had expected, the pope decided for the Studites and against Joseph. Following the earlier decree of St. Tarasius, the patriarch deposed Joseph again. Now the whole unpleasant affair was closed, to the relief of nearly all but the hapless Joseph.[250]

After so easily making peace with the Franks and peace in the Church, the emperor received news of a victory against the Arabs. In August the Arabs on the frontier had mounted a raid of moderate size on the Anatolic theme. The strategus Leo the Armenian, now more alert than he had been as strategus of the Armeniacs a year and a half before, learned of the raid in time to lead his troops against the raiders. Putting them to flight, he killed some two thousand and captured many of their horses and arms. Since the defeat of Arab raiders was a very rare event, this exploit must have restored Leo's tarnished reputation and even done something for Michael's. At approximately this time the Arab civil war gave the Byzantines an opportunity to destroy Camachum, the border fort betrayed by rebels in 793, which now seems to have been left deserted and in ruins.[251]

MICHAEL'S FALL

Meanwhile, the Bulgars had apparently completed their occupation of the border areas in Thrace settled since 780 by the Byzantines but recently abandoned. Krum, who was satisfied with defeating Nicephorus's invasion and rolling back the Byzantine border, sent an embassy to Michael under Dragomir, one of his Slavic lieutenants. Dragomir presented a written offer from Krum to revive an old peace treaty of the first half of the eighth century between the Bulgars and Byzantines. This had provided, first, that the Byzantine frontier in Thrace would be where it had been before Irene, a provision that seems to have required no further Byzantine withdrawal and may even have meant that the Bulgars would return some of the land that they had just occupied. Second, every year the Byzantines would give the Bulgars clothes and dyed skins worth the very modest sum of 2,160 nomismata, a gift objectionable only because it could be considered a kind of tribute. Third, traders were to be allowed to cross the frontier freely as long as they complied with Byzantine customs regulations, though if they did not their goods could be confiscated. Fourth, each power was to extradite any subjects of the other, even if they were wanted for treason at home. Apparently Krum was offering to return some prisoners taken in 811. Krum concluded his letter by threatening that if the Byzantines did not agree to his terms he would attack

30. Mesembria, showing the narrow isthmus that is the only entrance to the town by land. (Photo: Courtauld Institute, London)

Mesembria, the last frontier point that had not fallen. It was a port and customs station on the Black Sea that had been cut off by land since the fall of Anchialus and Develtus.

Michael submitted Krum's proposal to his advisers, who consisted of his principal civil servants, headed by the magister Theoctistus, and the leading clergy, headed by the patriarch Nicephorus and Theodore of Studius. Almost all opposed the peace. The main substantive objection they raised was against the requirement that the Byzantines hand over Bulgar deserters to Krum. Though there was some dispute over how many if any would be affected, most of the clergy seem to have been worried about Bulgars who had joined the Byzantines and accepted Christianity. They quoted the words of Christ, "Him that cometh to Me I will in no wise cast out" (John 6:37). The secular officials were probably more disturbed at the prospect of recognizing the losses of territory and accepting the humiliation of peace on Krum's terms, especially because the Byzantines still had many more troops than the Bulgars. The emperor deferred to his advisers' judgment and rejected Krum's offer of peace.

Krum accordingly put Mesembria under a siege, which he continued throughout the month of October. The Bulgars used siege engines designed by an expert Arab engineer who had first deserted to the Byzantines and accepted baptism, then deserted to the Bulgars when he was punished by Nicephorus. He may have been the engineer named Eumathius who fled to Krum in 809 after Nicephorus refused to grant him immunity from punishment. Since Mesembria was obviously hard pressed, on November 1 the emperor again called his advisers together in the hope that they would let him make peace. By now the patriarch and some other bishops had changed their minds, but Theodore of Studius, joined by Theoctistus and the other civil officials, still refused to accept Krum's terms.

Four days later, after the appearance of a comet that many took to be a harbinger of disaster, the news reached Constantinople that the Bulgars had taken, looted, and destroyed Mesembria. They had found it well stocked with household goods, silver, and gold, and had also captured some Greek fire, the incendiary substance that was the Byzantines' secret naval weapon. They had already found some of the siphons used for shooting the fire when they had taken Develtus the previous spring. At about this time Krum seems to have executed all the Byzantines taken captive in 811 who refused to renounce Christianity, though the details of their fate never became known at Byzantium. The opportunity for peace had passed.[252]

Since the campaigning season of 812 had also passed, Michael had time to prepare to fight the next year. Fortunately for him, the Arabs posed no problem, because the forces of Ma'mūn were besieging Amīn in Baghdad, while Syria was divided among warring factions supporting the two claimants to the caliphate. Michael did what he could to help the Christian war refugees from Syria who managed to reach Cyprus, welcoming some of them to Constantinople and giving their monks a monastery there, and appropriating 7,200 nomismata for the relief of the rest. With no idea of intervening in Syria himself, however, he had scarcely any need for troops in Asia Minor, and could transfer most of its thematic armies to Thrace to fight Krum in the spring.[253]

In early February of 813, two Christian refugees from Bulgaria, probably Byzantines captured by Krum, brought a report that Krum was planning a surprise attack on the troops that the Byzantines had assembled near Adrianople. Acting quickly, Michael led out the tagmata on February 15 and took Krum by surprise in his turn, killing some Bulgars and driving Krum's force from Adrianople. Though it was not a major victory, it was Michael's first in his own right and he savored it. He was back in Constantinople for the feast of St. Tarasius on February 25, which he and his wife, Procopia, celebrated along with his success by having the late patriarch's tomb plated with 95 pounds of silver. With a new enthusiasm for warfare, Michael began to gather all available soldiers for a decisive blow at the Bulgars. He called up large contingents from all the themes, including recent recruits and some that usually stayed behind to guard the frontier with the Arabs, and ordered them to arrive in Thrace by the beginning of spring.

This army was probably too big, and assembled too early. The Anatolian troops grumbled against Michael, especially those from the frontier areas of the Armeniac and Anatolic themes, who were unaccustomed to long service so far away from their homes. Since the Byzantines easily outnumbered the Bulgars, these soldiers from the Arab frontier were hardly needed; and since Michael did not even begin operations until May, the soldiers would have been better occupied supervising the spring planting on their land grants than idly sitting in Thrace for over a month, exhausting their provisions. At the beginning of May, Michael set out for Thrace with the tagmata, stupidly taking his wife, Procopia, along for the first stage of the march as he had done a year before. A solar eclipse on May 4 demoralized many of the troops, who took it as a bad sign. Though Michael tried to buy favor by distributing donatives to the troops and gifts to the officers, Procopia did not help Michael's reputation by giving a parting speech urging the soldiers to keep her husband safe in battle. The troops took the money but ridiculed the emperor.

Relying on his advisers from the clergy and civil service, who had little military experience, Michael advanced no farther than the region of Adrianople, well short of the old border. He encamped at Versinicia and waited for the Bulgars to attack him. As the Byzantines had already nearly exhausted their supplies, they were reduced to pillaging the Thracian countryside. On June 7 Krum appeared with his army opposite the Byzantine camp, but when he saw that the Byzantines substantially outnumbered his force he too encamped and waited. Leo the Armenian, strategus of the Anatolics, and John Aplaces, strategus of Macedonia, both wanted to attack the Bulgars, but Michael would not allow it. The two armies remained facing each other.[254]

Michael's dithering offered an opportunity to those who might want to overthrow him. The Anatolics, who were particularly discontented with the emperor and had a possible candidate for the throne in their vigorous commander Leo, seem to have begun plotting treachery at this time; Leo may even have come to an agreement with Krum to discredit Michael by assuring his defeat. Back in Constantinople, the emperor's latest demonstration of indecision and incompetence encouraged the growing group who favored Iconoclasm. This group included those whom Michael had discharged from the tagmata the year before for agitating against him and plotting on behalf of the blinded sons of Constantine V.

While Michael stayed encamped opposite the Bulgars in June, some of the discharged soldiers in the capital staged a rather ingenious demonstration. Before the patriarch was to lead the citizens in a litany in the Church of the Holy Apostles, the plotters secretly pried open the locked doors that led from the church to the adjoining imperial mausoleum. They arranged these doors in such a way that an inconspicuous blow could open them. When the service began, the congregation saw the doors fly open with a crash as if propelled by a miraculous force. The plotters immediately rushed into the mausoleum, threw themselves upon the tomb of Constantine V, and shouted to their dead hero, "Arise, and help the state that is perishing!" As others entered, the plotters claimed that they had seen Constantine appear on horseback and ride off against the Bulgars. Clever though it sounds, this plan does not appear to have worked very well in practice, and the city prefect arrested its perpetrators at once and forced them to admit what they had done. They were paraded about the streets, repeatedly proclaiming their fraud to remove any doubts in the minds of the credulous.[255]

After the Byzantine and Bulgar armies had kept their positions for fifteen days in the increasing heat and the Byzantines had run short of both food and water, Michael's generals forced the issue. Protesting that the Byzantine force was ten times as large as the Bulgars', John Aplaces demanded a battle. He proposed to begin combat with the wing under his command, composed of the themes of Thrace and Macedonia. He exhorted Michael, who apparently commanded the tagmata in the center, to follow. Leo the Armenian, commanding the Anatolics and other Asian themes on the other wing, assured the emperor that he would press home the victory. Michael had to agree. Though by now he may well have suspected that Leo was disloyal, the only reasonable choices left him were to attack quickly or to retreat in dishonor. The Byzantines attacked on June 22.

The imperial camp was on higher ground, from which Aplaces led his wing down for his initial charge. He engaged the Bulgars opposite him and drove them back with some loss, but Michael hesitated to join him, and Leo's wing with the Anatolics started to flee for no apparent reason. Seeing the Eastern themes in flight, Michael's forces began to flee after them, and no one reinforced Aplaces and the Western themes. By themselves, these were too few to sustain their attack and began to fall back. When they realized that they had been left alone, they too turned to flight, but by this time many were unable to escape.

Aplaces and many of his men were killed, and Michael, who seems to have hesitated even to flee, was almost left behind. The Bulgars, afraid of an ambush, did not pursue at once, but the fleeing Byzantines trampled each other, and mistook their compatriots behind them for the enemy. A number of the horses, left weak from too little water and fodder, soon fell and died, and many of the soldiers abandoned their arms and armor.

While the Bulgars followed cautiously to gather the arms and baggage and round up the stragglers, some Byzantines took refuge in nearby forts, perhaps Versinicia, Scutarium, and Probatum, only to be captured when the forts fell. Except among the troops of Macedonia and Thrace, however, the army does not seem to have suffered very large losses, and aside from Aplaces no high-ranking officers or dignitaries are reported to have died.[256]

Leo the Armenian was widely and reasonably suspected of treachery, though no absolute proof came to light. After his own poor performance, Michael was thoroughly dispirited. While he cursed his troops, he mainly blamed his defeat on his own sins and those of his father-in-law, Nicephorus. Leaving Leo in command of the army, he decamped for Constantinople, which he reached on June 24. He seems already to have been thinking of abdicating. By entrusting the army to Leo he had put himself in Leo's power anyway, and the commander of the city garrison, the count of the Walls John Hexabulius, told him as much.

The soldiers in Thrace were indignant that, as they saw it, Michael had fled home to his wife, and they were ready to acclaim Leo emperor. Though Leo protested his loyalty to Michael, probably because he wanted to conceal his treachery as much as he could, Krum's advance made such tact inopportune. Michael the Amorian, an old comrade of Leo's who had joined and deserted the revolt of Bardanes Turcus with him, became exasperated enough to threaten to kill Leo if he did not accept the troops' acclamation. Leo therefore accepted on the grounds of the extreme need of the state, and wrote to the patriarch Nicephorus to give assurances of his Orthodoxy and ask for his blessing.

Never eager for a fight, the emperor Michael now definitely wanted to abdicate to avoid bloodshed, including his family's and his own. The patriarch counseled abdication for the same reason. Reportedly Michael even sent Leo the imperial regalia in secret. Michael's wife and advisers, however, were reluctant to lose their influence, and opposed the abdication. The magister Theoctistus and the domestic of the Schools Stephen, who had joined to make Michael emperor in the first place, wanted him to remain. Procopia was particularly indignant at the idea of giving up her place to Leo's wife Barca, whom she considered unworthy of it.

Indecisive to the last, Michael put off abdicating until Leo and his troops actually arrived at the capital on July 11. Then he, Procopia, and their three sons and two daughters were tonsured and clothed as monks and nuns in the Church of Our Lady of the Pharus in the palace. Leo exiled Michael to a monastery on the nearby island of Plate. The former emperor was accompanied by his two younger sons, though Leo took the precaution of sending the eldest son, Theophylact, to another island and castrating all three of them. Leo confined the empress Procopia to a monastery that she had founded in Constantinople and dedicated to her patron, St. Procopia. On July 12 the patriarch Nicephorus crowned Leo emperor in St. Sophia.[257]

CONTRIBUTIONS OF NICEPHORUS'S REIGN

Contemporaries naturally regarded Nicephorus's reign as a failure. He had died in a catastrophic defeat, and his dynasty had lost the throne after his son and son-in-law had reigned only briefly and unsuccessfully. The same hostile contemporary who observed that Michael Rhangabe had spent all of Nicephorus's carefully accumulated gold also added that Krum had taken all of Nicephorus's carefully reclaimed territory, leaving the impression that nothing whatever remained of the haughty and parsimonious emperor's achievements. The story of Nicephorus's dynasty seemed to follow the Parable of the Rich Fool, who heaped up wealth for himself only to find that one night his soul was required of him, and others would enjoy his goods.[258]

It is true that Nicephorus's two successors accomplished little before they were deposed. One can hardly blame young Stauracius, who reigned for just four months, mortally wounded and surrounded by courtiers anticipating his death, and nonetheless showed a certain amount of spirit. With much less excuse, Michael Rhangabe scarcely ruled at all. His reign was simply a series of blundering attempts to find the most popular course and follow it. Though later Leo the Armenian undermined Michael's position, the throne he sought to occupy was then almost vacant anyway. If Michael's extravagance and military incapacity did not cripple the empire for a generation, the reason is merely that Nicephorus had left the empire too strong to be wrecked in just two years.

Nicephorus himself also did things that turned out to be mistakes. Sometimes he seems to have courted unpopularity needlessly. At least twice his soldiers' discontent took him by surprise, in the revolt of Bardanes Turcus and the mutiny at Serdica. He evidently underestimated the trouble reinstating Joseph of Cathara to the priesthood would ultimately cause with the Studites, and so mishandled the case. When he raided Cilicia and Melitene, fomented a rebellion in Cyprus, and contemplated annexations at the expense of the caliphate, he misjudged the power and determination of the Arabs, and the Byzantines soon paid for his error. Finally, of course, he led his troops into a trap in Bulgaria from which he could not extricate himself. All these mistakes, however, would have been difficult to avoid without either knowing more than Nicephorus could have known or consistently avoiding doing anything unpopular. The latter course, as Michael Rhangabe found, had its own dangers. Apart from the final disaster in Bulgaria, Nicephorus was able to recover from his miscalculations, and in other cases he handled his foreign and domestic enemies skillfully. On the whole, the enterprises in which Nicephorus failed probably seemed at the time at least as promising as those in which he succeeded.

Nicephorus's most obvious achievement, the lasting reclamation of the Greek peninsula for the empire, was no easy task. The real test of it came after Nicephorus's death, when Krum threatened the Balkans and Michael Rhangabe was not about to stop either a Slavic uprising or a return of the colonists to their original homes. Except for the settlers on the Strymon, who fled from a particularly exposed position along with less recent settlers, Nicephorus's colonists stayed where they had been put scarcely two years before. And except perhaps for the Slavs in western Thrace, who soon became independent again, no Slavic tribes appear to have taken advantage of the empire's troubles to rise against the Byzantine rule that Nicephorus had so recently established. New though most of them were, the themes of Peloponnesus, Hellas, Cephalonia, and Thessalonica were sound enough to survive. The territorial losses to Krum were in the old themes of Thrace and Macedonia, where the expansion of Byzantine territory had taken place, largely under Irene, with less careful planning. It was only because Nicephorus's enemies practically ignored his gains in the Greek peninsula, where he had planned the expansion from the start, that they could pretend that everything he had gained had been lost.

Another of Nicephorus's achievements that his enemies almost ignored was his expansion of the army. This was probably vital to the retention of the new themes in Greece and to the recovery of Venetia and Dalmatia, because civilian settlers, though necessary, were not sufficient. In 807, when Nicephorus had brought some civilians into the western Peloponnesus without sending in additional troops, the Slavs rebelled with such ferocity that the Byzantines of Patras attributed the rebellion's defeat to a miracle. In 812 no miracle saved the parts of Thrace and Macedonia where settlers had been brought in without permanent protection from new soldiers. On the other hand, as soon as Nicephorus had increased the Byzantine armies in the Greek peninsula from 2,000 to 8,000 men, that region became for most purposes secure. Many of these troops, like Nicephorus's new tagma of the Hicanati, could soon be used in foreign campaigns as well.

Perhaps Nicephorus's greatest accomplishment, which his opponents described only to decry, was his reorganization of the empire's system of taxation. Our sources so meticulously and admiringly record Michael's many benefactions that they would scarcely have failed to mention his restoring tax exemptions, destroying tax rolls, or dismissing tax inspectors if he had done any of these on a large scale. Instead Michael seems to have been content to receive the new revenues and give them back, perhaps because he realized that most taxpayers are more grateful for what they receive than for what they are merely permitted to keep. Any exemptions that Michael did grant would have been easy for his successors to cancel as long as the government maintained accurate records and efficient inspectors. After Nicephorus the empire went through some serious trials, many of which cost it large sums, but for years to come its system of taxation seemed to be an almost inexhaustible gold machine. Despite Michael's reckless munificence, when Leo the Armenian took over the government he faced no known financial problems, nor did a shortage of cash trouble the Byzantine government at any other time during the following half-century.

The extent to which Nicephorus's reforms positively stimulated the Byzantine economy, beyond swelling the state treasury, is difficult to judge. Opening a large new area in the Balkans to cultivation undoubtedly expanded agriculture, and the emperor's compulsory loans to shipowners would have forced some expansion of trade. His settling new ports on the Greek coast, like Patras, Methone, and Corone, and his policing the Adriatic with the army and fleet of the Theme of Cephalonia, should have made trading easier. Collecting the taxes more equitably reduced the tax burden of the poorer and less influential farmers, who were then less likely to go bankrupt and more likely to buy extra oxen or seed to increase their crop yields. Population growth, which Nicephorus's colonization stimulated, ensured that the empire would gradually become richer.

On the other hand, Nicephorus plainly increased the proportion of the empire's wealth that went to the state, leaving a smaller proportion to be invested in agriculture or trade. Often Nicephorus put the money he collected to productive use, as when he paid troops to defend the Balkans or made maritime loans; and Michael returned a good deal of the surplus to the private sector. But many state expenditures were not very beneficial to the economy, and state hoarding, always a temptation for a cautious Byzantine sovereign, did little if any good. Further, the tax inspectors' vigilance reinforced the Byzantines' prejudice against economic enterprise, and encouraged them to hoard and hide their money if they had much of it.

On balance Nicephorus's financial measures probably did little either to speed or to retard the gradual growth of the empire's wealth. What Nicephorus primarily did was to make sure that the government gained an ample share of the new riches—on which, given the empire's continuing defensive problems, it had a legitimate claim. To judge from the extent of Nicephorus's reforms and the outcry against them, under Irene the state had become lax in collecting its revenues. Nicephorus reversed this dangerous trend.

Even though efficiency and honesty in tax collection may not be an unmixed blessing, in most respects efficiency and honesty are good things, and Nicephorus's government seems to have provided more of them than the empire had seen for a long time. Though the extent of the change is, on the available evidence, almost impossible to measure, it would be strange if Nicephorus, who demanded such a high standard of service from those who collected state money, had demanded any less from those who spent it. A case in which his administrators appear to have performed particularly well was in the transportation and settlement of the new colonists in the Balkans. Nicephorus's ambassadors, notably Bishop Michael of Synnada and Arsaphius the Protospatharius, also accomplished difficult assignments with distinction. The army and its officers seem generally to have performed somewhat better under Nicephorus than they had under Irene and Constantine VI. When Leo the Armenian fell short of Nicephorus's standards as strategus of the Armeniacs, he found himself promptly dismissed. Through his special court of the Magnaura Nicephorus seems to have tried to keep a check on his officials' honesty, evidently with some success.

Under Nicephorus, then, the empire's officials gave a fairly good account of themselves after their rehabilitation by Irene. As always, they are hard to distinguish as individuals, but we know something about the patriarchs Tarasius and Nicephorus, and of course about the emperor himself, who had been an official for most of his life. Exceptional though the abilities of these three men were, in some ways they appear to have been representative of their class. Like most of their fellows, they were iconophiles by conviction, showed more than conventional piety, and admired and associated with monks. Despite the patriarch Nicephorus's temporary and perhaps hastily conceived enthusiasm for killing extreme heretics, all three were reasonably tolerant men, as one would expect of those used to holding responsible posts; none went out of his way to persecute iconoclasts, for example. Yet fear of making mistakes and enemies did not render them or other officials of the time unduly cautious, as many bureaucracies are and as the Byzantine bureaucracy had been under the iconoclasts. Irene had favored her bureaucrats for political and religious reasons, and the emperor Nicephorus had served among them and understood them. Thirty years of such leadership seem to have brought out the best in the empire's religious, civil, and military officials.

During these years the officials continued their revival of learning, which brought with it a revival of writing. While much of the literature of the time is now lost and most is difficult to date exactly, it is plain that learned Byzantines soon went beyond assembling and copying passages on icons from the Church Fathers and wrote on their own. At first, not surprisingly, they found it harder to restart Byzantine literature after an interruption of sixty years than it had been to restore icons. After organizing the patristic research for the Council of Nicaea of 787, the patriarch Tarasius composed scarcely any formal writing during the remaining twenty years of his patriarchate. But several less prominent authors warmed to the task of celebrating the former resistance to Iconoclasm.

Several such writers now revived Byzantine hagiography. In 806 Stephen, a deacon of St. Sophia, wrote a biography of St. Stephen of Mount Auxentius, a monk who had been lynched by iconoclasts in 764. Probably a little earlier, Bishop Constantine of Tius in the Bucellarian theme composed the story of the relics of St. Euphemia, miraculously saved from Constantine V's attempt to destroy them and rediscovered by 796. Other iconophile heroes commemorated in biographies at this time include St. Anthusa of Mantineum, an abbess under Constantine V, and Theophanes the Cubicularius, a chamberlain under Leo IV. The latter two texts survive only in part, like some others that probably are roughly contemporary with them. Admittedly, none of these authors is a literary genius. Probably the best of them, Stephen the Deacon, leans heavily on a sixth-century saint's life as a model, from which he borrows phrases and themes to make sure that he is composing in the proper manner.[259]

At the same time, and also with some hesitation, some iconophile officials were reviving Byzantine historiography. At least one iconophile history, apparently the earliest, is now lost and known only from two surviving histories that drew upon it. The first of these, already mentioned, is the patriarch Nicephorus's short history extending from 602 to 769, probably the first work of the time written in classicizing Greek. The second, almost certainly the period's longest book, was mostly the work of George, syncellus under the patriarch Tarasius, who was probably deposed for complicity in the conspiracy of 808. George planned and collected material for a massive chronicle from the Creation to his own times, but only finished the part up to the year 284 before his death. On his deathbed he asked his friend Theophanes, abbot of a monastery in Bithynia, to complete the chronicle from the materials that he had prepared, and Theophanes did so by 814. This chronicle, composed by George and Theophanes from a variety of sources that they copied closely and sometimes clumsily, is mostly a simple work of reference, but it is a vitally important one. By assembling the facts that linked ninth-century Byzantines with the days of Justinian and Heraclius it reinforced an otherwise vague

31. Theodore of Studius, from an eleventh-century mosaic in the Monastery of Nea Mone, Chios. (Photo: Benaki Museum Photographic Archive, Athens)

and tenuous awareness of the past. Ever since, the chronicle attributed to Theophanes has been the main source of Byzantine history for the two hundred years before 813.[260]

Though most of this literature looked backward, one author of the time did not: Theodore of Studius. His writings, a good many of which date from after 813, include letters, sermons, poetry, and rules for the monks under his direction. Under him other Studites wrote literature too, notably his brother Joseph, intermittently metropolitan of Thessalonica, whose homilies survive. Theodore differs from most other authors of his time in that he not only quotes authorities and follows models but also expresses and defends his own views, which he often put into practice. Though he grew up in a family of civil servants, Theodore never held civil office; when Irene came to power in 780 Theodore was just 21, and took advantage of the new regime to become a monk at once. He did more than anyone else to rebuild monasticism as an independent force in Byzantium—something the civil service could hardly be.

We have already seen how his independence brought him and the Studites to clash with the emperors Constantine VI and Nicephorus. Idealistic though he could be, however, Theodore did not disdain public life. He probably wanted to be named patriarch of Constantinople in 806, and at that time he praised Nicephorus for "setting the empire right when it was in a bad state" as well as for his piety. While he abhorred Nicephorus's leniency toward Joseph of Cathara, he apparently favored the emperor's annexations in the Balkans, which after all spread Christianity. Under Michael Rhangabe Theodore became an influential adviser of the emperor and, among other things, had a decisive voice in continuing the war with the Bulgars. He was as intelligent, fearless, and impatient for reform as the emperor Nicephorus, though they may have been too much alike to make good allies.[261]

At the start of Nicephorus's reign the Byzantine upper class was better educated and more respected than at any time in memory, and it presided over a richer and more peaceful empire. Naturally many prominent Byzantines hoped for nothing better than a consolidation of their power after its disruption by Iconoclasm. Nicephorus wanted more. He hoped to enrich, enlarge, and strengthen the Byzantine state, and had no use for officials and monks who pursued their own interests at the state's expense. Not surprisingly, some officials and monks, as remarks in the chronicle of Theophanes show, considered Nicephorus's efforts vicious meddling. Though the emperor imposed his will successfully for most purposes, his plans strained Byzantine resources and sentiments so much that sooner or later something was likely to go fatally wrong, and so it did. Nicephorus was a man ahead of his time; but, like many such men, he forced his time a long way forward.

CHAPTER FOUR

The Struggles of Leo V and Michael II, 813-829

Leo the Armenian was throughout his career a man of versatile talents and flexible principles. He was born in Armenia, probably around 775, so that he began to rule in his late thirties. Since his father Bardas was of an Armenian princely family, probably the Gnuni, Leo would have spent his childhood acquiring the basic knowledge and manners of a cultivated man. When he was in his teens, however—most likely in 788, when some 50,000 Armenians of every rank are known to have fled Muslim persecution—his parents brought him to the empire. His father apparently received a military land grant in a village called Pidra in the Anatolic theme, where Leo came of age in much poorer and meaner circumstances than he had been raised to expect. Leo himself enrolled in the army of the Anatolics sometime in the 790's.[262]

Leo's chance to mend his fortunes came in 802, when Bardanes Turcus became commander of all five themes of Asia Minor with his headquarters in the Anatolics. Bardanes, who seems to have been on the lookout for promising young men, liked Leo. Though the young soldier was short, he was handsome and powerfully built, with curly hair, a luxuriant beard, an impressive voice, and a self-confident manner. It can have done Leo no harm that his general, like him, had Armenian blood, and must have recognized the name of Leo's distinguished family. Bardanes appointed Leo as one of his spatharii, or personal bodyguard, and gave his daughter Barca to Leo in marriage. Leo thus joined Bardanes' inner circle, which included two other spatharii: Michael the Amorian, to whom Bardanes married another of his daughters, and Thomas the Slav. The preeminence of these three spatharii may indicate that one of them, perhaps Leo, was centarch of the company, while the others were its two pentecontarchs.[263]

32. Leo V (r. 813–20). Mutinensis graecus 122, fol. 155ʳ. Note the particularly long beard. (Photo: Biblioteca Estense, Modena)

Despite the great favor that Bardanes had shown to his two new sons-in-law, when he rebelled against the emperor Nicephorus in 803 they deserted him in mid-rebellion. As we have seen, Nicephorus rewarded both Leo and Michael handsomely, making Leo turmarch of the Federates, the second-ranking officer in the Anatolic theme. This was probably the time when Michael Rhangabe, Nicephorus's son-in-law, stood godfather for Leo's son Symbatius and so bound Leo more closely to the imperial house. By 811 the emperor had promoted Leo to strategus of the Armeniacs for distinguished service.

In that year, however, Nicephorus dismissed and exiled Leo for negligence after Arab raiders had surprised him and taken his headquarters at Euchaïta. Luckily for Leo, Nicephorus met his end soon thereafter. Michael I, the godfather of Leo's son, recalled Leo later in 811 and made him strategus of the Anatolics, the empire's highest-ranking military post. Nonetheless, Leo was almost certainly behind his troops' desertion of Michael on the battlefield in 813, after which he overthrew the emperor. By the time of his accession, therefore, Leo had betrayed or disappointed each of his three major patrons—Bardanes Turcus, Nicephorus, and Michael Rhangabe. His military record was also mixed, though he had won one notable victory against the Arabs in 812.[264]

After his coronation on July 11, Leo speedily made some important appointments. Though he was not harsh to the appointees of Michael Rhangabe, he must have been wary of two high officials who had engineered Michael's accession and dominated his administration. Of these the mastermind was Theoctistus the Magister, while Stephen the Domestic of the Schools had generally used his powerful command to collaborate with Theoctistus. Later in Leo's reign Theoctistus was a monk and Stephen was magister, and it was most likely at the start that Leo deposed Theoctistus and shifted Stephen to the former's prestigious but not intrinsically powerful post.

Yet the emperor chose a partisan of Michael's to fill the empire's most important command, strategus of the Anatolics, which his own proclamation had left vacant. The new strategus was Manuel, who though probably still in his twenties had been serving as protostrator, head of the imperial stables. An Armenian like Leo, Manuel was to prove unusually able in the course of the military career on which Leo now launched him, giving him the rank of patrician. Leo also rewarded his two fellow guardsmen from his days with Bardanes Turcus. One, Thomas the Slav, whose loyalty to Bardanes seems to have blighted his career for ten years, Leo made turmarch of the Federates, and so Manuel's second-in-command in the Anatolic theme. The other, Michael the Amorian, who had been serving under Leo as a leading officer of the Anatolics, received the command of the Excubitors, the second-ranking tagma. At the same time Leo gave Michael the rank of patrician and stood godfather for the Amorian's little son Theophilus.

These favors were ostensibly signs of confidence in Michael the Amorian, but they may actually betray some anxiety about him. After all, Michael might have seemed to have a better claim on the more powerful command of the Anatolics than Manuel, who had been loyal to Michael Rhangabe to the end; or the Amorian could have received the command of the first-ranking tagma of the Schools, which Leo gave to someone whose name we do not know. Not long before, however, the Amorian had threatened to kill Leo unless he hastened his plotting against Michael Rhangabe; and Leo may already have decided to repudiate his wife Barca, the sister of Michael the Amorian's well-loved wife Thecla.

While Leo cannot have wanted to offend the Amorian by breaking their connection by marriage, in some way Barca was an embarrassment to the new emperor. The former empress Procopia had been scandalized at the idea of Barca's becoming empress, and since Barca was of good family the scandal seems to have been about her behavior. Presumably because of the objection that Procopia hinted at, Barca is never heard of after Leo's accession, and Leo was soon free to remarry. As Leo neither proclaimed nor buried Barca as an empress, he apparently divorced her on the only legal ground, adultery. Divorcing an adulterous wife was difficult, but it would have been easier for an emperor than for a man of lesser rank, especially if the adultery was notorious and tended to discredit the imperial office. As Barca's brother-in-law, Michael the Amorian privately pronounced Leo's marital conduct "unholy," and he bore a grudge against the emperor thereafter. Even so strict a moralist as Theodore of Studius, however, raised no objection.[265]

Leo's relations with the patriarch Nicephorus were delicate. While still outside the capital Leo had sent a letter affirming his Orthodox beliefs to the patriarch. When the new emperor arrived in the city and Michael Rhangabe abdicated, Nicephorus had sent a delegation of bishops to Leo. They brought a prepared statement of Orthodoxy and a promise not to introduce new doctrines, which they invited Leo to sign. He heartily assured the bishops that he agreed with everything in the document and would sign it. Though he did not sign on the spot, the delegates could not tactfully insist on that. Leo managed to overlook the matter until his coronation the next day. Then he declined to sign.

This naturally disturbed the patriarch, but he had lost his principal means of pressuring Leo as soon as the coronation had taken place. To make an issue of the signature would show distrust of the new ruler, probably offend him, and even imply that unless he signed he was free to introduce innovations in the Church. The patriarch seems rather to have taken the position that Leo was bound by his original letter to maintain church doctrine, and Leo did not dispute this. Nonetheless, the emperor's care to avoid committing himself formally is a fairly clear sign that from the start he was thinking of reintroducing Iconoclasm. For the time being he let this implied threat stand without elaboration. He would have found it useful for intimidating the patriarch in such matters as obtaining a divorce.[266]

With Michael Rhangabe and his family Leo was as magnanimous as it was politic to be. As we have seen, he took the precaution of exiling Michael and having his sons castrated. Perhaps as a further precaution, and doubtless as an addition to the imperial revenue, Leo confiscated all Michael's property, including his ancestral Palace of the Mangana near the Great Palace and large stretches of farmland in Thrace. Leo kept both the palace and the lands as imperial property, placing them under the jurisdiction of an imperial curator of the Mangana. In compensation, Michael received a yearly pension from the treasury. The conditions of his and his family's monastic exile do not seem to have been at all harsh.[267]

Leo had little leisure to settle domestic affairs at the start of his reign, because a Bulgar attack was imminent. While Leo was taking power, the khan Krum had invested Adrianople, which was full of refugees from the surrounding countryside. Leaving his brother to besiege the city, Krum advanced on Constantinople with the main Bulgar army. As soon as he was crowned Leo had to order hurried preparations for a siege, and he spent much of his first week as emperor in inspection tours of the city walls, trying to encourage the anxious defenders. Six days after Leo's accession, on July 17, Krum and his troops arrived before the fortifications of the capital.

Though Krum's victory at Versinicia was mostly the result of the desertion of Leo's Eastern themes, his success and the Byzantines' failure had now taken on a momentum of their own. Apart from the heavy losses among the Western themes, the Byzantine forces were disorganized and discouraged by their defeat and by the recent overthrow of Michael Rhangabe. The mere sight of the Bulgars beginning a siege of Constantinople was a shocking demonstration of Byzantine helplessness. Krum tried to heighten the impression and the insult as much as possible. He marched from one end of the land walls to the other to show off the size of his army. In front of the Golden Gate he sacrificed men and animals to his gods, simultaneously frightening and outraging the Byzantines. Within view of the walls he went wading in the nearby Sea of Marmara and splashed water at his men, probably as part of another ceremony. He had his harem of concubines brought out and received their prostrations and praise. He demanded that the Byzantines stick his spear into the Golden Gate as a sign of submission to Bulgar power. Byzantine observers found it particularly galling that no one was able to stop Krum's insolent behavior.

Making as if to put the city under siege, Krum then had a ditch dug outside the land walls and briefly manned it. Like his other demonstrations, however, this was mostly bravado. With neither a fleet nor a full battery of siege engines, Krum was powerless to storm the land walls or to besiege the city on the seaward sides, and he seems to have known as much. If the ditch had any military purpose, it was to prevent sallies by the Byzantines while the Bulgars sacked the outskirts of Constantinople, as they proceeded to do. Krum's evident aim was to force Leo to come to terms in order to end this humiliation and destruction of Byzantine property. Soon the khan stated his demands: a substantial tribute to be paid in gold, robes, and maidens for his harem.

Leo agreed to talk about the terms. For the conference, he proposed that Krum come with three unarmed retainers to the seashore near the Blachernae Gate, where Leo would arrive by boat with three unarmed men of his own. From the first, Leo had no intention of negotiating with Krum, but rather hoped to kill him. The night before the meeting, Leo secretly sent armed men to a house by the place agreed upon, with orders to attack Krum when the sign was given. The next day Krum duly arrived, accompanied by a Bulgar official, a Byzantine deserter who had married Krum's sister, and the deserter's son by her. The emperor approached by boat with his men, among them the count of the Walls John Hexabulius. As the imperial party landed, Krum dismounted and sat on the ground, entrusting his horse to his half-Byzantine nephew, who stood nearby. As soon as the khan had seated himself at a little distance from his horse, John Hexabulius, who had apparently been wearing a helmet, uncovered his head. This was the signal for the ambushers to attack Krum.

Unknown to the Byzantines, however, according to Bulgar custom uncovering one's head seems to have been a sign of disrespect for the khan. Krum took instant offense and made for his horse, thereby gaining a few crucial seconds. When the Byzantines watching from the city walls saw Krum being helped onto his horse by his retainers, they alarmed him still more by prematurely shouting, "The Cross has triumphed!" By the time the Byzantines who had been waiting in ambush had run to the spot, Krum was already fleeing on horseback. They shot arrows after him, and they thought that they had wounded him, but he escaped to his main army. Meanwhile, men from the imperial boat fell upon Krum's retainers, killing the Bulgar official and capturing the Byzantine deserter and his son. The Byzantines had not hurt Krum seriously; quite possibly they had not wounded him at all. It was the affront to his honor that the khan remembered for the rest of his life, and immediately sought to avenge upon whatever Byzantine subjects and property he could seize.[268]

THE BULGAR WAR

The next day, abandoning any idea of negotiation, Krum ordered his men to lay the suburbs of Constantinople utterly waste. The Bulgars destroyed the suburban monasteries, along with several sizable churches that Irene, Nicephorus, and Michael had recently restored, and palaces, houses, and farms in the same area. They then made an excursion to the north to the suburban imperial palace of St. Mamas, which they thoroughly sacked. Everyone they captured was killed; the animals they found were slaughtered. They stripped the emperor's private racetrack at St. Mamas of its bronze lion and bear and some marble statues, and denuded the palace cistern of its ornamental dragon and even the lead pipes; all these were packed in wagons and shipped back to Bulgaria. The Bulgars smashed the columns of the palace and burned the rest. Their troops then fanned out along the Bosporus and devastated and plundered both the coast and the area inland. Next they returned to the Golden Gate and began devastating and plundering the coast to the west as far as the farthest suburb of Rhegium. All the European environs of the capital, where the emperor and the urban aristocracy had many palaces and estates, suffered severely.

Leaving the vicinity of the capital in ruins, Krum devoted himself to methodically wrecking the part of Thrace that was not already in his hands. His army made its way rapidly along the entire northern shore of the Sea of Marmara, seizing and looting most of the seaports in turn, though all were fortified. The Bulgars destroyed the fort of Athyra and its stone bridge, leveled the walled town of Selymbria with its churches and houses, and pulled down the fortress of Daonium. When they were unable at the first attempt to storm Heraclea, a larger town, they contented themselves with burning the buildings outside its walls; but they took the next walled town, Rhaedestus, burned its houses and churches, and killed its defenders.

The next place, Panium, had a large garrison and resisted, so the Bulgars impatiently burned its suburbs and went on to take the nearby fort of Aprus. For ten days they used Aprus as a base for hunting out the Byzantine peasants who had taken refuge on nearby Mount Gannus with their families and flocks from all over the lowlands of Thrace. Less careless than they had been at St. Mamas, the Bulgars butchered the men but spared the livestock, women, and children, whom they sent back to Bulgaria. They then burned Aprus and raided the Thracian Chersonese nearly to the end of the peninsula. Finally, they returned to the Hebrus River valley and advanced along it, sacking every settlement as far as Adrianople, large and small, including the town of Didymoteichus. In about a month, the Bulgars had laid waste the best part of the theme of Macedonia.[269]

During all this time Adrianople, the capital of the theme, had been under siege by Krum's brother. Some 40,000 men, women, and children were within the walls, probably including as many refugees from other places as citizens of the town. Though they had ample water from the Hebrus, during the month's siege this large number of besieged had, not surprisingly, exhausted their food supplies; yet the city still held out when Krum and his men arrived. He brought up some siege engines, probably prepared by the engineer Eumathius who had deserted to him under Nicephorus, and began a bombardment.

Though Krum did not breach the walls at once, his show of determination was enough to intimidate the defenders, who saw no prospect of a relieving army and wanted to save their families' lives. Toward the end of August, they surrendered the city. Presumably in compliance with the terms of surrender, Krum did not kill any of the 40,000 captives, but deported them to a part of his khanate beyond the Danube, probably between the mouths of the Danube and the Dniester. Their colony in Bulgaria came to be called "Macedonia," and in fact Krum had put there a considerable part of the population of the Macedonian theme. Then the Khan withdrew to the north.[270]

During the entire Bulgar invasion Leo had remained behind the walls of Constantinople and concentrated on keeping himself alive and on the throne. Humiliating though the invasion had been for the emperor, his three predecessors had failed so dismally against the Bulgars that Leo's subjects seem to have been slow to condemn him. Besides, in the capital the soldiers from the Eastern themes who had just proclaimed Leo may not have impressed the Bulgars but would surely have intimidated potential rebels.

Leo moved to increase his support by making some new domestic arrangements. By now he was free from his former wife, Barca, and he soon selected a new bride. His choice fell on Theodosia, the daughter of Arsaber the Patrician, the man who had led an abortive conspiracy of clergy and civil servants against the emperor Nicephorus in 808. With this marriage Leo managed to dissociate himself from the deposed and largely discredited ruling family while reassuring the iconophile intelligentsia. Theodosia was a devout iconophile, and enjoyed the confidence of both the patriarch Nicephorus and Theodore of Studius. Her reputation and family were good, she was an Armenian like Leo, and Leo seems to have liked her.[271]

On the other hand, at Christmas of 813, soon after his remarriage perhaps, Leo made a gesture that could only have been unsettling to iconophiles. He crowned his eldest son, Symbatius, who was no more than ten years old, as his co-emperor. So much was standard practice. At the same time Leo summoned whatever troops he had in and near the capital to receive a donative. Leo's controversial measure was to rename his son Constantine at the time of the coronation, and then to instruct the newly paid troops to acclaim him and his son as "Leo and Constantine." Any reasonably alert Byzantine of the time would have realized that this was the same acclamation addressed almost a century before to Leo III and Constantine V, and renewed in 776 for Leo IV and Constantine VI. By thus comparing his family to the Isaurian dynasty, Leo V was declaring his intention to repeat the Isaurians' victories against the Bulgars. At the same time, how-

33. A nomisma of Leo V and his son Symbatius-Constantine, shown three times actual size. (Photos: Dumbarton Oaks Byzantine Collection, Washington)

ever, he was implying to many that he approved of the Isaurians' Iconoclasm and shared the feeling that the Bulgars' victories were a divine punishment for the restoration of the icons. Although Leo did not officially take this position, and could assure iconophiles that he meant merely to emulate the Isaurians' military campaigns, only the naive would have believed him.[272]

Soon after the coronation of Symbatius-Constantine, Krum made the need for Isaurian-style military measures evident once more. About January of 814, when the winter weather was clear and the rivers were low, the khan sent a force of 30,000 armored Bulgars to devastate the part of northern Thrace that the previous raid of the southern coast had mostly spared. This expedition probably began by seizing Sozopolis, the northernmost port still in Byzantine hands, and the inland town of Bizya. The Bulgars proceeded to the capital of the theme of Thrace, Arcadiopolis, and took that, then forded the shallow Rhegina River, apparently in pursuit of the fleeing inhabitants. South of the Rhegina they captured a large number of Byzantines, bringing the total taken to some 50,000 men, women, and children.

Then, however, heavy rains came, the river rose rapidly, and the Bulgars found themselves unable to recross with their prisoners. For fifteen days they were stranded, outnumbered by their captives, cut off from retreat, and not far from a substantial Byzantine force at Constantinople; but Leo did not risk attacking them. Finally the rains abated, and the Bulgars forced their captives to build a makeshift wooden bridge over the river. They sacked the town of Burtudizum on their way back, if they had not done so earlier. Along with the 50,000 Byzantines, the Bulgar army returned to their khan with large herds of sheep and cattle and a useful stock of saddlecloths, rugs, and bronze utensils.[273]

Apparently just after these raids, Krum organized some of the Byzantine borderlands as a province of the Bulgar khanate. He entrusted this province to his brother, presumably the same man who had besieged Adrianople while the main Bulgar army had gone to Constantinople and ravaged southern Thrace. Krum's brother had as a subordinate a "strategus" named Leo. The new Bulgar province was subdivided into a "Right Side," to the west of the Tonzus River, and a "Left Side," to the river's east. The Right Side, including Beroea-Irenopolis and probably Philippopolis and Serdica, was administered by a Bulgar boyar named Tuk, with the subordinate "strategi" Bardanes and John under him. The Left Side, including Develtus, Anchialus, and Sozopolis—but not Mesembria, which Krum had destroyed earlier—was placed under the boyar Irataïs, whose subordinates were the "strategi" Cordyles and Gregoras.

The Byzantine names and titles of the "strategi" indicate that some Greeks remained in this formerly Byzantine territory, which Krum intended to keep. To the south, Krum seems not to have planned to occupy such places as Adrianople and Arcadiopolis permanently. He had therefore deported their populations in order to weaken Byzantium and strengthen Bulgaria, as he had done with the populations of Mesembria and Develtus before he had decided to hold their territory. An inscription set up at Constantia, northwest of Adrianople, probably marked the frontier of the organized Bulgar province in early 814. No secure Bulgar occupation of the land farther south was possible as long as the Byzantines held Constantinople.[274]

Surprisingly, however, Krum was ready to follow up his many victories with a determined assault on the Byzantines' practically impregnable capital. He assembled a large army, conscripting many Slavs and recently conquered Avars along with his Bulgars. He put the Byzantine engineers who had deserted him to work devising a variety of siege machines on a far grander scale than those he had used against Adrianople. The arsenal included rock throwers, fire throwers, arrow throwers called "scorpions," catapults for artillery balls and for spiked missiles called "briers," battering rams, and penthouses called "tortoises" to protect the soldiers manning these engines. He also collected more mundane slingshots, pickaxes, and siege ladders. To carry this equipment the Bulgars built 5,000 wagons fireproofed with iron plate and gathered 10,000 oxen to pull the wagons. The khan reportedly planned to throw his men and machines against the wall around Blachernae, the weakest part of the land wall and the only segment where it was not double.[275]

34. The wall of Leo V, Constantinople, showing how it was joined to the earlier city wall. It was built between 814 and 816. (Photo: Warren Treadgold)

Spies soon informed Leo of all these preparations. Krum could scarcely have concealed most of them, and he may have wanted them to be known, because he had already learned to use fear as a weapon against the Byzantines. Leo began massing his own troops, and started building a second wall outside the existing one around Blachernae. Work was still under way in April, when Krum could be expected to begin his campaign in order to allow himself a long stretch of good weather to pursue his siege. About the beginning of April Leo sent an embassy to Charlemagne to ask him to help against the Bulgars, presumably by attacking their rear. In fact, Charlemagne had died on February 29, though the news had not yet reached Constantinople. When the embassy finally arrived at Aachen in July, Charlemagne's son and successor, Louis the Pious, received the ambassadors graciously, but by then the embassy had little to do but confirm the existing treaty between the two powers, because the Bulgar danger had become far less pressing.[276]

As Krum was completing his preparations to attack Constantinople, on April 13, 814, the irascible Bulgar suddenly suffered a cerebral hemorrhage. Blood flowed from his ears, nose, and mouth, and he was dead. The throne passed to a new khan, Dukum, who was probably the same as Krum's trusted brother, the besieger of Adrianople and the governor of the Bulgars' new frontier province. Dukum at least postponed the expedition against Constantinople. As it happened, he himself died within a month or two, and was succeeded as khan by a certain Ditzevg, possibly Krum's cousin. These rapid changes of ruler naturally threw the Bulgars off balance. They entirely abandoned Krum's plan for a siege of the Byzantine capital and did not take the field again for more than a year.[277]

Leo claimed credit for Krum's death, alleging that the khan had died from the effects of the wound that Leo's ambushers had supposedly inflicted on him the year before. Though Leo's Fabian tactics did seem to have been justified by the outcome, they had allowed Krum to do appalling damage to the themes of Macedonia and Thrace, which had been devastated from end to end with the exception of a few fortified ports. While these themes' armies had been severely reduced at the battle of Versinicia, Leo still had most of the tagmata and the themes of Asia, which surely outnumbered the Bulgars. Of course, the troops were disorganized, depleted, and demoralized by their defeats, had been poorly led since 811, when most of their best officers had died, and had mutinied against Nicephorus even before that. Such weaknesses could offset numerical superiority. Any field campaign against the Bulgars would therefore have been risky, and though the risk might have been justified for the good of the empire it was not the safest way for Leo to stay on the throne. If Leo wanted to establish himself as the new Leo III or Constantine V, his most promising course was probably to blame the Bulgars' victories on the icons, rebuild the numbers, discipline, and morale of the army at his leisure, bring back Iconoclasm, and then resort to arms under conditions that he could choose. That is what he eventually did.[278]

THE RENEWAL OF ICONOCLASM

Since the time of his proclamation, when Leo had avoided signing a promise not to change church doctrine, he must at least have been considering a return to Iconoclasm. After Krum died, when the Byzantine government was finally able to catch its breath, Leo confided his intention to ban the icons to some of his official advisers. His main argument was practical, not theological. The pagans, he said, had recently been defeating the Christians. (This was mostly true as far as the Bulgars and Arabs went, and the Byzantines were always less impressed by victories over the Slavs, important though those had been.) Why, he asked, were the Byzantines losing?

Leo's answer was that they lost because they were venerating icons. He pointed out that the emperors who had venerated icons had come to a bad end, either slain in battle or overthrown. (Though only Nicephorus I had died in battle, Constantine VI, Irene, Stauracius, and Michael I had all been deposed, as had the last six emperors before Iconoclasm; that made eleven out of eleven iconophile rulers over 130 years.) By contrast, Leo observed, all the emperors who had not venerated icons had died natural deaths while still reigning, and had enjoyed honorable burial among the imperial tombs in the Church of the Holy Apostles. (This was true of the three iconoclast emperors, Leo III, Constantine V, and Leo IV, except that Leo IV's death may not have been as natural as was generally believed.) Therefore, Leo concluded, he should imitate the successful emperors and abolish the icons, so that he and his son could also live long lives and their dynasty could last "until the fourth and fifth generation." Since the Isaurian dynasty had reigned for four generations, by this choice of words Leo was again comparing his family to it. The select body of officials to whom he spoke did not openly disagree with him.[279]

Leo's argument was easy to understand. Its assumption that God gave material rewards and punishments for men's behavior was almost universally shared by Byzantines. Of course, convinced iconophiles would have protested that matters were not so simple, that the iconophile rulers had not always failed and had deserved punishment for quite different reasons, and that the iconoclast rulers had suffered setbacks too. In 814, however, after three years of military disasters, Leo's argument would have seemed to have force to most Byzantines without strong feelings about icons. Leo himself, a foreigner who had arrived in the empire only when Iconoclasm was being condemned, probably believed in what he said. On the other hand, even to those with no interest in icons, the obvious argument against Iconoclasm was that it would stir up violent controversy about something that had ostensibly been settled. Beyond this, most clergy and many civil servants did hold definite views on the question, and favored the icons. Leo therefore proceeded slowly and deviously.

One serious problem for Leo was that the majority of the educated men of the time believed that Iconoclasm was based upon theological ignorance and misconstruction. The emperor was therefore fortunate to find an ally who, though young, already had a reputation for piety, learning, and intelligence. This was John Morocharzanius, abbot of the Monastery of Sts. Sergius and Bacchus, which adjoined the Great Palace. Probably born about 785, he was the son of a certain Pancratius, who to judge from his name was at least part Armenian. John was in school when the iconophile revival of learning was under way. Since he was later known as "the Grammarian," he had evidently been a schoolteacher himself for a short time, but by 813 he had entered the Monastery of the Hodegetria in Constantinople, where his main task seems to have been to paint icons. Early in Leo's reign, John became abbot of Sts. Sergius and Bacchus, but at this time he was still known as an iconophile, and corresponded with Theodore of Studius on friendly terms. For one reason or another, however, John had secretly turned against the icons, and he planned with the emperor for their abolition.[280]

On Pentecost of 814, which fell on June 4, Leo put John at the head of a commission that was to collect and study books from the monasteries and churches of Constantinople to find passages favorable to Iconoclasm. The official version was that John and his colleagues were conducting inquiries because Leo was anxious over the length of his reign. This may have been a deliberately obscure allusion to Leo's observation that iconoclasts reigned longer than iconophiles.

At first the commission consisted only of John and two of Leo's allies in the civil service, the protoasecretis Eutychianus and another official, John Spectas. These three began collecting books and within a month submitted some preliminary findings to the emperor. Leo showed their hastily assembled references to the patriarch and invited his comments. Nicephorus coolly pointed out that the passages condemned pagan idols, not Christian icons. Equally coolly, Leo accepted the explanation. John, who was ill at the time, had to send Nicephorus a letter disowning his attempt to use the passages to support Iconoclasm and begging the patriarch's absolution, which he received.

After this embarrassment, on the advice of John and his colleagues Leo expanded the commission to include two monks, Leontius and Zosimas, and a particularly learned bishop, Anthony Cassimates of Syllaeum. Anthony, who was plainly a good deal older and better grounded in theology than John, had begun his career as a notary and schoolteacher. He had then entered a monastery in Constantinople, become its abbot, and eventually been made bishop of the small town of Syllaeum in southwestern Asia Minor. Summoned by Leo, he arrived in the capital in July. With his help, the commissioners settled down in quarters in the Great Palace to prepare a more careful report. They soon discovered a copy of the acts of the iconoclast council held by Constantine V in 754, which cited many passages from the Fathers that the members of the commission looked up. By early December their research was complete, and they presented a carefully documented and frankly iconoclast report to the emperor.[281]

Armed with this new report, Leo again summoned the patriarch, who had shown great patience with Leo's ill-disguised flirtation with Iconoclasm of the past year and a half. Leo did not ask Nicephorus to approve Iconoclasm, and did not even profess it openly himself. He rather stated that the soldiers were objecting to the veneration of icons and blaming it for the victories of the Bulgars and Arabs. Leo therefore proposed, as a compromise, to remove only the portable icons that were hanging in low positions, where they could be touched and kissed. Nicephorus would not agree. The emperor then asked him what the grounds were for venerating icons, since the Scriptures did not mention the practice. The patriarch replied that for the veneration of icons and much else the Church relied on traditions handed down from the apostles and Church Fathers. This was what Leo had been waiting for. He observed that the members of his research commission had now found passages "in ancient books" explicitly opposing the veneration of icons, and he invited Nicephorus to discuss their findings with them.[282]

The patriarch soon sent several iconophile bishops and abbots to state their beliefs and to answer Leo's questions, but this was not what Leo wanted. He demanded that they debate the questions with John the Grammarian, Anthony Cassimates, and their fellow researchers. This demand the iconophiles refused, insisting that the ecumenical council of 787 had already settled the issue. Their refusal exasperated the emperor, though he still claimed to have an open mind about the icons. As the opposing positions hardened, Leo's soldiers gathered before the main gate of the Great Palace, the Chalce, and pelted the icon of Christ above it with rocks and mud, shouting iconoclast slogans. No doubt according to a prearranged plan, the emperor ordered the icon to be taken down on the pretext of protecting it from desecration. Everyone knew that when the empress Irene had restored the icons she had set up this image to replace one removed by Leo III, as she had declared in an inscription visible over it. The icon of the Chalce was therefore a symbol whose significance everyone understood. Leo V had now shown, even though he had not yet said, that he was bringing back Iconoclasm.[283]

Thoroughly alarmed, the leading iconophile clergy, monks, and laymen of the capital met in the patriarchal palace adjoining St. Sophia on Christmas Eve of 814. The patriarch presided. Also in attendance were several important iconophile bishops within several days' journey, including Joseph of Thessalonica, Peter of Nicaea, Theophylact of Nicomedia, Aemilianus of Cyzicus, Michael of Synnada, Eudoxius of Amorium, and Euthymius, former bishop of Sardis. The number at the meeting was reportedly 270. Theodore of Studius was present; his uncle Plato had died the previous April. Nicephorus ordered the report of John's commission to be read aloud to the group. Frequently he interrupted to refute the commission's iconoclast arguments, and asked, "None of you agrees with anything in these, do you, Brothers?" All shouted back assurances of their Orthodoxy. Afterward all those present signed a pledge to remain united against Iconoclasm and to oppose it at the price of their lives. Finally the group moved next door to St. Sophia, where they passed the night praying for the empire to be spared a return to Iconoclasm.[284]

Such an outpouring of iconophile sentiment was hard to ignore, and Christmas Day was not an opportune time to force a change in church doctrine. On Christmas morning, Leo summoned the participants in the prayer vigil to the nearby imperial palace. There they found the members of the iconoclast commission, along with other courtiers and the officials who formed the senate. The emperor first spoke with the patriarch in private. Apparently during this interview, Nicephorus showed Leo the written pledge signed by the Orthodox and told Leo to dismiss him as patriarch if he wished, but never to compromise the faith. Leo protested that he had no idea of dismissing Nicephorus or of compromising the faith, and pointedly pulled out the little cruciform icon hung around his neck and kissed it.

When the emperor and the patriarch joined the others, Nicephorus reaffirmed his rejection of Iconoclasm and Leo reaffirmed his Orthodoxy and venerated his little icon again. But Leo observed that John and his colleagues held different views and had arguments for them. The emperor therefore proposed a debate between the two parties, in which he would act as mediator. Michael of Synnada objected that Leo had already shown his preference for John's group, particularly by quartering them in the palace. While Leo insisted that he wanted only to discover the truth, several iconophile bishops protested that he would not give them a fair hearing, and Theodore of Studius bluntly told him to leave church affairs to the clergy. Nonetheless, Leo avoided an open breach. When he went to Christmas Mass at St. Sophia he venerated an altar cloth with a Nativity scene embroidered upon it.[285]

Though Leo had compromised to avoid a confrontation on Christmas, just twelve days later the emperor took back his concession by attending Mass on Epiphany without venerating the same altar cloth. Then Leo set to work separately on the iconophiles who had supported Nicephorus when they were together, and by one means or another he won most of them over to his plan for removing the icons that were hung low. In the meantime, Nicephorus wrote to the two strong iconophiles closest to the emperor, the empress Theodosia and the general logothete Democharis, asking them to use their influence with Leo to avert Iconoclasm. He also wrote to the protoasecretis Eutychianus—who had actually served on the original iconoclast commission but may have been wavering—exhorting him to change his ways and save his soul.

Whatever effect these letters may have had on their recipients, Leo was not deterred. Through some of those who had joined his party he informed the patriarch that Nicephorus too would have to agree to the removal of low-hanging icons or be deposed. When Nicephorus refused, Leo constrained him further by deposing and exiling the members of his staff in St. Sophia and appointing as the new sacristan an iconoclast layman, the patrician Thomas. The patriarch escaped immediate deposition because he had become gravely ill, probably partly from strain and distress, and the physicians gave him little chance of recovery. Pending the outcome of this illness, Leo put Thomas in effective control of the patriarchate.[286]

Sometime in February of 815 Nicephorus rallied, only to be faced by new trials. Leo sent Theophanes the Spatharius, the brother of the iconophile empress Theodosia, to the patriarch's sickbed to ask him to answer the arguments of the iconoclasts. Nicephorus agreed to do so only if Leo stopped persecuting iconophiles. Then Leo had several bishops from Constantinople and its environs meet in a synod to try Nicephorus, apparently for not replying to the iconoclasts' arguments. The synod summoned him to answer the charges. On March 13, the first day of Lent, a delegation of clerics arrived to deliver the summons at the patriarchate, along with a mob of soldiers shouting iconoclast slogans. The iconoclast sacristan Thomas managed to keep the mob out of the patriarchate, but he admitted the clerics, who read a letter from the synod to Nicephorus. Nicephorus in turn pronounced the members of the synod deposed on the valid canonical ground that they had no right to convene without their patriarch's permission. He did not, however, cling to office. That very day he made his way over to St. Sophia to bid farewell to his congregation and sent a letter of abdication to the emperor. That night the emperor's men took him out of the patriarchate on a litter, and brought him by boat across the Bosporus to a monastery he had founded himself, where he was to remain in exile.[287]

The next day Leo called a meeting of his ministers and announced that Nicephorus, unable to present arguments in defense of venerating icons, had abdicated. The emperor opened discussion about Nicephorus's successor, proposing John the Grammarian. The leading ministers objected on the ground of John's youth and obscurity, and asked rather that the new patriarch be someone mature and distinguished. Ever flexible about means, Leo agreed to appoint Theodotus Melissenus, the son of a brother-in-law of Constantine V. Theodotus was old and well born enough to suit Leo's ministers and iconoclastic enough to suit Leo, though he was a layman of no particular education or piety. He was rushed through orders so that he could be consecrated on Easter and hold a council shortly thereafter.

By now everyone must have realized that the council would reintroduce Iconoclasm. With Nicephorus in exile, Theodore of Studius assumed leadership of the resistance, and organized most of his fellow abbots. Most of the secular clergy seem already to have been exiled, intimidated, or won over to the other side. On Palm Sunday, March 25, Theodore had his monks process solemnly around the grounds of his monastery of Studius, singing iconophile hymns and each holding up an icon. But on Easter, April 1, Theodotus was duly enthroned, celebrated with a merriment that some found unseemly, and speedily called his council. Theodore wrote a letter on behalf of the principal abbots of the empire refusing Theodotus's invitation to attend.[288]

Nothing unexpected happened at the council, which was held at St. Sophia. The new patriarch presided, and Leo's son Symbatius-Constantine, then about eleven years old, was the emperor's ceremonial representative. In the first session the council endorsed Iconoclasm officially, recognized Constantine V's Council of Hieria of 753 as the Seventh Ecumenical Council, and accordingly repudiated the Second Council of Nicaea of 787. The next day, in a second session, the council forcibly summoned several recalcitrant Orthodox bishops, and when they would not recant anathematized them, deposed them, and handed them over to the secular authorities for imprisonment. The remaining bishops then drew up a decree that forbade the veneration of icons, though it did not positively mandate their destruction and avoided calling their veneration idolatry. Various citations from the Fathers were added to support this decision. Although many of the members of the council were not happy with the decree, all signed it. By gradual but effective steps, Leo had restored Iconoclasm.[289]

While the emperor clearly wanted to avoid persecution whenever possible, he could not ignore the refusal of the iconophile bishops to subscribe to his council's decree. Shortly after the council, he had them brought from their prison and gave them another opportunity. When they refused, he sent them into exile in different places to make it difficult for them to organize resistance. At the same time, he changed Nicephorus's place of exile to a monastery somewhat farther from the capital. Though he seems to have won over the majority of bishops, he had to exile most of those of the highest rank, including the patriarch Nicephorus, Joseph of Thessalonica, and the metropolitans of Amorium, Ephesus, Miletus, Nicaea, Cyzicus, and Nicomedia. The lower-ranking bishops sent into exile included the highly respected Michael of Synnada and Euthymius, ex-bishop of Sardis.

Otherwise Leo for the present behaved as if those not openly against him were for him, even in the case of iconophile abbots who had refused to attend his council. He obviously had to exile Theodore of Studius, who was unignorable, and Leo promptly sent him to Metopa in the Opsician theme. The emperor chose Leontius, a Studite monk who had broken with Theodore over the Moechian affair, as the new abbot of Studius,

35. The martyrdom of Byzantine captives by the Bulgars in 815. Vaticanus graecus 1613, p. 345. Painter: Nestor. (Photo: Biblioteca Apostolica Vaticana, Vatican
City)

avoiding a general dissolution of the monastery. In exile Theodore determinedly set about organizing an underground opposition. No matter
how carefully Leo minimized the iconophile resistance, it was a serious
problem that could be expected to worsen in the short run. Leo now had
to show that Iconoclasm could provide benefits to the empire that would
outweigh the dissension it caused.[290]

LEO'S SUCCESSES

After Krum's death, the Bulgars had not bothered the Byzantines much
during the rest of 814. The reigning khan, Ditzevg, however, was a harsh
man hostile to Christians. He demonstrated this amply in January of 815
by having the arms of Manuel, the captured archbishop of Adrianople,
cut off, his body cut in two, and the pieces thrown to the dogs. Soon afterward, to Christian satisfaction, Ditzevg went blind, apparently as the
result of an illness, and since a blind man was unfit to lead an army the
khan's retainers killed him. The next khan, Omurtag, a son of Krum,
liked Christians no better than his predecessor. By the summer of 815, at
the start of his reign, Omurtag ordered the death by torture of all the
Christians under his rule who would not renounce their faith. Most of

those captured in Krum's campaigns had already been settled north of the Danube in their new colony of "Macedonia," where Krum's order may not have had much effect. Many doubtless decided that apostasy was a sin that one could repent of later, whereas death was permanent. But some 380 became martyrs, including George, archbishop of Develtus, Leo, bishop of Nicaea in Thrace, and Leo and John, both "strategi" of the Bulgars' newly acquired border provinces. Nevertheless, the Bulgars did not attack Byzantine territory during this time.[291]

Most of the refugees from Byzantine Thrace and Macedonia took advantage of this respite to return to their homes south of the frontier established by Krum, rebuild their houses, and plant crops for 815. Leo must also have arranged to replace dead and missing soldiers in the usual way, though to what extent he redeployed troops in the two ravaged themes is uncertain. By the fall of 815, Omurtag judged that the border regions had recovered enough to be worth raiding and led an expedition into them. The Bulgars destroyed and plundered crops, took prisoners and livestock, and burned down houses before returning to Bulgaria without meeting significant Byzantine resistance. When Leo sent an embassy to Omurtag to ask for peace, the khan rebuffed him. Leo had little choice but to prepare for a campaign against the Bulgars that would put the merits of Iconoclasm to the test of battle.[292]

Before dealing with the Bulgars, Leo took further measures to establish Iconoclasm firmly. He replaced the bishops who had held out for the icons, and so filled most of the empire's principal sees with his own men. He reinstated some defrocked clergy who would join him, among them Joseph of Cathara, whose return was a particular affront to Joseph's old enemy Theodore of Studius. Then the emperor ordered many icons removed or destroyed, along with liturgical vessels that were decorated with religious images. The persecution gradually broadened as some protested the destruction of icons and others abstained from communion with the emperor's new patriarch and bishops and were denounced by informers. Leo and his supporters tried to make the resisters accept communion from Theodotus by imprisoning and flogging them, but the emperor failed with most of this group of recalcitrants, who were mainly abbots, monks, and nuns. He briefly exiled them, like the earlier group of bishops, to different remote spots. During the first two months of 816, however, Leo recalled the exiled bishops and abbots, and called to Constantinople some iconophiles who had not yet been exiled, ostensibly so that they might pray together for the success of his coming expedition against the Bulgars. They were to be kept at the capital in custody during the expedition, apparently in the hope that its success would convince them of the error of their views.[293]

With his whole reputation staked on this campaign, Leo took as few chances as he could. Before he left he completed the work on the addition to the walls of Constantinople that he had begun when Krum threatened the city. Having thus protected his rear, he set out with a large force, probably near the beginning of Lent, which fell on March 3. Marching quickly along the Black Sea coast and leaving the Bulgars no time to mass against him, he arrived at the ruined town of Mesembria near the original frontier with Bulgaria. Not far from there, where the Balkan Mountains meet the sea and the Byzantine navy could support him, he carefully fortified a camp and stocked it with ample supplies. Soon a Bulgar force arrived and encamped nearby, but the Bulgars did not wish to attack Leo's strongly entrenched position. Since the place was barren, after some days they began to suffer from a lack of provisions.

One night toward the beginning of April 816, Leo secretly took a large contingent of picked men, left the main army, and stationed himself behind a nearby hill where he could not be seen. The next day the Bulgars saw that Leo and his men were missing. The remaining Byzantines managed to give the Bulgar spies the impression that the emperor had deserted them. At this news, the Bulgars became highly confident, and the following night they relaxed their vigilance, expecting an easy victory the next day. Then, according to plan, the main Byzantine force attacked the enemy camp and, taking the Bulgars asleep, unarmed, and unprepared, killed and captured a great many. As the survivors fled, Leo's contingent emerged from its ambush behind the hill and finished them off. The emperor then led the victorious Byzantines on a brief retaliatory raid into the neighboring part of Bulgaria, where they plundered the land and killed many civilians, particularly children. For years to come the Bulgars referred to the site of the ambush as "Leo's Hill," and to the battle as a disaster.[294]

The battle of Leo's Hill, though not won in a particularly glorious way, effectively crippled and demoralized the Bulgars and encouraged the Byzantines, putting an end to five years of apparent Bulgar supremacy. The triumphant emperor returned to Constantinople by Easter, April 20, able to claim that God had rewarded his Iconoclasm on the battlefield. After celebrating Easter and his victory, Leo made a fresh attempt to persuade the recalcitrant iconophiles to accept communion from the patriarch Theodotus. To that end, with the help of the newly reinstated Joseph of Cathara, John the Grammarian tortured a little and persuaded a little. In aid of the cause, the patriarch Theodotus declared that he was himself an iconophile by conviction. Leo's victory, however, was probably the most effective argument, because it seemed to show that God did not oppose Leo's policies. Several leading iconophiles, including Archbishop Peter of Nicaea and Abbot Nicetas of Medicium, took communion from Theodotus and were released. Though both soon repented of their lapse, it was another victory for Leo, and shows his prestige at the time. Those who held firm he imprisoned or exiled again, trying to disrupt their cohesion by simultaneously moving their leader Theodore of Studius farther off, to Boneta in the Anatolic theme.[295]

Best of all for Leo, the khan Omurtag agreed to negotiate a peace treaty on acceptable terms. The peace was to last for thirty years, renewable at ten-year intervals. Prisoners were to be exchanged, the soldiers man for man, the commanders and civilians for ransom. Of the lands annexed by Krum, the Bulgars gave up the southeastern portion, including the towns of Sozopolis and Develtus. The frontier was set at a line running from Develtus to the Bulgar forts of Constantia and Macrolibada in the upper Hebrus valley. This was approximately the same as the Byzantine frontier at the beginning of Irene's reign, except that Leo had conceded control of the ruins of Mesembria, perhaps to reassure the Bulgars that he planned no further raids from that region. The Bulgar frontier was then to turn north to the Balkan Mountains around Serdica, while to the south the Byzantines were to leave the Slavs formerly subjected by Irene and Constantine VI independent.

The Byzantines had therefore recognized the loss of all their gains in Thrace since 780, including the link by land between Byzantine Thrace and Greece. On the other hand, all this territory was out of their hands anyway at the time, and the treaty allowed them to reoccupy peacefully a considerable area that they had lost. Unlike earlier Bulgar-Byzantine agreements, the treaty does not seem to have called for any tribute from the Byzantines. It was ratified in the latter half of 816, perhaps at the beginning of the indiction on September 1. Leo's enemies attacked him for blasphemously ratifying the peace amid Bulgar pagan rituals and having the Bulgars ratify it with Christian rites; but they did not deny that the terms he had obtained were favorable ones under the circumstances.[296]

During the rest of his reign Leo paid particular attention to restoring the devastated themes of Thrace and Macedonia. The peace with the Bulgars held; in fact, the Bulgars, reminded of Byzantine power by Leo, seem to have spent their energy in building an earthwork to defend their own border rather than in raiding Byzantine territory. Leo had the ruined towns and forts rebuilt, leading troops into the region to maintain security and to help in the construction. Though the Macedonians whom Krum had deported across the Danube stayed where they were, Adrianople, Arcadiopolis, Bizya, and the other old settlements began to rise again by 817. The Thracian and Macedonian themes regained their old structure and had their armies brought up to their former strength. Most of the territorial gains of Irene and Nicephorus to the west that Leo had written off

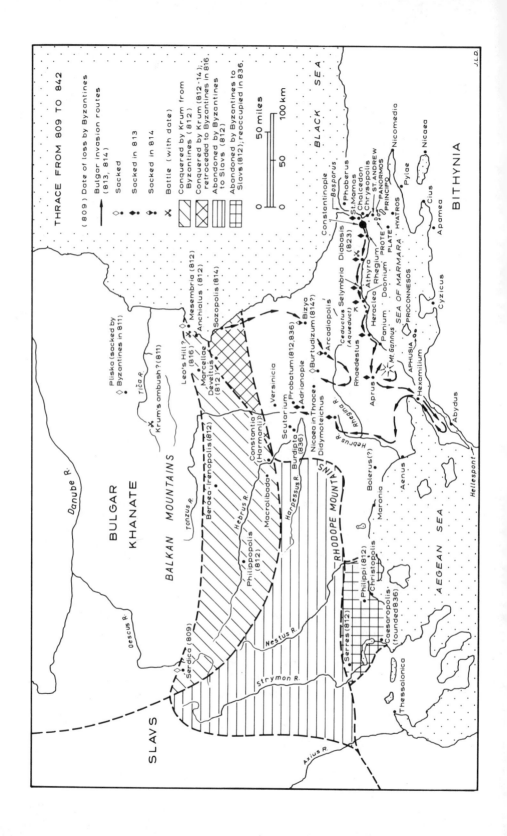

THRACE FROM 809 TO 842

(809) Date of loss by Byzantines

Bulgar invasion routes
(813, 814)

◇━━━◇ Sacked

◆━━━◆ Sacked in 813

◇━━━◇ Sacked in 814

✕ Battle (with date)

▨ Conquered by Krum from Byzantines (812)

▧ Conquered by Krum (812-14); retroceded to Byzantines in 816

▥ Abandoned by Byzantines to Slavs (812)

▦ Abandoned by Byzantines to Slavs (812), reoccupied in 836.

0 ___ 50 miles

0 __ 50 __ 100 km

SLAVS

BULGAR KHANATE

Danube R.

Oescus R.

Ticha R.

Krum's ambush? (811)

Pliska (sacked by Byzantines in 811)

BALKAN MOUNTAINS

Tonzus R.

Serdica (809)

Beroea-Irenopolis (812)

Hebrus R.

Philippopolis (812)

Harpessus R.

Macrolibada

Constantia (Harmani?)

Scutarium

Nestus R.

RHODOPE MOUNTAINS

Strymon R.

Serres (812)

Philippi (812)

Christopolis

Caesaropolis (founded 836)

Thessalonica

AEGEAN SEA

Axius R.

Hellespont

Leo's Hill? (816)

Mesembria (812)

Anchialus (812)

Marcellae

Develtus

Sozopolis (814)

Versinicia

Probatum (812,836)

Adrianople

Burtudizum (814?)

Bizya

Arcadiopolis

Ceaducus

Selymbria

Diabasis (823)

Burdipta

Nicaea in Thrace

Didymoteichus

Hebrus R.

Melas R.

Boleros (?)

Maronia

Aenus

Constantinople

Bosporus

St.Mamas

Chalcedon

Chrysopolis

Heraclea

Rhegium

Athyra

Panium

Daonium

Mt.Gannus

Rhaedestus

Apros

Hexamilium

PLATE

ST.ANDREW

PANORMOS

PROTE

PRINCIPO

HYATROS

APHUSIA

PROCONNESOS

SEA OF MARMARA

Abydus

BLACK SEA

Phoberus

Nicomedia

Nicaea

Pylae

Cius

Apamea

Cyzicus

BITHYNIA

J.L.D.

cannot ever have been very well populated or garrisoned, since they had not been systematically settled like Nicephorus's new lands in Greece. Leo had recovered the most fertile part of the Thracian plain. Before long, it was as prosperous as ever.[297]

In the fall of 816, Leo sent another embassy to the Frankish emperor Louis the Pious at Aachen. Though in general relations between the Franks and Byzantines were good, a local dispute had arisen over the delimitation of Byzantine, Frankish, and Slavic possessions in Dalmatia. The purpose of Leo's embassy was to complain about supposed encroachments on Byzantine territory by Cadolah, the Frankish governor of the region. The emperor Louis did what he could to satisfy Leo by sending a mediator of his own to Dalmatia along with Cadolah and the Byzantine ambassador Nicephorus, but no very satisfactory solution appears to have been forthcoming. When Leo sent Louis another embassy on the same subject in the spring of 817, Louis dismissed it with impatience. At the same time, Paschal I, who had become pope in January, refused to receive envoys from Leo's patriarch Theodotus Melissenus, and corresponded on friendly terms with Theodore of Studius and the iconophile underground. Perhaps because the Byzantines needed no more trouble on their western frontiers, Leo carefully cultivated the friendship of the Venetian duke Agnellus, to whom he sent the body of St. Zacharias and money and workmen to build a convent to house it.[298]

By early 817 Leo had the idea of using his peace with the Bulgars to exploit the continuing chaos in the caliphate. At this time the caliph Ma'-mūn was in faraway Khurāsān and rebellions were raging in parts of Iran and Iraq and most of Syria and Egypt. While Leo was not ready for a full-scale war, under the circumstances limited raids on Syria and Egypt looked neither difficult nor dangerous. Leo seems to have taken three measures against the Arabs early in 817. First he ordered a Byzantine trade boycott of Egypt and Syria, ostensibly because Arab rebels had profaned Christian sanctuaries in Jerusalem. Since these sanctuaries had first been profaned in 812, some five years earlier, his actual motive may have been to put Byzantine traders and ships out of reach of retaliation before he attacked the Arabs. Then Leo sent a fleet that raided the Egyptian port of Damietta. Most impressively, Leo himself set out for the east with an army, apparently in March, making his second Lenten campaign in two years. Though he did not provoke the Arabs unduly, he appeared on the Armenian frontier, secured the border fort of Camachum which the Byzantines had destroyed five years before, and rebuilt and garrisoned it before returning to Constantinople.[299]

So, after banning the icons in 815, Leo had defeated and made peace with the Bulgars in 816 and strengthened the Arab frontier by acquiring

an important stronghold in 817. An iconophile source disparagingly remarks that Leo "had kicked up his heels against the Bulgars and Arabs,
and been seized by unconquerable conceitedness." But even these words
do not imply that Leo was the only person impressed by his accomplishments. God seemed to be on his side, and his prospects for founding a
long-lasting dynasty looked excellent, especially since his new empress,
Theodosia, had already borne him at least one more son, Basil, and soon
bore him two more, Gregory and Theodosius. The iconophiles were on
the defensive, and Leo was understandably proud of himself.[300]

LEO'S FALL

During the three years after 817, Leo devoted himself to domestic affairs with an energy that the empire had not seen since the death of the
emperor Nicephorus. Leo worked along the lines that Nicephorus had set
down, and he seems to have found much of Nicephorus's work still in
place. Aside from the devastated themes of Macedonia and Thrace, which
Leo had already begun to restore, the empire was evidently peaceful and
prosperous. The reorganized themes of the Greek peninsula had become
an established part of the state, untroubled by major revolts among the
native Slavs, desertions by the Byzantine colonists, or outside raids. The
other themes had had time to adjust to the loss of the settlers in Greece
and to the other disruptions caused by Nicephorus's reforms. Certainly
Leo had plenty of money in his treasury, despite the damage and expense
of the Bulgar wars. The quality and honesty of the civil service, however,
may have been less well maintained. Michael I had been a weak and lax
administrator, and Leo, who during the first few years of his reign had
behaved with necessary circumspection, could not have afforded to offend
many officials merely because they were incompetent or corrupt.

Once he felt securely in power, Leo was more scrupulous than before.
He took care to appoint civil and military officials of ability and education, and concerned himself particularly that they not take bribes. He
made no attempt to purge the civil service of iconophiles as long as they
were loyal and kept their opinions to themselves. Even after several years
of official Iconoclasm, most of Leo's chief officials were iconophiles and
even friends of Theodore of Studius: Stephen the Magister, Leo the Sacellarius, the postal logothete John Hexabulius, the general logothete Democharis, and Pantoleon, probably the military logothete. Leo confidently put the exiled iconophile ringleaders in such men's custody; the
iconophile Zacharias, Leo's administrator of the estates of the Mangana,
guarded Abbot Nicetas of Medicium when Nicetas resumed his resistance to Iconoclasm.

On the other hand, Leo showed himself willing to punish even allies and iconoclasts. He convicted of adultery and slit the nose of Zosimas, a monk who had served on the iconoclast research commission of 814. In a case that became well known, Leo acted on a complaint that a commoner's wife had been abducted by a civil official of Constantinople whom the city prefect had refused to prosecute. After an investigation showed the charge was true, the emperor both punished the guilty official and cashiered the prefect. On the model of the emperor Nicephorus, who had heard cases in the Magnaura palace, Leo dispensed justice personally in the room of the Great Palace called the Lausiacus. Unlike Nicephorus, Leo was not accused of rapacity.[301]

Open iconophilism, of course, Leo had outlawed. Since he faced an extremely determined opposition and did not want to make martyrs, his enforcement of Iconoclasm was erratic, in most instances lenient, and in the difficult cases ineffective. Under the leadership of Theodore of Studius, the iconophiles were in constant communication by letter, recognized the bishops of their party as the real hierarchy, enjoyed recognition from the pope and the Orthodox patriarchs of Alexandria, Antioch, and Jerusalem, steadfastly refused communion with iconoclasts, and demanded strict penance from any of their members who lapsed. Everywhere Theodore and the other clergy who led the resistance could depend upon broad support from the laity. They repeatedly found a sympathetic layman or laywoman in the right place or with the right influence to circulate their letters, to hide them when they were in flight, and to help them when they were in government custody. Like their leaders, many ordinary iconophiles secretly venerated icons and avoided iconoclast communion.

Though the emperor must have known the sympathies of many lay iconophiles, he evidently thought that they were too many and too well placed to prosecute. Theodore once congratulated a certain Gregoras, an exceptionally outspoken iconophile, for being the only layman to suffer flogging for the cause. Leo usually restricted his penalties to clergymen and nuns who resisted actively. Even so, after imprisoning them in places of exile, which he often shifted, he did not go beyond having them whipped. This was the penalty for particularly open opposition, suffered by a number of monks and nuns, among them Theodore. For the nuns the main punishment seems to have been the shame of being stripped before their beatings while men looked on; but two Studite monks died after severe floggings, though their deaths were probably not intended by the emperor. These measures utterly failed to break up the iconophile underground, which under Theodore exercised such influence that it brought back many who had lapsed into Iconoclasm for a time, even including Leontius, Leo's hand-picked abbot of Studius. Leo contented himself with the outward submission of the official church hierarchy and the outward acceptance of the laity.[302]

Only within the army was Leo's Iconoclasm a partial success. The army had harbored some convinced iconoclasts ever since the first period of Iconoclasm. It had not cared much for Irene, Nicephorus, or Michael Rhangabe, and it had found in Leo's victories reasons for liking both Leo and Iconoclasm. Leo had led his soldiers to victory twice; throughout his reign he supervised their drilling. Though the army had its iconophiles, they did not predominate, and Leo was able to use the power of military discipline against them. Presumably on Leo's orders, commanders began to have iconoclast priests lead the troops in singing hymns and bless the food that the whole army ate. This made the soldiers go beyond what Theodore of Studius normally allowed iconophiles to do; but even he had to admit that it was a difficult case, and few if any soldiers seem to have resisted. Leo probably applied greater pressure to military commanders than to civil servants to accept iconoclast communion. A friend of Theodore's, the strategus Theodotus, was one of the few iconophile officials to yield. Of course, the emperor could hardly expect adherence to Iconoclasm under such circumstances to be sincere or lasting.[303]

Early in 819 Leo put all five of the regular themes of Asia Minor under a single strategus, Manuel the Armenian, who had served him as commander of the Anatolics a short time before. Leo does not seem to have meant for Manuel to fight the Arabs. Though soon after his appointment Manuel received a letter from an Arab rebel in Syria proposing an alliance, this was an unsolicited offer, and the negotiations continued after Manuel's tenure. The emperor appears rather to have wanted Manuel to deal with internal discontent. He ordered Manuel, as one of his first acts, to transfer Theodore of Studius from Boneta in the Anatolic theme to Smyrna in the Thracesians. At Boneta Theodore had led the iconophile resistance by means of an unstoppable stream of letters, in spite of Leo's repeated orders to Craterus, the strategus of the Anatolics before Manuel's appointment. Apparently Leo hoped that a change of prison and a stricter guard would finally silence Theodore.[304]

By early 820 Leo had dismantled Manuel's extraordinary command, but he seems still to have been on his guard against rebellions, since he put one or two key themes under members of his family. A relative named Bardas was assigned to command the Thracesian theme and so to guard Theodore of Studius in his exile there; the emperor could not have anticipated that Bardas would soon become ill, request Theodore's prayers, and die. At the same time, Leo may have made his nephew Gregory Pterotus count of the Opsician theme, which as the nearest Asian theme to the capital needed to be especially secure.

Leo then broke up the Armeniac theme by detaching its northwestern and northeastern turmae and making them respectively the new theme of Paphlagonia and the ducate of Chaldia. Of the Armeniacs' original force of 14,000, 2,000 were assigned to Chaldia and 3,000 to Paphlagonia. Leo's primary motive for this division may have been to reduce the power of suspected rebels among the Armeniacs. Though the Armeniacs' opinion of Leo is not specifically attested, they had suffered a humiliating defeat through Leo's negligence in 811; they often took a position opposed to the Anatolics, who were Leo's strongest supporters; and in the crisis that came a year later they sided with Leo's enemies.[305]

Even so, the fact that Paphlagonia and Chaldia were both on the Black Sea coast suggests that their creation had a strategic purpose as well. These smaller jurisdictions made the defense of the coast more flexible, putting it under the control of local commanders instead of a strategus whose overriding concern was the defense of the land frontier with the Arabs. Perhaps from the start, the strategus of Paphlagonia had on his staff a ca-tepan, who was a naval official. The commander of Chaldia, whose head-quarters were at the port of Trebizond, at first had the title not of strategus but of duke, traditionally used for coastal commands. Though for centuries the Black Sea had been a peaceful Byzantine lake, at about this time the Vikings known as the Rus were beginning to reach it from southern Russia. The creation of these two new jurisdictions may well be a sign that the devastating raids of the Russians had already begun, calling forth a typically vigorous response from Leo.[306]

Leo was not only worried about plotters in the provinces. Probably in 820, his spies uncovered a conspiracy against him in Constantinople. A number of conspirators were convicted summarily. Leo ordered them to be blinded or deprived of their hands or feet, which were hung up in the streets of the capital as a warning to others. Even though some of those punished may have been innocent, Leo certainly had his share of enemies, as was only natural after his reintroduction of Iconoclasm and his efforts to root out corruption.

His most formidable opponent had a personal motive as well. Michael the Amorian, domestic of the Excubitors, still resented Leo's remarriage at the beginning of his reign. Leo is said to have known for some time how Michael felt—perhaps because he had protested openly when Leo divorced Barca—and had even warned Michael not to air his views, which few others shared. Nonetheless, overlooking this private resentment as he overlooked the iconophilism of other officials, Leo kept the Amorian in his post. Until 820 Michael took no hostile action, but by then the emperor had accumulated enough enemies that Michael could organize a conspiracy, apparently gaining followers by criticizing Leo's Iconoclasm.

The conspiracy was detected just before Christmas 820 by John Hexabulius, now the postal logothete, whose duties included internal security. Hexabulius's agents caught Michael, but found no evidence against anyone else of importance. The Amorian confessed his own guilt without implicating others. Leo, who was understandably furious at his trusted comrade's treachery, sentenced him to be burned alive and ordered the sentence to be carried out at once, on Christmas Eve. He was only dissuaded by his empress, Theodosia, the woman whose marriage Michael so resented, who may have felt some guilt about her position. She urged her husband to postpone the execution until after the Christmas season, both to avoid profaning the feast and to gain time to discover whether there were more conspirators. Leo reluctantly agreed.

Unluckily for him, there were indeed undetected conspirators. Worst of all, they included the papias, the custodian of the Great Palace, who was related to Michael. This man kept the keys of the palace, including those to the room where Michael was chained. At nine o'clock that night, when Michael asked for a priest, the papias entrusted the arrangements to Theoctistus, a eunuch who had apparently been a subordinate of Michael's. Through Theoctistus the prisoner sent word to the other conspirators that if they did not rescue him immediately he would denounce them to Leo. This message quickly persuaded the papias and the others to extemporize a plan to murder the emperor.

At four o'clock on Christmas morning Leo was to hear Mass in the palatine chapel of St. Stephen in Daphne, of course without his bodyguards. That very night the plotters assembled a select band of armed men, dressed them in clerical garb, and brought them to the palace, where the papias admitted them and led them to the chapel. When the emperor came in, the supposed clerics took him wholly by surprise. Despite his desperate attempts to defend himself with a candelabrum, they easily hacked off his arms, legs, and head. They then brought Michael from his prison, pulled imperial robes over his leg-irons—which they could not remove at once—and acclaimed him emperor.

The murderers dragged Leo's truncated corpse out of the palace and into the Hippodrome, where they stripped it and tied it to an ass, which they drove around the racecourse. Then they rounded up Leo's wife, mother, and four sons, put them on a boat with Leo's body, and sent them to a monastery on the nearby island of Prote. There they castrated all four sons, as Leo had castrated the sons of Michael Rhangabe, but less gently. The youngest, Theodosius, died from the operation, and the second son, Basil, became temporarily mute. As the three youngest boys were under seven and the eldest, Symbatius-Constantine, was about seventeen and unmarried, that was the end of Leo's dynasty.

Such was the conspirators' work, effective but needlessly brutal. Its beneficiary Michael, having been in prison during the murder, made what use he could of his alibi to disclaim knowledge of the plot and to express disapproval of the assassins. Scarcely anything about them became public knowledge, except that an enormous man named Crambonites had struck the death blow. The original conspirators too remained largely anonymous, except for Michael, Theoctistus, and the papias, who may have been Michael's cousin Catacylas. Nevertheless, they reportedly had wide support in the palace, no doubt among the Excubitors and the palace staff.

In general, the sanguinary murder of this able emperor seems to have caused fewer regrets among the capital's troops and civil servants than might have been expected. When the exiled patriarch Nicephorus heard of Leo's death, he thoughtfully remarked, "Then the Roman Empire has lost a great, although impious, protector." But there was no public mourning in Constantinople. John Hexabulius released Michael from the irons into which he had just put him, remained postal logothete, and became Michael's trusted adviser. Early that afternoon Leo's patriarch, Theodotus, without requesting a penance or reassurance of any sort, crowned Michael in St. Sophia.[307]

THE CONTESTED SUCCESSION

Michael II the Amorian was a less cultivated man than Leo V, and in fact was the first emperor in over a century to come from an obscure family. Apparently somewhat older than Leo, he might have been born about 770 and been 50 or so when he became emperor. His birthplace was in or near Amorium, headquarters of the Anatolic theme, where he is said to have spent his youth in poverty, raising horses and other livestock. Nonetheless, he acquired the rudiments of literacy and by 803 seemed to Bardanes Turcus, commander of all Anatolia, a fit person to make his aide and son-in-law along with the well-born Leo the Armenian. Therefore Michael's penury appears to have been exaggerated, and his father Leo may well have been an army officer with a good-sized ranch on his military estate. Plausible reports connect Michael's family with Athingan heretics, an austere sect sharing certain practices with Jews that was strong around Amorium; but Michael outwardly professed conventional Christianity. He had probably criticized Leo's Iconoclasm before, and he had a close relative who was an iconophile.

After deserting Bardanes Turcus's rebellion with his comrade Leo, Michael had been made count of the tent of the Anatolic theme by Nicephorus I and given a house in Constantinople. He remained in this post until 811, when Leo became strategus of the Anatolics and so Michael's im-

36. Michael II (r. 820–29). Mutinensis graecus 122, fol. 159ʳ. Note the prominent wrinkles and gray beard. (Photo: Biblioteca Estense, Modena)

mediate superior. When Leo became emperor, as has been seen, he promoted Michael to domestic of the Excubitors and stood godfather for Michael's son. Nonetheless, Michael never forgave Leo for his remarriage. Perhaps because of his Athingan upbringing, Michael was a strict moralist of abstemious habits, solicitous of his wife Thecla and his young son Theophilus. With rough manners, only an elementary education, plain looks, and a pronounced stammer, he had little use for the high society of the capital. The urban aristocracy knew that this bluff rustic would never be one of them, but they evidently preferred him to the innovating foreigner who had preceded him. In particular, many of them hoped that the new ruler would restore the icons.[308]

At the beginning of his reign Michael proclaimed a partial amnesty for prisoners and exiles. The main beneficiaries were those punished by Leo V on suspicion of plotting against him or for openly opposing Iconoclasm. The amnesty included Theodore of Studius, who hopefully journeyed back from Smyrna toward the capital, soon joined by his brother Joseph of Thessalonica and other iconophiles. Michael avoided taking an official position on the icons at first, but then so had Irene, who had waited longer than he before she recalled iconophile exiles. For the present the new emperor, still unsure of his position, avoided alienating any possible supporters. Very soon after Michael's accession, probably in January 821, the iconoclast patriarch Theodotus died, making it easier to restore the deposed patriarch Nicephorus if the emperor chose. For some time Michael left the see vacant and did not commit himself.[309]

Whether or not he was sincerely dismayed by the savagery of Leo's murder and the castration of Leo's sons, Michael tried to give an impression of kindness to the former imperial family. He confiscated only part of Leo's property, assigning much of it for the support of the late emperor's mother, widow, and sons in their monastic retreats. Leo's young cousin Bardas, who was not the same as the late strategus of the Thracesians and appears not to have been an important person, Michael left at liberty but downcast, perhaps because of the loss of his rank and property. More dangerous was Leo's nephew Gregory Pterotus, an older man who had served as a strategus more than once and at the time may have been commanding the nearby Opsician theme. When Gregory came to acknowledge Michael as emperor, his feelings overcame him and he began upbraiding the Amorian for his part in Leo's murder. For the moment Michael said mildly that he understood the depth of Gregory's grief, but two days later he took the precaution of having Gregory arrested and sent into exile on the island of Scyros off Euboea.[310]

From this time the count of the Opsician theme was Michael's own faithful kinsman, his cousin Catacylas. If he was the same relative as the papias of the palace who had helped make Michael emperor, he had certainly earned an important reward. Michael also rewarded Theoctistus, the eunuch who had delivered the crucial message, with the high court position of chartulary of the inkpot. Otherwise Michael seems to have been slow to make new appointments as he tried to determine whom he could rely upon.

In the capital and in Europe the empire's military commanders supported him. Leo's principal civil officials, most if not all of whom were iconophile, welcomed Michael's accession and remained in office. In Asia the Opsician theme was secured by Catacylas. The uneventful recall of Theodore of Studius from Smyrna shows that at first Michael's control extended to the Thracesians, where the strategus, Leo's relative Bardas, had just died. The Armeniacs, whose loyalty Leo seems to have suspected when he had divided their territory, were favorable to the new emperor

under their strategus, Olbianus. Michael also tried to gain allies from outside the empire by promptly pursuing the negotiations with Arab rebels
begun under Leo in 819. Probably by way of the Armeniacs, he sent envoys to the rebel leader Naṣr in northern Syria to conclude the proposed
alliance. But Naṣr's followers refused to ally themselves with Christians
and forced him to put Michael's representatives to death.[311]

In the rest of Asia Minor, the results of Leo's recent campaign to assure
his subjects' loyalty appear to have outlived him. At any rate, when the
officers and army of the Anatolic theme learned that Michael had overthrown Leo, they refused to acknowledge the new ruler. Instead they proclaimed another emperor, Thomas the Slav, an old comrade of Leo's who
declared himself his avenger. As turmarch of the Federates, Thomas was
only the second-ranking officer of the Anatolics, but he was based at their
headquarters in Amorium and their strategus seems not to have opposed
his proclamation. The Anatolics proclaimed Thomas emperor so quickly
after Leo's murder that Michael was able to claim in the capital that
Thomas had rebelled while Leo was still ruling.

In reality, however, Thomas had taken his chance before Michael could
make his authority felt in the Anatolic theme. There Thomas actually was
what he claimed to be, the immediate successor of Leo V. He was joined
by the civil officials, including the local tax collectors, and within a short
time he was also recognized by the commanders and soldiers of the Bucellarians, Paphlagonia, and the Cibyrrhaeots, in some or all of which he
may have assumed control before Michael did. When the Thracesians
eventually followed, two-thirds of the army of Asia Minor was backing
Thomas. The tax collectors of these provinces, who had probably begun
their collections at the beginning of the indictional year in September and
had not yet forwarded their receipts to the capital for the annual payments
in Lent, turned over their revenues to Thomas. He could therefore pay his
troops on time with money left over as a reserve.

To explain the strength and durability of Thomas's uprising is easier
than most modern scholars have believed, because it was not, as many
have thought, a challenge to the established government. Michael had no
better right to the throne than Thomas had. Indeed, since Michael was
implicated in Leo's murder and Thomas was not, Thomas had a great advantage with Leo's former supporters, who must have been a strong
group in Asia Minor. Those who did not care much who was emperor,
always a majority when there was no clear heir, had to choose between
two candidates practically from the start. For those who were nearer
Amorium than Constantinople, Thomas was the easier choice. While
both Michael and Thomas claimed that they were innocent of Leo's murder and that their opponent had rebelled against him, Michael's claims

were false and Thomas's claims were true. In the strict sense, Thomas was not a rebel at all.[312]

Like Michael II and Leo V, Thomas had first gained prominence in the bodyguard of Bardanes Turcus before Bardanes rebelled in 803. Evidently the bodyguard of the strategus of the Anatolics was a good place to start climbing to the throne, and of course acquaintance with a previous emperor helped too; but Thomas had fewer advantages than his two comrades. He was rather older, born into a Slavic family long settled in the town of Gaziura in the Armeniac theme. Bardanes had not favored him with the hand of one of his daughters; and Nicephorus had not rewarded Thomas later, because he had stood by Bardanes to the end. He had, however, continued serving with the senior turma of the Armeniacs, the Federates, and when Leo became emperor he had made Thomas their turmarch and kept him in the post up to 820.

By then Thomas's hair was white, but he was still a vigorous man and might have been about 60. Despite his age and a lame leg, he was a capable and valiant soldier, well-spoken and clever, and popular among his troops, who had served with him, and liked him, for many years. At Amorium Thomas had a far better reputation than Michael, whose long residence and service there had merely won him ridicule for his stammer, suspicion of sharing his relatives' Athinganism, and contempt for his performance in battle.[313]

Nonetheless, Michael held the capital, and with it the tagmata, the central bureaucracy and treasury, and the most obvious tokens of legitimacy, including coronation by the patriarch of Constantinople. He also held the European themes and two of the main themes of Asia Minor, the Opsician and the Armeniacs, besides the ducate of Chaldia and, at first, the Thracesian theme. Though the Armeniacs and Chaldia were cut off from the rest except by sea, as long as Michael kept control of them he could communicate with the Arabs, as he had already done without positive results, and threaten Thomas's base in the Anatolics. Apparently in an effort to crush Thomas early, Michael sent a force from the Armeniacs against him. Thomas fought a battle with Olbianus, strategus of the Armeniacs, put him and his troops to flight, and marched through Armeniac territory to Chaldia. This victory gave Thomas all of the ducate of Chaldia and the part of the Armeniac theme along the frontier.

Olbianus still remained in control of the rest of the Armeniac theme with a large part of its army and enough of its seaboard to keep open his contacts with Constantinople, probably through the ports of Amisus and Sinope. Before Thomas could attack Olbianus again, he learned that the Arabs had taken advantage of the division among the Byzantines to launch a major raid by sea on the Cibyrrhaeots and by land on the Anatolic theme itself, where Thomas had left few troops behind. To defend the homes and families of his men, he was obliged to interrupt his operations against Olbianus, but he retained the ducate of Chaldia, and apparently set up the part of the Armeniacs that he had taken as a new "ducate of Armenia" under a commander loyal to his cause. While Thomas fought the Arabs, probably during the spring of 821, Michael II enjoyed a respite from civil warfare, though nearly half the empire acknowledged Thomas as its ruler.[314]

With his hold on the empire so insecure, Michael was more anxious than ever to avoid making enemies by taking a position on icons. He had never venerated them himself, perhaps not so much from agreement with iconoclast emperors as because of his familiarity with Athinganism, which like Judaism avoided religious images. In political terms, if Michael continued Iconoclasm he would not need to issue an edict or to hold another church council that would reopen this sensitive issue yet again. On the other hand, keeping Iconoclasm seemed to require appointing a new iconoclast patriarch in opposition to the deposed patriarch Nicephorus and alienating a powerful and numerous group of iconophiles.

Even before reaching Bithynia, Theodore of Studius had marshaled his forces to urge Michael to abandon Iconoclasm. Shortly after Leo's murder Theodore had sent a letter to the emperor to that effect, at the same time writing to enlist the influence of his own iconophile friends in the bureaucracy, including the magister and the three principal logothetes. One of these, the general logothete Democharis, had already defended the icons openly against the leading iconoclast, John the Grammarian. Even if some of these men did not press their opinions upon Michael, it made little difference. From several years' experience in the Great Palace the emperor knew what they thought, and he knew that at the Byzantine court silent opponents could be as dangerous as vocal ones.[315]

Trying to find a way to compromise, Michael proposed that the iconophile bishops and abbots who had just returned from exile meet with the incumbent hierarchy to discuss the matter. This, however, was unacceptable to Theodore of Studius, who led the iconophile abbots and bishops. On their behalf Theodore sent a respectful letter to Michael declaring them unable to discuss the icons with iconoclasts and proposing that the pope arbitrate instead. Since the pope openly opposed Iconoclasm, Michael was stymied.

The emperor's obvious reluctance to offend iconophiles apparently encouraged the deposed patriarch Nicephorus to break his silence and write to Michael asking that the icons be restored. Hoping to reach a compromise without a discussion, Michael expressed his admiration for Nicephorus's eloquence and offered to reinstate him as patriarch, provided that

Nicephorus would agree to set aside the iconoclast council of Constantine V, the iconophile council of Irene and Constantine VI, and the iconoclast synod of Leo V, and take no position for or against icons. These were major concessions that the emperor offered, unworkable though they would have been in practice. Without flatly rejecting them, Nicephorus asked Theodore and his followers to speak with Michael, evidently as his representatives. One of the iconophile officials, perhaps Leo the Sacellarius, arranged a meeting with the emperor, who, even if he was reluctant, could not easily avoid it.[316]

When Theodore and the other leading iconophiles came to the palace, Michael again asked them to discuss the issues with the iconoclasts, this time offering to appoint arbitrators who were known to favor icons, probably from among the government officials. Theodore and the others again refused, since they were unwilling to meet with heretics, to submit to secular judgment, or to accept the proposals for mutual toleration that Michael doubtless had in mind. Instead they answered the iconoclasts' arguments in detail and defended the icons uncompromisingly. After hearing them out, the emperor told them that their words were well and good, but he had never venerated icons himself and had decided to leave the Church as he had found it at his accession. He declared, however, that he would tolerate their iconophile views and practices as long as they lived outside Constantinople. With that, he dismissed them from the palace, and they left for Bithynia.[317]

Quite apart from his personal distaste for icons, by this time Michael must have felt that he had little choice but to continue Iconoclasm. Although the iconophile clergy would not compromise, the iconoclasts would be as tolerant as he told them to be. Besides, as long as Thomas the Slav was growing stronger and posing as Leo's avenger, Michael's chosen strategy was to claim to be Leo's rightful successor, and abandoning Leo's Iconoclasm could only undermine that claim. To temporize any longer would simply annoy iconoclasts and make all the incumbent clergy nervous.

Once Michael had decided to keep Iconoclasm, he had nothing to gain by leaving the patriarchate vacant. The most dedicated iconoclast candidate, and probably the ablest, was John the Grammarian, abbot of the Monastery of Sts. Sergius and Bacchus. Six years of promoting Iconoclasm had made him better known than he had been in 815, when he had missed being chosen patriarch because of his obscurity and youth; but he had also made himself particularly hated by the iconophiles, whom Michael wanted to antagonize as little as possible. Therefore the emperor chose the next most dedicated candidate, Bishop Anthony Cassimates of Syllaeum, a learned man who had been John's most useful collaborator on

37. A nomisma of Michael II and his son Theophilus, shown three times actual size. The type is only slightly different from those of Nicephorus I, Michael I, and Leo V with their own adolescent sons (see Figs. 24, 29, 33). (Photos: Dumbarton Oaks Byzantine Collection, Washington)

the iconoclast research commission of 814. Anthony was consecrated patriarch toward the spring of 821, perhaps on Easter, March 27, since major church feasts were the usual times for such consecrations and the absence of a patriarch at the celebration would have been conspicuous.[318]

Though he had not chosen John the Grammarian patriarch, Michael had great respect for John's learning. He put John in a place where he could lend the imperial family some much-needed intellectual respectability, by making John tutor to his son and heir, Theophilus. Michael crowned Theophilus his co-emperor soon after he had declared his preference for Iconoclasm, probably on Pentecost, May 12. Theophilus was then eight years old, and apparently Michael's only child. He grew up under John's influence to be admiring of his tutor and a good deal like him: cultured, clever, a little too self-confident, and a convinced iconoclast.[319]

In the meantime Thomas the Slav had been dealing with the Arabs. Though forced by their raids to interrupt his advance into Michael's territory in Chaldia and the Armeniacs, Thomas did not give up the initiative. Instead of returning to the Anatolics to drive out the raiders or attacking the Syrian frontier province from which they came, he marched straight across the frontier into Arab-held Armenia, which was highly vulnerable. The Arab governor of Armenia was also in charge of Azerbaijan, where the religious sect of the Khurramites was in full rebellion under their leader Bābak and had soundly defeated the governor's forces a few months before. Thomas brushed aside the forces that opposed him and seized Theodosiopolis (Erzurum), well inside Armenia. With Bābak stronger than ever in Azerbaijan and other rebels under Naṣr still holding out in northern Syria, the caliph Ma'mūn wanted no more enemies. Besides, he had no reason to oppose Thomas's war against the emperor reigning in Constantinople. When Thomas sent an embassy toward the end of spring to propose peace, Ma'mūn was receptive.[320]

The result was not merely a peace but an alliance. Thomas apparently agreed to pay the caliph a moderate tribute. For his part, Ma'mūn recognized Thomas's claim to the Byzantine throne and offered him moral and material support. Under the caliph's protection Thomas traveled to Antioch in Arab Syria, where the Orthodox patriarch Job crowned him emperor. Highly irregular though the coronation was, it allowed Thomas to wear a crown and to appeal implicitly to iconophiles, since Job and the Orthodox patriarchate of Antioch had not accepted Iconoclasm. Besides strengthening Thomas's claim in this way, Ma'mūn allowed his new ally to recruit volunteers for his army from Abbasid territory. Apparently most of these recruits were Christians from the northern frontier region, who may already have joined Thomas when he invaded Armenia. Now Thomas was free to devote all his energies to toppling Michael II.[321]

Thomas made efforts to attract more Byzantine backing as well. Especially for a would-be emperor as old as Thomas, it was a weakness not to have an heir. Thomas accordingly adopted a younger man, whom he gave the name of Constantius and crowned junior emperor. The name hinted at the story, which Thomas's partisans began to circulate, that he was not really a Slav named Thomas but rather Constantine VI, the son of Irene, who contrary to popular belief had not been blinded and had not died. If he had been alive, Constantine would have been 50, rather younger than Thomas; but the story was not an official claim and was not really expected to stand critical scrutiny. It might win some favor among the credulous, might remind others that Michael II had no better hereditary right to rule than Thomas did, and, like the coronation by the patriarch of Antioch, could imply that Thomas was an iconophile without formally committing him. Though as former adherents of Leo V most of Thomas's men doubtless accepted Iconoclasm, his studied ambiguity on the icons also attracted some iconophile volunteers. Thomas could be all things to all men until he had conquered the whole empire, and then he would have time enough to disappoint some of his followers.[322]

At Constantinople Michael saw the danger clearly enough, and did what he could to strengthen such support as he had. After making Anthony patriarch of Constantinople, the emperor tried to conciliate iconophiles by choosing as archbishop of Ephesus his own iconophile relative, also named Michael. This appointment was particularly calculated to help the emperor Michael's cause among iconophiles in the Thracesian theme, which then seems to have been wavering between Michael and Thomas. But the prospective archbishop proved to be too good an iconophile to accept consecration from an iconoclast patriarch, and the Thracesians joined Thomas the Slav.[323]

Michael was particularly annoyed when, in the late spring, after he had decided to continue Iconoclasm, a Syracusan monk named Methodius arrived as a legate from Pope Paschal I. Since news had arrived at Rome that the new emperor was undecided about the icons, Methodius had hoped to arrive in time to persuade Michael on behalf of the papacy and the rest of Orthodox Christianity to restore both the icons and the patriarch Nicephorus. Instead Methodius found that Michael considered his mission to be not merely foreign interference in Byzantine affairs but positively disloyal, since as a Sicilian Methodius was an imperial subject. With uncharacteristic harshness, the emperor ordered Methodius to be imprisoned indefinitely in a tiny cell on an island near Constantinople. Michael showed similar and understandable resentment when the patriarch of Antioch Job crowned Thomas the Slav, since like the pope the Eastern patriarchs were supposed to respect the Byzantine emperor's authority over Christendom. Apparently Michael had the patriarch of Constantinople Anthony excommunicate Job for his presumption.[324]

To preserve his control over the two Anatolian themes that still stood by him, Michael took a step that was sure to be popular. For the year of the indiction that began on September 1, 821, he remitted half the hearth taxes of the Opsician and Armeniac themes, ostensibly as a reward for their loyalty but presumably more as an incentive to stay loyal. This measure would have cut taxes in these themes by approximately a quarter, a reduction that Michael could make up by drawing on the central treasury but that Thomas, who depended on current revenues, could not easily imitate. Finally, Michael strengthened the walls of Constantinople, realizing that Thomas was preparing to march on the capital.[325]

THE WAR BETWEEN MICHAEL AND THOMAS

Thus far Thomas had won most of Asia Minor without a fight, worsted Michael's forces in the Armeniacs and Arab forces in Armenia, concluded an alliance with the Arabs, and gained a number of volunteers, all without suffering a single defeat of importance. But to win the war he had to take Constantinople, with its magnificent walls, its many tagmatic troops, its ample treasury, and the usual assumption that whoever held it was the true emperor. Thomas almost certainly had partisans inside the capital who would work to betray it to him if he put it under siege. Though he had not completed the conquest of Asia Minor, to do so he would have to overcome determined opponents without even then being sure of final victory. Appearing before Constantinople might win him the war quickly; and, if a long siege was needed, the sooner it started the better chance Thomas would have. If Thomas took too long to secure Constantinople, he could expect his troops to melt away.

Thomas planned to lead an expedition on both land and sea against the capital. He already had control over the fleet of the Cibyrrhaeots, with some 70 ships, but since Michael controlled the Imperial Fleet of the capital, with about 100 ships, this did not seem enough. The western themes had small fleets, but, still uncertain who was going to win the war, they apparently sent Thomas no more than a formal submission. Thomas therefore set about building himself more ships. He also had a large number of siege engines built, and stockpiled provisions for the troops. The fleet was supposed to meet at Lesbos when it was ready, and then to join in the advance of the land forces. Even if Thomas did not fully control the theme of Hellas, his fleet gave him control of its offshore islands, including Scyros, where Michael had interned Gregory Pterotus, nephew of Leo V and recently deposed strategus. When he was released, Gregory was happy enough to join Thomas in fighting Michael, and Thomas was pleased to have the aid of a man who lent color to his claim to be the avenger of the murdered emperor. Thomas accordingly named Gregory the commander of his fleet, which had assembled on Lesbos by October with 10,000 soldiers.[326]

Though Michael's cousin Catacylas still held the Opsician theme, which lay between Thomas's territory and Constantinople, Thomas's plan was to mass his army in the Thracesian theme and then march along the Opsician coast to Abydus on the Hellespont. There he could meet his fleet, be ferried across the strait, and proceed to stir up rebellion against Michael in the themes of Macedonia and Thrace as he advanced on Constantinople. Michael was plainly aware of this plan and worried about it. He led an army out from Constantinople through the two threatened themes to encourage his allies and to make the towns as secure as possible. He also changed his orders to Theodore of Studius and the other iconophile bishops and abbots. Instead of forbidding them to live in the capital as before, he now commanded them to come to it, fearing that otherwise they would join Thomas and further increase his appeal to iconophiles. Theodore was in fact not at all impressed by Thomas, probably because of his association with Leo V, and his followers seem to have shared his view. They all obediently moved to Constantinople.

When Thomas began his advance on the capital, he put his adoptive son

Constantius in charge of an army in Asia Minor that was supposed to deal with Olbianus, Michael's strategus of the Armeniacs. When Constantius advanced against Olbianus, however, he fell into an ambush, and though his troops did not suffer greatly he himself was killed. After Thomas had marched unopposed to Abydus and met his fleet, he received Constantius's severed head, forwarded by Michael from Olbianus. Though Thomas had not lost a true son or evidently much of a general, Olbianus was clearly going to remain a problem for him. Nonetheless, Thomas's main force was undefeated and held both sides of the Hellespont. On a moonless night, probably in November, he sent out contingents to land at several points on the coast of the theme of Macedonia, then made the crossing himself.[327]

Michael's cause in the European provinces collapsed as soon as Thomas's army landed. If any part of the empire had reason to revere the memory of Leo the Armenian it was the region of Thrace, which his treaty with the Bulgars had delivered from utter devastation and to which his reconstruction had restored a semblance of urban life—all no more than five years before. Thomas enjoyed an enthusiastic reception and soon was master not only of the themes of Macedonia and Thrace up to the suburbs of Constantinople but also of the theme of Thessalonica, which was now cut off from the capital. These new territories sent Thomas more volunteers, even including Slavs from outside the empire, who may have hoped that their fellow Slav would be especially generous to them. Thomas now claimed to have 80,000 troops, and in fact he had at least nominal control of nearly 60,000 of the empire's soldiers, without counting his volunteers.

By contrast, Michael, who had retreated ignominiously from Thrace, had at most 35,000 troops who were still loyal to him, all in the tagmata and the Opsician and Armeniac themes. The tagmata gathered in the capital, and the two themes sent reinforcements to Constantinople after Thomas's departure and Constantius's death lessened the military threat to them. Michael also had the Imperial Fleet, but few if any other ships. Plainly he considered both his army and his fleet inferior to those of Thomas, and prepared only a passive defense. He apparently anchored his ships safely in the fortified harbors of the Sea of Marmara on the southern side of the city. To guard the Golden Horn to the north he relied on the usual defense, an iron chain stretched across the bay's mouth to the suburb of Galata on the opposite shore. He then waited for Thomas with his army, and Gregory Pterotus with his fleet.

Gregory came first. He sailed up to the chain and, unhampered by Michael's ships, broke or unfastened it. Then he brought his forces up the Golden Horn past the city, and waited with them at the mouth of the river Barbyses at the far end of the Horn until Thomas arrived. Before joining

Gregory near the capital, Thomas hastened to adopt and crown a new junior emperor and heir to replace the dead Constantius. Though Gregory would have been the logical choice as Leo V's nephew, the same logic could suggest that he was the rightful emperor; so it was probably by design that Thomas sought to close the issue before he and Gregory met. Thomas's choice was a man named Anastasius, said to be a former monk but otherwise as obscure as Constantius had been. With him, Thomas marched to Constantinople in early December, hopeful that after seeing the size of his army and navy the citizens would open the gates to him without a fight.[328]

In this Thomas was disappointed. Many in the provinces may have liked Leo V, but few in the capital had shown dismay when Michael overthrew him. All the soldiers defending the city had had ample opportunity to desert to Thomas earlier if they had been so inclined, and the tagmata, especially the Excubitors, whom Michael had led before his accession, could hardly expect Thomas to trust them if he won. The walls were strong and recently put in order, supplies were adequate, and across the Bosporus the territory of the Optimates and the Opsician theme were still held by Michael's cousin, who could send in more men and provisions by sea. When Thomas showed himself outside the land walls, the defenders jeered at him. He accordingly encamped near the quarter of Blachernae on the hill of Cosmidium by the Golden Horn to prepare for a siege. His forces seized all the remaining outposts around Constantinople on the European side. To encourage the defenders, Michael had his young son, Theophilus, lead a procession of the city's clergy around the walls, carrying the wood of the True Cross and the clothing of the Virgin and singing a litany. The emperor also set a great battle flag over the Church of St. Mary of Blachernae, where both armies could see it.

Even if he did not expect to be able to storm the city by main force, Thomas hoped to attack it vigorously enough to demoralize the defenders and to take advantage of any attempt to betray it to him. His plan was to direct the main attack against the quarter of Blachernae, where the wall was slightly weaker, while his junior emperor, Anastasius, led troops against the rest of the land wall to the south and Gregory Pterotus and his navy assaulted the sea wall from different sides. The land forces were well supplied with catapults, rams, and scaling ladders, while Gregory's fleet had both seagoing catapults and a store of the Byzantines' secret incendiary substance, Greek fire. Thus Thomas's forces could exploit signs of weakness or disloyalty anywhere along the walls.

This triple assault began according to plan. By Blachernae, Thomas's contingent brought out their catapults and rushed up to the wall with their ladders. But they were driven off by Michael's own artillery, which

38. The obverses of two folles of Michael II and Theophilus, shown twice actual size. Like all the nomismata of the reign, the follis at left, which is of the usual type, shows Theophilus without a beard. The follis at right shows him with a beard and mustache; because it is the only known specimen of its type it seems to have been minted only at the very end of Michael's reign, in 829. If this was the date at which Theophilus grew his first beard, the coin confirms indications that he was baptized in June 813 and was born shortly before that date, so that he would have been sixteen in 829. (Photos: Dumbarton Oaks Byzantine Collection, Washington)

prevented them from bringing their catapults and rams close enough to be effective. Anastasius had no better success, while unfavorable winter winds dispersed Gregory's ships before they accomplished anything of importance. Thomas concluded that it was too late in the season for naval operations, and on land alone there was little he could do. As the weather was becoming cold, he sent his men into winter quarters nearby. He continued to hold all Thrace outside the walls and apparently kept up patrols so that the siege continued on land, but he did not try to keep up a full blockade by sea.[329]

When the spring of 822 began, Thomas again prepared for a land and sea assault. This time, with less hope of help from inside the city, he decided to concentrate his forces on Blachernae alone, which his army would attack from its camp and his fleet would attack from the Golden Horn. Just before the operations were to start Michael appeared on the Blachernae walls and announced an amnesty for any of the opposing troops who would join him. This speech merely encouraged Thomas's forces to think that their enemy was desperate; but before they had had time to mock Michael properly the gates opened, his soldiers sallied out, and his fleet appeared in the Horn. The sallies, taking Thomas's army by surprise, had some success, but the main blow was to his fleet. Thomas's ships, many of which were tied together to serve as platforms for cata-pults, were prepared for a land assault rather than a sea battle. When the sailors saw the enemy fleet bearing down upon them, some actually fol-lowed Michael's invitation and deserted, and the rest confusedly put to shore without resisting. It was Thomas's first personal defeat. Though he retained his military superiority and kept up a strict blockade of the city by land, his fleet was no longer much stronger than Michael's.

This setback had the greatest effect on Gregory Pterotus, who was probably still the naval commander and so most humiliated by it. Already he had felt neglected by Thomas, anxious about his wife and children, whom Michael held in the city, and inclined to drink heavily. After the naval defeat he was more depressed than ever, and decided to desert to Michael. He left the camp by night with a small squadron whom he had persuaded to join him. Without trying to pass the besiegers and enter the city, he struck out into Thrace, where he might gain adherents who had admired his late uncle. Though Gregory tried to let Michael know of his defection by sending a Studite monk to him, Thomas's blockade was so complete that the monk could not get through. Thomas himself learned about Gregory's desertion soon enough, and, setting out at once with a detachment of picked men, speedily defeated and killed Gregory.

Thomas made skillful use of this much-needed victory, declaring everywhere that he had beaten Michael's forces on both land and sea. In particular, he wrote to Hellas and the other western themes to announce his success and to demand more ships and supplies to complete the con-quest of Constantinople. This time the Westerners were ready to believe that Thomas was winning the war, and sent ships with both men and grain. When this new fleet put in at the harbor of Byrida on the Sea of Marmara just west of the capital, Thomas's fleet is said to have reached the mighty total of 350 vessels. It probably outnumbered Michael's by more than two to one.[330]

By now it must have been summer. Thomas was eager to attack again with his strengthened fleet, which was so immense that under favorable conditions it might well be able to storm some part of the sea wall. Re-alizing the danger, Michael sent his own navy against the ships from the west before they could join those on the Horn. It caught them in their harbor, shot a wall of Greek fire against them, and destroyed many of them with their crews. Of the ships that escaped, a few managed to join Thomas on the Golden Horn, but the rest surrendered to Michael. With his naval reinforcements now largely in the hands of his enemy, Thomas no longer had naval superiority, though he continued to besiege the city.

Michael's troops made occasional sallies, but scored only minor successes. The war seemed to have arrived at a stalemate, in which Thomas could not take the capital but Michael was too weak to force him to raise his siege.[331]

Michael needed more troops, and finally he hit upon a plan for getting them. The Byzantines' treaty of 816 with the Bulgars still held, and to the Bulgar khan Omurtag the man who held Constantinople was naturally the true emperor. Invoking the treaty, Michael appealed to Omurtag to attack Thomas, apparently offering an early renewal of the treaty, which if unrenewed would expire in four years, and perhaps suggesting that the Bulgars reward themselves by plundering Thrace and Macedonia. Omurtag accepted. By November of 822 the Bulgars had invaded. News of the invasion forced Thomas virtually to raise the siege of Constantinople and to march with his whole army against the Bulgars, leaving only his fleet in the Golden Horn. The two armies clashed at the aqueduct near Heraclea in Thrace, called "Ceductus" by the Latinless Byzantines. Thomas's army, which was evidently the larger, killed a great number of Bulgars and drove them back to Bulgaria, but seems itself to have suffered heavy casualties. At Constantinople Michael was able to claim so persuasively that Thomas had lost that Thomas's fleet surrendered. Making no attempt to resume the siege, Thomas went into winter quarters at Arcadiopolis in Thrace.[332]

Little chance remained that the siege could succeed after the loss of the fleet, and Thomas's troops probably had little heart for it. Yet when Thomas abandoned his siege of Constantinople, he practically admitted that he could not win the war, even though he still controlled the greater part of the empire. During the winter some of his partisans began to realize that his cause was desperate, and deserted in small bands to Michael. It is an impressive proof of the loyalty that Thomas inspired that most of his troops did not desert him. His only hope now was to lure Michael into an open battle, which Thomas might win.

In the spring of 823 Thomas encamped on the plain of Diabasis, about 30 miles west of Constantinople, and began supplying himself by raids on the neighboring territory, which Michael had evidently reoccupied during the winter. Doubtless he needed the food and fodder, and probably he wanted to provoke Michael to come out against him; but the best reason for Michael to attack was Thomas's newly evident weakness. For a month or two Michael bided his time, but by the beginning of May he had massed his troops, including Olbianus and Catacylas and forces from their themes, and marched out against his enemy.

Thomas, who even this late in the war retained a numerical advantage, formed a stratagem that he hoped would assure him of victory. To play on the confidence of Michael's troops that their opponents would be demoralized, Thomas ordered his men to pretend to flee after their first contact with the enemy, then to turn on them and surprise them as they pursued. This might have been a good plan if many of Thomas's troops had not been fully as demoralized as Michael's men expected them to be. As it was, after they began to run and found Michael's army bearing down on them, they forgot to stop. In the end they dispersed in an utter rout. Many surrendered to Michael, and the remainder took refuge in four of the fortified towns of Thrace. The largest group returned with Thomas himself to their former quarters at Arcadiopolis, others escaped with Anastasius to Bizya, and still others went to Panium and Heraclea.[333]

Always cautious, Michael decided to blockade the towns and starve his adversaries out. By proclaiming that he did not want to shed any more Christian blood, he played on the war-weariness of both sides, and in fact he had no reason to wish to spend more lives in storming these places. Reportedly he also wished to avoid showing the nearby Bulgars how walled cities could be taken by storm, since they might use the lesson against him later. He therefore invested Arcadiopolis carefully, digging and manning a ditch around it but making no use of catapults or rams. Reckoning that his most important objective was to subdue Thomas and what was left of his main army, Michael kept his troops together in Thrace and ignored Thomas's few partisans still in Asia Minor. These, too weak to render Thomas effective aid themselves, in the summer of 823 gave free passage to Arab raiders from the caliphate, who might draw Michael away from Thrace. The Arabs ravaged Michael's territories in the Opsician theme and the territory of the Optimates, from which they drove out Theodore of Studius, who had recently been allowed to return there from Constantinople. But they did not attempt to cross the Bosporus, and Michael let their raid run its course.

In the besieged towns of Thrace, Thomas's men again proved remarkably loyal despite their recent sharp defeat. Most of them held out for months when they could easily have deserted or surrendered on favorable terms. They first sent out the unserviceable animals, and then the old or disabled soldiers; they let their horses starve, then ate the horses, and finally ate skins and leather. Some did desert to Michael, but others managed to slip through the blockade to Bizya, where things were less desperate, in the hope of arranging Thomas's rescue with the help of his adopted son, Anastasius. But before they could act it was too late.

At last, after five months of siege, in mid-October part of the surviving garrison at Arcadiopolis opened negotiations with Michael and agreed to surrender Thomas and the town in return for a pardon. The bargain concluded, Thomas was brought, bound and on an ass, to Michael, who put his foot on his head. Thomas's only words were, "Have mercy on me, True Emperor." When Michael started to interrogate his captive about his relations with Michael's men, John Hexabulius, the postal logothete, advised the emperor not to believe the testimony of enemies against friends. Finding the advice good, Michael dropped the questioning, to which Thomas had not responded. He immediately had Thomas's hands and feet amputated and his body impaled. After the garrison of Bizya learned of Thomas's execution, they quickly surrendered the city and their leader, Anastasius, whom Michael punished in the same fashion.[334]

While Thomas had been besieged, his partisans in the provinces seem not to have deserted him in large numbers. As soon as he was dead, most of them probably submitted, including the armies of the western themes that had always been somewhat cool to him; but even then some resisted, perhaps because they doubted the reports of his death. On the coast of the theme of Macedonia, Panium and Heraclea held out for almost four months while Michael pacified the rest of Thrace. Finally, by February of 824, an earthquake damaged their walls. At Panium the destruction was so severe that the defenders surrendered at once; but at Heraclea the shaken walls were still defensible, and Michael compelled surrender only by landing troops on the sea side.

The last of Thomas's great expeditionary force had now given up, and Michael returned victorious to the capital by the beginning of March 824. He seems not to have punished at all those who had submitted early or on terms. Among those he captured later, he executed the volunteers from the caliphate and perhaps the Slavs; but most of the Byzantines he merely displayed in the Hippodrome with their hands tied behind their backs. Then he relegated the ones he considered most guilty to remote spots and released the rest. Michael wisely recognized that the numbers of his former opponents guaranteed most of them impunity.[335]

Meanwhile, not without difficulty, Michael's power had been secured in Anatolia. Most of the officers and soldiers left behind by Thomas probably submitted peacefully to the government, but for months some held out as little better than brigands or pirates. Among the Cibyrrhaeots many continued to resist, and evidently kept some degree of organized control over the theme's territory. In the Anatolic theme an officer of Thomas's named Choereas had his headquarters at the fort of Caballa near Iconium, and in the Bucellarian theme Gazarenus Coloniates, another officer, was based at the town of Saniana, not far from Ancyra. These two, who may have served Thomas as strategi of their themes, still commanded troops and apparently cooperated in raiding the rest of the countryside. In the Thracesians too former soldiers of Thomas were roaming about, raping and pillaging. Under the circumstances the regular troops of these themes, most of whom had recently fought for Thomas and were just returning home exhausted, were not the best people to restore order.

Michael adopted various expedients. He sent the Imperial Fleet to the Cibyrrhaeot theme, which could only be controlled from the sea. Its commander took possession of the theme's headquarters at Attalia and began the work of pacification. On his advice, Michael entrusted the theme to an acting strategus, John Echimus, a Palestinian who had lived at Attalia for years as a private citizen. John showed extraordinary military talent, and soon hunted down the outlaws and punished them by confiscating their military lands, thus dismissing them from the fleet. Michael tried to win over Choereas and Gazarenus shortly after Thomas's execution by offering them not only pardons but the rank of magister, higher even than the patrician's rank usually given to senior strategi. Even this they refused, preferring to continue their rebellion rather than rely on Michael's promises.

After failing with the leaders, Michael's envoys sought to persuade the inhabitants of the two towns, who would clearly benefit from peace, to close the gates on the warlords while they were off raiding. Michael's agent, a certain Guberius, had a peasant musician convey a message to a churchman in Saniana, offering to make him metropolitan of Neocaesarea if he would use his influence in the emperor's interest. With the help of this man, who was delighted to accept, the people of Saniana shut out Gazarenus, and those of Caballa were similarly persuaded to shut out Choereas. Finding themselves excluded from their strongholds, the leaders joined forces and set out for Arab territory, but troops loyal to Michael apprehended and crucified them on their way. Then order gradually returned. By the spring of 824, more than four years after his proclamation, Michael seems for the first time to have taken fairly complete possession of the empire.[336]

The conflict between Michael and Thomas shows the worst that could come from a disputed succession at Byzantium. By late 821 no one had a very plausible claim to the throne except by right of conquest, and by that right two candidates had roughly equal claims. After the murder of Leo V, Thomas had established much the firmer grip on the provinces, but Michael securely held the capital. Although Thomas had made steady progress, Michael's position was practically impregnable. Within his territory Michael successfully branded Thomas as a rebel and exploited the dislike that many in the capital and the Armeniacs had felt for Leo V. Elsewhere Thomas successfully depicted Michael as the murderer and himself as the avenger of Leo, whose reputation in the thematic army and in Thrace was generally a good one.

Normally civil conflict at Byzantium dissipated before it reached the point of civil war because one side had, or soon gained, an evident advantage. Then those who were undecided hastened to join the stronger side, and by so doing brought it a speedy victory. The victory then justified itself, because it was widely attributed to the will of God. This time, however, it was very hard to tell which side was the stronger and better, and different groups came to different conclusions. Once sides had been chosen and defended for some time, they were not easily abandoned, and the war dragged on. Worst of all, when God gave no clear sign and the empire continued to suffer, the suspicion grew that neither side was really in the right, which in dynastic terms was perfectly true.

Therefore the war caused a general malaise, which lingered after the fighting was over. At first there had been a rough division of opinion between those who felt that Leo V was an unscrupulous character who had unwisely raked up Iconoclasm and those who felt that he had restored the empire to capable rule and right belief; the former view predominated in the capital and the latter was widely held in the provinces. After the war it was not so much that these positions had hardened as that both had been weakened, because Leo's rule had been much better than what followed but the attempt to avenge him had been a disastrous failure. Nonetheless, except in part of Thrace, the war had not caused much destruction of property. The long sieges and few battles would have killed rather few men, and not many soldiers had even been dismissed. Only the navy had suffered major losses. All this could be repaired or forgotten in a few years, though unfortunately the navy turned out to be needed before it had completely recovered.

MICHAEL'S RECONSTRUCTION

After this inauspicious beginning, Michael II made an effort to convert his subjects' exhaustion and resignation into more positive feelings about himself and the dynasty he hoped to found. Even before the end of the war Michael's propagandists had been at work to establish his legitimacy and to blacken Thomas's reputation. By the time the war was over, they had managed to combine the absolutely undeniable facts with some skillful distortions and falsehoods to produce an ingenious official version of what had happened.

Thomas, according to them, had during the reign of Irene seduced the wife of his commander Bardanes Turcus and fled to the Arabs. He had remained in the caliphate for 25 years, apostatizing from Christianity. Late in Leo's reign, however, he had declared himself to be Constantine VI, made a pact with the caliph to subject the empire to the Arabs, and gathered a force of volunteers from Arab territory. Then he had invaded

Chaldia and the Armeniac theme, defeating the strategus of the Armeniacs. Concluding that Leo was unable to defeat Thomas, some conspirators in Constantinople overthrew Leo, and the chief officials and the patriarch chose Michael as his successor. Thomas's rebellion continued to spread, and he took over additional provinces and besieged Constantinople for a year. Then the Bulgar khan Omurtag, despite Michael's efforts to prevent him from invading, attacked and defeated Thomas on Byzantine soil. Finally, Michael defeated Thomas at Diabasis and slowly put the rebellion down with a minimum of bloodshed. This account was used for official purposes and apparently was turned into a long iambic poem entitled *Against Thomas* by Ignatius the Deacon, a church official on the staff of St. Sophia.

Though the very highest officials, early supporters of Thomas, and well-informed people in the Armeniac and Anatolic themes would have known this story to be false, it seems to have successfully imposed upon many others. Even most of the educated people in Constantinople and the West had never heard of Thomas before 821, could easily believe that Leo V had suppressed reports of a rebellion in the East, and had no knowledge of the details of Leo's murder and Michael's accession, or of Michael's negotiations with the Bulgars. Many had heard another version of the facts; but, especially if it included the naive story that Thomas was Constantine VI, that version was not clearly preferable to Michael's, which was coherent and backed up by his God-given victory in the war. So Michael's version soon became the standard one, and must have gone far to shore up his legitimacy by making his accession seem guiltless and by stigmatizing Thomas as a rebel against Leo V.[337]

Of course, Michael still had trouble with the iconophiles. When he returned to Constantinople early in 824, he tried once again to persuade them to compromise by having a leading iconophile in his service, Leo the Sacellarius, approach Theodore of Studius. Theodore replied to both Leo and the emperor that he could agree to no compromise, because matters of the faith were to be decided by the spiritual authorities of both East and West, and first and foremost by the pope. As before, when the emperor had agreed to drop his request for a debate between iconophiles and iconoclasts, he exploited any opening for an agreement. Having nothing to lose by sending an embassy to the pope, he decided to do so.

To improve his chances for a favorable hearing, Michael first sent ambassadors to the Frankish emperor, Louis the Pious, who was far less committed to icons than the pope was, with a cordial letter requesting Louis to support Michael's cause at Rome. The letter included the official account of Thomas's uprising and a cautiously worded statement opposing excessive attention to icons. The ambassadors brought Louis a gift of luxurious fabrics. To show Michael's respect for Louis's authority, they took with them Fortunatus, patriarch of Grado, who had fled to Constantinople in 821 when Louis had summoned him to answer a charge of plotting with the Croats. Michael chose his ambassadors tactfully. Their head was the strategus Theodotus, probably of Sicily, a friend of Theodore of Studius who was an iconophile in communion with the iconoclast hierarchy; but with him was Theodore Crithinus, steward of St. Sophia and a convinced iconoclast. The embassy left for the Frankish court in April of 824 and was to proceed afterwards to Rome. For the time being, at least, Michael had dexterously revived the idea of a compromise with the iconophiles.[338]

Late in the civil war Michael's wife Thecla had died. He had buried her in the Church of the Holy Apostles and declared himself too grief-stricken ever to marry again. His declaration proved unwelcome to his chief officials and their wives, who found court society dull without an empress, probably the more so because Thecla had been from a rich Constantinopolitan family whereas Michael was a simple provincial. When Michael saw that his celibacy was unpopular and that remarrying might bring political advantages, he met with the officials and let them urge him to remarry. He agreed to do so on condition that they sign an oath to defend and obey his new wife and any children she might have, even after his death. As such an oath could scarcely be refused, the officials gave this new support to Michael's dynasty.

The best wife from a political point of view was a member of a previous dynasty, but unfortunately all the women of the three most recent imperial families had been relegated to convents at one time or another for political reasons. Sure of the obedience of his church hierarchy, Michael decided to risk the scandal of having a princess released from her monastic vows. If he took that chance, he could do no better than one of the two daughters of Constantine VI and his first wife, Maria of Amnia. The Isaurian dynasty had been on the throne long enough and had won enough victories to gain real legitimacy; iconoclasts favored the family because it had started Iconoclasm, and iconophiles liked it because it had brought back the icons. Now that his views on icons were newly ambiguous, Michael obtained the consent of Constantine's younger daughter, Euphrosyne. She was then in her early thirties and a nun in the convent founded by her grandmother Irene on the island of Principo. Though Euphrosyne was an iconophile and Theodore of Studius had been on friendly terms with her, Theodore was outraged at her disregard for her vows and tried to persuade her mother, Maria, not to accompany her to the palace. Others, including iconophiles, seem to have cared much less than Theodore, however, and on balance probably thought better of Michael because of the marriage. Since Euphrosyne remembered her convent fondly and Michael was a puritan who regretted his first wife and already had an heir, their union, which remained childless, may have been a marriage in name only.[339]

With his reputation on the rise, Michael sought a victory over a foreign enemy. The Arabs had given him ample reason for retaliation by their aid to Thomas, and their own civil troubles still weakened them, especially in the border territories. Probably in the summer of 824, Michael sent an army to northern Syria, the very region where the Arab authorities were still trying to subdue the rebel Naṣr. The Byzantines swept down upon the city of Sozopetra and destroyed it, driving off the local livestock as booty. At the same time Michael sent ships, apparently from the Imperial Fleet, to raid the coast of Syria. Aside from rebuilding and refortifying Sozopetra, the caliph took no immediate countermeasures. The emperor therefore had his revenge and his victory, and had shown that civil war had not crippled the army of Asia Minor.[340]

Even Michael's embassy to the West was a partial success. In November 824 Louis the Pious received the ambassadors cordially, sent them on to Rome with his blessing, and showed signs of agreeing with Michael's views on icons. If the ambassadors accomplished little at Rome, as seems to be the case, at least Theodore of Studius did not use the pope's reply to stir up iconophile opposition to Michael. When the ambassadors returned to Constantinople about the spring of 825, its two leaders, the iconophile Theodotus and the iconoclast Theodore, were at odds, with the emperor inclined to take Theodore's part. Theodore of Studius anxiously appealed to his friend Pantoleon, now perhaps general logothete, to intercede for Theodotus, and under the circumstances was careful not to offend the emperor.[341]

Probably at about this time, Michael felt sure enough of his position to promulgate some legislation on ecclesiastical matters. Most of it, like his variety of Iconoclasm, was of an austere and puritanical sort. He decreed that in Lent the fast should be kept on Saturdays, as was the Western practice but not the Eastern, and that legal oaths should be taken in God's name alone, and not in the names of the saints. He is also said to have decreed that children should not be taught from either pagan or patristic texts, which may mean that he wanted their education to begin with the Bible; that he forbade them ever to study other works is quite incredible. Two of his other laws showed a tolerant spirit. He abolished the head tax on Jews of one nomisma a year, a measure that many of course attributed to his supposed Athinganism. He also reportedly forbade the word "Saint" to be written on pictures of saints, a measure that shows he did not forbid the pictures to be painted.[342]

Toward the end of the spring of 825, Michael sent an embassy to the caliph al-Ma'mūn to propose a peace treaty, now that the Byzantines had shown that they could raid Arab land again and the Arabs still had internal difficulties. Ma'mūn, however, had finally come to terms with the rebel Naṣr and pacified Syria, and he was in no mood to let Michael's raids go unavenged. He refused the offer of peace and that summer dispatched a large raiding expedition across the frontier, which advanced as far as Ancyra. Michael sent troops that defeated the raiders twice, at Ancyra and at Corum, killing the Arab commander. The caliph also sent a fleet to raid the Cibyrrhaeot theme and attack its headquarters at Attalia. The Cibyrrhaeots' fleet, which does not seem to have been back at full strength since the civil war, offered no effective opposition; their acting strategus, John Echimus, negotiated with the Arab commander who was besieging Attalia and simply bought him off. This raid exposed a weakness of the Byzantines on the sea that was soon to be exploited by the Arabs, though not by those under the caliph's authority.[343]

THE ARAB INVASION OF THE ISLANDS

The Byzantine islands had never been very well defended. The largest and most exposed of them, Sicily, had a strategus who commanded a thousand troops on the island and was the superior of the duke of Calabria, who commanded another thousand on the mainland. The fleet of the theme of Sicily seems to have been of modest size. The islands of the Aegean Sea were under the jurisdiction of the strategus of the Cibyrrhaeots, whose headquarters were at Attalia on the southern coast of Asia Minor. He had a subordinate, titled the drungary of the Dodecanese or of the Aegean Sea, who was probably based at Rhodes; this drungary commanded a thousand men and about half the Cibyrrhaeots' fleet, some 35 ships when it was at full strength.

The Cibyrrhaeot theme did not include Crete, which had its own archon. He presumably commanded only the hundred-man guard that was the prerogative of all strategi and archons, as well as a handful of ships. Cyprus, which also had its own archon, was shared uneasily with the Arab authorities. The smallness of the forces defending the islands in comparison with the army on land shows the Byzantines' lack of interest in sea power—an indifference that until this time had largely been shared by the Arabs, since the caliphate was even more predominantly a land power than the empire was. Only during the reign of Michael II did Arabs first make a serious attempt to take and hold the islands.[344]

The trouble began in Sicily. Late in the spring of 826, Michael II named Constantine Sudes strategus of Sicily, perhaps to replace Theodotus, the

SICILY AND CALABRIA

Croton City represented at
Council of Nicaea (787)
⊙ Capital of a theme
○ Capital of a ducate
• Other town

friend of Theodore of Studius. When Constantine arrived in his new province, he put his turmarch, Euphemius, at the head of the theme's fleet. Euphemius was an energetic man. Before the good sailing weather was over, he led a long naval raid on the African coast (then part of the Aghlabid emirate, which was independent of the caliph), captured some Arab merchants, and took considerable booty. Before he returned to the theme's headquarters at Syracuse, however, Euphemius learned that his commander was preparing to arrest him. The brothers of Euphemius's wife had protested to the emperor that Euphemius had abducted their sister from a convent and married her against her will. Michael had therefore ordered the strategus Constantine to try Euphemius and, if he was guilty, to cut off his nose.

To avoid standing trial, the enterprising turmarch persuaded the officers of his fleet to join him in a conspiracy against Constantine. When his fleet arrived at Syracuse, Euphemius used it to seize the city. Constantine, who had either been away from Syracuse or had fled from it, gathered some troops on the island and attacked Euphemius, but Euphemius defeated him and forced him to take refuge in Catana. When Euphemius sent an army against him there, Constantine fled again, but was captured and killed. By this time Euphemius had hopelessly compromised himself with the imperial government, and to justify his independence had himself proclaimed emperor, evidently before the end of 826.

Although he held Syracuse and Catana, Euphemius had not secured the entire island. He seems to have entrusted the task of winning over the western part of it to a confederate named Plato, possibly an Armenian, whom he made commander of part of his troops. Euphemius probably chose Plato in the hope that he would win over his cousin Michael, the commander of Panormus (Palermo) which was the chief city of western Sicily. Instead Plato promptly joined his cousin in espousing the cause of the government in Constantinople, collected more troops, and attacked his patron as a rebel. These self-proclaimed loyalists defeated Euphemius and drove him to Syracuse, where he embarked with his remaining forces just as his enemies were entering the city. He then sailed to Africa, sent legates to the Aghlabid emir's capital at Qayrawān, and appealed to the emir, Ziyādat-Allāh I, for help.[345]

After taking counsel with his court, the emir agreed to an alliance. He recognized Euphemius's title and committed to the enterprise 70 ships, 700 cavalry, and 1,000 infantry, certainly a match for the loyalist remainder of the thousand regular troops of Sicily. In return, the self-styled emperor recognized the emir as his suzerain and promised him a large share of the Sicilian revenues. The combined fleet was more Arab than Byzantine, and Euphemius had decidedly less control over it than the Arab leader, Asad ibn al-Furāt. It sailed from Susa on June 14, 827, and three days later landed at Mazara on the western shore of Sicily. When the local Byzantine troops attacked the expeditionary force, Asad captured them easily, though he released them after they prudently declared themselves partisans of Euphemius. He did not, however, trust any of the Byzantines much, and told Euphemius and his men to stay out of future fighting.

Plato, who was still acting as strategus of Sicily, must already have asked for help from the emperor, but none had yet arrived. He therefore assembled as many troops as he could from the vicinity, perhaps including reinforcements from Calabria, and marched to the west of the island in July. The Arabs came out to meet him and attacked. After fierce fighting, the Byzantines fled with heavy loss. Plato escaped to Henna, a stronghold in the center of the island. From there he passed over to Calabria, where he presumably hoped to gather troops but instead was killed.

After Plato's defeat the duke of Calabria, a regular imperial appointee, may have chosen to regard the self-appointed strategus as a rebel who had helped overthrow Constantine Sudes. Legally Plato's position was certainly irregular, but he had performed a necessary function. After his death his cousin Michael continued to hold Panormus, but otherwise Byzantine resistance crumbled. Asad took towns and forts all over Sicily with little opposition, collecting prisoners and booty as he went. Even the Syracusans sent him a nominal submission, hostages, and tribute. They did not, however, admit his troops within their walls, following the advice of Euphemius, who had found his Arab allies stronger than he wished.

Michael II must first have heard of the trouble in Sicily in early 827, when Plato was in precarious control of the whole island. By summer the emperor assembled a small fleet, including a contingent levied from the Venetians, and sent it to Sicily, but by then the island was in chaos. The Syracusans apparently sent back this inadequate force to avoid antagonizing Asad. Nonetheless Asad, always distrustful of Byzantines, correctly suspected that the Syracusans were using the time they had gained by their supposed submission to strengthen their walls and to put in provisions for a siege. Probably before the end of 827, he had marched to Syracuse, brought his fleet there, and besieged the city by land and sea.[346]

In the meantime the empire was acquiring another seagoing Arab enemy. In March of 827 Ma'mūn's general 'Abd Allāh laid siege to Alexandria, which had been seized by a band of exiled Arabs from Spain. Cut off by land in the town's seaside citadel, the Spanish Arabs opened negotiations with 'Abd Allāh and suggested that they might settle somewhere in Byzantine territory with their wives and children. Perhaps in June, with the general's leave, they sent out ten to twenty of their ships to reconnoiter Crete under their leader Abū Ḥafṣ. Abū Ḥafṣ found the island without any naval defenses, perhaps because its little squadron had not been replaced after the civil war, and took ample plunder and prisoners. Nonetheless, when he returned to Alexandria he made no move to transfer his people to Crete permanently. The siege there dragged on until December, when Abū Ḥafṣ's band ran out of provisions and submitted to 'Abd Allāh, proposing to purchase houses near Alexandria and live there peacefully. Only when the Alexandrians refused to sell property to them—understandably, in view of the devastation that they had brought to the town—did Abū Ḥafṣ and his followers decide to go to Crete. They set sail, aboard 40 ships, in the spring of 828.[347]

No doubt Michael II and his government assumed that the expedition of Abū Ḥafṣ in 827 was a mere raid, because they devoted all their energy at the beginning of 828 to outfitting a large fleet to send to Sicily. Michael applied to the Venetians and had them send more ships, but he was not content with this. He seems to have gathered nearly every vessel he had, including the Cibyrrhaeot fleet with its strategus. Only the flotilla of the Anatolic theme, which had a short coastline adjoining the caliphate, and part of the Imperial Fleet certainly remained behind. The emperor would hardly have left the Aegean so denuded of ships if he had anticipated an invasion there, but his anxiety about Sicily was well founded. The North African base of the Aghlabid emir was much nearer to Sicily than Constantinople was, and if the Arab invaders took Syracuse, with its strong fortifications and superb harbor, the Byzantines would have little hope of expelling them later.[348]

Syracuse was in grave danger at the time. Early in the spring of 828, Asad received reinforcements by sea from Africa and even from the Umayyad caliph of Spain. The only significant Byzantine force left on the island was the garrison of Panormus, under the command of Michael, the loyal cousin of the sometimes loyal but now deceased Plato. As the Syracusans seemed to be losing heart, Michael led a force out of Panormus in an attempt to relieve them. He found Asad's men in a siege camp protected by a ditch, awaiting his assault. When the Byzantines charged, many of them fell into concealed pits dug by the Arabs outside the ditch, and after suffering heavy losses were compelled to retire. Asad now tightened the blockade around the Syracusans, who offered to surrender in return for a guarantee of their freedom, lives, and property. Asad was ready to accept the terms; but his troops, disdaining a victory without spoils, would not agree.[349]

The siege was difficult for the Arabs as well. Because the Syracusans had stripped the neighborhood of provisions, the besiegers began to suffer from famine, and were reduced to eating their horses. Many of the soldiers demanded to return to North Africa and only calmed down after Asad had their ringleader gently flogged. Then disease broke out in the Arab camp. At the beginning of summer, Asad himself died, either of the disease, or of the effects of wounds he had received, or of both. At the time of his death, the Byzantine hostages whom he had been keeping, probably ever since the Syracusans had made their nominal submission, escaped. With no time to send back to Qayrawān for orders, the Arab army elected a new leader, Muḥammad ibn Abī'l-Jawārī. Just when Syracuse seemed within his grasp, the great fleet sent by Michael II appeared.[350]

Beset by hunger, sickness, and a fleet much larger than their own, now all the Arabs wanted to go back to North Africa. They took to their ships in the harbor and tried to sail out of its narrow mouth. The Byzantines, who might have done well to let them leave, instead blocked the entrance and trapped them inside. The Arabs therefore burned their ships to deny them to the Byzantines and withdrew into the interior.

Though the siege of Syracuse was now broken, the Arab army took advantage of its leisure to reduce inland towns that remained in Byzantine hands. The Arabs besieged the hill town of Menaenum, which fell after just three days, and then took the city of Agrigentum. The Byzantine fleet should have had enough men to move inland and at least challenge the Arabs; perhaps a few men were dispatched. By midsummer, however, Michael II desperately needed ships to send against Abū Ḥafṣ on Crete, and had had time to send for them. Although a small part of the armada may have stayed in Sicily, the Venetians went home and the Cibyrrhaeots returned to the Aegean to fight their new enemy.[351]

Sometime in the spring Abū Ḥafṣ and his 40 ships had landed on Crete to meet, as in the previous year, no opposition of any consequence. Their ships might have held some 12,000 men, women, and children, of whom perhaps 3,000 were seasoned fighting men, enough to conquer the island if no defenders arrived from outside. They anchored at Suda Bay in northwestern Crete. Abū Ḥafṣ left 800 men behind to guard the fleet, and with the rest plundered the island for twelve days. He realized, however, that he would need to be ready to defend himself against the Byzantines. Since the island evidently had no properly fortified port, Abū Ḥafṣ promptly began work on a fortified settlement by the sea, surrounded by a moat. The Arabs called the town Khandaq, or "Trench," after its moat; the Greeks called it Chandax, and Westerners came to call it Candia. It had a good harbor, was centrally located in order to dominate the island, and was on the north side in order to threaten the whole Aegean. Thus far Abū Ḥafṣ had not troubled to take most of the established towns on Crete.[352]

Michael soon learned, probably in a dispatch from the helpless archon, that the Spanish Arabs were building a base on Crete. Since the Cibyrrhaeots—and apparently most of the the Imperial Fleet and the fleets of themes—were away in Sicily, the emperor asked the strategus of the Anatolics, Photinus, to sail to Crete with the few ships he had and to take appropriate measures. On his arrival in Crete Photinus discovered how many invaders there were, and reported their number to Michael, requesting a force adequate to rid the island of Arabs. But the emperor did not have a truly adequate force.

Nonetheless, he scraped together such ships as he could, found troops for them, put them under the protostrator Damianus, the head of the imperial stables, and sent this makeshift fleet to Crete. Photinus combined his forces with those of Damianus and attacked the Arabs on land near their unfinished stronghold, probably at the beginning of summer. Dam-

ianus fell wounded in the first assault, the Byzantines took flight, and the
Arabs were victorious. After losing most of his ships, Photinus escaped
by boat to the island of Dia off Chandax, from which he proceeded to
Constantinople to give the emperor the bad news. Apparently under-
standing that his armament had been too weak, Michael did not blame
Photinus for his failure.[353]

Now that Syracuse had been relieved and there might still be time to
prevent Crete from becoming another Sicily, Michael must have recalled
most or all of the Sicilian expeditionary force, including the Cibyrrhaeots
with their strategus. Because this took time, Abū Ḥafṣ had most of the
summer to continue work on Chandax and to conquer the towns of
Crete. These he took one by one, destroying their fortifications and treating their people harshly. Most Cretans seem to have fled, converted to
Islam, or been enslaved, except in one town that surrendered on terms; its
inhabitants were permitted to keep their freedom and their religion. Since
the island was reasonably small, Abū Ḥafṣ decided that he could and
would make it predominantly Muslim and rid himself of religious divisions at home.[354]

Michael now assigned the task of retaking Crete to Craterus, the strategus of the Cibyrrhaeot theme, who by autumn of 828 landed on the
stricken island with his entire force of 70 ships and 2,000 marines. This
should have been enough. If Craterus had arrived before Abū Ḥafṣ had
established himself, Crete would almost certainly have remained Byzantine. As it was, Craterus had the better of the Arabs in a day-long battle,
after which they fled the field. But the Byzantines celebrated their victory
with too much wine, and slept too soundly afterwards. The Arabs surprised them during the night and butchered them. Craterus himself fled
in a ship to the island of Cos in the Dodecanese. Two Arab ships caught
up with him there, seized him, and crucified him.[355]

In contrast with these disastrous reverses on Crete, the Byzantine position on Sicily was improving. The main Arab army that had left Syracuse sought to continue its conquests by taking the extremely strong
mountain fortification of Henna (the later Castrogiovanni). The Arabs
entrusted the negotiations to the "emperor" Euphemius, to whom the
people of Henna promised to make a formal submission if he would send
the main Arab army away. When Euphemius arrived with a few of his
men, the delegation that came to meet him stabbed him to death. The Arabs cannot have regretted his loss very much, but his assassination was a
sign that the Sicilians were gaining confidence in the imperial cause, perhaps because they had heard that the emperor Michael was preparing to
send out a strategus whom they could trust, along with a large army.[356]

Early in the spring of 829, Michael sent out none other than Theodotus,

Theodore of Studius's friend, who had apparently been strategus of Sicily before he had served on the embassy to Louis the Pious that had nearly brought his downfall. Theodotus therefore knew the country, which he had governed in the peaceful days, not long past, before the revolt of Euphemius. At this point Michael appears to have given the defense of Sicily priority over the recovery of Crete, which was the less rich island and seemingly the more difficult to retake. With the Cibyrrhaeots out of commission for the time being, Michael probably sent part of the Imperial Fleet along with Theodotus, who also brought new soldiers for the thematic army of Sicily. After he landed, Theodotus led his troops against the Arabs, who were still near Henna. The Byzantines attacked, only to be defeated by the Arabs, who killed many of them and took 90 officers prisoner. Theodotus and the rest of his troops escaped into Henna. Very soon thereafter, however, perhaps in April, the Arab leader Muḥammad ibn Abī'l-Jawārī died, and the man elected to replace him, Zuhayr ibn Gawth, had less success than his predecessor.[357]

After this election Theodotus and his men surprised an Arab raiding party and defeated it. The next day, when the entire Arab army came to avenge the loss, the Byzantines won the ensuing battle, killed many Arabs, and pursued the rest to their fortified camp, which Theodotus besieged. Without sufficient supplies to hold out for long, the Arabs tried a night attack on the Byzantines; forewarned, the Byzantines ambushed their attackers and cut them to pieces. The remnant of the strong army that had besieged Syracuse and Henna made its way to Menaenum, the last Arab outpost in the east of the island. There Theodotus besieged them again. The nearest point still in Arab hands was Agrigentum; but when its garrison learned what had happened to the main army they destroyed their post and decamped for Mazara in the west, the Arabs' original beachhead. As the soldiers inside Menaenum were once again reduced to eating horses and even dogs, the Byzantines had the upper hand in Sicily by the autumn of 829. They could expect to clear the island of invaders before long if all went well.[358]

At the same time Michael was not ignoring the Arabs of Crete. After they had practically annihilated the army of the Cibyrrhaeot theme and killed its strategus, they had started to overrun the next islands to the north, the Cyclades. These formed part of the Cybyrrhaeot theme, which was defenseless until the marines killed on Crete could be replaced and new ships built. By now the Arabs of Crete were so formidable that service in the Cibyrrhaeots was not very attractive. Especially in the drungus of the Aegean Sea, where much of the land for soldiers was in Arab hands, no one was likely to enlist.

After the defeat of the Cibyrrhaeots and the death of their strategus,

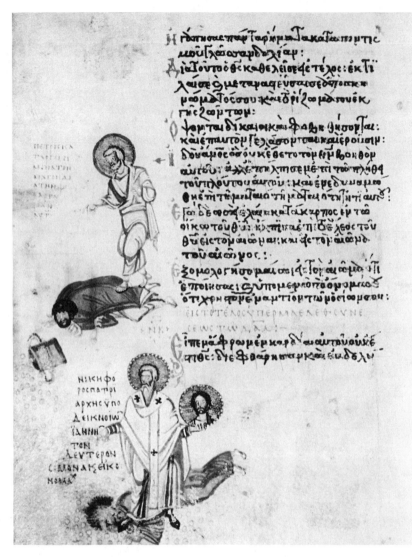

39. *Top*, St. Peter trampling Simon Magus; *bottom*, the patriarch Nicephorus trampling John the Grammarian. State Historical Museum, Moscow, add. 129, fol. 51ᵛ, a ninth-century manuscript of the Psalms. The text illustrated is Psalms 52:6–7: "The righteous also shall see, and fear, and shall laugh at him: 'Lo, this is the man that made not God his strength; but trusted in the abundance of his riches, and strengthened himself in his wickedness.'" The legend of the bottom illustration is "The patriarch Nicephorus pointing out Jannes, the second Simon [Magus] and iconoclast." In later Byzantine tradition John is often nicknamed "Jannes" (after the Egyptian magician of 2 Tim. 3:8; cf. Ex. 7:11) as an allusion to his dabbling in the occult. The coins are probably an allusion to the luxury in which John lived as patriarch of Constantinople (838–43). Nicephorus actually died fifteen years before John was condemned at the restoration of the icons in 843. (Photo: Professor Kurt Weitzmann, Princeton University)

Michael II appointed a certain Oöryphas to raise new marines, empowering him to offer his recruits a bonus of 40 nomismata, which was more than six years' regular pay. With this inducement Oöryphas was able to sign up a sizable company, who because of the bonus received the nickname of Tessaracontarii, or "Fortyers." Ships were quickly built or requisitioned over the winter, and in the spring of 829 Oöryphas and his men descended upon the Cyclades. By now the never very numerous Arabs were overextended, and the new marines easily cleared and garrisoned the islands. Reportedly they even landed on Crete, but had to withdraw after meeting with fierce resistance. The Tessaracontarii probably became most of the regular garrison of the Aegean Sea, while other men took the vacant places for Cibyrrhaeot marines on the mainland. At least the empire had finally defeated the Cretan Arabs and repaired its defenses against them, though both the defeat and the repair work were by no means complete.[359]

Except for Sicily, Crete, and the Cyclades, in the years after the civil war Michael II gave the empire a much-needed rest from domestic upheavals and foreign adventures. The treaty with the Bulgars had been renewed until 836, unaffected by the fact that not long before the renewal took effect in 826 some Byzantine captives had escaped from Bulgaria surreptitiously. Michael prudently chose not to retaliate for the land and sea raids sent out in 825 by the caliph Ma'mūn, who in return left the empire alone as he reestablished his authority in Egypt and struggled with the Khurramite rebels in Azerbaijan. In mid-827 Michael again sent Theodore Crithinus with an embassy to the Frankish emperor Louis the Pious. Louis, who had already taken a conciliatory position on Iconoclasm at his church council in Paris in 825, gladly received the embassy and its gift of a splendid manuscript of Pseudo-Dionysius the Areopagite. He reciprocated with ambassadors of his own in February 828.[360]

Within the empire Michael continued to treat iconophiles with a moderation that gradually reduced ill feeling over Iconoclasm. As before, he left iconophiles undisturbed if they stayed outside Constantinople, and perhaps even if they did not. The iconophiles lost both their greatest champion and their leader when Theodore of Studius died on November 11, 826, and the former patriarch Nicephorus died on April 5, 828. After years of official Iconoclasm, old age was slowly overtaking the iconophile bishops and abbots, who were those most publicly committed to their cause and had the best claims to lead it. Nevertheless, profound iconophile sentiment remained widespread, while iconoclast sentiment was remarkably shallow.[361]

During most of 829, and probably earlier, Michael suffered increasingly from kidney disease, which finally permitted him to do what no other Byzantine ruler had done since 780, and probably since 775. Unlike his predecessors, Michael II died of natural causes while he was still ruling, succumbing to his illness on October 2, 829. A moderate to the end, on his deathbed he declared a general amnesty for prisoners. His successor was his son Theophilus, then just sixteen years old. Because of his youth and the oath that the empire's chief officials had signed, Theophilus was at first to rule together with his stepmother, Euphrosyne, but would soon be of age to govern independently. Despite all the disasters of his nine-year reign, Michael appeared to have founded a dynasty with a good chance of lasting, which again was something that the empire had not seen for a good many years.[362]

LEO'S AND MICHAEL'S ACCOMPLISHMENTS

Bardanes Turcus had shown himself an excellent judge of talent when he appointed Leo the Armenian, Michael the Amorian, and Thomas the Slav to the elite guard of the Anatolics. From that position Leo had maneuvered his way to the imperial throne, survived and brought to an end a full-scale Bulgar invasion, and imposed Iconoclasm with a steady hand against strong opposition. Then Michael, when Leo seemed well established, had won the throne for himself while imprisoned under sentence of death, and had ridden out a civil war of more than three years with an opponent who controlled most of the empire. Thomas, with less luck and less treachery than his two old comrades, had made himself Leo's successor in nearly half the empire, would have become undisputed emperor if a single gate of the capital had been opened to him, and maintained a rival government and army that lasted until after his death. These feats required political skill of a high order; but unfortunately for the empire that skill was mostly directed against other Byzantines.

It is easy to make a case that Leo, Michael, and Thomas sacrificed the empire's interests to their personal ambition. Leo was largely to blame for the Bulgars' devastation of Thrace, which he brought on by deserting Michael Rhangabe in battle and allowed to continue because he would not risk attacking Krum. Leo's reintroduction of Iconoclasm, which for such a thoroughly political man does not appear to have been a matter of simple religious idealism, proved not even to be in his own best interest, and redivided a society that had almost recovered its religious cohesion. Michael could not justify the brutal overthrow of Leo either by his trivial private grievance or by any likely hope of reuniting the Byzantine people, whom he split more bitterly than ever. He could defend himself only with a set of falsehoods that put the blame for Leo's murder on others. Thomas undertook his own reckless enterprise with very dubious chances of success and, when it became virtually hopeless in 823, continued it at great cost to himself and others. While attempts to seize the throne were common at Byzantium, most of them, whether successful or not, had been far less destructive than those of these three men, not least because previous plotters, like Bardanes Turcus, had given up rather than fight to the bitter end.

Nevertheless, Leo V and Michael II were both outstanding managers, and when they had leisure to benefit the empire they did so. Leo put an end to the Bulgar threat, which had begun in 811 through no fault of his. His victory over Omurtag in 816 was much needed, and his treaty, which preserved most of the land colonized by Nicephorus I, brought many years of welcome peace on the Bulgar frontier. By defeating the Bulgars and Arabs, Leo restored Byzantine self-confidence when it had been seriously shaken. Although he could probably have accomplished this without reintroducing Iconoclasm, he thought Iconoclasm would help raise morale, and for some in the army it doubtless did. The latter part of Leo's reign brought military, administrative, and judicial reforms whose nature and benefits are not very clear today; but if even Leo's enemies praised his work, it presumably did some good.

Then Michael II, even while he fought Thomas and continued Iconoclasm, did reduce the amount of hostility that iconophiles felt toward the government. Again, by his mercy to the former partisans of Thomas the Slav, Michael probably hastened the empire's recovery from the civil war. The general amnesty that Michael proclaimed on his deathbed was a rare act of clemency for a Byzantine ruler, and as such was sorely needed. Among those released in 829 was Methodius, the papal legate whom Michael had imprisoned for almost nine years on an obscure charge of iconophile propaganda; but the amnesty apparently came too late for Methodius's cellmate, a hapless wretch jailed since 797 for plotting against Irene, then left to rot by five emperors whom he had done no harm. Michael earned little glory in battle, but in his efforts to fight the remote and stubborn Arab invaders of the islands he showed his usual grim determination, which especially in Sicily did not go unrewarded.[363]

Although the loss of Crete and the beginning of an intractable war on Sicily would trouble the empire for many years to come, how much these were the fault of Leo, Michael, and Thomas may be disputed. In the course of Thomas's uprising and Michael's suppression of it many ships were destroyed and many experienced naval officers, oarsmen, and marines were killed. The fleet was probably back at full numerical strength by 828, but then the blunders of its officers and men look like evidence of inexperience in combat. The Spanish and African Arabs must have heard of the civil war, which would have encouraged them to attack the empire when they might expect it to be weakened and disunited. Although there is not a shred of evidence for the social or economic discontent that some modern scholars have wanted to make a cause of Thomas's uprising, the civil war did result in a general feeling that the empire was in disorder, which might slightly have weakened the resistance of the Sicilians and Cretans to the Arab invaders.

All these considerations, however, seem less important than the remoteness of Sicily, the absence of regular troops on Crete, the simultaneity of the attacks on both islands, and the government's long-standing lack of interest in sea power. Invasions of Crete and Sicily might well have been about as successful at any time in the previous two centuries. It should also be recognized that behind the Byzantines' excessive indifference to maritime defense lay the correct belief that the empire was essentially a land power. Arabs on Sicily and Crete were a major nuisance, but not a major threat to the empire's vital interests.

On the whole, the reverses that the empire suffered between 813 and 829, devastating though they were for those people who were directly affected, did little if any lasting harm to the Byzantine state and society. The Bulgars systematically pillaged Thrace in 813 and 814, but agriculture had recovered enough there to make the land worth raiding again in 815. The Thracian towns of Arcadiopolis and Bizya, which Leo rebuilt only after 816, were strong, well-provisioned, and populous by the time Thomas the Slav used them as bases in 822 and 823. Whatever trauma Leo's Iconoclasm caused to iconophile aristocrats did not prevent them from serving Leo as his highest civil officials to the end of his reign. The uprising of Thomas and its suppression probably caused less damage to Asia Minor than a major Arab raid, and certainly far less harm to Thrace than the recent Bulgar war.

As always, the army's casualties in the Bulgar and civil wars, which do not seem to have been terribly high, were replaced promptly as new recruits came forward to fill the vacant places and receive military lands and pay. The civil war was harder on the fleet, but Michael was able to raid Syria by sea in 824, the same year the war ended. Though the Cibyrrhaeot fleet offered no effective resistance to the Arabs a year later, it soon had its full complement of ships again. Only when invaders actually conquered territory that included military lands, as the Arabs did in Sicily and the Cyclades, did Michael need to transport soldiers from the East to Sicily or to offer a bounty for recruits to fight in the Aegean.

No doubt all this warfare cost money, either spent on campaigns, new ships, and fortifications or lost through tax exemptions and the actual loss of taxable land. Yet the governments of Leo and Michael never showed signs of financial strain. Even Thomas the Slav, who had no access to the imperial treasury in Constantinople, had no trouble sending the caliph tribute, outfitting great fleets, and paying about two-thirds of the empire's army for three years out of his provincial revenues. He resorted to raiding only at the end of the war, and no source reports that any of his troops deserted because they had not been paid. Evidently the reformed revenue system of Nicephorus I continued to work beautifully all over the empire.

Whereas the first period of Iconoclasm had affected Byzantine culture adversely, the second did nothing of the sort. Leo V not only failed to silence the strongest iconophiles but gave them a reason to write more passionately than ever. Theodore of Studius wrote dozens of letters from prison under Leo, and dozens more under Michael II, when he also prepared sermons regularly for his community in Bithynia. Though the patriarch Nicephorus stayed out of politics after he was deposed, he wrote two treatises against Iconoclasm before his deposition and five afterward; these constitute the most important body of iconophile theology of the period. Other iconophiles also wrote theology, and probably some lives of iconophile saints.[364]

Leo V could take more direct credit for the fact that there was now a group of iconoclast intellectuals. Their leaders were John the Grammarian, abbot of Sts. Sergius and Bacchus and later tutor to Michael's heir, Theophilus, and Anthony of Syllaeum, appointed patriarch by Michael in 821. Even though their only known literary work at this time was the report of the iconoclast commission of which they were the principal members, both were learned and influential. There were also writers who were not clearly iconoclasts but were in communion with the official hierarchy. They included Ignatius the Deacon, sacristan of St. Sophia, who about 824 wrote the poem against Thomas the Slav already mentioned, and perhaps Nicetas of Amnia, a monk who was the grandson of St. Philaretus the Almsgiver and wrote a life of his grandfather in 822. Though the amount of literature lost since Byzantine times always makes comparisons somewhat risky, literary activity appears to have been on the rise during the reigns of Leo and Michael. It follows that Byzantine education was performing its functions, the chief of which was to supply the government with competent civil servants.[365]

Admittedly, during the years from 813 to 829 Byzantium's reverses were much more obvious than its advances. The empire, which had gained considerable territory under Irene and especially under Nicephorus I, had to cede all Irene's acquisitions and part of Nicephorus's. It also lost some of Sicily, which it had held since the reign of Justinian, and all of Crete, which had remained unconquered since the days of the Roman Republic. Worse yet, Crete became a haven from which Arab pirates could raid the whole Aegean Sea. Through this time domestic order was often poorly kept, and governmental stability was not well maintained. The most encouraging thing about the disasters of these years was that the empire weathered them with so little damage, and with no signs of real disintegration. Population growth and improvements in education continued in spite of war and Iconoclasm. Leo built upon, and Michael at least did not reverse, the reforms of the imperial administration begun by Irene and completed by Nicephorus. Theophilus inherited an empire in surprisingly good condition.

CHAPTER FIVE

The Ambitions of Theophilus, 829-842

The sixteen-year-old emperor began his reign with infectious enthusiasm and energy. For years—practically for centuries—the Byzantine government had been struggling with crises, disasters, and disruptive attempts at reform. Every ruler since Leo IV had ascended the throne under questionable or tragic circumstances, and faced trouble almost at once. Michael II had started badly and ended little better, his reputation tarnished by the murder of his predecessor, the long civil war, and the continuing struggle with the Arabs over the islands. Never a very attractive personality, by the end he had been old, sick, and exhausted. By contrast, Theophilus inherited the empire without his father's limitations, guilt, or enemies, or any truly pressing problems. He himself appears to have seen his opportunity from the start, and to have set out to win a reputation for brilliance such as no emperor had had before.

Given his youth, Theophilus was exceptionally cultured and well educated. He was little like his simple and provincial father, who had entrusted his son's training to others. Though Theophilus was probably born at Amorium while his father was still stationed there, he had lived in the capital since his infancy. With the emperor Leo V for his godfather, a mother raised in polite society, and a father of high rank, he was one of the empire's more privileged children. Before his adolescence he was crowned junior emperor and began studying with one of the empire's most learned and intelligent men, John the Grammarian. After his mother Thecla died, Theophilus acquired a noble stepmother, Constantine VI's daughter Euphrosyne, who by his father's wish became his co-emperor in 829.[366]

Not every adolescent who became an emperor would have stayed on good terms with his former tutor and with his stepmother and co-ruler,

40. Theophilus (r. 829–42). Mutinensis graecus 122, fol. 164ʳ. Note the two long curls of the beard. He seems to be shown toward the end of his reign, when he was in his late twenties. (Photo: Biblioteca Estense, Modena)

but Theophilus was apparently fond of both John and Euphrosyne. The empress seems to have come to a friendly agreement with her stepson to retire as soon as he had chosen a wife from girls whom she would present to him. He certainly deferred to her social judgment in identifying suitably well-born and well-behaved candidates, and in arranging a proper bride show. Soon after his accession, Theophilus appointed John as his syncellus, the imperial representative at the patriarchate, and in so doing probably designated him as successor to the patriarch Anthony, who was much older than John.

   John, who continued to serve as abbot of the Monastery of Sts. Sergius and Bacchus, was the leading exponent of intellectual Iconoclasm, of which Theophilus was an avid partisan. The emperor was sincerely devout, showed particular devotion to the cult of the Virgin, and loved and even wrote hymns; but to him icons were marks of ignorant superstition. If he knew that his stepmother was an iconophile, he decided to overlook the fact as a feminine foible. While he was far tougher than her father, Constantine VI, she was much milder than her grandmother Irene, and she never disputed that Theophilus was going to rule in his own right, and as an iconoclast. Though he accepted Euphrosyne as his social adviser at first and adopted John the Grammarian as his permanent theological counselor, Theophilus definitely thought for himself.[367]

From his accession, for example, he thought of building on a grand scale. For over a century most emperors had had money enough to build, but except for Irene they had mostly spent it on strengthening fortifications and restoring what had been destroyed by the enemy. Irene had been the first to build important new structures, the Palace of Eleutherius and St. Sophia at Thessalonica. Both were presumably the work of artists and artisans from the capital, who, to judge from the clumsiness of St. Sophia, were still learning their trade when its construction began about 784. From that time on, the growth of the capital's population and the recovery of monasticism would have helped workmen develop the skills needed to build and decorate houses and churches. When Theophilus embarked on great projects for restoring the city walls on the seaward sides and for expanding the Great Palace, he found men able to do work that would be admired for centuries to come. However, perhaps because such men were not many, he continued these projects slowly throughout his reign.

The Great Palace already had ample room in two large complexes: the group of the Daphne and Magnaura, begun by Constantine I on the southeast side of the Hippodrome, and the newer group of the Bucoleon and Chrysotriclinus to the southwest, extending down to the shore of the Sea of Marmara. The last great builder on the palace grounds, Justinian II (r. 685–95, 705–11), had joined the Daphne and Magnaura with the Bucoleon and Chrysotriclinus by constructing two long halls down the hill by the side of the Hippodrome. Theophilus sought to build on the vacant part of the hillside between the two groups of palaces, which was open to the sun and sea breeze and had a fine view of the Sea of Marmara and the palace reservoir and gardens.

Very soon after his accession the emperor started work on the first part of the complex he planned, a structure facing east which he called the Pearl. It was to serve as Theophilus's own residence, and had three main rooms. The first was a rectangular hall with eight columns of mottled rose marble supporting its roof. To its south was a summer bedchamber with a dome set on four dark marble columns, which opened onto two green-pillared porches to the south and east. The walls of both rooms were decorated with colored mosaics of animals, reminiscent of the mo-

41. A tower of the sea walls, Constantinople, rebuilt by Theophilus. The lower inscription should read "Tower of Theophilus, in Christ Emperor," but when the inscribed pieces were fitted into the wall the "Emperor" was placed after the "in" by mistake. The upper inscription dates from a later Byzantine restoration. (Photo: Dumbarton Oaks Byzantine Collection, Washington)

saics commissioned by Constantine V, and the bedchamber's dome was studded with gold points like stars. There was another bedchamber to the north, protected from the wind, for use in winter. Though it must have made a delightful private residence, the Pearl was also meant to be seen by Theophilus's courtiers and talked about as proof of the refinement of his taste. Never slow to take credit for his building, Theophilus marked the sea walls that he restored with inscription after inscription bearing his name.[368]

The young emperor also wanted to be known for his justice. Nicephorus and Leo V had held their own law courts in the palace that were open to all, but Theophilus went farther than they had. Early in his reign he announced that every week he would ride out from the Great Palace across the city to pray at the Church of St. Mary of the Blachernae. As he rode, he would stop to listen to the complaints of any who waited along his path, and he would visit the markets to make sure that the merchants were not overcharging their customers. All complaints were to be investigated. The emperor let it be known that he would show no favor to miscreants of high rank or great wealth, even if their accusers were poor and obscure.

So seriously did Theophilus take his intention to right wrongs that at the beginning he seems to have forgotten that even those of high rank can be falsely accused. Soon after his accession, he heard complaints from former marines of the Cibyrrhaeots that five years earlier their acting strategus, John Echimus, had wrongly confiscated their property. Theophilus summoned John, who was now the monk Anthony, from a monastery on the Bithynian Mount Olympus. Anthony explained that he had confiscated the marines' property because they had been partisans of Thomas the Slav and had continued their disorder after the civil war. Theophilus, rejecting this explanation, handed the accused over to his minister for petitions, Stephen, who by intermittent imprisonment and flogging tried to force Anthony to repay money that he no longer possessed. When five months later Theophilus changed his mind and released the monk, he then became angry with Stephen, whom he punished by beating, tonsure, confiscation, and exile. At about the same time as Anthony was arrested, the emperor exiled the former bishop Theophilus of Ephesus, who like Anthony was an iconophile. Evidently the bishop was accused of misappropriating alms for the poor. Probably the emperor was inclined to believe the worst of those who rejected Iconoclasm, though as yet he did not punish anyone on that ground alone.[369]

Also at the start of his reign, Theophilus listened to an accusation by his postal logothete Myron that Manuel the Armenian, the distinguished former strategus of all Asia Minor, was plotting to seize the throne. Apparently the charge was slanderous, as the protovestiarius Leo Chamodracon assured Theophilus, and the emperor seems to have been uncertain whether to believe it or not. The accused, however, did not wait for the emperor to make up his mind. As soon as he learned of Myron's accusation, Manuel slipped out of Constantinople and used his authority to travel east at top speed by the carriages of the imperial post, which Myron had not thought of denying him. Arriving at the border of the caliphate, he sent word to the Arabs that he was fleeing the wrath of the emperor and would offer them his services in return for a pledge of safety and a promise that he would be allowed to remain a Christian. They gladly accepted, and Manuel soon received a warm reception from the caliph al-Ma'mūn at Baghdad.[370]

Since by this time Chamodracon and John the Grammarian had convinced Theophilus of Manuel's innocence, the young emperor was greatly distressed by his general's flight. He appears to have dismissed Manuel's accuser Myron as postal logothete and replaced him with Arsaber, John the Grammarian's brother. John now proposed a plan for bringing Manuel back. John himself would go on an embassy to Baghdad, ostensibly to announce Theophilus's accession, to present gifts to the caliph, and to visit Byzantine captives in Ma'mūn's prisons, but actually to offer Manuel the emperor's full pardon if he would return. Theophilus agreed, and sent John off with four hundred pounds of gold and other lavish presents. When John arrived at Baghdad, probably late in 829, the caliph accepted the gifts with pleased surprise and allowed the ambassador to visit the prisons and to provide the Byzantine captives with funds. No doubt it was some of John's money that persuaded one of the caliph's chief officials to allow John to meet Manuel privately. Manuel was receptive to the terms he was offered, though his escape would obviously take time. Without raising any suspicion, John returned to Constantinople with presents from the caliph and one hundred ransomed prisoners.[371]

Despite the emperor's generous gifts to him, Ma'mūn was preparing to lead an expedition against the empire in person for the first time in his caliphate. According to one report, Manuel had himself suggested an expedition when he arrived in Baghdad. Ma'mūn wanted to perform the pious act of a Holy War and may have interpreted John's gifts as a sign that the emperor was weak and afraid to fight, since he had already accepted Manuel's desertion and one defeat by Arabs in battle. In October of 829, some Byzantine ships, apparently from the Imperial Fleet on its way back from Sicily, had been destroyed by the Arabs of Crete, who had resumed raiding the recently pacified Cyclades; yet Theophilus, with few ships left, had done little or nothing. So the caliph confidently made his preparations and left Baghdad for the empire late in March of 830. In April, however, he interrupted his progress to celebrate the marriage of one of his daughters. Thereafter he advanced at such a slow pace that the Byzantines may well have concluded that he was not serious about his invasion.[372]

In the meantime, Theophilus had mourned his father for six months, and was ready to select a bride. After Irene had held a bride show for Constantine VI, and Nicephorus another for Stauracius, a show was expected. Euphrosyne, whose mother had been chosen for her father in the first show, naturally continued the custom. She had sent out to every theme to collect beautiful and well-born candidates, who arrived in Constantinople by May 830. The show was held in Theophilus's newly completed hall of the Pearl, which the ceremony may well have inaugurated. Theophilus was to make his selection by presenting the maiden he chose with an apple of gold. The place and the golden apple seem to reflect the taste of the ostentatious and literary Theophilus more than that of his stepmother, a former nun who was even then planning to return to a convent. After Euphrosyne had escorted the contestants into the Pearl, she handed Theophilus the apple and invited him to give it to whichever one he pleased.

The story of what happened was told soon after the event and may be essentially authentic. If it was invented, at any rate the inventor made the participants behave in character. According to our account, the emperor, already known as a connoisseur of beauty, paused in front of a breathtaking young woman named Cassia. Though he marveled as he looked at her, Theophilus remained conscious of his dignity. Using a verse that he had perhaps prepared beforehand, he commented aloud, "Yet / Through a woman evils came to man." Modestly but readily, Cassia replied, in a verse of her own, "But / Through a woman better things began." The solemn young ruler was utterly taken aback, passed by Cassia, and gave his apple to another girl named Theodora. Cassia then founded a convent in Constantinople, where she became a nun and wrote hymns and epigrams.[373]

Of the two contestants we know, Theophilus doubtless chose the one who suited him better. Probably born about 808, Cassia was a few years older than the emperor, well born, strong-willed, and an iconophile. Before 821, when she was a mere child of perhaps twelve, she had corresponded with Theodore of Studius, who had praised her precocious intelligence and writing style and exhorted her to enter a convent when the persecution was over. About 825, however, Theodore had written to rebuke her for trying to deny communion to a lapsed iconophile on his deathbed. She would have made a troublesome wife for a pompous iconoclast like Theophilus.

Theodora was milder in temperament, presumably younger, and certainly very beautiful, with black eyes that were especially striking. Though she came from the theme of Paphlagonia, where her late father had been turmarch, her family was wealthy and splendidly connected in the capital. She was the niece of the patrician Manuel who had recently fled to the Arabs, and she was related by marriage to Manuel's accuser, the former postal logothete Myron. She was also somehow related to the patrician Nicetas Monomachus, and her sister Calomaria had probably already married the patrician Arsaber, the brother of John the Grammarian. Unknown to Theophilus, however, Theodora was, like Cassia, an iconophile. On Pentecost, June 5, 830, the emperor crowned Theodora Augusta in the Church of St. Stephen in Daphne and married her in St. Sophia.[374]

LEADING ARISTOCRATIC FAMILIES

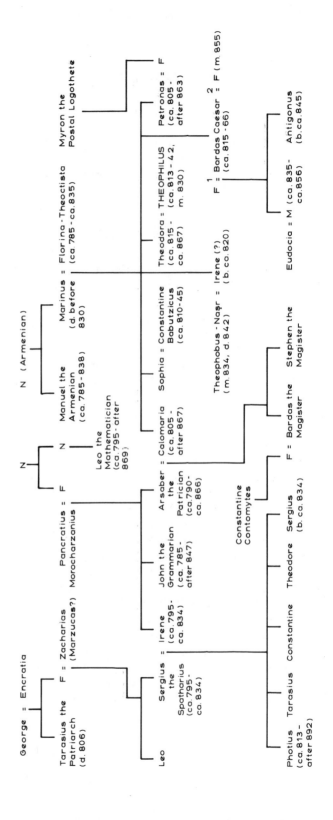

Soon afterward the empress Euphrosyne, having provided her stepson with a consort, resigned her co-emperorship and once again entered a convent—but not the convent on Principo where she had grown up. Instead she bought a house called the Gastria in the outlying part of Constantinople and converted it into a monastery of her own, where she was nearer to Theophilus and the wife she had helped him choose. Euphrosyne appears to have been a friend of Theodora's widowed mother, Theoctista, whom Theophilus honored with the new rank of girdled patrician. Apparently not long after Euphrosyne's retirement Theoctista entered the Gastria herself. Euphrosyne had purchased the building from a Nicetas the Patrician who was probably the same as Theoctista's relative Nicetas Monomachus, now an iconophile monk. Euphrosyne's mother Maria, with whom Euphrosyne had spent most of her life on Principo, was from Paphlagonia and had Armenian connections, like both Theoctista and Nicetas.

Apart from these bonds of acquaintance, race, and homeland, however, the strongest tie between Euphrosyne and the family of Theodora was devotion to icons. Euphrosyne had probably selected only iconophiles for Theophilus's bride show, and Cassia would have served her religious purpose as well as Theodora. But the empress may have spoken warmly to her stepson about Theodora and influenced his choice. On the whole Theophilus was happy with his wife, but her opposition to Iconoclasm was as steadfast as Euphrosyne could have wished.[375]

Euphrosyne's retirement freed Theophilus to take a measure that he had evidently been postponing as long as she ruled with him. At the time of the next chariot races in the Hippodrome, the emperor made a new display of ruthlessly impartial justice. When the races were over, while he still sat in the imperial box surrounded by his chief officials, he ordered his protovestiarius, Leo Chamodracon, to produce a grisly relic. It was the broken candelabrum with which Leo V had tried to protect himself ten years before, when the conspirators had cut him down in the palatine chapel of St. Stephen on Christmas morning. The emperor asked the officials who formed the Byzantine senate, "What does a man deserve who enters the Lord's temple and kills the Lord's anointed?" The senators, who could hardly tell their emperor that they approved of murdering emperors, duly answered, "He deserves death, Sire." Theophilus immediately ordered the city prefect to have the men who had attacked Leo brought out and beheaded at the end of the Hippodrome, in full view of the spectators. Some of the officials heard the unfortunate men rightly protest that Theophilus would not have been emperor if they had not killed Leo, but the summary sentence was carried out.

These executions effectively freed Theophilus from any responsibility for the murder that had established the Amorian dynasty, and may also have helped deter future conspiracies against him. Though Michael II had dissociated himself from the murderers, no knowledgeable Constantin-opolitan believed him; for him to do what his son later did would have shown such shameless hypocrisy that it would probably have done him more harm than good. For Theophilus, the step did not reflect well on his father's memory, which is presumably why he waited to take it until his father's widow was no longer ruling with him. Yet Theophilus was per-sonally guiltless of the murder, and seems to have had genuine respect for Leo, who had been his godfather, the champion of Iconoclasm, and the patron of his teacher John the Grammarian. Since Theophilus had estab-lished a reputation for total impartiality of judgment, he was able to make an act that might have seemed a cynical exercise in propaganda look like an act of idealism.[376]

After almost four months of desultory progress toward the Byzantine frontier, the caliph al-Ma'mūn was now ready to begin his campaign. Manuel had persuaded him to divide his forces. One army, led by Ma'-mūn's son al-'Abbās and accompanied by Manuel, some Arab officers, and a group of Byzantine captives who had volunteered for the expedi-tion, was to attack the Khurramites of Azerbaijan. These rebels, under their leader Bābak, had been little disturbed since they had defeated the caliph's forces in 828. They needed punishing, and al-'Abbās—who was probably only the nominal head of the expedition that Manuel would ac-tually lead—needed some military glory. This army left by way of the town of Melitene for the east. The main expedition, that against Byzan-tium, was led by Ma'mūn with the help of one of his best generals, the ex-slave Ashinās, and some others. Ma'mūn passed through the Cilician Gates and entered Byzantine Cappadocia in mid-July of 830.

Ma'mūn intended only a raid—but a raid in overwhelming force. The garrisons of the local forts, without aid from other Byzantine troops, were hopelessly outnumbered, and those that were besieged surrendered within days. After taking the little fort of Magida, whose people he al-lowed to go free, Ma'mūn moved on to Corum, the seat of the turmarch of Cappadocia. When he began to storm it, its garrison and inhabitants capitulated on July 21. The caliph let his soldiers sack and destroy the town and take prisoners, but he then bought the prisoners from their cap-tors and released each Byzantine with a nomisma of pocket money. He sent Ashinās to take Soandus, apparently the seat of a drungary who was the most important officer in Cappadocia outside Corum; the drungary also surrendered his town. Other generals easily captured another fort, and one apparently pushed on to take the fort of Semaluus just inside the Armeniac theme. Such as they were, these forts were the caliph's chosen goals, and he sent a letter from Corum to Baghdad to announce his victory. On September 9, he left Byzantine territory to spend the winter at Damascus.[377]

Meanwhile Manuel and al-'Abbās had fought a cautious campaign against the Khurramites and killed some of them. Bābak's Khurramites were not very numerous, and the main key to fighting them was to avoid falling into an ambush in the mountainous region they controlled. This Manuel had done, and even if his success was modest, Ma'mūn still expressed great pleasure when he heard of it. His son could claim a victory, and the Khurramites were slightly humbled. A determined attempt to root Bābak and his men out of their mountain sanctuaries would probably have posed too great a risk to the caliph's prestige and to his son's safety to suit Ma'mūn. Manuel and the Byzantine prisoners he had brought along had therefore won the confidence of the caliph, and of the Arab officers whom the caliph had sent along to keep an eye on Manuel in Azerbaijan.

As the army marched back to join Ma'mūn at Damascus, it took the route that led to the Pass of Adata, and approached Byzantine territory. Manuel proposed to the Arab officers that at this point he and 'Abbās take part of the army, apparently including the Byzantine captives, and raid Cappadocia as the caliph's troops had just done. Though the Arab officers should have suspected something, Manuel was apparently so persuasive that they raised no objection. In early November, when they had crossed the border, Manuel suggested that he and 'Abbās go off hunting. While they were alone with a few of their men, he told the youth that he was returning to the empire, kissed him goodbye, and left him shedding tears of confusion and shame.

With the help of the Byzantine captives who were with him, Manuel absconded with the arms of 'Abbās and his attendants, who nonetheless made their way safely back to their fellows. All the Arabs shamefacedly returned to northern Syria by the Pass of Adata. Manuel made good his escape, and soon arrived at Constantinople. There Theophilus received him with joy, and demonstrated his trust in him by making him domestic of the Schools. Later the emperor stood godfather for Manuel's children. By now, of course, Theophilus was married to Manuel's cousin, and Manuel's accuser was out of office. Manuel thus became Theophilus's leading general.[378]

Meanwhile the war in Sicily had not gone as well as might have been expected. It had taken an abrupt turn for the worse in the summer of 830, when a large Arab fleet arrived from Spain to raid the unlucky island. The Byzantine strategus Theodotus did not try to prevent the Spanish Arabs from ravaging Byzantine territory, but continued to concentrate on finishing off the famished remnant of the North African army that he held besieged in Menaenum. The men at Menaenum put out an appeal for help to the Spanish raiders, who agreed to join them on condition that the Spanish Arab leader, Asbagh ibn Wakil, should lead the joint Arab forces. When the North Africans at Menaenum conceded this, Asbagh and his raiders, joined by other Arabs newly arrived from Africa, marched on Menaenum, raiding as they went.

Unable to face this strong relicf force, Theodotus was robbed of his victory. In August, he retreated to Henna, and Asbagh entered Menaenum to the joy of the recently besieged Arabs. Also in August, the North Africans of Mazara, whom their new Spanish allies had reinforced and encouraged, began besieging Panormus. The troops that had just united at Menaenum burned and abandoned the place and began a siege of another town, probably Calloniana to the east.

When they began this siege, however, they suffered the same fate as at the earlier Arab siege of Syracuse in 828. Disease broke out in their camp, killing Asbagh and many others. Though the Arabs took the town before the fall of 830 was over, they were gravely weakened, and decided to retreat. Seeing his chance, Theodotus and his Byzantines pursued them. He killed so many in a series of skirmishes that the Spanish Arabs, except for those still besieging Panormus, returned to their ships and sailed for Spain. Yet Theodotus himself was also killed. By January of 831 both sides were weak and had lost their leaders. The Arabs still held the western end of the island and besieged Panormus, but the rest of Sicily, while horribly devastated, was clear of Arabs.[379]

On the whole, Theophilus's debut as emperor was a considerable success. He had dazzled his subjects with unusually punctilious justice, a luxuriously appointed bride show, magnificent building, and ostentatious wealth; yet he had avoided looking frivolous and had shown himself a competent ruler. Unlike Michael II and Leo V, he relied a good deal on his advisers, particularly his syncellus John the Grammarian; but he was not merely his advisers' creature, as Michael I had been. By bringing back Manuel he had demonstrated a willingness and ability to correct his mistakes. For a man of barely eighteen it was a very creditable performance. The enthusiasm about Theophilus evident in the sources that survive today was doubtless felt by many people at the time in Constantinople and elsewhere. Under him, more than in the first years of Irene and much more than at any time since, the empire appeared even to contemporaries to be growing stronger and richer.

THE NEW ICONOCLASM

In the spring of 831, Theophilus learned that an army drawn from the Arab military settlements of Cilicia had crossed the border, probably by the Pass of Adata, and entered the Armeniac theme. No doubt the Cilicians were fewer than Ma'mūn's raiders of the previous year, but after seeing that the caliph had met no significant opposition they were confident that they could safely raid farther than he had. Theophilus wanted to put a stop to this sort of humiliation before the Arabs made a habit of it. Assembling his troops quickly, he set out together with Manuel, his new domestic of the Schools. He and Manuel caught up with the Cilician Arabs near the fort of Charsianum, took them by surprise with superior numbers, and defeated them utterly. About 1,600 were killed, up to 7,000 were taken prisoner, and the rest fled.

On his return to Constantinople Theophilus received a hero's welcome from the officials of the senate and from the Augusta Theodora, who was probably then already pregnant with his first child. He arranged to enter the city from the west, by the Golden Gate, the traditional entrance to the city for imperial victors. There followed a triumphal procession down a main street decorated with flowers and streamers, prayers of thanks in St. Sophia, and ceremonial presents and acclamations for the emperor, who in return gave gifts to both the senate and the people. Finally Theophilus held races in the Hippodrome, where the Arab prisoners were displayed. When the domestic Manuel presented an Arab captive who could ride while wielding spears in both hands, the spectators had the satisfaction of seeing the man unhorsed by a gallant Byzantine eunuch, Theodore Craterus, whom Theophilus had dared to challenge the Arab.[380]

Though Theophilus's attack on the Cilician raiders had been amply provoked, the news of it aroused the caliph Ma'mūn in Damascus, who immediately prepared a retaliatory campaign. When he had come as far as Adana in Cilicia, he found that Theophilus had sent him 500 Arab prisoners as a goodwill gesture; but the caliph was not propitiated. He entered Cappadocia through the Cilician Gates on July 4, accompanied by his son 'Abbās and his brother and heir, Mu'taṣim. The three marched together with a large army to Heraclea, which probably had not recovered fully from its sack in 806 and submitted without resistance. There Ma'mūn, Mu'taṣim, and 'Abbās each took part of the army and set off to raid separately.

Since the two main Cappadocian forts of Corum and Soandus had been destroyed the previous year and the other important fort of Lulum held out through the season, the Arabs had little to prey upon. Ma'mūn contented himself with sacking the underground shelters where the hapless

Cappadocian peasants had taken refuge. Mu'taṣim captured every pathetic little place he could find, first allowing the inhabitants to surrender. 'Abbās, who after being tricked by Manuel the previous year had a reputation to restore, received the capitulation of one fort of some consequence, Tyana. While he was looking for more glory, he met up with Theophilus, who had arrived to show the Byzantine flags. 'Abbās defeated the emperor in a skirmish and took some better spoils than usual. The Arabs had had enough of raiding by September 24, when they returned to northern Syria.[381]

In Sicily, which had become as much a battleground as Cappadocia was, Theophilus needed to act if he was to save Panormus. Yet he sent no reinforcements, probably because he lacked the necessary ships as long as the Cibyrrhaeots were fully occupied in fighting off the Arabs of Crete and the Imperial Fleet was recovering from its massive losses of October 829. Panormus, whose commander Michael had apparently been replaced by Symeon the Spatharius, withstood a siege of a year until, after supplies were exhausted and there was no hope of relief, Symeon surrendered on terms in early September of 831.

The Arabs allowed a safe departure to Symeon, the bishop of Panormus Luke, and a few others, probably including the garrison. The conquerors enslaved the others in the city, who had been reduced during the blockade to fewer than 3,000. Panormus now became the capital of the Arab holdings in Sicily, which formed a compact colony in the west of the island, the part nearest to the African coast. The African emir sent a new governor to Sicily around March of 832. Fortunately for the Byzantines, however, his arrival brought dissension between the Arabs from Africa and those from Spain, which interrupted Arab progress on Sicily for three years.[382]

His defeat in Cappadocia and the news of the fall of Panormus would already have shocked Theophilus when, early in December of 831, he learned that some iconophiles were circulating a pamphlet predicting his death. Ominously, this was only the latest of three such iconophile pamphlets. The first had prophesied Leo V's death eight months before it happened, and the second had foretold Michael II's demise five months in advance. Theophilus, enraged by what seemed to him not so much a prophecy as an iconophile plot, was determined to identify and punish those who were responsible. The gravest suspicion fell on Methodius, the Sicilian legate of the pope whom Michael II had imprisoned until his deathbed amnesty. Methodius had evidently chosen his monastic name in honor of St. Methodius of Olympus, generally believed to be the author of a celebrated book of prophecies. The pamphlet prognosticating Leo's death had appeared under the name of Methodius. The second pamphlet—if it is indeed the one attributed to the prophet Daniel that survives in a Slavonic translation—is based on the prophecies attributed to Methodius of Olympus and shows an overriding interest in the fate of Syracuse, the home town of the Sicilian Methodius. Thus Theophilus had some reason to think that Methodius had written all three pamphlets.

The emperor ordered the arrest of Methodius and of Methodius's friend Euthymius, former bishop of Sardis. Imprisoned on the island of St. Andrew, near Constantinople in the Sea of Marmara, the two men were questioned about their associates by the postal logothete—probably Arsaber, the brother of John the Grammarian—who was accompanied by the chartulary of the inkpot Theoctistus. Euthymius seems to have mocked Theoctistus and would name only one of his visitors: Theoctista, the mother-in-law of both the logothete and the emperor! Theophilus had both Euthymius and Methodius beaten soundly. While Methodius, who was just over 40, could endure it, the 77-year-old Euthymius died from his injuries on December 26 and became an iconophile martyr. The empress Theodora was reportedly so upset at Euthymius's death that she told Theophilus that God would desert him for what he had done. Methodius remained closely confined on St. Andrew. Another suspect arrested at the same time was Joseph of Thessalonica, the brother of the late Theodore of Studius, who was exiled to Thessaly until his death seven months later. This was also the time when Theophilus forbade the iconophile monk Nicetas Monomachus to live near Constantinople, perhaps especially because he was related to Theodora and Theoctista.

Though Theophilus had doubtless distrusted iconophiles from the start, from his point of view they were the ones who started open hostilities by attacking him. Before this he had been tolerant enough of suspected iconophiles to rule jointly with one and to choose another as his wife. He had freed Anthony, an iconophile monk charged with misappropriating land. He had evidently ignored the matter of the iconophile tract prophesying his father's death. Although the prediction seems to have been that Michael would be executed rather than die of kidney disease, this was the sort of thing that Byzantine governments took seriously; yet Theophilus had left the prime suspect, Methodius, at liberty until the prophecy of Theophilus's own death appeared. Hitherto, though a less moderate man than his father, Theophilus had tolerated iconophiles exactly as his father had.

Even now, for the time being, Theophilus punished only individual iconophiles who were suspected of conspiracy. The incident of the prophecy, however, troubled him greatly, particularly because it involved relatives of his wife, who were well represented among his highest officials. Besides the postal logothete Arsaber and the domestic of the Schools

43. Nicetas Monomachus the Patrician holding an icon of Christ. Vaticanus graecus 1613, p. 94. Painter: Menas. (Photo: Biblioteca Apostolica Vaticana, Vatican
City)

Manuel, these officials included the drungary of the Watch Petronas, who
was Theodora's brother, and the quaestor Eustathius Monomachus, who
was also a relative of the exiled monk Nicetas. Although the emperor was
unwilling to blame his wife's whole family, he blamed the icons, and from
this time on his dislike and fear of iconophiles increased.[383]

Ma'mūn's newfound enthusiasm for raiding Byzantine territory seems
to have baffled Theophilus, as indeed it might anyone not familiar with
the Muslim concept of Holy War. Whatever paltry plunder the caliph
might wring out of Cappadocia could hardly cover the expenses of his
expeditions, and surely could not justify his neglecting his many problems at home, of which the Khurramites were but one. From February to
April of 832 the caliph had to go to Egypt to put down a Coptic revolt
that could not be neglected any longer. When he returned to Damascus,
he found a Byzantine ambassador, possibly John the Grammarian again,
with a letter from Theophilus requesting peace. Because in the greeting
the emperor had named himself before the caliph, Ma'mūn sent the letter
back without reading it and used it as a pretext for a new invasion of
Cappadocia.

As Lulum was the only Cappadocian fort of consequence that the Arabs had not taken recently, Ma'mūn concentrated his efforts on it. In May 832 he began a siege, but Lulum, well provisioned and fortified and stoutly defended, withstood him for three months. Finding that the campaign no longer amused him, the caliph had two fortifications built near the walls of the Byzantine stronghold, left a large army under his general 'Ujayf ibn 'Anbasa with enough supplies to besiege Lulum for a year, and returned to the caliphate. After Ma'mūn's departure, however, the resourceful defenders of Lulum managed to capture 'Ujayf by trickery.

By this time, apparently in September, Theophilus had finally responded to the defenders' appeals for help and arrived with an army. Though their leader was a captive in Lulum, the Arabs from the two forts attacked the emperor, put him to flight, and plundered his camp. When he saw Theophilus defeated, the Byzantine commander at Lulum made an agreement with 'Ujayf to release him if he would arrange a safe departure for those in the fort. 'Ujayf kept his word, and the Arabs entered and garrisoned the place. The raids on Cappadocia were beginning to look like a conquest, since the Arabs had driven most of the Byzantine resistance out of the country, had established a strong base, and were preparing to winter on the Byzantine side of the Cilician Gates.

Theophilus soon sent another letter to the caliph asking for peace, this time naming Ma'mūn first. He requested the return of the forts conquered by the Arabs and a truce of five years, in return for which he would pay 100,000 nomismata and return the 7,000 Arab prisoners he held, most of them presumably taken in his victory near Charsianum in 831. The emperor contrasted the futility of continuing the war with the benefits of peace, which would bring security to the frontiers and allow trade to flourish. He threatened to attack Arab territory if Ma'mūn did not agree to his proposals. Ma'mūn wrote back indignantly disclaiming any interest in peace or commerce, proposing that the Byzantines convert to Islam, and demanding an annual head tax if they did not. Though the emperor had himself offered to pay Ma'mūn to obtain a truce, apparently his pride would not allow him to pay a head tax as if he were a Christian subject of the caliph. In any case, he did not reply.[384]

The winter of 832–33 was unusually cold, and the late spring brought the beginning of a plague of locusts in Asia Minor. Much worse were the threats of the caliph Ma'mūn. Assembling a great army in northern Syria, he announced his intention to conquer the entire empire, establishing Arab military colonies at regular intervals as he marched by way of Amorium to Constantinople. On May 25, 833, the caliph's son 'Abbās crossed the frontier, and soon began to build the first of these colonies on the site of the Cappadocian town of Tyana, which the Arabs had destroyed in 831. 'Abbās brought both soldiers and workmen and laid out a walled city a mile square with four gates. Ma'mūn was to follow shortly with the main army. He could not be defeated; he would not make peace. The immediate future looked bleak for the Byzantines and for Theophilus, whose luck seemed to have deserted him after his triumph two years before.[385]

In these straits Theophilus lashed out against the iconophiles, probably not so much because they wished him ill as because he wanted to win God's favor by ending the toleration of people whom he considered heretics. The emperor had the patriarch Anthony hold a new synod that evidently reaffirmed the condemnation of icons by Leo V's council of 815, which since 820 had almost been in abeyance. In June 833, Theophilus issued a formal edict against iconophiles, ordering the arrest of the surviving iconophile clergy and monks who were not in communion with the official hierarchy and providing that anyone who sheltered them would have his property confiscated by the state. Others whom Theophilus regarded as heretics seem to have been included in the edict as well, among them Paulicians, who were condemned to death.

Since after eighteen years most of the old iconophile bishops were dead, the main weight of the emperor's edict fell on iconophile monks. Among the many arrested and imprisoned were the former abbots Hilarion of Dalmatus, John of Cathara, and Macarius of Pelecete. Michael Syncellus and the brothers Theodore and Theophanes, monks from Jerusalem who had arrived and been imprisoned under Leo V, seem also to have been victims of this persecution. Theophilus confined these monks and others on the island of Aphusia in the Sea of Marmara, except for Michael, who was kept in the capital. Three monks from the Monastery of the Abrahamites in Constantinople who openly protested the edict were beaten so severely that they died, on July 8. The emperor seems not to have meant for their beating to be fatal, since he had already confined them not to prison but to the Monastery of St. John the Baptist in Phoberus, at the northern end of the Bosporus. Another monk who remonstrated with Theophilus was able to dispute at length with John the Grammarian after a beating, and then to escape to the Bithynian hills. Many other iconophile monks, like the abbots Peter of Atroa and Nicetas the Patrician, hid themselves in the hills of Bithynia and other places to avoid arrest.

Probably among those who had their property confiscated for harboring outlawed iconophiles was the wealthy dignitary Sergius the Spatharius. Sergius was the brother-in-law of John the Grammarian and had probably hoped that his connections would protect him. But Theophilus was no respecter of persons. He ordered Sergius led around the market by a rope around his neck as an example. Sergius, his wife Irene, and their children were then sent into exile, where Sergius soon died. Though The-

ophilus's stepmother Euphrosyne, now a nun, was one of the few iconophiles who were safe, she managed only with difficulty to have food and
clothing delivered to Michael Syncellus in prison. The persecution of Leo
V had been no more stringent. If God was afflicting the empire because it
tolerated iconophiles, these measures were well calculated to appease
Him.[386]

The efficacy of Theophilus's edict was soon put to the test. On July 9,
as fear began to spread throughout Asia Minor, Ma'mūn crossed the frontier into Cappadocia with his forces and encamped at Podandus, just inside the Cilician Gates. There he met an emissary from Theophilus who
offered him repayment of all the expenses of his expedition, return of all
Arab captives, and reparations for whatever harm the Byzantines had
done the Arabs, if only he would agree to a truce. The caliph brushed the
terms aside and expressed his determination to pursue the war, no matter
how much Theophilus might offer to pay.

Ma'mūn toured Cappadocia to collect the submissions of some remaining forts, then returned to Podandus to receive more capitulations
before resuming his advance farther into Byzantine territory. But suddenly he fell ill. According to one report, he had eaten tainted dates; another version has it that he caught cold after being splashed with icy water
from a mountain stream. In any case, he died on August 7, and his successor, al-Mu'taṣim, faced a rebellion and wanted to consolidate his
power. He called off the invasion, ordered the destruction of the Arabs'
new base at Tyana, and evacuated Byzantine territory.[387]

For Theophilus, as for any convinced iconoclast, God's message could
scarcely have been clearer. When Leo V had persecuted iconophiles, he
had been able to defeat the Bulgars and Arabs and enjoy peace. When Michael II had killed Leo and tolerated iconophiles, civil war had broken out
and the Arabs had defeated the Byzantines in Crete and Sicily. While Theophilus had continued his father's toleration, the Arabs had defeated him
and threatened to destroy the empire. But the moment that he had heeded
the divine warning and begun persecuting iconophiles again, God had
struck down his enemy Ma'mūn and stopped the Arab invasion. The lesson was that official Iconoclasm alone was not enough; the iconophiles
had to be punished. Obviously committed iconophiles could not accept
any such interpretation, and even some people with little use for icons
must have been uneasy at the prospect of unending persecution. From this
time on, however, Theophilus was sure that his mission was to be God's
instrument in stamping out iconophile heresy, and equally sure that if he
did so he would both bring his empire the highest form of justice and
guarantee his reign the immortal fame he desired.

BRILLIANCE AT HOME

Early in the year 834 Theophilus enjoyed another stroke of luck. The new caliph, al-Muʿtaṣim, in planning to restore order to the caliphate, decided to prepare an expedition to put down the Khurramite rebels. Members of this renegade sect had for years held much of Azerbaijan under Bābak and had recently organized a large army in the Zagros Mountains of northwestern Persia, under another chieftain named Naṣr. In the fall of 833 Muʿtaṣim sent a general to take defensive measures in Azerbaijan who was able to defeat one of Bābak's raiding parties. In November the caliph made a much greater effort against Naṣr, whose stronghold was uncomfortably close to Baghdad, and sent a substantial force to attack him on his home ground.

Perhaps because Naṣr was too bold, the caliph's army dealt him a crushing defeat by December 25. About 60,000 Khurramites are said to have been massacred, and most of the surviving women and children seem to have been enslaved. A few of the survivors may have fled to Bābak. But 14,000 soldiers, without most of their wives and children but with their leader Naṣr and his father, made the difficult trek over the highlands of Armenia in midwinter and reached Byzantine territory in the Armeniac theme. Seeing that he had no hope of reestablishing himself in the caliphate but that the Byzantines were pleased to receive him and his men, Naṣr was prepared for the drastic but logical step of converting to Christianity. His religious authority over his men was evidently so great that they were willing to follow his example.

Naturally Theophilus was delighted at the prospect of this mass conversion of infidels and of increasing the Byzantine army by almost a sixth with loyal soldiers who hated the Arabs. When Naṣr came to Constantinople for his baptism, he took the name of Theophobus ("God-fearing"), on the pattern of Theophilus ("God-loving"). The emperor gladly gave the newly christened Theophobus the rank of patrician and made him his brother-in-law by marrying him to one of the empress Theodora's sisters. Thus raised to a position of the greatest honor, Theophobus took up residence at Constantinople in a palace by the Golden Horn. After the other Khurramites were baptized, Theophilus enrolled them as Byzantine soldiers in special companies under their own officers. These were called the Turmae of the Persians, though most Khurramites were actually Kurds. The emperor dispersed his new soldiers among the different themes of both Asia and Europe, where by imperial edict he required widowed or unmarried Byzantine women to marry them.

Though they were not enrolled in the regular armies of the themes, the "Persians" drew regular military pay, and since the women who were required to marry them appear to have been from military families, they would have gained shares of military land through their wives. In return, the women's families seem to have received generous compensation, because they positively encouraged such marriages. The Persian turmae were to serve primarily on campaigns, when their soldiers would be called up from their homes and assembled into a single company commanded by Theophobus. They therefore formed a new type of unit, settled in the provinces like the troops of the themes but essentially mobile like the troops of the tagmata. By this arrangement Theophilus evidently hoped to assimilate the Khurramites gradually while using them to strengthen his central striking force. Though the new soldiers needed to settle down and learn Byzantine ways before they were ready for service, the emperor had high hopes for them. As the news of their warm reception spread in the caliphate, it would become an open invitation for some of the other Khurramites under Bābak to join the Byzantines.[388]

Theophilus probably had still more good fortune in 834. Theodora had borne him three children in about three years, all of them girls. He had named the eldest Thecla, in tribute to his mother, and the other two, who may have been twins, Anna and Anastasia. He was so proud of all three that he quickly crowned them and took the extraordinary step of striking coins showing their portraits, putting himself, Theodora, and Thecla on the obverse and Anna and Anastasia together on the reverse. Naturally, however, he wanted a son and heir, and about 834 Theodora gave him one. Theophilus did not name the child for his father, Michael, as might have been expected, but chose the name Constantine. While this was a highly appropriate imperial name, Theophilus doubtless recalled that it was also the name that Leo V had chosen for his son in honor of the Isaurian dynasty's Constantine V. Theophilus crowned Constantine as an infant, as he had crowned his daughters, and celebrated his son's birth by minting new coins showing only himself on the obverse and little Constantine on the reverse.[389]

Theophilus's high spirits at the time seem to show in his lavish redecoration of the throne room in the Magnaura palace, which easily surpassed his previous efforts at opulence. Since he wished the empire's vast gold reserve to be seen, he decided to put some of it directly on display in a memorable fashion. He ordered the archon of the gold smelter, who served under the special secretary, to produce a varied array of ornaments of solid gold. When the archon was done, an audience with the emperor was literally a dazzling experience. Two great organs of gold studded with semiprecious stones and crystal sounded as guests were ushered in or out. Two lions of hammered gold on pedestals guarded the throne, which was shaded by a golden plane tree with golden birds perched on its branches.

44. The five types of nomisma struck by Theophilus, all shown actual size. These coins give important clues about the growth of Theophilus's family, but modern scholars have found them difficult to interpret, largely because of an unfounded modern conjecture that Theophilus was married not in 830 but in 821. The following dates seem the most likely. *First row,* The type issued from 829 to ca. 833: *obverse,* Theophilus alone; *reverse,* a cross with the legend "Lord, help Your servant." *Second row,* The type issued ca. 833: *obverse,* Theophilus with his wife Theodora on his right, and his first daughter Thecla on his left; *reverse,* Theophilus's second and third daughters Anna and Anastasia. Since the appearance of consorts and daughters on Byzantine coins is extremely uncommon, this coin shows Theophilus's particular pride in Theodora and in his first three daughters, who had probably been born very recently. The type is extremely scarce today, indicating that it was issued only during a brief period. *Third row,* The type issued from ca. 834 to ca. 835: *obverse,* Theophilus; *reverse,* his son Constantine. Since apparently Constantine had just been born, Theodora and the daughters have been dropped to make the type the usual one for an emperor and his son and heir (cf. Figs. 24, 29, 33, 37). This type too is extremely scarce today and was presumably issued only for a short time. *Fourth row,* The type issued from ca. 835 to 840: *obverse,* Theophilus; *reverse,* his son Constantine with Michael II. Constantine is paired with Michael II to indicate that he, like Michael, was now dead. This is much the most common type of the reign. *Fifth row,* The type issued from 840 to 842: *obverse,* Theophilus; *reverse,* his son the future Michael III. Now that Michael had been born, the commemoration of Theophilus's first son Constantine has been dropped. This type is also very rare today, probably because so many nomismata of the previous type had been issued that new nomismata were not needed. (Photos: Dumbarton Oaks Byzantine Collection, Washington)

By means of mechanical devices the lions could open their jaws and the birds their beaks, and after the organ played they roared and chirped in harmony with music conveyed by hidden pipes. The emperor and empress also had new ceremonial robes woven of gold thread, so that they would be as golden as everything else in the room. It all took well over 20,000 pounds of gold, but everything could be melted down again in an emergency.

The imperial gold smelter also produced the Pentapyrgium, a gold display case in the form of a sort of doll house with several stories and five towers. Its open compartments held imperial regalia, plate, and other treasures that would otherwise not be seen or be seen very seldom, such as imperial wedding garments and wedding crowns. Since it was portable, the Pentapyrgium could be placed in the Magnaura or the Chrysotriclinus as it was wanted. While the emperor obviously enjoyed such objects in themselves, he was particularly careful to put them where every important foreign or Byzantine visitor could see them and marvel at the emperor's and the empire's riches.[390]

Amid his pleasure at the evaporation of Ma'mūn's invasion, the arrival of the Khurramites, the birth of his son, and the redecoration of his throne room, Theophilus rested from military measures. While to avoid provoking Mu'taṣim for the time being was only good sense, there was little excuse for not taking advantage of peace in the East to fight the Arabs on Crete and Sicily. The Arab pirates from Crete were still at large in the Aegean, though when Theophilus sent some converted Khurramites to the Aegean islands he may have helped matters somewhat. On Sicily the internecine fighting among the Arabs died down by 834, when the Aghlabid emir's governor, Abū Fihr, sent raiders into Byzantine territory in central Sicily in the late winter and early spring. The Byzantine garrison of Henna twice attacked the raiders, only to be driven back to its fortifications. During this time Theophilus was apparently rebuilding the Imperial Fleet after its disaster of 829, but with little of the urgency or extravagance of his work on the Great Palace. Having missed his opportunity to attack the Arabs at their most disunited, he prepared his first naval expedition to Sicily as a tardy response to the raids of 834. It was not ready to leave until the middle of 835.

Meanwhile the beleaguered Byzantine forces on Sicily continued to fight gallantly and the Arabs, though stronger than they, continued to behave like squabbling brigands. Early in 835, when the Arab governor led another raid on central Sicily in person, the Byzantine strategus of Sicily led his own troops in a counterattack. The Arabs won again, this time plundering the Byzantine camp and capturing the strategus's wife and son. Later that spring, Abū Fihr sent out more raiders, who pillaged the region of Tauromenium on the east coast of the island. But dissension among the Arabs smoldered still. Some of these raiders on their return to Panormus assassinated Abū Fihr and then deserted to the Byzantines.

Quicker to react than Theophilus, the Aghlabid emir dispatched a new governor, who by summer had raided around Syracuse and begun a second raid, probably in central Sicily. The dogged Byzantine strategus marched out to meet the Arabs and actually succeeded in driving them off into mountainous terrain covered with thick scrub, where he could not pursue them further for fear of an ambush. After waiting for a time, he withdrew; but as soon as his army expected no battle the Arabs attacked it and put it to flight. The strategus, repeatedly wounded, was carried off by his men, while the Arabs, as usual, concentrated on collecting the Byzantines' arms, horses, and baggage.

Toward the end of the summer of 835 much of the rebuilt Imperial Fleet appears finally to have arrived in Sicily from Constantinople. Before the Byzantines had had a chance to use their new strength, however, the Aghlabid emir sent out another fleet with yet another governor, Abū'l-Aghlab, a member of the emir's own family. The Byzantine fleet strongly contested his passage, sinking or capturing many of his ships before he put in at Panormus on September 12. Nonetheless, he had enough ships to avenge himself by attacking the Byzantine fleet in force, capturing most of it, and beheading all the prisoners he took. With the Arabs' supremacy restored, he conducted a sea raid on Pantellaria and a land raid on the area of Tauromenium, where his men burned the harvests, massacred the inhabitants, and, of course, took booty. Theophilus had yet to solve his problems with Sicily and with his navy.[391]

In 835 the caliph Mu'taṣim continued trying to assert full control over the caliphate by various measures. He sent a partly successful campaign against the Khurramite Bābak and transferred his capital from Baghdad up the Tigris to Samarra, which he refounded and rebuilt. Though he himself did nothing against the Byzantines, the frontier troops in the region of Melitene undertook to raid the Armeniacs on their own under their leader 'Umar, probably in the summer. Theophilus, who had won his previous victory under similar circumstances, hastened to catch the raiders before they left, and he did in fact inflict a defeat upon them; but 'Umar regrouped, attacked again, and defeated the Byzantines with heavy loss. Theophilus and his men fled, abandoning their camp, which 'Umar took, carrying the emperor's bed and wardrobe back to Melitene as trophies. There was no occasion for a new triumph when the emperor returned to his capital, still with a military record that fell short of the luster to which he aspired.[392]

Theophilus suffered another blow at about the same time. Apparently his infant son Constantine, in a moment when he was not watched closely enough as he crawled or toddled in the gardens next to his father's new palace of the Pearl, fell into the reservoir and drowned. The emperor buried his son in a little coffin among the imperial tombs in the Church of the Holy Apostles, and had the fatal reservoir drained and filled. He tried to console himself by laying out a new garden on the terrace he thus created, where he could enjoy the sun and the view of the Sea of Marmara and sometimes dine outdoors, remembering his son.

Throwing himself into his favorite occupation of building, he constructed three stories of new apartments forming an angle with the Pearl and connecting it with the empress's quarters further down the hill. On the highest story, the largest new room, the Camilas, was of the same richness as the Pearl, which it adjoined. It had a ceiling supported by six columns of green marble and studded with starlike gold points, walls decorated with more green marble below and with mosaics of figures picking fruit above, and a floor paved with white marble. Adjacent to the Camilas was a chapel dedicated to the Virgin, Theophilus's chosen patroness, and to the Archangel Michael, his father's patron saint. The story below held a dining room, quarters for eunuchs, and some rooms decorated with painted scenes that may have been a nursery for the emperor's young daughters. From this story stairs descended to a large veranda with colonnades overlooking the seaward sides, which was divided into two open rooms adorned with inlays of colored marble; one of these was called the Musicus because its inlays fitted so harmoniously. From this veranda two more staircases joined by a foyer led down to the Porphyra, the empress's bedchamber in the Chrysotriclinus. The five flights of stairs separating the bedchambers of the emperor and empress seem not to have bothered the youthful Theophilus, who obviously enjoyed looking at the rich decoration on his way. Probably before all this was completed, the emperor found better consolation in the birth of yet another daughter, whom he named Maria after his patron saint and pronounced his favorite.[393]

After Constantine's death Theophilus made a major change in his coinage. The important difference was not in the gold nomisma, on the reverse of which the emperor rather touchingly added a commemorative portrait of Michael II to Constantine's to show that his son, like his father, was dead. The change in the form of the copper follis was more dramatic. Ever since the follis had been introduced in 498, its reverse had been marked with an M, the Greek symbol for 40, signifying that it was worth 40 of a tiny copper coin called the nummus. In 538 the reverse of the follis had begun to show the regnal year of the current emperor in abbreviated Latin. After some four centuries, the significance of the M had been forgotten, since the nummus was no longer struck, and even the smallest de-

45. Folles of Theophilus from before and after the changes of ca. 835, shown actual size. *Left*, The type issued between 829 and ca. 833: *obverse*, Theophilus; *reverse*, meaningless symbols that had long been miscopied from a type introduced in the sixth century. *Right*, The type issued between ca. 835 and 840: *obverse*, Theophilus; *reverse*, the legend "Theophilus Augustus, you conquer." This follis was minted in unusually large quantities. (Photos: Dumbarton Oaks Byzantine Collection, Washington)

nomination, the half-follis, was marked with an M (technically it should have been a K, for 20 nummi). As Latin passed from normal use, what had been the regnal year also lost its meaning and turned into an ornamental arrangement of letters. Now Theophilus dropped all these meaningless marks from the back of the follis and replaced them with the legend "Theophilus Augustus, you conquer." Although he had not had much success in battle since his triumph of 831, he was planning on having more, and anyhow the inscription would make a good impression on those who used the coin. This change in the form of the follis shows that Theophilus, unlike his predecessors who had cared mostly about gold coins, had begun to pay some attention to his copper coinage.

He paid it so much attention that he began to mint an enormous number of these folles. During the five years after 835 he struck them at something like six times the previous rate. A very rough modern estimate indicates that over that time he flooded the empire with some hundred million new folles and half-folles, which might have been about 40 for every family in the empire. No source reveals his motive for this remarkable increase. Publicizing his boast of military conquest hardly seems an adequate reason. Because government salaries, donatives, and all other important payments were made in gold, no state expenditure seems to lie behind the minting. Although the state did turn a profit from its copper coinage by exchanging it for gold, even without counting the cost of the copper and the minting 100,000,000 folles would have made not quite 350,000 nomismata, perhaps 2.5 percent of the government's normal revenue for the years when the folles were issued. In any case, since Theophilus seems to have had more gold than he knew how to use, the minting was not needed as a source of revenue. The most likely explanation is that during his regular visits to the marketplace in Constantinople Theophilus had found that his subjects did not have enough copper coins, the only sort that were small enough for everyday business transactions. To identify such an obvious inconvenience would have required no profound knowledge of economics. Once Theophilus had recognized the problem, his celebrated solicitude for his subjects' welfare would have dictated the remedy: orders to mint more copper.

Since if anything Michael II seems to have minted more copper coins than before, an evident scarcity of them under Theophilus probably indicates that commerce was expanding. Theophilus's earlier letter to Ma'-mūn stressing the commercial benefits of peace also indicates that Theophilus was aware that the empire's economy was growing and might be made to grow more. At Constantinople his restoration of the city walls and improvements in the palace gave employment to many ordinary laborers and important business to the capital's architects, masons, carpenters, jewelers, and artists. The building boom extended beyond these imperial projects and even made land scarce in some quarters, to judge from the fact that the emperor's brother-in-law Petronas simultaneously built a palace so high and close to his neighbor's house as to cut it off from the light. When Theophilus had the miscreant flogged and razed the palace, the vacant lot was valuable enough to compensate the neighbor. This incident does not of course mean that Theophilus disapproved of private building in general, any more than another story that he ordered the destruction of a merchant ship belonging to Theodora means that he was opposed to commerce that did not compromise the dignity of the imperial family. Unlike the former report, the latter may well be invented, but that it was told at all suggests a growth of trade at the time.[394]

BRILLIANCE ABROAD

About the winter of 836 Theophilus took the extraordinary step of proclaiming the engagement of his youngest daughter Maria, then not even a year old, to a worthy young man of noble Armenian ancestry. The emperor's prospective son-in-law was Alexius Musele, certainly a relation and perhaps the grandson of the Alexius Musele whom the Armeniacs had elected their strategus when they rebelled against Irene in 790, and whom Constantine VI had blinded when he put down the conspiracy of 792. All this was well in the past. The younger Alexius was strong, handsome, and wealthy, had evidently distinguished himself as a military officer, and lived in his forebears' palace on the acropolis of Constantinople. At his betrothal Theophilus made Alexius a patrician, and probably also the heir to the throne if the emperor died without a son, because the betrothal makes little sense otherwise. It was a very tentative way to provide for the succession, as Maria would not reach legally marriageable age for over eleven years and Theophilus was only 23, in good health, and begetting children at a great rate. The betrothal did, however, reduce Theophilus's dependence on his wife's powerful family, which had iconophile associations and included Petronas, whom Theophilus had just had whipped and deprived of his house. Since Theophilus had fared ill in his recent military campaigns, it was also useful to him to have a presumptive heir who might fight with better success, or would at least discredit the dynasty less if he lost.[395]

After the death of the caliph Ma'mūn, with the Khurramites becoming ready for service in the army, Theophilus had new freedom and new resources with which to wage war. He also had several possible fronts on which to fight. One was the eastern front, where Mu'taṣim had not yet subdued Bābak and where Theophilus seems always to have meant to use his new corps of converted Khurramites. By late spring of 836 the emperor received a curious letter, dated to April, purporting to be from a great Easter synod held at Jerusalem by the Orthodox patriarchs of Antioch, Jerusalem, and Alexandria. Though Theophilus was presumably annoyed by the attempts in the letter to persuade him to repudiate Iconoclasm, its praise for his justice, congratulations for his triumph of 831, and expressions of hope that he might soon return Syria, Palestine, and Egypt to Byzantine rule were welcome flattery. Then the islands certainly needed help, especially Sicily, where the Arabs were raiding so furiously that the price of Byzantine slaves had plummeted. By summer Theophilus seems nearly to have finished repairing the Imperial Fleet after its heavy losses on Sicily the previous year, with a speed that suggests he planned a new expedition to the West. Finally, Leo V's 30-year treaty with the Bulgars came up for its second 10-year renewal in late 836, and Theophilus received an appeal for help that was best answered before the treaty was renewed.[396]

Ever since 813, when the Bulgar khan Krum had deported 40,000 Byzantines from the theme of Macedonia, the captives and their descendants had lived in a Bulgarian province known as "Macedonia." This province was apparently located as far from Byzantine territory as possible, in the area between the mouths of the Danube, which were swampy and nearly impassible, and the Dniester, which served as the frontier between the Bulgars and the Magyars. The leader of these exiled Byzantines was the "strategus" Cordyles, a Byzantine Armenian who had earlier served as a subordinate "strategus" of the ephemeral Bulgar province of the Left Side, which had been set up by Krum in 814 and mostly ceded back to the empire by Omurtag in 816. Cordyles and the exiles he led had now lived for 23 years in their "Macedonia," and must have renounced Christianity during Omurtag's persecution of 815 in order to save their lives. Nonetheless, they still wanted to go home to Byzantium, and they hoped that the coming renewal of the treaty might give them an opportunity.

About the summer of 836, Cordyles left his son Bardas to govern "Macedonia" and traveled secretly, probably by boat, to Constantinople. There he asked Theophilus to send ships to rescue the long-lost Macedonians. The emperor was eager to help, but wanted to avoid formally breaking the treaty if possible. Since the people of "Macedonia" were not mentioned in the treaty, he decided to send ships, doubtless including the newly repaired Imperial Fleet, which would wait just across the Dniester—in Magyar rather than Bulgar territory—until Cordyles and his people could cross the river to meet them. Cordyles returned to "Macedonia" to put this plan into effect.

The Bulgar khan Persian-Malamir, however, seems soon to have learned of Theophilus's preparations for a naval expedition on the Black Sea and not unreasonably guessed that its purpose was to raid Bulgar territory. As he did not yet have proof of a treaty violation and in any event had no fleet capable of opposing the Byzantines on the sea, he apparently sent his general Isbul to the region of Thessalonica to foment a rising of the local Slavs against the Byzantines. There Isbul caused devastation and bloodshed without directly involving the khan.

Persian-Malamir cannot have suspected what Cordyles and his people intended, because the departure of much of the Bulgar army to the south actually made their escape easier. When they began to ferry their possessions across the Dniester, the Bulgar commander of the region discovered what they were doing and tried to stop them, but his forces were inferior to those of the Macedonians, who were led by Cordyles and another Armenian named Tzantzes. After fighting a battle with the Bulgars and killing many of them, the Macedonians completed crossing the river with their property. The Bulgars, who could not cross in pursuit without invading the territory of their neighbors, appealed to the Magyars, many of whom arrived to relieve the fugitives of their goods. But the Macedonians were numerous enough to defeat the Magyars twice, and made their escape with property intact to the imperial ships that awaited them. Theophilus received his new subjects with honor in the capital and sent them to their old homes in the theme of Macedonia, making their leader Tzantzes strategus of the theme.[397]

Though the Byzantines had not broken the letter of the treaty, the Bulgar khan declared that they had depopulated his lands, which was in effect true, and retaliated with his own troops. He and his general Isbul invaded the border region near Adrianople and sacked the small forts of Probatum and Burdipta before returning to Philippopolis on Bulgar territory. In response, Theophilus gave Alexius Musele the new title of Caesar, which in the absence of a co-emperor made him heir to the throne, and sent him to Thrace with an army. The new Caesar was accompanied by the magister, probably Arsaber, the brother of John the Grammarian.

Alexius's objective seems to have been less to fight the Bulgars than to use the war as an excuse to seize the coast between the Nestus and Strymon rivers, which the treaty of 816 had left in the hands of independent Slavs. The new Caesar evidently had little difficulty in conquering the coastal strip, and secured the new territory by founding a town, named Caesaropolis after himself, before he returned to Constantinople. These infractions on both sides notwithstanding, Persian-Malamir and Theophilus renewed the treaty when the time came. The emperor had easily got the better part of the bargain, having rescued the Macedonians and restored Byzantine control over the whole land route from Thrace to Thessalonica.[398]

This maneuvering in the Balkans on land and sea had, however, made it impossible for Theophilus to send the Imperial Fleet to Sicily or an army to the East during 836. By the end of the year, the situation in Sicily had improved slightly. Earlier in the fighting season, in addition to the Sicilian Arabs' successful raiding of the area around Mount Aetna, a fleet had brought more raiders from North Africa who had taken still more booty. When they had taken all they wanted, however, the North African Arabs had returned home, and the Byzantines had twice defeated the Arabs of Sicily, the second time, near Henna, inflicting heavy casualties upon them. The Byzantines' subsequent defeat in a naval battle in which they lost eleven ships showed how much they continued to need reinforcements, and reports from his troops on the island must have kept the emperor aware of their plight. But Sicily was far away, and fleets sent there had tended to disappear without accomplishing anything. Theophilus had more enthusiasm for a campaign against the caliphate, and gave it precedence over another Sicilian expedition.[399]

For two years the caliph's general Afshīn had been methodically closing in on the Khurramite rebel Bābak in Azerbaijan. In the spring of 837 Muʿtasim sent substantial reinforcements to Afshīn's already huge army. As Bābak's position grew desperate, he sought to create a diversion. Keeping his sense of humor in adversity, he wrote to Theophilus that the caliph had sent even his tailor and his cook against the rebels (a pun on the names of two of the caliph's commanders), so that the emperor could attack the caliphate without fear of opposition. Bābak did not exaggerate much, as the Byzantines were probably able to confirm from other sources. Theophilus decided to seize the opportunity, which was especially favorable because while the Arabs' border troops were fighting Bābak most of the soldiers of the Asian themes could be spared from their defensive duties to join an invasion. The emperor was also ready to test his new Persian Company of converted Khurramites. He therefore called up most of the Asian themes, the Persian Company under Theophobus, and the tagmata under the domestic of the Schools Manuel, and set out for the east. The Arabs estimated, in round but plausible numbers, that his army totaled some 70,000 soldiers and 30,000 servants and baggagemen, figures that indicate he left behind about 18,000 thematic troops to guard Asia Minor. No Byzantine army this large had taken the field for centuries, and few Arab armies had been so big.[400]

Theophilus planned to raid the region of Melitene, whose troops had raided the empire and defeated him in 835, and then to pass through part of Arab Armenia. Before he began the raid he sent to the Armenians to warn them of his arrival and to demand tribute. Then, in the summer of 837, he crossed into Arab territory, apparently by the Pass of Melitene but bypassing Melitene itself, and reached the nearby town of Sozopetra. When it did not surrender at once, the immense Byzantine army easily took it by storm. Making an example of the town to induce others to surrender, Theophilus spared the Christians but had all the Muslim men he captured killed, the Muslim women and children taken prisoner, and the city plundered and burned. A few Khurramites exceeded their orders and raped and disemboweled some of the women. All this made the impression Theophilus desired on the inhabitants of the neighboring regions, who either paid him tribute or fled to the south. Though one Christian from Edessa encouraged the Byzantines, most local Christians were afraid of Muslim reprisals later, and had noticed that the Christians of Sozopetra had lost all their property in the sack.

Then the Byzantines turned east, ravaging the territory of Melitene and taking prisoners whom they sent back to imperial territory, and reached and besieged the town of Arsamosata. Though most of the available Muslim troops were fighting Bābak, the garrison of Melitene and some others tried to help Arsamosata's defenders; but the Byzantines defeated them, killing some 4,000 in the battle, and took and burned the town. After this Theophilus devastated the part of Armenia north of Arsamosata, plundering and destroying several settlements. By this time he had made his point. The Armenians of Theodosiopolis to the northeast sent the tribute he had demanded, while the Armenian prince of Syspiritis, which adjoined the Byzantine ducate of Chaldia, agreed to become a Byzantine client.

Finally the emperor turned back again on Melitene, which he threat- ˋ

46. The basement of the palace of Theophilus, Bryas, Bithynia, built in 837.
(Photo: Dumbarton Oaks Byzantine Collection, Washington)

ened to destroy like Sozopetra if it did not submit. The people of Melitene
mollified him by making a nominal submission, giving him gifts, returning the prisoners that they had taken two years before, and handing over
hostages to assure that they would not raid imperial territory again. Since
Melitene was strongly fortified and he was beginning to worry that the
caliph might eventually send an army against him, Theophilus decided to
be satisfied with his achievements thus far. Taking with him about a thousand prisoners and having cropped the ears and noses of others and set
them free, the emperor returned to Byzantine territory through the Pass
of Melitene, laden with booty. A small Arab army of 4,000 men did arrive just as he left, but he easily destroyed it.[401]

On his return, before he crossed the Bosporus to Constantinople, Theophilus ordered the construction of a new palace as a memorial of his victories. He chose a site at Bryas, on the Asian shore of the Sea of Marmara
just southeast of Chalcedon. The Bryas palace was to resemble an Arab
palace of Baghdad, and John the Grammarian drew on his experience
from the embassy of 829 to advise the architect, Patrices the Patrician, on
how the work should be done. The only exceptions to Arab forms were
to be a chapel dedicated to the Virgin next to the emperor's bedchamber
and a three-apsed church dedicated to the Archangel Michael and several
female martyrs. The Virgin was of course Theophilus's chosen patroness
and the patron saint of Maria, his favorite daughter; St. Michael was his

father's patron, and the female martyrs were probably Thecla, Anna, and Anastasia, the patron saints of his mother and his other three daughters. The palace was to be surrounded with parks and amply supplied with water.

After arranging for this construction, the emperor made his triumphal entry into the capital as elaborately as in 831 and with much the same ceremonies. Greeted by boys crowned with flowers, he displayed his booty and prisoners in a procession accompanied by the Caesar Alexius Musele, who appears to have gone along on the expedition. Finally, Theophilus himself competed in the races in the Hippodrome, wearing the color of the Blues. Since the other charioteers tactfully allowed him to win, the people could acclaim him simultaneously for both his military and his athletic triumph.[402]

As a piece of theater, Theophilus's campaign was admirable enough. After several humiliating defeats, he had gained a real victory at the expense of the people who had worsted him most recently, the garrison of Melitene. He had collected prisoners who would be useful for future exchanges and booty that made a fine show at his triumph; he had doubtless improved the morale of his troops; and he had impressed the people of the border region with Byzantine power. Though the tribute he had collected in Armenia and northern Mesopotamia could be expected to be paid only once, the client state of Syspiritis was a more permanent gain. Theophilus seems to have raised Chaldia in rank from a ducate to a theme in order to give its commander more authority to deal with this new vassal.

Although the expedition did not save Bābak, who was captured by the caliph's troops in September 837, it probably encouraged many of Bābak's troops to follow the example of their fellow Khurramites and flee to Byzantine territory. There seem to have been about 16,000 soldiers among them, since they brought to about 30,000 the total number of Khurramites in the emperor's service. Theophilus evidently entrusted Theophobus with the task of integrating them into the Persian Company. Gaining the services of this new band of Khurramites was more important than any of Theophilus's actual victories in the campaign. It could justify even the great risk of retaliation by the caliph, who was beside himself with rage at the Byzantines' temerity. Early in 838 he sent a winter raid into Byzantine territory that took a few captives and some livestock, but he was not likely to consider this sufficient revenge.[403]

Theophilus, however, showed little concern about the risk he ran. For the next campaigning season, he prepared not to meet the caliph's troops but rather to send reinforcements to Sicily for the first time since 835, a measure that he had postponed in favor of operations in the Balkans in

836 and his eastern campaign in 837. Sicily badly needed reinforcing. In the winter of 837 Arab raiders from Panormus had taken advantage of the carelessness of the garrison of Henna to occupy the town, though the loss proved temporary because the Byzantines, who had kept control of the citadel, managed to buy the raiders off. During the rest of the year the Arabs had raided the western part of the island again and taken their usual booty.

Hoping to add the relief of Sicily to his victories, Theophilus prepared to dispatch a good-sized army under the Caesar Alexius Musele. The Imperial Fleet presumably carried the troops, whose number might have equaled the fleet's capacity of 4,000 passengers. The emperor allegedly had another motive for sending Alexius, because he suspected the Caesar of plotting to seize the throne; but even if this is true, and Theophilus meant to disrupt a possible conspiracy and to test Alexius's loyalty, the size of the expedition shows that it was not a sham. Alexius probably left at the beginning of the spring of 838.[404]

When he sent off Alexius, Theophilus had reasons for optimism. Ever since his iconoclastic edict of 833, his reign had prospered, except for the death of his son Constantine and some minor reverses on Sicily. But he could reasonably hope for the success of Alexius's expedition and for the eventual birth of another son, since his marriage was remarkably fecund. His latest child was, however, a girl, whom he named Pulcheria, presumably after the sainted empress who had founded the Church of St. Mary of Blachernae, to which he made his weekly pilgrimages.

His iconoclastic edict had caused less trouble than might have been expected, because time was claiming the last of the native Byzantine leaders of the iconophile party. Of these, the abbots John of Cathara, Macarius of Pelecete, Nicetas the Patrician, and Peter of Atroa had all died by 837; Abbot Hilarion of Dalmatus lived on in exile. The other leading iconophiles who survived in prison were Methodius, Michael Syncellus, Theodore, and Theophanes, who as former legates of the pope and of the patriarch of Jerusalem could be considered outside agitators. To be sure, many Byzantines continued to hold iconophile convictions, among them numerous monks, some imperial officials like the long-serving sacellarius Leo and the chartulary of the inkpot Theoctistus, the empress Theodora, and the retired empress Euphrosyne; but the officials and the women of the imperial family had to be discreet, and no monk had a position of leadership comparable to that of Theodore of Studius before his death. Many people without strong opinions on the subject must have thought that Theophilus's Iconoclasm was being rewarded by God with obvious temporal success.[405]

THE ARAB INVASION

Early in April of 838, the patriarch of Constantinople Anthony died, probably after an illness of several years. The succession of his long-time assistant, Theophilus's old tutor John the Grammarian, was almost automatic, and John was consecrated on April 21, the Sunday after Easter. Though he had served Theophilus as an adviser and ambassador from the start, John gained more influence over church affairs when he became patriarch, and of course he stood for the strictest Iconoclasm. As it happened, shortly after John's consecration news reached Theophilus at his Bryas palace that Iconoclasm was about to be put to its severest trial since the Arab invasion of 833. Bent on revenge for the Byzantines' raid of the previous year, the caliph Mu'taṣim had left his new capital of Samarra on April 5 with an army of some 80,000 soldiers and the declared purpose of taking first Ancyra and then Amorium, which was the largest city of Asia Minor and apparently Theophilus's birthplace. As far as we can tell, the Byzantines had never defeated an Arab army of such size before. If Iconoclasm brought divine aid in military emergencies, this was the time for it.[406]

Though the emperor and his newly consecrated patriarch had the courage of their convictions, they wanted to make absolutely certain that their Iconoclasm was rigorous enough before the Arabs tested it. Apparently in May, when Theophilus was preparing to lead his troops against the Arabs, John held a synod in the emperor's favorite church, St. Mary of Blachernae, and explicitly anathematized all those who venerated icons. Even Leo V's council of 815, which had been reaffirmed by Theophilus's synod of 833, had not pressed its condemnation of iconophiles quite so far. In practice the action of John's synod made little difference, because by simply condemning icons the former councils had condemned iconophiles who did not communicate with the hierarchy, and refusing communion was the only way that a reasonably careful iconophile was likely to reveal himself.

Nonetheless, the anathema, which was applied by name to a number of prominent iconophiles, including the late patriarch Tarasius, marked a noticeable stiffening of the iconoclast position. After this second synod Theophilus issued a second iconoclast edict, ordering that all icons be either destroyed or plastered over. This again was more than Leo V had done, though by now few icons can have remained in public places and no effort seems to have been made to look for those in private hands. Still, the beating and imprisonment of the monk Lazarus, a famous painter of icons, seems to have resulted immediately from this edict. Regardless of the practical effects of the council and edict, Theophilus's main purpose

was surely to demonstrate both to God and to his people that his Iconoclasm was of the purest sort, so that the One would aid the empire against
the Arabs and the others would understand that it was Iconoclasm that
provided the help.[407]

Early in June the emperor set out for Asia Minor, accompanied by the
cavalry tagmata under the domestic of the Schools Manuel, the Persian
Company under Theophobus, and probably troops from the themes of
Thrace and Macedonia, which were not threatened by the invasion. Theophilus seems to have called few of the soldiers of the other themes to join
the main army, evidently judging that they were needed to defend their
homelands. When he arrived at Dorylaeum, near where the road to Amorium branched off, the emperor had to decide what to do about the defense of the city, which he knew to be the caliph's final objective. Theophilus was planning to use his largest force to block the road from the
Cilician Gates to Ancyra, which the Arabs were most likely to take if they
kept to their plan to sack Ancyra first. But he had to consider the possibility that part or all of the Arab army would take the direct road from
the Cilician Gates to Amorium.

The emperor's advisers suggested that he simply evacuate the population of Amorium, a step that might possibly deter an Arab attack and
would at least make it unnecessary to divide the army to guard the city.
Theophilus, however, was confident of victory and rejected this advice as
cowardly. Instead he reinforced Amorium. Apparently he reinforced the
Anatolics, who were commanded by their strategus Aëtius, by sending
them the Excubitors, whose domestic was probably the protospatharius
Theophilus, and the Watch, whose drungary was Theodora's brother-in-
law Constantine Babutzicus. The emperor then proceeded to Cappadocia
and took up a position where the road from the Cilician Gates to Ancyra
crossed the Halys, probably at Saniana. There he hoped to stop the Arabs
from crossing the river.

By thus dividing his forces, Theophilus had left his main army dangerously weak. The previous year he had apparently been able to muster a
united force of some 70,000 troops, only 10,000 fewer than the entire
Arab invasion force that he now faced. By not making use of most of the
soldiers of the themes and by sending half the soldiers of the tagmata to
Amorium, he had reduced his main army to about 40,000 men. Of these
probably 10,000 were the Schools under Manuel, the Hicanati under their
domestic Theodore Craterus, and the Optimates. The remaining 30,000
would have been in the Persian Company, of whom 16,000 were very recent refugees from the caliphate. Though the emperor had great confidence in Theophobus and his Persians, neither their fighting ability nor

their loyalty had yet been given much of a trial. Near the Halys, however, the emperor was probably joined by soldiers from the Bucellarian, Paphlagonian, and Armeniac themes, who were defending their own territory there. A month went by, but the caliph did not come.[408]

Mu'taṣim did in fact intend to take the road from the Cilician Gates to Ancyra, but his plans were more complex than Theophilus anticipated. During his slow advance, the caliph divided his own army into two parts. The smaller contingent was led by Afshīn, the general chiefly responsible for crushing the rebellion of Bābak the previous year; it was to pass by Melitene, join the emir of that city, 'Umar, and invade the Armeniac theme through the Pass of Melitene. This army, 30,000 strong, included 10,000 Turks and the whole army of Arab Armenia. The other army, of 50,000 troops, was divided into an advance guard led by Ashinās, who had accompanied Ma'mūn on his campaign of 830 against the empire, and a main army under the caliph himself; this force was to invade Cappadocia by the Cilician Gates, as the Byzantines expected. The various armies were then to meet at Ancyra, capture it, and proceed together to Amorium. The arrival of these contingents in the empire was scheduled so that they would arrive at Ancyra at nearly the same time. Afshīn and 'Umar, with a slightly longer distance to cover, would therefore have invaded a few days before Ashinās, who followed on June 19, and Mu'taṣim, who came on June 21.

After they had entered Byzantine territory the Arabs continued to advance slowly, but with considerably better intelligence of the Byzantines' movements than the Byzantines had of theirs. Soon after crossing into Cappadocia Mu'taṣim captured and killed a party of Byzantine scouts and learned that Theophilus lay in wait at the Halys, so that the caliph was able to warn Ashinās and his vanguard to gather more information before they advanced farther. Ashinās sent a scouting party to the region of the recently rebuilt headquarters of the turmarch of Cappadocia at Corum. In the meantime, the eastern Arab army under Afshīn had advanced to the region of Dazimon, well inside the Armeniac theme, and encamped there, probably to gather supplies before proceeding to Ancyra.

Only in the middle of July did Theophilus learn of the existence of Afshīn's army, which was threatening to cut him off from the rear. If the emperor was quick, however, he might be able to defeat Afshīn before the caliph's main army came up. Theophilus therefore left most of the thematic troops near the Halys under the command of a cousin of his, who was perhaps the strategus of the Bucellarians, and departed for Dazimon with his original force of 40,000 men, which easily outnumbered Afshīn's force of 30,000. The scouts of the principal Arab army, who had avoided an ambush set by the turmarch of Cappadocia and captured several Byzantine soldiers, brought word of the emperor's departure to Ashinās. He tried to warn Afshīn, but Theophilus arrived at Dazimon before the warning did.[409]

In the plain of Dazimon, near a village called Anzen, the emperor and his men came within sight of Afshīn's army on July 21. Afshīn had learned of the Byzantines' approach, probably from his scouts, in time to draw up his troops in battle formation, but his forces were obviously inferior. Rejecting the advice of both Manuel and Theophobus to attack the Arabs during the night, Theophilus followed the counsel of his other officers and attacked at dawn on July 22. The Byzantines soon routed most of the enemy infantry, killing some 3,000, but the 10,000 Turkish cavalry stood fast.

Around noon the Turks counterattacked, showering arrows upon the Byzantines in an astonishingly unbroken stream. Under this hail of arrows the Byzantine army began to break up, and most of it fled, leaving the emperor isolated among a band of 2,000 Persians along with Manuel and some other tagmatic officers. The Turkish archers had surrounded the emperor's party and were closing in when a sudden rainstorm wet their bowstrings and interrupted the fighting, but when the rain stopped Theophilus and his men were still trapped. The frightened Persians began to plot among themselves in their own language, which was probably Kurdish, to save themselves by betraying Theophilus to Afshīn.

Fortunately for Theophilus, Manuel understood them. Thinking quickly, he grasped the bridle of the emperor's horse and led him away, and when the bewildered Theophilus tried to resist threatened him with his sword. Manuel and some of the other officers then fought their way through the surrounding Turks and brought Theophilus to safety in the plain of Chiliocomum by nightfall, though Manuel was severely wounded. By then, most of the rest of the army, thinking that the emperor was dead, had dispersed in panic. Theophobus and his Persians had fled north, while the others had decamped in the direction of Constantinople. Afshīn was master of the field, while the Byzantine army, though it had not suffered many casualties, had almost disappeared as a fighting force.

From Chiliocomum Theophilus hastened after the soldiers who had fled to the west. He soon caught up with a number of them, as well as with the army he had left behind under the command of his cousin. This cousin, evidently despairing of resisting the caliph's huge army, had stripped the route from the Halys to Ancyra of supplies, evacuated Ancyra, and withdrawn toward the northeast. As he had done so, however, most of his soldiers had deserted him, probably in order to defend their homes and families, and many had fallen into the hands of the Arabs. The enraged Theophilus had his cousin beheaded; but he had to deal fairly mildly with his other scattered troops and officers, since he was trying to reassemble an army that could oppose the Arabs. He immediately dispatched such troops as he had under Theodore Craterus to defend Ancyra, but when Theodore reported that it was totally abandoned the emperor sent him on to aid in the defense of Amorium, which was now exposed to attack. Theophilus himself withdrew to Dorylaeum, just northwest of Amorium. In the meantime, on July 27, Manuel died of the wounds he had received at Anzen.[410]

To add to his misfortunes, Theophilus received word, apparently from his stepmother Euphrosyne, that refugees from the army had spread the report of his death to the capital, where some officials wanted to proclaim a new emperor. She urged him to come at once. He therefore ordered the troops stationed at Amorium to hold the city, and hurried to Constantinople. After proving that he was alive he faced no real conspiracy among his officials: they had thought of proclaiming another emperor only while they had believed that Theophilus had died with no heir but the Caesar Alexius, who was far away in Sicily. Nonetheless, Theophilus dealt out punishments, apparently forcing the tonsure of a relative of his named Martinacius, who had been mentioned as a possible emperor, and perhaps executing the military logothete George for conspiracy and confiscating his property. Theophilus may have removed his postal logothete as well, because this is the first time the eunuch Theoctistus, the old ally of Michael II and long the chartulary of the inkpot, is known to have been logothete. The emperor also made one of his famous rides to Blachernae, in the course of which he learned from a petitioner that the horse he was riding had been misappropriated by the count of the Opsician theme. The emperor had the count flogged.[411]

While Theophilus punished officials in the capital, Asia Minor was in chaos. The Persian Company had regrouped at Sinope on the coast of the Armeniac theme, but understandably feared Theophilus's wrath, knowing he had discovered that some of them had plotted to betray him. They therefore proclaimed their leader Theophobus emperor. Theophobus had little enthusiasm for the rebellion and did not try to extend his authority even into the neighboring theme of Paphlagonia. But he, too, thought that the emperor might blame him, and with as many as 30,000 troops found himself in a strong position to resist the rest of the empire's disorganized army. Theophilus was in great fear that Theophobus might join the caliph, but since the caliph had even more reason to distrust the former

Khurramites than Theophilus had, that was never likely. For the present Theophobus simply held the region of Sinope and deprived the emperor of the Persians' services.[412]

Meanwhile the Arabs had quickened the pace of their invasion. About five days after the battle of Anzen a Byzantine prisoner had led some of the soldiers of Ashnās to the salt mines where the people and garrison of Ancyra had taken refuge. After a brief resistance the Ancyrans had surrendered to their attackers, who after taking their supplies had let them go and moved on to Ancyra itself. Ashinās came to Ancyra about July 26, and within the next two days the caliph and Afshīn joined him. Realizing that the Byzantines were no longer capable of active resistance, the Arabs lost little time in sacking Ancyra and ravaged only cursorily as they advanced to Amorium, which they put under siege on August 1.[413]

Though Amorium was well fortified and defended by a substantial force under the strategus of the Anatolics Aëtius and the commanders of three of the four tagmata, Theophilus had little confidence that it could hold out for long against the caliph's great army. He again left Constantinople and rode through Nicaea back to Dorylaeum, but his troops were far too weak to attack the Arabs. Instead he sent ambassadors to the caliph, assuring him that the previous year's atrocities at Sozopetra had been committed contrary to his orders. He offered to have his own men rebuild Sozopetra at his own expense, to free all the Arab prisoners he had taken there and elsewhere, and to surrender those responsible for the atrocities to the caliph for punishment. He also promised gifts and tribute in return for peace. The caliph was not interested, however, and detained the Byzantine ambassadors to watch the progress of the siege.[414]

The Arabs were well equipped with siege engines, but so were the defenders of Amorium. For some days the two sides traded missiles across the walls, which were extremely strong. In one place, however, water had undermined the wall, and the damage had been only superficially repaired. An Arab who had been taken prisoner by the Byzantines earlier and converted to Christianity deserted to the caliph and revealed the weak spot. Mu'taṣim directed his machines there and opened a breach, which the Byzantines had great difficulty in defending. In desperation the strategus Aëtius decided to try to flee through one of the gates by night with as much of the garrison as he could; but when he wrote to inform Theophilus of his straits and his plan the letter was intercepted by the caliph, who kept a close watch over the gates and prevented any escape. As the siege continued, the Arabs made several major assaults without success, but they pressed the defenders of the breach very hard.

After two weeks of siege, on August 15, the officer charged with defending the breach, a certain Boïditzes, despaired of withstanding the Arabs much longer and slipped out of the town to negotiate with the caliph, ordering his men not to fight until he returned. While Boïditzes spoke with the caliph, however, the Arabs assaulted the breach and entered Amorium unopposed. Some soldiers made a stand in a large monastery, and died when the Muslims burned it. Aëtius and a number of his men took refuge in a tower, but had no choice except to surrender. Of the roughly 70,000 people in Amorium when it fell, the Arabs killed some 30,000 men, most of them probably soldiers, while the Turks raped over a thousand women. The Arabs pillaged the town very thoroughly, collecting all its soldiers, inhabitants, and movable property and dividing and selling them methodically, except for a group of officers and notables who were reserved for the caliph. Theophilus's ambassadors were allowed to leave safely to bring the terrible news back to the emperor. Finally, the caliph burned the city, destroying it almost entirely except for its walls, which survived the fire.

The caliph advanced a day's march in the direction of Dorylaeum and might well have continued the campaign if he had not learned of a rebellion in the caliphate in favor of Ma'mūn's son 'Abbās, who had partisans even in Mu'taṣim's expeditionary force. The caliph was consequently forced to leave Amorium on August 15 and return to his domains as soon as possible, without completing the destruction of the walls at Amorium or of the neighboring town of Polybotus. He took the shortest route, through the central Anatolian desert to the Cilician Gates, despite its lack of water. On the way a number of Arab soldiers died of exhaustion and thirst. Many Byzantine prisoners escaped, and the caliph ordered 6,000 others beheaded, saving only the group of notables with the strategus Aëtius and the tagmatic commanders Theophilus, Constantine Babutzicus, and Theodore Craterus. At last the army passed through the Cilician Gates and left Byzantine territory, as the caliph hurried to put down the revolt of 'Abbās.[415]

Theophilus roused himself from his shock sufficiently to send another embassy after Mu'taṣim in an effort to rescue the leading prisoners. Aëtius, after all, was his highest-ranking commander now that Manuel was dead, and the commanders of the tagmata, always close associates of the emperor, included Theodora's brother-in-law Constantine Babutzicus. Theophilus assigned the mission to Basil, the turmarch of Charsianum in the Armeniac theme, perhaps because he was the officer stationed nearest to the caliph, who by then would have been in Cilicia or northern Syria. Basil brought the caliph gifts and a letter from Theophilus, offering in exchange for peace and the release of the captives not only to free all the

Arab prisoners but to pay the immense sum of 20,000 pounds of gold, or 1,440,000 nomismata. When Muʿtaṣim asked for the return of Manuel and Theophobus as well, Basil answered that this was impossible, as indeed it was, because Manuel was dead and Theophobus was in rebellion and out of the emperor's control. The caliph then ridiculed Theophilus for offering just 20,000 pounds of gold, saying that he would not be satisfied even with 100,000 pounds, an almost impossible sum. Anticipating a possible refusal, Theophilus had kept enough dignity to give Basil a second letter for the caliph, filled with reproaches and threats. While these did no good, they at least allowed the emperor the satisfaction of angering his enemy, who sent back the gifts with Basil. But Muʿtaṣim may have taken his revenge by executing Aëtius.[416]

By this time, Theophilus had fallen ill from the impact of this avalanche of disasters. He took little comfort from the rebellion of ʿAbbās, which according to one report he had himself encouraged, and which certainly had been helpful to the Byzantines. In his despondency Theophilus contracted a high fever, from which he sweated profusely. Even after it passed, his heart and digestion were permanently weakened. Though he was still only 25, the emperor would be in indifferent health for the rest of his life, and never fully regained his self-assurance.[417]

Devastating though it appeared at the time, Muʿtaṣim's invasion was not a catastrophic blow to the empire. Except for Amorium, the Byzantine towns and countryside had suffered little more than in countless previous raids, and except for the troops killed and captured at Amorium there had been rather few Byzantine casualties. At Anzen most Byzantines had fled rather than died, and at Ancyra the Arabs had freed the population and garrison and damaged the city so little that the headquarters of the Bucellarian theme were reestablished there almost at once. Though Amorium itself was a heap of ashes, its great walls remained standing to await a future reconstruction. The headquarters of the Anatolic theme were temporarily transferred to Polybotus, which cannot have suffered much damage. While the revolt of the Persian Company was a major annoyance, the rebels posed no real threat to Theophilus's rule and had nowhere to go outside the empire.[418]

The Byzantine reverses were not even an indication that the empire would be at the Arabs' mercy in the future. Amorium would probably have withstood the siege had it not been for a single badly repaired part of its wall. Theophilus's troops had been winning at Anzen with somewhat superior numbers until the Turks had driven them off with special archery tactics that the Byzantines had never seen before and were not to see again for two centuries. Otherwise, Theophilus's division of his

troops and the Persian Company's revolt had left the Byzantines outnumbered by the Arabs everywhere for the rest of the campaign, while the
concentration of so many men at Amorium, along with the Persians' revolt, had deprived the Byzantines of much of their capacity for local defense. Nonetheless, no important forts but Ancyra and Amorium seem to
have fallen, not even Corum in Cappadocia or Dazimon in the Armeniacs, both of which the Arabs had passed by in force at a leisurely pace.
Theophilus had relied too much on the Persians, been overconfident, and
seen the defense of Amorium and other places in terms of his personal
prestige rather than practical strategy. But such mistakes did not need to
be repeated.[419]

The only lasting casualty of the Arab invasion was the idea that strict
Iconoclasm guaranteed divine aid. For that, appearances were what mat-
tered, and nothing could disguise the fact that the iconoclast emperor had
suffered a defeat unparalleled in its humiliation since Nicephorus I had
died fighting the Bulgars. The outcome did not exactly prove that Iconoclasm was wrong, because the iconophiles had had many reverses of
their own, Nicephorus's among them, but it did rob the iconoclasts for all
time of their most persuasive argument to the undecided, that Iconoclasm
won battles. Theophilus's realization of what his defeat implied was probably the main cause of his physical and nervous collapse.

THEOPHILUS'S DEPRESSION

For months after the Arab sack of Amorium the unlucky emperor followed the only sensible course of taking as little military action as possible. Though the Byzantine system of military recruitment as always replaced casualties almost automatically, this time it had to replace most of
the 30,000 troops in the Anatolic theme and in three of the cavalry tagmata. Some soldiers from these units, particularly the garrisons of various towns in the Anatolics, must have avoided capture, and many of
those captured had escaped, but at least half of the 30,000 men killed at
Amorium and of the 6,000 killed later must have been soldiers. There had
also been some losses at Anzen. The new recruits took time to enroll and
to train, and until this had been done even putting down the revolt of the
Persian Company, let alone taking revenge on the caliph, would have to
be postponed.

Although Theophilus could have recalled the Caesar Alexius and his expeditionary force from Sicily, the Imperial Fleet appears to have returned
already, and the Caesar's remaining troops were too few to make
much difference in the East. Furthermore, they were having a gratifying

amount of success where they were. In the spring Alexius had arrived in time to force the Arabs to raise a long siege of the town of Cephaloedium, some 40 miles to the east of Panormus, which the Arabs would certainly have garrisoned and kept if they had taken it. The Caesar then went on to defeat the Arabs several times, and apparently to capture the leader of one of their raids and kill many of his men. This sort of good news was particularly welcome to the emperor in the fall of 838, even though Alexius was a good deal short of ousting the well-entrenched Arabs from the island.[420]

Theophilus consoled himself with his favorite pastime of building, which increased his pleasure and prestige without risks. He commissioned great new bronze doors for St. Sophia, with inscriptions invoking the help of God the Father for himself, of the Virgin for Theodora, and of Christ for the patriarch John, perhaps as a thank-offering for his escape from death at Anzen. He also began building a new complex of ceremonial buildings in the Great Palace, within the right angle formed by his two residential buildings of the Pearl and the Camilas.

The new complex had two main parts whose design recalled the palace architecture of late antiquity. One, called the Triconch, was a hall with half-domed apses, or conches, in three of its four walls, so that its floor plan resembled a three-leafed clover. Its roof was gilded. The eastern and central conch was supported by four porphyry columns, probably connected by a door with the Pearl behind it, and clearly intended for the emperor's throne. Opposite it was a silver door opening onto a vestibule that led into the second part of the complex, a hall called the Sigma because it was shaped like the lunate form of that Greek letter, which is the same as a Roman *C*. The roof of the Sigma was supported by fifteen columns of colored marble, and both the Sigma and the Triconch had walls decorated with marble inlays. Beneath them were another two halls of similar shape, the one under the Triconch being called the Mysterium because a secret whispered in one of its conches could be clearly heard in the conch across from it. Theophilus was delighted with the structures on their completion, and made the Triconch his usual place of business.

On the other side of the Sigma from the Triconch, Theophilus laid out a great courtyard. In the center of the Sigma's concave facade was a platform for a golden throne, flanked by bronze lions. The lions' mouths spouted water that filled a semicircular pool within the arms of the Sigma, on the far side of which was a terrace with another fountain. This fountain was of bronze rimmed with silver, and its spout was a golden pine cone. Beyond it was a stage surmounted by a marble arch set on slender columns. After the courtyard was complete, Theophilus began a ceremony

47. Two episodes from the story of Leo the Mathematician. Matritensis graecus 26-2, fol. 75ʳ, a twelfth-century manuscript of the chronicle of John Scylitzes. *Left,* At the caliph's court in Samarra, three Arab geometers marvel at the geometric proofs given by a Byzantine prisoner who had studied under Leo the Mathematician. *Right,* In Constantinople, three messengers deliver a letter from the caliph to Leo, inviting him to come to the Arab court to teach. (Photo: Biblioteca Nacional, Madrid)

there called the Saximodeximum, or "Dancing Reception," at which he sat on the golden throne and watched performers from the Blues and Greens dance and sing on the stage and parade their horses on the terrace to musical accompaniment, while the golden pine cone spouted spiced wine and the basin of the fountain was filled with mixed nuts. Thus the troubled emperor began to regain some of his enjoyment in life.[421]

Theophilus also developed his interest in scholarship as an indirect result of the sack of Amorium. Among the noble Byzantine prisoners taken there was a young man with an extraordinary knowledge of geometry and astrology, who greatly impressed the caliph. When Muʿtaṣim learned that the youth had been taught by the schoolmaster Leo the Mathematician, a cousin of the patriarch John, he sent another Amorian captive to Constantinople with a letter for Leo, inviting the scholar to his court and promising him a distinguished position there. On receiving the letter Leo, fearing that the emperor might learn of it and consider him disloyal, passed it on to the postal logothete Theoctistus, who showed it to Theophilus. Though the emperor must have known all along that his close associate John had a learned cousin, the caliph's letter greatly enhanced Leo's merits in his eyes. Summoning Leo to court, he commissioned him to teach students under imperial patronage in quarters at the Magnaura palace, with a generous salary and a staff of teaching assistants. In this manner Theophilus founded the first public school known to have existed at Byzantium in over two centuries.[422]

From this time on the emperor's enthusiasm for learning grew, though this interest seems to have had much to do with the occult. It was not strange for a ruler who had been surprised as brutally as Theophilus was by the Arab invasion to become obsessed with trying to learn what might happen next. When John the Grammarian became patriarch, his brother Arsaber the Patrician had built him a laboratory in a suburban palace on the European bank of the Bosporus, where the patriarch soon attempted to predict the future for the emperor by divination. Leo the Mathematician had, and used, a knowledge of astrology; a contemporary rumor had it that his pupil had attracted the caliph's attention by predicting the day Amorium would fall.

Nonetheless, before long Leo made an entirely scientific and practical contribution to defense against the Arabs by inventing an optical telegraph linking Constantinople with the Arab frontier. Employing the well-known system of signal fires set on mountaintops at intervals, Leo devised two synchronized clocks, one at the capital and one at the Cappadocian fort of Lulum. A list of twelve messages was then drawn up, each of which corresponded to an hour of the day or night. A fire set at a particular hour conveyed a specific message, which was relayed to the other end of the telegraph before the hour was up. The system was not only of obvious military value but could partly soothe the emperor's anxiety about the Arabs' intentions.[423]

Theophilus himself began to pore over books in the palace library, consulting John and Leo when he found a text obscure. Soon he discovered a book that neither John nor Leo could explicate, and was so tormented by curiosity that he lost his appetite. Finally an imperial chamberlain named John suggested that he consult the iconophile monk Methodius, who had been confined for seven years on the island of Aphusia on suspicion of predicting Theophilus's death. The emperor took the advice and sent the chamberlain to Aphusia with the book. Methodius easily explained the text, possibly because it contained Latin, which he knew well but John the Grammarian and Leo probably did not, or perhaps merely because he was a more accomplished prophet. When the chamberlain brought the written reply to the emperor, Theophilus was so pleased that he immediately had Methodius brought from his cell. The learned monk was assigned quarters in the recently completed Sigma, presumably on the lower floor, where the emperor questioned him daily on a variety of subjects, doubtless including future events. Though the emperor remained an iconoclast and Methodius was still a prisoner, the two also discussed the Scriptures and theology.[424]

Near the beginning of 839 Theophilus received what seems to have been the first peaceful embassy sent by the Russians of Kiev, who had been raiding the northern coast of Asia Minor for years, probably as early as 819. Now they had been cut off from the Black Sea by hostile tribes, evidently the Magyars and Khazars, against whom they appear to have wanted Byzantine help. Though the Magyars had battled the Byzantine refugees from Bulgaria less than three years before, they, like their allies the Khazars, had traditionally been friendly with the Byzantines, and threatened the empire much less than the seagoing Russians did. Theophilus was probably pleased that the Magyars and Khazars had made it impossible for the Russians to raid the empire, and he certainly owed the Russians nothing. He therefore avoided any military action; but, not wanting to offend the Russians when they appeared more favorably disposed than usual, he arranged for their ambassadors' safe passage home. Since at just this time he was preparing to dispatch ambassadors of his own to the Frankish emperor Louis the Pious, he sent the Russian envoys along on that embassy, asking Louis to have them guided back to their own land.

The main purpose of the embassy to Louis was to secure Frankish aid in fighting the Sicilian Arabs. The chief ambassador was the patrician Theodosius Babutzicus, who was apparently the brother of Theodora's unfortunate brother-in-law Constantine, one of the captives taken by the Arabs at Amorium. In his letter to Louis, Theophilus asked for a renewal of the long-standing peace between the Byzantine and Frankish empires, and gave thanks to God for the victories that he had recently won against his foreign enemies, doubtless meaning the Arabs of Sicily. He then requested that a Frankish force be sent to complete the defeat of the Arabs, whose continued presence on Sicily might lead to raids on the Frankish possessions in central and northern Italy. Frankish assistance was actually needed more than Theophilus then knew, because at about this time the African emir had dispatched substantial reinforcements to Sicily. When the embassy arrived at Ingelheim on June 15, Louis the Pious was polite, but no reinforcements were forthcoming. When Louis found that the Kievan ambassadors were Vikings, a people who had already raided his domains, he detained them indefinitely, tactfully concealing his action from the Byzantine emperor.[425]

Apart from this embassy, for almost a year after the fall of Amorium Theophilus appears to have taken little interest in administration, or indeed in much of anything else besides his hobbies of building and scholarship. It was apparently in this period of listlessness that he began an affair with a beautiful female attendant of Theodora, though before this he had been a scrupulous moralist and very fond of his wife. Theodora quickly learned of the affair, and though she did not mention it her gloomy and anguished manner was enough to show that she knew. Stricken with remorse, he admitted his lapse, swore that this was the only time he had been unfaithful to her, and begged her pardon. As a gesture of contrition, he built a new palace for their daughters, called the Carianus, which took its name from its stately steps of Carian marble. It was joined to the Triconch on the south and to the winter bedchamber of the Pearl on the east, and thus completed the palace complex on the hillside between the Palace of Daphne and the Chrysotriclinus.[426]

At approximately this time Theophilus made an unpleasant discovery. By now he was of course aware of the iconophile sympathies of his stepmother, Euphrosyne, and of Theodora, the wife whom Euphrosyne had encouraged him to choose. Euphrosyne and Theodora—like Theodora's mother, Theoctista, who had probably died before 839–had helped mitigate the persecution of iconophiles when they could. Nevertheless, the emperor tried not to be a respecter of persons, and he must have demanded that the women of his own household obey his edicts. They were hardly able to avoid communion with the iconoclast hierarchy or personally to conceal fugitive iconophiles in violation of the iconoclast edict of 833; and Theophilus presumably expected them not to venerate icons in accordance with the iconoclast edict of 838, even if they had previously done so. He was naturally sensitive about any exposure of his five daughters to a practice that he considered heretical.

Though Theodora may have been too discreet to keep icons in the palace, she often sent her daughters to Euphrosyne's Monastery of the Gastria in the outlying part of Constantinople. There Euphrosyne gave the girls presents, fed them fruit, and secretly taught them to venerate icons, which she kept carefully concealed in a chest. The children were naturally told to keep the veneration of the icons a secret, especially from their father. One day in early or mid-839, however, when Theophilus asked his daughters what they did at the Gastria, he discovered the truth. The youngest, Pulcheria, who was then about two years old, told him that Euphrosyne kept many dolls in a box, which she held close to their faces for them to kiss. The emperor flew into a rage, and forbade his daughters to be taken to his stepmother again. He probably even forced Euphrosyne to leave the Gastria, since he could scarcely prevent his children from visiting the tomb of their grandmother Theoctista, which was located there. Euphrosyne built herself another monastery, the Monastery of Euphrosyne, nearby.[427]

Theophilus's anger at this incident may show in two particularly savage measures he took to persecute individual iconophiles. On July 8, 839, he

48. The supposed Church of the Gastria, Constantinople, now the Sancaktar Mosque. Although the identification of the building is not certain, it is supported by signs that this was a secular structure converted into a church, because the Gastria was a house belonging to Nicetas Monomachus that the empress Euphrosyne converted into a monastery in 830. (Photo: Irina Andreescu Treadgold)

summoned from the iconophile prison camp on Aphusia the Palestinian brothers Theodore and Theophanes. Theophilus suspected them of having been sent by the Orthodox patriarch of Jerusalem to oppose the Iconoclasm of Leo V. In fact, their mission had been to try to obtain relief from Arab depredations at Jerusalem in 812. Nonetheless, the emperor knew that the patriarch of Jerusalem had sent them and that they had been opposing Iconoclasm since Leo's reign, and he would not listen to their respectful explanations. Sympathetic questioning by the postal logothete Theoctistus finally established the key point that they had first come under Michael I, but the emperor still had them beaten by the city prefect. When they refused to accept iconoclast communion, on July 18 their faces were tattooed with twelve verses declaring that they had been branded for coming from Jerusalem to propagate heresy. On the advice of the patriarch John, Theophilus then exiled them to the town of Apamea in the Opsician theme.[428]

Probably at roughly the same time, the emperor summoned the painter Lazarus, who he had heard was painting icons again in prison. This time Theophilus had Lazarus's hands branded with hot iron plates and returned him to prison in a pitiable condition. The empress Theodora and some of the emperor's other associates, probably including Theoctistus, managed to persuade the emperor to allow Lazarus to recover at the Monastery of St. John the Baptist at Phoberus, which apparently served as a more comfortable place of detention for iconophiles than prison. Although twice before this Theophilus had had iconophiles beaten so severely that they died, his torture of Theodore and Theophanes and of Lazarus reveals a more sadistic frame of mind, probably the result of frustration at his military failures of 838 and his increasingly obvious inability to suppress the veneration of icons.[429]

The Caesar Alexius Musele also suffered from the emperor's bad temper. After a promising start on Sicily, he had been defeated by the recently reinforced Arabs. Back in Constantinople, his betrothed Maria, Theophilus's daughter, had just died at about age four. She was buried by her grieving father in a magnificent little silver-plated tomb in the Church of the Holy Apostles, next to her brother Constantine. The engagement was therefore over. The Caesar had been suspected of plotting before, and now some Sicilians came to Constantinople to charge that he was betraying the Byzantine cause to the Arabs and planning to make himself emperor. This time Theophilus believed the charges and decided to recall Alexius, but since the Caesar was far away with a sizable army and near to potential allies recalling him was a delicate business. As it happened, the archbishop of Syracuse, Theodore Crithinus, was in the capital at the time, and as a staunch iconoclast appointed under Theophilus he seemed a trustworthy person to deal with Alexius. Telling the archbishop to bring back Alexius under a pledge of immunity, the emperor sent him to Sicily.[430]

THEOPHILUS'S REFORMS

In the summer of 839 Theophilus regained his health and spirits enough to lead out an army in an effort to prevent another Arab raid. If the Arabs had planned one, he succeeded in deterring them, and returned home without mishap. The Persian Company still held the region of Sinope and acknowledged Theophobus as their emperor, but their rebellion was sustained only by their fear of what Theophilus might do to them if they submitted, and they stayed where they were. Theophobus was reportedly in secret communication with the emperor, and had assured him that he had been proclaimed against his will and was doing everything he could to persuade the Persians to end their revolt. For the present, therefore, Theophilus left the Persians alone in the hope that Theophobus would eventually bring them around. Yet the Persians did not trust the emperor, and Theophobus cannot have been entirely confident about Theophilus's mercy either. Just as they had lived for years as rebels against the caliphate in Azerbaijan and the Zagros, the Persians were now prepared to live as rebels against the empire in the northern Armeniac theme for a long while.[431]

Soon after his return from his preventive expedition against the Arabs, Theophilus received an embassy from the khan of the Khazars, the empire's half-forgotten allies to the east of the Black Sea. They were apparently having trouble with the Russians. The khan asked the emperor's help in building a fort to defend the lower Don, down which the Russians could sail to threaten not only the Khazar khanate but the Byzantine archontate of Cherson in the Crimea. Granting the request, Theophilus sent out the spatharocandidatus Petronas Camaterus with engineers and some ships from the Imperial Fleet and the thematic fleet of Paphlagonia. After putting in at Cherson, Petronas proceeded to the site selected by the Khazars, where he supervised the construction of a strong fort that the Khazars named Sarkel, or "The White House."[432]

In the meantime the Caesar Alexius Musele had returned from Sicily to Constantinople, relying on the imperial safe-conduct conveyed to him by Theodore of Syracuse, who had accompanied him back to the capital. Theophilus had scrupulously honored similar assurances that he had given to Manuel the Armenian in 830, but since the traumatic events of 838 the emperor was a suspicious and embittered man. He had Alexius beaten, imprisoned, and stripped of his rank and property as a rebel. On his next weekly visit to the Church of St. Mary of Blachernae with his officials, Theophilus found Theodore of Syracuse standing by the altar in his episcopal robes as a petitioner against injustice, boldly accusing the emperor of violating the safe-conduct he had given Alexius. In a blind fury Theophilus had the archbishop dragged from the altar, beaten, and exiled.

When Theophilus next went to St. Sophia, however, the patriarch John the Grammarian himself reproached him for his conduct, and asked him to recall Theodore. This reproof from his old tutor, long-time ally, and spiritual mentor seems finally to have reawakened Theophilus's sense of justice. The emperor recalled Theodore and returned him to the post he had once held as steward of St. Sophia, though apparently he did not trust him enough to send him back to Syracuse. Then Theophilus released Alexius and restored his property and rank of Caesar, implicitly admitting that the charges against him had not been well founded.[433]

At nearly the same time Theophilus offered a full amnesty to Theophobus and the whole Persian Company if they would end their rebellion. When they hesitated to accept, the emperor gathered an army and proceeded to the theme of Paphlagonia, which directly adjoined the region of the Armeniac theme that they held around Sinope. Rather than risk a battle, the Persians came to terms with the emperor. Under their agreement, the Persian Company was to be broken up; those Persians who had already been settled in the themes were to return to their homes and wives as regular soldiers of the thematic armies; and the others were to be distributed among fifteen themes and other districts, so that each would have 2,000 Persians. Theophobus would return to Constantinople as before and presumably would lead some Persians on occasional campaigns, and some Persians would rank as turmarchs as before and head Persian turmae within the themes; but there would no longer be an independent and unified Persian command. This sensible arrangement was carried out during the winter. The Byzantine army had evidently assumed its new shape by the spring of 840, when the troops were paid.[434]

The broad outlines of the integration of the Persians into the regular army can be conjectured with some confidence from a contemporary description of the army as it was immediately after the change. At the end of 839 the government apparently prepared an official manual with all the principal facts about the new system, including the boundaries, headquarters, troop strengths, and fortified places of each theme, the command structure, and the pay scale. Evidently this manual was distributed to Byzantine military officers to inform them of the new state of affairs. Somehow it found its way into the hands of an Arab prisoner of war named Muslim al-Jarmī, who soon returned to the caliphate and incorporated its information into a book of his own, from which excerpts survive today. These reveal a careful plan adopted by Theophilus to disperse the Persians and to reform the Byzantine army in the process.[435]

Though there were fifteen Byzantine themes in 839, Theophilus did not simply send 2,000 Persians to each of them. He sent no more Persians to the six small themes of the Western class, each of which had only 2,000 soldiers to begin with and most of which did not need their forces doubled. Sicily could have used as much help as it could get, but the emperor seems to have been too wary of a new rebellion to trust the Persians there, and besides had plans for another Sicilian expedition by the Imperial Fleet. He therefore assigned contingents of Persians only to each of the nine existing themes in the East, including Thrace and Macedonia. A tenth Persian contingent was incorporated into the Optimates, who at 2,000 were too few to transport the baggage of the larger Byzantine armies that were now taking the field. Except for the Optimates, in most cases the assignment would merely have meant adding the Persians who already had wives, homes, and lands in the theme to the rolls of the regular thematic troops. Aside from reducing the danger of a future Persian revolt and increasing the power of the strategi somewhat, this part of the distribution did not change the army greatly.

Beyond this, however, Theophilus created three new districts on the frontier in order to concentrate the Persians where they were most needed, without making them a clear majority of the troops in any region. These new districts and their armies were known as "cleisurae," or mountain passes, because their main task was to guard the most vulnerable points on the mountainous Arab frontier. The cleisura of Charsianum defended the Pass of Melitene and the cleisura of Cappadocia the Pass of Adata and the Cilician Gates, while the cleisura of Seleucia guarded the Lamis River, which defined the border between the empire and Arab Cilicia. Previously Charsianum had been a turma of the Armeniacs and Cappadocia and Seleucia turmae of the Anatolics, but as cleisurae all were separate commands. Their generals, the cleisurarchs, ranked lower than strategi but did not need to report to any other headquarters before calling up troops and sending them into action.

Theophilus thus added flexibility to the Byzantine response to Arab raids. More important, he added manpower. In the previously existing themes the Persian contingents brought forces of 60,000 men up to 78,000, and in the area of the cleisurae the Persians nearly doubled the size of the regular army, increasing it from 7,000 to 13,000. The only established themes to grow so much were the fairly recent creations of Chaldia and Paphlagonia, of which the former was also on the frontier and the latter was vulnerable to Russian raids. The Persians increased Chaldia's army from 2,000 to 4,000, and Paphlagonia's from 3,000 to 5,000.

As these two themes and the cleisurae were on the whole sparsely populated, finding the Persians military lands in them would not have been difficult, though to bring idle land under cultivation would have taken some time and money, for which the Persians probably received an allowance. The cleisurae, Chaldia, and Paphlagonia were probably the regions of the Persian turmae, largely Persian troops headed by Persian turmarchs, who served under strategi and cleisurarchs who were probably not Persian. Whereas most of the original soldiers of these areas had served as garrisons of forts, the intended role of the Persians was to oppose Arab raiders in the field—at least if their behavior in the next few years is any guide.

Just when the Persian revolt had come to an end, Petronas Camaterus returned from building Sarkel to report that the archontate of Cherson was in danger, presumably from the Russians, and to recommend that Theophilus create a new theme there. With Persian troops to spare, Theophilus acted on the recommendation at once, creating a theme called the Climata ("the Districts"). He appointed Petronas himself as the first stra-

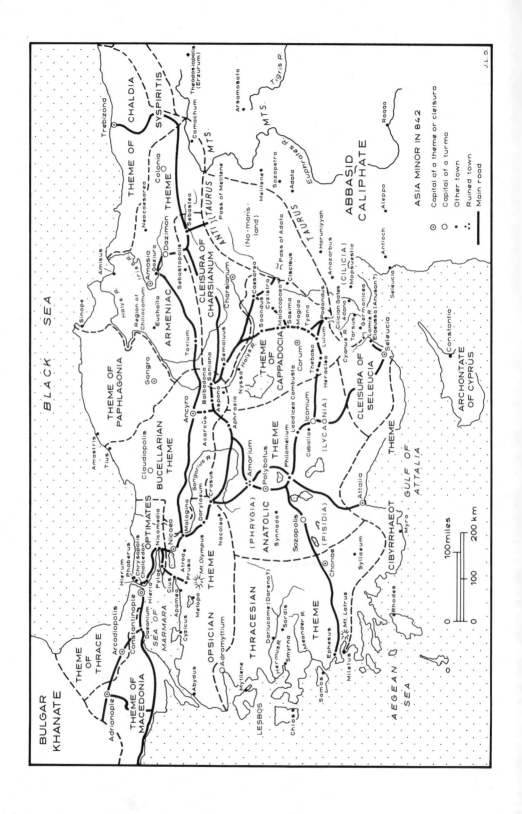

ASIA MINOR IN 842

⊙ Capital of a theme or cleisura
○ Capital of a turma
• Other town
∴ Ruined town
▬ Main road

BULGAR
KHANATE

BLACK SEA

THEME OF CHALDIA

SYSPIRITIS

ABBASID
CALIPHATE

THEME OF PAPHLAGONIA

DAZIMON THEME

ARMENIAC THEME

CLEISURA OF CHARSIANUM

ANTI (TAURUS) MTS.

TAURUS MTS.

BUCELLARIAN THEME

THEME OF CAPPADOCIA

CLEISURA OF SELEUCIA

ARCHONTATE OF CYPRUS

OPTIMATES

ANATOLIC
(PHRYGIA)
THEME

(LYCAONIA)

(PISIDIA)

SEA OF MARMARA

OPSICIAN THEME

THRACESIAN
THEME

CIBYRRHAEOT THEME

GULF OF ATTALIA

THEME OF THRACE

LESBOS

AEGEAN SEA

THEME OF MACEDONIA

Trebizond
Theodosiopolis (Erzurum)
Camachum
Arsamosata
Tigris R.
Colonia
Neocaesarea
Sebastea
Melitene
Sozopetra
Adata
Amisus
Sinope
Amasia
Gaziura
Euchaita
Sebastopolis
Charsianum
Pass of Melitene
(No-mans-land)
Pass of Adata
Raqqa
Aleppo
Antioch
Constantia
Seleucia
Germanicea
Anazarbus
Mopsuestia
Adana
Tarsus
Cilician Gates
Podandus
Lulum
Tyana
Magida
Sasima
Cyzistra
Soandus
Caesarea
Malacopaea
Ciscisus
Haruniyyah
Euphrates R.
Sozopolis
Neocaesarea
Region of Chiliocomum
Amastris
Tius
Gangra
Claudiopolis
Ancyra
Acarcus
Sargarius R.
Crasus
Malagina
Dorylaeum
Nacolea
Amorium
Polybotus
Philomelium
Iconium
Caballae
Corum
Thebasa
Heraclea
Loamis R.
Elaeussa (Anusun?)
Seleucia
Attalia
Syllaeum
Rhodes
Myra
Samos
Chios
Smyrna
Sardis
Ephesus
Miletus
Mt. Latrus
Chonae
Laodicea Combusta
Tyavium
Saniana
Balbadona
Aspona
Nyssa Halys R.
Aphrazia
Semaluus
Halys R.
Iris R.
Sargarius R.
Arcadiopolis
Adrianople
Constantinople
Chalcedon
Chrysopolis
Hierum
Phoberus
Pylae
Datonium Hieria
Nicomedia
Nicaea
Atroa
Prusa
Cius
Apameo
Cyzicus
Metopa
Abydus
Mytilene
Adramyttium
Mt. Olympus
Dariucome (Dareno?)
Hermus R.
Meander R.
Syannada
Nacolea
Sozopolis
Colonia

100 miles
200 km

tegus, promoting him to the rank of protospatharius, since he had performed his mission well and was familiar with local conditions. Apparently at the same time, Theophilus decided to strengthen his links with Venice and Sicily by elevating the archontate of Dyrrhachium to the status of a theme.

Both the Climata and Dyrrhachium, which as archontates had had only token garrisons, received contingents of 2,000 men. In these cases, however, Theophilus is not likely to have taken the risk of sending an undiluted force of Persians to such remote spots, where rebellion would be easy. On the other hand, some Persians had previously been settled in some western themes, like Hellas, that were not due to receive additional troops. In those themes either the Persians or some of the regular soldiers needed to be transferred in order to leave each theme with its original strength of 2,000 men. The most promising and likely solution would have been to enroll the Persians in place of some of the regular troops, then to transfer those regular troops and their families to the Climata and Dyrrhachium. When the new themes were set up these troops probably took some additional territory from the Albanians around Dyrrachium and the Goths in the Crimea, and some Albanians and Goths may even have come to work as tenants or hired hands on the cavalrymen's military estates. Beyond this, providing soldiers with military lands in such half-deserted regions would have required only the usual time and money necessary to open new land for agriculture.[436]

As soldiers were shifted and new themes and cleisurae created, Theophilus appears also to have changed the organization of the themes. At least since the early eighth century, and probably since the system of themes had begun, the smallest territorial division of the empire had been the drungus, commanded by the drungary, with its corresponding military unit of 1,000 soldiers. In the tagmata, and perhaps in thematic armies when they were drawn up for battle, there was also a division of 200 soldiers called the bandum, or standard, but this had not corresponded to any territorial district. In 839, when the enrollment of the Persians was in any case making it necessary to shift all the boundaries of drungi for the first time in perhaps a century and a half, Theophilus apparently used the opportunity to subdivide the newly defined drungi into districts called banda, with 200 soldiers apiece.

These banda had their own commanders, who were titled counts and had their own headquarters. Just as each drungary probably commanded 200 cavalry and 800 infantry, each new count, taking a fifth of a drungus, probably commanded 40 cavalry and 160 infantry, distributed over the whole district he commanded. To accommodate this change, the centarchs were made to command not 100 but 40 men each, so that each bandum had one cavalry centarch and four infantry centarchs. The result was a proliferation of commanders with responsibility for the defense of specific districts with specific troops. This permitted better control of the troops and a better defense against raiders.[437]

Although many of these changes would have been unpopular in the army—particularly those that required soldiers to move to remote regions and perhaps to share their military allotments with Persian newcomers—one additional military reform had a universal appeal. The emperor practically doubled the soldiers' pay. The old pay scale seems to have been one nomisma for the first year of service, two for the second, three for the third, and so on until pay reached six nomismata for the sixth and all later years. Six nomismata per year was the maximum unless the soldier was made an officer. The new pay scale continued the annual increases up to the twelfth year of service, so that the maximum pay for a soldier was twelve nomismata. Previously the troops had been paid at intervals ranging from one year to six years, but now the interval seems to have been set at three years, when troops would receive whatever was due them since their last payday. Though the soldiers drew their livelihood primarily from their military lands, additional pay of six nomismata represented roughly the price of a horse or a yoke of oxen, and was not to be despised. It would have raised the soldiers' morale, encouraged them to improve their equipment, and increased their loyalty to the emperor and his government. It also raised the annual payroll from about 900,000 nomismata to 1,440,000, but the government was awash in gold and could afford it.[438]

By 839 Theophilus had evidently learned from the military disasters of 838. Until then he appears to have felt that the main thing he needed to do to win battles was persecute iconophiles. After the collapse of the Byzantine army in the face of the Arab invasion, he had to recognize that Iconoclasm alone was not enough, and either he or his advisers eventually looked for practical reasons for the military failure. That the Persian Company needed to be broken up was a fairly obvious conclusion. But the rest of the army had not performed very well or obediently either, particularly when the defeated troops at Anzen and the force that Theophilus had left under his cousin had simply dispersed. And, in retrospect, the Byzantine defenders of Cappadocia had not been very successful in repulsing Ma'mūn's raids before the caliph died in 833.

In 839, therefore, when someone conceived a plan for concentrating the Persians on the Arab frontier and improving local control over the troops by appointing commanders over smaller regions, Theophilus implemented it. Finally, after years in which he had thought of money mostly as something with which to build and decorate luxury buildings, Theophilus came to realize that it might also be used to make his army more loyal and effective. Though the enthusiasm of the troops for their increase in pay could be expected to begin at once, the full effects of these military reforms would take several years to be felt. Yet they could scarcely fail to be of benefit in the long run.

THEOPHILUS'S LAST YEARS

Before Theophilus's military reforms had been fully implemented, Theodora gave birth to a son on January 9, 840. This time Theophilus followed Byzantine custom and gave his father's name to the boy, who became Michael III. Now that the emperor had a son and heir, the Caesar Alexius Musele received imperial permission to retire to a monastery, which he built on land given him on the Asian bank of the Bosporus. Having the succession definitely settled on a son would both have pleased the emperor and lessened the danger of plots against him by aspirants to the throne. The succession was the more important because the emperor's health was failing. He was becoming prematurely bald, and after his expedition to quell the Persian revolt he seems never to have led an army again, though he was still quite capable of governing.[439]

Some of his confidence was also returning. After he had appointed Leo the Mathematician to teach in the Magnaura palace, the emperor had permitted Leo to answer a letter from the caliph consulting him on various problems of geometry and astrology. Doubtless as Theophilus had intended, Leo's replies set Mu'taṣim afire with envy. Toward the beginning of 840 the caliph sent to Theophilus to offer him 2,000 pounds of gold (144,000 nomismata) if he would only allow Leo to come to Samarra for a short time. The emperor refused, saying that it would be senseless to impart to others the knowledge of the universe for which the empire was famous.

As an expression of his esteem for Leo, Theophilus soon had him ordained and consecrated archbishop of Thessalonica by the patriarch John the Grammarian, so that Leo joined his cousin John as one of the empire's leading ecclesiastics. Theophilus thus deprived his new School of the Magnaura of its head less than a year and a half after it had been founded, and made a bishop of a man with few theological interests. In a sermon that has been preserved, the consecrated mathematician is reduced to discussing the Pentecost in terms of the properties of the numbers 1, 7, 8, 49, and 50. But Theophilus doubtless felt that he was giving the Church the wisest man he could find. In the process he was advertising the connection between knowledge and Iconoclasm, because Leo was of course appointed as an iconoclast.[440]

In the spring of 840 Theophilus roused himself to combat the Sicilian

49. The continuation of the story of Leo the Mathematician (see Fig. 47). Matritensis graecus 26-2, fol. 75ᵛ. *Right,* The caliph, disappointed that Leo has declined his offer of a teaching position and accepted a professorship from Theophilus, sends an ambassador to the emperor with a letter. *Center,* The ambassador journeys to Constantinople. *Left,* Theophilus receives the letter, which asks him to send Leo to the caliphate for a brief period. (Photo: Biblioteca Nacional, Madrid)

Arabs once again. They had been intervening more and more in southern Italy, where the duchy of Naples had formed an unholy alliance with them against the declining power of Benevento. They captured a base for themselves at Tarentum in Apulia, and began raiding Byzantine Calabria, besides harrying what was left of Byzantine Sicily. Familiar with the difficulties of waging war at such a distance with only his own resources, the emperor tried to collect allies. As before, he applied to Venice, where he sent the patrician Theodosius Babutzicus, recently returned from the court of Louis the Pious, to grant the doge the rank of spatharius and to ask the Venetians for naval assistance. Theophilus also had the original, if somewhat unrealistic, idea of getting help against the Sicilian Arabs from the distant Umayyad caliph at Cordova, and dispatched an embassy to him with presents. The emperor's offer was ostensibly to help the caliph of the West overthrow the Abbasid caliphate in the East; but before the Umayyad caliph could fight the Abbasids he would first have needed to subdue the Aghlabids of North Africa, the sponsors of the Sicilian Arabs.

Naturally without waiting for a response from Cordova, Theophilus sent the Imperial Fleet to the West to join the Venetians, who had prepared 60 ships to fight the Arabs. Apparently before the Imperial Fleet arrived, the Arabs defeated the Venetians in a battle off Tarentum, capturing or killing nearly all the Venetian crews. The Imperial Fleet seems just to have reached Calabria before it too was defeated by the Arabs and returned in disorder to Constantinople. For the time being the Arabs were left masters of the western seas. A number of small Byzantine forts in the west of Sicily then surrendered to the Arabs, whose domains henceforth extended to the Halycus (Platani) River. Outside the territory that they actually held, no part of the island or of Calabria was safe from their raids.[441]

Perhaps in the summer of 840, Theophilus sent an expedition to compel the Christian kingdom of Abasgia to recognize Byzantine suzerainty, which its separation from the empire by Arab-held Armenia had allowed it to repudiate. The expeditionary force was of some size and probably included Persians, because its leader was Theophobus. The emperor appointed as an associate commander Theodora's brother Bardas, presumably to serve as a check on the reformed rebel. Like Theodora, Bardas was probably still in his mid-twenties, because despite his high connections and later prominence this is the first active part that he is known to have taken in state affairs. Although Theophobus stayed loyal, the expedition was repulsed with heavy loss, probably by the Arabs in Armenia before it had even reached Abasgia. Its defeat may be a sign that Theophilus had tried to use his reformed army too soon, before it had become accustomed to its new system of organization.[442]

Evidently later in the summer, after Theophobus had returned to Constantinople, the caliph sent his recently appointed governor of the frontier regions, Abū Saʿīd, to raid the empire. Abū Saʿīd and his main army set out from Aleppo while he sent the Arab troops of Cilicia ahead of him under their general Bashīr, the commander of Mopsuestia. Both forces were to pass through the Cilician Gates and raid through Cappadocia in the direction of Ancyra. Bashīr crossed Cappadocia collecting livestock and captives in the usual fashion; but near the border that Cappadocia shared with the Bucellarians he met an unusual amount of opposition. A force of former Khurramites appeared, probably those Persians settled in the new cleisura of Cappadocia, led by their Persian turmarch, whom the Arabs mistook for Theophobus. These Persians drove off Bashīr and freed all his captives. Before long, however, the main army under Abū Saʿīd came up, reinforced Bashīr, and attacked the Persians near the fort of Acarcūs, some distance inside the Bucellarian theme.

Though the Persians seem to have been vastly outnumbered and their leader fell early in the battle, they fought on grimly to the last man. Since Abū Saʿīd believed, or pretended to believe, that he had killed Theophobus and his chief lieutenants, the Arab governor ordered the heads of the dead men to be preserved in salt and sent back to the caliph by way of Mopsuestia. Yet Abū Saʿīd appears to have lost so many of his own troops in the battle that he abandoned his expedition and returned as he had come. As it turned out, when the salted heads were sent through Mopsuestia the women there discovered that most of them were the heads of their own husbands, who had been killed fighting for Bashīr and mis-identified as Persians. The head supposed to be Theophobus's, however, convinced the caliph Mu'taṣim, and he rewarded Bashīr handsomely.

In fact, Byzantine resistance had been much stiffer than the Arabs had expected. The Persians stationed on the frontier had shown themselves, even at this early stage, to be formidable defenders of Byzantine territory. It may well have been in recognition of their bravery that Theophilus now raised Cappadocia from a cleisura to a full theme. The emperor apparently took revenge for Abū Sa'īd's raid by having the Cibyrrhaeot fleet raid Seleucia, the port of Antioch, taking booty and captives and forcing Mu'-taṣim to build more fortifications there. Theophilus's military reforms seemed therefore to be taking effect, though they could not be expected to work miracles against greatly superior enemy forces.[443]

The emperor was in a good mood when an ambassador arrived from the Umayyad caliph of Cordova, probably that autumn, bringing a present and rather vague proposals for an alliance. The emperor kept the ambassador with him for an extended visit and found him a very amusing young man, particularly when he declared himself unable to listen to conversation while Theodora was in the room because her beauty was so distracting. (Theophilus may not have realized that Arabs were unaccustomed to seeing women without veils.) But the alliance never brought any practical advantages.[444]

At around this time Theophilus officially crowned his son Michael in St. Sophia, probably on Christmas, when Michael was not yet a year old. Theophilus was so proud of his son that for the ceremony he had the patriarch John's name rubbed off the bronze doors of St. Sophia and the name of the new emperor Michael added in the space. The emperor continued to make his weekly rides to Blachernae, and he still loved to build. When on one of the rides the nuns of the Convent of St. Isidore appealed to him to restore the roof of their refectory, the structure pleased him so much that he rebuilt, refounded, and endowed the whole complex as a magnificent hospice named for himself, moving the nuns to another convent.[445]

During the campaigning season of 841 Theophilus did not try to mount another expedition against the Sicilian Arabs, who were wreaking general havoc. In the spring they raided the Adriatic, including Dalmatia as far north as Istria and the Italian coast as far north as the mouths of the Po. They sacked Ancona, and captured a number of Venetian merchantmen, which were helpless before their numbers. On Sicily, the Arabs again raided the region of Henna, ravaging, plundering and taking prisoners as usual, though they made no new conquests. Probably only a large Byzantine fleet with strong support from the Italian powers had any hope of stopping the Arabs, and Theophilus had learned by now that anything

50. The bronze doors of St. Sophia, Constantinople, which were originally dedicated in 838 but had their monograms altered in 840 after Theophilus crowned his son Michael. The monograms are to be interpreted (starting at the top and reading from left to right): "Lord, help | Theophilus the ruler. | Mother of God, help | Theodora the Augusta. | Christ, help | Michael the ruler. | The year from the creation | of the world 6349, indiction 4 [840/41]." (Photos: Dumbarton Oaks Byzantine Collection, Washington)

less merely provided the enemy with more booty. Not ready to make a major effort, he postponed attending to Sicily and concentrated on his eastern front.[446]

Apparently in the spring, the Arab governor Abū Saʿīd again raided Cappadocia and took captives, but this time he met even stronger opposition than before. Either the Persian soldiers killed the previous year had been replaced or soldiers from the neighboring cleisurae of Seleucia and Charsianum came to the Cappadocians' aid. The Byzantine forces pursued Abū Saʿīd's army through the Cilician Gates onto Arab soil, defeated him, and recovered all the prisoners he had taken, whom they returned to their homes.

Humiliated by the presumption of the Byzantines, who were spoiling the game of Holy War that the Arabs had played for centuries, Abū Saʿīd made a second attempt to raid, probably in the summer and with more troops. This time he tried invading the cleisura of Charsianum through the Pass of Melitene, but the Byzantines were even better prepared for him. A Byzantine army chased his troops through the pass in disorder and carried their pursuit deep into Arab territory. As the Arabs fled, the Byzantines raided the region of Melitene and captured the fortified towns of Adata and Germanicea, which seem to have been taken entirely by surprise. Without trying to hold the towns, the Byzantine forces returned with many prisoners. This was a victory almost comparable to that of Theophilus in 837, yet it was won without the emperor's participation and apparently without any help from the capital. Under their new system of organization, the provincial armies and especially the cleisurae were performing splendidly.

Theophilus thus found himself with so many Arab prisoners that he could hope to exchange them for the Byzantines taken at Amorium and elsewhere. Through an embassy he proposed the exchange to Muʿtaṣim. The caliph accepted the gifts the ambassadors brought and gave an ambiguous reply to the emperor's proposal. He said that he could not accept the idea of an exchange, which would imply that Muslims and Christians were of equal worth, but if the emperor would release the Arabs without asking anything in return the caliph might outdo him by releasing twice as many Christians. As a gesture of goodwill, he sent Theophilus fifteen camels loaded with gifts. Though the emperor understandably declined to act on the caliph's suggestion that he free his prisoners without guarantees, this exchange of presents was taken by both rulers as a sign that a truce existed between the two powers.[447]

Just as peace was reestablished with the caliphate, the Cretan Arabs, who had been fairly quiescent for some years, launched a new raid in the fall of 841. Taking practically their entire fleet, they raided the coast of the

Thracesian theme and landed near Miletus. They must have had little knowledge of the territory, because they struck inland not at a place from which they could reach some of the theme's many market towns but at Mount Latrus, a monastic community that was still at the stage of real poverty and offered only opportunities for slaughtering monks. As soon as the Arabs had left their ships and begun devastating the monasteries, the strategus of the Thracesians, Constantine Contomytes, gathered his troops and swept down upon them, annihilating the raiding party. Though the Arabs had not landed very far from the theme's headquarters at Chonae and pirates were naturally at a disadvantage fighting regular troops on land, Constantine's victory seems to indicate that the recent military reforms were improving local defense even in the Thracesians, where such defense was seldom needed. In any case, the Cretan Arabs were humbled, and soon the Byzantines began to think again of trying to reconquer Crete.[448]

The new military system may have had a less fortunate consequence in the theme of Peloponnesus, where in about the autumn of 841 the Slavs revolted. Though they had apparently remained quiet since their last revolt had been put down under Nicephorus I in 807, during that time the Byzantines had probably disturbed them very little. Theophilus's military reforms would have meant that apart from the two headquarters of drungi that already existed, presumably at Corinth and Patras, the government would have set up seven more headquarters of banda, thus establishing much tighter control over the Peloponnesus. Within two years the Slavs appear to have found this system oppressive. They temporarily succeeded in throwing off Byzantine rule in part of the theme and in raiding much of the rest, but the rebellion was soon to be quelled, probably in the following year.[449]

By this time Theophilus was seriously ill with dysentery. Once the Arab raids on Asia Minor had been curbed, the piece of unfinished business that galled him most was the war against the Arabs of Sicily. Again he thought of obtaining help from the Franks. Louis the Pious had provided no troops after the embassy of 839, but Louis had died in 840, and now his son Lothar was the Frankish emperor, with effective control over Italy. Theophilus therefore ventured an embassy to Lothar, led by his ambassador to the Franks and Venetians on earlier occasions, Theodosius Babutzicus. In return for Frankish support against the Sicilian Arabs, Theophilus offered to bestow one of his daughters, probably Thecla because at age eleven she was nearly old enough to marry, upon Lothar's son and heir Louis II. Theodosius departed at about the beginning of 842, and Lothar gladly accepted the Byzantine offer; but before the embassy returned both Theodosius and Theophilus had died. Theophilus had almost certainly realized that he would not live to see Sicily pacified, but he hoped that a Frankish alliance would leave his son and his widow a means of pacifying Sicily after his death.[450]

As his disease worsened, Theophilus held a secret meeting with his closest advisers, who evidently included the postal logothete Theoctistus and Theodora's brother Petronas, possibly domestic of the Schools. To them Theophilus expressed his fear that after he died the Persians and some of his officials would try to proclaim Theophobus emperor. With the death of Manuel and the retirement of Alexius Musele, Theophobus was the leading general of the empire, and commanded the deep loyalty of Persians settled all over the themes. Moreover, during his years of residence in Constantinople, and perhaps through his marriage with Theodora's sister, he had made some powerful friends in the capital, not least because he was said to have iconophile sympathies. As the junior emperor Michael was barely two years old, Theophilus thought his dynasty was vulnerable. His advisers apparently did not disagree. The emperor had Theophobus brought to the palace and detained there in such a way as not to arouse suspicion.

When he realized that his death was near, Theophilus summoned a group of leading officials and citizens to the throne room he had decorated in the Magnaura, where he was brought in on a couch to address them for the last time. He alluded to the youth and good fortune he was leaving behind, but his main concern was for his wife and son. He reminded his audience of the justice he had shown them, and asked them to repay him by aiding Theodora and little Michael. He thus made clear his desire to be succeeded by his widow as regent for their son. Even if her power was in principle to be absolute, she would be assisted by her two brothers, Petronas and Bardas, and especially by the logothete Theoctistus, a long-standing friend of the dynasty, who as a eunuch could associate with the empress without scandal and exercise power without suspicion of plotting to become emperor. Finally Theophilus bade his people farewell. They responded by weeping, probably for the most part sincerely.

Some Persians were beginning to inquire about Theophobus. One night, on the emperor's orders, Petronas and Theoctistus had the dangerous prisoner beheaded. The official story remained that Theophobus was with the emperor in the palace. The execution might have been justified, with difficulty, on the ground that Theophobus had been a party to a rebellion and his pardon had been granted under duress; but killing him was of course a political act. The execution may well have spared the empire another Persian revolt, and in any case it relieved some of the dying emperor's anxieties about the future. Theophilus may also have lived long enough to learn of the death on January 5 of the caliph Muʿtaṣim, who had inflicted on him the greatest humiliation of his reign. Theophilus himself died of dysentery on January 20, 842, shortly before or shortly after his twenty-ninth birthday.[451]

CONTRIBUTIONS OF THEOPHILUS'S REIGN

From his time to ours, Theophilus has enjoyed a fairly good reputation. The golden apple with which he chose his bride, and the roaring golden lions and twittering golden birds with which he decorated his throne room, entered the mythology of Byzantium and spread beyond it. Despite his Iconoclasm and his cruelty to many iconophiles, his efforts to do justice were remembered too; in the twelfth-century Byzantine satire *Timarion* he joins Minos and Rhadamanthus as one of the judges of souls in the underworld. Theodora, who was later canonized, helped to save him from being remembered as a persecutor of iconophiles by circulating the story that he had repented of his persecution on his deathbed, and by making sure that the council that restored the icons a year after his death did not condemn his memory.

In short, his propaganda had its effect. The impression made by his well-staged triumphs partly counterbalanced even his defeat at Amorium. Both Byzantine and modern scholars have admired his patronage of scholarship, and particularly of Leo the Mathematician, who became something of a legend in his own right. Byzantium had had rulers with little time for such things since Justinian I, and if Theophilus fell short of Justinian's éclat, he after all had a good deal less time, power, and money to work with. If Justinian is left aside, Theophilus seemed to outshine every other ruler of the four hundred years before his accession, none of whom was remembered so well or so fondly. On the surface, then, Theophilus was a success. On his deathbed he regretted not his failures, but that he was unable to enjoy his good fortune longer.[452]

Observers who have looked only a little closer have been less impressed. Golden apples, birds, and lions raise some suspicion of dilettantism; especially in the early part of his reign, Theophilus sometimes looks like a boy emperor playing with imperial toys. Though Theophilus's justice paid little heed to wealth or rank, too often it seems also to have disregarded the merits of the case. Theodora's story of his partial deathbed repentance was of course a pious fraud, and that she came to tell it at all emphasizes what a failure his Iconoclasm was. When Irene restored the icons, she had needed to prepare for years and to overcome armed opposition, and even so the restoration proved impermanent; when Theodora speedily abandoned Iconoclasm, she freed the Byzantine government from a political incubus and met with little opposition from anyone but the patriarch John the Grammarian. Theophilus's persecution mainly served to provide heroes for an iconophile movement that was running short of them, to make an unpopular doctrine particularly obnoxious to those who had found his father's diluted form of it barely tolerable, and to identify his reign so closely with Iconoclasm that his first major defeat was taken as proof that Iconoclasm was wrong.[453]

When Theophilus took the field his military record was, to put it charitably, disappointing. Not even his mostly glowing legend could efface the Byzantines' memory of the fall of Amorium and of the Arabs' martyring its remaining captives three years after Theophilus's death. Theophilus's patronage of scholarship did not prevent him from removing Leo the Mathematician from the classroom just created for him and misplacing him in a bishopric. Theophilus's admiration for learning was shot through with what even a number of educated Byzantines would have considered superstition. As far as learning, warfare, and religious harmony were concerned, things seemed to go a good deal better under Theophilus's successor Michael III, to the point where Theophilus might even appear to be the last ruler of Byzantium before its revival, if not a ruler who positively held the revival back.

Theophilus's obvious failures, however, were of no more lasting significance than his generally successful self-promotion. Though his persecution caused ill feeling during his reign, its aftereffects were surprisingly mild. The only major and permanent result of the Arab invasion of 838 was to discredit Iconoclasm so convincingly that Byzantium could regain its religious unity shortly thereafter and, for the first time in its history, keep that unity intact for centuries. No doubt Theophilus often acted frivolously and ill-advisedly, but the empire did not pay a very high price for his mistakes. One reason that Theophilus has seemed to many Byzantine and modern observers the most appealing of the emperors of the eighth and ninth centuries is that he showed an unusual capacity to learn and change during his reign. If he had reigned 50 more years, as was quite possible in view of his youth, he might well have become one of the greatest Byzantine rulers.

The two principal changes enacted by Theophilus's administration both contributed to the revival of the empire. The first was his reform of the army, which ranks with Nicephorus I's financial reforms as one of the two great administrative measures that helped revive Byzantium. Though in the first place Theophilus's chance to incorporate the Khurramites into the Byzantine army was simply the result of good luck, he seized his opportunity eagerly and in the end intelligently. His warm reception of Naṣr's men encouraged Bābak's to join him later. The manpower that these "Persian" troops provided soon enabled the themes to meet any but the largest Arab armies on an equal footing in both defensive and offensive warfare. The far-reaching changes in military organization and pay made in the winter of 840 not only reduced the danger of revolts by the Persians but gave the themes greater control over their territory and more flexibility in repelling and avenging enemy attacks. Theophilus left the Byzantine army with its numerical strength increased by a third, and its fighting effectiveness increased by still more. Only after his reorganization was it ready to become the army of conquest that would double the size of the empire by the eleventh century.

Theophilus's second important contribution was actually an effect of his superficial brilliance. Theatrical though his style was, it must have helped convince both Byzantines and foreigners that the empire's long struggle for existence had been won, and so established confidence in Byzantine power. After the empire rode out the Arab campaign against Amorium, no foreign ruler threatened Byzantium so seriously again for over 200 years. From Theophilus's time on, the Byzantines felt able to attend more to trade, which Theophilus encouraged by expanding the bronze coinage, and to art, letters, and the other occupations of peacetime, which he furthered as well.

Although the Byzantines' real fight for survival had been over since the reign of Leo III, such setbacks as the Bulgar war of 809–16 and the civil war of 821–24 had tended to disguise that fact. The different efforts of Irene, Michael I, and Leo V to convince their subjects that they were entering an era of renewed greatness had been frustrated by those rulers' own failures and by the bumbling of Constantine VI, the harshness of Nicephorus I, and the uncouthness of Michael II. The Bulgar and civil wars had particularly concealed the effects of the financial reforms of Nicephorus, of which the empire reaped the full benefits only under Theophilus. Theophilus was the first ruler to make clear to the Byzantines how wealthy and strong their empire had become since the eighth century. The expansionist spirit that many historians have dated to the beginning of the reign of Michael III was mostly the legacy of Theophilus.

CHAPTER SIX

The Empire in 842

What constitutes the revival of a state or a society? Though the concept may seem a subjective one, increases in economic prosperity, military power, and even literary education can be established as objective facts. The belief of a people that they are becoming more prosperous, powerful, and learned can also be real, and be shared by their neighbors. The Byzantines valued wealth, strength, and learning at least as much as modern men do. Since they lacked modern aspirations for things like advanced technology, social equality, and representative government, to expect progress toward any of those as part of a Byzantine revival would be anachronistic. The Byzantines did usually have most of the kinds of freedom they wanted, including the freedom to circulate criticisms of official doctrine, though they often lacked the particularly cherished freedom to impose their views on others; this situation never got much worse or better. The Byzantines tended to judge thinking by its correctness rather than its originality, and to wait to express new ideas until they had learned the opinion of the best ancient scholarship. Because until the eleventh century they were still rediscovering many earlier opinions, before that time they produced little original thought. For the present purpose, then, "revival" simply means the renewed growth of wealth, power, and knowledge, and of the benefits that follow from them.

The revival of a state, that is, of an administrative, military, and legal apparatus, does not need to accompany the revival of its society—that is, of the community of people belonging to the state. In Byzantine history the two kinds of revival occurred separately more than once. The fourth and sixth centuries were for the most part times when the Byzantine state grew larger and stronger while its subjects grew fewer and poorer. During much of the eleventh and twelfth centuries most Byzantines became richer, more urbanized, and more cultured, yet the state became progressively weaker. Eventually, it is true, either political or social weakness turned out to weaken Byzantium as a whole. Since the state drew its revenue and manpower from its subjects and the subjects relied on the state to keep out foreign invaders, defense required the cooperation of both state and subjects. After each of the one-sided revivals, in turn the Germans and Huns, the Persians and Arabs, the Seljuk Turks, and the Latins of the Fourth Crusade invaded the empire, doing grave harm to state and society alike.

Even in the years between 780 and 842, the demands of the government could conceivably have driven the empire's subjects to despair and economic ruin, as some charged Nicephorus I with trying to do; or the Byzantines could have become more prosperous without paying more taxes or fighting effectively for their country, as Nicephorus apparently feared they might. In the end, however, neither of these things happened. The revival of the state seems evident from the simultaneous growth of its territory, the efficiency of its administrators, the strength and loyalty of its army, and its government revenues. Meanwhile Byzantine society showed signs of revival by increases in population, general prosperity, trade, urbanization, and the level of education and culture.

In principle all these changes should be partly measurable, and despite the unsatisfactory state of our evidence some of them are. The empire's territorial gain during these years was probably about 10 percent. Surviving figures indicate that the army grew by half, and its members' loyalty was presumably strengthened by an average pay increase of some 62 percent. As the total army payroll rose by about 140 percent while the government still ran a surplus, the guess that the state revenue rose by about 60 percent cannot be very much too high. An increase in government revenue of this proportion, which by the end of the period raised no loud complaints about overtaxation, implies both a population increase and a rising standard of living. The roughly sixfold increase in the minting of bronze coins looks like evidence of a rise in trade, while the nearly sevenfold increase in the number of administrative centers indicates growing urbanization. As for education and culture, modern computations of the numbers of manuscripts copied and literary works written, approximate though they inevitably are, show a decided rise between 780 and 842. All these trends and figures are worth bearing in mind, for they show that the Byzantine revival was not only real but of surprising breadth and power.

How, then, could so many bad things have happened to the Byzantines between 780 and 842? While the army occasionally defeated the Arabs and Bulgars during this time, it lost more often, and achieved nothing against those enemies that made up for the devastation they inflicted on Byzantine territory. The Arab conquests of Crete and part of Sicily compromised Byzantine supremacy in the Mediterranean, and allowed those lands to become bases for future raids of yet more territory. The war between Michael II and Thomas the Slav was both harmful and demoralizing, and throughout this period there were serious revolts and conspiracies, six of them successful. Anyone who in 780 had hoped for dynastic stability, perhaps with a 70-year-old Constantine VI still ruling in 842, would have been cruelly disappointed. The bitter and inconclusive controversy over the icons also wasted much of the Byzantines' energy and sapped their morale. All of this hardly signaled a general advance of Byzantine society and the Byzantine state.

However, just as a strong state need not be reviving, a reviving state need not be very strong as yet. A state that is weak at first may be unable to avoid some humiliating defeats, yet may be reviving nonetheless. In fact, one indication of a state's growing power is its ability to endure reverses without permanent damage, whereas a state in decline tends to suffer severely from defeat and to gain little from victory. In absolute terms, the empire of Justinian was obviously stronger than the empire of Theophilus, but Justinian's reconquests did not prevent his state from becoming weaker, while Theophilus's defeats led to changes that made his state stronger. Defeat or victory in battle, or the occurrence of a conspiracy or revolt, does not necessarily depend on a state's underlying strength.

In the nature of things, moreover, revivals are usually slow, unlike some declines, which a foreign invasion or a natural disaster can bring on quite suddenly. It is hard to imagine an event that could have increased the Byzantine Empire's population and wealth as sharply as the plague of Justinian's time had decreased them, or strengthened the Byzantine army and urban culture as abruptly as the Persian and Arab invasions had weakened them. Heraclius had actually won back all the territory taken by the Persians and gained some reparations besides, but his victories left the empire a wreck. There was no quick and easy way for the Romano–Byzantine Empire to reverse a decline in territorial extent, demography, and general prosperity that had begun in the second century A.D. and continued with only temporary remissions for half a millennium. Recovery there was, but in the beginning it was gradual and inconspicuous.

Did the Byzantines themselves perceive the revival, or did they see only the reverses? Here the thinness of our contemporary source material makes an answer risky. The chronicle of Theophanes, compiled about 814, preserves some nearly contemporary opinions, regardless of whether they are those of its supposed author. It reflects a favorable and hopeful view of the first part of Irene's reign, though understandably more confused views of the years during and after Irene's struggle with

Constantine VI. The picture that Theophanes gives of Nicephorus I's reign is of a time of oppression and disaster, and the evident sympathy in the chronicle for Michael I does not go so far as to deny that his brief tenure turned out badly. The bits and pieces of other contemporary views that have been preserved, mostly in hagiography, tend to show that at least the iconophile churchmen and officials who produced those sources were also optimistic about Irene's reign before 789 and ambivalent about her later reign and that of Michael I. But they held opinions of Nicephorus's government quite unlike those in Theophanes' chronicle, ranging from ambivalent to strongly favorable.

For Leo V's reign we have opinions from one contemporary chronicle, known as the Scriptor Incertus, and some from another early chronicle preserved by Symeon the Logothete and George the Monk. There is also a fair amount of contemporary hagiography, other assorted scraps, and the somewhat deformed evidence in the much later chronicles of Genesius and Theophanes Continuatus. These sources depict the first three years of Leo's reign as a bad time, of course because of Leo's restoration of Iconoclasm but also because of the ruinous Bulgar war. Yet the little they say about the last four years of the reign suggests that, though Leo still had plenty of enemies, in most people's opinion things had taken a definite turn for the better. The scanty sources for the reign of Michael II (which except for the absence of the Scriptor Incertus are about the same as those for Leo V) make it clear that there was not much to like in that period of civil war and Arab piracy, though the iconophiles returned the emperor's tolerance of them by showing little malice toward him.

For the reign of Theophilus, the only nearly contemporary chronicle is that of George the Monk, but another early chronicle is summarized closely by Symeon the Logothete, and some of the information in Theophanes Continuatus and Genesius seems not to have been much altered from contemporary sources. Again, a fair amount of early hagiography survives. George the Monk and the saints' lives make nearly everything sound bad, but they are mainly interested in the emperor's persecution of iconophiles; when George describes how everything else went wrong, one of his principal examples is the Arab conquest of the islands, which he seems not to realize had happened earlier. The sources are surprisingly reluctant to blame Theophilus for the humiliating Byzantine defeats of 838. Apart from his persecutions, Theophilus's reign seems to have made a remarkably good impression on contemporaries. Despite his military defeats, even the iconophiles appear to have regarded his rule as a time of unprecedented wealth, learning, artistic activity, and justice. Part of the reason is doubtless that they were impressed by a lavish show; but by the end of Theophilus's reign most Byzantines also seem to have been enjoying a new peace and prosperity, for which they gave their ruler some of the credit.[454]

Of course, a number of Byzantines actually lived through most or all of the years between 780 and 842. Among the figures mentioned in this book who could have remembered the entire period was the former emperor Michael I, who was born about 775, fell in 813, and in 842 was still drawing his imperial pension as the monk Athanasius on the island of Plate near Constantinople. He died two years later, apparently after his immense property had been restored by the empress Theodora. The oldest surviving figure whom we know of was Joannicius, born into a Bithynian peasant family in 762, enrolled in the tagma of the Excubitors about 780, a deserter from the army after the defeat at Marcellae in 792, and then an iconophile hermit. In 842 he was already venerated as a living saint on Mount Olympus in the Opsician theme, and he saw the icons restored before he died in 846.[455]

Another who lived through the whole period was Ignatius the Deacon. He was born about 770, in time to study with the protoasecretis Tarasius, who as patriarch of Constantinople ordained him deacon. Ignatius served the patriarch Nicephorus as well, then conformed to Iconoclasm and before 842 became archbishop of Nicaea. After the icons were restored, he lived several more years as a penitent monk, trying by means of his writing to convince the church authorities that he had always been an iconophile at heart. Less opportunistic was Hilarion of Dalmatus, born in 776 under Leo IV as the son of the steward of the emperor's table, the third-highest palatine official. Hilarion became a monk under Irene and in 807 was elected abbot of Dalmatus against his will. After 815 his quiet but firm devotion to the icons caused him to be alternately imprisoned, freed, exiled, and whipped under Leo V, freed under Michael II, whipped and imprisoned again under Theophilus, and freed and restored to his abbacy under Theodora before his death in 846. Each of these men, and anyone else who was older than 65 in 842, could have given a firsthand judgment on how much better or worse things had got since the accession of Irene.[456]

No such firsthand judgment survives, unless we count the predictable satisfaction of Joannicius and other iconophiles when the icons were finally restored in 843. Ignatius the Deacon had once observed that through his own efforts scholarship had advanced greatly, but by 843 he was no longer in such a self-congratulatory mood as he contemplated the wreckage of his career. Anyone with a part in public life, even with the detached observer's part played by Joannicius, would have had some unpleasant memories of the abrupt changes in government and religious policy over the years, though these would have affected ordinary Byzantines a great deal less.

As usual in Byzantine history, our sources are not much interested in the provinces, the working classes, institutional reforms, economics, or statistics of any sort. The Byzantines' view of history emphasized how much their empire remained the same, not how it changed; nor can most contemporaries anywhere be expected to appreciate fully changes that occur gradually over two generations. While many Byzantines must have been aware of many of the differences between the empire of 780 and that of 842, the transformation was surely greater than the vast majority realized.

THE TERRITORY

The map of the empire in 842 was significantly different from what it had been in 780, and the map in 809 would have been different from both the others. In 809, before the Bulgars' surprise attack, the empire held both the conquests of Irene in western Thrace and the conquests of Nicephorus I in the Peloponnesus, northern Greece, and the valley of the Strymon River. The Byzantines had also gained effective control over Dalmatia by making it an archontate, while their only loss since 780 had been the border fort of Camachum on the Euphrates. After 809, the Bulgars and Slavs overran not only the new land in the region of the Strymon and western Thrace, but also much of the rest of Thrace that had been Byzantine far longer. They did not, however, take any of the new lands in northern Greece or the Peloponnesus. Then in 816 Leo V's treaty with the Bulgars reestablished the Thracian frontier of 780, except for abandoning the isolated port of Mesembria. The next year Leo reoccupied Camachum. At this point, therefore, in comparison with 780 the empire had registered very large gains and only one minor loss, though it had not been able to hold on to a large additional region that it had taken temporarily.

During the next 25 years Byzantine gains and losses were small, at least in area. The North African and Spanish Arabs who took part of Sicily in 827 and all of Crete in 828, despite various vicissitudes of war, did not hold significantly more or less land in 842. They then held a third of Sicily, which was about equal in area to the whole of Crete. Small though they were, however, these territorial losses caused annoyance to the empire that was out of proportion to their size. In 836 Theophilus retook from the Slavs the strip of Thracian coast by the mouth of the Strymon, thus restoring Byzantine control over the land route from Constantinople

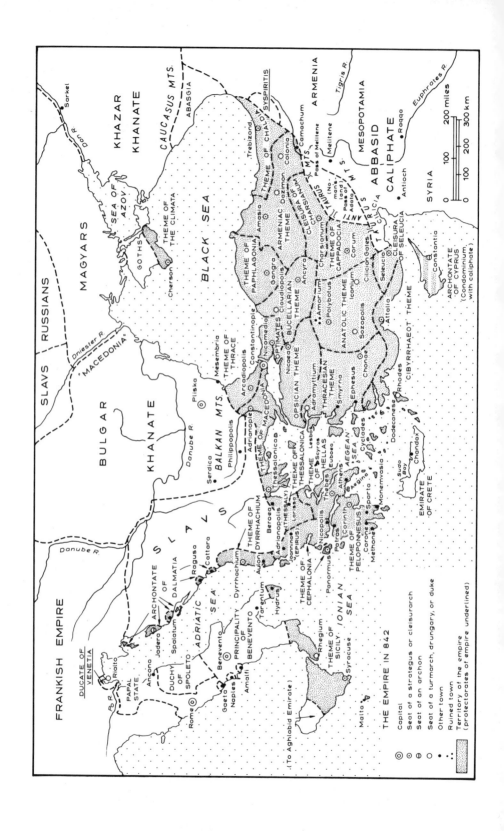

THE EMPIRE IN 842

◎ Capital
⊙ Seat of a strategus or cleisurarch
⊖ Seat of an archon
● Seat of a turmarch, drungary, or duke
• Other town
⊙ Ruined town
Territory of the empire
(protectorates of empire underlined)

FRANKISH EMPIRE

PAPAL STATE

DUCATE OF VENETIA

Rialto
Ancona
Jadera
Spalatum
ARCHONTATE OF DALMATIA
Ragusa
Cattara

Rome ◎
Gaeta
Naples ⊙
Amalfi
PRINCIPALITY OF BENEVENTO
Benevento ⊙
DUCHY OF SPOLETO

Tarentum
Hydrus
Otranto
THEME OF DYRRHACHIUM
Dyrrhachium
Aulon
THEME OF CEPHALONIA

Rhegium
THEME OF SICILY
Syracuse
(To Aghlabid Emirate)
Malta

SLAVS

ADRIATIC SEA

IONIAN SEA

Panormus
THEME OF PELOPONNESUS
Methone
Corone
Sparta
Monemvasia

Beroea
Larissa
THEME OF HELLAS (THESSALY)
Nicopolis
THEME OF EPIRUS
Aegina
Corinth
Patras
Thebes
Euboea

THEME OF MACEDON
THEME OF THESSALONICA
Thessalonica
Lesbos
Skyros
AEGEAN SEA
Cyclades
Smyrna
Ephesus
Chonae

SLAVS

RUSSIANS

"MACEDONIA"

Dniester R.

BULGAR KHANATE

Danube R.

Serdica
Philippopolis
BALKAN MTS.
Pliska ◎
Mesembria
Adrianople
Arcadiopolis
THEME OF THRACE
Constantinople
Nicomedia
Nicaea
OPSICIAN THEME
Adramyttium
THRACESIAN THEME

MAGYARS

Don R.
Sarkel

KHAZAR KHANATE

SEA OF AZOV

GOTHS

THEME OF THE CLIMATA
Cherson

BLACK SEA

CAUCASUS MTS.
ABASGIA

SYSPIRITIS
Trebizond
THEME OF CHALDIA
Colonia
Camachum
ARMENIA
Tigris R.
Euphrates R.

Amasia
Gangra
Claudiopolis
THEME OF PAPHLAGONIA
Dazimon
ARMENIAC THEME
CLEISURA OF CHARSIANUM
Charsianum
TAURUS MTS.
Camachum
Pass of Melitene
Melitene

BUCELLARIAN THEME
Ancyra
Amorium
THEME OF CAPPADOCIA
Polybotus
ANATOLIC THEME
Iconium
Corum
Cilician Gates
Seleucia
CLEISURA OF SELEUCIA
CIBYRRHAEOT THEME

Pimates
Tyana
Sozopolis
Attalia
Rhodes
Dodecanese

Suda Bay
Chandax
EMIRATE OF CRETE

ARMENIA

MESOPOTAMIA
ABBASID CALIPHATE
SYRIA
Antioch
Raqqa

(No-man's-land)
Adata
Pass of Adata
TAURUS MTS.
ANTI-TAURUS MTS.

Constantia
ARCHONTATE OF CYPRUS
(Condominium, with caliphate)

200 miles
300 km
200
100
100
200
100
0

to Greece. Then in 839 his establishment of the themes of Dyrrhachium and the Climata in the place of former archontates probably brought with them some annexations of land from the Albanians and Goths, as the new troops were moved in and given farms.

The overall result of the territorial changes since 780 was some weakening of the empire's position in the Mediterranean and a great strengthening of its position in the Balkans. This net gain takes on its full meaning only when one realizes that by 842 the reoccupation of Greece was the first case since the reign of Justinian in which the empire had retaken a significant amount of territory and continued to hold it for over 30 years. In fact, the reoccupation was to last for centuries, and the empire soon showed itself able to make and keep further conquests.

The other major change in Byzantine geography was a multiplication of provinces. In 780 the empire had had fifteen provinces, nine of them equivalent to themes. In 842 it had twenty-three, twenty-one of them equivalent to themes. In the interim four themes had been created by expanding former archontates, namely Thessalonica, Cephalonia, Dyrrhachium, and the Climata. A fifth theme, Peloponnesus, had been created by expanding a piece of another theme, Hellas, whose remaining territory was extended in turn. By 842 there were also four themes and two cleisurae that had been divided off from other themes: Macedonia from Thrace; Paphlagonia, Chaldia, and Charsianum from the Armeniacs; and Cappadocia and Seleucia from the Anatolics. While one archontate had been lost in Crete, another had been created in Dalmatia from territory that had previously been almost independent.

To understand the significance of the addition of twelve new themes and cleisurae within less than 60 years, one should realize that during the previous 130 years, as long as the themes had existed as the empire's main territorial divisions, only five new themes had been added. In geographical terms, the latest addition meant that for the first time the themes corresponded to distinct regions. The emperors had now broken up the vast areas of the Anatolic and Armeniac themes, which had included everything from seacoast to interior plain and mountain frontier.

The main reason for the creation of these new themes was, without much doubt, that the different regions they defined faced defensive problems of different sorts. Despite many signs that the empire was becoming stronger during this period, through most of it defensive problems abounded. In 842 each of the empire's 23 provinces, with the possible exception of the peculiar condominium with the Arabs on Cyprus, seems to have suffered some form of invasion within the previous twenty years. The great majority of the provinces had been invaded within the last six years, and in two themes, Peloponnesus and Sicily, fighting was actually going on at the time of Theophilus's death. The empire's adversaries had become more diverse since 780, when the Abbasid caliphate and the Bulgar khanate had been its only important enemies. Now they had been joined by the Sicilian and Cretan Arabs and the Russians, not to speak of the Slavs in the Peloponnesus. Each of these harried distinct regions.

Over this whole period, the themes of Macedonia and Thrace were among the worst sufferers from outside incursions. They had been almost completely devastated by the Bulgars between 812 and 815, when their headquarters at Adrianople and Arcadiopolis had both been sacked. They were also the scene of some of the worst fighting between Michael II and Thomas the Slav between 821 and 823. As recently as 836, the Bulgars had destroyed two of Macedonia's border forts just before the renewal of their treaty. Nonetheless, conditions in the two themes were probably rather good in 842. The real devastation of the land had ended in 815, and after that the 20-year treaty with the Bulgars, despite the one minor breach, had provided the population with an unaccustomed amount of security. Many of the Byzantines deported to Bulgaria in 813 had finally returned with their children in 836, when they almost certainly received money from Theophilus to aid in their resettlement. If Constantinople was growing, as it seems it was, the people of Macedonia and Thrace were best positioned to profit from supplying it with more food. The virtual doubling of the pay of imperial soldiers would also have had the greatest impact in this region because, as the home of most of the tagmata, it was the place where soldiers were most densely concentrated.

On the other side of the straits, the Opsician theme and the district of the Optimates would also have benefited from the increased prosperity of the capital and the tagmata. This area too had suffered during the civil war, especially in 823 when the Arabs had raided briefly in support of Thomas; but with this exception it had not been raided since 798, and was as secure as any part of the empire. Though there had been rumors that the region would be raided in 833 and 838, nothing had come of them. To the south, the Thracesian theme, always much the empire's richest, had escaped major raiding since 782. Along its coast the Arab pirates from Crete had been something of a nuisance, at least by making shipowners reluctant to venture out from the theme's ports. When the Cretan Arabs had actually raided on land in 841, however, their unfamiliarity with the terrain suggests that they had not raided often before. Their crushing defeat by the Thracesian army would discourage them from doing so again for some time.[457]

After the creation of the new coastal and frontier provinces, the Anatolic, Bucellarian, and Armeniac themes essentially corresponded to the interior of Anatolia. This area, nearly all of it plateau of moderate fertility and population density where livestock and some grain were raised, shared a common lot in the first part of the ninth century. The Anatolics, Bucellarians, and Armeniacs had all been raided a number of times under Irene and Nicephorus, and in 811 the Armeniacs had had their headquarters at Euchaïta destroyed. After 811, partly because of the Arab civil war, they had enjoyed almost 30 years of peace, broken only by a little fighting during the Byzantine civil war and one Arab raid in 825. Then, in 838, the Arabs had invaded all three, sacking the Bucellarians' capital at Ancyra and destroying the Anatolics' capital at Amorium. As has been seen, however, aside from the destruction of Amorium, the fast-moving Arab invasion of 838 did not cause very great devastation, certainly not in comparison with the repeated raids before 811. Though in 842 Amorium was still in ruins, and the Anatolic army would still have felt some of the effects of its heavy losses when Amorium was taken, otherwise life in these three themes had probably returned to normal.

The situation of Seleucia, Cappadocia, and Charsianum was quite different from that of the remainder of the Anatolic and Armeniac themes, from which they had been separated only in 839. Theophilus had made them cleisurae because they were the least defensible parts of the frontier with the Arabs. They were consequently the objectives of the great majority of the small-scale border raids that the Arabs had staged up to 812, again in 821 and 825, and beginning once more in 830. Even though our sources often fail to specify precisely where on the border the raiders went, it is clear that Cappadocia was raided much more than Charsianum and Seleucia, the last of which may have escaped rather lightly. In Cappadocia every fort of any importance had fallen to the Arabs at least once between 830 and 833, although most of the people and their livestock must have escaped, often by hiding in their elaborate underground shelters. The Arabs had gone on raiding up to 841, but since the recent creation of the cleisurae the raiders had met with unprecedented Byzantine resistance and in the last year with total defeat. After two centuries in which the borderlands had been Arab playgrounds, they finally had some hope of more security, a hope that was later to be fulfilled.

By 842 the empire had three themes whose main orientation was toward the Black Sea, all created since 819. These were Paphlagonia and Chaldia on the southern seacoast and the Climata in the Crimea to the north. It appears likely that the elevation of these districts to the rank of theme was at least partly a response to the raids of the Russians, which had begun—and reached Amastris in Paphlagonia—long before 842. On the other hand, these raids are extremely poorly documented. They must have stopped before 839, when a friendly Russian embassy told Theophilus that Russia was cut off from the Black Sea by hostile tribes, evidently the Khazars and Magyars. Later in 839 Theophilus helped the Khazars build a fort, presumably to ward off the Russians, and the officer sent to supervise the construction warned the emperor of a threat to the Byzantine possessions in the Crimea, again presumably from the Russians. Nevertheless, the Russians do not seem actually to have attacked the Byzantines at this time. Apart from the Russians, the only raids on the Black Sea region had been made by the Arabs more than 50 years before. In 842, therefore, Paphlagonia, Chaldia, and the Climata would have shown no very conspicuous signs of devastation, and the Black Sea remained safely under Byzantine control.[458]

In the Mediterranean, by contrast, the Cibyrrhaeot theme and the theme of Sicily faced quite serious threats from the Muslims ensconced on Crete and in western Sicily. The Sicilian Arabs, with a base in North Africa much closer than the Byzantines' sources of supply and reinforcements, were not only making annual raids in every part of the theme and beyond but had a real chance of conquering all Sicily eventually. The Cretan Arabs had at first tried to extend their conquests to the Aegean islands of the Cibyrrhaeot theme, but, being much closer to the Byzantine heartland and lacking support from outside, in 829 they were repulsed, and had to be content with Crete thereafter. Though from 829 their pirate vessels harassed Byzantine shipping in the Aegean, except for their abortive raid on the Thracesians in 841 they seem to have left the Aegean coast and even many of the islands undisturbed. With the loss of nearly all their fleet in 841, they were themselves dangerously exposed to a Byzantine assault, which indeed came in 843. By 842, then, the Aegean part of the Cibyrrhaeot theme would have recovered somewhat, while the Anatolian part, which had not been raided since 825, would have been essentially restored.[459]

The Byzantines' recent gains in the Balkans comprised the largest part of the five themes of Thessalonica, Hellas, Peloponnesus, Cephalonia, and Dyrrhachium, to which one might add the archontate of Dalmatia. These had suffered a little from sea raids. The Cretan Arabs had raided the island of Aegina in the theme of Hellas about 828, and in 829 had raided Mount Athos in the theme of Thessalonica; in 841 the Sicilian Arabs had pillaged one of the islands of Dalmatia. Probably a few more raids have passed unrecorded in our sources. There had also been two Slav revolts, one fomented by the Bulgars in 836 in the theme of Thessalonica and another that broke out in Peloponnesus in 841 and was not put down until the next year. But apart from these temporary disturbances the new Balkan territories had been at peace since the Byzantines had annexed them, a fact that is rather impressive in view of their wide extent and substantial Slavic population. They had surely strengthened Byzantine influence over

Venetia, which had drawn closer to the empire to fight the Sicilian Arabs. Without such a strong Byzantine presence nearby, Naples had drifted so far from its allegiance as to join the Arabs as allies.

In sum, certain appearances to the contrary, except in Sicily and the Aegean Sea the security of the empire was considerably better in 842 than in 780. The exceptions were of some importance, especially because they were very difficult for the Byzantines to remedy. Unlike the rest of the empire, Sicily was not really within the area that could best be defended from Constantinople; it was a relic of Justinian's sixth-century reconquests that the Byzantines had retained mostly because no strong sea power had previously appeared to contest it. Although Crete should not have been difficult to defend if the Byzantines had been ready to defend it, after it was strongly garrisoned by an enemy it could be retaken only by an elaborate amphibious assault of a sort that no premodern army could perform without great risk and expense. Unless Crete was retaken, wiping out petty piracy that came from it was practically impossible; even the ancient Romans had been unable to eliminate Mediterranean piracy before they took Crete. Nonetheless, fearsome though the Cretan and Sicilian Arabs were for Byzantine shipping in the Aegean and Adriatic and for the Byzantines on Sicily, the loss of Crete and part of Sicily made little if any difference to the vast majority of Byzantines, who lived elsewhere and had nothing to do with sea trade. The damage to the state was mostly to its pride. The trifling losses in revenue from the lost lands and lost trade was more than canceled out by even small improvements on the Anatolian and Balkan peninsulas.

Improvements there had been more than small. The peace treaty of 816 with the Bulgars and the reoccupation and resettlement of Greece had brought great benefits to the Balkans. The informal peace with the caliphate and the creation of the new border provinces had helped things in the East somewhat less, but even there the long-term trend was in the Byzantines' favor. While the empire had made gains in territory and population, by losing North Africa and Khurāsān the caliphate had lost something like 30 percent of its land and people. This meant that the emperor now ruled about a sixth as much land as the caliph instead of a tenth, and perhaps two-fifths as many people instead of a quarter. The revenue of the empire had increased from about 5 percent of the income of the caliphate in 780 to about 13 percent in 842. Though this may still look like a hopeless disparity, it did not prevent Theophilus from mustering an army of about 70,000 men in 837, almost as many as the 80,000 that a major effort by Mu'taṣim gathered in 838. The reviving empire and the disintegrating caliphate were moving toward approximate equality in strength at a rapid and accelerating pace.[460]

THE ADMINISTRATION

For the empire's central bureaucracy the years between 780 and 842 were for the most part a time of enhanced power and prestige, and of continuity in organizational structure and personnel. This was by no means, however, a time when the central bureaucracy was left free to do pretty much as it liked, as had apparently been the case during most of the eighth century. Then the iconoclast emperors' lack of respect for the civil service had been accompanied by a lack of interest in it. Irene's increased attention to the bureaucracy was soon followed by the efforts of her successors to make officials less corrupt and more effective.

These efforts did not involve adding many new officials. During this period just one new bureau seems to have been added to the thirteen departments of the central administration, and it did not last. This was the bureau of the curator of the Mangana, created by Leo V in 813 when he confiscated the Mangana palace and the sprawling estates in Thrace that had been the ancestral property of Michael I Rhangabe. Since the Rhangabe family's possessions appear to have been nearly as valuable as all the previous imperial palaces and estates combined, Leo did not put them with the others under the jurisdiction of the great curator, but gave them their own department, whose revenues may well have gone into a special fund. Though after Theophilus's death Theodora evidently abolished the department by restoring its property to Michael Rhangabe and his sons, as eunuchs the sons could have no heirs, and it was probably understood that when they died the Mangana would again pass under an imperial curator, as eventually it did.[461]

The other thirteen bureaus seem to have gained only such new members as were needed to administer and supervise new jurisdictions. Thus the bureau of the great curator received an administrator and inspector for Irene's Palace of Eleutherius, and the military logothete's office received paymasters and messengers for the new themes and tagma created during these years. The general logothete, postal logothete, and chartulary of the sacellium would have received about 40 more subordinates to help them administer, inspect, and tax the new provinces. Excluding the bureau of the Mangana, the central administration therefore grew from about 500 men to about 600. Nonetheless, as will appear, the real change in provincial administration must have been much greater than is evident from this modest increase in the number of officials in Constantinople. For one thing, the provincial tax collectors, who were essentially private businessmen, surely grew in number when Nicephorus expanded the tax base.[462]

The period's frequent changes in government, and the switches from

Iconoclasm to Orthodoxy and back again, did not greatly affect the staffing of the civil service. When Irene restored the icons the civil servants had mostly been iconophiles anyway, and she had already removed a few recalcitrant officials for conspiring against her in 780. When Constantine VI took power he did not even remove Irene's chief ally Stauracius as postal logothete for more than a moment, and certainly did not conduct a major purge of Irene's supporters in the bureaucracy. Nicephorus I's coup against Irene was staged by some civil servants on behalf of one of their own, and the character of the coup that put Michael I on the throne was much the same. Since few civil servants were inclined to defend Michael I or Leo V by the time they fell, their successors conducted no purges. Theophilus's execution of the murderers of Leo V does not seem to have touched the bureaucracy either. As a result, many civil servants, including very high ones, went on serving despite dramatic changes in government and church doctrine. Most of Leo V's chief officials were friends of Theodore of Studius who had presumably served under Michael I and were to go on serving under Michael II.[463]

Two examples seem particularly noteworthy. John Hexabulius, a friend and correspondent of Theodore's, as count of the Walls warned Michael I that Leo the Armenian was dangerously powerful in 813. Nevertheless, when Leo then became emperor he trusted John from the first, and as his postal logothete John detected the conspiracy of Michael the Amorian and jailed him in 820. Nevertheless, when Michael then became emperor, he retained John as postal logothete and in 823 took John's advice to execute Thomas the Slav without interrogating the prisoner about his collaborators.

Another man may even have succeeded in occupying the same high bureaucratic post all the way from the reign of Irene to that of Theophilus. Leo the Sacellarius, a eunuch from Sinope, was one of the conspirators who helped Nicephorus overthrow Irene in 802. He may well have been the same Leo the Sacellarius as the friend to whom Theodore of Studius wrote during Leo V's persecution of iconophiles about 818. This friend was certainly the same Leo the Sacellarius who corresponded with Theodore in an effort to reconcile him with Michael II in 824. Very probably it was the same Leo the Sacellarius who visited the iconophile hermit Joannicius to ask for his prayers under Theophilus, about 838. If Leo was then about Joannicius's age, he would have first appeared in his high financial office when he was around 40, but he could easily have been ten years younger. Such men, far from being unprincipled, found private faith in icons compatible with the public performance of their duties. Theodore of Studius, strict though he was, gladly made use of their influence whenever he could.[464]

Apart from the palace coups of 802 and 811, which removed rulers who were scarcely capable of ruling any longer, and the abortive maneuvers in 838 by people who believed that the emperor was already dead, the civil service mostly stopped plotting between 780 and 842, in marked contrast to its frequent conspiracies during the previous 60 years. Even the conspiracy of 808, which aimed to install Arsaber the Quaestor as emperor, was mainly led by monks and clergy, who after all could not put forward one of themselves as their candidate. Though some civil servants were involved as well, the conspiracy took place in the midst of financial reforms that affected the private interests of a number of wealthy people, some of whom incidentally held public office. During none of this period do the civil servants seem to have been seriously disaffected as a group.

While the reintroduction of Iconoclasm cannot have been welcome to most of the central bureaucracy, the iconoclast emperors of the ninth century, unlike those of the eighth, took some pains to avoid offense to their civil servants. Leo V first made his case for Iconoclasm to a trusted group of officials, two of whom he then appointed to his original commission of three to research the theology of icons. Later, when many officials objected to Leo's nomination of John the Grammarian as patriarch of Constantinople, Leo appointed someone acceptable to them instead. Michael II twice used his officials to negotiate with the iconophile monks and bishops. The second marriage of Leo V, to the daughter of Arsaber the Quaestor, and that of Michael II, to the granddaughter of Irene, were calculated to appeal to both civil servants and iconophiles. Theophilus consulted his chief officials before he executed the murderers of Leo V, and bade the senators a fond farewell on his deathbed. Since Byzantine historiography is mostly the work of bureaucrats, its generally favorable opinion of Theophilus's court probably mirrors the opinions of his officials. From Irene's reign on, then, the empire's civil servants enjoyed fairly stable tenure and much imperial favor, and their morale seems to have been better than in the preceding period.

It is not difficult to infer from some of Nicephorus I's reforms and from other bits of evidence that Irene had tolerated a certain amount of official corruption, evidently in the collection of taxes, and probably in the administration of justice. Nicephorus, Leo V, and Theophilus all tried to decrease corruption in the bureaucracy. Nicephorus proclaimed laws to curb tax evasion involving the connivance of officials, and Leo V strove to appoint unbribable men to office. To give subjects recourse against officials, Nicephorus held his special court in the Magnaura, Leo held his in the Lausiacus, and Theophilus heard complaints all the way from the palace to Blachernae and back. Although measures to correct abuses are always better evidence that the abuses existed than that they were corrected, bitter protests indicate that Nicephorus's reforms worked, and Leo and Theophilus are known to have punished some very high officials, including a city prefect and a minister for petitions. The Byzantine bureaucracy was so small that any significant effort to reform it should have had considerable impact; making examples of a few prominent cases would naturally have deterred others. When the young Methodius of Syracuse came to Constantinople to seek civil office from Nicephorus, he took with him a large sum of money, presumably for the bribes that had once been expected; but the information that Methodius had heard in Sicily may have been out of date, because after arriving he abandoned his plan and took the advice of an ascetic to become a monk.[465]

Along with at least some increase in the honesty of the bureaucracy went a definite increase in its efficiency. Since the virtual doubling of the state revenue between Irene and Theophilus is too great a change to be explained only by growing general prosperity, it must reflect more efficient, as well as more honest, assessment and collection of the taxes. The growth in the gold reserve surely began well before it reached the superabundance that became evident at the beginning of Theophilus's reign in 829. Nicephorus seems therefore to have succeeded in his strenuous efforts to raise tax receipts. After him the civil service must have continued to enforce his reforms.

From Nicephorus's reign on, the bureaucracy had to perform several extraordinary and difficult tasks, starting with the new census completed in 809 and probably begun in 807. No sooner had the bureaucracy finished this than it had to make arrangements for setting up the new themes in the Balkans, and for transferring many families from the rest of the empire to those themes. Under Leo V the officials had to arrange for the reoccupation and reconstruction of the almost entirely devastated themes of Thrace and Macedonia, and under Michael II they had to reestablish control over the provinces after the widespread disruptions caused by the war with Thomas the Slav. Under Theophilus, the civil service had to settle as many as 30,000 converted Khurramites in various parts of the empire between 834 and 838, providing them with wives, land, and arms, and in 836 it had to settle some 40,000 refugees from Bulgaria in Thrace. Finally, in 839 it had not only to resettle many of the former Khurramites but to redraw all the empire's internal administrative boundaries, add two entirely new themes, revise the army's command structure, and recalculate the soldiers' pay.[466]

Though so many complicated administrative arrangements could hardly have been made without mistakes, no mistakes are mentioned in the surviving sources, and in the end all of these operations achieved their purposes. Even if the former Khurramites and the Slavs of the Peloponnesus eventually revolted, those revolts cannot fairly be blamed on administrative failures and were soon put down. While the bureaucracy might well have been able to perform such difficult tasks before Nicephorus, performing them would itself have improved the census lists and muster rolls, and officials' ability to use them. So much radical intervention in the affairs of the provinces must have made the bureaucracy more familiar with provincial affairs and more capable of supervising them.

Although it is plain that the main reasons for the creation of new provinces during this period were military, it is also clear that the multiplication of provinces had consequences for civil administration. Whenever a new theme or archontate was created, it received the usual administrative, judicial, and secretarial officials who were independent of the strategus or archon, along with some members of the strategus's staff who had a civil as well as a military role. The more themes there were, and the more the giant Anatolic and Armeniac themes were split up, the better suited the provinces were to civil government and the easier it was to control the strategi from Constantinople. This result was partly accidental, but it was not entirely so. Already in the eighth century Constantine V had divided the Opsician theme to bring it to heel after its count had rebelled, and in 820 Leo V probably divided the Armeniacs as part of a campaign against his supposed enemies.

Even more important for administration than the multiplication of themes was the introduction in 839 of the bandum, the district garrisoned by 200 soldiers. Before 839 the smallest regular districts within themes had been the drungi, garrisoned by 1,000 soldiers, of which there were 70 throughout the empire. After 839 the themes and cleisurae were divided into 479 banda with their own headquarters and territory. Though the bandum, like the theme, began primarily as a military unit and at first had no civil officials of its own, it became the basic administrative division of the empire, the equivalent of an American county. When administrative documents referred to the provinces in the following period, they classified the territories not by cities or drungi but by banda. The drungus soon lost its status as a territorial division, and within 60 years banda were grouped into new themes and transferred from one theme to another without regard for their drungi. Most banda created in 839 seem to have kept the same boundaries for centuries. Some 600 years later, long after the military system that the banda represented had collapsed, they were still the basic Byzantine administrative districts.[467]

The government's preference for the banda is not surprising, because they formed much more manageable districts than drungi, which could be as far-flung as all the islands of the Aegean Sea, and they were much more evenly distributed than cities. Of all the provinces, only the relatively urbanized themes of the Thracesians, Cibyrrhaeots, and Sicily seem to have had more cities than banda, while such overwhelmingly rural provinces as the Armeniacs, Paphlagonia, and Charsianum had not even a third as many cities. Even though the commander of a bandum was a military official, he was still a permanent representative of the government who was in touch with the capital. He maintained a headquarters that could serve as a base for civil officials when they visited, and he commanded a garrison that could enforce the government's will. The bandum was an instrument that could be used to tighten Byzantine administration, and soon it was used as such.[468]

On the whole, therefore, this was a period in which the Byzantine administration worked better than it had for many years, and probably better than at any time since the old civil administrative system had broken down in the first half of the seventh century. Though the provincial government remained mostly military in character, the central bureaucracy in Constantinople came to have closer control over it, not least because the bureaucracy itself had become better disciplined and had gained in prestige. If the introduction of Iconoclasm in the eighth century had alienated and demoralized the civil service, the impact of the reintroduction of Iconoclasm in the ninth century was less adverse. A year after Theophilus died, most civil servants, headed by the postal logothete Theoctistus, welcomed the restoration of the icons. But probably few regretted that the memory of the late emperor was not condemned, because Theoctistus and most of the rest of them had served Theophilus and his father faithfully and well, and not unwillingly.

THE ARMY

While the quality of the civil service was improving, during most of the period from 780 to 842 the army did little to better its generally mediocre performance since the Arabs had defeated Heraclius. As usual, its most impressive ability was to survive military catastrophes without permanently losing either troop strength or territory. Though the empire's security improved markedly during this time, the improvement was more a result of the Bulgar treaty and the Arab civil war than of better defense by Byzantine soldiers. The army did win a few important victories in the field, including successful raids on Arab territory in 786, 805, and 837, and the battle in 816 that led the Bulgars to make peace. These victories, however, were less numerous than the defeats, and tended to occur only when the Byzantines were fully prepared and the enemy unprepared and probably outnumbered. The significant conquests of this period resulted from the Byzantines' moving into the lands of people, usually Slavs, who offered little if any resistance. Unless Byzantine troops had clear advantages over their adversaries, they usually lost; and in between losing they often revolted.

Though the system of the themes had never been good at stopping enemy raids, it had been quite good at stopping enemy conquests. This continued to be the case, despite the empire's loss of Crete, part of Sicily, and the territory acquired by Irene and Nicephorus in Thrace. The fall of Crete cannot be blamed on the themes, because Crete was outside the thematic system when it fell. By contrast, despite a vigorous attempt, the Cretan Arabs were unable to conquer any part of the neighboring Cibyrrhaeot theme for more than a few months. Although the conquests of Irene and Nicephorus were apparently attached to the theme of Macedonia, no garrisons with military lands seem to have got properly settled there before the Bulgars attacked. When peace was finally made, the empire ended up still holding virtually all of the territory where thematic troops had been established with lands. In Sicily, which was indeed an established theme, year after year the soldiers fought numerous adversaries doggedly with minimal reinforcements, exacting heavy enemy casualties for the little territory they gave up. The same was true in Cappadocia and the other areas on the Arab frontier, where there were no permanent losses of land. When the soldiers were actually defending their homes, they fought well. The themes did not, however, provide them with an effective means of defeating an enemy before it reached their homes—at least not until Theophilus's reforms of 839. There were too few troops on the border, and reinforcements could not be called up quickly enough.

In battle, the army showed two major weaknesses that accounted for most of its defeats: it was too often disaffected, and it was too easily caught off its guard. In 782 the disloyalty of the strategus Tatzates and his men had robbed the Byzantines of a victory against the Arabs, and in 813 the ambitions of Leo and his men probably caused Michael I to lose to the Bulgars. In 838 the Persian Company almost surrendered Theophilus to the Arabs at Anzen, and by revolting broke up the defeated army afterward; shortly thereafter, Amorium was betrayed from within. Again, Serdica was lost through treachery in 809. The disaffection of the Anatolic soldiers who had recently been discharged from the tagmata may have contributed to their defeat by the Arabs in 788, and there may be some truth in the story that the Cibyrrhaeot strategus Theophilus was betrayed to the Arabs by his colleagues in 790.

Though even very good armies can occasionally be taken by surprise, the Byzantines were surprised too often for a properly disciplined force. The Bulgars ambushed them in 788, in 809, and for practical purposes in 811, when the Byzantine troops were looting the Bulgarian countryside in some disorder. The Arabs ambushed them in 804, in 811, and on Crete in 828, when the Byzantines ate and drank too much in celebration of a nearly complete victory. Even when Byzantine armies were not ambushed, they were often ill prepared for battle, as in 788 against the Beneventans, in 792 against the Bulgars, again the same year against the Armeniac rebels, or in 832 against the Arabs. The army's shaky loyalty was probably related to its disorderly condition, because troops that are ready to revolt cannot safely be disciplined, as Nicephorus I learned from experience. If Nicephorus had been able to concentrate more on the Bulgars and less on keeping his soldiers contented, the catastrophe of 811 in Bulgaria might have been averted.

During this period the themes showed a reluctance to follow the lead of the government in Constantinople, and even the tagmata sometimes had a mind of their own. In 790 the themes of Asia Minor rose not only against Irene but against their own commanders, and in 792 the soldiers of the Armeniacs rebelled against both their strategus and Constantine VI. In 800 the troops in Cappadocia were ready to rebel in favor of Stauracius; in 803 all of the Anatolian themes but the Armeniac backed Bardanes Turcus; and in 813 the Anatolian themes put Leo V on the throne. The appointment of monostrategi over groups of themes in 802, 803, and 819 betrays the government's anxiety about the themes' loyalty. Even though the uprising of Thomas the Slav in 821 was not technically a rebellion, it indicates some weakness in the link between the capital and the themes. The Arab invasion of Sicily began because of the revolt of Euphemius in 826, which the revolt of Elpidius in 781 had foreshadowed. The dispersal of the army and the revolt of the Persian Company in 838 similarly showed a failure of the government to control its soldiers. Though tagmatic soldiers were under better control, some of them still forced Irene to dissolve her church council in 786, and they plotted against Constantine VI in 792 and Nicephorus I in 807. The tagmata mutinied while on campaign in 809 under Nicephorus and in 812 under Michael I, in the latter case causing the loss of much of Thrace.

This sort of behavior is not entirely surprising coming from the themes, because they were only a part-time force. Most of the time thematic soldiers were simply farmers who kept some military equipment in their storerooms. Most lived far from the headquarters of their drungary, who probably mustered and drilled them very seldom unless they were actually needed for military service. Except when they served on campaign with the emperor or the domestic of the Schools, as they rarely did, their only connection with the central government was to receive some very meager pay, at intervals that by 839 could be as far apart as six years. When there was an enemy raid, they fought under their drungary and tur-

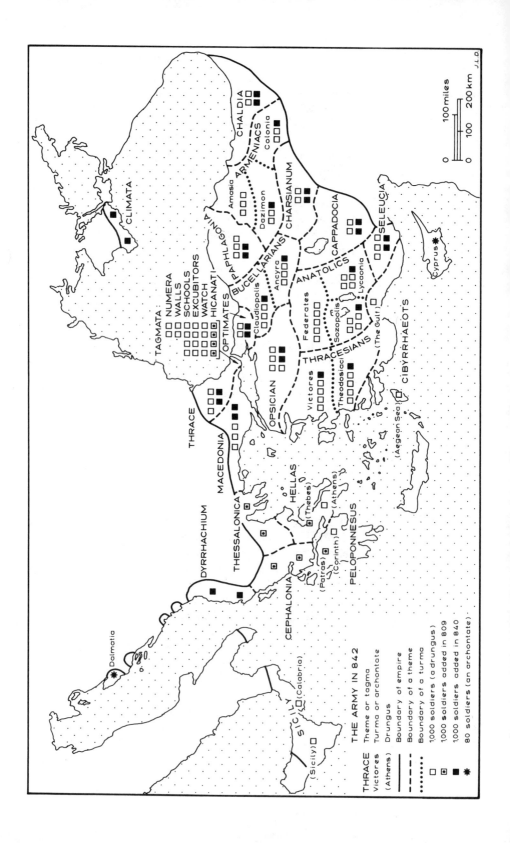

THE ARMY IN 842

THRACE   Theme or tagma
Victores   Turma or archontate
(Athens)   Drungus

☐   Boundary of empire
☐   Boundary of a theme
■   Boundary of a turma

☐   1,000 soldiers (a drungus)
☐   1,000 soldiers added in 809
■   1,000 soldiers added in 840
✳   80 soldiers (an archontate)

TAGMATA:
NUMERA
WALLS
SCHOOLS
EXCUBITORS
WATCH
HICANATI

CLIMATA

CHALDIA
Colonia
ARMENIACS
Amasia
Dazimon
CHARSIANUM
CAPPADOCIA
SELEUCIA
Cyprus

PAPHLAGONIA
OPTIMATES
BUCELLARIANS
Ancyra
ANATOLICS
Lycaonia
Claudiopolis
Federates
Sozopolis
(The Gulf)

OPSICIAN
Victores
THRACESIANS
Theodosiaci
CIBYRRHAEOTS
(Aegean Sea)

THRACE
MACEDONIA

DYRRHACHIUM
THESSALONICA
HELLAS
(Thebes)
(Athens)
PELOPONNESUS
(Corinth)
(Patras)

CEPHALONIA
(Calabria)
SICILY
(Sicily)

Dalmatia

0   100 miles
0   100   200 km

J.L.D.

march, and in some cases under their strategus, but scarcely ever did they receive reinforcements from the capital.

To be sure, the soldiers knew that in principle they held their lands in return for military service, and that if they did not appear when their drungary called them up they would be liable to lose their land. But they were most unlikely to lose it if they followed their drungary and turmarch in a revolt, whether or not the revolt succeeded. Only in 793, when Constantine VI confiscated the lands of the entire senior drungus of the Armeniacs and branded and exiled its soldiers, were ordinary thematic troops punished for rebellion. If the soldiers of the themes did not behave like fully professional troops, this was because they were not drilled, paid, or disciplined like professional troops.[469]

The tagmata behaved rather better because they were drilled regularly, fought more often, and were sometimes led by the emperor himself. Inevitably, however, with a near-monopoly of military power near the capital, they were occasionally tempted to use their position to impose their own wishes on the government. If anything, they did so less than might have been expected, probably because their six divisions had their own commanders and seldom acted together. They were also easier to discipline than the themes, since they were closer at hand; substantial numbers of their soldiers were discharged for insubordination by Irene in 786, by Nicephorus in 809, and by Michael I in 812. Nonetheless, when they campaigned along with thematic soldiers they could be infected by the indiscipline of the themes, as apparently happened in 812, and they were sensitive enough about their modest pay to mutiny in 809 when it was late.

Such were the defects of discipline, organization, and loyalty that Theophilus's military reforms of 839 must have been meant to address. Though the reforms had been needed much earlier, there were good reasons for their not coming much before they did. The arrival of the 30,000 Khurramites by 837 certainly made expanding the army easier, though Nicephorus had shown that thousands of new soldiers could be recruited within the empire if the government was determined to do it. A sizable budgetary surplus was necessary if more was to be spent on the army on a consistent basis, and though the surplus seems to have been large and regular since Nicephorus's tax reforms the government may have needed time to grow accustomed to the fact. The most important new element in 839, however, was the government's realization that changes were necessary, which was caused by crushing defeats at the hands of the Arabs in 838 and the revolt of the Persian Company. Only those shocks persuaded Theophilus that he should give up some of the gold that he was spending on buildings and furniture, and should alter troop dispositions and command structures that had been in place for most of two centuries.

The main features of the military reforms of 839 have already been out-lined. Apparently Theophilus increased the soldiers' full pay from six to twelve nomismata a year, payable every three years; disbanded the Persian Company of 30,000 men and settled its soldiers among the themes in fifteen contingents of 2,000 men each; created the three cleisurae of Charsianum, Cappadocia, and Seleucia on the Arab frontier, along with the theme of Dyrrhachium in modern Albania and the theme of the Climata in the Crimea; and reorganized all the themes into the smaller districts called banda, garrisoned by 200 soldiers each. Consequently, after 839 the regular army was better paid, larger, redistributed in the direction of the Arab frontier, divided into additional independent commands, and more tightly organized at the local level. Each change did something to correct the army's previous defects.

The increase in pay would have led not only to better morale but to improved preparedness and loyalty. Much of the soldiers' original pay must have gone to maintain their military equipment, which the state evaluated, and presumably sold from its warehouses, at a price of eighteen and a half nomismata per man. This sum probably applied to all soldiers, and did not include the cavalryman's horse, which would have cost another six nomismata or so if it was purchased. While arms, armor, and horse would under ordinary conditions have lasted a number of years, all could easily be lost or rendered unserviceable in a single battle, forcing the soldier to raise some three years' pay at once; each would also tend to need replacement all at once when it was worn out. Before 839 many soldiers must have been left with inadequate equipment that they lacked the money to replace, however much their farms produced in kind. After 839, this problem would have lessened considerably. Only after 839 could soldiers have accumulated significant savings from their pay above what they needed for equipment, and so been able to buy more land, livestock, and other goods that served to reward them rather than just to pay their expenses. Half a pound of gold every three years was the sort of income that would be likely to inspire some gratitude, and to make a soldier think twice before joining a rebellion that would jeopardize his pay.[470]

That an increase in the regular army from 90,000 to 120,000 men would have improved Byzantine offensive and defensive capabilities is obvious. What may be less obvious is that such an increase allowed the government to reinforce the Arab frontier without making many regular troops leave their established homes, and without giving large themes that were not on the frontier the impression that their needs for manpower were being ignored. Since more than half the former Khurramites had no established homes in the empire, they could be shifted to one place as readily as another. Moving them caused none of the outcry that Nicephorus I had pro-

TABLE I
Troop Strength of the Byzantine Army, 780–842

Army division	780	816	838	842
Themes and cleisurae				
Anatolic	18,000	18,000	18,000	15,000[a]
Armeniac	14,000	14,000	9,000	9,000[a]
Bucellarian	6,000	6,000	6,000	8,000[a]
Cappadocia	(to Anatolic)	(to Anatolic)	(to Anatolic)	4,000[a]
Cephalonia		2,000	2,000	2,000
Chaldia	(to Armeniac)	(to Armeniac)	2,000	4,000[a]
Charsianum (cleisura)	(to Armeniac)	(to Armeniac)	(to Armeniac)	4,000[a]
Cibyrrhaeot	2,000	2,000	2,000	2,000
Climata				2,000[a]
Dyrrachium				2,000[a]
Hellas	2,000	2,000	2,000	2,000
Macedonia	(to Thrace)	3,000	3,000	5,000[a]
Opsician	4,000	4,000	4,000	6,000[a]
Paphlagonia	(to Armeniac)	(to Armeniac)	3,000	5,000[a]
Peloponnesus		2,000	2,000	2,000
Seleucia (cleisura)	(to Anatolic)	(to Anatolic)	(to Anatolic)	5,000[a]
Sicily	2,000	2,000	2,000	2,000
Thessalonica		2,000	2,000	2,000
Thrace	6,000	3,000	3,000	5,000[a]
Thracesian	8,000	8,000	8,000	10,000[a]
SUBTOTAL	62,000	68,000	68,000	96,000
Special corps				
Persian Company			30,000	
SUBTOTAL			30,000	
Tagmata				
Excubitors	4,000	4,000	4,000	4,000
Hicanati		4,000	4,000	4,000
Numera	2,000	2,000	2,000	2,000
Optimates	2,000	2,000	2,000	4,000[a]
Schools	4,000	4,000	4,000	4,000
Walls	2,000	2,000	2,000	2,000
Watch	4,000	4,000	4,000	4,000
SUBTOTAL	18,000	22,000	22,000	24,000
TOTAL	80,000	90,000	120,000	120,000

NOTE: Total payrolls (in nomismata):

780: 600,000   816: 680,000   838: 900,000   842: 1,440,000

[a]Figures include 2,000 men added after dissolution of the Persian Company in 839 and reassignment of its members to the thematic armies and Optimates.

voked in 809 when he shifted settlers from Asia Minor to the Balkans. On the other hand, Theophilus's carefully balanced distribution of the Persians in equal lots (even though the creation of the cleisurae made the actual distribution far from equal) seems to show both concern for the real defensive needs of the recently invaded Armeniac, Bucellarian, and Anatolic themes and caution to avoid offense to any major thematic army that might cause trouble. The western themes, which knew that they were in a less important category and were in no position to begin a serious revolt anyway, received no reinforcement, and may well have had to make up for Persians already settled among them by sending some of their regular troops to the Climata and Dyrrhachium.

Though the resulting deployment of troops was not ideal, it did result in a significantly greater concentration of manpower in places where it was needed. Within the region of the Arab border—the three original cleisurae, the Armeniacs' turma of Colonia, and the theme of Chaldia— the gain was probably from 11,000 to 20,000 men, or practically double. The themes on the border with the Bulgars and Slavs, including the new theme of Dyrrhachium, grew from 10,000 to 16,000 men. If the themes of Paphlagonia, Chaldia, and the Climata were largely intended to ward off a threat from the Russians, as seems very likely, they now had 11,000 troops to perform this task instead of their previous 5,000. A good case can admittedly be made that the Opsician and Thracesian themes did not need their added contingents of 2,000 troops, which might have been better deployed in Sicily, the Cibyrrhaeots, or the Armeniacs' turma of Colonia. Nonetheless, the distribution of troops among the themes after 839 was much better suited to the empire's defensive needs than the previous distribution, which had been arranged hurriedly in the mid-seventh century and left virtually unchanged until Theophilus.[471]

The creation of Theophilus's new themes and cleisurae, and of the other themes of Irene, Nicephorus, and Leo V, was in itself beneficial to Byzantine security, as has already been noted. Especially in places subject to raids, having an independent commander on the spot, who could muster troops quickly and lead them on short notice, made defense far easier. By 839 every frontier theme except Sicily had been either created or divided since 789, and each section of the frontier had its own strategus or cleisurarch, except the turma of Colonia in the Armeniacs. This last exception is puzzling, particularly because Colonia's part of the frontier was rather vulnerable to Arab raids. In the subsequent period Arab raiders often passed through the area of Colonia to avoid the cleisurae, where resistance was stiffer. Perhaps Theophilus did not see the weakness, since few raiders seem to have crossed there earlier; perhaps he had some unknown resentment against the troops of Colonia, to whom on his deathbed he sent a turmarch who was in disgrace. Nevertheless, despite this gap in the system of frontier provinces, that system was much more nearly complete after 839 than before.[472]

Finally, the introduction of the bandum made the whole army both more flexible and more professional. The division of each drungus into five banda made soldiers answerable to a commander from their immediate area, the count, who evidently took over responsibility for mustering and drilling them. While the bandum, or "standard," seems always to have existed as a battlefield formation, after it became a territorial division soldiers who lived together fought together, and inevitably identified closely with each other and with their count. While under the previous system there had been no thematic officer permanently stationed at about two-thirds of the fortified places in the empire, after 839 every fortified place seems to have had at least a count in residence. Though not every count had a fort, each had a permanent headquarters of some kind and two scouts and two messengers at his disposal. A count could therefore learn of an enemy raid and summon his 200 troops to defend their district on very short notice, which was often the only notice that raiders gave.[473]

The new system may be illustrated by the example of the Thracesian theme, which has already been described as it was in 780 under Michael Lachanodracon. In 842 its strategus was probably still Constantine Contomytes, who shortly before had annihilated the Arabs from Crete raiding Mount Latrus, south of Ephesus. Not surprisingly in view of his theme's importance, Constantine was well connected; his daughter either had married or would marry the nephew of both the empress Theodora and the patriarch John the Grammarian. The theme he commanded was organized as it had been before 839 down to the level of the drungaries, of whom each turma now had five instead of four. Every drungary now commanded five counts, each of whom led 40 cavalry and 160 infantry. Then each count commanded five centarchs, who led just 40 men, though their title survived to show that they had formerly commanded 100. Of these centarchs, one evidently led a cavalry squadron while the other four led infantry. Under each centarch's command were four decarchs, who as before commanded ten soldiers apiece.[474]

All the counts, 50 in the whole theme, had separate headquarters, except two who seem to have been stationed together at the theme's capital of Chonae with the strategus. The presence of two counts and a double bandum at the capital follows from the fact that after 839 every strategus had not one but two commanders of guards, titled the centarch of the spatharii and the count of the hetaeria, apparently the leaders of cavalry squadrons from two different banda. When the command of a centarch was reduced from 100 men to 40, the guardsmen of the centarch of the spatharii were automatically reduced as well; since each new bandum had just 40 cavalry, two banda were needed at the capital to provide the strategus with 80 mounted guardsmen, which was still 20 fewer than he had

THE THRACESIAN THEME IN 842

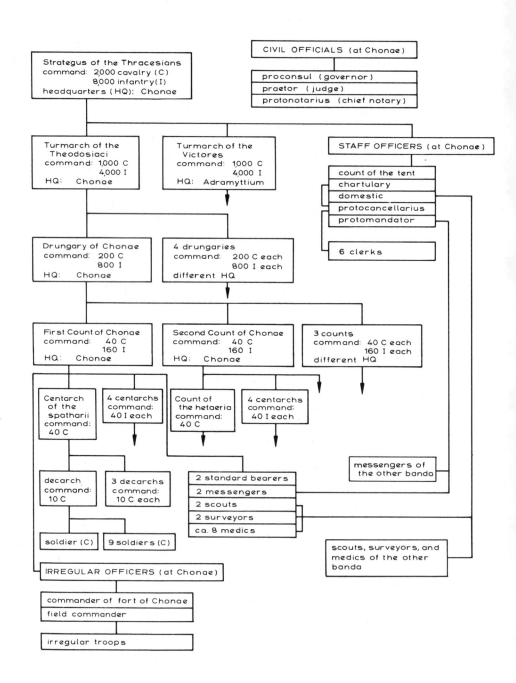

had before. This arrangement also assigned each theme's capital twice as many men as any other headquarters, so that the strategus had 400 soldiers in his immediate vicinity. In fact, the system of banda gave strategi much more additional power than this, because by working through the counts they could summon their other soldiers far more quickly and conveniently, especially from the banda near their capital. It was probably with such a force, assembled speedily from the banda between Chonae and the sea, that Constantine Contomytes caught the raiders of 841 before they reembarked for Crete.[475]

If the system of banda worked well in the Thracesian theme, where enemy raids were few, it was a greater boon in the frontier provinces, where raids were incessant. As long as Cappadocia had been a turma of the Anatolics, for example, it had had only 2,000 men under two drungaries to defend its large and exposed territory. Of its nineteen forts, only two, the capital at Lulum and the junior drungary's headquarters, probably at Soandus, had had regular commanders in residence. The other seventeen forts had made shift with irregular officers who could organize only the local civilians for defense. After 839, Cappadocia was at first a cleisura and soon a theme with 4,000 men, and each of its nineteen forts had a count able to call up the thematic troops stationed nearby. Cappadocia, as a district particularly open to raiders, was unique in Asia Minor in having all the headquarters of its banda fortified. Most of the counts in the much safer Thracesian theme had unfortified headquarters. But all ten Thracesian drungaries could have been accommodated in the theme's fifteen forts, leaving five for additional counts.[476]

Even though the system of banda was still very recent in 842, it had already begun to prove itself. In the years between 780 and 839, out of dozens of raids, only incursions in 781, 807, 812, and 831 had been defeated by the Byzantines, and defeating the first and last of these had required help from the capital. In 840, however, the Cappadocians had nearly fought off an Arab raid with their own forces. In 841 there were three raids, and all were utterly crushed by thematic armies fighting alone. Before the Thracesians' victory over the Cretan Arab raiders, the cleisurae had driven one Arab raiding party out of Cappadocia and well into Cilicia, and they then drove another group of raiders out of Charsianum and well past Melitene, in the process sacking the important Arab forts of Adata and Germanicea. This was a very impressive change. Although the Byzantine army was not yet able to end Arab raids in Asia Minor altogether, it would do so in just over twenty years. It would then begin reconquering the border region that the Arabs had taken so long ago.[477]

THE ECONOMY

How much did the Byzantine economy grow between 780 and 842, and in what ways? If complete archives survived, it would be possible to estimate rural population growth from hearth-tax records, and the expansion of the area under cultivation from land-tax records, in both cases rather reliably. These records would also indicate how often farmers who were unable to pay their taxes forfeited their land to their neighbors or received tax exemptions; this would provide a fair index of agricultural prosperity. Records of customs duties would also make it possible to estimate the volume of trade all over the empire in different years. The archives, however, have long since disappeared, leaving only the barest traces in sources that are preserved today. Those traces are nonetheless the necessary starting point for discussing the development of the Byzantine economy.

Some valuable figures survive that relate to the empire's situation in 842. First, the army payroll is said to have totaled 20,000 pounds of gold (1.44 million nomismata) about 867, when the army appears to have been essentially as it was established by Theophilus's military reforms of 839. The surviving descriptions of the army's troop strength, command structure, and pay scale as they were set in 839 can be used to calculate how much the payroll should have been then; the result of this calculation is almost exactly 1.44 million nomismata. Further, Theophilus is said to have left at his death a reserve in the treasury of 97,000 pounds of gold, or 6,984,000 nomismata. By 856, after fourteen years in which expenditure seems to have changed little since the army payroll had increased in 839, the gold reserve had risen to 109,000 pounds, or 7,848,000 nomismata. It can therefore be reckoned that around 842 the Byzantine government spent about 1.44 million nomismata a year on its army and ran an annual surplus of about 61,000 nomismata.[478]

Apart from these fairly secure numbers, only fragmentary evidence survives; but it seems good enough to show that the army payroll in 842 must have been roughly equal to all the other expenditures put together. The total expenditures would therefore have equaled something like 2.8 million nomismata, and total revenues, including the surplus, would have been around 2.9 million. The size of Theophilus's military pay increase in 839 can be deduced approximately from the payroll of the Armeniac theme that is recorded for 811, and fortunately we can keep track of how much the army had grown since 780. It can thus be calculated that in 780 the army payroll was about 600,000 nomismata. If we assume that other expenses were not very much lower than in 842 and that Irene kept her budget roughly in balance, we can estimate her expenditures and revenues at around 1.8 million nomismata. Though the estimates for revenue both in 842 and 780 could easily be raised or lowered somewhat, it is very hard to see how either could be wrong by more than 400,000 nomismata.[479]

This being said, a figure for revenue in 842 of 2.9 million nomismata, or even of 2.5 million, is remarkably high in comparison with both the revenue in 780 and that under Justinian I, three centuries before. Late in his reign, after the plague had begun but also after North Africa and Italy had been reconquered, Justinian's revenue has been estimated from abundant but incomplete evidence at between 5 and 7 million nomismata, with a recent estimate tending toward the bottom of that range. That the empire's revenue in the ninth century was as much as half that in the sixth seems the more likely because the gold reserve of 856 was over a third of the empire's record gold reserve of 320,000 pounds of gold (23.04 million nomismata) in 518, which was before the plague. It is also significant that by 842 the empire was maintaining an army only 30,000 men smaller than the 150,000 men of Justinian's day. Yet Justinian's expanded empire was about three times the size of Theophilus's, and included Egypt, which is generally considered to have been the richest land in the Mediterranean before modern times.

Admittedly, the Byzantine government's cash revenue was always a good deal less than its total revenue, and even that was far less than the empire's gross national product. The comparison of figures for cash revenue, however, can be misleading only if the government made considerably greater use of cash in the ninth century than in the sixth. This seems unlikely; in fact, the reverse is usually assumed to be true, though that assumption is questionable. The comparisons of total revenue can be misleading only if the government took a considerably greater share of its subjects' income in the ninth century than in the sixth. This too seems unlikely, particularly because under Justinian complaints of fiscal oppression are bitter and frequent, while from Michael I to Theophilus such complaints are practically unknown. Yet the amount of revenue raised from each subject under Theophilus seems to have been at least four-fifths of what it had been under Justinian. It is difficult to escape the conclusion that the empire of Theophilus was more prosperous than the empire of Justinian, and when the effects of the plague are taken into account this is not as surprising as it may at first appear.[480]

Using the estimates for state revenue to compare the prosperity of the empire under Irene and under Theophilus is more difficult, because it is highly probable that the government made more use of cash and took a larger share of the empire's wealth in 842 than it did in 780. On the other hand, increased monetarization is ordinarily either a sign or a cause of economic progress; and a government is likely to be able to take more of its subjects' income without provoking protests only if their income is rising. As has already been noted, part of the increase in state revenue between 780 and 842 must have been the result of more efficient and honest collection of taxes—but by no means all. The two estimates for revenue, whose margin for error is less when they are compared because they are liable to err in the same direction, imply important economic growth between these dates. Trade was such a small part of the economy that this substantial growth can be explained only by an increase in farm production.

Why would farm production have increased during these years? That the climate had been turning slightly warmer since the mid-eighth century has already been mentioned; this would have helped, though probably not a great deal. We have seen that conditions in the empire were on the whole more peaceful than before, at least in the period after civil war began in the caliphate in 809 and the treaty with the Bulgars was ratified in 816. Farmers obviously benefit if fewer crops are burned and fewer farm animals are stolen by raiders. Further, the empire's annexation of more cultivable land and pasture in Greece and elsewhere would have tended to increase agricultural production. But since land does not seem to have been particularly scarce in the empire in 780, more land would have been of limited use without more people to work it.[481]

Therefore the empire's population must have grown during these years. Existing evidence is so poor, however, that any population estimate must be very approximate, and no estimate of population growth can be more than illustrative. A recent attempt to estimate population at various dates in different parts of the world, which at least has the merit of putting much scattered evidence into context, indicates that the empire would have had about 7 million people in 780 and about 8 million in 842. If we reckon from the amount of state revenue that the empire's hearth and land taxes in 842 produced about 2.5 million nomismata, a population estimate of 8 million for that date would translate into about 2 million rural households, paying taxes on an average holding of some 36 modii apiece.

Despite the roughness of the calculation, its result seems fairly satisfactory. While the average holding at the time appears to have been something like 50 modii (10 acres or 4 hectares), allowance must be made for tax exemptions, especially of land recently ravaged by the enemy, and for some inefficiency and corruption in tax collection. By such reckoning, if we assume that the average holding on which taxes were actually paid was not under 25 modii or over 50, the Byzantine population of 842 should have been somewhere between 6.7 and 9.5 million, a range that leaves the estimate of 8 million comfortably in the middle.

For 780, before Nicephorus I had reformed the tax system, estimating the population from the tax revenue is considerably more problematic, because so much of the revenue that was theoretically due would have gone uncollected. If 1.6 million nomismata was the approximate yield of the land and hearth taxes in 780, an average taxable holding of 36 modii would imply a population of only about 5.1 million, which is plainly too low, with a population increase between 780 and 842 of about 60 percent, which is plainly too high. The population estimate of 7 million that has already been suggested for 780 would imply that taxation was then about a quarter less efficient than in 842, a proportion that is by no means impossible. On the other hand, this population estimate, like its corollary that the population grew by about 15 percent between 780 and 842, cannot be said to be confirmed by such a method. All one can reasonably say is that the population did grow substantially.[482]

Part of this increase was the result of immigration and annexation. Fifty thousand Armenians reportedly fled from the caliphate to the empire in 788, and this was only a particularly large group out of many Armenian emigrants who kept entering the empire. Then there were the 30,000 Khurramites, most of them probably Kurds, who arrived between 834 and 837. Emigrants from the caliphate during this period could hardly have been fewer than a hundred thousand, and were probably a good many more. It is true that the Bulgars deported 40,000 Byzantines from Thrace in 813, but an approximately equal number of survivors and descendants from this group returned to Byzantium in 836. When Nicephorus made his annexations in Greece and gained effective control over Dalmatia, and Theophilus made his own annexations in Albania and the Crimea, they took over native populations along with the lands: Slavs in Greece, Slavs and Latins in Dalmatia, Illyrians in Albania, and Goths in the Crimea. The Slavs in the Peloponnesus were numerous enough to mount annoying rebellions in both 807 and 841. Those revolts notwithstanding, the conquered peoples had to live with Byzantine rule in the end, and most of them seem to have accepted it from the start. All these non-Byzantines eventually became Byzantine and contributed to the empire's economy.

The native Byzantine population certainly grew as well, and probably by more than the ordinary rate of medieval increase. Civilian casualties in the wars of this time appear to have been negligible. Population growth normally rebounds after a period of plague, especially because overcrowding does not restrain the growth. The Byzantines had plenty of new territory to expand into, and Nicephorus forced them to settle it even if they were not so inclined. Within the empire's previous borders, too, land cannot have been scarce. In 809 the settlers who departed for the Balkans opened up farmland all over the empire, and land was still widely available in the 830's, or the Khurramites could not have been settled so easily over so many provinces. That there was vacant land for them in the frequently raided border region is not at all surprising; but even the relatively populous Thracesian and Opsician themes and the territory of the Optimates each had land for 2,000 new soldiers, whose holdings had to be considerably larger than average. With such a relative abundance of land, a growing population would have been expanding cultivation and grazing into fairly good plowland and pasture that had previously lain fallow only for lack of cultivators or herdsmen, or because it was raided too often. Under such circumstances, population growth would have stimulated agricultural production very strongly, and provided enough new wealth to benefit both the state and its subjects.

Some of this demographic and economic growth should have been felt in towns, not only because farmers sold some of what they produced there but also because some of them lived there, going out to their fields in the morning and coming back in the evening. Though population figures for Byzantine towns are so few and imprecise that they can show nothing about the growth of urban population over such a brief period, the process of setting up the new headquarters of banda in 839 is, once again, an important piece of evidence. These capitals were permanent posts, and could be maintained only at established settlements of some size. Even if they were more like forts than towns, they still had to be big enough to provide a refuge in wartime for 200 soldiers, their dependents, and some civilians. Well before 842 finding places for such headquarters would have been easy enough in districts that had more cities than there were to be banda, as in the Thracesians, the Cibyrrhaeots, and Sicily, or that had nearly as many cities, as in Macedonia and the Opsician. Outside Greece, however, no district apart from those five seems to have had even two-thirds as many cities as banda, and only one had more than half as many forts as banda. Nevertheless, by 839 it was possible to establish in each a full complement of bandum headquarters.

In the Armeniac theme of 839, for example, there were only seven cities that had sent bishops to the Council of Nicaea in 787, barely enough to provide bases for the theme's seven drungaries. There were just seventeen fortified places, probably including all seven cities. Yet 44 counts could be given permanent posts there. In the new cleisura of Charsianum, just three cities had sent bishops to the council, and a total of five fortified places existed. Yet nineteen headquarters of banda were established there. Even the Bucellarian theme had only fourteen cities represented at the council, and just one more fortified place than that; but it could provide 39 bases for counts.

To be sure, in 839 the government probably created a few of the settle-

TABLE 2
Provincial Cities, Fortified Places, and Headquarters, 787–842

District as in 842	Cities in 787[a]	Headquarters up to 839[b]	Fortified places in 839[c]	Headquarters after 839[d]
Anatolic	46	13	35	74
Armeniac	7	7	17	44
Bucellarian	14	6	15	39
Cappadocia	9	2	19	19
Cephalonia	4[e]	2	?	9
Chaldia	8	2	6	19
Charsianum	3	2	5	19
Cibyrrhaeot	43	2	?	9
Climata	1[e]	1	?	9
Cyprus	6	1	?	1
Dalmatia	0[e]	1	?	1
Dyrrhachium	1[e]	1	?	9
Hellas	7[e]	2	?	9
Macedonia	22	3	13[f]	24
Opsician	28	4	11	29
Optimates	10	2	3	19
Paphlagonia	7	3	5	24
Peloponnesus	4[e]	2	?	9
Seleucia	12	3	11	24
Sicily	13	2	?	9
Thessalonica	1[e]	2	?	9
Thrace	9	3	10	24
Thracesian	90	8	15[f]	49
TOTAL	345[e]	74	165	481

[a]Figures show the number of cities represented by bishops at the Second Council of Nicaea, which was presumably slightly lower than the total number of cities.

[b]Figures include headquarters of drungaries (which included all headquarters of strategi and turmarchs) and of archons.

[c]Figures taken from ibn Khurdādhbih, 77–80.

[d]Figures include headquarters of counts (which included all headquarters of strategi, turmarchs, and drungaries) and of archons.

[e]Note that after 787 territorial gains would presumably have added more cities to this total.

[f]Figure emended from the text of ibn Khurdādhbih.

ments or forts that it used for headquarters. When Dyrrhachium, which had been an archontate based on a single city with a garrison of about 100 men, was suddenly turned into a theme with 2,000 men, the foundation or refoundation of settlements as headquarters for some of its nine banda was presumably part of setting up the theme. In the new cleisura of Cappadocia, the coincidence that there were nineteen headquarters of banda and nineteen fortified places may well mean that the government ordered an extra fort or two to be added to the many already there, so that each headquarters in that frequently invaded land would be fortified.[483]

On the other hand, Theophilus could scarcely have contemplated introducing the system of banda if it had meant founding dozens of new settlements where none had existed before, and in any case no source mentions such foundations. As it happens, we know the names of fourteen banda in the semidesert region where the Armeniac and Bucellarian themes met the cleisurae of Charsianum and Cappadocia. All are described as the garrisons of specific places that must be settlements. Because several of these seem not to be attested before the ninth century, they may well be of fairly recent date, but none has a name that suggests it was a recent imperial foundation. They were apparently villages, not large but more than a mere cluster of huts, that had sprung up or been resettled before 839. No doubt their inhabitants made use only of the best land in the area, probably for pasturing livestock; but even this barren plain had more than the handful of migrant herders it would have had if its population had been extremely sparse. That any number of people were settled in such a region is some evidence that the rural population was growing, spreading, and gathering in towns.[484]

For the demography of Constantinople the only evidence seems to be anecdotal, and as such of little value. That Theophilus's brother-in-law Petronas built a palace that cut off the sunlight from a neighboring house presumably means that some part of the city was becoming more densely settled; but one piece of evidence should not be pressed too far. Probably better evidence is simply the impression given by the sources that at this time the capital was a lively place with a number of prominent and prosperous people in it, an impression that the sources for the preceding 60 years do not give. We have seen that more tax money was flowing into the capital than before, and money usually attracts people. There might also have been more money made from trade, and more traders present as a result.[485]

Was there more trade? Aside from further anecdotal evidence, there is one important change that bears on the question: the great expansion of the coinage beginning in the middle of Theophilus's reign. From this time on, Byzantine copper folles and gold nomismata become much more common in both Anatolia and the Balkans. The increased production of folles, which were chiefly used for private exchange, was ordered by Theophilus between 835 and 840; his aim was probably to relieve a shortage, which seems to show that trade had already increased. Theophilus would also have needed to mint a great many more nomismata in late 839 in order to pay the army in early 840 at nearly twice the previous rate. In fact, the type of nomisma that was minted between about 835 and 840 is extremely common today, much more so than the type minted during the scarcely shorter period between 829 and about 833. Nomismata paid to soldiers would have spread quickly all over the empire, including the newly annexed or pacified provinces on the frontiers. Because the soldiers' pay was raised while their taxes remained the same, most of the new no-mismata would have been spent in the private economy, joining the more abundant folles to enlarge the monetary economy. Whether or not Theophilus had any idea of stimulating commerce, his expanded coinage would have had that effect.[486]

The expansion of the money supply occurred, however, at a time when the Arabs based in Crete and Sicily were making sea trade more hazardous, and the only reasonably inexpensive way that goods of any bulk could be moved far was by sea. Before the Arabs invaded the islands, there had of course been an established Byzantine shipping industry. Nicephorus had probably helped it to grow somewhat by his policy of making maritime loans from the state gold reserve, though this may not have continued under his successors. It seems unlikely that many Byzantine shipowners simply went out of business when Arab pirates appeared in the Aegean and Adriatic, at a time when consumers had more money to spend than before.

In fact, the amount of Arab piracy can easily be exaggerated. Since the empire continued to hold nearly all of the coasts and the islands except for Crete and Sicily themselves and to operate important thematic fleets, the pirates could not hold secure bases near most of the empire's shipping. Spending much time on the open sea was as perilous for pirates as for any other sailors. Piracy was therefore very much a hit-or-miss affair, and trade went on in spite of it. Gregory the Decapolite, a monk who seems to have played some role in the iconophile underground during the 830's, traveled in several ships from Ephesus to the Sea of Marmara, from there to Aenus and Christopolis in Thrace, from Corinth to Rome by way of Rhegium and Naples, back to Thessalonica with stops at Syracuse and Hydrus, and later from Thessalonica to Constantinople. While he skirted both Arab bases, he met Arabs only on land, near Hydrus, though at Ephesus he did find that the many captains there were reluctant to sail for fear of a particular band of Arab pirates who were lurking nearby at the time, and at Corinth the seamen were similarly fearful of Arabs. Gregory's disciple Joseph the Hymnographer was not as lucky as Gregory, and spent some time in captivity on Crete after its pirates seized the ship in which he was traveling from Constantinople to Rome. If anything, however, the fact that shipowners kept up regular trade in the face of the Arab danger confirms that there was a good deal of money to be made in commerce at the time.[487]

Most trade, naturally, transferred inexpensive goods over short distances within the empire. The most necessary item was food, which the neighboring countryside had always supplied to the towns, Constanti-

52. The wealthy widow Danelis borne by her slaves in a luxurious sedan chair (shown without regard for perspective, as often happens in Byzantine art). Matritensis graecus 26-2, fol. 102ʳ. (Photo: Biblioteca Nacional, Madrid)

nople above all. If country dwellers themselves were becoming more prosperous, their demand should have been mainly for clothing, and one important case suggests that such demand was growing. At about this time one of the greatest fortunes of the middle Byzantine period was being amassed at Patras in the Peloponnesus from what appears to have been a weaving business. By 856 we find there a widow named Danelis in possession of vast estates and many slaves, including weavers, and producing clothing, rugs, and other woven goods. The business apparently raised sheep on the land in the interior of the peninsula and had female slaves weave the wool in the town. Because Patras had been Byzantine only since 805, the establishment must have been of fairly recent date; yet it must also have taken several decades to build up. Since Danelis's lands are said to have been of very great extent and she had huge amounts of coin and other movables as well, her wealth implies a wide market for textiles, even though part of her land may have been raising other things besides sheep. Trade on any large scale is particularly significant coming from a recently acquired province like the Peloponnesus, where any evidence of substantial trade is evidence for its growth.[488]

As always in the Byzantine economy, trade was much less important than agriculture, and the state, rather than commerce, dominated monetary transactions. This being said, the impression of wealth given by Theophilus's lavish spending does appear to parallel a real growth of prosperity throughout the empire. Most of this expansion was doubtless a matter of natural population growth, which had little or nothing to do with any state action. The state did not always help, as when it hoarded gold unproductively, a practice that Theophilus continued. The state did contribute, however, when it annexed and settled Greece, reformed the collection of taxes, expanded the coinage, and increased military pay, and it shares some of the credit for the economic revival.

SOCIETY

Apart from general indications that this was a time of increasing order and prosperity, we hear little about the condition of ordinary Byzantines, and that is probably a good sign. Nicephorus I, who was known for his concern for the poor, determinedly shifted more of the burden of taxation onto those best able to pay, and his reforms seem to have been kept up by his successors, to the benefit of the peasantry. There had been times in Byzantium, and would be again, when smallholders, including soldiers, were in financial straits and abandoning their land in large numbers; but evidently this period was not one of them. When land was plentiful and taxation not unduly oppressive, most small farmers could hold on to what they had, even if they were occasionally hit by a hard winter, a plague of locusts, or an enemy raid.

The soldiers' lands, which in the case of the infantry were reasonably typical small holdings distributed all over the empire, seem to have been well maintained, because each theme continued to have its full complement of soldiers. If some troops had to share their estates with the recently enrolled Persians, the estates were apparently large enough to accommodate everyone without much complaint. Though there were some unsettling changes in the countryside during this time, among them Nicephorus's transfer of population from Asia Minor to the Balkans, there is nothing to suggest any widespread rural crisis—certainly not in the efforts of some soldiers to install Thomas the Slav instead of Michael II as the successor of Leo V.

Although we know of the prosperity of the widow Danelis, we know little about the people in the provinces who would have bought the clothing, blankets, and rugs that her business produced. No doubt if our evidence for life in the country were better, we would find many peasants who increased their holdings at home, or started large farms in previously fallow land in Asia Minor or the recently enlarged Balkan territories. As it is, since our sources deal overwhelmingly with the upper classes in the capital, most of our evidence of social change applies to them. It shows a society in which previously unimportant people often became prominent, powerful, and rich in a short time.

As before, the ruling class in Constantinople remained a small group. Everyone knew almost everyone else, and a high proportion of the people who counted were related to each other by blood or marriage. Civil and military officials tended to stay in office most of their lives, either in the same post or in progressively higher ones. Great fortunes were seldom lost, unless by the possessor's being deposed as emperor or leading a failed conspiracy, and even then he and his relatives commonly kept something. Snobbery about parvenus certainly existed, as when Leo V's officials of senatorial rank complained that John the Grammarian was too obscure to be patriarch of Constantinople, and persuaded the emperor to choose a relative of the Isaurian dynasty instead. All this sounds very exclusive and conservative.[489]

But the upper class in Constantinople was itself mostly formed of people of provincial origins and foreign race. Irene had grown up at Athens, from which her relatives the Serantapechi later came to the capital to assume high positions. Nicephorus I, brought to the throne by the innermost circle of Irene's officials, had grown up in Cappadocia and was reportedly of Arab stock. Michael I was from an excellent family with a fine palace in Constantinople and estates in Thrace; but his surname, Rhangabe, can hardly be Greek and is probably Slavic. When Leo V wanted a well-born second wife, he chose the daughter of the former quaestor Arsaber, once the candidate for emperor of conservatives disgruntled with Nicephorus's reforms; but Arsaber, or Arsavir, is a classically Armenian name. When Theophilus wanted an heir in case he died childless, he chose the younger Alexius Musele, a wealthy man of the illustrious family of the Crenitae, who had another fine palace in the capital; that family was Armenian too. The best examples one can cite of leading men who were from good old Constantinopolitan families of Greek origin are Theodore of Studius and the patriarch Nicephorus; but their families and fortunes seem to have ended with them.

John the Grammarian was therefore looked down upon in 815 by many whose families had not been part of high society in the capital for very long, though of course social prominence can take a surprisingly short time to become second nature. John, however, was to have his turn as well. By 842 he had not only been named patriarch without controversy but had seen his brother Arsaber become the empress's brother-in-law and a magister, and his cousin Leo the Mathematician ordained archbishop of Thessalonica. In later sources, despite all the abuse that iconophiles heap upon John, his family of the Morocharzanii is numbered among the best, and so, within a generation or two, it was.[490]

Besides the families of Leo the Armenian, who had been born abroad, and of Michael the Amorian, whose rusticity was notorious, several other families gained lasting prominence at this time. Although their fortunes may have been founded on imperial favor, they usually continued to prosper without it. The family of Maria of Amnia, Armenians from Paphlagonia, obviously owed their position to Maria's marriage to Constantine VI in 788. Yet they did not vanish from sight after Constantine divorced her in 795. Maria's uncle John went on to become strategus successively of the themes of Hellas and the Armeniacs, and the family later disappeared from view only because it died out. Another Armenian family from Paphlagonia that prospered in the capital at this time was that of Manuel, who had made his name as protostrator and monostrategus well before his niece Theodora married Theophilus. Already very important under Theophilus, Theodora and her family were to dominate the government during most of the reign of her son Michael III. The families of both Maria and Manuel continued to be well aware of their racial and provincial connections, which may well have led the empress Euphrosyne, Maria of Amnia's daughter, to encourage Theophilus to marry Theodora.[491]

While the empire had been assimilating Armenians for centuries—and Arabs and Slavs had lived on the empire's borders for a long time—more exotic races were also climbing to the top of Byzantine society around 800. Bardanes Turcus's surname seems to identify him as at most a second-generation Khazar, which may mean that his father had arrived in Byzantium in the mid-eighth century, at about the same time as Leo IV's Khazar mother. Domestic of the Schools by 796, in 803 Bardanes commanded all the themes of Asia Minor, had immense wealth and a large palace in Constantinople, and was enthusiastically proclaimed emperor by his troops. Though he was then blinded, his son Bryenes was a high official in 813, and thereafter the family's fortune was made when Bardanes' sons-in-law became the emperors Leo V and Michael II. There is some reason to think that Sergius, the wealthy official exiled as an iconophile by Theophilus, was a Khazar too, since he is said to have been of foreign origin and his son Photius was nicknamed "Khazarface." After 842 Photius and his brothers evidently regained their father's wealth and had distinguished political and ecclesiastical careers.

One of the four patricians whom Irene chose to lead the horses that drew her carriage in 799 was Constantine Boïlas, whose last name identifies him as the descendant of a Bulgar boyar. Other distinguished Byzantines of this name appear later. Even a Russian family appears to have entered the highest society at this time, since we find a man named Inger (that is, Igor) as archbishop of Nicaea under Michael II. Inger was a relation of the Martinacius who was also related to the emperor Theophilus and was mentioned in 838 as a possible emperor. Inger's family, later called the Martinacii, had an illustrious future ahead of them in the person of Eudocia Ingerina, mistress of Michael III, wife of Basil I, and mother of Leo VI.[492]

In general, this was the period in which Byzantine family names became firmly established, and with them the beginnings of an aristocracy based partly on birth as well as on wealth and public office. The first of the great families of later Byzantine history appear now. The earliest known Monomachus is Nicetas, who was born about 762 in Paphlagonia and became a patrician and strategus of Sicily by 797. Though he was somehow related to the empress Theodora, he appears to have gained office before other members of his family, whom he may then have helped to rise. His parents had made Nicetas a eunuch to promote his career, but the family continued and prospered after him, and one of them eventually became the emperor Constantine IX.

The earliest known representative of another great family, the Scleri, came from the Armeniacs and had been made strategus of Hellas by 805, when he reconquered the Peloponnesus for Nicephorus. Petronas, appointed strategus of the Climata by Theophilus in 839, is the earliest known Camaterus; by the twelfth century the Camateri would rise to the top of the ecclesiastical and bureaucratic hierarchy. The first known member of the noble family of the Guberii appears as an official of Michael II in 824. Though the family seems to have come from Cappadocia, it was established in a position of wealth and influence at Constantinople before 855. While the Byzantine nobility was never extremely difficult to break into, the late eighth and early ninth centuries presented particularly good opportunities to begin a family that could be famous for hundreds of years.[493]

Acquiring influence in Constantinople almost always meant acquiring office, or at least having a relative in office, but this could be managed in several ways. Obviously luck played a part, as when officials helped their relatives gain preferment or when a beautiful young woman was chosen as an imperial bride in a bride show; yet the government appointed or chose remarkably few unsuitable people. If Theophilus made his wife's uncle Manuel domestic of the Schools, or his patriarch's cousin Leo the Mathematician head of the new public school, both appointments were amply justified by the men's abilities. A marriage could follow from merit, as seems to have happened when Bardanes Turcus married his daughters to his promising adjutants Leo the Armenian and Michael the Amorian. While wealth, social connections, and familiarity with power were naturally among the qualities that the government wanted in its officials, it did not ignore learning, intelligence, and honesty. In a changing society, where the emperor himself could be an outsider, ability had more than the usual chance to be recognized, and provincial or foreign origins or humble birth were no bar.

The ruling class in the capital was so open to provincials and members of the lower class that our evidence reveals something about those groups in spite of itself. It shows that such relatively poor and rural districts as Hellas, Cappadocia, and Paphlagonia had their wealthy families, who were certainly or probably landowners. The tendency for the largest Byzantine landholders to come from the poorest provinces seems therefore to start at least this early, probably because the rich were able to extend and maintain agriculture under conditions that would bankrupt smallholders. Rich provincials nonetheless felt a strong pull toward the capital, and were ambitious to have their children well placed there. For poorer provincials, like Leo the Armenian and Michael the Amorian, the most likely way to make one's fortune was in the army, where even common soldiers could rise to the top by attracting their superior's attention. In Constantinople, however, education was perhaps the best means of bettering oneself. John the Grammarian's father was apparently a weaver, and his cousin Leo is alleged to have been poor as well, but the cousins still reached the highest positions in the church hierarchy because of their learning.[494]

It is probably significant that the poor found it particularly easy to make an ecclesiastical career at this time, because unlike most other Byzantine institutions the secular church was in some confusion and disrepute. It had simply suffered too many upheavals. Since the discarding of Iconoclasm in 787 had been carefully prepared and moderately executed, it had caused less disruption than might have been expected, and in any case it allowed an eager new generation of principled iconophiles to gain bishoprics. The controversy over Constantine VI's second marriage, though of much less importance, was unfortunate for clerical prestige, because in the course of it the Church had to change its position three times, from approval in 795 to disapproval in 797, then to approval again in 806 and disapproval again in 812. Worst of all, of course, was the restoration of Iconoclasm in 815. Because the clergy had always tended to be iconophile, there was no body of convinced iconoclast clerics waiting to take office. Leo V had to pressure reluctant but flexible iconophile clergy to fall into line, and resorted to appointing not very spiritually inclined laymen to be sacristan of St. Sophia and patriarch of Constantinople. Michael II's flirtation with the iconophiles in 821 presumably undermined the position of the hierarchy further. Then Theophilus's progressively stricter enforcement of Iconoclasm would have discomfited the many clergy who were lukewarm about the doctrine.[495]

By 842 scarcely anyone, whatever his religious views, can have had a very high opinion of the integrity of most Byzantine bishops. Even Leo V's patriarch Theodotus apparently tried to persuade iconophiles to accept communion from him by professing to favor the icons. Inger, archbishop of Nicaea under Michael II, appears to have temporarily repented of his Iconoclasm when he was admonished by the hermit Joannicius. Ignatius, sacristan of St. Sophia and archbishop of Nicaea under the iconoclasts, wrote mournfully to his friends that he was unable to offer God fitting worship, and effusively repented of his Iconoclasm after 842. Leo the Mathematician, always a peculiar choice for archbishop of Thessalonica, mentions icons with approval in a sermon that he delivered just three months after Theophilus's death. John the Grammarian, at least, was a true believer, but when the restoration of the icons came in 843 he stood almost alone among the bishops in refusing to abjure Iconoclasm.[496]

For a time, a number of iconophile bishops survived who had been consecrated before 815, but few if any lived until 842. Though there were many more iconophile monks, after the death of Theodore of Studius in 826 they lost much of their cohesiveness, especially after Theophilus confined many of them on the island of Aphusia in 833. When Theophilus died in 842, the iconophiles were thus in some disarray. The patriarch chosen in 843 was Methodius of Syracuse, who though not exactly a foreigner was a Sicilian and had been an envoy from the pope. Among the confessors with the best reputations were the monk Theophanes, whom Theophilus had branded on the face, and Michael Syncellus, both Palestinians originally sent out by the patriarch of Jerusalem. Methodius appointed both to high church office, but he had trouble finding suitable Byzantine candidates. Although Iconoclasm vanished rapidly after 843, it left the Byzantine Church shaken and fragile, prone to internal divisions that would recur for years.

A certain amount of disruption, however, is to be expected in a time of change, and Byzantine society still showed a fundamental stability. Its ceremonies, institutions, and principles remained the same. If Michael II was too provincial to run his court with proper ceremony after his first wife died, his officials soon had him marry a second wife who would do what was called for. During the reign of Theophilus, a ruler who showed no trace of his father's humble origins, the capital saw a revival of ceremony, and of the races in the Hippodrome as well. The emperor retained his powers and prestige, whoever he might be, and the government remained strong, whoever manned it. Though Iconoclasm shook the

Church rather badly, in the process it created a generation of spiritual heroes soon venerated as saints, like Theodore of Studius and the patriarch Nicephorus, and it probably stimulated the underlying religious feeling that brought the restoration of Orthodoxy in 843.

CULTURE

In scholarship, more clearly than in any other field, the Byzantines recognized the progress that they had made by the middle of the ninth century. In a dedicatory epigram to one of his books, Ignatius the Deacon describes himself as "widely acquainted with learned poetry," and boasts that he has "brought to light the study of literature, which had lain hidden in the sea of oblivion." When Photius, writing to his brother probably in 845, considers why a work of ancient arithmetic was not in circulation, he dismisses the idea that it was too difficult, "because today many of our acquaintances have an exact knowledge of geometry, mathematics, and the other sciences"; the reason, he concludes, must be that few copies of the work had survived those earlier times when "the habit of not saving useful books took on a great and irresistible power." Although until 838 Theophilus had left Leo the Mathematician in obscurity and Methodius of Syracuse in prison, the emperor was jealously guarding them as learned assets by 840, when he refused to lend Leo to the caliph Mu'taṣim. While Byzantine sources may then make exaggerated claims of the superiority of Byzantine scholarship to Arab, the balance had plainly shifted in Byzantium's favor since the reigns of Irene and Hārūn, when no claims of superiority were made.

Doubtless Byzantine standards for scholarly progress differed somewhat from modern ones. To the Byzantines, real learning was familiarity with classical or patristic authorities, and the best writing was in Attic Greek and made frequent classical allusions. The writing style of Ignatius the Deacon is highly artificial and deliberately obscure, so that it is difficult to distill historical facts from his letters and saints' lives, let alone from the texts dependent on his propagandistic poem against Thomas the Slav. The ancient work that Photius trusted his learned contemporaries could understand was a bizarre amalgam of arithmetic and pagan mythology, which even Photius considered silly in itself but found useful to test its readers' erudition.[497]

Nonetheless, part of the game was really to understand what the ancients had meant. Leo the Mathematician's student is said to have surpassed Mu'taṣim's court geometers because he could explain the Euclidean proofs that they could only parrot. Imitation led to adaptation, and reading to experiment. Byzantines and most moderns would agree that more schooling, more copying of manuscripts, and more writing are good things, and that knowledge of the rules of grammar and mathematics is useful both as mental discipline and for practical purposes. Even if the Byzantines' most highly prized literary productions bore most modern readers, Byzantine scholarship still made some notable advances.[498]

One advance was in the schools. Until the beginning of the ninth century, though a number of elementary and secondary schools existed, one could acquire a higher education only with difficulty. Apparently there was no regular school of higher learning in Constantinople. Before 784, when he was protoasecretis, Tarasius seems to have taken time to teach Ignatius the Deacon as a personal favor accorded to a single pupil. Some twenty years later, after learning grammar and poetry in Constantinople, Leo the Mathematician received some higher education in rhetoric, philosophy, and mathematics from an unnamed man of learning, perhaps a monk, on an island probably in the Sea of Marmara; but this scholar could provide only the beginnings of Leo's real education, which the young man then pursued by private reading in monastery libraries, probably in Bithynia. Under such circumstances only a few determined or fortunate people could become really erudite.[499]

Ignatius, however, became a teacher himself for some time toward the beginning of the century, as did John the Grammarian. Both are mentioned specifically as schoolmasters, and seem to have offered a regular course of instruction, which they were capable of continuing to an advanced level. Though before long their ecclesiastical careers would have interrupted or at least interfered with their teaching, Leo the Mathematician soon opened his own school, which would have been in operation from about 820 to 838. By the latter date, Leo's student who was captured by the Arabs could say that there were many students like himself in Byzantium, and though he noted that there were few masters he did not speak of Leo as the only one.[500]

In 838, of course, Theophilus transferred Leo to the Magnaura palace, where Leo became head of the first public school of the middle Byzantine period. Although he taught there for just two years before he was made archbishop of Thessalonica, the emperor does not seem likely to have shut the new school at that time. Theophilus had decided that a public school in the palace was worth having; and there were others, qualified if not as well qualified, who could take Leo's place. In 843, when Leo was deposed from his archbishopric, he returned to the Magnaura as its professor of philosophy, joined by his student Theodore as professor of geometry, a professor of astronomy, Theodegius, and a professor of Greek, Cometas. The school is then described as a new foundation, and as far as the four professorships were concerned it probably was; but one of Leo's

three later colleagues may well have been tending the school while Leo
was at Thessalonica. The School of the Magnaura was to continue for
generations as a permanent institution of higher learning, the first in a
very long time to have a faculty of more than one professor. Students who
attended it could study with other leading scholars, such as Photius, who
reportedly ran a school after he returned from exile in 842.[501]

It might be argued that the civil service had no need for more men with
advanced training in philosophy, geometry, astronomy, and literature.
The post of protoasecretis at the head of the chancery and that of patriarch
at the head of the Church called for real learning; but the old educational
system had already provided a Tarasius to hold them both, just as Photius
was to hold them later on. The main function of the School of the Magnaura may well have been to train not officials, but teachers for secondary
schools. The better Byzantine education got, however, the better the civil
service was likely to get, particularly when it came to drafting complicated legal documents and to calculating state financial transactions. Although such tasks may not have required much creative thought, without
the aid of modern filing methods, complete dictionaries, double-entry
bookkeeping, and Arabic numerals Byzantine civil servants did need a
wide knowledge of Greek and mathematics and great powers of concentration—precisely what a good Byzantine school instilled. Learning to
enjoy boredom at school was ideal preparation for a career in the Byzantine bureaucracy, even if its effects on literature were rather deleterious.[502]

Though few seem to have agreed with John the Grammarian about the
intellectual merits of Iconoclasm, Theophilus's patronage obviously encouraged scholarship by people who would conform to official doctrine.
John himself wrote some theology, of which the pitiful fragments that
survive cannot give a fair idea; he also conducted scientific experiments,
which included divining the future but may not have been limited to that
purpose. It was under Theophilus that Leo the Mathematician devised his
optical telegraph between Constantinople and the Arab frontier; though
most of Leo's scientific and philosophical writings seem to date from after
842, some of them may be earlier, and he may well be the author of a
medical treatise written under Theophilus. The acquaintances whose scientific knowledge Photius esteemed so highly doubtless included his uncle John and his somewhat more distant relative Leo. Since Iconoclasm
did not affect scientific research in any important way, Photius could ad-
mire the expertise of John and Leo as Theophilus had admired that of
Methodius. By the same token, however, the scientific revival did not re-
dound greatly to the credit of Iconoclasm.[503]

Apart from Leo and John, the leading intellectual in the iconoclast establishment was Ignatius the Deacon, who was quite uncomfortable with

his role. Some of his meticulously formal letters date from his years as archbishop of Nicaea under Iconoclasm, though in the form in which he later edited them they include only iconophile sentiments. His brief dramatic poem on the Fall of Adam and Eve and his verse summaries of Aesop's *Fables* probably date before 842, like the literary work he began with his proud dedicatory epigram. The latter may be the same as an indirectly preserved dictionary on notable writers that is probably Ignatius's, which manages to refer to John of Damascus without mentioning that the celebrated theologian was an iconophile. Under Iconoclasm Ignatius wrote his life of George of Amastris, which, again, ignores the fact that George was an iconophile and even praises him in terms acceptable to iconoclasts, declaring that hagiography supplies "living images" of a godly way of life. Ignatius seems also to have written his lives of his former patrons the patriarchs Tarasius and Nicephorus under Iconoclasm, though they were such famous iconophiles that he must either have kept these works secret or conceivably have written them before the iconoclast edict of 833. Ignatius was an immensely learned man whose knowledge of classical literature is painfully evident from his contorted style; but the iconoclasts could not fairly claim him, even though the iconophiles rebuffed him after their doctrine triumphed.[504]

Despite their tribulations, the iconophiles produced some important literature under Theophilus. While Methodius may not have written the pamphlet predicting Theophilus's death in 831, he probably was responsible for those predicting Leo V's death in 820 and Michael II's death in 829. By then he had also written his life of Theophanes Confessor, the iconophile monk who had completed the great chronicle of George Syncellus. Soon afterward, in prison, Methodius wrote his life of St. Euthymius of Sardis, the former bishop and friend of Methodius who had been imprisoned with him in 831 and died after a severe flogging. One or two saints' lives by other hands also survive from this time, and more were probably written. Some of the poetry of Cassia, the rejected candidate at Theophilus's bride show, probably dates from Theophilus's reign. After her rejection she had become a nun and produced both secular epigrams and religious hymns. Though her surviving works do not refer to Iconoclasm, the letters that Theodore of Studius wrote to her when she was a girl make her iconophile convictions clear.[505]

At least one notable work of history was written by an iconophile at this time. It survives in two anonymous fragments, one recounting Nicephorus I's defeat in 811 and now known as the *Chronicle of 811*, and one on political and ecclesiastical affairs between late 811 and early 816, which is now called the Scriptor Incertus. Both sections, written in a somewhat careless but difficult style, give a detailed and vivid narrative, including

53. Methodius of Syracuse as patriarch of Constantinople (843–47). A drawing made between 1847 and 1849 by Gaspare Fossati of a mosaic in St. Sophia, Constantinople, that is now lost but was probably of the ninth century. (Photo: Archivio Cantonale, Bellinzona)

physical descriptions of Nicephorus I and Michael I. The chronicler was evidently a contemporary familiar with court circles. While the *Chronicle of 811* has been deliberately excerpted, the work of the Scriptor Incertus does not begin or end in a logical place and appears to derive from a mutilated manuscript. According to a plausible conjecture, the full original text of the Scriptor Incertus was used by a hagiographer in the 850's as a source for events extending as far back as 753 and as far forward as 825.[506]

These years fall within the period covered by the history of Sergius Confessor, which dealt with both political and ecclesiastical affairs between 741 and 828. Sergius was, as we have seen, an official who was exiled as an iconophile under Theophilus, probably at the time of the edict of 833. According to his son Photius, Sergius's style was simple and spontaneous, terms that a charitable critic could apply to the Scriptor Incertus. Though Sergius's history is today considered to be lost and the Scriptor Incertus to be unidentifiable, it is not at all likely that two such similar histories were written at this time. Sergius therefore seems to have been the Scriptor. In any case, what we have of the Scriptor Incertus marks a perceptible maturing of Byzantine historiography. Despite his hatred of Iconoclasm, the author shows an understanding of Michael I's weaknesses and of Leo V's political strategy that is much more sophisticated than anything in George Syncellus or Theophanes.[507]

In the years before 842, Sergius's son Photius, who shared his father's exile, must have begun to write on his own. Born about 813, Photius says himself that as a youth (hence around 830) he composed a lexicon. The *Lexicon* of Photius that survives today may well be a revised edition of this early effort. Good dictionaries were obviously needed if people were to write in a higher style and to read more widely than before, and Photius was a voluminous reader and writer from an early age. His mammoth *Bibliotheca*, a description of his reading that includes lengthy notes taken over a period of years, seems to date from 845, but much of it probably represents work done during and before his family's exile between 833 and 842. Photius's teachers, apart from his father, are unknown; like Leo the Mathematician, he plainly owed most of his knowledge to his own private research. Still, since Photius was almost as learned a man as Byzantium ever produced, the scholarly resources among which he was raised were presumably rich ones.[508]

As for art and architecture, Theophilus's program of building and decoration has already been described. The main group of palaces shows a coherent overall plan, though Theophilus completed it in stages. Its center was the Triconch, an audience hall whose three apses led the eye to the imperial throne in the central apse. The two arms of the Sigma formed a monumental entrance hall for the Triconch, with the terrace, pool, fountain, and arch outside enhancing the monumentality of the doors in the center and at the ends of the wings. The lower story of the Sigma may have been a study, since Theophilus installed Methodius there, while the lower story of the Triconch, the Mysterium, was probably a sort of lobby. As one entered the Triconch, the emperor's quarters were straight ahead in the Pearl, which had the best view over the palace gardens. To the right was the Camilas, with the dining room, the eunuchs' quarters, possibly the imperial nursery, and a passage to the empress's bedchamber; to the left was the Carianus, built for the emperor's daughters when they were older. Among other parallels with late antiquity, the overall plan rather resembles that of the Palace of Antiochus, a fifth-century residence just north of the Hippodrome that by Theophilus's time had been converted into the Church of St. Euphemia. The buildings were certainly meant to rival the richest creations of the early Byzantine period, when Constantinople's greatest monuments had been erected.[509]

Apart from this particularly striking group, we know of Theophilus's work on the sea walls, his hospice, his stupendous gold ornaments for the Magnaura, his bronze doors for St. Sophia, which still survive, and his imitation Arab palace at Bryas, whose substructures have been found. Of aristocratic commissions we hear only of the view-obstructing palace of Petronas, which was torn down, but this was certainly not all the private art of the time. Since Lazarus, whom Theophilus tortured, was a famous icon painter, there must have been considerable painting of icons, which Michael II had even permitted as long as the word "Saint" was not written on them. Under Theophilus, Lazarus is said to have painted one of his most celebrated works, an icon of John the Baptist for the monastery at Phoberus, whose patron saint the Baptist was. In the period after Theophilus, Byzantine building, painting, mosaic, and minor arts thrived. Although the restoration of the icons obviously stimulated religious art, the quality of its surviving specimens shows that it drew upon years of artistic experience and tradition. With so many new families rising to wealth and fame and establishing themselves in the capital, Petronas can scarcely have been the only one who wanted an elegant new house, decorated so as to emulate the splendid commissions of the emperor. If not much art of this time has been found to date—when Theophilus's buildings in the palace remain entirely unexcavated—the reason is hardly that this was a time of artistic poverty.[510]

In both art and literature, the Byzantines of the early ninth century tended to imitate late antiquity. There is nothing surprising about this, because the majority of literary and artistic models available to them dated from the second through the sixth centuries, the last period in which their society had produced much literature or art. Some of the borrowing from this store was very direct. Ignatius the Deacon adapted many passages from an oration of Gregory of Nazianzus for his own saints' lives, while Theophilus removed gilded coffering from a fifth-century mansion in Constantinople to adorn the ceiling of the Lausiacus in the Great Palace. Since the sixth century, late ancient literary and artistic traditions had partly survived at Byzantium, though the output of literature and art had been so small that these traditions had been partly forgotten. At first the Byzantines concentrated more on recovering what they had lost than on advancing beyond it. Already, however, Ignatius was drawing not only on late authors but on Sophocles and Euripides in his poetry, and Theophilus, with the help of John the Grammarian, had built a palace inspired by Arab architecture. Freer adaptation and more innovation were to come in the following period.[511]

CAUSES OF THE REVIVAL

In the Byzantine revival of the late eighth and early ninth centuries the empire showed a vigor that seems more typical of a new state than of the oldest state in the world. After all, even if there is no rule that empires should decline after a few centuries at most, the great majority of them have followed that pattern. The characteristics that allow a state to prosper at one time eventually become less advantageous as times change; but most old states lack the flexibility to transform themselves to meet new circumstances. By the ninth century the Eastern Roman Empire was an ancient polity living on in the Middle Ages, amid conditions utterly unlike those of its heyday. Its government was proud of its continuous tradition, and did not want to imitate its more recently arrived neighbors, which it considered inferior. That the empire even survived is astonishing enough. How could it actually have thrived?

Certainly demographic growth is one reason. Today, when there is a legitimate fear of overpopulation in many places, the benefits of population growth are easily overlooked. As long as there is land enough to accommodate more people comfortably, their arrival benefits nearly everyone, and the state most of all. Families have more children who can share their work, expand their farms and their production, put stockpiles away for future emergencies, and still pay more taxes. The government then finds it easier to collect its revenues and to recruit its soldiers, while wealthier and more contented subjects are less inclined to rebel. Such trends would have been reinforced by the somewhat problematic factor of climatic improvement. From all this Byzantium benefited.

But the Abbasid caliphate and the Carolingian kingdoms did not benefit, though to all appearances their territories gained in population and improved in climate just as much as the land ruled by Byzantium. Though the individual inhabitants of western Europe and the Middle East do seem to have been better off, this did not help their governments. At the start of the ninth century, the Abbasid and Carolingian states appeared much stronger than Byzantium; by the end of the same century, they were falling to pieces, and did not survive the next century in recognizable form. The Eastern Roman Empire was not only hundreds of years older than its neighboring powers around 800; it was to outlive them by hundreds of years more.

Of course the decline of the caliphate was itself a contributory cause of the Byzantine revival. Almost since Mohammed, the caliphate had been the empire's archenemy, the only power that seriously threatened Byzantium's existence and the only one that raided the really vital provinces of Anatolia. By comparison, the Bulgars and the Arabs of Crete and Sicily were unimportant. From the time of the Abbasids' civil war, the empire enjoyed markedly more peaceful conditions as a result of its enemy's troubles; even after the civil war was over, discord in the caliphate brought the Arab invasions of 833 and 838 to a premature end. The falling off of Arab invasions and raids undoubtedly contributed to Byzantine prosperity. Nonetheless, one might still ask why Byzantium, which had political divisions and a civil war of its own, did not decline along with the caliphate.

A Byzantine decline at this time is easy enough to imagine. Examples of a government that lost control while its subjects prospered are to hand not only in the ninth-century caliphate but in Byzantium itself in the eleventh century. Although richer subjects may not rebel, they naturally want to keep their new wealth for themselves, and as they gain more wealth and influence they become less dependent on the state and better able to resist its demands. A subtle shift in power, as the governed become more powerful but the government does not, is in the long run more dangerous to a state than an open rebellion. The tax evasion uncovered by Nicephorus I and the mutinous tendencies of the army throughout this period show that Byzantium did indeed face this sort of problem. How was it overcome?

To begin with, in the form in which the empire's army and administration emerged from the seventh century, they provided the state with practical means of protecting its power. The themes and tagmata were rigorously organized; even though the soldiers might be settled over a wide area, specific officers were responsible for all of them according to a definite chain of command. Taxation was in the hands of its own network of officials under contracts, and the taxes due from each household were clearly determined. If a soldier did not serve, his military land could be taken from him and given to someone who would take his place. If a farmer did not pay his taxes, his farm was to be given to a neighbor who would pay them instead. Officials in Constantinople kept written registers of soldiers, military lands, households, and farms, while officials in the provinces were charged with keeping the records up to date. If the system functioned properly, it was not oppressive, because each soldier was provided with enough land to support his service, and each farmer was assessed only the taxes that his resources enabled him to pay. These rules allowed the state, by means differentiated enough to be reasonably fair but simple enough to be workable, to take its share of its subjects' labors and production.

Although the system was not very difficult to maintain under the emergency conditions that gave rise to it, in more peaceful and prosperous times it required more care from the central government. As long as each part of the empire was raided frequently, the soldiers were called up to defend their home territory and kept in fighting trim without much need for drilling. When raids became fewer, however, the soldiers were liable to forget their training and to let their equipment deteriorate. As long as economic opportunities were few, the lot of a soldier was a fairly attractive one, and troops had little reason to desert and give up their land grants and modest pay. But when times turned better and new lands were becoming safe enough to settle, the temptation to throw off military obligations was greater.

As long as the population and the area under cultivation did not expand much, tax collection was simply a matter of determining which people were responsible for paying the set assessment of a village. When households were growing and fields were extended farther out, however, the village's assessment should have risen, and when new villages were settled they too should have been assessed. Yet for a tax collector with the usual one-year contract, it must often have been easier to collect the taxes that the government was accustomed to receiving and to accept a bribe to keep new lands, households, and villages off the rolls. During the tenth and eleventh centuries there is increasing evidence of these sorts of corruption and decline in the army and the system of taxation, and we have seen that it was already a danger in the late eighth and early ninth centuries.

We have also seen that by and large the state overcame these threats to its power, first through the constant efforts of its officials, but also because of measures taken by particular emperors. By ending Iconoclasm and relying heavily on her civil servants, Irene healed the breach between the emperors and their bureaucracy that had opened during the political and religious purges of the previous hundred years. Then Nicephorus I, while remaining allied with the civil service from which he had risen, employed it to reform the system of taxation and to extend Byzantine military power in the Balkans. Leo V and Michael II preserved most of Nicephorus's gains through a series of crises. Theophilus then found himself in possession of abundant wealth, which he eventually used to reform and expand the army.

Nicephorus seems to have understood pretty clearly what needed to be done. Irene and Theophilus appear to have been somewhat less perceptive, and Leo and Michael had immediate concerns that distracted them from the empire's long-term problems. Regardless of how much these rulers understood what they were doing, however, their actions made a large part of the difference between the stronger state that actually developed and the weaker state that would probably have emerged during, say, a prolonged reign by Michael I.

The advantages of demographic growth, Abbasid decline, a serviceable administrative system, and able rulers would still not have helped very much if Byzantine society had been as resistant to change as it is often said to have been. Always conservative in style, the Byzantines certainly could be conservative in substance; but they were seldom less so than in this period of economic expansion and social mobility. The catastrophic invasions of the seventh century had changed Byzantine society profoundly, reducing the urban superstructure and overextended frontiers that the empire could no longer afford. The invasions had also led the Byzantines to adopt still more changes that built a strong defensive reaction into the empire's military and administrative machinery. This state of preparedness outlasted the emergency, and the reforms forced by military necessity made the Byzantines readier to accept later reforms for which the need was less pressing. By the eighth century Byzantium was by no means a new state, but it showed much of the flexibility of a new society.

While the Byzantines' ill luck in the seventh century weakened their resistance to change, it did not destroy their confidence that their empire was favored by God. They realized that the Lord could be angry for a time, whether about their personal sins or about icons, Iconoclasm, or some other heresy; but they were sure that His wrath would not last forever. Even in desperate situations, the Byzantines were not much given to despair. When finally the empire's fortunes began to improve, first under Irene and Constantine VI and more convincingly under Theophilus, Byzantine self-confidence soon returned. This return of confidence was to continue with the restoration of the icons in 843, which quite typically was followed by a speedy assault on Crete to take advantage of divine approval for the change in doctrine. Since the Byzantines were willing to reform what they thought displeased God and hopeful of success if they did so, the Byzantine society of this time was not only capable of revival, but ready for it.

By 842 the Byzantines had a right to some self-confidence, because they had, more than at any earlier time, improved their own lot. Of course their empire was still an unbroken continuation of the Roman Empire, and their culture an unbroken continuation of ancient Greek culture. Until about 780, however, the most striking difference between the Byzantines and their ancient predecessors had been the large parts of their political and cultural heritage that the Byzantines had lost, while their main achievement had been not to lose the rest of it. The political, economic, and cultural advances of the subsequent Byzantine revival were the first important additions to what the Byzantines had inherited.

Because these advances were new, and not drawn from ancient sources, they began to make Byzantium culturally independent. The measure of this is that they made it more distinct from western Europe, which shared Byzantium's Roman past but was now undergoing changes of its own. Consequently, with little open hostility, the two became increasingly estranged from each other. The reintroduction of Iconoclasm in 815 caused less tension with the Western Church than the original adoption of Iconoclasm had in 730; the condemnation of Iconoclasm in 843 improved relations with the Western powers even less than its first condemnation in 787. By 843 the Byzantines were largely indifferent to Western opinions. For Byzantium the greatest future opportunities lay in the East, the center of its power, where its reformed army was to conquer the Arabs on its eastern border, and its ever more impressive civilization was to convert the Bulgars and Slavs to its north. But in order to expand on this scale, Byzantium had first needed to revive itself.

Afterword

Afterword
on the Sources

The sources for the years between 780 and 842 become steadily more abundant as the period goes on, but they also become more difficult for the modern historian to use. One reason for the abundance and the difficulty is the expansion of literature at the time, which produced more letters, saints' lives, and theological treatises that provide historical evidence in a context that is not historiographical. But the main reason for the multiplication of both sources and problems is that at 813 two long historical works begin that were composed more than a century later with a remarkable lack of historical sense. Fortunately, three reasonably sound narrative sources cover most of the period, though they leave a gap between 816 and 829.

For the period from 780 to 813, the principal source is the last portion of the chronicle of Theophanes Confessor. Since the chronicle was completed before 815, it is a contemporary source, though its voice is not always that of Theophanes himself. At the least Theophanes made extensive use of notes provided by his friend George Syncellus, who had died before he could finish his own chronicle. Up to 780 the chronicle of Theophanes depends on various literary sources, which even if they do not survive can be known from other histories that used Theophanes' sources without using Theophanes. Although the last such evidence of a literary source applies to 780, the existence of more literary sources for the reign of Constantine VI and Irene has recently been conjectured, mostly because Theophanes seems at some times to favor Irene and at other times to favor Constantine. Such arguments are not conclusive, however, because Theophanes or George Syncellus could easily have had divided loyalties, or even have recognized that neither ruler was all good or all bad.

Certainly this part of Theophanes' chronicle is far from being impartial. It shows great hatred of Iconoclasm, and rabid hostility to Nicephorus I. As far as can be judged from internal evidence and our scanty comparative material, however, its facts seem to be fairly reliable, as we would expect from a source writing soon after the events for a contemporary audience, which could hardly be deceived beyond a certain point. It is helpfully arranged year by year in annalistic entries, and its chronology for this period appears to be correct, except for an occasional day of the month that may have been corrupted by a later copyist.[512]

Most of the other sources for the years before 813 provide mere scraps of evidence, which supplement what Theophanes says but are not complete or reliable enough to provide a proper check on it. For internal Byzantine history, the main sources are the acts of the Council of Nicaea of 787 and references in some saints' lives and the earlier letters of Theodore of Studius. The hagiography contains so few historical facts amid so many conventional sentiments and miracles that the brief entries in the *Synaxarium*, a number of which give abstracts of lost saints' lives, are often about as valuable for the historian as the complete texts. For external affairs, there are incidental references in Arabic, Syriac, Armenian, and Latin chronicles, for all of which Byzantium is of secondary importance. The one most interested in the empire is Michael the Syrian, who draws on a lost Syriac chronicle by Dionysius of Tellmaḥre. But Dionysius, though he was a contemporary who died in 845, had such a vague idea of what was going on in the empire and made so many absurd mistakes about it that any uncorroborated report on Byzantium in Michael the Syrian is questionable, while any contradicted by a Byzantine source is practically worthless.[513]

Overlapping with the very end of Theophanes' chronicle are the two surviving fragments of the history that should probably be attributed to Sergius Confessor, the *Chronicle of 811* of Nicephorus I's last campaign and the Scriptor Incertus on the years from 812 to 816. This is an excellent source arranged in accurate chronological order, though the latter part is still available only in an antiquated edition that fails to correct many corruptions in its text. After it breaks off, a long period begins for which the main narrative sources date from the middle of the tenth century. The lone exception is the rather stupid chronicle of George the Monk, composed soon after 867, which includes a few facts in its denunciations of the second period of Iconoclasm. The much more informative tenth-century histories, obviously drawn from earlier sources that are now lost, divide into two groups of two, which frequently disagree with each other.[514]

In one group are the chronicles of Genesius and the so-called Theophanes Continuatus, both of which begin where Theophanes ends, in 813.

Both of these chronicles, especially the latter, are longer, more detailed, more colorful, and more elegantly written than their two competitors, and in consequence they have generally been more popular with modern historians. This popularity has largely persisted despite the efforts of the historian who spent the most time analyzing them, Henri Grégoire, who concluded about these chronicles, "They must be read with the most extreme distrust and believed capable of anything. They must constantly be suspected of replacing history with legend."

Though by reading Genesius and Theophanes Continuatus selectively one can extract a number of plausible-looking stories from them, they are filled with sweeping prophecies that always come true, elaborate fictions of a hagiographical character, and self-contradictory chronological data. For example, both recount in detail the exploits that Manuel the Armenian performed after the time when he had actually died, and both tell the story of the battle of Anzen again and again as if they were referring to a succession of battles at different dates. Genesius seems at least to have copied most of his errors from his sources, but Theophanes Continuatus appears to have felt free to alter his sources as he pleased, even reassigning the parts in events from one historical figure to another. Nonetheless, both clearly drew on some sources that contained correct information, though they sometimes misunderstand or distort it.[515]

The other two tenth-century texts are the chronicle of Symeon the Logothete and the so-called Pseudo-Symeon. While the latter is largely copied from the former, the Pseudo-Symeon had some additional sources, including a few that he shares with Theophanes Continuatus but transmits more accurately, and a somewhat better text of the Scriptor Incertus than the one extant today. The Pseudo-Symeon has also inserted into his interpolated text of Symeon some totally arbitrary dates, which have repeatedly deceived unsuspecting scholars who assume that such a reassuringly precise chronology must have at least a little value. The text of the genuine Symeon has, surprisingly, never been edited as such, though it survives in several manuscripts. The only printed texts from which it can be known reproduce plagiarizations of it by Leo Grammaticus and Theodosius Melissenus and sections of it that medieval compilers interpolated into the chronicle of George the Monk.

This absence of a proper edition had understandably confused modern users of the chronicle, and has given rise to the persistent misconception that Symeon's work is somehow a continuation of George's. In fact, both Symeon and George used an earlier, lost chronicle that paraphrased the work of Theophanes and continued it to 829; Symeon reproduced more of this work than George did. For the reign of Theophilus, Symeon used another lost chronicle, which was composed before 866 and recounted events in an accurate chronological sequence. Since this chronicle appears to have been highly reliable, this part of Symeon's chronicle is much the best source for the years from 829 to 842, though it has seldom been treated as such. Before 829 Symeon's account seems accurate enough, but so brief that it is mostly useful for identifying which of the contradictory versions in Genesius and Theophanes Continuatus is the better.[516]

These four narratives can be checked against a number of other sources for the period between 813 and 842. The return of Iconoclasm deserves much of the credit for these sources' composition, because it gave rise to the letters that Theodore of Studius wrote as the leader of the resistance and to hagiographical texts that describe what their saints did during the iconoclast persecutions. As before, there are various foreign sources, which become more important with the Arab conquests on Sicily and Crete and the great Arab campaign of 838. Particularly interesting is the material in the Arab geographers that seems to depend on a Byzantine government manual describing the army as it was in 839, and the *Tacticon Uspensky*, a rank-list of Byzantine officials that dates from 842 or 843.[517]

Such are the main literary sources, most of which are best evaluated in connection with the specific events that they report. The nonliterary sources are frustratingly scanty and hard to use. No archives appear to survive as such, though a very little of what must have been in them can be reconstructed. Byzantine inscriptions for this period are few and uninformative, and most are poorly published in places that are difficult to locate. Archeology has turned up little that is specifically applicable to this period, a fact that is not surprising in view of most archeologists' lack of interest in Byzantium and the small amount of building done at the time. Numismatics and sigillography have contributed more, and for both coins and seals serviceable catalogues are available.[518]

Under such circumstances, studying this period is not easy, and many of the conclusions one reaches are more or less open to question. On the other hand, problems that in isolation look insoluble can often be resolved with a fair degree of certainty if they are considered in context, using all the available evidence. Aside from Genesius and Theophanes Continuatus, few of these sources contain much deliberate deceit, and since even those two are more interested in telling a good story than in really sophisticated distortion, they can usually be caught out without too much trouble. Though there are many things about this time that we shall never know, it is not one of the truly dark ages of Byzantine history, like the century and a half before it.

Reference Matter

Notes

For the works cited here in short form, complete authors' names and publication data are given in the Bibliography, pp. 465–75. For abbreviations used in these notes, see the list on p. 465.

CHAPTER ONE

1. Theophanes, 444. Leo was then nineteen, and Irene is likely to have been a few years younger than he. On Irene's orphanhood, see her words at Theophanes, 478. She had an uncle and a cousin with the family name of Serantapechus, and at this time having a family name at all was an indication of some social standing (see Theophanes, 474). On her oath to Constantine V, see Cedrenus, 2: 19–20.

2. Theophanes, 444, 445.

3. Theophanes, 449, 451, 453.

4. Cedrenus, 2: 19–20, and Theophanes, 453, 454. On both passages, see Treadgold, "Indirectly Preserved Source," 69–76. Leo was born on January 25, 750 (Theophanes, 426).

5. For a good discussion of the theological problem, see Martin, 124–29. On Artabasdus, see Speck, *Artabasdos*; though I cannot agree with Speck's argument that this rebellion did not involve the restoration of icons, I accept his revision of its chronology.

6. Constantine's second wife, Maria, died in 752 (Nicephorus, *Breviarium*, 65). Constantine himself was born between September and November of 718 (Theophanes, 399–400). For the births of his fourth and fifth sons, Nicetas and Anthemius, in 763 and 769, see Nicephorus, *Breviarium*, 70 and 76 (note that Anthemius must have been born after April of 769, when Nicetas was still the youngest son according to Theophanes, 444). Anthusa was born about 758 and was the twin of either Christopher or Nicephorus—probably the latter, since he was old enough to head a conspiracy in 776 and was the younger of the two. See Mango, "St. Anthusa."

7. Theophanes, 443–44, 450; Nicephorus, *Breviarium*, 77; Cedrenus, 2: 18. On the passage from Cedrenus, see Treadgold, "Indirectly Preserved Source." On the revenue, see below, pp. 38 and n. 36.

8. Theophanes, 449–50, reading ἐν τέλει for ἐν τῇ πόλει at 449.13–14 (see Treadgold, "Unpublished Saint's Life," 241). On the timing of paydays, see below, n. 20.

9. Theophanes, 450–51. Note that Nicephorus was an ex-Caesar in 780: Theophanes, 454. On his age, see above, n. 6.

10. On the physical aspect of Thrace and Asia Minor, see Hendy, 21–68.

11. For the numbers of troops in each thematic army, see Treadgold, *Byzantine State Finances*, 16–18. A very rough idea of the relative populations of the themes may be gained from Map 3, which shows the distribution of the empire's cities as they were represented at the Council of Nicaea in 787, based on Mansi, 13: 380–87.

12. Cf. Theophanes, 440.

13. On Cyprus, see Jenkins, "Cyprus."

14. On revenues, see Treadgold, *Byzantine State Finances*, 3, 64–65, 86. (Mahdī's revenue must have been roughly equal to that of his nearly immediate successor Hārūn.) On populations, see the relevant estimates in McEvedy and Jones. On field armies, see Treadgold, ibid., 92.

15. Translations of Arab reports of the raids are conveniently available in Brooks, "Byzantines."

16. See Beševliev, *Protobulgarische Periode*, 145–228.

17. On Calabria, note that while only bishops from the toe of Italy (modern Calabria) happened to attend the Council of Nicaea in 787, on the heel (ancient Calabria) Hydrus (Otranto) was still in Byzantine hands; ca. 835 the central government's edict of 833 against iconophiles was being enforced there, and as there is no likely time for Hydrus to have been retaken in all likelihood it had never been lost (*Life of Gregory the Decapolite*, ch. 13, p. 58). On Sardinia, note that the archbishop of Sardinia was officially represented at the Council of Nicaea in 787 by a deacon from Catana in Sicily (Mansi, 13: 381).

18. On the Khazar marriage alliance, see Theophanes, 409.

19. The rebellions were those of 717, 721, 727, 729, 741–43, 766, and 775, apart from the recently discovered conspiracy earlier in 780, which had political implications.

20. For the payment of officials, see Liudprand, 6.10. On the banquets see Philotheus, in Oikonomidès, 165–235.

21. On all the officials of the capital see Oikonomidès, 302–29, and, particularly on their numbers and salaries, Treadgold, *Byzantine State Finances*, 40–49.

22. On the efficiency of the bureaucracy at this time, see Treadgold, "Revival," 1258–66.

23. On the warehouses, see Hendy, 626–34, 654–62.

24. On Constantine V's creation of the tagmata, see Haldon, 228–35.

25. Further on the tagmata and the other military departments, see Treadgold, *Byzantine State Finances*, 24–29, 32–33.

26. On Joannicius, see Petrus, 386, and Sabas, 333–37; cf. Mango, "Two Lives." On Anthony, cf. Theophanes, 442.

27. On the organization of themes, see Treadgold, *Byzantine State Finances*, 18–24.

28. On the turmae of the Thracesians, cf. Constantine VII, *De Ceremoniis*, 663 (referring to the year 935), with Jones, 2: 1418–19, 1429, who argues that the various Theodosiani and the Victores were raised between 384 and 395. For the head-

quarters of the turmarchs about 842, see Treadgold, "Notes," 283–84. I assume that the *De Ceremoniis* has listed the turmarchs of the Thracesians in the order of their rank, and that their "turmarch of the Seacoast" was the head of a division created between 842 and 935. On the spatharii, cf. below, pp. 355–57 and n. 475.

29. Cf. *Life of Philaretus*, 125–27. For the numbers of support corps for a bandum of 200 men (or thereabouts), see Leo VI, *Tactica*, 4.35 (2 standard bearers), 12.51 (8–10 medics), 12.56–57 (2 scouts and 2 surveyors), 12.119 (6–8 medics), and 12.120 (2 scouts, 2 messengers, and 2 standard bearers). These numbers should probably be multiplied by five to give a figure for the drungus of 1,000 men, which was later divided into five banda (cf. below, pp. 317–18 and n. 437). For the numbers of fortified places in the themes about 840, see Table 2 and ibn Khurdādhbih, 77–80 (on p. 78, four forts in the Thracesian theme apart from Ephesus is definitely too few, and I would emend the text to read "fourteen").

30. On Lachanodracon, see Theophanes, 445–46. Cf. Mansi, 13: 184E–185A, for a reference to iconoclasts' burning books at Phocaea in the Thracesian theme.

31. See the discussion in Hendy, 619–62, which independently and simultaneously arrived at the same conclusion about the origin of the themes expressed in my "Military Lands." My only important disagreement with Hendy is over his conjecture (pp. 645–51) that the pay of Byzantine soldiers in the middle period was a continuation not of the regular pay in the earlier period but of the quinquennial donative. Procopius says that Justinian let the quinquennial donative lapse in the sixth century, and all Hendy's examples of donatives after Justinian are accessional, not quinquennial, donatives (pp. 646–47). Hendy's explanation of the order of Constantine Porphyrogenitus's pay lists as "evolved" from "intermediate" and "primitive" pay lists requires "two major exceptions" and three that are scarcely less major out of a list of just twelve themes (pp. 648–49); in fact, the list simply gives the order of precedence of the themes' strategi in the contemporary treatise of Philotheus (see Oikonomidès, 137–39). Hendy's "intermediate" list fails the one historical test to which it can be put, since Theophanes, 484–85 and 489, makes clear that the army of Macedonia was paid in 809 and the army of the Armeniacs in 811, which cannot be reconciled with Hendy's conjectures. Finally, Hendy's reconstruction contradicts the most explicit evidence on military pay in the middle period, that in Arab sources that Hendy considers unreliable (p. 650) but I believe derive from a Byzantine government manual (see Treadgold, "Remarks").

32. Ya'qūbī (Brooks, "Byzantines," part 1, 735–36); Ṭabarī (ibid., 735–37); Bar Hebraeus, 117 (confused); Theophanes, 451–53. (At Theophanes, 451, the figure of 100,000 Byzantine troops is incredible; see Treadgold, *Byzantine State Finances*, 73.)

33. On military revolts in this period, see Kaegi, *Byzantine Military Unrest*.

34. On the plagues, see Biraben and Le Goff. On the change in climate, see Duby, 5–11.

35. On the gold-copper ratio, which is certain for a somewhat later date, and probably obtained as early as the eighth century, see Grierson, *Catalogue*, 3.1: 16–19. For the laborer's wage, see Jenkins, "Social Life," 86–87, though I believe Jenkins exaggerates the wretchedness of the life this wage would support. My calculation for the price of bread is based on Leo VI, *Book*, ch. 18, which allows bakers to add 60 folles profit and overhead to the price of the bread made from 10 nomismata's worth of wheat (on which the commercia, at 10 percent, amount to

1 nomisma). Ostrogorsky, 319–22, puts the normal price of wheat at 12 modii to the nomisma. At this price, one pound of bread (0.035 modius) would cost almost exactly one follis.

36. See Treadgold, *Byzantine State Finances*, 67–90.

37. On military pay, see Treadgold, *Byzantine State Finances*, 74.

38. The calculations of revenue per subject and per acre are based on a revenue of 7 million nomismata and a population of 16 million in the later sixth century, when the empire was about three times as large as in 780; see Stein, 155, and McEvedy and Jones. As above, the revenue in 780 is estimated at 1.8 million nomismata and the population at 7 million. Though all these figures are rough, the proportions cannot be very far wrong. On the gold panic of 767, see Nicephorus, *Breviarium*, 76, and Theophanes, 443. Note that in the sixth century the smallest coin was the nummus, worth 7,200 to the nomisma, and there were also 5-nummus and 10-nummus pieces. In the eighth century the smallest coin was the half-follis, worth 576 to the nomisma, which corresponded to 20 old nummi (the copper coinage had been subject to some inflation during the intervening period).

39. For cities with bishops in 787, see Darrouzès, whose findings appear in Map 3. On the population of Constantinople, see Jacoby. Mango, *Byzantium*, 80, puts the population below 50,000 at its nadir about 748, which seems to me too low; at any rate, the city had recovered substantially by 780.

40. To acquire some idea of how rough this rule of thumb is, we can apply it to the cities of Turkey in 1970 in the manner suggested below for Byzantium about 800. Our rough estimate for the largest city, of course Istanbul, would probably be 2 million (actually it was some 2,248,000). We might then guess the second city, Ankara (Ancyra), at 1 million (actually 1,209,000); the third, Izmir (Smyrna), at 667,000 (actually 521,000); the fourth, Adana (Adana), at 500,000 (actually 365,000); and the fifth, Bursa (Prusa), at 400,000 (actually 276,000). While these are substantial differences, for none of the top twenty Turkish cities would the difference be as much as 50 percent if they were ranked correctly, and for only five cities would it be as much as 33 percent. The average difference would be 22 percent, and for the total of the twenty cities, the difference between the actual and estimated figures less than 7 percent. In short, the rule could provide us with a fair guide to the urban population of Turkey in 1970. More elaborate formulas have been suggested, e.g., by Russell, but they yield little better results. On the population of Amorium in 838, see below, p. 303 and n. 415. The *Synaxarium*, 414–16, implies that refugees from at least as far away as Nicaea in Thrace were at Adrianople when the 40,000 were captured in 813; Symeon the Logothete (Moravcsik, "Sagen," 117) closely confirms this number for all the captives by noting that 10,000 adult males were taken. I have similarly assumed 25 percent adult males in extrapolating from the figure for Laodicea Combusta given by Ṭabarī (Brooks, "Byzantines," part 1, 734).

41. Mango, *Byzantium*, 62, estimates that in the early period "a large provincial city . . . may have had a population of about 50,000, while an average provincial city may have been in the 5,000–20,000 range." On the walls of Ephesus, see Foss, 106–7.

42. The main evidence about the guilds is in Leo VI, *Book*, 369–92.

43. For a discussion, which is almost certainly overoptimistic, see Lopez. Cf. Hendy, 626–34, esp. p. 627 n. 311.

44. With these reservations, one may get a vivid and mostly accurate idea of life in Byzantium from Jenkins, "Social Life."

45. The area of Constantinople was about 14 square kilometers, and that of fifth-century-B.C. Athens about 2.2 square kilometers.

46. On the Blues and Greens, see Cameron, 297–308. For unseemly performances of mime, see Theodore, *Eulogy of His Mother*, 885C; cf. Nicephorus, *Apologeticus*, 556A–B. Mango, "Daily Life," 341–51, discusses the middle Byzantine Hippodrome and mime in terms that I find too gloomy, though obviously both had declined since early Byzantine times. On private dinner parties, see *Life of Philaretus*, 145–49.

47. On Ephesus, see Foss, 104–15.

48. See Lemerle, *Agrarian History*, 27–85, and Bouras. On Amnia, see *Life of Philaretus*, especially 135.

49. On robbery, see *Life of Philaretus*, 115–17, and George the Monk, 765–66. On piracy, see Ashburner, 10–13, 20–21; cf. cxliii–cxlix. On brigands by the sea, see also the *Synaxarium*, 673 (referring to St. Hesychius, who died about 792 according to the *Synaxarium*, 515–16).

50. On Irene's family, see n. 1 above.

51. On average sizes of farms, see Treadgold, *Byzantine State Finances*, 62. On the importance of livestock, see *Life of Philaretus*, 113, 117–25, 125–27.

52. The figures for average family income and taxes are based on the data in Treadgold, *Byzantine State Finances*, 55–57.

53. See Ladner for a good treatment of the question of Iconoclasm, on which subsequent debate has steadily become less profitable. Cf. the remarks of Mango, "Historical Introduction," esp. n. 12.

54. See *Ecloga*, 17.20 (fornication outlawed), 2.1 (bride's consent for marriage), 2.13 (grounds for divorce), title (reference to "greater humanity"), 17.36 (abortion prohibited), 17 *passim* (penalties of death and mutilation), and 17.38 (homosexual acts punishable by death).

55. See *Ecloga*, 17.29 (seduction), 2.13 (adultery by wife), 17.19 (adultery by husband). On Constantine's sexual preferences, see Theophanes, 443. Byzantines seem to have been scarcely aware that lesbianism was possible.

56. On the purges, see Theophanes, 405, and Nicephorus, *Breviarium*, 52.

57. For a fuller description of the Byzantines' secondary-school readings, see Treadgold, *Nature*, 6–7. On Ignatius the Deacon's education, see his *Life of Tarasius*, 423.

58. See Browning, "Literacy."

59. On the books available at Constantinople, see Mango, "Availability," 31–35. A good indication is that about half of the material in the books described in the *Bibliotheca* of Photius, composed in the mid-ninth century, is lost today (Treadgold, *Nature*, 9).

60. See Kitzinger.

61. For a recent survey of art in this period, see Cormack, "Arts." For Constantine V's art, see *Life of Stephen*, 1120C (on St. Mary of the Blachernae), 1172A–B (on the Milium).

62. On Leo's repairs, see Theophanes, 412. On Constantine's repairs, see Theophanes, 440, and Nicephorus, *Breviarium*, 75–76.

CHAPTER TWO

63. On Leo's tomb, see Grierson, "Tombs," 54; cf. Constantine VII, *De Ceremoniis*, 645. On the coins, see Grierson, *Catalogue*, 3.1: 337–38.

64. Theophanes, 454. Note that Bardas was strategus of the Armeniacs in 772 (Theophanes, 445), but not in 778, when Caristerotzes held that post (Theophanes, 451).

65. The eldest brother, Christopher, in particular seems to have been quite passive throughout his life. One later source could even report that he had died during his father's reign: *Synaxarium*, 355 (not a very reliable source, since it makes Christopher the son of Leo III).

66. On Theodora, see *Synaxarium*, 354–56; this source is confused (see above, n. 65), but when it asserts that Theodora remained a virgin we can probably assume that she had no children, and there is no reason to doubt that she died in her convent. On Anthusa, see *Synaxarium*, 597–600, 613–14, and Mango, "St. Anthusa."

67. Stauracius's first appearance in the sources is at Theophanes, 456, where (in 782) he is already described as logothete and patrician, in control of everything.

68. Theophanes, 454.

69. Theophanes, 455. News of the discovery of the coffin even penetrated to Italy (Andrea Dandolo, 123) and Syria (Michael the Syrian, 10–11). See Mango, "Forged Inscription" (but on p. 205, line 6, Mango's date should be 795/96).

70. The quotation is from Theophanes, 455. While the author of these words may be George Syncellus, he as well as Theophanes was an iconophile monk. On the new monks, see Speck, *Kaiser Konstantin VI*, 113–14, mentioning the families of Theodore, Theophanes, John of Psicha, and Nicetas of Medicium, plus Nicephorus of Medicium. One might add John of Cathara (*Synaxarium*, 631) and still be sure that the movement included many others whom we do not know by name.

71. For Theodore's words, see his *Eulogy of Plato*, 824B. Note that Leo IV had strongly opposed Theophanes' early attempts to lead a monastic life; Methodius, 10–11. On the convent founded by Irene, see Theophanes, 478, and Treadgold, "Unpublished Saint's Life," 243–51.

72. On the families of Theodore and Theophanes, see Theodore, *Eulogy of Plato*, 808A–D, and Methodius, 11. On Constantine's opposition to monasticism, cf. Rouan, esp. 428–29, where she argues that Constantine martyred St. Stephen the Younger for trying to recruit prominent men in the court or army into monasteries and iconophilism.

73. Michael of Studius, 245A–B; Theodore, *Eulogy of Plato*, 817D–820B; Nicephorus the Sceuophylax, *Life of Theophanes*, 19; Theodore, *Panegyric of Theophanes*, 22; and *Life of Macarius of Pelecete*, 145.

74. *Life of John of Psicha*, 109–10; and see Alexander, *Patriarch Nicephorus*, 157–62.

75. On Paul, see Theophanes, 453, 457, and *Life of Tarasius*, 392; cf. *Life of John of Gotthia*, 168B, and Grumel, no. 348, pp. 11–12. On Euthymius, see *Synaxarium*, 345. Euthymius was born about 753, since he died in 831 at the age of 78; see Gouillard, "Oeuvre," 40–41.

76. Theophanes, 454–55. Cf. Ya'qūbī (Brooks, "Byzantines," part 1, 736).

77. Theophanes, 455; Ṭabarī (Brooks, "Byzantines," part 1, 737).

78. Theophanes, 455–56.

79. The sources for this entire campaign are Theophanes, 456–57; Michael the Syrian, 2; Bar Hebraeus, 117–18; Leontius, 152–54; Ya'qūbī, Ṭabarī, and the *Kitāb al-'Uyūn* (Brooks, "Byzantines," part 1, 737–39). For a discussion of the evidence, see Tritle.

80. On the earlier careers of Anthony and Peter, see Theophanes, 442.

81. On the sources, see Speck, *Kaiser Konstantin VI*, 121.

82. Theophanes, 455; John was certainly military logothete by 787 (Mansi, 12:999B and Theophanes, 464), and Constantine was in love with Rotrud by 789 (Theophanes, 463).

83. Theophanes, 456–57. On St. Sophia at Thessalonica, see Mango, *Byzantine Architecture*, 161–65, and Cormack, "Apse Mosaics."

84. Theophanes, 457; cf. 433.

85. On operations in Thrace in 786, see Mansi, 12:990C, and Theophanes, 462. For the frontier in 787, cf. Theophanes, 463.

86. Theophanes, 453, 457–58, confirmed and supplemented by Irene herself (Mansi, 12:1003D–1006A), *Life of John of Gotthia*, 168B–C, and *Life of Tarasius*, 397–98.

87. See Theophanes, 458–60, which as far as the text of the speech is concerned is virtually identical with Mansi, 12:986D–990B, though only the latter mentions the opposition to the council. In the *Life of Tarasius*, 398–402, Ignatius tells a similar story, but evidently had no access to the text of the speech and had to reconstruct it from memory. Tarasius's quotation is modified from 2 Tim. 2:9, "but the word of God is not bound."

88. There were also Monophysite patriarchs of Alexandria, Antioch, and Jerusalem acknowledged by the majority of Christians in the caliphate; but as heretics they were ignored by the Orthodox. Theophanes, 460–61, says that the peace with the Arabs had not yet been broken when the letters went out to the patriarchs of Antioch and Alexandria. Since he does not mention Jerusalem, the Byzantine government may already have known that its patriarch was unreachable, but the title of the letter (printed in Mansi, 12:1119D–1127A) says that it was also addressed to Jerusalem. The Eastern monks' reply and the enclosed letter are in Mansi, 12:1127C–1146C; on their representatives, cf. Theophanes, 461. I conjecture that the "desert" of which the monks speak was in Egypt because one of the legates, Thomas, was abbot of the Egyptian monastery of St. Arsenius (Mansi, 14:380D), while the other does not mention any specific Eastern affiliation when he signs the acts of the council. Thomas was familiar with current conditions at Alexandria (Mansi, 13:60D) and may have embarked from there for Byzantium. Here I take the two representatives' title of syncellus to mean not that they had held that formal church office, but simply that they had been associates of the patriarchs in some capacity.

89. Irene's letter is in Mansi, 12:984E–986C (emending to *indict. viii* at the end); cf. 1127A–B, where the pope's legates note that Tarasius's letter to the pope was about the same as that sent to the Eastern patriarchs. Hadrian's reply is in Mansi, 12:1056A–1072B.

90. On the restoration of icons, see Mansi, 13:462C. On Tarasius's monastery, see *Life of Tarasius*, 402–3. On Michael, cf. *Life of Theophylact*, 73–75, with Mansi, 12:994C, etc., where Michael is listed as bishop of Synnada.

91. On Dorus, see *Life of John of Gotthia*, 169D. The date seems to follow from the fact that John did not go to the council of 786 and that another bishop had been chosen in his place to go to Nicaea in 787. Thus the order of the chapters in the *Life* must mean that John's capture followed the patriarch Paul's abdication in 784 but not the Council of Nicaea, which the *Life* mentions only as a later consequence of Paul's abdication.

92. Ṭabarī (Brooks, "Byzantines," part 1, 739–40); since no hostilities by the

Byzantines are mentioned, their breach of the peace must have been their failure to pay the tribute, especially because Ṭabarī dates the breach to April, when the tribute was due. On Michael and his companions, see *Synaxarium*, 98; here "Alīm" is evidently Alī ibn Sulaymān, which provides the clue to the date.

93. Ṭabarī (Brooks, "Byzantines," part 1, 740); Balādhurī (ibid., part 2, 90–91); Michael the Syrian, 2; Bar Hebraeus, 118. The "patrician" mentioned in the Arab sources can only be the strategus of the Armeniacs, who in 790 was Nicephorus (Theophanes, 466); see below, pp. 95–96 and n. 118.

94. Mansi, 12:990B–991B, which generally seems a somewhat more detailed and reliable account than Theophanes, 461–62. On the date, see Mansi, 12:999D, where the authority is Tarasius himself. See also *Life of Tarasius*, 403–4, and Theodore, *Eulogy of Plato*, 828A.

95. For the dismissals, see Mansi, 12:991B–C, and Theophanes, 462. According to the *Life of John of Gotthia*, 168C, the only source to mention the exile of bishops, the soldiers numbered some 6,000 together with their families. On the soldiers who joined the Anatolics, cf. Theophanes, 463. Though some have suggested that Irene's new recruits became the tagma of the Watch, I believe that that tagma already existed before this, and Constantine of Tius, 97–98, explicitly says that Irene put her new recruits into the places vacated by the soldiers she had cashiered, rather than into a new unit.

96. On the legates of the pope and the East, see Theophanes, 462. For this and the following description of the council, see the acts in Mansi, 12:991–1154, and 13:2–486, in which the numbers of the bishops and abbots can be counted. For a convenient summary of the council with detailed references to Mansi, see Dumeige, 101–50. Tarasius's staff members appear repeatedly, mostly as readers of documents.

97. Mansi, 12:991D–1051A.

98. On Hadrian's letter, see Wallach, 3–26, arguing that, though the Greek translation as we have it has been tampered with to omit the pope's criticisms of Tarasius's election as a layman, the translation read at Nicaea was complete and accurate. On the council's reception of the letter, see Mansi, 12:1051A–1111E. On the council's third session, see Mansi, 12:1114A–1154E.

99. Mansi, 13:1A–156E.

100. Mansi, 13:157A–201E.

101. On the sixth session, see Mansi, 13:204A–364D, and on the seventh, Mansi, 13:364E–413A.

102. On the final session, see *Life of Tarasius*, 405, and Mansi, 13:413B–439E. For Tarasius's letter, see Mansi, 13:458B–462D. The emperors' letter is mentioned in the *Liber Pontificalis*, 1:512.

103. See the references to and commentary on the sources for the suspension of these clerics in Grumel, nos. 360–66, pp. 16–20.

104. On Justinian II, see Theophanes, 363, and Nicephorus, *Breviarium*, 362 (both texts give the age as sixteen, but inclusive reckoning for ages was normal). On Constantine V and his son Nicephorus, see above, p. 9 and n. 6. On Irene's embassy in 787, see *Annales qui dicuntur Einhardi*, 75; *Annales Laurissenses*, 168; *Annales Fuldenses*, 350.

105. On Charlemagne's refusal, see *Annales qui dicuntur Einhardi*, 83. On Charlemagne's attachment to his daughters, see Einhard, 62. On his relations with Benevento, see Einhard, 32; *Annales Regni Francorum*, 74; Erchempert, 235; *Annales*

Laurissenses, 168, 170; and *Annales Fuldenses,* 350. More generally on Beneventan history in this period, see Bertolini, and the old but still useful Poupardin.

106. The source for Irene's abortive alliance with Arechis is a letter of Pope Hadrian to Charlemagne: *Codex Carolinus,* 617–18. Adelchis had arrived in Constantinople in 775 and taken the Greek name of Theodotus: Theophanes, 449. On Grimoald's accession, see Erchempert, 236; *Codex Carolinus,* 620; *Annales Maximiniani,* 21; and *Annales Regni Francorum,* 82. Grimoald had to strike coins and issue documents in Charlemagne's name.

107. At least Theophanes, 463, believed that Irene broke off the marriage contract. On the bride show, see *Life of Philaretus,* 135–43.

108. See Treadgold, "Bride-Shows," 395–413, for a general discussion of the bride shows, though my treatment of the events leading up to the show of 787 is deficient and should be corrected by the account given here.

109. *Life of Philaretus,* 115–17 (I suspect that Philaretus lost his property in the raid of 780 that captured the nearby fort of Semaluus; see above, p. 34 and n. 32), 143–45; Theophanes, 463. On Philaretus's Armenian blood, see below, p. 271 and n. 375.

110. Theophanes, 463. Grégoire, "Autour de Digénes," 287–88, persuasively identifies Theophanes' "Copidnadus" with Podandus in Cappadocia (assuming a false reading in the Greek). The suggestion that Diogenes, presumably turmarch of Cappadocia, was the prototype of Digenes was first made by Grégoire, "Tombeau." Though the identification can hardly be proved, it has in its favor the name (deliberately transformed to "Digenes" to fit the hero's supposed double ancestry), the date, which leaves enough time for the development of the legend before the epic appeared, and the location in Cappadocia. The arguments presented against the identification tend to show only that it is not helpful for interpreting the poem, which considering the long growth of the legend (including many accretions of figures whose historical prototypes are of later date) is to be expected. See the discussion and bibliography in Beck, *Geschichte,* 63–97.

111. Theophanes, 463–64. The attack followed Constantine's marriage in November and preceded the campaign in Calabria, still in 788; see n. 112 below.

112. Theophanes, 464 (calling Adelchis "Theodotus," the Greek name he assumed); *Poeta Saxo,* 244–45; *Annales Regni Francorum,* 82; *Chronicon Moissiacense,* 298–99; *Annales Maximiniani,* 22; *Annales Sithienses,* 36. The date was after Constantine's wedding in November but before Christmas. I see no reason to share the skepticism of Speck, *Kaiser Konstantin VI,* 598 n. 34, that Adelchis was present as Theophanes says.

113. On the Armenian refugees, see Leontius, 162, who gives their number as about 12,000 men with their wives and children. On the alliance with Benevento, see Erchempert, 236, and *Life of Philaretus,* 113 (the former spells Euanthia's name "Wantia," and the latter has confused Grimoald with his father, Arechis). Since Constantine VI disliked Maria, he would have been unlikely to use her sister to make a marriage alliance after 790. On Constantine's proclamation in the capital, see Speck, *Kaiser Konstantin VI,* 230–34.

114. The date was probably about 789. Macedonia cannot have been a separate theme in 788, when the strategus of Thrace was operating on the Strymon, but it evidently was a theme by 792, when there were two strategi, Nicetas and Theognostus, in the area (Theophanes, 467–68). The division seems more likely to have occurred under Irene, who had a long-standing program of expansion in Thrace,

than in the tumultuous first year of Constantine VI's rule alone. The troop strengths are based on my deductions in *Byzantine State Finances*, 69–72.

115. Theophanes, 464–65.

116. See Kindī (Brooks, "Relations," 390). On the oath, see Theophanes, 465.

117. Theophanes, 465; *Synaxarium*, 433–34 (two accounts). Theophanes speaks of two strategi with fleets, and the only theme besides the Cibyrrhaeots that is known to have had a fleet and that existed at this time was Hellas (cf. Constantine VII, *De Ceremoniis*, 653). The second account in the *Synaxarium* speaks of three other strategi besides Theophilus, presumably including those of the nearby Anatolic and Thracesian themes.

118. Theophanes, 465–66; cf. Nicephorus, *Chronographicon*, 100. Among several textual variants, I adopt the form "Musele" for Alexius's name since it is the same as that of an Alexius Musele, certainly his relation and probably his grandson, who is known under the emperor Theophilus. That Alexius Musele is definitely identified as an Armenian. See below, pp. 289–90 and n. 395. On the location of Atroa, note Mango, "Two Lives," 394 n. 7.

119. Theophanes, 466–67. On the coins, see Grierson, *Catalogue*, 3.1: 336–39.

120. Theophanes, 467.

121. Theophanes, 467; cf. Yaʿqūbī and Ṭabarī (Brooks, "Byzantines," part 1, 710). The suggestion that the expedition was called off is made by Speck, *Kaiser Konstantin VI*, 239.

122. Theophanes, 467.

123. Theophanes, 467–68; Petrus, 386C–387A; Sabas, 337B–338A. The last source misdates the battle near Marcellae, probably for reasons of its own; see Speck, *Kaiser Konstantin VI*, 666, n. 68, and Mango, "Two Lives," 398–401.

124. Theophanes, 468–69. On Euchaïta as headquarters of the Armeniacs, see below, pp. 168–69 and n. 226.

125. That Constantine agreed to pay the Bulgars tribute seems to follow from the incident recorded by Theophanes, 470; see below, p. 106 and n. 133. On the loss of Camachum, see Balādhurī (Brooks, "Byzantines," part 2, 88); Michael the Syrian, 8; and Theophanes, 469.

126. Michael the Syrian, 8–9; Bar Hebraeus, 119 (where "Rabsāh" is obviously Thebasa); Theophanes, 469, 481 (the latter recording the rebuilding of Thebasa; see below, p. 138 and n. 179).

127. Ṭabarī (Brooks, "Byzantines," part 1, 741); Michael the Syrian, 9, like Bar Hebraeus, 119, is poorly informed on the Byzantine side of events, but their source, Dionysius of Tellmaḥre, had seen Arabs who had accompanied the expedition.

128. On the death of Philaretus, see *Life of Philaretus*, 151–65. Maria's daughters were named Irene and Euphrosyne. The former is known only from the mention of her tomb at Constantine VII, *De Ceremoniis*, 647, and from Theodore, *Letters*, 2.104 (1360D–1361C). On the latter, see below, pp. 246–47 and n. 339. On the relationship of Theodote to Theodore and Plato, see Michael of Studius, 253B.

129. *Life of Tarasius*, 408–12; Theophanes, 469. I reject the report of the *Narratio de Tarasio*, 1852D–1853A, that Constantine threatened Tarasius with a renewal of Iconoclasm to get a divorce. If a story this favorable to Tarasius were true, we would hear of it from an early source, and not only from this late and vague document.

130. Theophanes, 469–70. "Anusan" may possibly be the ancient Elaeussa in Isauria, quite near the Lamis.

131. Theophanes, 470; cf. Michael the Syrian, 9.

132. On the alliance of Theodore and Plato, see Michael of Studius, 249B. For early reactions to the marriage, see Theophanes, 470 (cf. 471 and 469); Theodore, *Eulogy of Plato*, 829A–832B; and Michael of Studius, 252B–253C.

133. Theophanes, 470.

134. On the relics of St. Euphemia, see Theophanes, 440, and Constantine of Tius, 103–4 (note at p. 83 that this text is liturgically associated with July 11, the feast of the Definition of the Council of Chalcedon, an association that would be easily explicable if the translation of the relics occurred on that day but is puzzling otherwise). On Constantine's attempts to meet Theodore and Plato, see Theophanes, 471, and Michael of Studius, 253B–C.

135. Theophanes, 471, 470–71; Theodore, *Eulogy of Plato*, 832B–833A; Theodore, *Letters*, 1.1–3 (904A–920C); Michael of Studius, 253C–256C (for the number of monks at Saccudium, see 248D). Theodore arrived in Thessalonica on March 25 (Theodore, *Letters*, 1.3 [917C]) after a journey of about 40 days.

136. On Anazarbus, see Balādhurī (Brooks, "Byzantines," part 2, 87). On Hārūn's raid and Constantine's response, see Yaʿqūbī and Ṭabarī (ibid., part 1, 741); Michael the Syrian, 10; and Theophanes, 471. On the location of the fort (al-Safṣāf in Arabic), see Hild and Restle, 268.

137. On Leo's death, see Theophanes, 471. For the Arab raid, see below, pp. 111–12 and n. 144.

138. Theophanes, 471–72. I adopt the reconstruction of the chronology (which Theophanes seems to have muddled) suggested by Speck, *Kaiser Konstantin VI*, 302–8, along with his explanation (pp. 308–21) of later reports that Constantine was still alive as reflections of the fairly effective concealment of his death.

139. Theophanes, 472, 468; Theodore, *Eulogy of Plato*, 833A; Michael of Studius, 256C–D.

140. On Justinian II's tongue, see Theophanes, 369. On Irene's coins, see Grierson, *Catalogue*, 3.1: 347–51. For her acts, see Zepos and Zepos, 1: 45–50.

141. On Theodote's retirement, see Symeon the Logothete (Georgius Interpolatus, 809), and Pseudo-Symeon, 645–46. On the recall of Plato and Theodore, see Michael of Studius, 256D–257D, and Theodore, *Eulogy of Plato*, 833A–D.

142. Irene's ally Bardanes was made strategus of the Thracesian theme by 799 (Theophanes, 474); the count of the Opsician theme was a certain John in 796 (Theophanes, 470), but was Paul the Patrician by 799 (Theophanes, 473); the strategus of Sicily was Nicetas the Patrician in 797 but Michael the Patrician in 799 (see introduction to *Life of Nicetas the Patrician*, 315–17).

143. Theophanes, 473.

144. On the earlier raids, see Michael the Syrian, 8, and Ṭabarī and Yaʿqūbī (Brooks, "Byzantines," part 1, 740); cf. Haldon and Kennedy, 111. On this raid, see Theophanes, 473, and Ṭabarī (Brooks, ibid., 741). Michael the Syrian, 12, and Bar Hebraeus, 120, mention a victory of Aëtius that must belong to this time.

145. Theophanes, 473 (on Constantine Serantapechus, cf. Theophanes, 474).

146. *Annales Laurissenses*, 182 (Constantine VI's embassy), 184; *Annales Regni Francorum*, 104; *Poeta Saxo*, 254; *Annales Fuldenses*, 351 (Constantine's embassy), 351–52; *Annales Lobienses*, 230.

147. Theophanes, 473; Ṭabarī (Brooks, "Byzantines," part 1, 741); Michael

the Syrian, 12; Bar Hebraeus, 120; Michael of Studius, 257D–260A; Theodore, *Eulogy of Plato*, 833D–836A.

148. Mas'ūdī, *Book*, 228, and Gouillard, "Oeuvre," 37, mentioning a successful embassy that can only be this one. Mention of it seems somehow to have dropped out of its chronological place in our text of Ṭabarī, though he refers to it later as if he had already mentioned it (Brooks, "Byzantines," part 1, 742–43). I do not subscribe to the doubts expressed by Brooks at n. 141 and think the problem may be somehow related to Ṭabarī's misdating of Irene's accession to 798, the apparent date of the peace. A peace treaty seems the logical explanation for the abrupt cessation of the aggressive Arab campaigns of 797–98. See Canard, 345 n. 1, who also believes in the treaty. Irene's own propaganda is probably behind the sources' frequent word play on her name, which means "peace" in Greek. Cf. Theophanes, 456, 457; Methodius, 13–14.

149. Theophanes, 473–74.

150. Theophanes, 474.

151. On Irene's failure to tax the Church's secular holdings, see below, pp. 151 and n. 197. The Arab raids are mentioned by Ya'qūbī (Brooks, "Byzantines," part 1, 742); the construction of Hārūniyyah in 799 is mentioned by Balādhurī (ibid., part 2, 87).

152. Michael of Studius, 260A–265B; Theodore, *Eulogy of Plato*, 833D–837A; cf. Theophanes, 481, whose figure of 700 monks seems more trustworthy than Michael's figure of just over 1,000 (at 260C). On Theodore's activities, see esp. Leroy. For Irene's foundation of the Principo convent, see Theophanes, 478, and Treadgold, "Unpublished Saint's Life," 243–51.

153. Theophanes, 474–75.

154. *Annales Laureshamenses*, 38; cf. *Vita Willehadi*, 381. For a good overview of the voluminous literature that discusses the scanty source material on the significance of Charlemagne's coronation, see Classen, 537–608. Like Classen, I reject the theory of Löwe, "Kölner Notiz," that Greek legates offered the imperial title to Charlemagne. If this improbable story that is so favorable to Charlemagne were true, it would be found in better Western sources than it is.

155. Theophanes, 475; cf. Theodore, *Letters*, 1.7 (929B–933C), esp. 932D on the taxation of up to a third (the value of one of a fisherman's three fish) and on inheritance taxes; cf. Theophanes, 487 (on their later restoration), and Methodius, 14.

156. Methodius, 14, speaks of an abundant supply of goods at the same time that he speaks of the exemptions. For Irene's largesse to her officials, see Theophanes, 476–77.

157. On Irene's embassy, see *Annales Regni Francorum*, 117; *Annales Fuldenses*, 352–53; *Annales Lobienses*, 230; and *Annales Xantenses*, 224. For the rest of the story, see Theophanes, 475, 478 (noting that Charlemagne's ambassadors were still in Constantinople on November 1). Those who find it incredible that such an unrealistic proposal could be seriously discussed should consider today's occasional proposals for the peaceful union of China and Taiwan or of East and West Germany. [Especially now that Germany has united!]

158. Theophanes, 476–77. I assume that the patrician Leo Serantapechus was a member of the same family as Theophylact Serantapechus, Irene's cousin (Theophanes, 474). On Gregory, see Theophanes, 451. On Peter, see the *Synaxarium*, 791–94.

159. Theophanes, 477–78 (completing the text from the *Life of Irene the Em-*

press; see Treadgold, "Unpublished Saint's Life," 241 n. 6); see Treadgold, ibid., 243–51.

160. On the Khazars' activities, see Kennedy, 122–23.

CHAPTER THREE

161. *Chronicle of 811*, 216.

162. On Nicephorus's origins, see Ṭabarī (Brooks, "Byzantines, part 1, 743); Michael the Syrian, 15; Bar Hebraeus, 120–21; and Alexander, *Byzantine Apocalyptic Tradition*, 66 and n. 21 (a contemporary Byzantine prophecy; see pp. 276–78 and n. 383 below). Cf. Theophanes, 488, who says that Nicephorus was from territory neighboring the Phrygians and Lycaonians, which Cappadocia does. For Elpidius's remark, see Michael the Syrian, 15–16, and Bar Hebraeus, 121; cf. *Chronicle of 1234*, 2. On Nicephorus's probable career as a strategus, see above, pp. 79 and 95–96 with nn. 93 and 118.

163. That Michael was the son of Theophylact Rhangabe (on whom see above, pp. 60–61 and n. 64) is the more likely because he named his eldest son Theophylact, and naming one's eldest son after his paternal grandfather was common practice. Young Theophylact (whose monastic name was Eustratius) was born about 793, since he was twenty in 813 (Theophanes Continuatus, 20); he was the second child, after his sister Gorgo (*Life of Ignatius*, 492A–B). Stauracius's youth follows from the fact that he is always shown beardless on his father's coins and married only in 807. Nicephorus's father's name is given by Mas'ūdī, *Book*, 228, 229, etc. That Nicephorus's wife died before his accession seems clear from the fact that the lists of imperial tombs do not mention her; her name was reportedly Procopia, so that her daughter was evidently named after her (see Grierson, "Tombs," 55, who, however, thinks the necrology that he is discussing has confused Nicephorus's daughter with his wife). That Nicephorus was logothete before 797 follows from the *Life of George of Amastris*, 52–53.

164. The only explicit mention of a plot is in two related sources of dubious reliability, Michael the Syrian, 12–13, and Bar Hebraeus, 120; but it seems to follow from Irene's removal to Lesbos in November to forestall a possible revolt (Theophanes, 479) and Aëtius's replacement by Bardanes. On Irene's transfer from Principo to Lesbos, see Treadgold, "Unpublished Saint's Life," 244.

165. On Bardanes, see n. 169 below; on Nicetas, see Theophanes, 479. Note that Sisinnius, like Aëtius, was with Nicephorus on his great expedition against the Bulgars in 811 (Theophanes, 491). On Peter the Patrician's appointment, which may possibly have been later than this, see *Menologium*, 517A; the *Synaxarium*, 792, says that Nicephorus made Peter domestic of the Hicanati, which probably means that he was the effective commander of that new tagma, nominally commanded by Nicephorus's grandson; see p. 162 and n. 212 below.

166. *MGH, Epistolae*, 4: 547; *Annales Regni Francorum*, 118; *Annales Mettenses Priores*, 89; *Annales Sithienses*, 37; *Annales Fuldenses*, 353; Andrea Dandolo, 125 (on Charlemagne's recognition of Byzantine rights in Venetia and Dalmatia).

167. See Theophanes Continuatus, 8; cf. Theophanes, 478.

168. On the court in the Magnaura, see Theophanes, 478–79, 489. On Nicephorus's love of the poor and cruelty to the rich, see *Life of Nicetas of Medicium*, ch. 31, xxiv, and Theophanes, 479, 487–88. On his asceticism, see *Life of George of Amastris*, 53–54; cf. Michael the Syrian, 15–16. On his hunting, see Theophanes Continuatus, 21. On his relative who was a monk, see Theodore, *Eulogy of Plato*,

837C, and Theophanes, 493 (giving the name). Symeon often served as an intermediary between Theodore and the emperor. On Nicephorus's restoration of churches, see Scriptor Incertus, 344.

169. The main source for the rebellion is Theophanes, 479–80, which can be supplemented by Genesius, 6–8; Theophanes Continuatus, 6–10; and the *Synodicon Vetus*, 129, the last of which supplies the connection of the rebellion with Irene, which its speedy collapse after her death tends to confirm. On al-Qāsim and 'Abd al-Malik, see n. 179 below. Bardanes' revolt is also mentioned by Andrea Dandolo, 132, and John the Deacon, *Chronicon*, 100, who seem to have thought that Bardanes' Thracesian theme was a fort or town named Tarsaricum or Tarsaticum.

170. On the location of Cathara, see Janin, *Églises*, 159–60; and on Joseph's role see *Synodicon Vetus*, 129. On Bardanes' marrying Leo and Michael to his daughters, see p. 196 and n. 263 below.

171. On Nicephorus's punishment of the rebels and rewards to Leo and Michael, see Theophanes, 480; Theophanes Continuatus, 9–10; and Genesius, 8. On Euthymius and his companions Theophylact of Nicomedia and Eudoxius of Amorium, see *Synaxarium*, 345, and Gouillard, "Oeuvre," 336–41; on the exiled monks, see *Annales Regni Francorum*, 124, which mentions the capture by the Arabs of 60 men from Pantellaria in 806, evidently also exiles. On Irene's burial, see Treadgold, "Unpublished Saint's Life," 245. On the Arab raiding, see Ṭabarī (Brooks, "Byzantines," part 1, 742); cf. Yaʿqūbī (ibid., 744), who has obviously misdated these same events to A.H. 188 (803/4).

172. Ṭabarī (Brooks, "Byzantines," part 1, 742–43); Michael the Syrian, 16; Bar Hebraeus, 121; *Chronicle of 1234*, 3 (misdated); Symeon the Logothete (Leo Grammaticus, 203–4); George the Monk, 772–73 (where the incorrect date seems to be an interpolation; see Treadgold, "Chronological Accuracy," 169); and cf. Canard, 345–79 (with translations of the letters not translated by Brooks on p. 350). Ṭabarī speaks of an immediate violation of the treaty by Nicephorus and a new invasion by Hārūn inspired by a poem, but, following Canard, I reject this, which is suspiciously folkloric and presupposes a blunder by Nicephorus that Theophanes would scarcely fail to mention.

173. Theophanes, 480, puts the date of the coronation in December, and it was a custom to crown successors only on great feasts of the Church; see Treadgold, "Chronological Accuracy," 166 and n. 34.

174. Theophanes, 480–81; at 480.22, I would insert the words recorded by de Boor in his apparatus, since even if they appear in only one manuscript and not in Anastasius Bibliothecarius's translation they make an unacceptable passage satisfactory, and they do not look like an interpolation.

175. Theophanes, 481; Ṭabarī (Brooks, "Byzantines," part 1, 744). On the location of Crasus, see Ramsay, 435.

176. Ṭabarī (Brooks, "Byzantines," part 1, 744); Masʿūdī, *Book*, 255–56; Michael the Syrian, 16 (misdated); cf. Canard, 355–56, and, on the general situation, Kennedy, 123–30.

177. *Chronicle of Monemvasia*, 16–18. With the scholion of Arethas (ibid., 25–27), I would read "a strategus was sent to the Peloponnesus," not "a strategus of the Peloponnesus was sent," as in the *Chronicle*, and would conclude that this was the strategus of Hellas, the only strategus in the area at the time.

178. *Chronicle of Monemvasia*, 9–10, with translation and commentary on 13–

16 and 17–20, and Lemerle's analysis of the scholion of Arethas on 25–27. On the fortifications of Patras and the predominantly Slavic character of the land soon after the conquest, see the semilegendary account in Constantine VII, *De Administrando Imperio*, ch. 49, pp. 228–33, with Lemerle's comments in *Chronicle of Monemvasia*, 37–40.

179. Theophanes, 481; Michael the Syrian, 16; and Bar Hebraeus, 122 (the last two both misdated). On the earlier Arab destruction of Thebasa and the Byzantine attack on Adata, see above, pp. 102 and 79 and nn. 126 and 93.

180. Theophanes 481; Ṭabarī (Brooks, "Byzantines," part 1, 745, where the account of the Byzantine raid is tacked on to the beginning of the account of the Arabs' retaliatory raid the next year, and so is technically misdated); Michael the Syrian, 16; and Bar Hebraeus, 121–22 (both misdated). On the attack on Melitene, see Balādhurī (Brooks, part 2, 89, dated only to Hārūn's caliphate; but note that it was followed by a major retaliatory raid, evidently that of 806). On the revolt of the Cypriotes, see Ya'qūbī (Brooks, part 1, 745) and Ṭabarī (ibid, 746, again added before reports of a retaliatory expedition).

181. Balādhurī (Brooks, "Byzantines," part 2, 85), where the text varies between A.H. 171 and A.H. 191, which would put the Byzantines' plans to occupy Tarsus in either 787/88 or 806/7. That Irene had any such plan in 787/88, or at any other time, seems incompatible with the policies she followed toward the Arabs, but such a plan (or a report of such a plan) makes excellent sense when attributed to Nicephorus in 806. I therefore believe that the rebuilding of Tarsus in A.H. 170 (786/87), mentioned by Ṭabarī (Brooks, part 1, 740), was a distinct event, though it was the work of the same man (Abū Sulaymān Faraj), who was an experienced rebuilder of cities and still active in the frontier area in A.H. 194 (809/10); see Balādhurī (Brooks, part 2, 85).

182. On the frontier districts in general, see Von Sivers, 71–77, and Haldon and Kennedy, 106–16.

183. Theophanes, 481; *Life of Tarasius*, 419–21. See Janin, *Géographie*, 481–82, on the monastery. Cf. *Life of Nicephorus*, 153–54.

184. Note that Tarasius died the week before Lent and was buried on February 26, Thursday of the first week of Lent (Theophanes, 481). For Theodore's letter, see Theodore, *Letters*, 1.16 (960A–961A). On Symeon's stylitism, see *Acts of David*, 220. On the voting, see Theodore, *Eulogy of Plato*, 837, and *Life of Nicephorus*, 154.

185. *Life of Nicephorus*, 142–52 (on the latter page, the statement that "the rulers," in the plural, granted Nicephorus his position dates the appointment after Stauracius's coronation at the end of 803). Nicephorus was born about 758, since he died at about age 70, thirteen years after his exile in 815 (*Synaxarium*, 725). On his career before 806 and on his history, see Alexander, *Patriarch Nicephorus*, 54–64, 157–62, and Mango, "*Breviarium*."

186. Theodore, *Eulogy of Plato*, 837C (where the monk is certainly to be identified with the Symeon the monk of Theodore's letters and Theophanes, 493); Theophanes, 481; *Life of Nicephorus*, 154–58; and *Catalogi Patriarcharum*, 291 (with the information that the emperor ordered the patriarch-elect to become a monk). On the location of Nicephorus's poorhouse, which could have been either of two poorhouses north of Constantinople, see Janin, *Géographie*, 569.

187. *Synodicon Vetus*, ch. 153, p. 128; Theodore, *Eulogy of Plato*, 837D–840A (on the date); Theodore, *Letters*, 1.24 (985B, on the number of bishops), 1.25

(989C–992A) and 1.43 (1065A–B) on Theodore's presence, silence, and subsequent actions, and 1.31 (1009B, on Joseph's restoration as steward; cf. Devreesse, 55).

188. Cf. Theodore, *Great Catechesis*, 631–32, with *Synaxarium*, 731–34 (showing that Hilarion was elected abbot of Dalmatus eight years before his deposition in early 815; I do not agree with Grumel, nos. 375, 376, p. 23, that this election necessarily took place before the council that restored Joseph). On Joseph's election, see Theodore, *Letters*, 1.23 (980D–981C).

189. *Annales Regni Francorum*, 120–21, 122; Andrea Dandolo, 131; John the Deacon, *Chronicon*, 102, 103. On the lands assigned to Pepin, see *MGH, Leges* 2: 126–30. On Nicetas, see *Life of Nicetas the Patrician*.

190. Theophanes, 482; Ya'qūbī and Ṭabarī (Brooks, "Byzantines," part 1, 745–46); Balādhurī (ibid., part 2, 85–86, on rebuilding Tarsus); Mas'ūdī, *Prairies* 2: 337–52 (especially on the advice Hārūn did not take); Michael the Syrian, 16 (garbled and misdated). On the whole campaign, see Canard. On the identification and location of the Byzantine strongholds involved, see Hild and Restle, 74–75, and their later entries on each. In view of Theophanes' extreme hostility to Nicephorus, I follow him on the amount of the tribute instead of Ṭabarī, who puts it at a somewhat higher 50,000 nomismata, including the six nomismata of head tax; presumably the 300,000 nomismata that Ṭabarī says Nicephorus was to pay eventually included several years' future payments. Since Michael is attested as bishop of Synnada in 787, 812, 814, and 815, and in 812 and probably in 803 served as an ambassador, it seems safe to identify him with the anonymous bishop of Synnada of 806 mentioned by Theophanes.

191. *Annales Regni Francorum*, 122 (on the blockade of the Frank-held port of Treviso), 124; Andrea Dandolo, 131; John the Deacon, *Chronicon*, 103–4.

192. Theophanes, 482; cf. pp. 148–50 and nn. 194 and 195 below.

193. Ya'qūbī, Ṭabarī, and *Kitāb al-'Uyūn* (Brooks, "Byzantines," part 1, 746–47); Balādhurī (ibid., part 2, 85–86, on the rebuilding of Tarsus); Michael the Syrian, 17–21 (on Hārūn's troubles in 807 with the Christians of northern Syria); Theophanes, 483 (on Ḥumayd's expedition), and Constantine VII, *De Administrando Imperio*, ch. 49 (on the Slav revolt with Arab help, a semilegendary account that fits conditions in 807 so well that it probably has a factual basis). Theophanes, 482, mentions an expedition sent by Hārūn when he learned that Nicephorus had rebuilt the forts but says that it took Thebasa again; since the Arab sources for the retaliatory expeditions indicate that the Arabs did not get so far, Theophanes seems to have intentionally or unintentionally misreported the facts.

194. See below, p. 157 and n. 205.

195. Theophanes, 482–83; cf. 486 (for the census), 485 (on Serdica's civilian population).

196. On Leo III's census, see Theophanes, 410 (referring only to Leo's counting male infants, but the tax increases in Sicily and Calabria suggest a wider reform, which Theophanes has distorted to fit his comparison of Leo to the pharaoh of Exodus).

197. Theophanes, 486–87, entered under 809/10, when I believe the census ended. These passages are much discussed; I myself have revised my view of them somewhat, and other interpretations differ somewhat from mine. See especially Bury, 212–18, and Bratianu, 195–211. On the sale of liturgical vessels and Nicephorus's unpopularity with the clergy, cf. Theophanes, 489, a general passage that cannot necessarily be dated to the year 811, under which it is entered; note

that it follows a general reference to the court of the Magnaura, which was set up in 802 or 803 (cf. Theophanes, 478–79).

198. Theophanes, 483.

199. Theophanes, 483–84; on George Syncellus, see Theophanes, 3–4, and Mango, "Who Wrote the Chronicle?"

200. Theodore, *Letters,* 1.31 (1009A–1013C, to the monks of Saccudium on Joseph's interview), 1.24 (981D–988B, Theodore's letter to Theoctistus), 1.26 (992B–993B, on his appeals to the patriarch, Symeon, and the emperor), 1.21 (969C–980C, Plato's letters to Symeon), and 1.23 (980D, on Joseph's appeal to the emperor).

201. On the expedition of Nicephorus and Stauracius, see Theodore, *Letters,* 1.26 (992D). On the truce and exchange of prisoners, see Mas'ūdī, *Book,* 256–57; Ṭabarī (Brooks "Byzantines," part 1, 747); and Michael the Syrian, 16 (garbled, but probably referring to this exchange). On Paul the Patrician's expedition, see *Annales Regni Francorum,* 127.

202. Theodore, *Letters,* 1.48 (1073B–C).

203. Theodore, *Letters,* 1.48 (1073C–D, 1072B–1073B). On the synod, see Henry, 509–19. On the exiles, see Theodore, *Eulogy of Plato,* 840C–841C, and Pseudo-Michael, 160B–161D.

204. See Theophanes, 484, on the Byzantines' awareness of Hārūn's death and the civil war, and Ṭabarī (Brooks, "Byzantines," part 1, 747), who says that the Arabs made no summer raid from 807 to 830, though in fact there seems to have been such a raid in 825 (see p. 248 and n. 343 below). On the civil war in general, see Kennedy, 135–62.

205. Theophanes, 484–85; on payment of Byzantine armies, see Treadgold, *Byzantine State Finances,* 12–31, 69–81.

206. Theophanes, 485–86. Though Theophanes insinuates that Nicephorus did not actually take Krum's palace, he is so hostile to the emperor that in the absence of a flat denial we should believe Nicephorus's word that he did so. On the payment of the soldiers of the tagmata during Holy Week, see Liudprand, 6.10 (the soldiers, of course, received less than a pound of gold).

207. *Annales Regni Francorum,* 127.

208. Theophanes, 486 and (on all ages' having to join the colonists) 487. On the Mardaïtes, cf. Theophanes Continuatus, 303–4, 311.

209. On the foundation and troop strengths of these and the other themes and tagma mentioned below, see Treadgold, *Byzantine State Finances,* 69–72, 16–18. A strategus of Peloponnesus (Leo Sclerus) is first mentioned in the sources in late 812, but as if one had existed before that date (Scriptor Incertus, 336). That Corinth had been the capital of Hellas seems evident from Constantine VII, *De Administrando Imperio,* ch. 49, p. 229 (though, probably through an anachronism, it is there called the capital of Peloponnesus) and from the *Chronicle of Monemvasia,* 10 (cf. 17–18 and 25–27), which says that before 805 the strategus (evidently of Hellas) had been sent to the eastern Peloponnesus. That Athens was the headquarters of the other drungus of Hellas seems likely, because it was there that the then-strategus of Hellas had interned the sons of Constantine V beginning in 797, and that some soldiers of Hellas had begun a conspiracy in their favor in 799. On Thebes as the later headquarters of Hellas, see Koder and Hild, 269–70. On Sparta, Methone, and Corone, see *Chronicle of Monemvasia,* 10.

210. Paul is not given the title of strategus of Cephalonia in late 808 and early

809, but by early 810, when he arrived in Dalmatia, he is; see *Annales Regni Francorum*, 127, 130. Though the Latin translation of Paul's title (*praefectus*) could also be used of an archon, heading an expedition of this importance and holding Paul's high rank of patrician are incompatible with the low status of an archon. On the transfer of the bishop and name of Nicopolis to Naupactus, see Soustal, 53–54, 213–14, though I would date the change to the time of the Slavic invasion rather than to that of an Arab raid under Michael II (in which I do not believe). Adrianopolis (Dryinopolis) was Byzantine by the time of the church council of 869 (Mansi 16:194C), and Joannina by the time of that of 879 (Mansi 17:377B); Nicephorus's reign seems the likely time for an extension of Byzantine control into this area. The archontate of Dalmatia was evidently created between 806, when there was still a virtually independent duke of Jadera (*dux Jaderae*), and 821, when an archon (*praefectus provinciae*), is attested; see *Annales Regni Francorum*, 120–21, 155–56; cf. *Tacticon Uspensky*, 57.

211. The theme of Thessalonica is first mentioned (together with the themes of Thrace and Macedonia) in a letter of Michael II to Louis the Pious, referring to the year 821 (Mansi, 14:418C–D). Beroea and Larissa were both Byzantine by 869 (Mansi, 16:194B, 191C), and, again, Nicephorus's reign seems the probable time for their region to have been annexed. On the settlers sent to the Strymon valley, see Theophanes, 496.

212. See *Life of Ignatius*, 492B, which says that Nicetas was ten when he became domestic of the new tagma. The text also says that Nicetas was fourteen when Michael I was deposed on July 11, 813, so that the tagma must have been created between July 12, 808, and July 10, 810. On the sons of the officers, see *Chronicle of 811*, 210. On Peter the Patrician's military career, see both the *Synaxarium*, 791–92, and the *Menologium*, 517A. These two entries seem to be independently abstracted from a common source, and I have accepted the (fully compatible) information in both. The *Synaxarium* says simply that Peter was domestic of the Hicanati, but if the explanation suggested here is correct, the contradiction with the *Life of Ignatius* is only apparent.

213. Theophanes, 486 and (on land given to the Paulicians) 488. On the population of Sparta, see the *Chronicle of Monemvasia*, 10 (cf. p. 20 and n. 28). On the people of Sisium, who arrived between 808 and 810, see Balādhurī (Brooks, "Byzantines," part 2, 86).

214. Theophanes, 486 and (on Nicephorus's motives) 487. The more favorable views of Nicephorus are in the *Chronicle of Monemvasia*, 10–11, and in Constantine VII, *De Administrando Imperio*, ch. 49, p. 230, the latter reporting "unwritten tradition" in the Peloponnesus.

215. *Chronicle of Monemvasia*, 10; Constantine VII, *De Administrando Imperio*, ch. 49, 230–32.

216. On the forced sales, see Theophanes, 487. At Theophanes, 486, where the two types of colonists are described, note that the description at the outset of Nicephorus as "having planned by means of these godless punishments to impoverish the army utterly" refers to the punishment of the mutinous troops of the tagmata in the spring of 809, described immediately before. It certainly does not refer to the program of colonization, as I and others, reading the passage out of context, have sometimes maintained. On the rapidity of the conversion of the Peloponnesian Slavs, see the *Chronicle of Monemvasia*, 10–11.

217. On the increase in the army payroll, see below, pp. 358–59 and n. 479.

218. Theophanes, 487–88.

219. Theophanes, 487. For a few examples of interest rates in the later medieval West, see Lopez and Raymond, 105 and n. 75 (30 percent, 43 percent, and 94 percent).

220. *Annales Regni Francorum*, 130, 132, 133–34; Andrea Dandolo, 132–33, 139–40; John the Deacon, *Chronicon*, 104–6; *Chronicon Altinate*, 52–54 (a partly legendary account); Constantine VII, *De Administrando Imperio*, ch. 28, p. 120 (only slightly inaccurate).

221. *Annales Regni Francorum*, 133–34. For the letter, see *MGH, Epistolae*, 4: 546–48.

222. Theophanes, 488.

223. Theophanes, 488.

224. Theophanes, 489; cf. *Chronicle of 811*, 210–12. On Nicephorus's supporters, see pp. 130–31 and n. 168 above.

225. On Nicephorus's intentions, see *Chronicle of 811*, 210.

226. Ṭabarī and Yaʿqūbī (Brooks, "Byzantines," part 1, 747, citing the latter twice); Balādhurī (ibid., part 2, 85); Theophanes, 489; Theophanes Continuatus, 10–11; Scriptor Incertus, 336. On the later location of the headquarters at Amasia, see ibn al-Faqīh (Brooks, "Arabic Lists," 76).

227. On the recall of the Studites, see Theodore, *Eulogy of Plato*, 841D–844A (implying plans to restore the Studite community), and Theodore, *Letters*, 2.109 (1369B) and Pseudo-Michael, 164A–C (though Theodore's prophecy of Nicephorus's death is clearly *ex eventu*).

228. On Nicephorus's tolerance of Paulicians, Athingans, and Nicholas the hermit, see Theophanes, 488–89. On the Athingans, see Rochow, "Häresie"; and on the Paulicians, see Lemerle, "Histoire."

229. Theophanes, 489–90. This general logothete was probably the same as the Nicetas the Patrician mentioned on p. 144 above. Mango, "Who Wrote the Chronicle?" 14–15, argues plausibly that Theophanes is most unlikely to have been in Constantinople to hear Theodosius say these words; but they seem to me so patently bogus that I find this a weak argument for attributing the passage to George Syncellus, as Mango would do.

230. See Theophanes, 490, 491; *Chronicle of 811*, 210.

231. Theophanes, 489 (for the date of departure), 490; the servant was named Byzantius. Theophanes, perhaps deliberately, overlooks the obvious purpose of the feints. At 490.11, our text of Theophanes appears to be at fault, because the *Chronicle of 811* twice (p. 212) says that Nicephorus spent fifteen days in Bulgaria, which indeed seems a minimum for all he did there, though if he entered Bulgaria on July 20 he would have been there only six days by the twenty-sixth. Therefore, emend from July 20 (κ') to 11 (ια'), a plausible copyist's error.

232. Theophanes, 490; *Chronicle of 811*, 210–12; and *Synaxarium* (on Nicholas the Monk), 343–44. Here the *Chronicle* speaks of a garrison of 12,000 and a relief force of 50,000, while the story of Nicholas speaks only of a force of 15,000, "a bit more or less." Since these forces were reportedly annihilated, the Byzantines should have been able to make a reasonably accurate body count, yet the figure of 50,000 for the second force is incredible. Without claiming any certainty, I would conjecture that the 50,000 of the *Chronicle* is an error for the 15,000 mentioned in the story of Nicholas. On the victory banquet, see also *Menologium*, 556B (on the martyrs in Bulgaria).

233. Theophanes, 490; *Chronicle of 811*, 212.

234. Theophanes, 490–91; *Chronicle of 811*, 212–14. The *Chronicle*, like some commemorations in the *Synaxarium* (pp. 837–38 but not 846–48), dates the battle

to July 23; but by calling this a Saturday it shows its confusion (probably due to a copyist's error somewhere), since it was July 26 that was a Saturday. Otherwise, I would reconcile the apparent inconsistencies between Theophanes and the *Chronicle*, which both seem to be based on good firsthand accounts, by supposing that Theophanes drew his information from high officers (he quotes words Nicephorus addressed only to them) while the *Chronicle's* author relied on sources of lower rank, who were not told about the palisades. To those not informed of the alarming facts, it seemed that the emperor had suddenly become confused and incapable of action and was quarreling senselessly with his son and generals, though in fact the emperor was struggling with a desperate situation and trying to avoid panicking his army. During the battle, it seemed that the Bulgars had constructed their palisades while Nicephorus was doing nothing, though in fact Nicephorus's paralysis was a result rather than a cause of the Bulgars' building the barriers. After the battle, many of the survivors never learned or guessed the truth. The conjecture seems confirmed by the fact that Theophanes, much as he hates Nicephorus, never accuses him of the utter incompetence attributed to him in the *Chronicle*, but only of pride.

235. Theophanes, 491; *Chronicle of 811*, 212–14.

236. Theophanes, 491–92; *Chronicle of 811*, 214–16. Though Theophanes, writing before 815, believed that Peter the Patrician had died, in fact he seems to have been captured, escaped, and, evidently without his fate becoming generally known, retired to a monastery; see *Synaxarium*, 792, and *Menologium*, 517A.

237. On the Byzantines' replacement of their losses, cf. Scriptor Incertus, 336, 337, 340. On the desertions, see *Synaxarium*, 343–44 (Nicholas), 792 (Peter), and *Menologium*, 517A–B (also on Peter).

238. Theophanes, 492; the date for Stauracius's proclamation is deduced plausibly by Bury, 16 n. 2, from the length of Stauracius's reign as recorded by Theophanes, 495.

239. Theophanes, 492. On the rumor, which under the circumstances someone could scarcely fail to think of, see Michael the Syrian, 70; Michael is often unreliable but in this case cites a contemporary Byzantine source from Constantinople, who should at least have known what the rumors were.

240. Theophanes, 492–93 and (on Stauracius's death) 495. At 493.14, read (with Dölger, 47, no. 384) τυποῦσθαι for τύπτεσθαι, and at 493.30, read αὐτὸν for αὐτοῦ. On Michael's residence at the Palace of the Mangana, see Theophanes Continuatus, 12.

241. For Michael's appearance, see Scriptor Incertus, 341, incorporating the readings and emendations of Browning, "Notes," 407. On the name "Rhangabe," see Grégoire, "Rangabé."

242. Theophanes, 493–94 (quotation from 494); Scriptor Incertus, 335–36.

243. Scriptor Incertus, 336; Theophanes Continuatus, 12; Theophanes, 494.

244. Theophanes, 494; *Synaxarium*, 373 (on Gregory of Acritas); *Annales Regni Francorum*, 136; *MGH*, *Epistolae* 4:556 (Charlemagne's reply); and see the patriarch Nicephorus's letter to Pope Leo, *PG* 100: 169–200, esp. 196D–197B, where he mentions the emperor Nicephorus's preventing him from writing.

245. Theophanes, 494; Scriptor Incertus, 335.

246. Theophanes, 494–95; Theodore, *Letters*, 23 (p. 21 Cozza-Luzi) and 2.155 (1485C Migne); *Life of Nicephorus*, 158–59 (where "Jews" and "Phrygians" seem both to be ways of referring to the Athingans); and Peter the Sicilian, chs. 175–76, p. 65. See also the comments of Grumel, nos. 383 and 384, pp. 26–27, though

since I interpret the *Life of Nicephorus* differently from Grumel, I do not believe that real Jews were involved, but only the supposedly Judaizing Athingans.

247. On the new recruits under Michael, see Scriptor Incertus, 336. On Develtus, see Theophanes, 495.

248. Theophanes, 495–96; here at least some of the evil advisers can be identified with the Studites, because of the evidence given in n. 246 above identifying them as the evil advisers who stopped the executions of the Athingans and Paulicians; cf. Theodore's association with evil advisers at Theophanes, 498. On Michael's reputation for being dominated by his wife, see Scriptor Incertus, 335. On the fall of Serres, which is not specifically mentioned by Theophanes, see Beševliev, *Protobulgarische Inschriften*, no. 16, pp. 177–78.

249. Theophanes, 496–97. On the soldiers' discharge, see Nicephorus, *Antirrhetici*, 3.492A–493B, and *Apologeticus*, 556B–D, referring to a sizable group of iconoclast soldiers discharged from the tagmata before 815 whose discharge cannot plausibly be dated to any other time than 812. I cannot accept the rickety conjectures of Alexander, *Patriarch Nicephorus*, 111–25, to explain these passages. Probably the sons of Constantine had been imprisoned in a monastery on Panormos, which was later known as Antigone, and were later transferred to another monastery on Aphusia; see Janin, *Églises*, 63–65, 200–201, where the present references are omitted and the monasteries' foundations are therefore probably dated too late. Some of the Athingans were apparently transported to the Aegean islands, since some were soon to be found on Aegina; see *Life of Athanasia*, 213.

250. *Annales Regni Francorum*, 136; *Annales Fuldenses*, 355; *Poeta Saxo*, 264; *Annales Xantenses*, 224; MGH, *Epistolae*, 4: 555–56; Andrea Dandolo, 141, 125 (the latter mentioning an earlier proposal for peace in Venetia and Dalmatia that was ratified only now). On the pope's judgment, see Michael of Studius, 272D–273A; cf. Theodore, *Eulogy of Plato*, 844A–B.

251. Theophanes, 497; cf. Yaʿqūbī (Brooks, "Byzantines," part 1, 747). On Camachum, see Balādhurī (ibid., part 2, 88), who dates the Arabs' loss of the fort between October 810 and September 813; conditions in the empire make 812 the most likely year. The Byzantines finally secured and rebuilt Camachum in 817; see below, p. 219 and n. 299.

252. Theophanes, 497–99; Theophanes Continuatus, 12–13. On the fate of the Byzantine prisoners in Bulgaria, see *Synaxarium*, 838, 847–48, and *Menologium*, 556B–C, all of which speak about the martyrdoms in vague and conventional terms.

253. Theophanes, 499; cf. Kennedy, 141–48, 167–69.

254. Theophanes, 500–501; Scriptor Incertus, 336–37; Theophanes Continuatus, 13–14.

255. Theophanes, 501; on the identity of these soldiers see n. 249 above.

256. Scriptor Incertus, 337–39; Theophanes, 501–2; Theophanes Continuatus, 14–16; Genesius, 4. On the Bulgars' capture of Versinicia and Scutarium, see Beševliev, *Protobulgarische Inschriften*, nos. 18, 31, pp. 178–79, 185–86.

257. Theophanes, 502; Theophanes Continuatus, 16–20; Genesius, 4–6; Scriptor Incertus, 339–41; *Life of Ignatius*, 492; *Life of Nicephorus*, 163–64.

258. Theophanes, 494, 496. Though neither Theophanes nor the *Chronicle of 811* appears to make direct use of the Parable of the Rich Fool in Luke 12:16–21 and both accuse Nicephorus of worse sins than folly, to many who were less hostile to Nicephorus the parable must have seemed about right.

259. On the works of Tarasius, Stephen, and Constantine, see in the first place

Beck, *Kirche*, 489, 508, 546, and his references, though Beck slightly misdates Stephen's work (written 42 years after St. Stephen's death in 764; see *Life of Stephen*, 1072C–D) and Constantine's (written perhaps between 796 and 806; see Halkin's introduction to Constantine of Tius, 81–82, though Ševčenko, 124 and n. 87, disputes the date). On Stephen's use of his model, see Gill (including some other, less important debts). On Anthusa, see Mango, "St. Anthusa"; on Theophanes, see Treadgold, "Indirectly Preserved Source." A number of entries in the *Synaxarium* and *Menologium* probably derive from saints' lives written at this time, though this cannot be proved. The most likely candidates, aside from the entry discussed by Mango, "St. Anthusa," are *Synaxarium*, 62–64 (Hypatius and Andrew), 98 (Michael of Zobe; cf. *Menologium*, 80–81), 99–100 and 125–30 (Theophilus the Younger; cf. *Menologium*, 84), 173–78 (Anna-Euphemianus), 195–98 (Gregory of Alexandria), 310–12 (Bacchus the Younger; cf. *Menologium*, 212–13), 434 (Theophilus the Strategus; cf. *Menologium*, 286–87), 515–16 and 673–74 (Hesychius of Andrapa; cf. *Menologium*, 445–48), and 922 (George the Limnaeote; cf. *Menologium*, 604), and *Menologium*, 580 (Julian and companions).

260. On Nicephorus, George, Theophanes, and their lost predecessor, see Hunger, 1: 344–47, 331–32, 334–39, 345–46, and his references, supplemented now by Whitby and esp. Mango, "*Breviarium*." On the circumstances of Theophanes' taking over George's work, see Theophanes, 3–4.

261. On Theodore and his brother Joseph, see Beck, *Kirche*, 491–96, 505–6, partially updated by Frazee. For Theodore's praise of Nicephorus, see Theodore, *Letters*, 1.16 (960A). At *Letters*, 1.26 (992D–993A), he seems to look favorably upon "the expedition of our pious ruler" in 808, and his favoring war with the Bulgars later would be consistent with such a view. At *Letters*, 2.218 (1660B), Theodore notes that Nicephorus, though avaricious, was completely Orthodox.

CHAPTER FOUR

262. On Leo's origins, see George the Monk, 780–82; Genesius, 21; Theophanes Continuatus, 6–7; and Pseudo-Symeon, 603; cf. Toumanoff, 50 n. 228, who, differing with earlier scholars, explains the sources' references to Leo's parents as part-Assyrian parricides by identifying them as Gnuni rather than Artsruni. On the migration of the 50,000 Armenians to the empire, see above, p. 92 and n. 113.

263. On Leo's appearance, see Pseudo-Symeon, 603. That Leo's wife, Barca (cf. Genesius, 5, and Theophanes Continuatus, 18), was Bardanes' daughter is an inference, but an almost certain one. Genesius, 22–23, and Theophanes Continuatus, 44–45, both tell the story that Michael the Amorian won his first wife when he was in the service of a strategus of the Anatolics who, having learned through a prophecy that Michael and another of his aides would become emperors, married two of his daughters to them. The strategus and the other aide are not named, but Michael came to prominence only about 802 under Bardanes, who was then strategus of the Anatolics, and the only other aide of Bardanes' who became an emperor is Leo the Armenian. Both Genesius, 6–7, and Theophanes Continuatus, 7–8, record separately that when Bardanes was strategus of the Anatolics (802–3) he heard a prophecy that Michael and Leo would become emperors. Such prophecies are presumably fictions produced after the fact, but this is all the more reason for believing that what they prophesied is factual. (Bury, 79–80, failing to make

this connection, can only conclude that the prophecy was partly wrong.) Note also that in Petrus, ch. 16, 392B–C, Leo is called the ἐξάδελφος of Bardanes' son Bryenes, a word that usually means "cousin" or "nephew" but here makes far better sense as "brother-in-law." That Leo, Michael, and Thomas were spatharii rather than staff officers seems clear from Theophanes Continuatus, 6–7, where they are called Bardanes' "spear carriers and assistants," and from the fact that later when Leo was made turmarch and Michael count of the tent these were clearly promotions.

264. On Michael's sponsorship of Leo's son, see Theophanes Continuatus, 24, where Leo is described as a "fellow father" with Michael. Leo can hardly have sponsored a son of Michael's, because Michael's youngest son, Nicetas, was born in 799, when Leo was still an unknown soldier; cf. *Life of Ignatius*, 492A–B. Admittedly, the same *Life of Ignatius*, 492C, states that Leo had sponsored Michael's children (in the plural!), but I take this statement to be a mistaken deduction by the late author of the *Life*, probably based on a correct but vague reference like that cited here from Theophanes Continuatus. Since Leo could only have married Barca late in 802 or early in 803, Symbatius was born no earlier than 803; since he attended a church council in 815 (to be sure, in a ceremonial capacity; see Scriptor Incertus, 360), he was probably not born much later. That Leo and Barca had no more children over some eleven years may itself be an indication that all was not well with their marriage; cf. n. 265 below.

265. On Theoctistus's monastic retirement, see Pseudo-Michael, 220A; on Stephen as magister, see Theodore, *Letters*, 2.76 (1313A–1316A), where Theodore's close friendship with the addressee seems to confirm the identification with the former domestic of the Schools. On Leo's appointments of Manuel, Thomas, and Michael, see Genesius, 9–10, and Theophanes Continuatus, 23–24, 110. On Leo's standing godfather for Theophilus, see Treadgold, "Problem," 337–38. On Procopia's remark, see Genesius, 5, and Theophanes Continuatus, 18; Barca was evidently, as indicated above, the daughter of the patrician Bardanes Turcus. That Barca was neither buried nor proclaimed as an empress is shown by her absence from the list of imperial tombs in Constantine VII, *De Ceremoniis*, 642–49 (esp. 645), and from the list of empresses in Nicephorus, *Chronographicon*, 105 (note, by contrast, the presence of Thecla in both places, and Michael's deep grief at her death according to Theophanes Continuatus, 78). For Michael's comment on Leo's marriage, see Genesius, 15, and Pseudo-Symeon, 609–10, both specifically referring to Leo's marriage to Theodosia. For Theodore of Studius's view of this marriage, see his *Letters*, 2.204 (1620B–21D). Alexander, *Patriarch Nicephorus*, 132 n. 5, was the first to suggest that Leo had repudiated Barca before marrying Theodosia.

266. Theophanes, 502, mentions Leo's original letter with its assurances of Orthodoxy, and implies that Nicephorus considered it binding; this is evidently the written pledge of Orthodoxy referred to by the Scriptor Incertus, 340–41, 349, and Symeon the Logothete (Leo Grammaticus, 207). Leo's evasion of signing Nicephorus's formal pledge is recorded in the *Life of Nicephorus*, 163–64, and later by Genesius, 20, and Theophanes Continuatus, 29. In reconciling these apparently discordant accounts I follow Bury, 56–57.

267. On the confiscation, see Scriptor Incertus, 341; on Michael's earlier ownership of the Palace of the Mangana, see Theophanes Continuatus, 12; on the estates attached to it, which were later reorganized by Basil I, see Theophanes Continuatus, 337; and on the imperial curator, whose duties in Thrace imply that he

administered the estates as well as the palaces, see *Life of Nicetas of Medicium*, xxvi–vii. All these passages are discussed in Treadgold, "Bulgars' Treaty," p. 216 n. 17. On Michael's allowance, see Genesius, 6.

268. Theophanes, 503; Scriptor Incertus, 342–44; Pseudo-Symeon, 612–14; Symeon the Logothete (Leo Grammaticus, 207–8). Though I cannot prove that the Bulgars took uncovering the head to be a sign of disrespect for the khan, I cannot make sense of the incident on any other supposition.

269. Scriptor Incertus, 344, Pseudo-Symeon, 614–15; Theophanes, 503; Symeon the Logothete (Leo Grammaticus, 208, 231). Our only fixed dates are that Krum arrived before Constantinople on July 17 and evidently took Adrianople by August 31, since Theophanes records its fall under A.M. 6305, which ended then. The raid on St. Mamas would have occurred roughly on July 20, beginning raids that lasted until August 20 or so. That Didymoteichus was taken by the Bulgars seems clear from Beševliev, *Protobulgarische Inschriften*, no. 21, pp. 180–81, and its location on the Hebrus indicates that it would have been taken at this time.

270. Scriptor Incertus, 344–45; Pseudo-Symeon, 615; Theophanes, 503; Theophanes Continuatus, 216–17; *Synaxarium*, 414–16; *Menologium*, 276; Symeon the Logothete (Leo Grammaticus, 208, 231; but on the numbers taken, see above, p. 41 and n. 40). On this Bulgarian "Macedonia," see the perceptive explanation of Bury, 356 and n. 5, 370 and n. 3. On its location, see below, pp. 290–91 and n. 397.

271. On Theodosia's parentage, see Genesius, 15, and Theophanes Continuatus, 35, passages that also indicate Leo was on good terms with his wife in 820 and was willing to take her advice even against his better judgment. On Arsaber, patrician and quaestor, whose name (Arsavir) is Armenian, see pp. 153–54 and n. 199 above. Theodosia was well established as empress by the end of 814 or beginning of 815, when Nicephorus showed his confidence in her by appealing to her on the issue of Iconoclasm (*Life of Nicephorus*, 189). Theodore of Studius praises her iconophilism in a letter to her and her son Basil written about 823 (Theodore, *Letters*, 2.204 [1620B–1621D]). Basil was old enough to talk in 820, since when he was castrated he temporarily lost the ability to speak (Pseudo-Symeon, 619, and Theophanes Continuatus, 46–47, where Basil is carelessly confused with Symbatius-Constantine). Especially because Pseudo-Symeon indicates that Basil had two younger brothers, Gregory and Theodosius, both born by 820, it seems likely that Basil was born by 815 and Theodosia married to Leo by early 814. An attempt to reassure iconophiles makes more sense before Leo crowned and renamed his son on Christmas 813, showing an inclination toward Iconoclasm. The right date for the marriage may therefore be late in 813, just after a speedy divorce.

272. Scriptor Incertus, 346; Pseudo-Symeon, 616.

273. Scriptor Incertus, 346–47; Pseudo-Symeon, 616–17; and, for the captures of Sozopolis, Bizya, and Burtudizum, which seem most likely to be connected with this expedition, see Beševliev, *Protobulgarische Inschriften*, nos. 28, 27, 20, pp. 184, 179–80.

274. For the inscription at Constantia (Harmanli), our source for these administrative measures, see Beševliev, *Protobulgarische Inschriften*, no. 47, pp. 220–29. For the reasons stated, I doubt that the missing part of the inscription for the Left Side included Adrianople. Philippopolis and Serdica, on the other hand, were even farther from Constantinople than Beroea, and together with it they would make a province similar in importance to that of Develtus, Anchialus, Sozopolis, and the unknown town of "Ranuli."

275. Scriptor Incertus, 347–48; Pseudo-Symeon, 617 (giving the number of oxen correctly, though the text of the Scriptor Incertus is defective here).

276. Scriptor Incertus, 348; Pseudo-Symeon, 617–13. For a description of the surviving part of Leo's wall, see Meyer-Plath and Schneider, 2: 119–20. On the embassy, see *Annales Regni Francorum*, 140–41; *Annales Laurissenses Minores*, 122; *Annales Xantenses*, 224; *Vita Hludowici*, 619.

277. Scriptor Incertus, 348; Pseudo-Symeon, 618. On the Bulgarian succession, see *Synaxarium*, 415.

278. Scriptor Incertus, 348; Pseudo-Symeon, 618–19. Leo's contention that he had gravely wounded Krum was conveyed by his ambassadors to the West, where it was believed; see *Annales Regni Francorum*, 139, and Andrea Dandolo, 140 (cf. John the Deacon, *Chronicon*, 106), where the fall of Adrianople is put before Leo's accession and Leo appears as the vanquisher of Krum.

279. Scriptor Incertus, 349.

280. On John's commission, see Scriptor Incertus, 352. On John's family name, see Theophanes Continuatus, 154, and Pseudo-Symeon, 649 (reading Μωροχαρζανίων with John Scylitzes, 84). On John's birthdate, note that he was considered "young and obscure" by some in 815 (Scriptor Incertus, 359), and that he had a brother, Arsaber, who was still alive in 865 (Theophanes Continuatus, 156–57, referring to a time when Basil the Macedonian was paracoemomenus, which he was only from 865 to 866; see Mango, "Eudocia," 22–24), though he died before 867 (cf. Theophanes Continuatus, 175, assuming that the editor has wrongly supplied the words in line 4; see Bury, 156 n. 1). John's Armenian origin follows from the names of his father (apparently Bagrat) and his brother (certainly Arsavir). For John's association with the Monastery of the Hodegetria in 813, see the *Interpolated Letter to Theophilus*, 368A–B, and Janin, *Géographie*, 199–200; this is the only plausible time to date John's activity as an icon painter, mentioned by Photius, *Homilies*, 15.1, 140. On his promotion to abbot of Sts. Sergius and Bacchus, see Theophanes Continuatus, 154, and Pseudo-Symeon, 649. That he was already abbot before 815 is plain from Theodore, *Letters*, 2.168 (1532C), where Theodore addresses him cordially as "Your Holiness"; like this one, Theodore's other letters to John (2.194, 2.211) show John's reputation for intellectual and spiritual distinction. For a fuller discussion of John, see Lemerle, *Premier Humanisme*, 135–46, who for reasons I do not find persuasive dates John's birth as early as the 770's.

281. Scriptor Incertus, 350–52; *Life of Nicetas of Medicium*, ch. 31, xxiv; Pseudo-Symeon, 606–7; *Life of Nicephorus*, 165 and (for the fact that Eutychianus was protoasecretis) 189–90. The story of John's recantation, told in the *Interpolated Letter to Theophilus*, 372A–B, and Photius, *Homilies*, 15.1, 140, must come after the appointment of the commission on Pentecost and before Anthony arrived in July. Though it is slightly odd that the Scriptor Incertus does not mention the incident, he does say that the commissioners at first found nothing helpful for their purpose, and Photius (who was John's nephew; see below, p. 280–81 and n. 386) is a reliable source and supports the less reliable *Interpolated Letter*. Since the Scriptor Incertus loathes John and Anthony (as he shows by pejorative rhetoric and gossip about them, which I have omitted here), he may not have wished to record that Nicephorus had put up with them so patiently when their intentions were so plain.

282. Scriptor Incertus, 352–53.

283. Scriptor Incertus, 353–55; unlike Alexander, *Patriarch Nicephorus*, 129 and n. 1, I believe that the two references to a meeting of the Orthodox in the Scriptor Incertus, 354, 355, refer to a single meeting, just as the Scriptor Incertus, 350, 352, refers twice to Leo's appointment of John to collect iconoclastic references in old books.

284. Scriptor Incertus, 354, 355 (on which see n. 283 above); *Life of Theophylact*, 77–79; *Life of Nicetas of Medicium*, ch. 32, xxiv; *Interpolated Letter to Theophilus*, 373B–C. In the last source cited, I am inclined to accept the figure of about 270 "fathers" for all those present, differing with Grumel, no. 393, p. 31, who thinks that the number refers only to the bishops and consequently finds it dubious; however, I too doubt whether the assembly anathematized Anthony of Syllaeum, as the *Interpolated Letter* says, since the other sources do not say this and it would have been a more direct challenge to Leo than the iconophiles seem to have been ready to make at that point. The presence of Theodore of Studius and Peter of Nicaea at the meeting follows from their being mentioned by the *Life of Nicetas of Medicium*, chs. 34–35, xxv. On the death of Plato on April 4, 814, see Pargoire, "À quelle date?"

285. Scriptor Incertus, 355–57; *Life of Nicetas of Medicium*, chs. 32–35, xxiv–xxv. I have harmonized these two perfectly compatible reports, leaving aside the heavily rhetorical account in the *Life of Nicephorus*, 167–89.

286. Scriptor Incertus, 357; *Life of Nicephorus*, 189–90. In the latter text, for the identification of the general logothete (whose title is given periphrastically) cf. Theodore, *Letters*, 2.82 (1324A–D), addressed to Demochares under that title and praising his efforts against Iconoclasm. For the identification of the iconoclast patrician named as sacristan, cf. Scriptor Incertus, 358. On the exile of the staff of St. Sophia, see the *Life of Nicetas of Medicium*, ch. 36, xxv.

287. Scriptor Incertus, 357–59; *Life of Nicetas of Medicium*, ch. 36, xxv; *Life of Nicephorus*, 190–201. The first of these texts mentions the first day of Lent as the date when the delegation arrived at the patriarchate, while the second text (and the *Synaxarium*, 534) mentions it as the date of Nicephorus's abdication. Both are presumably correct. See also *Life of Nicholas of Studius*, 880C–881A.

288. Scriptor Incertus, 359–60; *Life of Nicetas of Medicium*, chs. 36, 37, xxv. On Theodore's procession and other activities, see Pseudo-Michael, 185B–188C; and, for Theodore's letter, see his *Letters*, 2.1 (116C–120A).

289. Scriptor Incertus, 360–61; *Life of Nicetas of Medicium*, ch. 37, xxv; *Life of Nicephorus*, 202–5. For the decree of the council, see the edition in Alexander, "Iconoclastic Council," 58–66.

290. On the exile of the bishops in general, see Scriptor Incertus, 361. For the names of individual bishops, various sources must be consulted. On Nicephorus's move, see *Life of Nicephorus*, 201. On Joseph of Thessalonica, Theophilus of Ephesus, Ignatius of Miletus, and Peter of Nicaea, see Theodore, *Letters*, 1 (pp. 1–2 Cozza-Luzi), 2.70 (1300A–C Migne), 4 (p. 5 Cozza-Luzi), and 151 (p. 133 Cozza-Luzi, relating that the bishop of Nicaea, previously exiled, had lapsed; cf. Pargoire, "Saints," 352). On Aemilianus of Cyzicus and Michael of Synnada, see the *Synaxarium*, 875, 703–4. On Theophylact of Nicomedia, see the *Life of Theophylact*, 80, and on Eudoxius of Amorium cf. pp. 77–79 with 80 in the same text. On Euthymius of Sardis, see Gouillard, "Oeuvre," 38–39. On Theodore of Studius, see Michael of Studius, 288B–C, and Pseudo-Michael, 188C–189B. On Theodore's replacement, Leontius, see Theodore, *Letters*, 2.31, 2.37 (1204B–C, 1229B–C Migne).

291. *Synaxarium*, 414–16; cf. Follieri and Dujčev. The date of January 22 given in the *Synaxarium* is presumably that of the death of Manuel, the martyr mentioned first and most prominently, and since this happened after Krum died the year must be 815. That Omurtag was Krum's son follows from Beševliev, *Protobulgarische Inschriften*, no. 13, 156.

292. Theophanes Continuatus, 24; Genesius, 10. For the date, see Treadgold, "Bulgars' Treaty," 217–19.

293. Scriptor Incertus, 361–62; *Life of Nicetas of Medicium*, chs. 38, 39, xxv–xxvi; Methodius, 29; *Life of Nicephorus*, 205–6. For Joseph's recall, cf. Theodore, *Letters*, 2 (p. 3 Cozza-Luzi) with 152 (pp. 134–35 Cozza-Luzi). On Theodore's places of exile, see Pargoire, "S. Théophane," 69–71.

294. Theophanes Continuatus, 24–25; Genesius, 10.

295. *Life of Nicetas of Medicium*, chs. 40–42, xxvi; Theodore, *Letters*, 2.9 (1140B–1141A Migne), 188 (p. 160 Cozza-Luzi). For Peter's lapse and repentance, see Pargoire, "Saints," 352–53.

296. The treaty is mentioned by Genesius, 20–21, 29; Theophanes Continuatus, 31–32, 65; *Life of Nicephorus*, 206–7; *Life of Nicetas of Medicium*, ch. 45, xxvii; and Michael the Syrian, 26. Much of the text is preserved in an inscription; see Beševliev, *Protobulgarische Inschriften*, no. 41, 190–206. For the date, see Treadgold, "Bulgars' Treaty," 214–20. That the coast between Thrace and Greece was partly controlled by Slavs about 833 is clear from the *Life of Gregory the Decapolite* 54–55, referring to the area around Christopolis.

297. Genesius, 21; Theophanes Continuatus, 30. Stephen of Taron, 107, dates the reconstruction of Arcadiopolis and Bizya to the year ending May 6, 817. On the Bulgars' border earthwork, much of which still exists and is probably to be dated to this time, see Bury, 361–62, and Beševliev, *Protobulgarische Periode*, 476–77.

298. On Leo's earlier embassy to Louis, see *Annales Regni Francorum*, 145; *Vita Hludowici*, 621; and *Annales Xantenses*, 224. On his later embassy, see *Annales Regni Francorum*, 146, and *Annales Fuldenses*, 356. On Theodotus's legates to the pope, see Theodore, *Letters*, 2.13 (1153D–1156A). On Leo's sending the body of St. Zacharias to Agnellus, see Andrea Dandolo, 142–43, and Tafel and Thomas, 1–3.

299. For Leo's boycott, see Andrea Dandolo, 144, and *De Sancto Marco*, 356A; on the earlier profanation of the holy places, see Theophanes, 499. On the raid on Damietta, see Maqrīzī, ch. 61.9, p. 40. This I would translate: "And when there was dissension between the brothers Muḥammad al-Amīn and ʿAbd Allāh al-Maʾmūn, and [subsequently] there were dissensions in the land of Egypt, the Byzantines had designs on the towns and attacked Damietta in the year 200 and a bit [more]." This apparently refers to the year 201 A.H. (July 30, 816–June 20, 817). Since peace was just being made with the Bulgars in the fall and the winter was unsuitable for naval operations, the Byzantine raid probably took place in the spring of 817. The raid led by Leo is mentioned by Theodore, *Letters*, 213 (pp. 180–81 Cozza-Luzi), referring to Leo's coming departure on campaign and almost certainly written soon before Easter 817 (April 12); on the date, see Pargoire, "S. Théophane," 76–77. Leo's capture and restoration of Camachum are mentioned by the Armenian chroniclers Samuel of Ani, 421, and Stephen of Taron, 107; the latter dates the event between May 6, 816, and May 6, 817 (year 265 of the Armenian Era). Honigmann, 57 and n. 3, finding a contradiction between these statements and Balādhurī's report (Brooks, "Byzantines," part 2, 88) that the Arabs lost Camachum between 810 and 813, thinks that at the later date some

other place is meant; but if between the two dates the fort remained deserted and ruined (and so in need of rebuilding), no contradiction arises. Further on this date, see Treadgold, "Bulgars' Treaty," 219–20 and nn. 27 and 28.

300. Genesius, 13. On Leo's sons by Theodosia, see n. 271 above.

301. Genesius, 14; Theophanes Continuatus, 30–31. On the high officials, see the letters Theodore wrote early in 821, just after Leo's death, exhorting them to urge the new emperor to abandon Iconoclasm: *Letters*, 2.76 (1313A–1316A, to Stephen), 2.80 (1320A–D, to "John the Logothete," whom Genesius, 22, identifies as John Hexabulius, the postal logothete), 2.82 (1324A–D, to Democharis), and 2.81 (1321A–1324A, to "Pantoleon the Logothete," who by process of elimination appears to be military logothete, since the low-ranking logothete of the herds probably had little influence with the emperor). Leo had chosen Stephen as magister to replace Theoctistus, Michael I's ally, who became a monk and abbot (Pseudo-Michael, 220A). See also Theodore, *Letters*, 2.56 (1268D–1269C), 2.129 (1416A–1419B), both to Leo the Sacellarius, one written under Leo V's persecution, and the other in 824. On Zacharias and Zosimas, see the *Life of Nicetas of Medicium*, ch. 43, xxvi, ch. 31, xxiv.

302. On Gregoras, see Theodore, *Letters*, 2.55 (1268B–D). On the nuns who were stripped and whipped, see the *Life of Nicephorus*, 206. On Theodore's whipping, and the deaths of the two Studite monks Thaddaeus and James, see Theodore, *Letters*, 2.38 (1229D–1232B), 2.5 (1124C–1128A), and 2.100 (1353B–1356B). On Leontius, see Theodore, *Letters*, 2.56 (1292C–D). For somewhat fuller accounts of the persecution, see Martin, 173–83, and Bury, 71–76.

303. On Leo's drilling of the army, see Theophanes Continuatus, 30. On iconoclast priests in the army and Theodotus's acceptance of iconoclast communion, see Theodore, *Letters*, 2.174 (1544C–D Migne), 2.136 (1436A–1437A Migne, of which the beginning is completed by *Letters*, 292 [pp. 241–42 Cozza-Luzi], which corrects the name from "Theodore" to "Theodotus").

304. Theodore, *Letters*, 2.63 (1281A–1284C), shows that he was transferred from Boneta to Smyrna when a single strategus ruled "the five themes." Michael of Studius, 296B–C, records that on February 23 (819) Craterus, then strategus of the Anatolics, had Theodore whipped. On this date and the date of the transfer in late May or early June, see Pargoire, "S. Théophane," 71 and n. 10. Michael the Syrian, 36–37, records that the Arab rebel Naṣr wrote to Manuel the Patrician offering an alliance when news came that the caliph Ma'mūn was moving to Baghdad (though the Byzantines did not respond to the offer until the reign of Michael II). While Ma'mūn may have decided to leave Merv as early as the start of 818, he was still not out of Khurāsān by that fall and did not arrive in Baghdad until August of 819; see Kennedy, 161–62. Therefore Naṣr's offer presumably dates from early 819, when Manuel already held his command, which must have been that over the five themes. On Leo's harshness to suspected plotters after 817, see Genesius, 13.

305. On Bardas, see Pseudo-Michael, 204B–205C. On Gregory, see below, p. 227 and n. 310. Paphlagonia and Chaldia were not yet separate jurisdictions in early 819, when Manuel commanded "the five themes" (Anatolics, Armeniacs, Thracesians, Bucellarians, and Opsician). On the other hand, Chaldia was a separate jurisdiction by late 820, as is clear from Michael II, 417E–418A. Paphlagonia is attested as a theme before Theodore of Studius's death in 826 if the miracle in Michael of Studius, 309C, is not posthumous. It seems impossible that Michael II made Paphlagonia a theme in the few days before the uprising of Thomas the Slav,

during the uprising, or after it; since the Armeniacs were his supporters, he had no reason to break up their territory and in fact reduced their taxes as a reward. I therefore conclude that Paphlagonia was made a province at the same time as Chaldia, in late 819 or early 820. On Paphlagonia's separation from the Armeniacs (rather than the Bucellarians, as has been maintained) and Chaldia's being originally commanded by a duke, see Treadgold, "Notes," 286–87, 280.

306. The title of duke was otherwise used for the governors of Calabria, Dalmatia, Venetia, Amalfi, Naples, and Gaeta. For the catepan of Paphlagonia, see Theophanes Continuatus, 123 (referring to the year 839), and Philotheus, 231.25. On the location of Chaldia's capital at Trebizond, see Constantine VII, *De Thematibus*, 73. The earliest mention of raids by the Rus is in the *Life of George of Amastris*, 64–68. The *Life* seems to have been written before 842, and by that time it says that the Rus were well known as raiders; on the *Life*, the date, and the controversy over the first appearance of the Rus, see Ševčenko, 120–25. Cf. Mango, "Eudocia," 17–19, who argues that a Russian named Inger (Igor) was a Byzantine bishop by the 820's.

307. On Leo's punishment of alleged conspirators, see George the Monk, 787–88; Genesius, 13; and Theophanes Continuatus, 25–26. The fairly reliable sources for the conspiracy of Michael and Leo's death are Symeon the Logothete (Leo Grammaticus, 210–11); Pseudo-Symeon, 609–10, 619–20; George the Monk, 788–89; the *Life of Nicephorus*, 207–9; and the *Acts of David*, 229 (the last locating the murder in St. Stephen in Daphne). The *Life of Ignatius*, 493A–B, contradicting the earlier and more reliable *Acts of David*, says that Leo was murdered in the Church of Our Lady of the Pharus, but this is almost certainly incorrect. Genesius, 15–20, and Theophanes Continuatus, 33–41, give an elaborated account that seems to be largely fantasy, though its mentions of the names of Theoctistus and Crambonites inspire some confidence and Leo's use of a candelabrum to defend himself is corroborated by Symeon (Leo Grammaticus, 214). For more on the fate of Leo's mother and his son Basil, see Theophanes Continuatus, 46–47. For Nicephorus's praise of Leo, see Genesius, 14; and, for Michael's condemnation of the murderers, see Michael II, 418. On Catacylas, see Genesius, 25.

308. George the Monk, 792; Genesius, 22–23; Theophanes Continuatus, 42–46; cf. the remarks in n. 263 above on Michael's marriage. The names of his father (Leo) and grandfather (George) are recorded by Ṭabarī (Vasiliev et al., 1: 311). Michael the Syrian, 72, says that Michael's grandfather was a converted Jew, probably because he is mistaking Athinganism for Judaism. Our only evidence for Michael's appearance is his portrait among the clumsy marginal illustrations in the Modena Zonaras, where he looks coarse and ugly even by the low standards of that manuscript. On Michael's iconophile relative, see the uninterpolated *Letter to Theophilus*, 359–60.

309. On the amnesty, see Michael of Studius, 304B–C: Pseudo-Michael, 205D–208B; *Life of Nicholas of Studius*, 889B–C; Theodore, *Letters*, 2.74, 83, 86, 90, 92; *Life of Nicetas of Medicium*, ch. 47, xxvii; *Life of Nicephorus*, 209; George the Monk, 792; and Symeon the Logothete (Leo Grammaticus, 211). On the death of Theodotus, see *Synodicon Vetus*, 130, which seems to make it almost simultaneous with the death of Leo V.

310. On the pensions for Leo's family, see Theophanes Continuatus, 46–47. On Bardas, see *Life of Nicephorus*, 201. On Gregory, see Genesius, 27, and Theophanes Continuatus, 57–58. Four seals survive that bear the name of Gregory, count of the Opsician, and are datable to an indeterminate time in the early ninth

century; Zacos and Veglery, nos. 1961, 1962, 1963, 3113A. At least one is likely to belong to Gregory Pterotus, perhaps from more than one appointment. Note that after Leo's murder Gregory came quickly but not immediately to Michael, and that the post of count of the Opsician is the only command to which Michael seems to have made a new appointment at the start of his reign.

311. On the chief civil officials, see pp. 220–21 and n. 301 above. Stephen the Magister, however, seems to have lost his largely honorific post by 822 (cf. n. 331 below), though he lived on till 842, by which time his son Euthymius, a former spatharius, had become a monk (Petrus, chs. 63, 65, 466A, 466C). On Catacylas and Olbianus, see Genesius, 23–24, and Theophanes Continuatus, 53–54. Olbianus seems to have been appointed by Leo, since Michael scarcely had time to install him there before Thomas was proclaimed. The Opsician theme, much nearer the capital, was a different case. On Theoctistus's appointment, see Genesius, 17–18, and Theophanes Continuatus, 38. On Michael's envoys to Naṣr, see Michael the Syrian, 36–37.

312. Genesius, 23–24; Theophanes Continuatus, 52–54. For an astute analysis of the sources for the uprising of Thomas, see Lemerle, "Thomas," with which I am in almost total agreement. Lemerle has shown that the more accurate of the two traditions about Thomas is the one that puts Thomas's proclamation after the death of Leo V. For Michael's version of the start of the "revolt," see Michael II, 417C–418B. For a recent restatement of the old view of Thomas's "revolt" as a sign of provincial discontent with the central government, see Köpstein, who includes references to earlier secondary literature.

313. On Thomas, see Genesius, 23, and Theophanes Continuatus, 6–7, 52–53. On p. 7, Genesius says, following a clearly legendary source, that Thomas was Armenian; but he contradicts himself on p. 23 by saying that Thomas was "Scythian," evidently meaning Slavic, and this is supported by Theophanes Continuatus. The fact that Leo, Michael, and Thomas had all got their start as guards of Bardanes Turcus in 802–3 inevitably led to later myths about prophecies at that time of their eventual destinies; see Genesius, 6–7, and Theophanes Continuatus, 7–8. The account of Thomas given in Michael II, 417C–E (followed by Genesius, 25–26; Theophanes Continuatus, 50–51; and other sources) is plain slander (cf. below, pp. 244–45 and n. 337).

314. See Michael II, 417E–418A; cf. *Acts of David*, 232, describing how Thomas first fought imperial troops in the Armeniac theme, and Theophanes Continuatus, 55, vaguely describing an early clash between the troops of Michael and Thomas in Asia Minor. Lemerle, "Thomas," 286–87, persuasively dates this campaign in the Armeniacs to the very beginning of Michael's reign, but Lemerle's interpretation of Michael II's "Armeniae Ducatum" as the Armeniac theme is not fully convincing. In the first place, Michael says that Thomas conquered the *whole* "Armeniae Ducatum," but a short time later we find Michael reducing the taxes of the Armeniac theme as a reward for its loyalty (Theophanes Continuatus, 53–54) and the Armeniacs' commander Olbianus defeating some of Thomas's forces in Asia Minor (Genesius, 26–27). Then it is not easy to see why Michael II should write "Armeniae" for "Armeniacorum," when he uses the latter term correctly later in the same sentence, and it is also peculiar that he should use the word "ducatum" in the same phrase both for Chaldia, which actually was a ducate, and for the Armeniacs, which were a full theme. Yet it is clear that Thomas did defeat the Armeniacs' commander and did take part of the Armeniac theme, since he could have reached Chaldia only by marching through Armeniac territory. I

therefore conjecture that there really was a ducate of Armenia, created by Thomas in the part of the Armeniacs bordering on Armenia that he had conquered, in order to reduce the power of the remaining Armeniacs. Though Michael would naturally have abolished this command when he retook the area, he is not minimizing Thomas's success in this part of his letter and had no reason to pretend that such a command had never existed. On the Arabs' raids on Thomas's territory soon after his uprising began, and therefore at this very time, see Genesius, 24, and Theophanes Continuatus, 54.

315. On Michael's avoidance of icons, see Michael of Studius, 317C, and Pseudo-Michael, 221B. For Theodore's efforts, see his *Letters*, 2.74 (to Michael II), 2.75, 2.76, 2.80, 2.81 (to various officials), and 2.82 (to Democharis, mentioning his arguing with John).

316. For Michael's proposal for a discussion between iconophiles and iconoclasts and the iconophiles' refusal, see Theodore, *Letters*, 2.86 (1329B–1332B). Since this letter does not mention the ex-patriarch Nicephorus, he apparently sent his own letter only afterward; for it, and Michael's response, see *Life of Nicephorus*, 209–10, and Theophanes Continuatus, 47–48. Once he had involved himself in the issue, Nicephorus seems to have gone on to propose the meeting of the emperor with Theodore and the other iconophiles. The *Life of Nicholas of Studius*, 892A–B, mentions Nicephorus's proposal, along with the part of an unnamed iconophile official in arranging the meeting, which is also mentioned in Michael of Studius, 317A–B. Theodore, *Letters*, 2.129 (1417B, addressed to Leo the Sacellarius), seems to make Leo a likely candidate to be identified with this official. Note that I would put these events in a slightly different order from Bury, 113–14 (esp. 114 n. 3), who puts Nicephorus's letter first and Michael's unsuccessful proposal for a discussion second (with Michael's actual meeting with the iconophiles third, where it certainly belongs).

317. Theodore, *Letters*, 2.129 (1417B–C); Michael of Studius, 317B–D; Pseudo-Michael, 221A–B; *Life of Nicholas of Studius*, 892A–893A, 897D–900A (an account that appears to be reworked to make Theodore appear more defiant than he was); cf. Symeon the Logothete (Leo Grammaticus, 211), and Pseudo-Symeon, 520, evidently referring to the same meeting.

318. On Anthony's consecration, see Pseudo-Symeon, 620–21. On patriarchal consecrations in general, note that Theodotus had been consecrated on Easter 815, Nicephorus on Easter 806, and Tarasius on Christmas 784. Symeon the Logothete (Leo Grammaticus, 211) indicates that Michael made his decision for Iconoclasm before he crowned his son Theophilus, probably on Pentecost (May 12), and no later than May (see n. 319 below). Since consecrating a patriarch and crowning a son on the same day would tend to devalue both ceremonies, Anthony was presumably consecrated earlier. Note that St. Symeon of Lesbos had an interview with a firmly iconoclast patriarch of Constantinople who must be Anthony not very long after Michael's accession: *Acts of David*, 230–31 (at n. 5 the editor wrongly identifies the patriarch as Theodotus). Note also that when Methodius arrived from Rome in late spring Michael had made up his mind about Iconoclasm (see p. 234 and n. 324 below).

319. On John's tutoring of Theophilus, see Theophanes Continuatus, 95–96, 154–55. On Theophilus's coronation, see Symeon the Logothete (Leo Grammaticus, 211), and Pseudo-Symeon, 621; on its date, see Treadgold, "Chronological Accuracy," 166–67, and cf. Van de Vorst, "Petite Catéchèse," 49–50, showing that it was no later than May.

320. For Thomas's campaign, see Genesius, 24; Theophanes Continuatus, 54; and Samuel of Ani, 421 (misdated, but noting that Thomas arrived at Erzurum-Theodosiopolis-Carin). On conditions in the border regions of the caliphate at this time, see Kennedy, 168–69, 171–72.

321. On Thomas's treaty, see Genesius, 24, and Theophanes Continuatus, 54–55; also see, on his coronation, Michael the Syrian, 75 (misdated and garbled), and, on the troops he assembled, Michael the Syrian, 37 (confused as usual), and Michael II, 417E–418A (mentioning Arabs, Persians, Georgians, Armenians, and Abasgians, the last three of whom were Caucasian and Christian). Cf. the analysis of these sources in Lemerle, "Thomas," 287–88, 285–86.

322. On Constantius, see Genesius, 26, and Theophanes Continuatus, 51–52. On Thomas's supposed claim to be Constantine VI, see Michael II, 417D; George the Monk, 793; Symeon the Logothete (Leo Grammaticus, 211–12); Pseudo-Symeon, 621; Michael the Syrian, 37, 75 (both times garbled); Genesius, 25; and Theophanes Continuatus, 51. In view of the fact that this story is reported even by the usually reliable sources of the Logothete tradition (Symeon the Logothete and Pseudo-Symeon), which otherwise do not follow the falsified version of Michael II, I am unwilling to follow Lemerle, "Thomas," 283–84, in regarding this claim as a complete fabrication by Michael, especially because it might have been quite useful to Thomas as a way of gaining support from ordinary people. For iconophiles who joined Thomas, see *Life of Peter of Atroa*, 141–43, 149–53.

323. On Michael's abortive appointment of his relative, see the uninterpolated *Letter to Theophilus*, 359–61 (the event seems to belong to a time when Michael's official decision in favor of Iconoclasm was a new one).

324. On Methodius, see *Life of Methodius*, 1248B–1249A; Genesius, 35; Theophanes Continuatus, 48; *Acts of David*, 237; and Gouillard, "Oeuvre," 44–46 (the date follows from the time it would have taken for news of Michael's accession to reach Rome and for Methodius then to travel to Constantinople). On Job's excommunication, see Michael the Syrian, 75, and Bar Hebraeus, 133 (a confused report, but the excommunication is highly credible in itself).

325. On the remission of taxes, see Theophanes Continuatus, 53–54; on hearth taxes in general, see Treadgold, *Byzantine State Finances*, 52–58 and esp. n. 209. On the walls, see the inscription in Meyer-Plath and Schneider, 2: 141, no. 64, and the interpretation in Treadgold, "Chronological Accuracy," 166.

326. Genesius, 26 and (on Gregory) 27; Theophanes Continuatus, 55 and (on Gregory) 57–58; Michael II, 418C. On the Cibyrrhaeots' fleet, see Genesius, 34, and Theophanes Continuatus, 79, both of whom say that the whole fleet of the Cibyrrhaeots was 70 ships in 828; cf. Constantine VII, *De Ceremoniis*, 652–53, listing a total of 32 dromons and 35 pamphyli for the three themes of the Cibyrrhaeots, Samos, and the Aegean Sea in 911/12, all of which were part of the Cibyrrhaeots earlier (see Treadgold, *Byzantine State Finances*, 18 and n. 54). The same source lists 60 dromons and 40 pamphyli for the Imperial Fleet. That Hellas made only a nominal submission at this time and waited to send help until it was surer Thomas would win seems to follow from Genesius, 29 (where "all the islands" probably includes Peloponnesus, Cephalonia, and Sicily), and Theophanes Continuatus, 63–64.

327. Genesius, 26–27; Theophanes Continuatus, 55–56; Michael II, 419A (on Constantius). For Michael's orders to the iconophiles, see Pseudo-Michael, 222C; Michael of Studius, 317D–320A; and *Life of Nicholas of Studius*, 900A. For Theo-

dore's opinion of Thomas, see Theodore, *Letters*, 2.129 (1416C–D); note that the other iconophile texts show him no favor.

328. Genesius, 27; Theophanes Continuatus, 56–57, 58; Michael II, 418C–D. I count as Michael's only the tagmata (though some of them may have defected to Thomas in Thrace), the Opsician theme, and the Armeniac theme (though since Thomas held the western Opsician theme and the eastern Armeniac theme, he may have had some of their soldiers as well). As noted above, Thomas's control over Hellas, Peloponnesus, Cephalonia, and Sicily seems to have been minimal.

329. Genesius, 24 (where the account is misleadingly telescoped), 27–28; Theophanes Continuatus, 58–61; Michael II, 418C–D. George the Monk, 797, and Symeon the Logothete (Leo Grammaticus, 212) confirm that Thomas besieged the city by land and sea for one year, which Michael's letter shows began in December of 821; therefore the siege was not interrupted for the winter. The blockade was very tight on land but necessarily less so by sea; cf. *Life of Peter of Atroa*, 141–43, and the comments on this passage by Lemerle, "Thomas," 293 and n. 133.

330. Genesius, 28–29; Theophanes Continuatus, 61–64. On Byrida, whose exact location is unknown, see Lemerle, "Thomas," 276 n. 83.

331. George the Monk, 795; Genesius, 24, 29; Theophanes Continuatus, 64. The last source says that the sallies were led at different times by Michael, Theophilus, Olbianus, and Catacylas. But Michael was a cautious man not likely to risk his life in a sally; Theophilus was nine years old; and Olbianus and Catacylas had remained in their respective themes at the beginning of the siege and were probably needed more there than in the capital, where they are otherwise known to have been only in 823 when Michael finally marched out against Thomas. Here I suspect that Theophanes Continuatus has made careless use of the material in Genesius, 24–25. There, in his drastically summarized and quite misleading initial account, Genesius vaguely praises Theophilus for sallying out at the start of the siege, though other, more detailed accounts say that there were no sallies and Theophilus simply led a votive procession on the walls at the time; then Genesius says that those chiefly responsible for quelling Thomas's uprising were Olbianus, Catacylas, and an otherwise unknown Christopher the Magister with his two sons Barsacius and Nasar the patricians. Though the last three may perhaps have led sallies, I suspect that in Theophanes Continuatus's source no leaders of sallies were named, as is the case with the mentions of sallies in the spring of 822 at Genesius, 28–29, and Theophanes Continuatus, 62.

332. Here I follow the persuasive analysis of Lemerle, "Thomas," 290–91 (cf. 279–80), who accepts the early but sketchy testimony of George the Monk, 797, and believes that the accounts of Genesius, 29–30, and Theophanes Continuatus, 65–66, reporting that the Bulgars came on their own initiative and defeated Thomas, are part of the distortions perpetrated by Michael II and his government. The late date of the Bulgar treaty for which I have argued (Lemerle, "Thomas," 280 and n. 103, inclined toward an earlier one) tends to confirm that Omurtag would not have spontaneously approached Michael about renewing the treaty at this time; and George the Monk's account is probably based on a reliable chronicle even earlier than he, dating from ca. 850 (see Treadgold, "Chronological Accuracy," 168–70, 194).

333. George the Monk, 797; Genesius, 30; Theophanes Continuatus, 66–68; Michael II, 418D–419A. The date of the battle of Diabasis follows from the fact that the siege of Arcadiopolis lasted five months (Michael II, 419A) and ended in the middle of October (Genesius, 31, and Theophanes Continuatus, 69–70).

334. George the Monk, 797; Genesius, 30–31; Theophanes Continuatus, 68–71; Michael II, 419A; *Acts of David*, 237. On the Arab raid, see Theodore, *Letters*, 2.127 (1409D–1412A), and Van de Vorst, "Petite Catéchèse," 40–41. This is probably the Arab raid mentioned by the *Life of Peter of Atroa*, 153.

335. Genesius, 31–32; Theophanes Continuatus, 71; Michael II, 419B–C. Michael the Syrian, 37, and Bar Hebraeus, 129, may reflect a distorted report of Michael II's punishment of Thomas's volunteers from the caliphate who were captured. On the date of Michael's return to the capital, see Van de Vorst, "Petite Catéchèse," 50–51.

336. On Choereas and Gazarenus, see Theophanes Continuatus, 71–73, where the musician's song reveals Guberius's name (cf. below, p. 370 and n. 493). For Saniana's location in the Bucellarian theme at this time (the borders were shifted later), see Constantine VII, *De Administrando Imperio*, ch. 50, 236. Cf. Belke, 222 (Saniana), 182–83 (Caballa). On brigands in the Thracesians at the end of the civil war, see *Life of Peter of Atroa*, ch. 41, 155–56. On the Cibyrrhaeots and John Echimus, later known as St. Anthony the Younger, see *Life of Anthony the Younger*, 193–95, 209, and the comments thereon by Lemerle, "Thomas," 291–93 (the assumption that the lands were military lands is mine; it follows from the evident fact that the men were soldiers). Otherwise on this *Life*, see Halkin, 187–225, who notes on pp. 195–98 that John became a monk in 825 after restoring order in his theme, spending ten months in Constantinople, and then dealing with an Arab raid; plainly John had restored order by mid-824 (though Halkin puts John's stay in Constantinople in "823–824" in his chronological table, he himself writes on the previous page that John cannot have left for the capital before the end of February of 824). Michael evidently felt fairly secure by April 10, 824, the date given in Michael II, 422B.

337. The story is told most clearly by Michael II, 417C–419C, and in Genesius, 25–32, who begins by citing the *Against Thomas* as his source. On Ignatius's authorship of this work, see *Suda*, 2: 1607–8, and Vasiliev et al., 1: 46 and n. 1. On the whole official version, see Lemerle, "Thomas," 255–84.

338. For Michael's proposals and Theodore's replies, see Theodore, *Letters*, 2.129 (1416A–1420B), 2.199 (1600B–1612C). The embassy brought along Michael's *Letter to Louis*, which at 419D–E names the ambassadors and at 422B mentions the gifts and the date. The embassy is also mentioned by the *Annales Regni Francorum*, 165, which at 155 describes Fortunatus's flight; cf. John the Deacon, *Chronicon*, 107, 108. On Theodotus (not "Theodorus," as in our text of Michael II), see Theodore, *Letters*, 2.189 (1577B–C; cf. p. 222 and n. 303 above on his communion with iconoclasts). On Theodore Crithinus, see Gouillard, "Deux figures," 387–401, esp. 398–400.

339. On Thecla's tomb, see Constantine VII, *De Ceremoniis*, 645. On Michael's remarriage, see Theophanes Continuatus, 78–79; Genesius, 35; Pseudo-Symeon, 621; Michael the Syrian, 72; and Bar Hebraeus, 129 (the last two, despite the absurd rumors they retell, apparently give the right date for the marriage). Theodore, *Letters*, 2.104 (1360D–1361C), implies by the order of the names in his heading that Euphrosyne was younger than her sister Irene and shows his benevolence to both; for his reaction to the marriage, see Theodore, *Letters*, 2.181 (1560B–1561A, to Maria), and his *Lesser Catecheses*, no. 74, 175–77. Note, however, that other contemporary iconophile sources do not mention the marriage at all.

340. On the capture of Sozopetra, see Balādhurī (Vasiliev et al., 1: 269). On the naval raid of Syria, cf. *Life of Anthony the Younger*, 199–200; this passage refers to

the Arab raid on Attalia in 825, but the Arab leader's words show that he was retaliating for a recent Byzantine raid, which Anthony's words indicate was sent out
directly by the emperor.

341. See *Annales Regni Francorum*, 165, and Theodore, *Letters*, 2.189 (1577A–
C). As recently as 821 Theodore's close friend Demochares had been general logothete and Pantoleon probably military logothete (see n. 301 above); but Demochares lost his post and then died sometime between then and Theodore's own
death in 826 (Theodore, *Letters*, 2.110 [1369D–1372D]; cf. Mango, "Observations," 407–8). The fact that Theodore did not appeal to Demochares in 825 may
well indicate that he had already been succeeded by Pantoleon, whom Theodore
approaches with obvious hesitation. Two seals attest that Pantoleon did become
general logothete (Laurent, *Corpus*, 2: nos. 305, 306, pp. 146–47), evidently as a
promotion from his similar but lower-ranking office.

342. See Theophanes Continuatus, 48–49, 99 (on the labeling of pictures of
saints, a measure also attributed to Leo V, with little probability). Generally on
the head tax on Jews, see Treadgold, *Byzantine State Finances*, 61.

343. On Michael's proposal for a treaty and the Arab land raid that followed,
see Balādhurī (Vasiliev et al., 1: 269). On Michael's defeat of the raiders at Ancyra
and Corum, see Stephen of Taron, 107. Though the Arabs claimed victory, Balādhurī's admission that their leader was killed supports Stephen's account. For the
sea raid on the Cibyrrhaeots, see *Life of Anthony the Younger*, 199–200. This passage is to be dated to 825, since it immediately precedes John's conversion to monasticism in that year; see Halkin, 195–99, who, however, dates the Arab raid to
824 for no particular reason.

344. Unlike some others, I do not believe that Crete was a theme before 828;
see Treadgold, "Notes," 277–80.

345. Theophanes Continuatus, 81–82; ibn al-Athīr (Vasiliev et al., 1: 356–57);
John the Deacon, *Gesta*, 429 (calling the strategus of Sicily not Constantine but
"Gregory"); Nuwayrī (Vasiliev et al., 1: 379–80). The account of the *Chronicle of
Salerno*, 498, seems poorly informed. I disagree with the interpretation of Vasiliev
et al., 1: 70–71, that the Arab sources' Balāṭa is probably a palatine title granted
by Euphemius rather than a name. Since this man revolted almost at once against
Euphemius and declared his loyalty to the imperial government, neither side is
likely to have referred to him by any title that Euphemius had given him. As the
Arab sources, who in this case seem relatively well informed about Greek names,
also render the Greek πλατεῖα by Balāṭa (for which Blāṭa would be an equally
easy reading), the corresponding name for a man in Greek would be Plato, which
is perfectly acceptable.

346. Theophanes Continuatus, 82; John the Deacon, *Gesta*, 429–30; Riyāḍ al-
Nufūs (Vasiliev et al., 1: 340–42, with absurdly high troop numbers and various
romantic touches); *Cambridge Chronicle* (ibid., 344–45, where "July" should be
corrected to "June" to agree with the other sources); ibn al-Athīr (ibid., 356, 357);
ibn al-ʿIdhārī (ibid., 374); Nuwayrī (ibid., 380–81). For Michael's naval expedition of 827, see Andrea Dandolo, 146.

347. Here I have tried to reconcile the accounts of Genesius, 32; Theophanes
Continuatus, 73–75; Michael the Syrian, 60; Bar Hebraeus, 131; Ṭabarī (Vasiliev
et al., 1: 287); and Kindī (ibid., 394). Both Byzantine sources say that the Arab
conquest of Crete occurred during the civil war, apparently because they mis-
understood a report that it came when the empire was still distracted and disrupted
by the war; cf. Symeon the Logothete (Leo Grammaticus, 212) and Pseudo-

Symeon, 621. Theophanes Continuatus makes it clear that the Arabs' first expedition to Crete, when they did not stay, occurred in the year before their occupation, which came in the spring. Michael the Syrian reports, apparently on firsthand authority, that the Spanish Arabs were besieged in Alexandria for nine months, from May to December of 827, and even then tried briefly to stay in Egypt before giving up and leaving. (Bar Hebraeus gives a slightly mangled version of the same account.) Ṭabarī speaks of their vague proposal to ʿAbd Allāh that they go to some Byzantine territory, made before they went to Crete, and Kindī says that they left for Crete in June 827. The easiest way of reconciling these data is to postulate that Abū Ḥafṣ proposed to depart for Byzantine territory early in the siege; bought time by leaving with some of his men in June 827 for Crete to reconnoiter; on his return did not follow up his proposal in the hope of being able to stay in Egypt; but finally departed for Crete with his people in the spring of 828 when he had no other choice. This reconstruction cannot, of course, be considered certain. For somewhat different reconstructions, see Brooks, "Arab Occupation," 431–32, and Vasiliev et al., 1:49–55. For a full bibliography on the subject, see Christides, though his own views on the date of the conquest are bizarre and unsubstantiated.

348. For the Venetians' contribution, see Andrea Dandolo, 148, and John the Deacon, *Chronicon*, 109. For the size of the fleet when it arrived, cf. ibn al-Athīr (Vasiliev et al., 1:358) and Nuwayrī (ibid., 382). That the Anatolic flotilla and part of the Imperial Fleet did not go to Sicily, while the Cibyrrhaeots did, seems apparent from the use of the former, but not the latter, in the two expeditions against Crete before the Sicilian expedition returned.

349. Ibn al-Athīr (Vasiliev et al., 1:357–58; cf. 356–57 for Michael's name); on Asad's reinforcements, see also ibn al-ʿIdhārī (ibid., 374), and Nuwayrī (ibid., 381), who also mentions the Syracusans' offer to surrender.

350. Riyāḍ al-Nufūs (Vasiliev et al., 1:342, 340); ibn al-Athīr (ibid., 358); ibn al-ʿIdhārī (ibid., 374); Nuwayrī (ibid., 381–82). Riyāḍ al-Nufūs, the earliest of these sources and the one most interested in Asad, says that Asad died (of wounds) in late June or early July of 828, and this date appears to fit best with the sequence of events in both Sicily and Crete. Of the others, ibn al-Athīr simply says that Asad died (of disease) in the year between March 828 and March 829, ibn al-ʿIdhārī that he died (cause not specified) in late September or early October of 828, and Nuwayrī that he died (of disease) in late October or early November of 828. Vasiliev et al., 1:81 n. 5, express no view of their own about the correct date.

351. Ibn al-Athīr (Vasiliev et al., 1:358); Nuwayrī (ibid., 382). On the Venetians, who understandably were not impressed with the success of the expedition, see Andrea Dandolo, 148, and John the Deacon, *Chronicon*, 109. That the other troops were recalled is my deduction, based on events on Crete.

352. Genesius, 32–33; Theophanes Continuatus, 75–76; Pseudo-Symeon, 622–23; Balādhurī (Vasiliev et al., 1:270). The Greek sources' story that Abū Ḥafṣ left the Arabs' wives and children behind, burned the ships after the landing, and bade his men take new wives on Crete is quite incredible, especially in view of the Arabs' power on the sea soon afterwards. Brooks, "Arab Occupation," 438–40, argues conclusively that a supposed confirmation of this tale in an Arab source, which no one today can find, is the result of an old misunderstanding, though strangely some doubts about his argument appear in Vasiliev et al., 1:55 and n. 3. Note that the capacity of a dromon, the standard Byzantine fighting ship and

probably much like the Arabs' pirate vessels, was 300 men (Constantine VII, *De Ceremoniis*, 652–53, and cf. Ahrweiler, 410–13). For the identification of Suda Bay, see Vasiliev et al., 1: 55 and n. 2.

353. Theophanes Continuatus, 76–77. The strategus of the Anatolics would hardly have been sent if the strategi of the Cibyrrhaeots, Peloponnesus, or Cephalonia had been available, nor would the protostrator have led a fleet out of Constantinople if the drungary of the Imperial Fleet had not been absent. Thus it seems clear that Crete was invaded while most of the empire's navy was in Sicily.

354. Theophanes Continuatus, 77–78; Genesius, 33–34; Pseudo-Symeon, 623, 624; Balādhurī (Vasiliev et al., 1: 270). De Boor argues convincingly that the Greek sources have mistaken the early Christian martyr Cyril of Gortyn for a martyr under the Arabs.

355. Genesius, 34; Theophanes Continuatus, 79–81; Pseudo-Symeon, 623 (where 200 ships is clearly an exaggerated figure).

356. Ibn al-Athīr (Vasiliev et al., 1: 358); Nuwayrī (ibid., 382). Theophanes Continuatus, 82–83, reports the story in a confused form, putting the assassination at Syracuse.

357. Ibn al-Athīr (Vasiliev et al., 1: 358); Nuwayrī (ibid., 382). The latter puts Muḥammad's death at the beginning of A.H. 214 (March 11, 829 – February 27, 830), thus dating the events. That Theodotus sailed with most of the Imperial Fleet is indicated by the fact that the fleet and its drungary were not available for the operations in the Aegean in early 829, which were entrusted to a newly levied force under a special commander.

358. Ibn al-Athīr (Vasiliev et al., 1: 358–59); Nuwayrī (ibid., 382–83).

359. Genesius, 35; Theophanes Continuatus, 81; Pseudo-Symeon, 623–24 (the only source to say that the Tessaracontarii attacked Crete). That the islands left unnamed by Genesius and Theophanes Continuatus were the Cyclades seems plain not only from the geography but from Symeon the Logothete (Leo Grammaticus, 212–13) and Pseudo-Symeon, 621.

360. Genesius, 29, says that the Bulgar khan Omurtag sent an embassy in the fall of 822 to negotiate the renewal of the treaty for another ten years, but even if this is true (cf. n. 332 above) the renewal would have taken effect only when the second decade began in late 826. Sabas, 359B–360A, relates that in 825 Joannicius miraculously liberated some Byzantines held prisoner in Bulgaria. Mango, "Two Lives," 404 and n. 30, understandably finds this episode suspicious; but he also argues (398–400) that Sabas drew his chronology from the complete text of the Scriptor Incertus, which would thus presumably have reported that prisoners were indeed liberated from Bulgaria in that year, just before the treaty was to be renewed. Note that Byzantine prisoners also escaped from Bulgaria just before the treaty was to be renewed for a second time in 836 (see below, pp. 290–91 and n. 397). On Michael's embassy of 827 to Louis, and Louis's embassy of 828 to Michael, see *Annales Regni Francorum*, 174; *Vita Hludowici*, 631; and the letter of Abbot Hilduin to Louis in *MGH*, *Epistolae*, 5: 330 (cf. Gouillard, "Deux figures," 398–400, for the identification of the steward or oeconomus of St. Sophia as Theodore Crithinus). On Louis's council at Paris, see Martin, 251–61.

361. On the date of Theodore of Studius's death, see Michael of Studius, 321D, who puts it in November of the twelfth year of his third exile (826); cf. Naucratius, 1845A–B, who records that Theodore died on a feast of St. Menas the Martyr (November 11) that fell on a Sunday, a combination that did occur in

826. On the date of the death of Nicephorus, see *Synaxarium*, 725, which puts it in the thirteenth year of his exile (the year beginning March 13, 828), and the *Life of Nicephorus*, 213, which dates it to Easter (April 5, 828).

362. George the Monk, 792; Genesius, 35; Theophanes Continuatus, 83–84; Pseudo-Symeon, 624; Symeon the Logothete (Leo Grammaticus, 213). For the exact date of Michael's death, see Grierson, "Tombs," 56. On Michael's amnesty, see *Life of Methodius*, 1249B.

363. On Methodius's cellmate, cf. *Life of Methodius*, 1248C–1249B, with Gouillard, "Oeuvre," 44–45, noting that the man had been in jail for 24 years in 821. On the plot of 797, see above, p. 112 and n. 145. The *Acts of David*, 237, indicates that this prisoner died in the cell before 829.

364. For basic facts and bibliography, see Beck, *Kirche*, 491–95 (on Theodore), 489–91 (on Nicephorus), 496 (on the theology of Nicetas of Medicium), and 510 (on the encyclical of Theodore's disciple Naucratius). On Theodore's sermons to his community, see esp. Van de Vorst, "Petite Catéchèse." On Nicephorus's theological works, see especially Alexander, *Patriarch Nicephorus*, 162–88. The biographies of Theophanes Confessor (by Methodius) and of John of Gotthia may date from Michael II's reign; see Ševčenko, 115, 118.

365. On Ignatius and Nicetas, see Ševčenko, 120–25, 126. Nicetas was in exile in the Peloponnesus in 822, when that region was under the loose control of Thomas the Slav, but the reason for his exile is quite uncertain. Perhaps he was a partisan of Michael II.

CHAPTER FIVE

366. George the Monk, 797, Genesius, 45, 49, and Theophanes Continuatus, 124, imply that Theophilus was born at Amorium.

367. On John's appointment as syncellus, see Theophanes Continuatus, 154–55 (John was syncellus by the time of his embassy; see p. 268 and n. 371 below). On the office of syncellus, see Oikonomidès, 308 and n. 114, with his references. That John continued to be an abbot after he became syncellus is clear from his seal; see Laurent, *Corpus*, 5.3, no. 1917, p. 221. On Theophilus's piety and his love of hymns, see Theophanes Continuatus, 87, 106–7.

368. On the workmanship of St. Sophia at Thessalonica, see Mango, *Byzantine Architecture*, 161–65. The date of the Pearl follows from the fact that Theophilus had it ready for his bride show in May 830. On its construction, see Theophanes Continuatus, 143–44; cf. Guilland, 94–115, esp. 101–2. On the Great Palace in general see Guilland, and Miranda, *Palais* and *Étude*, none of which is very satisfactory. On Theophilus's restoration of the walls, see Genesius, 53; Theophanes Continuatus, 94–95; and Pseudo-Symeon, 627. On his inscriptions on the walls, see Mango, "Byzantine Inscriptions," 54–57; they seem to date from all parts of his reign.

369. On Theophilus's arrangements to hear complaints and inspect markets on his way to the Blachernae, see Theophanes Continuatus, 87–88. On the charge against John Echimus, see *Life of Anthony the Younger*, 209–11. On Theophilus of Ephesus, see Gouillard, "Oeuvre," 39; note that he, like Anthony, was later venerated as a saint (see *Synaxarium*, 77).

370. Symeon the Logothete (Leo Grammaticus, 218–19; cf. 214 for Leo Chamodracon's surname); Pseudo-Symeon, 632; Genesius, 44 (badly garbled); Theophanes Continuatus, 118 (taken out of context); Michael the Syrian, 74, Bar He-

braeus, 132, and *Chronicle of 1234*, 16 (all three misdated because just before this their common source has wrongly inserted Theophilus's campaign of 837 at the start of his reign). On the date, see n. 371 below.

371. On the embassy, see Symeon the Logothete (Leo Grammaticus, 219, to be completed from Georgius Interpolatus, 796–97); Pseudo-Symeon, 632–33; Genesius, 44 (again garbled); Theophanes Continuatus, 95–98 (not mentioning Manuel), 119 (mentioning Manuel, but as if reporting another embassy and with legendary touches). Though Symeon does not explicitly say that the embassy went to Baghdad, his references to the caliph's court and prisons imply it, and Theophanes Continuatus confirms it. Since Ma'mūn was last in Baghdad in March of 830, the embassy must have been before then; there is no reason to reject Theophanes Continuatus's statement that John connected it with Theophilus's recent accession, which implies that it left in the autumn. The time of an emperor's accession was also a frequent occasion for conspiracies or allegations of conspiracies against him. I would tentatively date Manuel's flight to October, John's departure to November, and John's arrival at Baghdad to December of 829. For earlier views, all based on a lower estimate of the value of the Logothete than mine, see Rosser and his references. I now think that in "Chronological Accuracy," 176–77, I dated Manuel's flight and John's embassy somewhat too late. As for the position of postal logothete, in the fall of 831 the postal logothete was persecuting iconophiles and shared a mother-in-law (by then Theoctista, the mother of Theodora) with the emperor Theophilus; see Gouillard, "Oeuvre," 39–40, 41 (for the date), 43. One of the two possible candidates is Arsaber, who had very probably married Theodora's sister Calomaria by this time, presumably held some high office when he acquired his high rank of patrician (he became magister only later), and as John's brother was likely to be an iconoclast; the other candidate is Constantine Babutzicus, first heard of as drungary of the Watch in 838 (see pp. 298–99 and n. 408 below), who may well not have been married yet in 831, probably had a purely military career, and would not have been canonized as one of the martyrs of Amorium in 845 if he had been known as a persecutor of iconophiles. Arsaber therefore seems much the likelier of the two. In any case, Myron was no longer postal logothete in 831.

372. On the battle off Thasos and its aftermath, see Theophanes Continuatus, 137, referring to "the Romans' fleet," evidently the Imperial Fleet. For the beginning of Ma'mūn's expedition, see Michael the Syrian, 74, and *Chronicle of 1234*, 16 (both mentioning Manuel's advising the caliph to invade Byzantium); Ṭabarī (Vasiliev et al., 1:287–88); Ya'qūbī (ibid., 272); *Kitāb al-'Uyūn* (ibid., 370); and ibn Ṭayfūr (ibid., 391–92).

373. Symeon the Logothete (Leo Grammaticus, 213–14); Pseudo-Symeon, 624–25. On the story's date, which has been doubted, see my "Problem," and, on its source, cf. my "Chronological Accuracy," 193–96, arguing that this portion of Symeon's work was based on a chronicle written about 860 by a writer connected with court circles under Theophilus.

374. See Theodore, *Letters*, 142, 270 (pp. 125–26, 217 Cozza-Luzi), and 2.205 (1621D–1624C Migne). Cf. Rochow, *Studien*, esp. pp. 3–5 (on the form of Cassia's name), 5–19 (a discussion rejecting the story of Theophilus's bride show as unhistorical, which I believe to be mistaken), and 20–26 (a discussion of the three letters, with which I essentially agree). Note that if I am correct in dating the Logothete's source (see n. 373 above), Cassia died before ca. 860, since the Logothete (Leo Grammaticus, 214) can say that she lived all her life in her convent. On Theo-

dora's beauty, even ten years and seven children later, see Maqqarī, 2: 115. On Theodora's parents, see Theophanes Continuatus, 89. Theophanes Continuatus, 174–75, records that one of Theodora's brothers was Petronas, the son-in-law of Myron by late 829 (cf. Symeon the Logothete [Leo Grammaticus, 218]), and that one of her sisters was Calomaria, wife of Arsaber the Patrician, who since his brother John the Grammarian was born about 785 (see above, pp. 208–9 and n. 280) was probably married before 829. Theophanes Continuatus, 148, records that Manuel was Theodora's paternal uncle. The synaxarium entry published with the *Life of Nicetas the Patrician*, 325, which is evidently based on the partly preserved contemporary biography (cf. ibid., 309, 312–33), says that Nicetas was a relative of the empress Theodora (for ἀπόγονον read or understand σύγγονον); the fact that both were from Paphlagonia supports this, though since Nicetas was evidently not Armenian he was probably related to the empress on her mother's side.

375. On Theophilus's marriage and Euphrosyne's retirement, see Symeon the Logothete (Leo Grammaticus, 213–14), and Pseudo-Symeon, 625, 628. Theophanes Continuatus, 86, states that Theophilus expelled Euphrosyne from the palace and sent her back to her original convent, and at p. 90 declares that it was Theoctista who had purchased the Gastria and turned it into a monastery. See Treadgold, "Problem," 333–34, 338–39, for a demonstration that here Theophanes Continuatus has substituted Theoctista for Euphrosyne out of disapproval for Euphrosyne as a lapsed nun. Still, Theoctista was buried in the Gastria (Constantine VII, *De Ceremoniis*, 647–48) and the apparent fact that she changed her name from Florina to Theoctista (Theophanes Continuatus, 89) indicates that she became a nun. I am therefore inclined to think that Theophanes Continuatus was at least right to place her at the Gastria, though not to make her its founder instead of Euphrosyne, who retained higher rank and was presumably the abbess. For Theoctista's rank of belted patrician, see Theophanes Continuatus, 89–90. The Armenian connection of Theodora's relatives is clear from Manuel's being an Armenian, while Arsaber too was an Armenian. Euphrosyne's family is usually considered to be Armenian because Theophanes, 463, describes her mother Maria as coming from the Armeniacs and because she had a cousin with the Armenian name of Bardas (*Life of Philaretus*, 141, 155), but this is not conclusive. Better evidence occurs in Theodore, *Letters*, 2.113 (1376D–1380C). Speck, "*Graikia*," in an effort to identify the father of another nun named Euphrosyne, to whom Theodore addressed this letter in 823, has established that he was (1) married to a woman named Irene, who died after him but before 823, (2) Armenian, (3) related to an emperor, and (4) a patrician and strategus first of Hellas and then of the Armeniacs, both around 800. I would identify this man with Maria's uncle John, father of her cousin Bardas, and through her related to Constantine VI. John's wife was indeed named Irene, and he had already begun a military career as a spatharius and member of the emperor's guard by the time his father Philaretus died in 792 (*Life of Philaretus*, 141, 145, and 155; 151 shows that Philaretus lived four years after Maria's marriage in 788). Speck, "*Graikia*," 87 and n. 59, finds no place for his anonymous strategus in Philaretus's family tree, apparently because John is not said to have had a daughter named Euphrosyne in 788 (*Life of Philaretus*, 141); but probably Euphrosyne was born later, perhaps by 792, when she would still have been too young to ask for her dying grandfather's blessing along with her two older sisters (*Life of Philaretus*, 159). "Euphrosyne" was, of course, a name that her presumed niece, the daughter of Constantine VI, also bore, and the two Eu-

phrosynes must have been born within a few years of each other. Given, then, that Philaretus's son John was Armenian, so was the entire family.

376. Symeon the Logothete (Leo Grammaticus, 214–15); Pseudo-Symeon, 625. Genesius, 36, and Theophanes Continuatus, 85–86, have a version of the story that appears to have been reworked to make Theophilus seem less ruthless and more just, since they give the conspirators a proper trial in the Magnaura palace.

377. On the caliph's raid of Cappadocia, see ibn Ṭayfūr (Vasiliev et al., 1: 391–92); Ṭabarī (ibid., 288); *Kitāb al-ʿUyūn* (ibid., 370); ibn Miskawayh (ibid., 347); Yaʿqūbī (ibid., 272, where "Anqira" is evidently an error for Qurra = Corum); ibn Qutaybah (ibid., 268, where Charsianum seems to be an anticipation of a raid in 831; see p. 275 and n. 380 below); Michael the Syrian, 74; Bar Hebraeus, 132; and *Chronicle of 1234*, 16–17 (showing confusion about Manuel's role and the date). Only Yaʿqūbī, ibn Qutaybah, and the *Chronicle of 1234* mention Samalū (Semaluus). See Vasiliev et al., 1: 100–103, who identify Corum and Soandus. See also Hild and Restle, 216–17 (Koron), 282–85 (Soandus), 276–77 (Sēmaluos), and 243–44 (Nakīdā = Magida). The Greek name for Sinān, the fourth place taken by the Arabs, seems not to be identifiable; see Hild, *Byzantinische Strassensystem*, 50 and n. 176. Ṭabarī mentions a "governor" at Soandus, a term unlikely to be applied to an official of lower rank than a drungary; before 839 there were only two drungi in Cappadocia (see below, p. 357 and n. 476), one of which was naturally based at Corum. For Manuel's campaign against the Khurramites, see Symeon the Logothete (Leo Grammaticus, 219, identifying them only as "the peoples of a certain enemy" of the caliph's, evidently Bābak); Pseudo-Symeon, 633 (identifying them as "Persians," a word customarily used by Byzantines for the Khurramites); Genesius, 50–51 (placing the campaign in Khurāsān, which is too far east); and Theophanes Continuatus, 118 (identifying the enemies as "Kormati" = Khurramites, though again locating them in Khurāsān). Symeon, the only source to relate these events in order, puts Manuel's campaign soon after the embassy of John the Grammarian, so that it must have been simultaneous with Maʾmūn's raid on Cappadocia; and Ṭabarī (Vasiliev et al., 1: 288) and ibn Ṭayfūr (ibid., 392) indicate this by reporting that ʿAbbās departed from Melitene at the same time Maʾmūn was invading Cappadocia. No army heading for Cappadocia would have gone from northern Syria through Melitene, because that route led farther east, either to the Armeniac theme or to Armenia and Azerbaijan.

378. Symeon the Logothete (Leo Grammaticus, 219–20); Pseudo-Symeon, 633–34; Genesius, 51 (where "Geron" seems to be a mistake for Corum in Cappadocia); Theophanes Continuatus, 118–21; ibn Ṭayfūr (Vasiliev et al., 1: 392, giving a version slightly less embarrassing to ʿAbbās); Yaʿqūbī (ibid., 272, saying that Manuel fled from "Anqira," his mistaken form of Qurra = Corum); Michael the Syrian, 74, Bar Hebraeus, 132, and *Chronicle of 1234*, 17 (all somewhat confused). Though the Arab sources understandably say as little about Manuel's exploits as possible, the fact that his supposedly great victory left Bābak about as strong as before indicates that the Byzantine sources have exaggerated its importance. On Bābak, see Rekaya, though he does not refer to Manuel's expedition, which is mentioned only in Greek sources.

379. Ibn al-ʿIdhārī (Vasiliev et al., 1: 374–75, where the figure of "about" 300 ships for Asbagh's fleet looks exaggerated); ibn al-Athīr (ibid., 359, where that total for all the new Arab ships is little more credible); Nuwayrī (ibid., 383); *Cam-*

bridge Chronicle (ibid., 345). The last source seems to be wrong by a few weeks when it puts the relief of Menaenum in the year beginning September 1, 830, but it is presumably right that Theodotus was killed in that year, because Nuwayrī makes it clear that he retreated safely from Menaenum. I assume that he died in one of the bloody engagements mentioned by ibn al-ʿIdhārī, though the defeated Arabs may not have been aware of his death. For a slightly different reconstruction, and for the probable identification of Calloniana (the modern Caltanissetta), see Vasiliev et al., 1: 127–29.

380. Theophanes Continuatus, 114–16 (where the speech of the domestic of the Schools, at this time Manuel, indicates that he had been present on the campaign); Ṭabarī (Vasiliev et al., 1: 288); ibn Miskawayh (ibid., 347); *Kitāb al-ʿUyūn* (ibid., 370); ibn Ṭayfūr (ibid., 392); Constantine VII, *De Ceremoniis*, 503–8. None of these six sources says that Theophilus actually went to Cilicia, but only that he fought Arabs who came *from* Cilicia; according to Theophanes Continuatus, he fought near Charsianum on Byzantine soil. Yet Vasiliev et al., 1: 103–4, state that Theophilus invaded the caliphate and postulate a separate campaign near Charsianum. The number of prisoners given by Theophanes Continuatus, 25,000, is plainly too high; for the figure of 7,000, see below, p. 279 and n. 384. Ibn Qutaybah (Vasiliev et al., 1: 267), evidently through a confusion with this campaign, says that Maʾmūn took Charsianum in 830. His muddled report does not seem sufficient reason to conclude that in 831 Charsianum actually fell. On the triumph, see Treadgold, "Problem," 331–32, for the view that though most of the description of the triumph in Constantine VII, *De Ceremoniis*, 503–8, refers to both 831 and 837, as it indicates, the mention of the Caesar (presumably the later Caesar Alexius Musele) has nothing to do with 831, applies only to 837, and has been included simply to provide a more complete set of precedents for the behavior of various officials at triumphs. Taking issue with this view, Mango, "On Re-Reading," 639–43, argues that the description properly belongs only to 831, because it implies that the Caesar took part in the campaign and that the magister, whom he identifies with Manuel, did not; Mango finds "no indication" that Alexius campaigned in 837, while Manuel is known to have campaigned then. However, Mango errs in saying that Manuel and Alexius are the only magistri attested at this time, since Arsaber, brother of John the Grammarian, is also mentioned as a magister and probably held the office in 837 (see below, n. 398). Symeon the Logothete indicates that Manuel was domestic of the Schools from 830 to 838, and as such Manuel seems to have gone on the campaigns of both 831 and 837. If there is "no indication" that Alexius went on the campaign of 837, as I believe he did, there is equally none that he went on the campaign of 831; for 831 there are such strong counterindications that no one has been able to show how his being Caesar then could be squared with the evidence (Mango does not try).

381. *Kitāb al-ʿUyūn* (Vasiliev et al., 1: 371, giving what seems to be the best account); Yaʿqūbī (ibid., 272); Ṭabarī (ibid., 288–89); ibn Miskawayh (ibid., 347); ibn Ṭayfūr (ibid., 392–93); Michael the Syrian, 74, and Bar Hebraeus, 132 (both with the month apparently wrong); *Chronicle of 1234*, 17. Cf. the account of Vasiliev et al., 1: 109–12.

382. Ibn al-Athīr (Vasiliev et al., 1: 359, where 70,000 is absurdly high for the original population of Panormus, though 7,000 would do nicely); ibn al-ʿIdhārī (ibid., 375); Nuwayrī (ibid., 383, where A.H. 220 is an error for A.H. 216); *Cambridge Chronicle* (ibid., 345); John the Deacon, *Gesta*, 430. The *Cambridge Chronicle*

dates the fall of Panormus after September 1, 831, and ibn al-Athīr dates it before September 12. Cf. the account of Vasiliev et al., 1: 129–30.

383. On the pamphlets and Euthymius's death, see *Acts of David*, 238 (which, however, has these events confused with the persecution of 833), and Gouillard, "Oeuvre," 39–41, 43–45. On Pseudo-Methodius of Olympus, and on the Slavonic text that I believe is a translation of the second pamphlet, see Alexander, *Byzantine Apocalyptic Tradition*, 13–60, 61–72 (Alexander, without himself making the identification, supposes the text was composed by a Sicilian between 827 and 829). Unfortunately, the work summarized and analyzed by Gouillard, Methodius's *Life of Euthymius of Sardis*, remains unedited. For the identification of the logothete as Arsaber, see above, n. 371. The chartulary of the inkpot is not named, but Theoctistus seems to have held that post continuously from 821 to 856. On Joseph of Thessalonica, who is also mentioned in this text, see also Van de Vorst, "Translation," 46 and 58. On Nicetas, see *Life of Nicetas the Patrician*, 327. In the latter, p. 319, the editor would date Nicetas's expulsion to about the beginning of 830 for reasons that I do not find persuasive. After Nicetas's expulsion his *Life* mentions his spending two Easters, the first at a suburban retreat near Constantinople (p. 327) and the second at Panteichium (p. 329), then describes his hurried travels to Ruphinianae, Catabolum, and back to Panteichium before Theophilus's edict against iconophiles (pp. 327, 329), which I would date to June of 833 (see below, pp. 280–81 and n. 386). I believe that the two Easters are those of 832 (March 24) and 833 (April 13), so that Nicetas was expelled about the beginning of 832. For Theophilus to have taken measures against an iconophile because of his iconophilism at the beginning of 830, or even of 831, would be quite unparalleled. On the offices of Petronas and Eustathius Monomachus, see Symeon the Logothete (Georgius Interpolatus, 793, since there is a lacuna in Leo Grammaticus, 215–16). Note that Monomachus was the surname of Nicetas the Patrician (*Life of Nicetas the Patrician*, 316–17); cf. n. 374 above on his relation to Theodora.

384. Ya'qūbī (Vasiliev et al., 1: 272–74); Ṭabarī (ibid., 289–91); ibn Miskawayh (ibid., 347); *Kitāb al-'Uyūn* (ibid., 371–72); ibn Qutaybah (ibid., 267); Michael the Syrian, 74–75; Bar Hebraeus, 132. These sources generally agree on the course of hostilities, but disagree about the dates of Theophilus's letters requesting a truce. The later Arab sources, ibn Miskawayh and the *Kitāb al-'Uyūn*, mention only one letter (which the caliph would not read because in it Theophilus named himself first), sent in 832; Ṭabarī mentions such a letter sent in 831, and gives the texts of a second letter and the caliph's reply to it, dated to 832; Ya'qūbī dates the first letter to 831 and apparently dates the second to later the same year, but since he says that Theophilus asked for the return of his forts, which the Arabs only garrisoned in 832, that must be the right date; Michael the Syrian mentions only a letter that the caliph did read, evidently the second, and dates it to the year ending October 1, 832. I conclude that the two later Arab sources have confused the content of the first letter with the date of the second, while the other sources are essentially correct. This is approximately the conclusion of Vasiliev et al., 1: 112–21.

385. On the harsh winter, see Michael the Syrian, 78–79, and Bar Hebraeus, 133 (for the date); and George the Monk, 798, and Theophanes Continuatus, 137 (for the impact on Byzantium of the cold winters of the time). On the plague of locusts, see Michael the Syrian, 78 (showing that the locusts were in Syria in 832), and *Life of Nicetas the Patrician*, 335 (showing that they had reached Bithynia by about the fall of 833, obviously by way of the intervening regions of Asia Minor).

On Ma'mūn's plans and the construction of the base at Tyana, see Ya'qūbī (Vasiliev et al., 1:274); Ṭabarī (ibid., 291); Mas'ūdī, *Prairies* (ibid., 329); ibn Miskawayh (ibid., 347–48, misdated to 832); Michael the Syrian, 75–76; and *Chronicle of 1234*, 19.

386. On the council, see the uninterpolated *Letter to Theophilus*, 359, dating it not long before the letter was written in April 836; the only plausible context for it is immediately before the edict. On Theophilus's edict, see *Life of Peter of Atroa*, 187–89; *Life of Nicetas the Patrician*, 327, 329; Sabas, 365; *Life of Gregory the Decapolite*, 53–54; *Synaxarium*, 733–34 (on Hilarion of Dalmatus); Theophanes Continuatus, 99–101 (including mention of the Abrahamites); Symeon the Logothete (Leo Grammaticus, 215, completed by Georgius Interpolatus, 791); and Pseudo-Symeon, 625. The *Acts of David*, 237–39, have mixed up this persecution with the martyrdom of Euthymius of Sardis in 831 and the branding of Theophanes and Theodore in 839. As for the date, the *Life of Peter of Atroa* puts the edict in the fourth year of Theophilus (October 2, 832–October 1, 833). More precisely, the *Life of Nicetas the Patrician* puts it at least a month or so after an Easter that must be that of 833 (April 13) and when an Arab invasion was expected in Bithynia, therefore roughly between the Arabs' first crossing of the frontier on May 25, 833, and Ma'mūn's death on August 7. The Roman Martyrology commemorates on July 8 the martyrdom of the three Abrahamite monks, who according to Theophanes Continuatus, 101, died as a result of their protests just after the edict (*Martyrologium Romanum*, 276). The edict should therefore be dated to June 833. The other monk who protested did so on the same occasion, according to Theophanes Continuatus, 102 (I do not agree with Laurent in his preface to the *Life of Peter of Atroa*, 42 n. 1, that the fact that Peter of Atroa was not then in charge of Calonorus indicates that he was dead, since the *Life*, 187–89, indicates that Peter was at St. Porphyrius at this time).

Note that Hilarion of Dalmatus, who was imprisoned on Aphusia at the time of the edict, was released at the start of 842 after eight years of confinement (*Synaxarium*, 733–34). John of Cathara was imprisoned with other iconophile clergy on Aphusia early in the reign of Theophilus, then died after two and a half years of confinement on a February 4 (*Synaxarium*, 633–34; see 444 for what seems to be the right death date); probably he died on February 4, 836, and was imprisoned about July of 833. The *Life of Macarius of Pelecete*, 157–60, says that Macarius was confined to Aphusia at a time that seems to be early in Theophilus's reign, after being briefly confined in Constantinople with Paulicians who had been condemned to death. The *Life of Michael Syncellus*, 240, notes that Theodore and Theophanes were confined to Aphusia, but at p. 238 reports that Michael was imprisoned in the fifth year of Theophilus, or 834/35. Since the chronology of this *Life* is utterly unreliable (see Treadgold, "Chronological Accuracy," 188–89 and n. 139), it seems likely that Michael was imprisoned at the same time as the others. The author of the *Life* appears unaware of Euphrosyne's identity, though this seems to follow from her influence and impunity.

On Sergius Confessor, see *Synaxarium*, 682, 681–84; his connections follow from his identification as the father of Photius by Mango, "Liquidation," 135–39. There, however, the "Genealogical Tree: Alternative 1" diagrammed by Mango is improbable on textual grounds and invalidated by the fact that it leaves no sister of Theodora to marry the Khurramite refugee Theophobus; see Symeon the Logothete (Leo Grammaticus, 215). I would therefore adopt the second alternative, assuming that Theophobus married Theodora's sister Irene (if the editors are right that that name should be restored at Theophanes Continuatus, 174–75, on the basis of John Scylitzes, 98). Sergius's exile and death should be dated early, because Photius stresses that his father and mother died young (Photius, *Epistolae*, 2: 152, no. 234), and as Photius was born before Michael of Synnada, Hilarion of Dalmatus, and other iconophile clergy were exiled in 815 (see Pseudo-Symeon, 668–70, and cf. Mango, "Liquidation," 138–39) his father cannot have been born long after 795. The fact that one of Photius's brothers was named after his father (Photius, *Epistolae*, 2: 97, no. 200), which was unusual in Byzantium, may well mean that he was born after his father's death. Finally, that Sergius was punished by the confiscation of his property fits well with Theophilus's edict of 833. (Pseudo-Symeon, 673–74, may mean that Photius and Sergius's surname was Marzucas and that it was of Khazar origin, but this is far from certain.)

387. Mas'ūdī, *Prairies*, 7: 94–101 (with the story of Ma'mūn's cold, which Vasiliev et al., 1: 329–30, omit); Ṭabarī (Vasiliev et al., 1: 291–92); Ya'qūbī (ibid., 274); ibn Miskawayh (ibid., 348); *Kitāb al-'Uyūn* (ibid., 372); ibn Qutaybah (ibid., 267); Michael the Syrian, 76, 83–84; Bar Hebraeus, 133; *Chronicle of 1234*, 19–20 (slightly misdating the caliph's death). On fears of an Arab invasion in Bithynia, see *Life of Nicetas the Patrician*, 329.

388. Symeon the Logothete (Leo Grammaticus, 215), gives the only reliable Byzantine account; Pseudo-Symeon, 625–27, Genesius, 37–40, and Theophanes Continuatus, 110–12, depend mostly on legendary elaborations and cannot be trusted. On Theophobus's palace, see Treadgold, "Chronological Accuracy," 189–90 and n. 149. The main Oriental sources on this band of Khurramites are Michael the Syrian, 84, 88; Bar Hebraeus, 132, 135; Ṭabarī (Vasiliev et al., 1: 292, 294), and Mas'ūdī, *Book* (ibid., 333–34); but see Rekaya for additional references (and at p. 45 and n. 4 a correction of the text of Ṭabarī at Vasiliev et al., 1: 294, to say not that the Khurramites were led by a "Bārsīs" but that they were called "Bārsīs," meaning "Persians"). Though Rekaya has established that Naṣr's movement was mostly independent of Bābak's, he appears to me to go somewhat too far in emphasizing that independence and much too far in minimizing the importance of the forces of both groups of Khurramites. For Theophilus's decree requiring widows and unmarried women to marry Khurramites, cf. Theophanes Continuatus, 112, with *Life of Athanasia*, 212, which describes how the decree led to the remarriage of Athanasia, the widow of a soldier of Aegina who had been killed defending the island against the Arabs of Crete. The latter passage suggests that the Khurramites were settled all over the empire and that the decree applied only to women from military families. Since Athanasia's parents pressed the marriage upon her, they must either have been well compensated if she complied or subject to a penalty if she did not; the former case seems more likely in view of Theophilus's well-known wealth and generosity, and because otherwise the decree would have caused dangerous discontent in the army and been very difficult to enforce.

389. For the birthdates of Theophilus's children and the chronology of his coinage, see Treadgold, "Problem," 333–35. Otherwise on the coins, see Grierson, *Catalogue*, 3.1, 406–16.

390. Symeon the Logothete (Leo Grammaticus, 215); Pseudo-Symeon, 627; cf. Pseudo-Symeon, 659; Theophanes Continuatus, 173, 257 (for the melting down of most of these ornaments later); Constantine VII, *De Ceremoniis*, 566–70, Liudprand, 6.5, 154–55 (both describing the manner in which the restored organ, lions, and tree were used in the tenth century); and Constantine VII, *De Ceremoni-*

is, 582 (on the articles displayed in the Pentapyrgium in the tenth century), 595 (on a throne made for Theophilus, but in the tenth century not located in the Magnaura). For the date of these creations, see Treadgold, "Chronological Accuracy," 172, 175, showing that it was between 834 and 836; as the date is presumably that at which they were put on display, work probably began no later than 834.

391. On Arab pirates off Ephesus in the Aegean, see *Life of Gregory the Decapolite*, 53–54; the reference to Theophilus's edict dates the passage to 833. That Khurramites were sent to the shore of the Aegean again follows from the *Life of Athanasia*, 212 (see n. 388 above). On affairs in Sicily, see ibn al-Athīr (Vasiliev et al., 1: 359–61) and ibn al-ʿIdhārī (ibid., 375); cf. ibid., 131–33.

392. Michael the Syrian, 84–85; Bar Hebraeus, 134. On the campaign against the Khurramites, see Rekaya, 52–53.

393. On Constantine's death, see Theophanes Continuatus, 88, which evidently refers to it; on his tomb, see Constantine VII, *De Ceremoniis*, 645; and on the date of Constantine's death and Maria's birth, see Treadgold, "Problem," 329–35. Both Symeon the Logothete (Leo Grammaticus, 216) and Theophanes Continuatus, 107, record that Maria was Theophilus's favorite. On the buildings Theophilus built after his son drowned, see Theophanes Continuatus, 88, 144–46.

394. On the earlier history of the follis, see Grierson, *Byzantine Coins*, 59–62, 154. On Theophilus's "reformed" and expanded coinage, see Grierson, *Catalogue*, 3.1, 412–15, with 94–97 on its quantity, giving figures on which I have based my rough calculations, adjusting for the redating of the coins as in my "Problem," 333–35, 340–41; see also Metcalf, "How Extensive Was the Issue?" esp. 309–10. For the state revenue at this time (about 2.9 million nomismata a year), see p. 341 and n. 460 below. For the incident of Petronas's palace, see Symeon the Logothete (Leo Grammaticus, 215–16, supplemented by Georgius Interpolatus, 793) and Pseudo-Symeon, 627–28; for the date, between 834 and 836, see my "Chronological Accuracy," 172, 175. For the story of Theodora's ship, see Pseudo-Symeon, 628; Genesius, 53; and Theophanes Continuatus, 88–89, the last source dating the story to 835 or later by noting that Theophilus saw the ship while sitting on the terrace built on the site of the reservoir after Constantine drowned.

395. Symeon the Logothete (Leo Grammaticus, 216); Pseudo-Symeon, 630; Theophanes Continuatus, 107–8. All three sources seem to think that there was a formal marriage, which I doubt; see my "Problem," 329–35. The betrothal would have taken place after Constantine's death, long enough before the Macedonian campaign for Alexius to have been patrician for a while before becoming Caesar, and probably before it was clear that Theodora was pregnant again, as it turned out with Pulcheria, who was born no later than 837.

396. Theophilus's plans for the former Khurramites follow from his use of them in 837. Cf. the uninterpolated *Letter to Theophilus*, 225 (for the title and date), 232 (for the praise, congratulations, and hopes). Gouillard, "Deux figures," 396–400, has questioned the authenticity of this document and pointed out that according to it Archbishop Theodore (Crithinus) of Syracuse had died before the letter was written in 836, while he is known to have still lived in 869. By itself, this would only show that the Eastern patriarchs were misinformed about events in faraway Syracuse. Nonetheless, despite its wealth of specific and plausible information, and the fact that it praises Theophilus as few iconophiles would have done after 842 and seems really to have been intended to sway him, it is still an extraordinarily pro-Byzantine document for so many clerics in the caliphate to have subscribed to in this form. I suspect it is a contemporary Eastern forgery. Cf.

Vasiliev, "Life," 216–25, and Mango, *Brazen House*, 61 n. 160, both of whom suspect interpolations. On the Arab raids in Sicily, see ibn al-Athīr (Vasiliev et al., 1: 361). That the Fleet was nearly repaired by summer follows from its use on the Black Sea coast by the autumn.

397. The source for the escape of the Macedonians is Symeon the Logothete (Moravcsik, "Sagen," 117–19; cf. Leo Grammaticus, 231–33). Its date of 836 follows from the fact that Basil the Macedonian, the future emperor, was 24 at the time (25 by the Byzantines' inclusive reckoning) and had been born under Michael I, and so about 812 (Symeon, 116); nearly all scholars justifiably assume that such maneuvers could only have taken place before the Bulgar treaty came up for renewal, which was in the fall of 836. The location of the Bulgarian "Macedonia" follows from its being (1) "beyond the Danube," (2) near the Black Sea coast, where the fleet from Constantinople came, and (3) next to a river that formed the boundary between Bulgar and Magyar territory, evidently the Dniester (the Danube being too marshy at its mouths to be crossed in the manner described). On the Slavic revolt around Thessalonica, see *Life of Gregory the Decapolite*, 61–62, and Beševliev, *Protobulgarische Inschriften*, no. 14, 164–65, and note Symeon's reference to the expedition of "Michael the Bulgar" to that region, apparently an error for Isbul; see Grégoire, "Sources épigraphiques," 756–73, with 773–84 for the conclusion that Persian and Malamir were the same ruler. For a rather different interpretation of these events, distinguishing Persian and Malamir, see Beševliev, *Protobulgarische Periode*, 292–94.

398. On Malamir's campaigns and his complaint about the depopulation of his lands, see Beševliev, *Protobulgarische Inschriften*, no. 13, 156. On Alexius's campaign, see *Life of Gregory the Decapolite*, 62–63, describing the activities soon after the troubles at Thessalonica of the "Caesar," the "magister," and their men (first they were at Christopolis and then at Bolerus, the latter presumably on their way back to Constantinople). Theophanes Continuatus, 175, says that Arsaber held the office of magister after his marriage to Theodora's sister Calomaria, which in view of his age was probably before 830, and as John's brother he is not very likely to have been trusted with such a high post after the restoration of the icons in 843. On Caesaropolis, see Grégoire, "Sources épigraphiques," 785. Mango, "On Re-Reading," 639–43, discusses these events while making no mention of the Bulgar treaty, rejecting the Logothete's evidence about Basil I's early history on the basis of the extremely feeble arguments of Adontz and others (see Treadgold, "Bulgars' Treaty," 215 and n. 14), and identifying the "magister" as Manuel, I believe wrongly (see n. 380 above).

399. Ibn al-Athīr (Vasiliev et al., 1: 361).

400. On Bābak's position at this time, see Ṭabarī (Vasiliev et al., 1: 293) and cf. Rekaya, 52–55, who successfully disposes of some previous scholars' theory that there had been an alliance between Bābak and Theophilus before 837. Ṭabarī (Vasiliev et al., 1: 293–94) gives the Arab estimates for Theophilus's army, which included the former Khurramites and presumably Theophobus; at this time the Asian themes totaled 50,000, the former Khurramites 14,000, and the tagmata 24,000 soldiers with 24,000 servants and 2,000 Optimate baggagemen, for a grand total of 88,000 soldiers and 26,000 noncombatants; presumably there were at least 4,000 more noncombatants to serve the thematic armies and the Khurramites. Symeon the Logothete (Leo Grammaticus, 220–21, supplemented by Georgius Interpolatus, 797) reports that Manuel was present, and his authority and that of Ṭabarī therefore corroborate the somewhat confused reports of Genesius, 36–37

(saying both Manuel and Theophobus were present), and Theophanes Continuatus, 124 (saying Theophobus was present).

401. Michael the Syrian, 73–74 (a misdated doublet), 88–89 (the best and fullest account); Bar Hebraeus, 135–36, 132, and *Chronicle of 1234*, 15 (the last two accounts paralleling Michael's doublet); Stephen of Taron, 107–8, and Samuel of Ani, 423 (but on both Stephen and Samuel, cf. Vasiliev et al., 1: 139 n. 2); Ṭabarī (Vasiliev et al., 1: 293–94, the best Arab account); Ya'qūbī (ibid., 274–75); Balādhurī (ibid., 269); Mas'ūdī, *Prairies* (ibid., 330–31); Symeon the Logothete (Leo Grammaticus, 220–21, supplemented by Georgius Interpolatus, 797–98); Genesius, 44–45, 46–47; Theophanes Continuatus, 124; *Acts of the Martyrs of Amorium IV*, 40–42. The Greek sources' improbable report that either Sozopetra or Arsamosata was the caliph's birthplace seems to have been circulated because Mu'taṣim later retaliated by sacking Amorium, which apparently was Theophilus's birthplace (see above, n. 366). Vasiliev et al., 1: 138–41, give a somewhat different account of this campaign, supposing for no reason I can see that Theophilus actually entered Melitene. I cannot now agree with Rekaya, 56–57 and n. 5, in dating Theophilus's campaign to March and April of 837, though I did so in "Chronological Accuracy," 177 and n. 76. Rekaya's date depends on an arbitrary redating of a passage in Mas'ūdī, *Prairies* (Vasiliev et al., 1: 331), describing the preparations for Mu'taṣim's campaign of the following year, and on rejecting Michael the Syrian's explicit statement that Theophilus's campaign took place in the summer.

402. Symeon the Logothete (Leo Grammaticus, 221); Theophanes Continuatus, 98–99; Constantine VII, *De Ceremoniis*, 503–8 (cf. Treadgold, "Problem," 331–32). The fact that Theophanes Continuatus's description of the Bryas palace provides for no chapel dedicated to a patroness of Theophilus's fifth daughter, Pulcheria, whose name is not that of a martyr, seems a reason, though hardly a conclusive one, for supposing that she was not yet born in the summer of 837.

403. The date of 837 for the creation of the theme of Chaldia was first suggested by Bury, 223 and n. 2, 261. *Acts of the Martyrs of Amorium VII*, 65, records that there were seven themes in 838, which would mean that Chaldia was then a theme; this should probably be accepted. If so, the mention of the duke of Chaldia in the *Tacticon Uspensky*, 53, is five or six years out of date and dates the prototype used by the redactor of the *Tacticon* to 837 or earlier; cf. Treadgold, "Notes," 280. On the Khurramites, note that Symeon the Logothete (Leo Grammaticus, 215) says that 14,000 Khurramites fled to Theophilus in 834, while Genesius, 41, and Theophanes Continuatus, 125, say that by 839 the Khurramites had increased to 30,000. Symeon's figure seems reliable, both because he is a reliable source and because medieval sources seldom underestimate armies; but the other two writers also seem to be correct, both because they are aware that the Khurramites had once been fewer and because their statement that 2,000 Khurramites were sent to each of fifteen districts in 839 is corroborated by facts otherwise known (see Treadgold, *Byzantine State Finances*, 69–73). Michael the Syrian, 90, and Bar Hebraeus, 136, say that Bābak, by the end of his revolt in September 837, saw that most of his men had fled to the empire and tried to flee there himself. This cannot plausibly be considered a reference to the flight of Naṣr (Theophobus) and his men three and a half years earlier, particularly because Naṣr's men had not even then been subject to Bābak; cf. Rekaya, 58–60. Note that Mas'ūdī, *Book* (Vasiliev et al., 1: 333–34), says that by 838 Khurramites from *both* Azerbaijan and the Zagros were fighting with the Byzantines and numbered "many thousands." It follows that two bands of Khurramites fled to the empire in succession, first Naṣr's in 834

and then Bābak's (though without Bābak himself) in 837. Theophanes Continuatus, 124, is probably referring to the reception of the latter group into the empire when he says that when Theophilus returned to the capital after his summer campaign of 837 he assigned Theophobus "to manage the affairs of the Persians" (though the chronicler then goes on mistakenly to connect this with the Khurramite revolt against Theophilus a year later). On the Arabs' winter raid, see Michael the Syrian, 89.

404. On the temporary capture of the town of Henna, see ibn al-Athīr (Vasiliev et al., 1: 361–62), and, on the subsequent raids, see ibn al-ʿIdharī (ibid., 375; the encounter described on 375–76 perhaps belongs to 838). On Theophilus's sending Alexius, see Symeon the Logothete (Leo Grammaticus, 216), and Pseudo-Symeon, 630; cf. Theophanes Continuatus, 107–8, who however says incorrectly that Alexius went to "Lombardy" (i.e., the Lombard principality of Benevento). On the arrival of the Byzantine expedition in Sicily, see ibn al-Athīr (Vasiliev et al., 1: 362); on Sicily, anything over a thousand troops would be "numerous." On the capacity of the Imperial Fleet, note that it carried 4,200 soldiers in 912; cf. Constantine VII, *De Ceremoniis*, 652 (counting 60 dromons with 70 soldiers each).

405. On Pulcheria's birth, see Treadgold, "Problem," 333–35, and cf. n. 402 above. On the foundation of the Church of St. Mary of Blachernae by the empress Pulcheria in the fifth century see Janin, *Géographie*, 161. John of Cathara probably died on February 4, 836; see n. 386 above. Nicetas the Patrician died on October 6, 836; see *Life of Nicetas the Patrician*, 345–47, and cf. 314. Peter of Atroa died on January 1, 837; see *Life of Peter of Atroa*, 223. Macarius of Pelecete died not very long after his imprisonment on an August 18, probably in 834; see *Life of Macarius of Pelecete*, 159–62. On Leo the Sacellarius, see Petrus, ch. 62, 425C, and Sabas, ch. 50, 378D–379A, and cf. p. 343 and n. 464 below.

406. On John's accession, see Symeon the Logothete (Leo Grammaticus, 221), Pseudo-Symeon, 635, and Theophanes Continuatus, 121, and cf. Treadgold, "Chronological Accuracy," 178–79; in addition to the arguments given in that article against accepting the interpolation at Theophanes, 362, as a reliable source for the length of John's patriarchate, note that the interpolation wrongly assigns Nicephorus a patriarchate of eight years (it should be nine), and thus fails the only certain test to which we can put it. On Anthony's illness, which began between 833 and 836, see the uninterpolated *Letter to Theophilus*, 359, though it is not quite certain that this disease was later the cause of the patriarch's death. For the date of Muʿtaṣim's departure, see Yaʿqūbī (Vasiliev et al., 1: 275; cf. 145 and n. 3). For the arrival of the news at Bryas, see Symeon the Logothete (Leo Grammaticus, 223–24). On the number of the Arabs' troops, see Michael the Syrian, 94–95; the hesitant statement of Masʿūdī, *Prairies* (Vasiliev et al., 1: 331) that the army was variously estimated at between 200,000 and 500,000 is no reason for questioning Michael the Syrian's detailed and plausible (though rounded) figures, which include 30,000 baggagemen, 50,000 camels, and 20,000 mules accompanying the main army of 50,000 men (the other army of 30,000 presumably had its own baggage train). Michael's total of 80,000 seems to be confirmed by Symeon the Logothete (Leo Grammaticus, 224), and Theophanes Continuatus, 113, though both think that this was the size of the smaller contingent alone. On Amorium as Theophilus's birthplace, see n. 366 above.

407. On the council, see *Synodicon Vetus*, ch. 155, p. 130, and on the edict, see Symeon the Logothete (Leo Grammaticus, 221), and Pseudo-Symeon, 635; cf.

Treadgold, "Chronological Accuracy," 179–80. Though the *Synodicon Vetus* is often wrong, and in fact says incorrectly that the council of 815 had anathematized iconophiles (ch. 154, p. 130), by 838 it has become a nearly contemporary document, and its account of the council of 843 (ch. 156, p. 132) is one of the best; cf. Mango, "Liquidation," 133–34, with 136–37 on the anathematization of Tarasius, which seems to be datable only to this occasion. That the Logothete does not mention a council at the time proves nothing, because the Logothete similarly fails to refer to a council when he mentions the edict of 833, though the uninterpolated *Letter to Theophilus* shows that there was a council then; see n. 386 above. On the painter Lazarus, whose production of icons violated the second edict rather than the first, see Theophanes Continuatus, 102–3, and cf. pp. 311–12 and n. 429 below.

408. On Theophilus's advance to Cappadocia, see Theophanes Continuatus, 109–10, 125–26; Genesius, 40; Symeon the Logothete (Leo Grammaticus, 222, 223–24); Pseudo-Symeon, 638; and Ṭabarī (Vasiliev et al., 1: 297, noting that Theophilus spent 30 days on the Halys). To these sources should be added Genesius, 65–66, and Theophanes Continuatus, 177, which purport to give an account of a battle fought near Dazimon in the late 850's under Michael III but are actually reworked accounts of the battle of Dazimon of 838; see Grégoire, "Manuel," 182–84, 201–4, and my "Chronological Accuracy," 180–83. Note that in this version the Arabs are led by ʿUmar of Melitene, who was a leader of the eastern contingent of the Arab army in 838, and have 30,000 troops, the very number this contingent had in 838; therefore this version's statement that the Byzantines had 40,000 troops, including many from Thrace and Macedonia, may well apply to 838 and be correct. As for the troops sent from Dorylaeum to Amorium, Theophanes Continuatus, 125–26, mentions that they were commanded by Theodore Craterus, Theophilus, and (Constantine) Babutzicus, while *Acts of the Martyrs of Amorium IV*, 46, 50, gives their dignities as protospatharius, protospatharius, and patrician respectively. Symeon (Leo Grammaticus, 224) says that at the fall of Amorium various "officers of the tagmata" were captured along with Constantine (Babutzicus) the drungary (evidently of the Watch, because this was the only non-naval drungariate nearly exalted enough to be held by a patrician). That the protospatharii Theodore Craterus and Theophilus were also tagmatic commanders is my conjecture, supported by the existence of a ninth-century seal of "Theophilus, Protospatharius and Domestic of the Excubitors" (Zacos and Veglery, no. 2517A) and the presence of Theodore Craterus in the capital in 831 as a familiar of the emperor (see Theophanes Continuatus, 115–16). Theodore was a eunuch, and, like Vasiliev et al., 1: 158 and n. 1, I believe that he was the eunuch who Ṭabarī (Vasiliev et al., 1: 300–301) says was one of the emperor's attendants (i.e., a tagmatic commander), first went with the main army to the east, and was then sent by the emperor to Amorium after being sent too late to defend Ancyra. (By process of elimination, he would have been domestic of the Hicanati.) It follows that Theophanes Continuatus must be wrong that Theophilus sent Theodore to Amorium at the start, though it is easy to see how this later reinforcement might have been confused with the earlier ones. (Note that the strange Greek text quoted in the commentary for *Acts of the Martyrs of Amorium*, 203, is not from *Acts of the Martyrs of Amorium VIII*, 84–85, as Nikitin says it is, and discredits itself by calling Theophilus strategus of the Anatolics and Aëtius a junior officer. I am unaware of its origin.)

409. Ṭabarī (Vasiliev et al., 1: 295–98); Michael the Syrian, 94–95; Bar Hebraeus, 136; *Chronicle of 1234*, 23–24; Genesius, 46–48; Theophanes Continuatus,

126–27. The general who according to Ṭabarī was the son of Theophilus's maternal uncle would have been the grandson of Bardanes Turcus and probably the child of Bardanes' only known son, Bryenes (see above, p. 196 and n. 263). His name is not known, though as he could have been named after his grandfather one might look for a strategus of the Bucellarians named Bardanes.

410. The accounts of the battle of Anzen as such are in Symeon the Logothete (Leo Grammaticus, 222, 224); Pseudo-Symeon, 636–37, 638; Genesius, 48–49; Theophanes Continuatus, 127–29; Masʿūdī, *Prairies* and *Book* (Vasiliev et al., 1: 331–32, 333–34); Ṭabarī (ibid., 299–301, 309); Yaʿqūbī (ibid., 275); Michael the Syrian, 95; Bar Hebraeus, 136; and *Chronicle of 1234*, 24. Cf. Genesius, 43–44, and Theophanes Continuatus, 113–14, 116–18, which describe a battle that purports to be earlier than Anzen but actually is Anzen; and Genesius, 65–66, and Theophanes Continuatus, 177, which describe a battle of Anzen that purports to date from ca. 858 but is actually that of 838. The date of Manuel's death is revealed by the *Synaxarium*, 851–52. On the extraordinary hagiographical fraud by which Manuel is revived after his death in Genesius and Theophanes Continuatus, see Grégoire, "Études," 520–24, and "Manuel" (though I do not fully share Grégoire's views on Theophobus). On the various versions of this battle, see Treadgold, "Chronological Accuracy," 180–83. The actions of Theophilus's cousin must be deduced from Ṭabarī (Vasiliev et al., 1: 297–301). He recounts that the cousin was left in charge of the forces near the Halys on the road to Ancyra; that the main Arab force then traveled that road easily, taking many prisoners but suffering severely from a lack of forage; that at the same time the inhabitants of Ancyra had fled; that when Theophilus returned from Anzen he found the army he had left under his relative (i.e., his cousin) well to the east of its original position and mostly dispersed; and that he consequently had the negligent commander beheaded.

411. The plan to proclaim another emperor is explicitly mentioned only by Michael the Syrian, 95, and Bar Hebraeus, 136, who say that Theophilus received the report of it from his "mother," by which they presumably mean Euphrosyne. Their often unreliable testimony gains support from Pseudo-Symeon, 635–36, Genesius, 49–50, and Theophanes Continuatus, 121–22 (note the mention of Theoctistus in the latter two); these say that at just this time, soon after the consecration of John the Grammarian and approximately when Amorium was taken, Theophilus made Martinacius a monk because the emperor had learned from an Arab prophetess captured in battle that Martinacius's family was destined to rule the empire, while Theophilus would be succeeded by his wife and a son, John would be deposed as patriarch, and the icons would be restored. The prophetess also told a certain Constantine Triphyllius and his son Nicetas, then the special secretary, that they would be tonsured later by an emperor named Basil, meaning Basil I (867–86), and George the Military Logothete that he would be executed in the Hippodrome and would have his property confiscated. Though all these prophecies are presumably *ex eventu*, Martinacius did exist and was related to Theophilus, and evidently was made a monk in 838 (see Mango, "Eudocia," 20–21, who however dates the prophecy to ca. 837, taking that to be the year of John's consecration); this fits well with Michael's statements. Though George could have been executed later, he could also be one of those whom, according to Michael, Theophilus executed for wanting to proclaim another emperor. Theophilus's prompt return to the capital also follows from Theophanes Continuatus, 124, and Genesius, 40, and from the report of Symeon the Logothete (Leo Grammaticus,

222–23; cf. Pseudo-Symeon, 637–38) about the misappropriated horse; cf. Theophanes Continuatus, 92–94, for another version of the story, and for the date see Treadgold, "Chronological Accuracy," 183–84.

412. Symeon the Logothete (Leo Grammaticus, 222, supplemented from Georgius Interpolatus, 802–3); Pseudo-Symeon, 637; Genesius, 40–41, 42–43; Theophanes Continuatus, 124–25. For indications that Theophobus did not hold Paphlagonia even in 839, see below, pp. 312–13 and n. 431.

413. Ṭabarī (Vasiliev et al., 1:298–302, 309) fits a remarkable amount of marching into the ten days between his dates for the battle of Anzen (July 22) and the beginning of the siege of Amorium (August 1). Allowing for as much marching time as possible, Ṭabarī's account can be reduced to the table below.

Ṭabarī's Chronology, July 22 – August 2

July 22	Battle of Anzen; Afshīn leaves Anzen
ca. July 25	Theodore Craterus finds Ancyra deserted
ca. July 26	Byzantine refugees from Ancyra and Anzen captured in salt mines; Ashinās arrives at Ancyra
ca. July 27	Muʿtaṣim arrives at Ancyra
ca. July 28	Afshīn arrives at Ancyra
ca. July 29	Ashinās leaves Ancyra
ca. July 30	Muʿtaṣim leaves Ancyra
ca. July 31	Afshīn leaves Ancyra; Ashinās arrives at Amorium
August 1	Muʿtaṣim arrives at Amorium, begins siege
August 2	Afshīn arrives at Amorium

This schedule would require the Arabs to have averaged travel of over 30 miles a day, since it is about 180 miles from Anzen to Ancyra and about 100 miles from Ancyra to Amorium. Though this speed is easy enough for cavalry (the Byzantine cavalry went twice as fast) and the infantry may have lagged behind, it is an indication of haste. The ravaging of the land between Ancyra and Amorium, mentioned by Ṭabarī, and the destruction of Ancyra, mentioned in a poem quoted by Masʿūdī, *Book* (Vasiliev et al., 1:334), must have been pretty perfunctory.

414. Genesius, 45, 49; Theophanes Continuatus, 129–30; Yaʿqūbī (Vasiliev et al., 1:275); Ṭabarī (ibid., 308–9).

415. The most detailed accounts of the siege are those of Ṭabarī (Vasiliev et al., 1:302–9), Michael the Syrian, 97–101, and Bar Hebraeus, 136–38; see also *Chronicle of 1234*, 24–25; Symeon the Logothete (Leo Grammaticus, 224); Pseudo-Symeon, 638–39; George the Monk, 797–98; Genesius, 45–46 (largely legendary); Theophanes Continuatus, 130–31 (again largely legendary); Balādhurī (Vasiliev et al., 1:269); Yaʿqūbī (ibid., 275); Masʿūdī, *Prairies* and *Book* (ibid., 332, 334); ibn Qutaybah (ibid., 268); *Synaxarium*, 279–80 (on the partial sack of Polybotus); *Acts of the Martyrs of Amorium I*, 1, 4 (erroneously saying that the strategi of all seven themes were captured, and calling the traitor Boödes), *II*, 11, *IV*, 42–44, *VII*, 65, 71 (again calling the traitor Boödes). The date of Muʿtaṣim's departure follows from Ṭabarī's statements that the caliph entered the empire on June 21 and turned back after 55 days (Vasiliev et al., 1:295, 309). Theophanes Continuatus, 130, gives the figure of about 70,000 for those in Amorium at the time it fell, and the figure seems quite possible if we count refugees from the neighboring area and note that the forces of the Anatolics, Excubitors, Watch, and Hicanati, whose commanders were in Amorium, totaled 30,000 soldiers. Masʿūdī, *Prairies* (Vasi-

liev et al., 1: 332), notes that 30,000 men were killed at the time of the sack, while Michael the Syrian, 99, mentions that over 1,000 nuns were raped (the *Chronicle of 1234*, 24, says over 4,000, probably through a textual error). Ṭabarī (Vasiliev et al., 1: 309) says that 6,000 male captives were killed on the way back to the caliphate. These numbers, though probably rounded upward, tend to support each other, and suggest that the normal population of Amorium had been on the order of 30,000 people.

416. Michael the Syrian, 96; Bar Hebraeus, 138; Genesius, 46; Theophanes Continuatus, 131. Genesius has the caliph say that he had spent more than 100,000 pounds of gold (7.2 million nomismata) on the expedition to Amorium; this is 24 times the cost of the most expensive Arab expeditions mentioned by Qudāmah, 193, and obviously a wild exaggeration. Theophanes Continuatus has the caliph say that Theophilus himself had spent 100,000 pounds on "ostentation and gift giving," which is in fact somewhere near the truth; see Treadgold, *Byzantine State Finances*, 85 and n. 355. Though neither source is very reliable and the remark would in any case be one of mockery, Theophanes Continuatus's version seems preferable. Mas'ūdī, *Prairies* (Vasiliev et al., 1: 332–33), indicates that Aëtius was executed not long after Bābak, and so probably in 838.

417. For Theophilus's alleged plot with 'Abbās, see Michael the Syrian, 101. On Theophilus's illness, see Genesius, 49, and Theophanes Continuatus, 131.

418. By 840 Ancyra was in use as headquarters of the Bucellarians, while the headquarters of the Anatolics were at Marj al-Shaḥm; see ibn al-Faqīh (Brooks, "Arabic Lists," 76, 74), and, for the date of this text's source, see Treadgold, "Remarks," 205–12. Marj al-Shaḥm is not identified in Belke, 203, except as an unknown fortress near Amorium; but its name ("Pasture of Fat") seems to be an Arabic rendering of the Greek Polybotus ("With Much Pasture"), which was one of the fortresses nearest to Amorium and not fully destroyed in 838 (see *Synaxarium*, 279–80).

419. On the Turks' archery tactics at Anzen, see Kaegi, "Contribution."

420. Like most scholars, I identify Alexius's force with the large Byzantine army whose success is mentioned by ibn al-Athīr (Vasiliev et al., 1: 362), and I suspect that it was also responsible for the defeat and capture of the Arab leader 'Abd al-Salām, mentioned by ibn al-'Idharī (ibid., 375–76). These victories are evidently those attributed to Alexius in the confused account of Theophanes Continuatus, 108, which are said to have increased his favor with the emperor. The Imperial Fleet was back in Constantinople and ready for another mission by the summer of 839; see below, p. 313 and n. 432.

421. On the date of the bronze doors of St. Sophia and their original inscriptions, see Mango, "When Was Michael III Born?" 253–54. On Theophilus's building in the palace at this time, see Symeon the Logothete (Leo Grammaticus, 225), Pseudo-Symeon, 640–41, and Theophanes Continuatus, 140–43; on the date, cf. Treadgold, "Chronological Accuracy," 187, and note that the Sigma must have been ready to accommodate Methodius by about the beginning of 839 (see p. 308 and n. 424 below).

422. Symeon the Logothete (Leo Grammaticus, 225); Pseudo-Symeon, 640; Theophanes Continuatus, 185–89 (wrongly identifying the caliph as Ma'mūn); cf. Treadgold, "Chronological Accuracy," 185–87.

423. On John's suburban laboratory, see Symeon the Logothete (Leo Grammaticus, 221), Pseudo-Symeon, 635, and Theophanes Continuatus, 156–57; cf. Treadgold, "Chronological Accuracy," 180. The rumors reported by Theophanes

Continuatus that John debauched beautiful women there (the text should be corrected from John Scylitzes, 86) are naturally not substantiated by the early source of the Logothete. On the prediction of Leo's student, see Symeon (Leo Grammaticus, 225), and Pseudo-Symeon, 640. On Leo's telegraph, see Pseudo-Symeon, 681–82, Theophanes Continuatus, 197–98, and Constantine VII, *De Ceremoniis*, 492–93; cf. Pattenden.

424. Pseudo-Symeon, 643–45 (who by noting that Methodius was imprisoned for seven years dates his release to the end of 838 or the beginning of 839); Genesius, 53; *Life of Methodius*, 1252B–1253A; Theophanes Continuatus, 116 (whose statement that Theophilus took Methodius along on the campaign of 838 is not supported by other sources and is incompatible with Pseudo-Symeon's statements about the length of Methodius's exile and his being housed in the Sigma).

425. On earlier Russian raids, see p. 223 and n. 306 above. On Theophilus's embassy to Louis, the Russians, their embassy, and their problems, see *Annales Bertiniani*, 19–20; Genesius, 50; and Theophanes Continuatus, 135. The Byzantine sources are likely to be right that the Byzantine ambassador Theodosius was a patrician, not metropolitan of Chalcedon as the *Annales Bertiniani* say; presumably the metropolitan was another ambassador, like Theophanes the Spatharius, also mentioned by the annals. Genesius's statement that Theodosius was a relative of Theophilus appears to indicate that he was Constantine Babutzicus's brother. On the Arab reinforcements sent to Sicily, see ibn al-Athīr (Vasiliev et al., 1: 362). On the military situation to the north of the Black Sea at this time, cf. below, p. 313 and n. 432.

426. Theophanes Continuatus, 95, 139–40, 144, and 160; Pseudo-Symeon, 653. The date of 839 seems to follow not only from Theophilus's depression but from the fact that the Carianus was apparently built after the Triconch (completed around the end of 838) and designed specifically for Theophilus's daughters, which implies that it was built before Michael III was born, if not necessarily before Maria died. The story fits best before the incident of the "dolls," which roused the emperor from depression to anger, and it may explain why he did not feel able to vent that anger on Theodora. Janin, *Constantinople*, 132, distinguishes *two* palaces called Carianus built by Theophilus, including one in the Quarter of Carianus near the Blachernae, which was for the daughters. The coincidence seems to me most improbable, apart from the fact that the daughters seem very young to be living so far from their parents at the time.

427. The story is told in its original form by Pseudo-Symeon, 628–29, and in an altered form by Theophanes Continuatus, 90–91, which replaces Euphrosyne with Theoctista for reasons of its own; see Treadgold, "Problem," 333–40, on the story and its date. The absence from the original version of Theoctista, who is in fact not heard of again after her visit to Euthymius of Sardis at the end of 831 (see above, pp. 277–78 and n. 383), appears to indicate that she was no longer living at the monastery, while her tomb is put there by Constantine VII, *De Ceremoniis*, 647–48 (of course, if she was still living there and was not involved, that would have been a reason for Theophilus to remove Euphrosyne so that his daughters could visit their grandmother). Theophilus's relegation of Euphrosyne to another convent at this time may be the source of the distorted statement at Theophanes Continuatus, 86, that he sent her back to her original monastery at the beginning of her reign; actually, she went to a new monastery that she founded herself and where she was buried—with, interestingly, Theophilus's daughter Anna, who had obviously become attached to her (Constantine VII, *De Ceremoniis*, 647). On the

monastery of Euphrosyne, see Janin, *Géographie*, 130–31. I do not believe the story, told just after the story of Pulcheria and the "dolls" in Pseudo-Symeon, 629–30, and Theophanes Continuatus, 91–92, that the court jester Denderis reported to Theophilus that he had seen Theodora playing with "dolls," and that she escaped Theophilus's wrath by saying the "dolls" were the reflections of herself and her servants in a mirror. One of the two stories is clearly copied from the other, and the second, which makes the iconophile Theodora outwit the iconoclast Theophilus, is much the more edifying and the less plausible. It may nonetheless be an invention of an early date, since Denderis looks like a historical person.

428. The best sources for the punishment of Theodore and Theophanes are Symeon the Logothete (Leo Grammaticus, 216–17), which reveals the date (see Treadgold, "Chronological Accuracy," 187–89); Pseudo-Symeon, 630–31; and especially Theodore's own letter to John of Cyzicus, referred to and quoted in the *Life of Theodore Graptus*, 669D–680A, which is the only source to reveal that the brothers had come to Constantinople under Michael I (676B) and that the postal logothete, at this time Theoctistus, was sympathetic to them (676B–C). The frequently erroneous *Life of Michael Syncellus*, 246, 232–33, says that they were branded in 836 and that they and Michael had come to Byzantium because of Arab oppression, which seems clearly to be that of 812 (see above, p. 185 and n. 253), but also that they came under Leo V; evidently the hagiographer, whose sense of chronology is very poor, assumed that Theophilus's belief that they had come under Leo V was correct. The error in the date of their arrival, though not in the date of their branding, is also made in the main text of the *Life of Theodore Graptus*, 661B–664C—which, however, explicitly connects their departure with the devastation of the Monastery of St. Sabas, an event that certainly happened in 812 (Theophanes, 499)—and in the *Encomium of Theodore Graptus*, chs. 14–18, pp. 120–25. The latter two texts, like Theophanes Continuatus, 104–6, attribute to Theodore lengthy anti-iconoclast arguments that he makes no mention of in his own letter and are presumably fabrications. On the whole question, cf. Treadgold, "Chronological Accuracy," 187–89 and esp. n. 139.

429. Theophanes Continuatus, 102–4, mentions the torture of Lazarus just before the torture of Theodore and Theophanes, and the two do seem to belong together, but the date of mid-839 for Lazarus's branding cannot be considered secure. On Lazarus, see Mango, "Documentary Evidence," 396–97. On the monastery of Phoberus, cf. pp. 280–81 and n. 386 above, and see Janin, *Églises*, 7–8 (though unlike Janin I see no reason to doubt that a place where iconophiles could be detained was not only a church but already a monastery, as it surely was later). The iconophiles previously beaten to death were Euthymius of Sardis and the monks of the Monastery of the Abrahamites; see pp. 277–78 and n. 383, and pp. 280–81 and n. 386, above.

430. For Arab victories on Sicily at this time, see ibn al-Athīr (Vasiliev et al., 1.362). On Maria's death and Alexius's recall, see Symeon the Logothete (Leo Grammaticus, 216–17, where the reference to the stripping of the silver from Maria's coffin by Leo VI must be an addition by Symeon to his source); Pseudo-Symeon, 630–31; and Theophanes Continuatus, 108 (where the chronicler seems to have altered the facts either out of sympathy for Theophilus or through confusion). For the location of Maria's tomb, see Constantine VII, *De Ceremoniis*, 645. Note that Maria was still alive at the time of the incident of the "dolls" (see p. 310 and n. 427 above) and that Alexius must have been recalled several months

before he actually arrived at Constantinople (see p. 313 and n. 433 below). On Theodore Crithinus's consecration, which apparently occurred shortly before the iconoclast synod of 833, see the uninterpolated *Letter to Theophilus*, 358–59 (cf. p. 290 and n. 396 above).

431. On Theophilus's preventive expedition against the Arabs at this time, see Theophanes Continuatus, 122; this is admittedly not a very reliable work, but here it is evidently copying a good source, which went on to give accounts of the Khazar embassy and the foundation of the theme of the Climata that can be independently confirmed. On Theophobus's secret communication with Theophilus, see Genesius, 40–41, and Theophanes Continuatus, 124–25.

432. Constantine VII, *De Administrando Imperio*, ch. 42, pp. 182–84; Theophanes Continuatus, 122–23 (giving the date as the year after the consecration of John the Grammarian and the forced tonsure of Martinacius, both of which were in 838, and the same year as the foundation of the theme of the Climata, which was late 839). Here I have accepted the very plausible view of Vasiliev, *Goths*, 108–12, that Sarkel was built as a defense against the Russians, though some other scholars believe that the Magyars were the enemy. See recently Obolensky, 128–29. (Note that Vasiliev and Obolensky both believe that Sarkel was built about 833, because they accept the erroneous date of 832 for John the Grammarian's consecration.) It seems likely that the Khazars wanted Sarkel built as a defense against a new enemy. While the Magyars had been occupying the southern Ukraine for at least a century in amity with the Khazars, the Russian embassy to Constantinople of early 839 seems to show hostility between the more recently established Russians and their two southern neighbors (see p. 309 and n. 425 above). At Theophanes Continuatus, 122, the reference to the Pechenegs looks like an addition by the chronicler, since it is not in the *De Administrando Imperio*. That this Petronas was not the same as Theophilus's brother-in-law and the former drungary of the Watch seems clear from his relatively low rank of spatharocandidatus, if not necessarily from his surname, Camaterus.

433. Symeon the Logothete (Leo Grammaticus, 217–18); Pseudo-Symeon, 630–32; cf. Theophanes Continuatus, 108, which apparently mitigates Theophilus's harshness in this case on the assumption that his daughter Maria had really married Alexius and was still alive, and out of a general tendency to emphasize Theophilus's justice. On the other hand, the Logothete has apparently distorted the story by making Theodore Crithinus an iconophile, perhaps because the chronicler wanted to claim Theodore's courage for the Orthodox side and had trouble imagining that Theophilus would have dealt so harshly with an iconoclast. Cf. Treadgold, "Chronological Accuracy," 194–95 and n. 174.

434. Symeon the Logothete (Georgius Interpolatus, 802–3, since there is a lacuna at Leo Grammaticus, 222); Pseudo-Symeon, 637; Genesius, 40–41; Theophanes Continuatus, 124–25. There are inferior accounts in Genesius, 42–43 (who says that Theophilus also sent a naval expedition against the Persians at Amastris and that he immediately broke his word and had Theophobus executed by the drungary of the Watch Oöryphas), and in Theophanes Continuatus, 135–36 (who says the same and muddles matters further by making Oöryphas the head of the naval expedition, though the drungary of the Watch commanded cavalry). The Logothete confirms that Theophobus was executed two years later and that the Persians were at Sinope in the Armeniacs and not at Amastris in Paphlagonia. That the Persians did not hold Paphlagonia is clear from the fact that Theophilus could go to Paphlagonia without confronting them and could send the Paphla-

gonian fleet to Cherson with Petronas Camaterus at this very time. Samuel of Ani, 429, may be confusedly referring to Theophilus's ending the Persian revolt when he says that the emperor took Trebizond and expelled the "Tadzhiks." The redistribution of the Persians among the themes is mentioned only by the better accounts in Genesius and Theophanes Continuatus; the Logothete simply says that the Persians were returned to their original places, which he has already said were in different themes in "Persian turmae" (Leo Grammaticus, 215). The date of the end of this rebellion follows from the Logothete's statement that it occurred just before the birth of Michael III, which was on January 9, 840 (see below, p. 319 and n. 439). Cf. Treadgold, "Chronological Accuracy," 183, which, however, fails to reject the inferior accounts in Genesius and Theophanes Continuatus.

435. On this hypothetical manual, and on the Arab prisoner and author al-Jarmī, see Treadgold, "Remarks."

436. For a reconstruction of the manner in which the Persians were distributed among the themes, cleisurae, and Optimates, see Treadgold, *Byzantine State Finances*, 69–73. On the previous status of Charsianum and Cappadocia as turmae, see Constantine VII, *De Administrando Imperio*, ch. 50, p. 236. Seleucia must earlier have been a turma of the Anatolics, the only non-naval theme that it adjoined; since its soldiers were not marines, none of them could have come from the Cibyrrhaeots. For ex-Khurramites on the Arab frontier later, see below, pp. 321–22 and n. 443. On the creation of the theme of the Climata, see Constantine VII, *De Administrando Imperio*, ch. 42, p. 184, and Theophanes Continuatus, 123–24.

437. On the introduction of the bandum and its implications for the cavalry, see Treadgold, *Byzantine State Finances*, 73–75, 80–81.

438. On the pay cycle and the increase in pay, see Treadgold, *Byzantine State Finances*, 14–15, 75–77, and below, pp. 358–59 and n. 479; cf. ibn Khurdādhbih, 84. For the price of Byzantine farm animals, see Ostrogorsky, 326–33.

439. On Michael's birthdate, see Symeon the Logothete (Leo Grammaticus, 222, supplemented by Georgius Interpolatus, 803), Pseudo-Symeon, 637, and Theophanes Continuatus, 108; cf. Treadgold, "Chronological Accuracy," 183, and esp. Mango, "When Was Michael III Born?" On Alexius's retirement, see Pseudo-Symeon, 632, and Theophanes Continuatus, 108–9; on his monastery, see Janin, *Églises*, 17–18. For Theophilus's baldness, see Theophanes Continuatus, 107, though the statement there that Theophilus consequently ordered other men to cut their hair short looks like an elaboration.

440. See Theophanes Continuatus, 189–92; Symeon the Logothete (Leo Grammaticus, 225); and Pseudo-Symeon, 640; and cf. Treadgold, "Chronological Accuracy," 185–87 and esp. n. 127. Theophanes Continuatus also says that the caliph offered a perpetual peace, which is absurd. For Leo's sermon, see Laurent, "Homélie."

441. For Arab raids on Calabria, the arrival and defeat of the Imperial Fleet, and the surrender of the Sicilian forts, see *Chronicle of Salerno*, 508, and ibn al-Athīr (Vasiliev et al., 1: 362). On the general situation in southern Italy, see Vasiliev et al., 1: 179–82. On the embassy to Venice and the Venetians' battle with the Arabs, see Andrea Dandolo, 150, and John the Deacon, *Chronicon*, 113–14. On the embassy to Cordova, see Maqqarī, 2: 114–15.

442. Theophanes Continuatus, 137. The date of this expedition may be guessed by process of elimination, on the assumptions that Theophilus made no important military moves on the Arab frontier between 834, when Theophobus arrived, and the expedition of 837 against Sozopetra; that in 837 and 838 Theo-

phobus's activities are well known; that in 839 Theophobus was in revolt; and that the Arabs could scarcely have believed he was dead in 841 if he had undertaken a major campaign then. An approximate *terminus ante quem* for Bardas's birthdate follows from the fact that in 856 the elder of his two sons married and was able to exercise responsibility over troops according to Symeon the Logothete (Leo Grammaticus, 238); the son might then have been about twenty, and if Bardas had married at about the same age he would have been born about 815. He would therefore have been roughly the same age as his sister Theodora, whose rival he was to become.

443. See Michael the Syrian, 96, Bar Hebraeus, 138, and the poets Abū Tammām (Vasiliev et al., 1: 399–402) and Buḥturī (ibid., 403–4); for the location of Acarcūs, see Vasiliev et al., 1: 408. All these sources share the Arab view that the Byzantine leader was Naṣr, the name of Theophobus before his baptism. Vasiliev et al., 1: 175–76, 415–16, also accept this view, though it is contradicted by all the Byzantine sources, including the very early source of the Logothete, which say that Theophilus had Theophobus executed in Constantinople at the beginning of 842. The Byzantine sources were far better positioned to know the truth than the Arabs, who moreover had every reason to claim that the salted head was Theophobus's even if it was not. See Treadgold, "Chronological Accuracy," 189–90, though it now seems clear to me that Michael's date for the battle of Acarcūs need only be no earlier than 838 (the year 1149 of the Seleucid Era; Michael the Syrian, 94) and no later than 841 (the year 1152; Michael the Syrian, 102). Since the battle plainly involved former Khurramites, who were in revolt until the end of 839, it must have occurred in 840. So probably did the Byzantine sea raid on Antioch, mentioned by Michael the Syrian, 101, and Bar Hebraeus, 139, because Theophilus is not likely to have risked provoking the caliph in 839. On the elevation of Cappadocia from cleisura to theme, which certainly occurred before 842/43 and almost certainly under Theophilus, see Treadgold, "Remarks," 207.

444. On the Umayyad ambassador, al-Ghazzāl, see Maqqarī, 2: 115.

445. For Michael's coronation, see Symeon the Logothete (Leo Grammaticus, 227); Pseudo-Symeon, 645; and Photius, *Homilies*, 18.3, who states that Michael had been crowned "in the cradle." Mango, "When Was Michael III Born?" 253–54, 258, notes that the bronze doors of St. Sophia were altered to take note of Michael's imperial title no earlier than September 1, 840, but then goes on to date Michael's coronation to "towards September 840," on the strength of a Western chronicle so confused that it makes Michael Theophilus's brother. In every known case between the seventh and the tenth century, emperors crowned their sons on Christmas, Epiphany, Easter, or Pentecost. See Treadgold, "Chronological Accuracy," 166 and n. 34 (though because of the evidence of the doors I would now alter my opinion, expressed in "Chronological Accuracy," 189, that Michael was crowned on Pentecost 840). Christmas was the first likely date after September, and then Michael could still reasonably be said to be in his cradle. This date seems to be late enough to explain the rarity of nomismata showing both Theophilus and Michael III, though such miliaresia are more common; see Grierson, *Catalogue*, 3.1, 416. On Theophilus's hospice, see Symeon the Logothete (Leo Grammaticus, 227, supplemented by Georgius Interpolatus, 809), Pseudo-Symeon, 645–46, and Theophanes Continuatus, 95 (the last confusing Theophilus's foundation with Leo III's); cf. Janin, *Géographie*, 263, 558–59. Note that if Michael was crowned on Christmas 840 the Logothete's order would date the foundation of the hospice to 841.

446. On the raids in the Adriatic, see Andrea Dandolo, 150, and John the Deacon, *Chronicon*, 114–15; note the reference of both to the sack of Apsorus (Osor in Yugoslavia) on the island of Crexi (Cres) off Istria just after Easter, which fell on April 17 in 841. For differing opinions on the date of these events, see Vasiliev et al., 1: 183 and n. 1. On the raids in Sicily, see ibn al-Athīr (Vasiliev et al., 1: 362).

447. Michael the Syrian, 102; Bar Hebraeus, 139. The destination of the first expedition is clear from the fact that the Byzantines pursued it into Cilicia, and the destination of the second from the Byzantines' pursuit into the area of Melitene and then to the southwest. That Theophilus did not participate in these campaigns seems clear from the silence of the Byzantine sources about them. The same silence suggests that the tagmata were not involved, while the Arabs' belief that Theophobus had died in 841 would presumably have been shaken if he had taken part in either expedition.

448. Theophanes Continuatus, 137. I cannot agree with Vasiliev et al., 1: 89–90, who date this raid to 829, just before the Cretan Arabs' defeat of the Byzantines off Thasos. Theophanes Continuatus clearly states that the raid on the Thracesians occurred at roughly the time of the execution of Theophobus, and the Cretan Arabs could hardly have annihilated a strong Byzantine fleet just days after their own fleet had been virtually destroyed. The raid on the Thracesians probably occurred in the fall of 841, since the weather would have been unfavorable for raiding after winter began. On Mount Latrus, see Janin, *Églises*, 217–20. Note the weak opposition of the Arabs of Crete to Theoctistus's expedition against them in 843, which is recorded by Symeon the Logothete (Leo Grammaticus, 229, supplemented by Georgius Interpolatus, 814–15); cf. Vasiliev et al., 1: 194–95.

449. Constantine VII, *De Administrando Imperio*, ch. 50, p. 232, dating the revolt to the reign of Theophilus with Michael III, and therefore almost exactly to 841; the fact that no measures were taken against it until after Theophilus's death indicates that the revolt came rather late in that year. Cf. Jenkins, ed., *Commentary*, 185, suggesting that "the cause of the revolt may well have been discontent at . . . an unwonted display of Byzantine authority in the province," of which there is archeological evidence, chiefly numismatic; Theophilus's "reformed" folles are found at Corinth in large numbers (see n. 394 above).

450. Genesius, 51; Theophanes Continuatus, 135; Andrea Dandolo, 151; *Annales Bertiniani*, 28 (recording Lothar's favorable reception of the embassy at Trier in the middle of 842), 43 (noting that the betrothal did take place, though the marriage never did).

451. On the secret meeting, Theophobus's fate, and Theophilus's death, see Symeon the Logothete (Leo Grammaticus, 227–28, supplemented by Georgius Interpolatus, 809–10); Pseudo-Symeon, 646–47; Genesius, 42, 43 (attributing the execution of Theophobus to Oöryphas, drungary of the Watch), 54 (apparently misdating Theophilus's death to January 24); Theophanes Continuatus, 136 (a partly legendary account), 139; and George the Monk, 797; cf. Grierson, "Tombs," 57 and n. 175. For Theophobus's Orthodoxy (i.e., iconophilism) as a cause of his popularity, see Symeon the Logothete (Georgius Interpolatus, 803). My guess that Petronas may have been domestic of the Schools is based on his prominence at this time and on the possibility that Genesius and Theophanes Continuatus, who accept the story that the former domestic of the Schools Manuel was still alive, may have suppressed information that contradicted that belief (perhaps they substituted Oöryphas for Petronas as Theophobus's executioner because

the former held Petronas's old post of drungary of the Watch). For Theophilus's final address in the Magnaura, see Genesius, 51–52, and Theophanes Continuatus, 138–39. Though each quotes different words, their speeches agree in substance and plainly go back to a common paraphrase, which since it noted that Theophilus was quite young, a fact of which no late source is aware, was presumably early. The statements of Genesius, 55, and Theophanes Continuatus, 148, that Theodora was to share power with Theoctistus and Manuel (the latter adds Bardas) are discredited by their revivification and exaltation of the dead Manuel (cf. n. 410 above), though since their source could not suppress the importance of Theoctistus it apparently had to make him another regent. The list of prominent advisers of Theodora in 843 given by the *Acts of David*, 245–46, mentions Theoctistus, Petronas, Bardas, and Sergius Nicetiates, the last a prominent relative of Theodora's (cf. *Synaxarium*, 778) who as he is not heard of before Theophilus's death may have gained real prominence only when Theodora became regent. The *Acts of David*, written between 863 and 865 (Kazhdan, 185–88), say nothing about these men's being regents.

452. On Theophilus's legend, see Diehl; cf. *Timarion*, chs. 29, 32–33, pp. 76, 78–79. The earliest source for the story of Theophilus's deathbed repentance is *Acts of David*, 244; cf. Pseudo-Symeon, 650–51, and Theophanes Continuatus, 152–54. On the restoration of Orthodoxy in general see Gouillard, "Synodikon," 119–29. On Leo the Mathematician's legend, which is often confused with that of the emperor Leo VI, see Mango, "Legend."

453. On the rapidity of the collapse of Iconoclasm, see Mango, "Liquidation," 133–40, who convincingly dismisses the view of some scholars that iconoclasts remained a threat for some time after 843.

CHAPTER SIX

454. On the sources in general, see the Afterword, below. The misdated mention of the Arab conquests in Sicily, Crete, and the Cyclades is in George the Monk, 798.

455. On the date of Michael I's death, January 11, 844, see Theophanes Continuatus, 19–20 (emending A.M. 6302 to 6352; see Ševčenko, 118 n. 42), where I assume that the 32 years that Michael lived after his abdication are counted inclusively. On the probable restoration of Michael's property, see Treadgold, "Bulgars' Treaty," 216 n. 17. On Joannicius, see Mango, "Two Lives."

456. On Ignatius, see Mango, "Observations." On Hilarion, see *Synaxarium*, 731–34, noting that Hilarion died at age 70 on a June 6 three years after the restoration of Orthodoxy (March 11, 843).

457. On the Arab pirates from Crete, see above, pp. 285–86 and n. 391, and below, p. 340 and n. 459.

458. On the Russian raids, see p. 223 and n. 306 above.

459. Exaggerated ideas of how much damage the Cretan Arabs caused at this time have recently been criticized by Lydia Carras in her preface to the *Life of Athanasia*, 203–5; that *Life* itself mentions only one Arab raid (p. 212), probably datable to 828 and certainly before Theophilus's edict of 834 that provided for unmarried women to marry the former Khurramites. Similar and generally persuasive arguments are presented by Kazhdan, 176–82 (though I disagree with his acceptance of the date of 828/29 for the raid on the Thracesians that was defeated by Constantine Contomytes). On the other hand, the *Life of Gregory the Decapolite*,

53–54, 63, refers to Arab pirates off Ephesus in 833 and to unnamed enemies, very probably Arab pirates, who were a peril off the Thracian coast near Maronia in 836, though they are not actually said to have done anything in either case. The *Life of Joseph the Hymnographer*, ch. 6, p. 6 notes that Arab pirates captured Joseph as he was sailing from Constantinople to Rome and took him to Crete shortly before Theophilus's death in 842. The Cretan Arabs seem therefore mostly to have plundered ships and not land.

460. The figures for the population of the empire and the caliphate are adapted from the relevant estimates in McEvedy and Jones, and the figures for the revenue of the empire in 780 and of the caliphate at both dates are taken from Treadgold, *Byzantine State Finances*, 2–3, 86–90. In *Byzantine State Finances*, 50, my estimate of the empire's revenue in 842 has been thrown off by my accidentally misrecording the sources' figure for the treasury reserve of 856 as 190,000 rather than 109,000 pounds of gold (ibid., 10–11). The correct figure, equivalent to 7,848,000 nomismata, means that between 842 and 856 Theodora saved 864,000 nomismata for an average annual surplus of about 61,000 nomismata. In consequence, my estimate that the annual expenditure was about 2.8 million nomismata implies that the revenue, including the surplus, was about 2.9 million nomismata, or between 2.5 and 3.3 million. At *Byzantine State Finances*, 61, I would retain my estimate of 400,000 nomismata for miscellaneous revenues and change my estimate of the revenue from hearth and land taxes to 2.5 million nomismata, a figure that tends to support the population estimates of McEvedy and Jones against those of J. C. Russell, which I tentatively adopted in *Byzantine State Finances*, 54–55 (see n. 482 below). The table below shows the comparative numbers, which as they are both approximate and rounded should not be pressed too far.

*Resources of Abbasid Caliphate
and Byzantine Empire, 780 and 842*

Category	Caliphate	Empire
Non-desert land (km²)		
780	7,000,000	700,000
842	5,000,000	800,000
Population		
780	30,000,000	7,000,000
842	21,000,000	8,000,000
Largest army		
ca. 780	95,793[a]	20,000[b]
ca. 842	80,000[c]	70,000[d]

[a]782 [b]797 [c]838 [d]837

461. On the Mangana, see Treadgold, "Bulgars' Treaty," 216 n. 17.

462. Besides those named in the text, the categories of officials that would have been expanded were the general logothete's chartularies of the arclae, epoptae of the themes, commerciarii, and dioecetae; the military logothete's chartularies of the themes, chartularies of the tagmata, legatarii and mandators, and optiones; the postal logothete's chartularies of the post, episceptetae, diatrechontes, and mandators; and the chartulary of the sacellium's protonotarii of the themes. Cf. Treadgold, *Byzantine State Finances*, 40–49, 111–14, on the numbers of the bureaucracy in 842.

463. On the officials of Leo and Michael who were friends of Theodore, see above, pp. 220–21 and n. 301.

464. The references to Leo the Sacellarius are in Theophanes, 476–77; Theodore, *Letters*, 2.56, 2.129, 2.187 (1268D–1269C, 1416A–1420C, 1573A–C); Petrus, 425; and Sabas, 378–79.

465. See *Life of Methodius*, 1245 B–C. Methodius had then just attained manhood, and he was born shortly after 787; see Gouillard, "Oeuvre," 43–45.

466. There could conceivably have been a new census starting in 837, a first year of the indiction (the civil war would have made one impractical in 822). Though such a census would have made the reforms of 839 easier, no evidence survives to attest it.

467. For a paraphrase of an administrative document of the reign of Leo VI (886–912) mentioning transfers of banda, see Constantine VII, *De Administrando Imperio*, ch. 50, 236. For a convenient presentation of the banda in the empire of Trebizond ca. 1432, see the frontispiece map in Bryer and Winfield, vol. 1, which shows seven banda and an additional "Theme of Greater Lazia," with three more conjectural banda and conjectural themes of Chaldia and Cheriana. These districts covered an area about half as large as the ninth-century theme of Chaldia, which had a total of 24 banda, quite possibly including all of those of ca. 1432.

468. See Table 2, comparing the numbers of cities in 787 with the numbers of headquarters from 839.

469. On the intervals at which soldiers were paid, see Treadgold, *Byzantine State Finances*, 14–15.

470. The figure of eighteen and a half nomismata for military equipment follows from Theophanes, 486, where it is stated that this was the amount assessed to equip each of Nicephorus's new soldiers in 809; see above, pp. 160–61 and n. 208. The average price of a horse is estimated by Ostrogorsky, 328–30.

471. Here I rely on the figures in Table 1, assuming that the turma of Colonia, as one of three turmae in a theme of 9,000 men, had 3,000 men of whom 1,000 were recently arrived Persians. These assumptions seem the most likely ones, since we should reckon in terms of complete drungi of 1,000 men, but they might be modified by 1,000 men either way without altering the overall picture much. On the original deployment of troops in the mid-seventh century, see above, pp. 32–33 and n. 31.

472. For the distrusted turmarch of Colonia, an iconophile named Callistus whom the Arabs later martyred, see *Acts of the Martyrs of Amorium II*, 27–28.

473. On the numbers of forts with drungaries before 839 and those with counts after 839, compare in Table 2 the number of forts with the number of capitals up to 839 and the number of capitals after 839. It seems safe to assume that as a rule counts were assigned fortified capitals whenever possible.

474. On the marriage of Contomytes' daughter to Bardas, a son of Theodora's sister Calomaria and John's brother Arsaber the Patrician, see Theophanes Continuatus, 174–75, omitting the words added by the editor and noting that Constantine was strategus of Sicily either before or after he was strategus of the Thracesians.

475. That the centarch of the spatharii and the count of the hetaeria commanded guards is clear from the names of their commands; and that their guardsmen were ordinary thematic troops seems clear from the absence of any special category of guardsmen in the complete rank-list of Philotheus, 143–61. The title of the centarch of the spatharii identifies him as a centarch, and since the count of the hetaeria ranked just below him in Philotheus, 109–11, he appears to have been

another centarch rather than a count of a bandum (there were several other kinds of count in any case). If the argument presented here is correct, in Treadgold, *Byzantine State Finances*, tables 1 and 4, each theme is assigned two centarchs too many and total pay that is 36 nomismata too high, since the centarch of the spatharii and the count of the hetaeria took the places of two ordinary centarchs. The resulting change in the estimated totals for the army is, of course, insignificant.

476. For the identification of Soandus as the junior drungary's headquarters in Cappadocia before 839, see above, pp. 272–73 and n. 377. Note that before 2,000 Persians were added to the rolls of Cappadocia in 839 it would have had 2,000 soldiers, and therefore two drungaries.

477. The most detailed account of Byzantine warfare with the Arabs in the subsequent period is in Vasiliev et al., 1: 191–264 and vol. 2, part 1.

478. On the army payroll in 867, mentioned by Theophanes Continuatus, 173, and Pseudo-Symeon, 659, see Treadgold, *Byzantine State Finances*, 12–31. On the gold reserve in 842 and 856, mentioned by Theophanes Continuatus, 253, 172, and Genesius, 64, see Treadgold, *Byzantine State Finances*, 9–12, and n. 460 above.

479. The payroll of the Armeniacs in 811 is recorded by Theophanes, 489. For the overall budget estimates, see Treadgold, *Byzantine State Finances*, and n. 460 above. At *Byzantine State Finances*, 74, I expressed the view that before 839 soldiers were probably paid 1 nomisma for each year of service up to six and thereafter 6 nomismata a year, while officers were paid the same as later; but I estimated payrolls before 839 by computing them at the later rate and taking 56 percent of the result. On the whole, however, it seems better to compute the payrolls at the supposed earlier rates. These would be an average of about 5.5 nomismata apiece for the common soldiers, with all officers' salaries the same as later except for the decarchs, who were presumably paid the maximum soldier's pay of 6 nomismata, and perhaps for the drungaries, who may earlier have been paid the salary of 72 nomismata that later went to the counts, since otherwise a gap would be left in the pay scale. The Armeniacs' payroll in 811 would therefore be as shown in the table below.

Payroll of the Byzantine Armeniac Armies in 811

Rank	Number of men	Rate of pay (nomismata)	Payroll (nomismata)
strategus	1	2,880	2,880
turmarch	6	216	1,296
count of the tent	1	144	144
chartulary	1	144	144
domestic	1	144	144
drungary	14	72	1,008
centarch of spatharii	1	36	36
protocancellarius	1	36	36
protomandator	1	36	36
centarch	139	18	2,502
decarch	1,400	6	8,400
common soldier	14,000	5.5	77,000
TOTAL	15,601		93,626

By this method of reckoning, the total army payroll would have been about 600,000 nomismata in 780, 680,000 nomismata in 816, and 900,000 nomismata in 838, estimates that are about 10 percent higher than those suggested in *Byzantine*

State Finances. The difference is too small to affect my overall budgetary estimate for 780–802.

480. The estimates for Justinian's budget are made by Stein, 141–60, and recently by Hendy, 164–73. For the gold reserve in 518, see Procopius, 19.7. On the size of the army under Justinian, see Agathias, 5.13.7. On the revenue per subject under Justinian, see p. 39 and n. 38 above, with n. 460 above for the figures from which the revenue per subject under Theophilus can be calculated.

481. The climatic change is mentioned above, p. 36 and n. 34. On the availability of land up to 780, see above, pp. 48–49 and n. 51.

482. As before, the estimates for the empire's population in 780 and 842 are adapted from McEvedy and Jones. In *Byzantine State Finances*, 52–58, I attempted a calculation of the revenue from hearth and land taxes in the belief that in 842 they yielded a revenue of about 2.9 million nomismata annually, and I then argued that the population of the empire was about 10 million, its rural households numbered about 2.5 million, and the average holding on which taxes were paid was about 30 modii. I now realize that my estimate of the revenue was about 400,000 nomismata too high (see n. 460 above), which indicates that I also overestimated either the population, or the average taxable holding, or both. Because no scholar has brought forward evidence that would justify an appreciably lower figure for the average holding, I am inclined to abandon the population estimate of 10 million that I adapted from J. C. Russell in favor of the estimate of 8 million that follows from the more recent work of McEvedy and Jones. Assuming an urban population of about 5 percent and an average household size of about 3.8, this estimate implies a total of 2 million rural households, which might have paid taxes as follows (figures in nomismata unless otherwise noted):

Hearth tax (0.5×2 million hearths)	1,000,000
Land tax (0.015×36 modii× 2 million plots)	1,080,000
SUBTOTAL	2,080,000
Surcharge (20%)	416,000
TOTAL	2,496,000

My other calculations also assume a 5 percent urban population, an average household size of 3.8, and tax rates as in these calculations.

483. For all the relevant figures, see Table 2 and its references.

484. For the banda, see Constantine VII, *De Administrando Imperio*, ch. 50, 236. The names attested earlier are Bareta, Balbadona, Aspona, Eudocias, Aphrazia, Verinopolis, Tabia (Tavium), Nyssa, and Caesarea; the others are Acarcūs, St. Agapetus, Myriocephalum, Holy Cross, and Comodromus.

485. On Petronas's house, see above, p. 289 and n. 394.

486. On the expansion of coinage, see above, pp. 287–89 and n. 394, and Metcalf, *Coinage*, 17–47. On the commonness of the types of Theophilus's coinage, see Grierson, *Catalogue* 3.1, 408–10; on their date, see the arguments in Treadgold, "Problem," 333–35.

487. On Gregory's travels, see *Life of Gregory the Decapolite*, 53, 54, 55–56, 58, and 63; and Mango, "On Re-Reading." On Joseph's capture, see n. 459 above.

488. On Danelis, see Theophanes Continuatus, 226–28, 316–21. The date follows from the fact that Basil the Macedonian met Danelis when Bardas was Caesar, and so not before 856, though before Basil came to Michael III's attention

about 858. The nature of Danelis's business is astutely surmised by Hendy, 206–7, who suggests that Danelis may have been of Slavic origin.

489. On John's rejection by Leo's officials, see Scriptor Incertus, 359, an early and reliable source. For relationships by blood and marriage among people mentioned in this book, see Fig. 42, which cannot be complete because certain connections are not precisely clear. For example, Theophano, the wife of Nicephorus's son Stauracius, was somehow related to the empress Irene, and Theodote, the second wife of Constantine VI, was somehow related to Theodore of Studius.

490. On the later reputation of John's family, see Theophanes Continuatus, 154, and Pseudo-Symeon, 649 (where the family name is misspelled in our text).

491. On Maria of Amnia's family, see above, p. 271 and n. 375.

492. On Bryenes, see Petrus, ch. 16, 392B–C. On Sergius's foreign origin, see Pseudo-Symeon, 668; and on Photius's nickname, see Pseudo-Symeon, 673–74 (where "Marzucas" may well be the family name, though its derivation is extremely obscure). On the name "Boïlas," see Moravcsik, *Byzantinoturcica*, 2: 93–94. On Inger, Martinacius, and Eudocia Ingerina, see Mango, "Eudocia."

493. On the beginning of the Byzantine nobility at this time, see Patlagean, and her references. On Nicetas Monomachus, see the preface to the *Life of Nicetas the Patrician*, 316–17. On the Scleri, see Seibt, esp. 19–20. On the Camateri, see Polemis, 125 and n. 6, and his references. On the Guberii, see Theophanes Continuatus, 72, and *Life of Irene the Younger*, 603C–604F (where the editor has not capitalized the name Guberii, though he strongly suspects that it is a name).

494. On the tendency for large landholders to come from poor and rural provinces, see Hendy, 100–108. On John the Grammarian's father, see Scriptor Incertus, 349–50 (for the meaning of the Greek word σκιαστής, see Lemerle, *Premier Humanisme*, 135–36 and n. 110). On Leo's supposed poverty, see Theophanes Continuatus, 185–86, 187–88.

495. On Leo's appointments of laymen to church office, see above, pp. 211–12 and n. 286, and pp. 212–13 and n. 288.

496. For Theodotus's profession of Iconoclasm, see *Life of Nicetas*, ch. 41, xxxiB. For Inger's temporary repentance, see Petrus, 406B–C, and Sabas, 360A–B. On Ignatius's distress at having to conform to Iconoclasm, see Mango, "Observations," 406–10; on his biography of George of Amastris, see Ševčenko, 120–25 (though Ševčenko may go somewhat too far in suggesting that the work is iconoclast in its ideology). For the reference to icons in Leo the Mathematician's sermon, see Laurent, "Homélie," 286–87 (for the date), 299.

497. Ignatius's epigram is in the *Anthologia Palatina*, 15.39. Photius's remarks are in his *Bibliotheca*, codex 187, 142b–145b, as emended in Treadgold, "Photius," 172–75.

498. On Leo's student and the Arab geometers, see Theophanes Continuatus, 186–87.

499. On Ignatius's education, see his *Life of Tarasius*, 423. On Leo's education, see Theophanes Continuatus, 191–92, where the printed text says the island was Ἄνδϱον, and the manuscript reads Ἄντϱον; de Boor, in his unpublished edition, suggests that this may be Hyatros in the Princes' Isles. The island was opposite a mainland that had many monasteries with libraries, and it is hard to identify this with any region but Bithynia at this time. Another island off Bithynia is also possible, perhaps the unknown Androte mentioned in Ignatius the Deacon's letters; cf. Mango, "Observations," 408 and n. 2.

500. On Ignatius's teaching, see the references of Browning, "Ignace," 407–8 (though I do not believe in the existence of a patriarchal school at this date, on which Browning does not insist). That John the Grammarian was a teacher is clear from his epithet, and of course he is known to have served as Theophilus's tutor. On Leo's private teaching, see Theophanes Continuatus, 185–86; Symeon the Logothete (Leo Grammaticus, 224, 225); and Pseudo-Symeon, 638, 640; cf. Treadgold, "Chronological Accuracy," 185–87.

501. On the reconstitution of the School of the Magnaura in 843, see Theophanes Continuatus, 185, 192; cf. Treadgold, "Chronological Accuracy," 187. On Photius's school, see Treadgold, *Nature*, 3, 28.

502. On the practical importance of bureaucrats' education, see Treadgold, "Revival," 1259–66.

503. For what survives of John's theology, see Gouillard, "Fragments." On Leo's writings, see Lemerle, *Premier Humanisme*, 167–76; and Hunger, 1: 18–19, 2: 227, 237–38, and 305, in the last place noting the possibility that Leo is the same as the Leo Medicus who wrote under Theophilus.

504. On Ignatius, see Browning, "Ignace"; Mango, "Observations"; Beck, *Kirche*, 511–12; and Hunger, 2: 143–44. On the biographical dictionary, see Treadgold, *Nature*, 31–32, 53–66, and the dictionary's biography of Ignatius himself in the *Suda*, 2: 607–8. If the dictionary's silence about the theology of John of Damascus is indeed a sign that it was composed under Iconoclasm, then (despite my remarks in *Nature*, 31–32) the works it attributes to Ignatius must have been written before 843. It mentions Ignatius's poetry, including his poem *Against Thomas*, his lives of Tarasius and Nicephorus, and his letters. Though in the form we have them the two last works date from after 843, Mango has shown that many of the letters date from Ignatius's episcopate, and there are rather clear signs that the *Life of Nicephorus* was originally composed before 843 and later revised (see Ševčenko, 125 and n. 92). On the *Life of George of Amastris*, see n. 496 above.

505. On Methodius's works, see Gouillard, "Oeuvre," 43–46, and n. 383 above. Ševčenko, 118–19, attributes to iconophiles writing at about this time the anonymous *Life of Nicephorus of Medicium* and the *Life of Nicholas of Myra* by a certain Michael; he also mentions Theosterictus's *Life of Nicetas of Medicium*, which seems to date from just after 842, and a letter by Theodore Graptus that doubtless does date from soon after his branding in 839 but is not really a work of hagiography. On Cassia, see Beck, *Kirche*, 519, Hunger, 2: 168, and p. 269 and n. 374 above.

506. On the Scriptor Incertus, see Hunger, 1: 333–34, and esp. Mango, "Two Lives," 395–400 (where note that in Sabas's *Life of Joannicius* the first date by an emperor's regnal year is 753/54, while after the regnal year 825 there follows a period of very vague chronology until the actual year of Joannicius's death, which Sabas knew from the work of his predecessor Petrus).

507. See Photius, *Bibliotheca*, codex 67, 33b; and Mango, "Liquidation," 135–39, who does not, however, suggest the identification of Sergius Confessor with the Scriptor Incertus.

508. Photius's mention of his composing a lexicon is in Photius, *Amphilochia*, no. 12, 153C. On its date, the date of the *Bibliotheca*, and the reading notes incorporated into the latter, see Treadgold, *Nature*, 4 and n. 15, 16–36, 37–51, and 88–96. Now also see Theodoridis's edition of Photius, *Lexicon*. On scholarship at this time in general, see Wilson, 61–119.

509. On the Palace of Antiochus, see Naumann and Belting, 13–44; the palace had a sigma-shaped entrance, but a penteconch rather than a triconch at its center.

A triconch with an "ovoid" entrance similar to a sigma is found in the fourth-century palace at Piazza Armerina in Sicily; see most recently Carandini et al., 293–325.

510. On Lazarus's icon of John the Baptist, see Theophanes Continuatus, 103; cf. pp. 311–12 and n. 429 above.

511. On Ignatius's borrowings from Gregory of Nazianzus, see Ševčenko, 123. On Theophilus's appropriation of coffering from the former palace of Basiliscus, the usurper who seized the throne briefly in 475–76, see Theophanes Continuatus, 147. On Ignatius's borrowings from Greek tragedy, see Browning, "Ignace," 405–7.

AFTERWORD

512. On Theophanes in general, see Hunger, 1: 334–39. For the view that the chronicle is almost entirely the work of George Syncellus, see Mango, "Who Wrote the Chronicle?" For an analysis of Theophanes' account of the years from 780 to 802 on the assumption that it is drawn from several literary sources, see Speck, *Kaiser Konstantin VI*, 389–97.

513. Ševčenko, "Hagiography," provides a convenient guide to the saints' lives of the time. On these and other sources, cf. pp. 192–95 and nn. 259–61 above. On the unreliability of Michael the Syrian, see Treadgold, "Chronological Accuracy," 161–62 and nn. 13, 15.

514. On Sergius Confessor and the Scriptor Incertus, see above, pp. 376–78 and nn. 506–7. On George the Monk, see Hunger, 1: 347–51.

515. On Genesius and Theophanes Continuatus, see Hunger, 1: 351–54, 339–43. For Grégoire's view of them and a sampling of their faults, see his "Manuel" (the sentences quoted here are on p. 204). Cf. Theophanes Continuatus, 90–91, with Pseudo-Symeon, 628–29, where the former has substituted Theophilus's mother-in-law Theoctista for his stepmother Euphrosyne (see Treadgold, "Problem," 333–34, 338–40).

516. On Symeon and Pseudo-Symeon, see Hunger, 1: 354–57, 349–51, and Treadgold, "Chronological Accuracy."

517. On the Arab geographers and the *Tacticon Uspensky*, see Treadgold, "Notes," and Oikonomidès, 41–47.

518. The coins are most conveniently published by Grierson, *Catalogue*, 3.1: 336–451; and the seals by Zacos and Veglery and by Laurent, *Corpus*.

Glossary

archon (*archōn*). Governor, especially of a province inferior in rank to a theme and called an archontate (*archontia*).

Augusta (*Augousta*, Latin *Augusta*). Title of honor bestowed upon some empresses.

bandum (*bandon*, Latin *bandum*). Originally a battle standard, later a troop of 200 men fighting under such a standard in the themes or tagmata, and from 840 the territorial district within which such a troop was settled, commanded by a count.

Caesar (*Kaisar*, Latin *Caesar*). Highest honorary title after that of emperor, carrying with it the presumptive right of succession in the absence of an emperor.

centarch (*kentarchos*, Latin *centurio*). Commander of a company of 100 soldiers, or from 840 of a company of 40 soldiers in the themes.

chartulary (*chartoularios*, Latin *chartularius*). Keeper of records. The chartulary of the inkpot (*chartoularios tou kanikleiou*) was an imperial adviser who kept the pen and purple ink used in signing official documents. Other chartularies headed the government departments of the sacellium and the vestiarium and kept the muster rolls of the themes and tagmata.

city prefect (*eparchos tēs poleōs*, Latin *praefectus urbi*). Civil governor of Constantinople.

cleisura (*kleisoura*). From 840, frontier province and its garrison, commanded by a cleisurarch (*kleisourarchēs*).

commercia (*kommerkia*, Latin *commercia*). Trade duties, normally 10 percent of the value of the merchandise traded.

consul (*hypatos*, Latin *consul*). Fifth-highest honorary title normally granted outside the imperial family, ranking just after spatharius.

count (*komēs*, Latin *comes*). Military officer of one of several sorts. Counts commanded the Opsician theme and the tagma of the Walls, and the banda within themes. The count of the stable (*komēs tou staulou*, Latin *comes stabuli*) headed the department that distributed horses and mules to the tagmata. The count of the tent (*komēs tēs kortēs*) was the principal aide of a strategus of a theme. From 840 the count of the hetaeria (*komēs tes hetaireias*) commanded one of the strategus's two troops of bodyguards, the other being the spatharii.

cubicularius (*koubikoularios*, Latin *cubicularius*). Chamberlain, especially of the emperor.

curator (*kouratōr*, Latin *curator*). Manager of an imperial palace or estate.

curopalates (*kouropalatēs*). Third-highest honorary title after that of emperor (just below nobilissimus), granted only to members of the imperial family.

decarch (*dekarchos*). Commander of a troop of ten men in the themes or tagmata.

domestic (*domestikos*, Latin *domesticus*). Military officer, either the commander of the tagma of the Schools, Excubitors, Hicanati, or Numera, or the supervisor of a theme's support corps.

drungary (*droungarios*, Latin *drungarius*). Military officer, either the commander of the tagma of the Watch or of the Imperial Fleet, or in the themes the commander of a drungus.

drungus (*droungos*, Latin *drungus*). Troop of 1,000 men, and the district in a theme within which such a troop was settled.

duke (*doux*, Latin *dux*). Commander of a ducate (*doukaton*, Latin *ducatum*), either a region of a theme, as for Calabria in Sicily or Chaldia in the Armeniacs, or an autonomous outlying province, as for Venetia, Jadera, Naples, Amalfi, and Gaeta. The latter three ducates came to resemble the entirely independent duchies in the West, like the duchy of Spoleto.

emperor (*basileus*, Latin *imperator*). Title not only of the chief ruler of the empire but of his joint rulers (co-emperors) and presumptive heir (junior emperor).

exarch (*exarchos*). Governor of Byzantine Italy (with his capital at Ravenna) or of Byzantine Africa, before those provinces were lost.

Excubitors (*Exkoubitoi*, Latin *Excubitores*). Second-ranking tagma, which with the senior tagma, the Schools, formed a mobile strike force of cavalry.

Federates (*Phiberatoi*, Latin *Foederati*). Senior turma of the Anatolic theme, and so outranking all other turmae of themes.

follis (*phollis*, Latin *follis*). Principal copper coin, exchanged at 288 to the gold nomisma. The normal price of a pound loaf of bread was one follis.

general logothete (*logothetēs tou genikou*). Chief finance minister of the empire.

great curator (*megas kouratōr*). Minister in charge of imperial estates and palaces (except for the Great Palace, which was the responsibility of the papias).

Hicanati (*Hikanatoi*). Tagma founded in 809 by Nicephorus I, to which the adolescent sons of some military officers were usually attached.

logothete (*logothetēs*). Principal government minister. The term when used alone generally applies to the postal logothete. The others were the general logothete, the military logothete, and the lower-ranking logothete of the herds (*logothetēs tōn agelōn*), who was in charge of requisitioning horses and mules for the tagmata.

magister (*magistros*, Latin *magister*). High-ranking adviser to the emperor, sometimes employed on special missions.

master of ceremonies (*epi tēs katastaseōs*). Official in charge of court ceremonial.

miliaresion (*miliarēsion*, Latin *milliarense*). Principal silver coin, valued at 24 copper folles, or one-twelfth of a gold nomisma.

military logothete (*logothetēs tou stratiōtikou*). Minister responsible for distributing pay to the army and navy.

minister for petitions (*epi tōn deēseōn*). Official in charge of transmitting petitions to the emperor.

monostrategus (*monostratēgos*). A single strategus commanding more than one theme at the same time.

nobilissimus (*nōbelissimos*, Latin *nobilissimus*). Highest honorary title after those of emperor and Caesar, granted only to members of the imperial family.

nomisma, *pl.* nomismata (*nomisma*, Latin *solidus*). Principal gold coin, struck at 72 to the pound of gold, valued at 12 miliaresia or 288 folles, and equivalent to about eighteen days' wages for a manual laborer.

Numera (*Noumera*, Latin *Numeri*). Infantry tagma, serving with the Watch and the Walls as a garrison and police force for Constantinople.

Optimates (*Optimatoi*, Latin *Optimates*). Military support corps of muleteers charged with carrying the baggage of the army on campaigns, and otherwise settled in a district in Bithynia.

orphanotrophus (*orphanotrophos*). Administrator of the imperial orphanages in Constantinople.

papias (*papias*). Administrator of the Great Palace in Constantinople.

patriarch (*patriarchēs*). Ecclesiastical title of the archbishops of Rome, Constantinople, Alexandria, Antioch, and Jerusalem, the five highest-ranking bishops of the Church.

patrician (*patrikios*, Latin *patricius*). Honorary title, the highest normally granted outside the imperial family.

pentecontarch (*pentēkontarchēs*). In the themes before 840, commander of a troop of 50 men.

postal logothete (*logothetēs tou dromou*). Minister in charge of the imperial post (*dromos*), and consequently of diplomacy and internal security.

primicerius (*primikērios*, Latin *primicerius*). Honorary title granted only to eunuchs, ranking just after protospatharius.

protoasecretis (*prōtoasēkrētis*). Head of the chancery that drafted and kept imperial records.

protocancellarius (*prōtokankellarios*). Subordinate of a strategus, in charge of drafting administrative documents for a theme.

protomandator (*prōtomandatōr*). Subordinate of a strategus, supervising a theme's corps of messengers (*mandatōres*).

protospatharius (*prōtospatharios*). The second-highest honorary title normally granted outside the imperial family, ranking just after patrician.

protostrator (*prōtostratōr*). Keeper of the emperor's private stable.

protovestiarius (*prōtobestiarios*). Custodian of the emperor's private treasury.

quaestor (*kouaistōr*, Latin *quaestor*). Minister of the judiciary, responsible for drafting laws.

sacellarius (*sakellarios*, Latin *sacellarius*). Supervisor of the secretarial departments of the bureaucracy.

sacellium (*sakellion*, Latin *sacellium*). State treasury for coined money, headed by the chartulary of the sacellium, who also supervised most imperial charitable institutions.

Schools (*Scholai*, Latin *Scholae*). Highest-ranking tagma, which with the second-ranking tagma of the Excubitors formed a mobile strike force of cavalry.

senate (*synklētos*, Latin *senatus*). Group of the main imperial officials and dignitaries, which as a body had a chiefly ceremonial role.

spatharius (*spatharios*). Either the fourth-highest honorary title normally granted outside the imperial family, ranking just after spatharocandidatus, or a member of the bodyguard of a strategus known as the spatharii.

spatharocandidatus (*spatharokandidatos*). The third-highest honorary title normally granted outside the imperial family, ranking just after protospatharius.

special secretary (*eidikos*). Administrator of the imperial factories.

strategus (*stratēgos*). Military governor and commander of a theme.

syncellus (*synkellos*). Chief assistant of a patriarch of Constantinople, Alexandria, Antioch, or Jerusalem. The syncellus of the patriarch of Constantinople was appointed by the emperor and represented the emperor's interests in the Church.

tagma, *pl.* tagmata (*tagma*). Primarily mobile army unit based in or near Constantinople. The tagmata were reorganized and greatly strengthened by Constantine V (r. 741–75).

theme (*thema*). Both a main province of the empire and the army unit settled in such a province. Lesser provinces were called archontates.

turma (*tourma*, Latin *turma*). Division of a theme, representing both a territorial district and the troops settled in the district, commanded by a turmarch (*tourmarchēs*).

vestiarium (*bestiarion*, Latin *vestiarium*). The state treasury for objects other than coined money, headed by the chartulary of the vestiarium, who also supervised the imperial mint and arsenal.

Walls (*Teichē*). Infantry tagma serving with the Watch and the Numera as a garrison and police force for Constantinople.

Watch (*Bigla*, Latin *Vigilia*). Cavalry tagma normally stationed in Constantinople along with the Numera and the Walls to serve as a garrison and police force, but occasionally used on campaigns.

Bibliography

This bibliography includes only works cited in the notes, none of which appeared after 1986. It uses the following abbreviations:

AnalBoll. *Analecta Bollandiana*
ASB *Acta Sanctorum quotquot toto orbe coluntur,* ed. J. Bolland
BMGS *Byzantine and Modern Greek Studies*
BZ *Byzantinische Zeitschrift*
DOP *Dumbarton Oaks Papers*
EHR *English Historical Review*
GRBS *Greek, Roman and Byzantine Studies*
JÖB *Jahrbuch der Österreichischen Byzantinistik*
MGH *Monumenta Germaniae Historica*
  SS   *Scriptores*
PG *Patrologiae Cursus Completus, Series Graeca,* ed. J.-P. Migne
REB *Revue des Études Byzantines*
TM *Travaux et Mémoires*
ZRVI *Zbornik Radova Vizantinološkog Instituta*

Acts of David. I. Van den Gheyn, "Acta Graeca SS. Davidis, Symeonis, et Georgii." *AnalBoll.* 18 (1899), 209–59.
Acts of the Martyrs of Amorium. Ed. and comm. V. Vasilievskij and P. Nikitin. Zapiski Imperatorskoj Akademii Nauk po istor.-filol. otděleniju, 8th ser., 7.2. St. Petersburg, 1905.
Agathias. *Historiae.* Ed. R. Keydell. Berlin, 1967.
Ahrweiler, H. *Byzance et la mer.* Paris, 1966.
Alexander, P. *The Byzantine Apocalyptic Tradition.* Berkeley and Los Angeles, 1985.
———. "The Iconoclastic Council of St. Sophia (815) and Its Definition (*Horos*)." *DOP* 7 (1953), 35–66.
———. *The Patriarch Nicephorus of Constantinople.* Oxford, 1958.

Andrea Dandolo. *Chronica*. In L. Muratori, ed., *Rerum Italicarum Scriptores*, new ed., vol. 12.1, ed. E. Pastorello, 9–327. Bologna, 1939.

Annales Bertiniani. E. G. Waitz. Hanover, 1883.

Annales Fuldenses. In *MGH, SS* 1: 343–415.

Annales Laureshamenses. In *MGH, SS* 1: 22–39.

Annales Laurissenses. In *MGH, SS* 1: 134–218.

Annales Lobienses. In *MGH, SS* 13: 224–35.

Annales Maximiniani. In *MGH, SS* 13: 19–25.

Annales Mettenses Priores. Ed. B. Von Simson. Hanover, 1905.

Annales qui dicuntur Einhardi. In *Annales Regni Francorum* (q.v.), 3–115.

Annales Regni Francorum. Ed. F. Kurze. Hanover, 1895.

Annales Sithienses. In *MGH, SS* 13: 35–38.

Annales Xantenses. In *MGH, SS* 2: 219–35.

Anthologia Palatina [*Anthologia Graeca*]. Ed. H. Beckby. 2d ed. 4 vols. Munich, 1957–58.

Ashburner, W. *The Rhodian Sea Law*. Oxford, 1909.

Bar Hebraeus, Gregorius. *The Chronography of Gregory Abû'l Faraj*. Vol. 1. Tr. E. A. W. Budge. Oxford, 1932.

Beck, H.-G. *Geschichte der byzantinischen Volksliteratur*. Munich, 1971.

———. *Kirche und theologische Literatur im byzantinischen Reich*. Munich, 1959.

Belke, K. *Tabula Imperii Byzantini*. Vol. 4, *Galatien und Lykaonien*. Vienna, 1984.

Bertolini, O. "Carlomagno e Benevento." In *Karl der Grosse* (q.v.), 1: 609–71.

Beševliev, V. *Die protobulgarische Inschriften*. Berlin, 1963.

———. *Die protobulgarische Periode der bulgarischen Geschichte*. Amsterdam, 1980.

Biraben, J. N., and J. Le Goff. "La Peste dans le Haut Moyen Âge." *Annales* 24 (1969), 1484–1510.

Bouras, C. "City and Village: Urban Design and Architecture." *JÖB* 31 (1981), 611–53.

Bratianu, G. *Études byzantines d'histoire économique et sociale*. Paris, 1938.

Brooks, E. W. "The Arab Occupation of Crete." *EHR* 28 (1913), 431–43.

———. "Arabic Lists of the Byzantine Themes." *Journal of Hellenic Studies* 21 (1901), 67–77.

———. "Byzantines and Arabs in the Time of the Early Abbasids." Parts 1, 2. *EHR* 15 (1900), 728–47; *EHR* 16 (1901), 84–92.

———. "The Relations between the Empire and Egypt from a New Arabic Source." *BZ* 22 (1913), 381–91.

Browning, R. "Ignace le Diacre et la tragédie classique à Byzance." *Revue des Études Grecques* 81 (1968), 401–10.

———. "Literacy in the Byzantine World." *BMGS* 4 (1978), 39–54.

———. "Notes on the *Scriptor Incertus de Leone Armenio*." *Byzantion* 35 (1965), 389–411.

Bryer, A., and D. Winfield. *The Byzantine Monuments and Topography of the Pontos*. 2 vols. Washington, D.C., 1985.

Bury, J. B. *A History of the Eastern Roman Empire from the Fall of Irene to the Accession of Basil I (AD 802–867)*. London, 1912.

Cameron, A. *Circus Factions*. Oxford, 1976.

Canard, M. "La Prise de Heraclée." *Byzantion* 9 (1962), 345–79.

Carandini, A., et al. *Filosofiana: The Villa of Piazza Armerina*. Palermo, 1982.

Catalogi Patriarcharum. F. Fischer, "De Patriarcharum Constantinopolitanorum Catalogis." *Commentationes Philologae Ienenses* 3 (1884), 263–333.

Cedrenus, Georgius. *Historiarum Compendium*. Ed. I. Bekker. 2 vols. Corpus Scriptorum Historiae Byzantinae. Bonn, 1838–39.

Christides, V. *The Conquest of Crete by the Arabs (ca. 824)*. Athens, 1984.

Chronicle of 811. I. Dujčev, "La Chronique byzantine de l'an 811." *TM* 1 (1965), 205–54.

Chronicle of Monemvasia. P. Lemerle, "La Chronique improprement dite de Monemvasie: Le Contexte historique et legendaire." *REB* 21 (1963), 5–49.

Chronicle of Salerno. In *MGH, SS* 3: 467–561.

Chronicle of 1234. A. Abouna, tr., *Anonymi Auctoris Chronicon ad A.C. 1234 pertinens*. Vol. 2. Louvain, 1974.

Chronicon Altinate. In *MGH, SS* 14: 1–69.

Chronicon Moissiacense. In *MGH, SS* 1: 280–313.

Classen, P. "Karl der Grosse, das Papsttum, und Byzanz." In *Karl der Grosse* (q.v.) 1: 537–608.

Codex Carolinus. In *MGH, Epistolae* 3: 476–653.

Constantine VII. *De Administrando Imperio*. Ed. G. Moravcsik. Tr. R. J. H. Jenkins. Washington, D.C., 1967.

———. *De Ceremoniis*. Ed. J. Reiske. Corpus Scriptorum Historiae Byzantinae. Bonn, 1829.

———. *De Thematibus*. Ed. A. Pertusi. Vatican City, 1952.

Constantine of Tius. *Discovery of the Relics of St. Euphemia*. In F. Halkin, *Euphémie de Chalcédoine*, 81–106. Subsidia Hagiographica, 41. Brussels, 1965.

Cormack, R. "The Apse Mosaics of St. Sophia at Thessaloniki." *Deltion tēs Christianikēs Archaiologikēs Hetaireias* 10 (1980–81), 109–26.

———. "The Arts during the Age of Iconoclasm." In *Iconoclasm* (q.v.), 35–44.

Darrouzès, J. "Listes épiscopales du Concile de Nicée (787)." *REB* 33 (1975), 5–76.

de Boor, C. "Ein falscher Bischof." *BZ* 13 (1904), 433–34.

De Sancto Marco: Historia Translationis. In *ASB*, April 3: 353–56.

Devreesse, R. "Une Lettre de S. Théodore Studite relative au Synode Moechien." *AnalBoll*. 68 (1950), 44–57.

Diehl, C. "La Légende de l'empereur Théophile." *Seminarium Kondakovianum* 4 (1931), 33–37.

Dölger, F. *Regesten der Kaiserurkunden des oströmischen Reiches*. Vol. 1. Munich, 1924.

Duby, G. *The Early Growth of the European Economy*. Tr. H. B. Clarke. Ithaca, N.Y., 1974.

Dumeige, G. *Nicaea II*. Paris, 1978.

Ecloga. In Zepos and Zepos (q.v.), 2: 11–62.

Einhard. *Vita Karoli Magni*. Ed. L. Halphen. 4th ed. Paris, 1967.

Encomium of Theodore Graptus. J. Featherstone, "The Praise of Theodore Graptos by Theophanes of Caesarea." *AnalBoll*. 98 (1980), 93–150.

Erchempert. *Historia Langobardorum Beneventanorum*. In *MGH, Scriptores Rerum Langobardicarum*, 234–64.

Follieri, E., and I. Dujčev. "Un' Acolutia inedita per i martiri di Bulgaria dell'anno 813." *Byzantion* 33 (1963), 71–106.

Foss, C. *Ephesus after Antiquity*. Cambridge, 1979.

Frazee, C. "St. Theodore of Studius and Ninth Century Monasticism in Constantinople." *Studia Monastica* 23 (1981), 27–58.

Genesius, Joseph. *Regum Libri Quattuor*. Ed. A. Lesmüller-Werner and J. Thurn. Berlin, 1978.

George the Monk. *Chronicon.* Ed. C. de Boor. 2 vols. Leipzig, 1904.

Georgius Interpolatus. *Vitae Recentiorum Imperatorum.* In Theophanes Continuatus (q.v.), 761–924. Bonn, 1838. [Ed. as Georgius Monachus.]

Gill, J. "The Life of Stephen the Younger." *Orientalia Christiana Periodica* 6 (1940), 114–28.

Gouillard, J. "Deux figures mal connues du second iconoclasme." *Byzantion* 31 (1961), 371–401.

———. "Fragments inédits d'un antirrhétique de Jean le Grammarien." *REB* 24 (1966), 171–81.

———. "Une Oeuvre inédite du patriarche Méthode: La Vie d'Euthyme de Sardes." *BZ* 53 (1960), 36–46.

———. "Le Synodikon de l'Orthodoxie: Édition et commentaire." *TM* 2 (1967), 1–316.

Grégoire, H. "Autour de Digénes Akritas." *Byzantion* 7 (1932), 287–302.

———. "Études sur le neuvième siècle." *Byzantion* 8 (1933), 515–50.

———. "Manuel et Théophobe, ou La Concurrence de deux monastères." *Byzantion* 9 (1934), 183–204.

———. "Rangabé ou Forte-Main." *Byzantion* 9 (1934), 793–94.

———. "Les Sources épigraphiques de l'histoire bulgare." *Byzantion* 9 (1934), 745–86.

———. "Le Tombeau et la date de Digénes Akritas." *Byzantion* 6 (1931), 498–99.

Grierson, P. *Byzantine Coins.* Berkeley and Los Angeles, 1982.

———. *Catalogue of the Byzantine Coins in the Dumbarton Oaks Collection and the Whittemore Collection.* Vols. 2, 3. Washington, D.C., 1968, 1973.

———. "The Tombs and Obits of the Byzantine Emperors." *DOP* 16 (1962), 1–63.

Grumel, V. *Les Regestes des actes du patriarcat de Constantinople.* Vol. 1, *Les Actes des patriarches.* Part 2, *715–1043.* Chalcedon, 1936.

Guilland, R. *Études de topographie de Constantinople byzantine.* 2 vols. Berlin, 1969.

Haldon, J. F. *Byzantine Praetorians.* Bonn, 1984.

Haldon, J. F., and H. Kennedy. "The Arab-Byzantine Frontier in the Eighth and Ninth Centuries." *ZRVI* 19 (1980), 79–116.

Halkin, F. "S. Antoine le Jeune et Petronas le vainqueur des Arabes en 863 (d'après un texte inédit)." *AnalBoll.* 62 (1944), 187–225.

Hendy, M. *Studies in the Byzantine Monetary Economy, c. 300–1450.* Cambridge, 1985.

Henry, P. "The Moechian Controversy and the Constantinopolitan Synod of January A.D. 809." *Journal of Theological Studies,* n.s., 20 (1969), 495–522.

Hild, F. *Das byzantinische Strassensystem in Kappadokien.* Vienna, 1977.

Hild, F., and M. Restle. *Tabula Imperii Byzantini.* Vol. 2, *Kappadokien.* Vienna, 1981.

Honigmann, E. *Die Ostgrenze des byzantinischen Reiches.* Brussels, 1935. [= Vasiliev et al. (q.v.), vol. 3.]

Hunger, H. *Die hochsprachliche profane Literatur der Byzantiner.* 2 vols. Munich, 1978.

ibn Khurdādhbih. *Kitāb al-Masālik.* In *Bibliotheca Geographorum Arabicorum,* ed. and tr. M. J. de Goeje, 6: 1–143. Leiden, 1889. [Page numbers in notes refer to translation.]

Iconoclasm. Ed. A. Bryer and J. Herrin. Birmingham, 1977.

Interpolated Letter tò Theophilus. In *PG* 95: 345–85.

Jacoby, D. "La Population de Constantinople à l'époque byzantine." *Byzantion* 31 (1961), 81–109.

Janin, R. *Constantinople byzantine.* 2d ed. Paris, 1964.

———. *Les Églises et les monastères des grands centres byzantins.* Paris, 1975. [=Janin, *Géographie* (q.v.), part 1, vol. 2.]

———. *La Géographie ecclésiastique de l'empire byzantin.* Part 1, *Le Siège de Constantinople et le patriarcat oecuménique.* Vol. 3, *Les Églises et les monastères.* 2d ed. Paris, 1969.

Jenkins, R. J. H. "Cyprus between Byzantium and Islam." In *Studies Presented to D. M. Robinson* 2: 1006–14. St. Louis, 1953.

———. "Social Life in the Byzantine Empire." In *The Cambridge Medieval History,* 2d ed., 4.2: 78–103. Cambridge, 1967.

———, ed. *Constantine VII Porphyrogenitus: De Administrando Imperio.* Vol. 2, *Commentary.* London, 1962.

John the Deacon. *Chronicon Venetianum.* In *Cronache veneziane antichissime,* ed. G. Monticolo, 1: 57–171. Rome, 1890.

———. *Gesta Episcoporum Neapolitanorum.* In *MGH, Scriptores Rerum Langobardicarum,* 424–35.

Jones, A. H. M. *The Later Roman Empire 284–602: A Social, Economic, and Administrative Survey.* 2 vols. Norman, Okla., 1964.

Kaegi, W. E. *Byzantine Military Unrest 471–843: An Interpretation.* Amsterdam, 1981.

———. "The Contribution of Archery to the Turkish Conquest of Anatolia." *Speculum* 39 (1964), 99–102.

Karl der Grosse. Ed. H. Beumann. 4 vols. Düsseldorf, 1965.

Kazhdan, A. "Hagiographical Notes (II)." *Byzantion* 54 (1984), 176–92.

Kennedy, H. *The Early Abbasid Caliphate: A Political History.* London, 1981.

Kitzinger, E. "The Cult of Images before Iconoclasm." *DOP* 8 (1954), 83–150.

Koder, J., and F. Hild. *Tabula Imperii Byzantini.* Vol. 1, *Hellas und Thessalia.* Vienna, 1976.

Köpstein, H. "Zur Erhebung des Thomas." In H. Köpstein and F. Winkelmann, *Studien zum 8. und 9. Jahrhundert in Byzanz,* 61–87. Berlin, 1983.

Ladner, G. "Origin and Significance of the Byzantine Iconoclastic Controversy." *Medieval Studies* 2 (1940), 127–49.

Laurent, V. *Le Corpus des sceaux de l'empire byzantin.* Vols. 2, 5. Paris, 1963, 1981.

———. "Une Homélie inédite de l'archevêque de Thessalonique Léon le Philosophe sur l'Annonciation." In *Mélanges Eugène Tisserant* 2: 281–302. Vatican City, 1964.

Lemerle, P. *The Agrarian History of Byzantium.* Galway, 1979.

———. "L'Histoire des Pauliciens d'Asie Mineure." *TM* 5 (1973), 1–144.

———. *Le Premier Humanisme byzantin.* Paris, 1971.

———. "Thomas le Slave." *TM* 1 (1965), 255–97.

Leo VI. *Book of the Prefect.* In Zepos and Zepos (q.v.), 2: 371–92.

———. *Tactica.* In *PG* 107: 669–1120.

Leo Grammaticus. *Chronographia.* Ed. I. Bekker. Corpus Scriptorum Historiae Byzantinae. Bonn, 1842.

Leontius [Ghévond]. *Chronicle.* Tr. G. Chahnazarian. Paris, 1856.

Leroy, J. "La Réforme studite." In *Il Monachesimo orientale,* 181–214. Orientalia Christiana Analecta, 153. Rome, 1958.

Letter to Theophilus. L. Duchesne, "L'Iconographie byzantine dans un document grec du IXe siècle." *Roma e l'Oriente* 5 (1912–13), 222–39, 273–85, 349–66.

Liber Pontificalis. Ed. L. Duchesne. Vol. 1. Paris, 1884.

Life of Anthony the Younger. In *Syllogē Palaistinēs kai Syriakēs Hagiologias*, ed. A. Papadopoulos-Kerameus, 1: 186–216. St. Petersburg, 1907.

Life of Athanasia. L. Carras, "The Life of St. Athanasia of Aegina." In *Maistor: Classical, Byzantine and Renaissance Studies for Robert Browning*, 199–224. Canberra, 1984.

Life of George of Amastris. In V. Vasilievskij, *Trudy*, 3: 1–98. Petrograd, 1915.

Life of Gregory the Decapolite. F. Dvornik, *La Vie de Saint Grégoire le Décapolite et les Slaves macédoniens au IXe siècle*. Paris, 1926.

Life of Ignatius. In *PG* 105: 487–574.

Life of Irene the Empress. In Treadgold, "Unpublished Saint's Life" (q.v.), 244–45. [Partial edition.]

Life of Irene the Younger. In *ASB*, July 6: 600–634.

Life of John of Gotthia. In *ASB*, June 7: 167–72.

Life of John of Psicha. P. Van den Ven, "La Vie grecque de Saint Jean le Psichaïte." *Le Muséon*, n.s., 3 (1902), 97–125.

Life of Joseph the Hymnographer. Ed. A. Papadopoulos-Kerameus. Zapiski Imperatorskago Universiteta, istor.-filol. fakul'teta, 50.2: 1–14. St. Petersburg, 1901.

Life of Macarius of Pelecete. I. Van den Gheyn, "S. Macarii Monasterii Pelecetes hegumeni Acta Graeca." *AnalBoll.* 16 (1897), 140–63.

Life of Methodius. In *PG* 100: 1244–61.

Life of Michael Syncellus. F. I. Smit, "Vita Michaelis Syncelli." *Izvěstija Russkago Archeologičeskago Instituta v Konstantinopolě* 11 (1906), 227–59.

Life of Nicephorus. In *Nicephori Opuscula Historica*, ed. C. de Boor, 139–217. Leipzig, 1880.

Life of Nicetas of Medicium. In *ASB*, April 1, appendix, xviii–xxviii.

Life of Nicetas the Patrician. D. Papachryssanthou, "Un Confesseur du second iconoclasme: La Vie du patrice Nicétas." *TM* 3 (1968), 309–51.

Life of Nicholas of Studius. In *PG* 105: 863–925.

Life of Peter of Atroa. V. Laurent, *La Vie merveilleuse de Saint Pierre d'Atroa*. Subsidia Hagiographica, 29. Brussels, 1956.

Life of Philaretus. M. H. Fourmy and M. Leroy, "La Vie de S. Philarète." *Byzantion* 9 (1934), 85–170.

Life of Stephen. In *PG* 100: 1067–1186.

Life of Tarasius. I. Heikel, ed., *Vita Tarasii*. Acta Societatis Scientiarum Fennicae, 17. Helsinki, 1888.

Life of Theodore Graptus. In *PG* 116: 653–84.

Life of Theophylact. A. Vogt, "S. Théophylacte de Nicomédie." *AnalBoll.* 50 (1932), 67–82.

Liudprand of Cremona. *Antapodosis*. Ed. J. Becker. Hanover, 1915.

Löwe, H. "Eine kölner Notiz zum Kaisertum Karls des Grossen." *Rheinische Vierteljahrsblätter* 14 (1949), 7–34.

Lopez, R. "The Role of Trade in the Economic Readjustment of Byzantium in the Seventh Century." *DOP* 13 (1959), 67–85.

Lopez, R., and I. Raymond. *Medieval Trade in the Mediterranean World*. New York, n.d.

McEvedy, C., and R. Jones. *Atlas of World Population History*. Harmondsworth, 1978.

Mango, C. "The Availability of Books in the Byzantine Empire." In *Byzantine Books and Bookmen*, 29–35. Washington, D.C., 1975.

———. *The Brazen House: A Study of the Vestibule of the Imperial Palace of Constantinople*. Copenhagen, 1959.

———. "The *Breviarium* of the Patriarch Nicephorus." In *Byzantium: Tribute to Andreas N. Stratos*, 539–52. Athens, 1986.

———. *Byzantine Architecture*. New York, 1976.

———. "The Byzantine Inscriptions of Constantinople: A Bibliographical Survey." *American Journal of Archaeology* 55 (1951), 52–66.

———. *Byzantium: The Empire of New Rome*. London, 1980.

———. "Daily Life in Byzantium." *JÖB* 31 (1981), 337–53.

———. "Documentary Evidence on the Apse Mosaics of St. Sophia." *BZ* 47 (1954), 395–402.

———. "Eudocia Ingerina, the Normans, and the Macedonian Dynasty." *ZRVI* 14–15 (1973), 22–23.

———. "A Forged Inscription of the Year 781." *ZRVI* 8 (1963), 201–7.

———. "Historical Introduction." In *Iconoclasm* (q.v.), 1–6.

———. "The Legend of Leo the Wise." *ZRVI* 6 (1960), 59–93.

———. "The Liquidation of Iconoclasm and the Patriarch Photios." In *Iconoclasm* (q.v.), 133–40.

———. "Observations on the Correspondence of Ignatius, Metropolitan of Nicaea (First Half of Ninth Century)." In *Überlieferungsgeschichtliche Untersuchungen*, 403–10. Texte und Untersuchungen, 125. Berlin, 1981.

———. "On Re-Reading the Life of St. Gregory the Decapolite." *Byzantina* 13 (1985), 635–46.

———. "St. Anthusa of Mantineon and the Family of Constantine V." *AnalBoll.* 100 (1982), 401–9.

———. "The Two Lives of St. Ioannikios and the Bulgarians." *Harvard Ukrainian Studies* 7 (1983), 393–404.

———. "When Was Michael III Born?" *DOP* 21 (1967), 253–58.

———. "Who Wrote the Chronicle of Theophanes?" *ZRVI* 18 (1978), 9–17.

Mansi, G. D., ed. *Sacrorum Conciliorum Nova et Amplissima Collectio*. Florence and Venice, 1759–98. [Reprint: Paris, 1901–.]

Maqqarī. *The History of the Mohammedan Dynasties in Spain*. Tr. P. de Gayangos. 2 vols. London, 1840–43.

Maqrīzī. *Khitat*. Part 2. Ed. G. Wiet. Mémoires publiés par les membres de l'Institut français d'archéologie orientale, 49. Cairo, 1923.

Martin, J. *A History of the Iconoclastic Controversy*. London, 1930.

Martyrologium Romanum. In *ASB, Propylaeum ad Acta Sanctorum Decembris*.

Mas'ūdi. *Book of Admonition and Reflection*. Tr. B. Carra de Vaux. Paris, 1896. [Or in Vasiliev et al. (q.v.), if so specified in notes.]

———. *Les Prairies d'or*. Tr. C. Barbier de Meynard. 9 vols. Paris, 1861–77. [Or in Vasiliev et al. (q.v.), if so specified in notes.]

Menologium Graecorum [*Menologium of Basil II*]. In *PG* 117: 19–614.

Metcalf, D. M. *Coinage in the Balkans, 820–1355*. Thessalonica, 1965.

———. "How Extensive Was the Issue of Folles during the Years 775–820?" *Byzantion* 37 (1967), 270–310.

Methodius. *Life of Theophanes*. Ed. V. V. Latyšev. Zapiski Rossijskoj Akademii Nauk po istor.-filol. otděleniju, 8th ser., 13.4. Petrograd, 1918.

Meyer-Plath, B., and A. M. Schneider. *Die Landmauer von Konstantinopel.* Vol. 2. Berlin, 1943.

Michael II. *Letter to Louis the Pious.* In Mansi (q.v.), 14: 417–22.

Michael of Studius. *Life of Theodore.* In PG 99: 233–328.

Michael the Syrian. *Chronique de Michel le Syrien.* Vol. 3. Tr. J.-B. Chabot. Paris, 1905.

Miranda, S. *Étude de topographie du Palais sacré de Byzance.* Mexico City, 1976.

———. *Les Palais des empereurs byzantins.* Mexico City, 1964.

Moravcsik, G. *Byzantinoturcica.* 2d ed. 2 vols. Berlin, 1958.

———. "Sagen und Legenden über Kaiser Basileios I." *DOP* 15 (1961), 59–126.

Narratio de sanctis patriarchis Tarasio et Nicephoro. In PG 99: 1849–54.

Naucratius. *Encyclica de obitu S. Theodori Studitae.* In PG 99: 1825–50.

Naumann, R., and H. Belting. *Die Euphemia-Kirche am Hippodrom zu Istanbul und ihre Fresken.* Berlin, 1966.

Nicephorus [Patriarch]. *Antirrhetici tres adversus Constantinum Copronymum.* In PG 100: 206–534.

———. *Apologeticus pro sacris imaginibus.* In PG 100: 533–834.

———. *Breviarium.* In *Nicephori Opuscula Historica,* ed. C. de Boor, 2–77. Leipzig, 1880.

———. *Chronographicon Syntomon.* In *Nicephori Opuscula Historica,* ed. C. de Boor, 81–135. Leipzig, 1880.

Nicephorus [Sceuophylax]. *Life of Theophanes.* In Theophanes (q.v.), 2: 13–27.

Obolensky, D. "The Crimea and the North before 1204." *Archeion Pontou* 35 (1979), 123–33.

Oikonomidès, N. *Les Listes de préséance byzantines des IXe et Xe siècles.* Paris, 1972.

Ostrogorsky, G. "Löhne und Preise in Byzanz." *BZ* 32 (1932), 293–333.

Pargoire, J. "À quelle date l'higoumène S. Platon est-il mort?" *Échos d'Orient* 4 (1900–1901), 164–70.

———. "S. Théophane le Chronographe et ses rapports avec S. Théodore Studite." *Vizantijskij Vremennik* 9 (1902), 31–102.

———. "Saints iconophiles." *Échos d'Orient* 4 (1900–1901), 347–56.

Patlagean, E. "Les Débuts d'une aristocratie et le témoignage de l'historiographie." In *The Byzantine Aristocracy: IX to XIII Centuries,* ed. M. Angold, 23–43. Oxford, 1984.

Pattenden, P. "The Byzantine Early Warning System." *Byzantion* 53 (1983), 258–99.

Peter the Sicilian. *History of the Manichaeans.* C. Astruc et al., "Sources grecques pour l'histoire des Pauliciens d'Asie Mineure," *TM* 4 (1970), 3–67.

Petrus. *Life of Joannicius.* In *ASB,* November 2.1: 384–435.

Philotheus. *Treatise.* In Oikonomidès (q.v.), 81–235.

Photius. *Amphilochia.* In PG, vol. 101.

———. *Bibliotheca.* Ed. R. Henry. 8 vols. Paris, 1959–77.

———. *Epistulae.* Ed. B. Laourdas and L. G. Westerink. 3 vols. Leipzig, 1983–85.

———. *Homilies.* Ed. B. Laourdas. Thessalonica, 1959.

———. *Lexicon.* Ed. C. Theodoridis. Berlin, 1982–.

Poeta Saxo. In *MGH, SS* 1: 227–79.

Polemis, D. *The Doukai: A Contribution to Byzantine Prosopography.* London, 1968.

Poupardin, R. "Études sur l'histoire des principautés lombardes de l'Italie méridionale, II." *Le Moyen Âge*, 2d ser., 10 (1906), 256–71.

Procopius. *Historia Arcana.* Ed. J. Haury and P. Wirth. Leipzig, 1963.

Pseudo-Michael. *Life of Theodore of Studius.* In *PG* 99: 113–232.

Pseudo-Symeon. *Chronographia.* In Theophanes Continuatus (q. v.), 601–760. [Ed. as Symeon Magister.]

Qudāmah ibn Jaʾfar. *Kitāb al-Kharaj.* In *Bibliotheca Geographorum Arabicorum*, ed. and tr. M. J. de Goeje, 6: 144–208. Leiden, 1889. [Page numbers in notes refer to translation.]

Ramsay, W. M. *The Historical Geography of Asia Minor.* London, 1890.

Rekaya, M. "Mise au point sur Théophobe et l'alliance de Bābak avec Théophile." *Byzantion* 44 (1974), 43–55.

Rochow, I. "Die Häresie der Athinganer." In H. Köpstein and F. Winkelmann, *Studien zum 8. und 9. Jahrhundert in Byzanz*, 163–78. Berlin, 1983.

———. *Studien zu der Personen, den Werken und dem Nachleben der Dichterin Kassia.* Berlin, 1967.

Rosser, J. "John the Grammarian's Embassy to Baghdad and the Recall of Manuel." *Byzantinoslavica* 37 (1976), 168–71.

Rouan, M.-F. "Une Lecture 'iconoclaste' de la Vie d'Étienne le Jeune." *TM* 8 (1981), 415–36.

Russell, J. C. *Medieval Regions and Their Cities.* Newton Abbot, 1972.

Sabas. *Life of Joannicius.* In *ASB*, November 2.1: 332–84.

Samuel of Ani. *Chronological Tables.* In *Collection d'historiens arméniens*, tr. M.-F. Brosset, 2: 339–483. St. Petersburg, 1876.

Scriptor Incertus [Sergius Confessor?]. *Historia de Leone Bardae Armenii Filio.* In Leo Grammaticus (q. v.), 335–62.

Scylitzes, John. *Synopsis Historiarum.* Ed. J. Thurn. Berlin, 1973.

Seibt, W. *Die Skleroi.* Vienna, 1976.

Ševčenko, I. "Hagiography of the Iconoclast Period." In *Iconoclasm* (q. v.), 113–31.

Soustal, P. *Tabula Imperii Byzantini.* Vol. 3, *Nikopolis und Kephallēnia.* Vienna, 1981.

Speck, P. *Artabasdos.* Berlin, 1981.

———. "*Graikia* und *Armenia*: Das Tätigkeitsfeld eines nicht identifizierten Strategen im frühen 9. Jahrhundert." *JÖB* 16 (1967), 71–90.

———. *Kaiser Konstantin VI.* 2 vols. Munich, 1978.

Stein, E. *Studien zur Geschichte des byzantinischen Reiches.* Stuttgart, 1919.

Stephen of Taron. *Armenian History.* Tr. H. Gelzer and A. Burckhardt. Leipzig, 1907.

Suda [*Suidae Lexicon*]. Ed. A. Adler. 5 vols. Leipzig, 1928–38.

Symeon the Logothete. *Chronographia.* Ed. [as specified in notes] as Leo Grammaticus, as Georgius Interpolatus, or in Moravcsik, "Sagen" (qq. v.).

Synaxarium Ecclesiae Constantinopolitanae. In *ASB, Propylaeum ad Acta Sanctorum Novembris.*

Synodicon Vetus. Ed. and tr. J. Duffy and J. Parker. Washington, D.C., 1979.

Tacticon Uspensky. In Oikonomidès (q. v.), 46–63.

Tafel, G. L. F., and G. M. Thomas. *Urkunden zur älteren Handels- und Staatsgeschichte der Republik venedig.* Vol. 1. Vienna, 1856.

Theodore of Studius. *Eulogy of His Mother.* In *PG* 99:883–902.

———. *Eulogy of Plato.* In *PG* 99:803–49.

———. *Great Catechesis.* Ed. A. Papadopoulos-Kerameus. St. Petersburg, 1904.

————. *Lesser Catacheses.* In A. Mai, ed., *Nova Patrum Bibliotheca*, vol. 9.1, ed. G. Cozza-Luzi. Rome, 1888.

————. *Letters.* Books 1 and 2, in *PG* 99:903–1669. Nos. 1–284, in A. Mai, ed., *Nova Patrum Bibliotheca*, vol. 8.1, ed. G. Cozza-Luzi, 1–236. Rome, 1871.

————. *Panegyric of Theophanes.* C. Van de Vorst, "Une Panégyrique de S. Théophane le Chronographe par S. Théodore Studite." *AnalBoll.* 31 (1912), 11–23.

Theophanes. *Chronographia.* Ed. C. de Boor. 2 vols. Leipzig, 1883. [References in notes are to vol. 1 unless specified otherwise.]

Theophanes Continuatus. *Chronographia.* Ed. I. Bekker. Corpus Scriptorum Historiae Byzantinae. Bonn, 1838.

Timarion. Ed. R. Romano. Naples, 1974.

Toumanoff, C. "Introduction to Christian Caucasian History, II." *Traditio* 17 (1961), 1–106.

Treadgold, W. "The Bride-Shows of the Byzantine Emperors." *Byzantion* 49 (1979), 395–413.

————. "The Bulgars' Treaty with the Byzantines in 816." *Rivista di Studi Bizantini e Slavi* 4 (1984), 213–20.

————. *The Byzantine State Finances in the Eighth and Ninth Centuries.* New York, 1982.

————. "The Chronological Accuracy of the *Chronicle* of Symeon the Logothete for the Years 813–845." *DOP* 33 (1979), 159–97.

————. "An Indirectly Preserved Source for the Reign of Leo IV." *JÖB* 34 (1984), 69–76.

————. "The Military Lands and the Imperial Estates in the Middle Byzantine Empire." *Harvard Ukrainian Studies* 7 (1983), 619–31.

————. *The Nature of the Bibliotheca of Photius.* Washington, D.C., 1980.

————. "Notes on the Numbers and Organization of the Ninth-Century Byzantine Army." *GRBS* 21 (1980), 269–88.

————. "Photius on the Transmission of Texts." *GRBS* 19 (1978), 171–75.

————. "The Problem of the Marriage of the Emperor Theophilus." *GRBS* 16 (1975), 325–41.

————. "Remarks on the Work of Al-Jarmī on Byzantium." *Byzantinoslavica* 44 (1983), 205–12.

————. "The Revival of Byzantine Learning and the Revival of the Byzantine State." *American Historical Review* 84 (1979), 1245–66.

————. "The Unpublished Saint's Life of the Empress Irene." *Byzantinische Forschungen* 7 (1982), 237–51.

Tritle, L. "Tatzates' Flight and the Byzantine-Arab Peace Treaty of 782." *Byzantion* 47 (1977), 279–300.

Van de Vorst, C. "La Petite Catéchèse de S. Théodore Studite." *AnalBoll.* 33 (1919), 31–51.

————. "La Translation de S. Théodore Studite et de S. Joseph de Thessalonique." *AnalBoll.* 32 (1913), 27–62.

Vasiliev, A. A. *The Goths in the Crimea.* Cambridge, Mass., 1936.

————. "The Life of St. Theodore of Edessa." *Byzantion* 16 (1942–43), 165–225.

Vasiliev, A. A., et al. *Byzance et les Arabes.* 2 vols. Brussels, 1935–68.

Vita Hludowici. In *MGH, SS* 2:607–48.

Vita Willehadi. In *MGH, SS* 2:378–90.

Von Sivers, P. "Taxes and Trade in the 'Abbāsid Thughūr, 750–962/133–351." *Journal of the Economic and Social History of the Orient* 25 (1982), 71–99.

Wallach, L. *Diplomatic Studies in Latin and Greek Documents from the Carolingian Age.* Ithaca, N.Y., 1977.

Whitby, L. M. "The Great Chronographer and Theophanes." *BMGS* 8 (1982–83), 1–20.

Wilson, N. G. *Scholars of Byzantium.* Baltimore, 1983.

Zacos, G., and A. Veglery. *Byzantine Lead Seals.* Vol. 1. Basel, 1972.

Zepos, I., and P. Zepos, eds. *Jus Graeco-Romanum.* 8 vols. Athens, 1931.

Index

In this index, "f" means a second mention on the next page; "ff" means separate references on the next two pages; two numbers with a dash between them mark a discussion spanning two or more pages; and *passim* denotes separate mentions on three or more pages in close but not necessarily consecutive sequence.

Library of Congress Cataloging-in-Publication Data

Treadgold, Warren T.
The Byzantine revival, 780–842 / Warren Treadgold.
   p.   cm.
Bibliography: p.
Includes index.
ISBN 0-8047-1462-2 (alk. paper) ISBN 0-8047-1896-2 (pbk)
   1. Byzantine Empire—History—527–1081.   I. Title.
DF581.T73 1988
949.5'02—dc19   87-37392
                                              CIP